This book, first published in Italian, is the leading study of the greatest composer of late Renaissance and early Baroque Italy. Monteverdi's contribution to secular, sacred and theatrical music in the period was unparalleled: his madrigals, church music and operas remain very much alive today. A large number of contemporary documents, including some 130 of his own letters, offer rich insights into the composer and his times, also illuminating the many and varied contexts for music-making in the most important musical centres in Italy. Fabbri uses these documents and other sources to present a rich narrative focusing on a composer who has perhaps rightly been called the 'father of modern music'. This translation of the newly revised text brings an indispensable book to a much broader readership, providing a vivid picture of a fascinating period in music history.

MONTEVERDI

MONTEVERDI

Paolo Fabbri

Translated by Tim Carter

CAMBRIDGE
UNIVERSITY PRESS

Published by the Press Syndicate of the University of Cambridge
The Pitt Building, Trumpington Street, Cambridge CB2 IRP
40 West 20th Street, New York, NY 10011–4211, USA
10 Stamford Road, Oakleigh, Melbourne 3166, Australia

Originally published in Italian as *Monteverdi* by E. D. T. Edizioni di Torino,
Turin 1985 and © E. D. T. Edizioni di Torino

English translation © Cambridge University Press 1994

First published in English by Cambridge University Press 1994 as *Monteverdi*

Printed in Great Britain at Woolnough Bookbinders Ltd, Irthlingborough,
Northants.

A catalogue record for this book is available from the British Library

Library of Congress cataloguing in publication data

Fabbri, Paolo, 1948–
[Monteverdi. English]
Monteverdi / Paolo Fabbri: translated by Tim Carter.
  p.   cm.
Includes bibliographical references and indexes.
ISBN 0 521 35133 2 (hardback)
1. Monteverdi, Claudio, 1567–1643.
2. Composers – Italy – Biography.   I. Title.
ML410.M77F213   1994
782'.0092 – dc20   93–11564   CIP   MN
[B]
ISBN 0 521 35133 2 hardback

To Patrizia

Contents

Foreword

Paolo Fabbri's *Monteverdi* (Turin, Edizioni di Torino, 1985) quickly established itself as a classic in the field of Monteverdi studies. Its rich documentation and powerful new insights into the life and work of so significant a composer in late Renaissance and early Baroque Italy changed fundamentally our view of the man and his music, and set a new standard for bio-bibliographical work in musicology. An English translation was clearly a must.

For the present edition, Professor Fabbri significantly revised his text (in 1988–9), removing much of his discussion of the music, given that it was designed for a specific Italian readership (present readers can find ample material in the rich bibliography in English on the composer). He also added new biographical and other information, and corrected a few minor errors in his original. Other changes have been occasioned by developments in the field. Fabbri's list of works has effectively been superseded by Manfred Stattkus's *Claudio Monteverdi: Verzeichnis der erhaltenen Werke* (Bergkamen, Musikverlag Stattkus, 1985) – there is a digest in English in Denis Arnold, *Monteverdi*, 'The Master Musicians', 3rd edition revised by Tim Carter (London, Dent, 1990) – and his long bibliographical note by the listings in K. Gary Adams and Dyke Kiel, *Claudio Monteverdi: a Guide to Research*, 'Garland Composer Resource Manuals', xxiii (New York & London, Garland, 1989). Thus we have not given a classified work-list here (although just about every work by Monteverdi is mentioned in the text and thus listed in the index), and the bibliography is limited only to specific works cited (by short-title reference) in the notes.

In the case of Fabbri's many documents concerning Monteverdi and his period, I have tended to translate things anew, with only two major exceptions (minor ones are cited in the notes): first, Denis Stevens's exemplary English edition of *The Letters of Claudio Monteverdi* (London, Faber & Faber, 1980); and second, the translations of documents by Monteverdi and Artusi in Oliver Strunk's *Source Readings in Music History* (London, Faber & Faber, 1952). I wish to thank Professor Stevens most warmly for his kind permission both to use his translations (including revisions for a much needed second edition forthcoming from Oxford University Press) and to make minor changes (in terms of styling and, very occasionally, of substance) as seemed necessary. Sadly, reasons of space have prevented giving the originals of the documents translated here, which could easily have doubled the length of the book (the one exception is the new addition (pp. 220–1) to the canon of Monteverdi letters). However, my tendency to favour somewhat literal translations – even at the expense of literary elegance – should help give a sense of the often tortuous nature of early seventeenth-century Italian prose in all its richness and vitality.

Paolo Fabbri himself read and commented on this translation, which in turn prompted further revisions and reinterpretations. I am indeed grateful to him, to John Whenham for help with the bibliography, to Francesca Chiarelli for her advice on numerous tricky passages in the Italian, and to Angela Cleall for her invaluable help in checking my manuscript.

Tim Carter

Preface

In preparing to add a new title to the already long list of studies on Monteverdi, I have first and foremost wanted my text to be both useful and usable, attempting to bring together all the facts and documents that can help achieve a historical understanding of the composer's output. I hope that my frequent recourse to long extracts from Monteverdi's letters, and also to other accounts of various kinds by his contemporaries, will be regarded by the reader not as tedious – or worse, a nuisance – but as an unparalleled source of information, offering direct access to material previously scattered here and there and now made available even independent of my own interpretations. I say this with a deep-seated belief in the vitality and power of historical documents of this kind.

I wish to thank Paola Chiarini Ricci, Oscar Mischiati, Livio Stanghellini, Elvidio Surian and Antonio Vassalli, who made suggestions, offered information and gave me help in various ways. Furthermore, I am indeed grateful to Tim Carter for his devotion to improving my work. Finally, I have long owed a particular debt to Lorenzo Bianconi, who has been generous to an extreme with advice and information, even to the extent of reading and commenting on my manuscript. If there is anything of value here, it is clearly thanks to him.

Paolo Fabbri

Notes on Monteverdi's texts

The attributions of the poetic texts set by Monteverdi in the listings here take account of the traditional literature, of the new information given in Nino Pirrotta's 'Scelte poetiche di Monteverdi' ('Monteverdi's Poetic Choices') – plus other sources cited as appropriate in the notes – and also of the results of the work of Lorenzo Bianconi and Antonio Vassalli on poetic sources used by musicians of the sixteenth and seventeenth centuries. Since these last attributions represent unpublished research (for which we gratefully acknowledge the generosity of Bianconi and Vassalli), we feel it useful to give full details here:

> *Madrigali spirituali* (1583). All the texts are taken from F. Rorario, *Rime spirituali* (Venice, 1581).
>
> *Canzonette* (1583). The common attribution of 'Io mi vivea com'aquila mirando' to Battista Guarini has no secure foundation. 'Corse a la morte il povero Narciso' is found anonymously in the *Ghirlanda di canzonette spirituali* (Venice, n.d.).
>
> *Madrigali . . . Libro primo* (1587). 'Amor, per tua mercè vatten'a quella' is in G. M. Bonardo, *Madrigali* (Venice, 1571); 'Se pur non mi consenti' is in L. Groto, *Rime* (Venice, 1587); 'Se nel partir da voi, vita mia, sento' is also in Bonardo's *Madrigali* (1571).
>
> *Il secondo libro de madrigali* (1590). 'Questo specchio ti dono' is in the *Gioie poetiche di madrigali del signor Geronimo Casone et d'altri celebri poeti* (Pavia, 1593).
>
> *Il quarto libro de madrigali* (1603). 'La piaga c'ho nel core' is in A. Gatti, *Madrigali* (Venice, 1614); 'Io mi son giovinetta' and 'Anima dolorosa che vivendo' are in the *Nuova scelta di rime di diversi eccellenti scrittori dell'età nostra*, i (Casalmaggiore, 1590).
>
> *Concerto: settimo libro de madrigali* (1619). 'Io son pur vezzosetta pastorella' is in the *Mostre poetiche dell'Incolto accademico Immaturo* (Venice, 1570; this perhaps explains Cicogna's remark concerning this collection (*Saggio di bibliografia veneziana*, p. 557) that 'there are various poems, some of which are said to have been set to music by

Claudio Monteverde'). 'O viva fiamma, o miei sospiri ardenti', often attributed to Alfonso Gesualdo, draws only its first line from Gesualdo's poem: the rest is different. We have no evidence for the common attribution of 'Se pur destina e vole' to Ottavio Rinuccini.

Scherzi musicali (1632). The common attribution of 'Armato il cor d'adamantina fede' to Ottavio Rinuccini has no secure foundation.

Madrigali guerrieri, et amorosi (1638). 'Se vittorie sí belle' is in F. Testi, *Rime* (Venice, 1613). The common attribution of 'Perché te 'n fuggi, o Fillide' to Ottavio Rinuccini has no secure foundation.

Introduction

In the decade following his death, Monteverdi's name remained prominent in the musical world. Publishers – and not just Italians – reprinted his works or, and preferably, presented hitherto unpublished music in anthologies and above all in single volumes wholly devoted to his compositions. There were revivals of his operas, as with the staging of *La coronatione di Poppea* in Naples in 1651 with the title *Nerone* (the libretto was printed there in the same year by Roberto Mollo) and perhaps elsewhere.[1] Nor do we lack acknowledgments of his standing by important musicians, such as the *maestro di cappella* of the French royal chapel, Thomas Gobert, who when writing to Costantin Huygens in 1646 could cite 'some madrigals composed by Monteverdi' as an example of the most enchanting 'Italian manner': Gobert particularly admired 'his search for and exploration of many beautiful chords and dissonances'.[2] Similarly, Heinrich Schütz, in the preface to his *Symphoniarum sacrarum secunda pars* (1647), made clear the personal debt arising from his having encountered the composer of the *Madrigali guerrieri, et amorosi*. And for the rest, it is an indication of Monteverdi's popularity in Austria and Germany – to which we shall return – that he was included in the *Tractatus compositionis augmentatus* by Schütz's pupil, Christoph Bernhard (1627–92). Here Monteverdi is cited together with his pupils Giovanni Rovetta and Francesco Cavalli in Chapter 43, 'Von der Imitation', as standing among the representatives of the 'stylus luxurians comunis' ('common luxuriant style') and of the 'stylus [luxurians] teatralis' ('theatrical luxuriant style').[3]

In Italy, and given the rapid decline of the madrigal, the genre which had made up so great a part of his output, Monteverdi was valued above all for the expressive quality of his writing for solo voice, particularly in a theatrical context:

> And in fact, if we examine the style called recitative, and which one would believe were better called monodic, tell me what displeases you in [the music of] Giulio Caccini, Iacopo Peri and Claudio Monteverdi (who is known to have emerged from that most fine Florentine school)? ... Thus one should also value ... the lament of Ariadne by Monteverdi, set to music with the assistance of the noble poet Ottavio Rinuccini ...[4]

So the *stylus dramaticus*, or recitative style, is associated usually as regards metre with comedies, tragedies and dramas in general, generally founding itself more on the affections used to express the poetic subject than on musical cadences and luxuriant vocalizations.

Among the chief celebrated musicians who practised this type of style[8] was Claudio Monteverdi, as his *Arianna* reveals.[5]

The excellent musician Claudio Monteverdi composed *Arianna* on the model of these two first operas [*Dafne* and *Euridice*], and having become *maestro di cappella* at St Mark's, Venice, he introduced there a certain manner of stage-works that have become so famous through the magnificence of theatres and of costumes, the delicacy of voices, the harmony of the instrumental ensembles, and the learned compositions of this Monteverdi, Soriano, Giovanelli, Teofilo and many other great masters.[6]

Monteverdi was firmly rooted in the world of late sixteenth-century polyphony, and particularly in those circles which had cultivated a type of madrigal destined for sophisticated listeners who accepted departures from classical compositional norms for specific expressive ends. He remained essentially faithful to his training as a contrapuntalist, seeking to render in music the poetic world of the affections. All the new techniques which he assimilated and developed for their own ends in the course of his career revolved around this nucleus, and it was during this career that he demonstrated the greatest openness towards the new, which was constantly and fruitfully grafted to the tree of the great polyphonic tradition.

With the change of taste towards a simpler style, one of show, inclined towards outward appearances and even playing to the gallery, it was inevitable that the greater part of Monteverdi's output should have been quickly consigned to the margins, even if it was admired for the learning it displayed. His fame as a composer of sacred music was more resilient, given the more severe adherence to stylistic norms in this repertory, but above all he was remembered as an opera composer because of the interest attracted by the new genre mixing music and theatre. But even here, his theatrical output was rendered obsolete by the omnipresent demand for new works, and particularly by the fluidity of his style, which was felt to be excessive and over-complicated in an age moving quickly towards the polarization of simple recitative and tuneful arias.[7]

For these reasons, we have to wait for academic historical writing of the eighteenth century to rekindle interest in Monteverdi's works. Already at the turn of the century, a number of theorists were citing Monteverdi, perhaps reflecting the enduring interest in the madrigal nurtured in particular Roman musical circles (witness the work of composers such as Michelangelo Rossi, Antonio Maria Abbatini, Domenico Dal Pane and Alessandro Scarlatti).[8] For example, in his *Guida armonica* (c.1690) Giuseppe Ottavio Pitoni chose an extract from 'Cor mio, non mori? E mori' (from Monteverdi's Fourth Book of madrigals) as an example of movement 'from a unison to a tenth';[9] and in his *Musico testore* (1706) Zaccaria Tevo revived the Artusi–Monteverdi controversy, demonstrating clear sympathy for the arguments of the Bolognese canon.[10] In addition to the notices in the theatrical listings of Bonlini (1731), Groppo (1745) and in the updated version of Leone Allacci's *Drammaturgia* (1755), Francesco Arisi gave biographical details of Monteverdi (and of his son, Massimiliano) – drawn from Caberloti's *Laconismo* – in the third volume of his *Cremona literata* (1741).[11] Similarly, in mid-century Francesco Saverio Quadrio recalled Monteverdi's activity as a madrigalist and opera composer,[12] and later (1783) Stefano Arteaga dusted the cobwebs off the famous *Lamento d'Arianna*.[13] Slightly earlier, Padre Martini had mentioned Monteverdi in his *Storia della musica*;[14] Martini later granted the composer full prominence in his practical treatise on counterpoint, where he reprinted in full two madrigals from the Third and Fifth Books ('Stracciami pur il core' and 'Cruda Amarilli, che col nome ancora') and the 'Agnus Dei' from the *Missa 'In illo tempore'* with extended analytical commentary preceded by general notes on the composer's music.[15]

Among English historians, both John Hawkins (1776) and Charles Burney (1789) offered biographical outlines of Monteverdi, focusing in particular on *Orfeo* and furnishing their discussions with numerous music examples.[16] Unlike Hawkins, a lawyer and musical dilettante, Burney, an organist and composer, was not content merely to refer to the controversy with Artusi: he also illustrated some of its details, following in the footsteps of Padre Martini, whom Burney had visited during his travels in Italy (moreover, he specifically cites Martini's *Esemplare* and himself reprints 'Stracciami pur il core'), dwelling on Monteverdi's somewhat incorrect (in Burney's view) part-writing. This criticism was to be revived a century later by Verdi, who, listing for Boito a series of composers suitable as didactic models for young musicians, included in his sixteenth-century group Palestrina, Victoria, Marenzio, Allegri 'and so many other good writers of that century, with the exception of Monteverdi, who laid out the parts badly'.[17] The entry on Monteverdi in the first edition of Ernst Ludwig Gerber's *Historisch-biographisches Lexicon der Tonkünstler* (1790) does not go much beyond what Martini, Hawkins and Burney had put together,[18] although it was enlarged with more recent information in the revised edition some 25 years later:[19] here the entry begins by calling Monteverdi 'the Mozart of his time'.

But dictionary-writers of the second half of the nineteenth century were able to note the new discoveries concerning Monteverdi made around the middle of the century by local historians such as Canal and Caffi. Also, more light was being cast on his period thanks to the renewed interest of some scholars of the first half of the century (Forkel, Kiesewetter, Thibaut, Baini, Winterfeld, Ambros) in composers and music of the sixteenth and seventeenth centuries. Although the last decades of the nineteenth century saw other important contributions from Italians (Canal, Davari, Guido Sommi and Giorgio Sommi Picenardi), significantly it was in the official journal of the new German musicology (the *Vierteljahrsschrift für Musikwissenschaft*) that Emil

Vogel's still fundamental biographical essay appeared (in 1887). That period also saw new editions of Monteverdi's music: the *Lamento d'Arianna* published by Gervaert in Paris in 1868, the madrigal '"T'amo mia vita" la mia cara vita' printed in London in 1883, and *Orfeo* issued by Robert Eitner in Berlin in 1881.

In the late nineteenth and early twentieth centuries, the number of editions of Monteverdi noticeably increased: the *Lamento d'Arianna* was republished by Parisotti (together with the Messenger's narration from *Orfeo*; 1885–1900), Solerti (1904) and Respighi (1910); d'Indy edited *Orfeo* (1905; the year before, his revision had been used for a performance of the opera in Paris) and *La coronatione di Poppea* (1908); and Torchi published the *Ballo delle ingrate* and the *Combattimento di Tancredi et Clorinda*. Similarly, *La coronatione di Poppea* was issued by Goldschmidt (1904) and Van den Borren (1914), *Orfeo* by Orefice (1910; the edition followed a concert performance the year before at the Milan Conservatory during the season of concerts presented by the Amici della Musica). Other editions included a selection of twelve five-part madrigals by Leichtentritt (1909) and Arnold Mendelssohn (1911), the *Sacrae cantiunculae* by Terrabugio (1910), and the Mass from the *Selva morale e spirituale* by Tirabassi (1914). But in that period, Monteverdi's fame, especially as an opera composer (and thanks to the first modern revivals), began to escape the narrow confines of musicological and scholarly circles, and in the refined aestheticism of those years the composer was also set up as a shining example of an archaic musical culture to be contrasted with the 'popular' tastes of modern times: witness the evocation of the 'divine Claudio' (the melancholic Mediterranean genius to be pitted against the barbaric Wagner) among the antique-Venetian bric-à-brac of D'Annunzio's *Fuoco* (1898), while a reflection of similar interests cultivated in French circles can be seen in the introduction to the *Traité d'harmonie théorique et pratique* by Dubois (1891).

These eager rediscoveries which slowly but surely brought Monteverdi back into the musical – and not just musicological – consciousness of the new century were to culminate in the publication of Monteverdi's complete works in 1926–32 (vols. I–XIV) and 1941–2 (vols. XV–XVI) edited by Gian Francesco Malipiero. Malipiero's edition appeared as part of a publishing programme ('Il Vittoriale degli Italiani'; 'The Triumph of the Italians') which one can ascribe to that climate of exalting national values which was always open to nationalist influences. In the case of the Venetian composer Malipiero, such notions – and likewise any hint of an archaicizing preciosity due to his direct contact with the ideas of D'Annunzio and his followers – were to some extent overtaken by his curious and admiring attention for a great predecessor who had worked in Venice several centuries before, using a language that was new but not revolutionary and who, indeed, had also been subject to censure from some of his contemporaries. Malipiero was searching for a personal style that leapfrogged Romanticism and therefore had a significant interest in the pre-Classical period: certainly in Monteverdi he was admiring one of the greatest musicians of that time, but perhaps he also felt some kind of affinity bonding him with that distant, lonely figure. In the short preface to the first volume of the complete edition, Malipiero announces his project to transcribe and publish all the 'works of one of Italy's *true* geniuses, not to resuscitate a dead man' but to demonstrate 'yet again how the great manifestations of art always remain *modern*'. He concludes by recalling the unfairness of the criticisms to which Monteverdi had been subjected and the later repentance of his critics: 'may this perhaps serve as a warning to the worthy descendants of the aforementioned persecutors of Claudio Monteverdi?'

From then on, editions, books and articles (and naturally, musical performances) focusing on Monteverdi multiplied still further, making him perhaps the most widely known composer of the period before Bach.

I

Cremona

1 Birth, family, surroundings

'15 May 1567, Claudio Zuan [= Giovanni] Antonio, son of Messer Baldasar Mondeverdo, godfather Signor Zuan Batista Zacaria, godmother Madonna Laura de la Fina'. Thus reads the entry, itself dated 15 May 1567, in the baptismal register of the church of SS. Nazaro e Celso in Cremona, recording the baptism of the first child of Baldassarre Monteverdi and Maddalena Zignani, who had been married towards the beginning of 1566.[1]

An apothecary, surgeon and doctor, Baldassarre had first kept a shop near Cremona Cathedral; only after his marriage did he move to the parish of SS. Nazaro e Celso in the Belfiore district of the Piazzano quarter. Claudio was born in this house, and was followed by Maria Domitilla and Giulio Cesare, baptized on 16 May 1571 and 31 January 1573 respectively. Maddalena died some time around 1576, but after Baldassarre remarried Giovanna Gadio in 1576–7 other children came to join those of the first marriage: Clara Massimilia (baptized 8 January 1579), Luca (baptized 7 February 1581) and Filippo (baptized January 1583). A third marriage (to Francesca Como, after 1583) seems not to have increased the family still further.

Cremona stood at the south-eastern edge of the state of Milan; for its economic and political importance it was the second city of the state after the capital. But Cremona was also close to the dominions of Venice (which stretched to the city), of the Gonzagas (the duchy of Mantua) and of the Farnese (the duchy of Parma). Less than ten years before Claudio Monteverdi's birth, the Treaty of Cateau-Cambrésis (1559) had sealed the legitimacy of the Spanish dominion over Milan – formerly a duchy ruled by the Sforzas – which in fact went back to 1535. Thus in political terms Cremona was dependent on Philip II of Spain, whose authority was transmitted through a Castellan who worked side by side with the local administration and who was responsible to the Governor of Milan.

Baldassarre Monteverdi had a degree of family wealth and was a man of some public significance: indeed, as well as owning several houses, archival documents record him among those who organized the Spanish census of 1576, and in April 1584 he is documented as being one of the founders of the Collegio dei Chirurghi (College of Surgeons) of Cremona, in whose statutes (approved and published in 1587) his name appears at the head of the list of those belonging to that professional body.

By 1584, his eldest child, Claudio, although not yet 20, could claim some reputation as a musician – at least in local circles – due chiefly to the fact that he had already published two books of music (the *Sacrae cantiunculae* of 1582 and the *Madrigali spirituali* of 1583), with a third on the way (the dedication of the *Canzonette a tre voci* is dated 31 October 1584). On the title-pages of these editions – as with all the later ones similarly dating from his years in Cremona (the *Madrigali a cinque voci* ... *Libro primo*, 1587; *Il secondo libro de madrigali a cinque voci*, 1590) – Monteverdi states clearly that he is a pupil of Marc' Antonio Ingegneri: 'Egregii Ingegnerii Discipuli' (*Sacrae cantiunculae*); 'Discepolo del Signor Marc'Antonio Ingegnieri' (*Madrigali spirituali*, *Canzonette* and *Madrigali a cinque voci* ... *Libro primo*); 'Discepolo del Sig.ʳ Ingegneri' (*Il secondo libro de madrigali a cinque voci*). Thus his teacher assumed responsibility for the dissemination of the works of a student who had not yet reached the age of majority and so was not permitted – in keeping with the civil statutes – to execute public contracts in his own name: this was not to be repeated in Monteverdi's *Terzo libro de madrigali a cinque voci* (1592), published by the composer when he was 25 and no longer resident in Cremona (Ingegneri in fact died a few days after Monteverdi signed the dedication).[2]

Ingegneri, born in Verona and a pupil of Vincenzo Ruffo, had moved to Cremona in around 1568, serving as a singer and organist at the cathedral: he seems to have been *maestro di cappella* by 1576.[3] The musical resources of the cathedral had been reorganized in the 1520s to make them suitable for the performance of modern polyphony in the Flemish style.[4] Normally there were a dozen singers plus an organist;[5] by the second half of the century, on particularly solemn occasions they would be joined ever more regularly by one or two instrumentalists. For example, from 1579–84, the cornett player Don Ariodante Regaini was taken on 'to play in all the *concerti*' alongside the choir; similarly, when it was decided in 1582 to 'lower the organ of the greater church by about a semitone', this was intended so as to adapt the instrument 'for the choir and for the *concerti* that are done and that will be done with all the types of musical instruments which will share in the choir and in the *concerto*'.[6]

But if Cremona's musical life was centred on the cathedral, around it were placed the parallel activities of other churches in the city. From the presence of organs, we know of music in S. Agostino (the composer Tiburzio Massaino was a member of its monastery at various times in the late sixteenth century), S. Anna, S. Francesco, S. Abbondio, S. Pietro, and S. Agata (where Rodiano Barera was *maestro di cappella*). And a little way outside the city, the Cistercian Benedictine, Lucrezio Quinziani, lived in the monastery of S. Maddalena. Musicians born, and sometimes trained, in Cremona, include Costanzo Porta, Antonio and Uomobono Morsolino, Agostino Licino, Carlo Ardesi, Lorenzo Medici and Benedetto Pallavicino: Monteverdi had direct dealings with some of them during his lifetime. As for secular music, permanent institutions included the *piffari* of the Comune – five players – and the musical resources of the Castello, groups focusing primarily on wind instruments. Nor would any even brief survey of music in Cremona be complete without mentioning the instrument-makers' shops which we know flourished there – among the organ-builders, the Maineri and Cristoforo Faletto, and among the makers of lute and string instruments, not least the Amati.[7]

But the most important figure in the musical life of Cremona in the second half of the sixteenth century was Marc'Antonio Ingegneri from Verona, who gained such fame in his adopted city that Alessandro Lami could include him among the distinguished Cremonesi surveyed in his *Sogno non meno piacevole che morale* (Cremona, Cristoforo Draconi, 1572). Lami devotes to Ingegneri part of the eleventh *ottava* of Canto III (with an unfortunate enjambment):

> La Fama poi che ne fur gionti a fronte
> cantando disse: 'Vedi l'Ingegneri
> Marcantonio, le cui virtú son conte
> ai Rossi, ai Caspi mari, agl'Indi e Iberi.'[8]

> Fame, since they had arrived before her, / singing said: 'See Ingegneri / Marcantonio, whose virtues are renowned / to the Red and Caspian Seas, to the Indies and Iberia.'

Similarly, Pietro Cerone from Bergamo, writing in Spain in the 1590s, includes Ingegneri among the modern 'practical composers' of madrigals whom one can 'imitate safely and without danger', together with 'Pedro Vincio, Philippe de Monte, Orlando de Lassus, Iuan de Maque, Costancio Puerta [Porta], Vicente Ruffo, Matheo Asula ... Franciso Guerrero, Thomas de Victoria [!?], Anibal Stabile, Ruger Iuvaneli [Giovanelli], Iuan Cavaccio, Luzasco Luzasqui, Lelio Bertani, Benito Palavicino, Lucas Marenzio, Iuan Baptista Mosto, Felix Anerio, Oracio Vecchi, Andres Dragoni, Iuan Fereti, Geronimo Conversi'.[9] Some of these musicians were well known to Monteverdi (consider Luzzaschi, Bertani, Pallavicino, Marenzio and Vecchi) and include individuals he met personally or knew through their works. For Cerone, Ingegneri was also to be included among the madrigalists – and among the founding fathers – of that subtle and artful style for an exclusive and initiated élite otherwise known as 'musica reservata':

> Philippe de Monte and Lucas Marenzio have written very beautiful and suave chromatic passages, or to describe them more properly, soft, lascivious and effeminate ones. Pedro Vincio and Marco Antonio Ingiñero were the first to distinguish themselves by the variety of their counterpoints, that is to say double, inverted, retrograde, at the tenth, at the twelfth, and in all the ways used today in Italy, of which one can almost say that they were the inventors. And be warned that the music governed by such counterpoints does not satisfy everyone, but only the professionals, and not the common people and those new to music; nor is it acceptable to the mere singer, given that it does not possess that sweetness and suavity that the natural ear desires. In fact, all its flavour rests in the artfulness of the parts and not in the euphony

of the voices, in the combination of counterpoints and not in the suavity of consonances. Hence a true judge can only be the capacity for technical understanding of the complete musician, and not someone or other's mere ear.[10]

Like his teacher, Monteverdi was to be a singer and string-player before becoming a composer.[11] His apprenticeship with Ingegneri has remained documented only by the title-pages of the printed music books dating from his years in Cremona. One can perhaps assume on the basis of the most typical musical careers of the period that the young Claudio was a boy-singer in the *cappella* of the cathedral, and later, perhaps when his voice broke, an instrumentalist working alongside the choir. Or he could have been a private pupil of Ingegneri in his house in the parish of S. Bartolomeo, like Camillo Gudazzi, who in 1606 edited the posthumous publication of his teacher's *Sesto libro dei madrigali a cinque voci*.[12] In the absence of any evidence, and however likely this may be, it all remains hypothesis.

Ingegneri arrived at Cremona when his own teacher, Ruffo, was in charge of music at the cathedral of nearby Milan. It is likely that he, too, was not unfamiliar with Milanese circles, given the close collaboration between, and the similar policies of, the prelates of both dioceses, Carlo Borromeo at Milan and Nicolò Sfondrato at Cremona. Sfondrato was Bishop of Cremona from 1560, and like his energetic mentor and colleague, and as so many other prelates of this period, he was an active supporter of the ideals developed and encapsulated in the resolutions of the Council of Trent (which ended its meetings in December 1563). To clarify these ideals and to hasten their implementation, Sfondrato convened three diocesan synods (in 1564, 1580 and 1583), while his frequent pastoral visits (in the period 1565–90) were intended to monitor the state of the parish churches and of ecclesiastical institutions and their pastoral activity. In 1566, Sfondrato founded the Cremonese Seminary for the education of the local clergy, and he began a strenuous campaign of repression against the abuses and privileges of the cathedral chapter. 'To promote the religious life of the people, as well as to combat deviations and abuses, he spread Christian doctrine through the schools, encouraged the creation of lay confraternities, supported charitable and welfare foundations, and introduced into some dioceses members of the new orders of regular clergy, such as the Barnabites, the Somaschi and the Theatines.'[13] Cremona and its territories had been among the most receptive in Lombardy to Protestant propaganda. From as early as the late 1530s, there were attempts to eradicate this thriving heresy, and around 1550 there was uncovered 'a true and complete community, soundly organized: the "ecclesia cremonensis", the first known example of a reformed church in the state of Milan, which had already been active for some time and in contact with other similar communities'.[14] Rooted in various social levels (from the nobility to artisans) and drawing its inspiration from Calvinism, this church, despite repression, was to make its influence felt even later through to the mid-1570s, when it was finally

eradicated. Both Carlo Borromeo and, in Cremona, Nicolò Sfondrato, com-
batted these infiltrations of protestantism, and Sfondrato's Counter-
Reformation zeal was rewarded by a secure and successful ecclesiastical career:
he was made a cardinal in 1583 and elected Pope in 1590, reigning until the
next year as Gregory XIV.

Marc'Antonio Ingegneri dedicated to Nicolò Sfondrato as bishop his
Sacrarum cantionum quinque vocibus liber primus (1576) and the *Liber secundus
missarum* (1587), and as pope, his six-voice *Sacrae cantiones* (1591); he also
dedicated the *Sacrarum cantionum cum quatuor vocibus . . . liber primus* (1586) to
Sfondrato's vicar, Don Antonio Maria Gabello. He further offered religious
works to Baron Paolo Sfondrato (Nicolò's brother) – not liturgical pieces like
the above but spiritual ones to texts by, for example, Vittoria Colonna – with
his *Secondo libro de' madrigali . . . a quattro voci* (1579), which opens with just
such a devotional text. This was evidently intended as a positive response to
the crusade against the indecency of profane madrigals undertaken by Carlo
Borromeo in his pastoral visit to the diocese of Cremona in the Holy Year of
1575.[15]

2 The *Sacrae cantiunculae tribus vocibus* (1582)

In a city so zealously committed to the post-Tridentine ideals of the Counter-
Reformation, it is not surprising that the young Monteverdi – he was only
fifteen – should have made his entrance into print with sacred and devotional
works. His *Sacrae cantiunculae tribus vocibus* was printed in Venice by Angelo
Gardano in 1582 (the dedication is dated 'Cremonae Kal. Augusti MDLXXXII',
i.e. 1 August). It contains 23 short motets for three voices (three divided into
a *prima* and a *secunda pars*)[16] to Latin texts taken for the most part from the
Vulgate, from the Roman and Ambrosian Breviaries and from the Roman
Missal. The first motet, for the Feast of St Stephen, was clearly an act of
homage to the canon Don Stefano Canini Valcarenghi, under whose protection 'Claudinus Monsviridus' – so the dedication is signed – made his debut in
print: we should not forget that dedicators and dedicatees were generally
joined by ties of patronage which, if not already in force, were at least desired.
The contents are:

1 'Lapidabant Stephanum', Response for Matins and Chapter for
   Nones for the Feast of St Stephen, first Martyr (26 December)
2 'Veni sponsa Christi', Magnificat antiphon for First Vespers of the
   Common of Virgins (the Feast of St Helen)
3 'Ego sum pastor bonus', Magnificat antiphon for Second Vespers for
   the Second Sunday after Easter

4   'Surge propera amica mea', *Song of Solomon*, ii: 10–12 (liturgical occasion not identified; for a Marian feast?)

5   'Ubi duo vel tres congregati fuerint', Magnificat antiphon for *Feria tertia* of the Third Week of Lent

6   'Quam pulchra es et quam decora amica mea', *Song of Solomon*, vii: 6, 2, 10, 14 (liturgical occasion not identified; for a Marian feast?)

7   'Ave Maria gratia plena', *Luke*, i: 28 (liturgical occasion not identified; for a Marian feast?)

8   'Domine pater et Deus', not identified

9a   'Tu es pastor ovium', Magnificat antiphon for First Vespers of the Feast of St Peter and St Paul, Apostles (29 June)

  b   'Tu es Petrus', fifth antiphon for Lauds for the Feast of St Peter and St Paul, Apostles (29 June)

10a   'O magnum pietatis opus', first antiphon for Lauds for the Feast of the Finding of the Holy Cross (3 May)

  b   'Eli clamans spiritum patri', *Mark*, xxvii: 46, 51; *Luke*, xxiii: 46; *John*, xix: 34 (liturgical occasion not identified; perhaps as 10a)

11   'O crux benedicta', Magnificat antiphon for Second Vespers for the Feast of the Exaltation of the Holy Cross (14 September)

12   'Hodie Christus natus est', Magnificat antiphon for Second Vespers for Christmas

13a   'O Domine Jesu Christe adoro te', not identified (meditation on Christ crucified)

  b   'O Domine Jesu Christe adoro te', not identified (meditation on Christ crucified)

14   'Pater venit hora clarifica filium tuum', antiphon for *Feria quarta in rogationibus* for the vigil of the Feast of the Ascension

15   'In tua patientia possedisti animam tuam', Magnificat antiphon for First Vespers for the Feast of St Lucy (13 December)

16   'Angelus ad pastores ait', third antiphon for Lauds for Christmas

17   'Salve crux pretiosa', first antiphon of Lauds for the Feast of St Andrew, Apostle (30 November)

18   'Quia vidisti me Thoma credidisti', antiphon for First and Second Vespers for the Feast of St Thomas, Apostle (21 December)

19   'Lauda Syon salvatorem', first and penultimate strophe of the sequence (attributed to Thomas Aquinas) for the Feast of Corpus Christi

20   'O bone Jesu illumina oculos meos', not identified (with a citation of *Luke*, xxiii: 46)

21   'Surgens Jesus Dominus noster', antiphon of Lauds for *Feria tertia in albis*

22   'Qui vult venire post me abneget se', Magnificat antiphon for Second Vespers of the *Commune unius martyris*

23   'Iusti tulerunt spolia impiorum', not identified

3 The *Madrigali spirituali a quattro voci* (1583)

The *Sacrae cantiunculae* were followed in the next year (1583) by the *Madrigali spirituali a quattro voci*, printed, according to the title-page, 'in Brescia by Vincenzo Sabbio, at the request of Pietro Bozzola, bookseller in Cremona'. Monteverdi signed the dedication to Alessandro Fraganesco 'from Cremona on the last day of July MDLXXXIII'. All the texts are taken from Fulvio Rorario's *Rime spirituali* (Venice, Guerra, 1581).

1	'Sacrosanta di Dio verace imago' (*ottava rima*)
2a	'L'aura del ciel sempre feconda spiri' (sonnet)
b	'Poi che benigno il novo cant'attende'
3a	'Aventurosa notte, in cui risplende' (sonnet)
b	'Serpe crudel, se i tuoi primier'inganni'
4a	'D'empi martiri e un mar d'orrori varca' (sonnet)
b	'Ond'in ogni pensier ed opra santo'
5a	'Mentre la stell'appar nell'orïente' (sonnet)
b	'Tal contra Dio de la superbia il corno'
6a	'Le rose lascia, gli amaranti e gigli' (sonnet)
b	'Ai piedi avendo i capei d'oro sparsi'
7a	'L'empio vestia di porpora e di bisso' (sonnet)
b	'Ma quel mendico Lazaro, che involto'
8a	'L'uman discorso, quanto poc'importe' (sonnet)
b	'L'eterno Dio quel cor pudico scelse'
9a	'Dal sacro petto esce veloce dardo' (sonnet)
b	'Scioglier m'addita, se talor mi cinge'
10a	'Afflitto e scalz'ove la sacra sponda' (sonnet)
b	'Ecco, dicea, ecco l'Agnel di Dio'
11a	'De' miei giovenil anni era l'amore' (sonnet)
b	'Tutt'esser vidi le speranze vane'

This new collection by Monteverdi placed itself in the context of a genre which found a space that has yet to be defined in the world of the Counter-Reformation in the late sixteenth century, the spiritual madrigal (on a vernacular text exploring a sacred, moral or devotional theme).[17] Within Petrarchism there came to dominate a lyric vein which no longer sought just to evoke a generic *gravitas* of tone and accent, but which was founded on an explicit religious impulse in terms of themes and on the need for pious edification. Spiritual subjects insinuated themselves into the short-breathed lyric poem, into instructional verse, and indeed into the epic proper: from Luigi Tansillo to Gabriel Fiamma, from Celio Magno even to Tasso, all reveal the flowering of devotional poetry. As regards music, this is matched (explicitly from 1563) by the spiritualization of so pre-eminently secular a genre as the madrigal, normally a forum for sentimental subjects played out against an amorous background. Philippe de Monte, Marenzio and Giovanni

Gabrieli – among others – were to publish spiritual madrigals in the 1580s, while the next decade saw in print similar collections by Palestrina and Orlando di Lasso (the composer of, among other things, the *Lagrime di S. Pietro* on Tansillo's *ottave rime*), and even a piece by Ingegneri (in the *Canzonette spirituali* published in Rome in 1591): moreover, some of Ingegneri's spiritual madrigals 'were already hidden within his books of madrigals for four and five voices' (but published later than Monteverdi's collection).[18]

All this suggests that the cultural climate of Cremona, and of Lombardy in general, at this time must have been particularly favourable for this kind of publication, and Monteverdi's volume, commissioned by the Cremonese bookseller and publisher Pietro Bozzola, 'joined in the programme of devotional music in the vernacular promoted by the Brescian publisher Vincenzo Sabbio in the 1580s [also including Lelio Bertani and Costanzo Antegnati's collection of 1585] following the stimulus of Borromeo's Counter-Reformation movement, which was most vigorous in Lombardy'.[19] Bozzola's interest in this new collection by the young Monteverdi, and the composer's connections with a member of the important Cremonese noble family, the Fraganeschi (Alessandro, the dedicatee, was a member of the city's Council of Ten in 1588),[20] seem to suggest that Monteverdi was well integrated into Cremona's civic life.

In the dedication, Monteverdi calls these *Madrigali* 'my first labours for four voices', having just referred to the enthusiasm with which Plato praises music, a common enough *topos* of the time. Printed as usual in four separate partbooks (one for each voice), they are now almost entirely lost – only the bass part survives – so that it is difficult to make any musical assessment of them.[21] As for the subjects of the texts – in the elevated forms of the *ottava rima* and the sonnet – if one excludes No. 2 (a greeting to a prelate) they are all

> drawn from the Old and New Testament, the first represented by the story of Judith [from Matins for the fourth week of September] (No. 8), and the latter by the crucifixion (to be more precise, by a meditation on the crucifix in *ottava rima* [suitable for Good Friday], No. 1), by Christmas (No. 3), the martyrdom of St Stephen [26 December] (No. 4), the Massacre of the Innocents [28 December] (No. 5), the conversion of Mary Magdalene [whose feast is on 22 July] (No. 6), the parable of Dives and the beggar [from the Gospel for the second Thursday of Lent; the fourth Sunday after Pentecost in the Ambrosian rite] (No. 7), and from the Baptism of Christ [from the Gospel for the third Sunday after Easter; the vigil of Epiphany in the Ambrosian rite] (No. 10).[22]

4 The *Canzonette a tre voci* (1584)

In 1584, the Venetian publishers Giacomo Vincenzi and Ricciardo Amadino issued the 'first' book (so called on the title-page, but it was to be the only one) of Monteverdi's *Canzonette a tre voci*. It was his third publication in the space of three years; in publishing one collection per year the seventeen-year-old composer perhaps betrays a somewhat frenetic desire to establish himself.

In the dedication, dated 'from Cremona, the last day of October, 1584', the composer offers these his 'first canzonettas for three voices' to Pietro Ambrosini, a member of a patrician family long established in Cremona.[23] The text of the opening canzonetta in fact alludes to the surname of the dedicatee, with verse concerning the plant Ambrosia of divine origin in so far as it was the mythical food of Olympus (and the mention in the first line of the second strophe of a 'verde ramo' – 'green branch' – seems to refer to Pietro Ambrosini's youth).

Alongside the history of the madrigal in the sixteenth century runs that of lesser forms in dialect or in other languages (napolitanas, villanellas, villottas, *canzoni villanesche* and the like). They certainly should not be seen as being directly opposed to the madrigal; on the contrary, they existed in a complementary relationship to it. These lesser forms were normally strophic and for a reduced number of voices (usually three), and for the cultivated composer and his public they constituted a moment of relaxation, freed from the need for expressiveness, tending towards facility and open to dance rhythms and to the comic and grotesque. They may have partaken of the popular, but this was always seen and controlled from above. The canzonetta was certainly more stylized and elegant in tone: it came into vogue around the late 1560s, and its blandishments seem designed to be associated with the madrigal, of which it constitutes a so to speak 'simple' version. 'It is natural that the texts of Monteverdi's *Canzonette a tre voci* of 1584 all remain anonymous, given the genre's absence of literary pretensions'.[24]

    1   'Qual si può dir maggiore'
    2   'Canzonette d'amore'
    3   'La fiera vista e 'l velenoso sguardo'
    4   'Raggi, dov'è il mio bene?'
    5   'Vita de l'alma mia, cara mia vita'
    6   'Il mio martir tengo celat'al cuore'
    7   'Son questi i crespi crini e questo il viso'
    8   'Io mi vivea com'aquila mirando'
    9   'Su, su, che 'l giorno è fore'
   10   'Quando sperai del mio servir mercede'
   11   'Come farò, cuor mio, quando mi parto'
   12   'Corse a la morte il povero Narciso'
   13   'Tu ridi sempre mai'
   14   'Chi vuol veder d'inverno un dolce aprile'
   15   'Già mi credev'un sol esser in cielo'
   16   'Godi pur del bel sen, felice pulce'
   17   'Giú lí a quel petto giace un bel giardino'

18 'Sí come crescon alla terra i fiori'
19 'Io son fenice e voi sete la fiamma'
20 'Chi vuol veder un bosco folto e spesso'
21 'Hor, care canzonette'

Of these texts, all typical of the canzonetta, 'more than half ... are gathered from other collections of the same type and especially from [the] *Canzonette ... Libro primo a quattro voci* (Venice, 1581) by Orazio Vecchi',[25] whence derive Nos. 2, 4, 7, 12, 19 and 20. No. 8 had already been set by Stefano Lando (Venice, 1566); No. 9 by Giacomo Moro (Venice, 1581); No. 11 by Gian Domenico da Nola (Venice, 1569) and Giovanni Zappasorgo (Venice, 1576); No. 12 by Gian Domenico da Nola (Venice, 1570 and 1572); and No. 13 by Alessandro Romano (Venice, 1579).

Thus while entering the field of secular music, Monteverdi again proceeded with caution, choosing the none too demanding genre of the three-voice canzonetta and laying out his texts, not without some ambition, 'as a mini-*canzoniere*, with a musical dedication ('Qual si può dir maggiore', which embroiders on the name of dedicatee), an invocation ('Canzonetta d'amore') and an envoi ('Hor, care canzonette')'.[26] But this plan remains entirely external to the collection, limited as it is to the outer sections; internally, the other canzonettas follow one after the other in random order, broaching subjects which are entirely typical of this lyric genre – the beauties and the cruelty of the beloved, pastoral games, more intense eroticism (in No. 16, with the theme of the flea on the breast of the beloved, typical also of the villanella), courtly gallantry and mythological preciosity. Sometimes there emerges, more or less cryptically, a woman's name (No. 5, 'ma ria voi sete' = Maria; No. 9, 'a la bell'alba onore' = Alba; No. 14, 'chiara / luce del mondo' = Chiara; No. 17, 'Giú lí a quel petto' = Giulia),[27] but there is no narrative or emotional development: the notion of a unified *canzoniere* remains unrealized.

But for that matter, such integration was rarely apparent even those volumes containing more demanding and better appreciated madrigal compositions, towards which the young Monteverdi soon sought to turn. Here he made his debut with a volume devoted entirely to his own music, without passing through the more modest stage – often adopted – of participating in an anthology or in a madrigal book belonging to a teacher.

5 The *Madrigali a cinque voci* ... *Libro primo* (1587)

The inevitable proving ground for any composer of the second half of the sixteenth century was the madrigal, normally for five voices. It was not only the secular genre *par excellence*, but compared with sacred music, it enjoyed a much richer stylistic flexibility and structural adaptability, thus permitting the exploration of techniques that were unthinkable in sacred repertories. And although the madrigal existed within a culture – and not only a musical culture – based on the notion of the 'excellent' (the ideal model) and on imitation, it also left room for more individual stylistic characteristics.

Monteverdi seems to have planned shrewdly his first attempts at a genre which was to take up so much time in, and to be so important for, his future career. He was prepared by the graded apprenticeship of the *Sacrae cantiunculae* and the *Canzonette* for three voices, and of the *Madrigali spirituali* for four. In his dedication (dated Cremona, 27 January 1587), too, Monteverdi seems to raise his sights, for the first time looking outside his native city. He found his dedicatee in the Veronese count, Marco Verità. In offering Verità his 'first madrigals for five voices' – 'compositions so youthful' that they do not merit 'any praise other than that which one is wont to give the flowers of spring as compared with that which one gives the fruits of summer and autumn' – Monteverdi refers to the 'so many kindnesses', to his 'obligation', and to the 'favours' received from the count. Although we know nothing more of these favours and kindnesses, certainly they suggest attempts by the composer, not yet twenty, to find a position outside Cremona.

We cannot be sure whether it was Ingegneri who directed his young pupil towards Verona – although Ingegneri had not lived in his native city for years, he had maintained associations and friendships there[28] – or whether it was the fame of a musical life which vaunted, among other institutions, the celebrated salon of Count Mario Bevilacqua (for whom in the 1580s music was also written by Orazio Vecchi, Orlando di Lasso, Philippe de Monte, the Cremonese Tiburzio Massaino, and Luca Marenzio) and the Accademia Filarmonica, to which were dedicated publications by Giaches de Wert (1571), Benedetto Pallavicino (from Cremona, 1579), Luca Marenzio (1582) and Ingegneri himself (his *Quinto libro de madrigali a cinque voci* of 1587, the same year as Monteverdi's First Book). We do not know whether Count Verità also moved in these circles, but he himself was certainly a poet and patron: his literary interests are apparent in collections of poetry from the beginning of the seventeenth century (the *Ghilranda dell'Aurora* of 1608 and Carlo Fiamma's collection of madrigals published in 1610–11),[29] while he is also the dedicatee of the *Giardinetto de madrigali et canzonette a tre voci de diversi auttori* edited by Paolo Bozi (Venice, Ricciardo Amadino, 1588), Agostino Bendinelli's *Sacrarum cantionum quatuor vocibus concinendarum liber primus* (ibid., 1592) and Paolo Fonghetti's *Capricci e madrigali . . . a due voci* (Verona, Francesco Dalle Donne & Scipione Vargnano, 1598), all by Veronese musicians (there is also an instrumental canzona titled *La Verità* in the *Musica* by Giovanni Cavaccio from Bergamo, printed in Venice in 1597).

The text opening Monteverdi's First Book also contains a veiled reference to one Camilla Verità (the christian name and surname can be extracted from lines 1 and 4; 'Ch'ami la . . .' = Camilla):[30]

Ch'ami la vita mia nel tuo bel nome
par che si legg'ogn'ora,
ma tu vuoi pur ch'io mora.
Se 'l ver porti in te scritto,
acqueta co'i begl'occhi il cor afflitto,
acciò letto non sia
ch'ami la morte, e non la vita mia.

That you love my life, in your fine name / it seems always clear to read, / but you wish me to die. / If you bear the truth written in you, / console with your beautiful eyes my afflicted heart, / lest should be read / that you love my death, and not my life.

The poet of this text remains unknown, as is also the case with some ten of the poems set here; the others are divided more or less equally between Battista Guarini, Antonio Allegretti, Giovanni Maria Bonardo, Alberto Parma, Luigi Groto, Giovan Battista Strozzi and Torquato Tasso, with no particular preferences. Monteverdi could find some of these texts in similar madrigal books by composers in a Brescia–Verona ambit, reflecting a selection that 'demonstrates how the young Monteverdi moved in cultural circles that were anything but cosmopolitan'.[31] To quote Pirrotta:

> Marenzio had already used the texts of 'Ardo sí, ma non t'amo' (Guarini), 'Questa ordí 'l laccio' (G. B. Strozzi), and 'A che tormi il ben mio'. 'Ch'ami la vita mia' and 'Tra mille fiamme' appear in *De floridi virtuosi d'Italia ... libro primo* (Venice, 1583), with music by Lelio Bertani and Orazio Vecchi, respectively. 'Baci soavi e cari' (Guarini) and, once again, 'A che tormi il ben mio' are found in the second and third volumes of the same series (Venice, 1585 and 1586) with music by Paolo Masnelli. 'La vaga pastorella' appears in *Il secondo libro di madrigali a quattro voci* (Venice, 1555) by Vincenzo Ruffo and, twelve years later, as a seven-voice dialogue in *Il primo libro de madrigali a sei voci* by Teodoro Riccio (Venice, 1567). With the exception of the star Marenzio, the composers from whom Monteverdi could obtain his texts all belonged to the Lombardo–Veneto circle centred around Brescia and Verona: Vincenzo Ruffo, who was Veronese and present in Verona from 1578 to 1580; Riccio, from Brescia and for a time *maestro di cappella* of that city; Masnelli, Veronese and organist first to the Bevilacqua counts and then to Guglielmo Gonzaga, later returning to Verona as organist of the Duomo and of the Accademia Filarmonica; Orazio Vecchi, present in Brescia in 1577 and then *maestro di cappella* of Salò, whose above-mentioned *Canzonette* are dedicated to Count Mario Bevilacqua of Verona; Bertani, 'master of the music at the Cathedral of Brescia'.
>
> Also from Verona was Ingegneri, whose texts, however, Monteverdi respectfully avoided repeating. Exceptions are 'Ardo sí, ma non t'amo' (Guarini) and 'Ardi e gela a tua voglia' (Tasso), which Ingegneri composed almost contemporaneously with his pupil and published in his *Quinto libro de madrigali a cinque voci* (Venice, 1587; dedicated to the members of the Accademia Filarmonica). The texts, in this case, were quite well known, having already been used by Vecchi in his *Madrigali a sei voci libro primo* (Venice, 1583) and by Masnelli in *Il primo libro de madrigali a cinque voci* (Venice, 1586). Marenzio limited himself to using just the first text, which

had served, however, as the given theme set to music by 28 different composers in the collection *Sdegnosi ardori* (Munich, 1585).[32]

Later, Guarini's *Canzon de' baci* ('Baci soavi e cari') was also set by Marenzio (1591) and Gesualdo (1594), and 'Filli cara et amata' by Benedetto Pallavicino (1594).

As for the contents of the First Book:

1   'Ch'ami la vita mia nel tuo bel nome' (madrigal)
2   'Se per avervi ohimé donato il core' (madrigal)
3   'A che tormi il ben mio' (madrigal)
4   'Amor, per tua mercé vatten'a quella' (Giovanni Maria Bonardo: madrigal)
5   'Baci soavi e cari' (Battista Guarini: madrigal)
6   'Se pur non mi consenti' (Luigi Groto: madrigal)
7   'Filli cara et amata' (Alberto Parma: madrigal)
8   'Poi che del mio dolore' (madrigal)
9a   'Fumia la pastorella' (Antonio Allegretti: madrigal)
  b 'Almo divino raggio'
  c 'Allora i pastor tutti'
10   'Se nel partir da voi, vita mia, sento' (G. M. Bonardo: madrigal)
11   'Tra mille fiamme e tra mille catene' (madrigal)
12   'Usciam, ninfe, omai fuor di questi boschi' (madrigal)
13   'Questa ordí il laccio, questa' (Giovan Battista Strozzi: madrigal)
14   'La vaga pastorella' (madrigal)
15   'Amor, s'il tuo ferire' (madrigal)
16   'Donna, s'io miro voi giaccio divengo' (madrigal)
17   'Ardo sí, ma non t'amo' (B. Guarini: madrigal)
18   'Ardi o gela a tua voglia', *Risposta* (Torquato Tasso: madrigal)
19   'Arsi et alsi a mia voglia', *Contrarisposta* (T. Tasso: madrigal)

The texts chosen for this book are all madrigals, that is, free mixtures of seven- and eleven-syllable lines without any strophic scheme or regular rhyme: the flexibility of the metrical structure aided the task of the composer, who could proceed with the desired freedom. All of these poems are also founded on matters of love, as was usual in sixteenth-century lyric poetry, and especially in the lighter genre of the madrigal:

> since the madrigal is granted the imitation of a courteous action, we should take care not to include in it any unfortunate event ... And in another poem rather than this should we turn to lamenting a very bitter thing lost, even though our betters have often done so; and in truth, reading a madrigal on so harsh an event, it seems to me like seeing one who amuses himself by laughing and joking when honest folk stand sighing and weeping, and especially when there are therein witticisms and word repetitions, and some frigid allusions. The carolling of nymphs, the singing of birds and the triumph of the meadows will be well placed therein, and in general, acts of

love will provide it with appropriate subject-matter, but with deaths and unfortunate events removed from it, for they are too worthy of tears.[33]

In a society marked by a return to closed oligarchic structures, as in sixteenth-century Italy, and with courts and academies practising the doctrine of aristocratic *otium*, we see the revival of both the poetics and the culture of the so-called *Dolce Stil Novo* for a courtly élite. Once more, the subject-matter turns chiefly on Love, focusing on the 'cor gentile' ('courteous heart'), where it finds its only worthy position. Following the popularization of neoplatonic ideas in the *Asolani* and after the establishment of Petrarch's *Canzoniere* as the ideal model for lyric poetry – both due to Pietro Bembo at the beginning of the sixteenth century – there flourished a tradition of love poetry (or just the poetry of gallantry) that in the latter part of the century permitted the increasingly intense infiltration of bitter sensuality, of pathos, of complacent witticisms and sentimental conceits: the privileged know and can live through uncommon psychological experiences, rejecting as banal descriptive clarity (antitheses and oxymorons were used to excess in this period). The musical madrigal applied itself to such poetry, disseminating and amplifying these dominant cultural models with the penetrative force granted by its being the most serious and best qualified genre of music for entertainment.

Most of the texts set by Monteverdi in his First Book are of this lyrical, amorous type: the exceptions are few, with narrative or descriptive texts in a pastoral vein (as Nos. 9, 12 and 14) according to the usual transformative convention. The shepherdess Fumia of No. 9 originated from one Eufemia, a Neapolitan gentlewoman whose 'masterly and utterly sweet way of singing and playing'[34] Allegretti had gallantly chosen to praise, and no less gallant is No. 1 in praise of Camilla Verità.

6 *Il secondo libro de madrigali a cinque voci* (1590)

The choice of texts in Monteverdi's *Secondo libro de madrigali a cinque voci* (Venice, Angelo Gardano, 1590) instead highlights a different kind of madrigal writing: dazzling, colouristic, inlaid with images reproducing a nature that is both vivid and bright. Lyric and emotional tones recede and are replaced by a tendency to description, to painting in sound, to light-footed grace and to erotic images.

Among the poets set here, the contemporary Torquato Tasso dominates, this time unequivocally: Tasso's lyric output had already found increasing favour among musicians for some fifteen years.[35] Of the texts chosen by Monteverdi, 'Non si levava ancor' (in two *partes*), 'Dolcissimi legami', 'Non sono in queste rive' and 'Donna, nel mio ritorno' were all included in the *Gioie di rime, e prose del Sig. Torquato Tasso* (Venice, 1587), while 'three other texts

['Mentre io mirava fiso', 'Se tu mi lassi' and 'Dolcemente dormiva'] had appeared a year earlier in *Delle rime et prose del Sig. Torquato Tasso. Parte quarta* (Venice, 1586) by the same publisher'.[36]

1a	'Non si levav'ancor l'alba novella' (Torquato Tasso: madrigal)
b	'E dicea l'una sospirando allora'
2	'Bevea Fillide mia' (Girolamo Casoni: madrigal)
3	'Dolcissimi legami' (T. Tasso: madrigal)
4	'Non giacinti o narcisi' (G. Casoni: madrigal)
5	'Intorno a due vermiglie e vaghe labbra' (madrigal)
6	'Non sono in queste rive' (T. Tasso: madrigal)
7	'Tutte le bocche belle' (Filippo Alberti: madrigal)
8	'Donna, nel mio ritorno' (T. Tasso: madrigal)
9	'Quell'ombr'esser vorrei' (G. Casoni: madrigal)
10	'S'andasse Amor a caccia' (T. Tasso: madrigal)
11	'Mentr'io miravo fiso' (T. Tasso: madrigal)
12	'Ecco mormorar l'onde' (T. Tasso: madrigal)
13	'Dolcemente dormiva la mia Clori' (T. Tasso: madrigal)
14	'Se tu mi lasci, perfida, tuo danno' (T. Tasso: madrigal)
15	'La bocca onde l'asprissime parole' (Enzo Bentivoglio: *ottava rima*)
16	'Crudel, perché mi fuggi' (Battista Guarini: madrigal)
17	'Questo specchio ti dono' (G. Casoni: madrigal)
18	'Non m'è grave il morire' (Bartolomeo Gottifredi: madrigal)
19	'Ti spontò l'ali, Amor, la donna mia' (F. Alberti: madrigal)
20	'Cantai un tempo, e se fu dolce il canto' (Pietro Bembo: sonnet quatrain)

This is the last of Monteverdi's printed collections in which the composer styles himself 'cremonese' and 'discepolo del sig. Ingegneri', and as with its predecessor, the Second Book bears a dedication to someone not from Cremona, the 'Most Illustrious Lord Iacomo Ricardi, President of the Most Excellent Senate, and of the Council of His Catholic Majesty in Milan'. If in the case of the dedication of the First Book to Marco Verità one can suggest an attempt to gain entrance into Veronese circles, now there is no doubt that Monteverdi was searching for a position outside his native city. Indeed, the dedication refers, amid the twisted locutions of a not entirely clear rhetoric, to a trip made by Monteverdi to Milan (perhaps in 1589, given that the dedication is dated Cremona, 1 January 1590) and to his having met, among others, Giacomo Ricardi, who was appointed president of the Milanese senate in that same 1589.[37] Monteverdi says that he had presented to Ricardi his First Book of madrigals and had also performed before him as a string-player, giving proof of his varied skills as a composer and instrumentalist:

> Thus I felt in the deepest part of my heart, my most illustrious lord and patron (I do not know from what influence), as soon as I was invited to come to bow before you, when I was in Milan, shoot rays of flaming respect

towards you, that I burned to dedicate myself to you; nor was it a marvel if, when I came under your gaze and you showered over me those so great and so humane and most illustrious words and manners, nay most precious pearls, I gained a thirst beyond all measure. And since by the singular proportion of your intellect I saw you fix your refined senses on the feeble movement of my hand on the *viola*, and to take delight in it, thus not knowing how to raise my weak fortune to such high sights except with tender reverence and with harmonic deeds, it was right, just as the first was freely shown to you by me, that so too also this new musical fruit of mine, such as it is, be consecrated to you...

II

Mantua

7 Mantua

It is clear that by the end of the 1580s, Monteverdi had more than once sought employment outside his native city, first in Verona, then in Milan. In the end, he found it in Mantua, at the Gonzaga court and as a string-player (he had presented himself to Giacomo Ricardi in that same capacity during his visit to Milan). We do not know for sure when Monteverdi began working in Mantua; however, it was after 1 January 1590, the date of the dedication of the Second Book of madrigals, which makes no mention of it. The first notice of his new position is in the dedication to Duke Vincenzo Gonzaga of Monteverdi's *Terzo libro de madrigali a cinque voci*, dated Mantua, 27 June 1592, where Monteverdi recalls 'that day, Most Serene Prince, when to my rare good fortune I came to serve Your Highness ... with the most noble practice of the *viola* which opened the fortunate gate of your service' and notes how 'my skill flowered for you in playing the *viola* ...'. In years to come, Monteverdi occasionally referred to the length of his stay in Mantua, but without resolving the matter once and for all. In a letter to Annibale Chieppio dated Cremona, 2 December 1608 (L.6),[1] he speaks of 'nineteen consecutive years'; and some days before, in a petition to Duchess Leonora dated Cremona, 27 November 1608, his father Baldassarre Monteverdi recalled the 'nineteen years in which he has found himself in the service of the Most Serene Lord Duke of Mantua' (see p. 100). But in another letter perhaps to Annibale Iberti dated Venice, 6 November 1615 (L.17), he mentions the 'course of 21 years' spent at court; and in the dedication of the *Selva morale e spirituale* (dated Venice, 1 May 1641), he refers to a 'period of 22 continuous years'. Given that Monteverdi left Mantua for good in July–August 1612, calculating backwards would suggest in the first and third cases that he assumed his post at the beginning of 1590, and in the second, 1591.

When Monteverdi arrived in Mantua around the age of 22, Vincenzo I Gonzaga, son and heir of Guglielmo Gonzaga and Leonora of Austria, was (from September 1587) the fourth duke (and the second of Monferrato). Guglielmo Gonzaga had demonstrated extreme skill and resolve throughout his reign, which lasted for just over 30 years (the previous duke, Francesco – Guglielmo's brother – had died in 1550, but given that the heir to the throne was a minor, Ercole Gonzaga had initially assumed the regency for several years). The separate and distant Marquisate of Monferrato had been finally acquired just a few years before, in practice from the Treaty of Cateau-Cambrésis (1559): Emperor Charles V had granted the fiefdom of the Paleologi family – whose male line had become extinct in 1533 – to the Gonzagas in 1536, despite the claims of Savoy and the Marquises of Saluzzo on the grounds of family ties. Guglielmo's constant concern, in the years to follow, was on the one hand to thwart the intrigues of Emanuele Filiberto of Savoy to take possession of Monferrato, and on the other, to establish the Gonzaga's absolute control over its recalcitrant subjects, and particularly the inhabitants of Casale. Acting with sagacity, and severely as needs be, Guglielmo succeeded in taming their insubordination, imposing the exemplary punishment of removing their municipal freedoms (in 1569). To sanction his new rule, Monferrato was elevated to the status of a duchy by imperial decree in 1575: thus as well as being third duke of Mantua, Guglielmo could call himself first duke of Monferrato.

Although the issue of Monferrato invoked various degrees of hostility – which at times flared up critically – in the case of Mantua, Guglielmo's rule was more magnanimous and prudent. Given that his foreign policy was founded on maintaining good relations with his neighbours (the Republic of Venice, adjoining Mantua to the north, the Dukes of Milan to the east, and the Farnese (Parma) and Estense (Ferrara) to the south), these were cemented where possible by shrewd dynastic marriages. Thus in the case of Guglielmo's children, Margherita married Alfonso II d'Este in 1579, and Vincenzo, the heir to the throne, married Margherita Farnese in 1581. Guglielmo himself had married the Habsburg Leonora of Austria in 1561, a wedding reflecting the Mantuan political allegiance to the Empire initiated by his father and uncles; and indeed his other daughter, Anna Caterina, married Ferdinand of Austria in 1582.

As for home affairs, Guglielmo began an extensive task of administrative reform with the aim of placing the remaining civic institutions of Mantua under the control of the ducal administration, while at the same time rendering more effective the operation of the Gonzaga's bureaucratic machinery: justice and financial matters were allocated to the newly instituted Senato di Giustizia (1571) and Magistrato Camerale (1573) respectively, the chancellery was made more efficient, the archive reordered, and the mercenary armed forces replaced by troops enlisted within the state. Guglielmo's intelligent protection of commerce and trade, and likewise his similar spirit of tolerance towards the hardworking Jewish community, permitted indirectly the enriching of the Gonzaga coffers through taxes and duties; and the duke did not hesitate to increase them still further by selling a number of feudal titles within the newly created Duchy of Monferrato.

Only in the case of papal interference, a reflection of post-Tridentine activity and of the Church's attempt above all to recover control of all the

Italian states, was the Duke of Mantua forced to submit to outside control; he also yielded to the installation of the Jesuits (in 1584), but not without having sought to defend his own sovereignty against the intrusion of the Inquisition. But the climate of the Counter-Reformation was apparent in Mantua even before the devotional and charitable activities cultivated by Guglielmo during the last years of his life (and probably encouraged by his wife): witness the output of figurative artists moving in court circles, whose work is predominantly based on sacred subjects or on moralizing allegories, reinforced by earlier Mannerist tendencies. The most time-consuming architectural work of the prefect of the ducal buildings, Giovan Battista Bertani (who held the post from 1549 to 1576), was also focused on the sacred: the Palatine church of S. Barbara was begun in early 1563 and was consecrated in the next year (although work continued on the building until 1570). Similarly, on 29 September 1582, a great procession headed by Carlo Borromeo placed in this church the relic of the patron saint's rib, which had been brought solemnly from Venice.

A true sovereign of the (albeit late) Renaissance, Guglielmo added to his well-rounded skills in government artistic interests developed both through commissions and patronage and through his own activities, given that he himself – as we shall see – was both a poet and a musician. Thus building activity at court continued at a hectic pace under Bertani's direction, who began the task of linking together various parts of the city built in different periods: this was systematically continued under Duke Vincenzo I by Antonio Maria Viani (prefect at the beginning of 1591 and then from 1595 until his death, which occurred between 1632 and 1637). Also, it was due to Bertani that the first fixed court theatre was constructed (in 1549), where troupes of actors frequently performed. Meanwhile, in another field of the arts the purchases for the ducal art gallery grew larger, with the collection increased by works by masters from both past and present: for example, Veronese and Tintoretto both had connections with Mantua. Nor did Guglielmo neglect to encourage local activity both in literary circles (as is witnessed indirectly by the flourishing of the presses of Ruffinello, Filoponi and Osanna) and in artistic ones: as a result, Vasari could rightly state, in the second edition of his *Vite*, 'In short, compared with when I saw Mantua before, now that I have seen it again in this year 1566, it is so much more adorned and beautiful that if I had not seen it, I would not have believed it. And what is more, artists have multiplied and continue still to multiply there.'[2]

In the year of Guglielmo's death (1587), Raffaello Toscano published at the press of Francesco Osanna his *L'edificazione di Mantova*, a poem which celebrated the epic story of the house of Gonzaga, and the men and the works of art bringing fame to a duchy which was then enjoying one of the most distinguished periods of its history. But if Guglielmo had founded the splendour of his reign on solid political and economic bases, his son Vincenzo was not to act in like manner: he was more inclined to a luxuriously chivalric lifestyle than to the art of government. Unlike his father, who had been hindered by physical deformity (he was a hunchback), Vincenzo repeatedly sought military glory, even if with only dubious success (witness the three campaigns in Hungary against the Turks from 1595 to 1601). But he certainly gained more distinguished results in amorous endeavours and in courtly life, which under his reign reached unparalleled heights of brilliance, if only at the expense of an ever more worrying depletion of the once rich (in Guglielmo's times) ducal coffers.

Vincenzo certainly acted according to his different character, but perhaps after his father's death the new duke was to some extent reacting against his authoritarian personality. In place of the cautious liberality of his father in matters artistic, Vincenzo initiated prodigious acts of patronage marked by his anxiety for pre-eminence. His wish to act 'in the grand manner' clearly dictated the protection offered to Tasso and the longlasting attempts to stage the most important theatrical work by another celebrated contemporary – Guarini's *Il pastor fido* – which finally bore fruit in 1598 with memorable results, so memorable as later to have the services of the ducal architect and scene-designer Viani sought outside Mantua. Similarly, witness the recruiting of painters such as Federico Zuccari together with Rubens and Pourbus, and the feverish round of entertainments (comedies adorned with splendid *intermedi*, tournaments, ballets) which would later find significant resonance in the 1608 wedding festivities. At the centre of Mantuan – but also Ferrarese – academic life, Vincenzo was to give a new impulse to the civic assembly of the Accademia degli Invaghiti, which he transferred to the court where it was to prepare its best-known and most important entertainment, the opera *Orfeo*, for which music was provided by the *maestro di cappella* of the ducal chapel, Monteverdi.

The Venetian ambassador, Francesco Contarini, presented the following account of Mantua to his senate on 3 October 1588.[3]

This city [of Mantua] is 4½ miles in circumference. It is surrounded by the lake formed by the River Mincio; although this lake produces bad air in the summer, nevertheless it acts as the greatest of fortresses. For its wealth of many beautiful and great palaces, the city is most pleasant, and particularly for its spacious streets, which are long and wondrously straight. It has 40,000 inhabitants, of which a fifth are Jews who, given that they are the providers of duties and merchandise, are of great utility and benefit to the lord duke, for the nobles, even though they are rich (and some of them have an income of up to 10,000 ducats per annum), do not wish to attend to such affairs. Its countryside is 30 miles long and 20 wide, all plentiful and inhabited, numbering therein 80,000 people, of which 6,000 are described as soldiers; although they do not achieve great success, the duke does not rest from exercising them so that they might overcome their native ineptitude ... His state adjoins Verona, Brescia, Mirandola, Ferrara and Parma ... From this duchy, which is an imperial fiefdom, the lord duke takes 200,000 ducats per annum, that is, 50,000 from his possessions, 20,000 from the mills and the rest from taxes. [The present duke] received on the death of his father, Lord

Duke Guglielmo, 1,700,000 doubloons ... I will only say that Vincenzo Gonzaga was the son of Duke Guglielmo, and he is the head of this family and is now duke of Mantua and Monferrato. Given that his exterior features are very well known to Your Most Excellent Lordships, I will speak only of his interior ones, among which shines forth principally his liberality and humanity, for which he has until now gained both the reputation of being the most splendid duke to have been in that city and the universal love as much of the nobles as of the people, having increased his bodyguard, made many gifts and lifted many taxes, also behaving towards his subjects with much affability, but in a manner that he is honoured, feared and revered by all. He listens with great patience to the requests and grievances of all, and to their supplications, which was not done by his father, and which therefore made him as disliked as the son is kind and pleasing. He delights greatly in hunting, in which he spends almost all his time, wishing to kill the wild animals with his own hands and not without personal danger, even though it is a matter of his own life. From this one can understand his own inclination towards the military, of which he is so enamoured that he does not think or speak of anything else, and thus he seeks the occasion to fulfil this his keenest desire ... He took for a wife the sister of the Duke of Parma, whom he loved so ardently that although for a whole year he could not consummate the marriage with her, he did not say a word to anyone, until his father, having heard that the princess had been treated by doctors on other occasions and interrogating her with his customary astuteness, revealed her impotence. Whenceforth, having tried all remedy through doctors and medicines (since she was happier rather to die than to be deprived of intimacy with her husband), with papal dispensation he joined in wedlock with the daughter of Grand Duke Francesco of Tuscany, with a dowry of 300,000 ducats, with whom he has had two male sons to his infinite delight, seeing his succession firm and fixed ... The lord duke possesses, as well as the duchy of Mantua, the marquisate of Monferrato, an imperial fiefdom located, like Meso-potamia, between two chief rivers, the Po and the Tanaro. It is most fertile and most populous, with 200,000 inhabitants, among which are 10,000 soldiers very ready to handle any kind of faction, of whom the lord duke expects much.

As for music (which the preceding duke, Guglielmo, had enjoyed and practised in person, even to the extent of publishing his own sacred and secular settings),[4] there were several institutions in Mantua devoted to composition and performance. The *cappella* of the cathedral (S. Piero Martire), of which Ippolito Baccusi was *maestro* (until 1592, then he was replaced by Ludovico Grossi da Viadana who was in post until 1600), stood alongside that of the court, which since 1565 had been under the direction of Giaches de Wert. Wert was also required to oversee music at the ducal church of S. Barbara, which had its own unique liturgy; Gian Giacomo Gastoldi was *maestro* here from 1582 (he stayed in this post until 1609) and Francesco Rovigo was organist (until 1597; he was replaced by Paolo Virchi, who held the post until his death in 1610).[5] The court musicians numbered about ten singers plus several instrumentalists, including an ensemble of six or seven *viole*, of which Monteverdi was initially a member (Alessandro Striggio the elder, Amante Franzoni and the violinist Salomone Rossi, the brother or husband of the singer Madama Europa, were also associated with the court).[6] In 1597, for example, the string-players were Giovan Battista and Orazio Rubini, Francesco Barberoli, Fabrizio Frolandi, Luigi Farina, Giacomo Cattaneo and Giovan Battista Barbimoli;[7] Monteverdi is not included among them probably because at the time he was used primarily as a singer and singing-master, as we are led to understand from a note by Giovanni Cossa dated 23 September 1594, which calls him a 'singer of His Highness'.[8] Whatever the case, Monteverdi soon also found the opportunity in Mantua to show off his skills as a composer, offering to the duke his Third Book of madrigals in 1592.

8 *Il terzo libro de madrigali a cinque voci* (1592)

Monteverdi's new collection, printed in Venice by Ricciardo Amadino, seems deliberately cast in a Mantuan vein. The dedication to Vincenzo Gonzaga is paralleled by a covert reference in the opening madrigal, celebrating the initiation of love. Its 'mischievous ambiguity'[9] would not have displeased the libertine duke.

> La giovinetta pianta
> si fa più bella al sole
> quando men arder suole.
> Ma se fin dentro sente
> il vivo raggio ardente,
> dimostran fuor le scolorite spoglie
> l'interno ardor che la radice accoglie.
>   Così la verginella
> amando si fa bella
> quand'amor la lusinga e non l'offende.
> Ma se 'l suo vivo ardore
> la penetra nel cuore,
> dimostra la sembianza impallidita
> ch'ardente la radice de la vita.

The young plant / grows fairer when the sun / burns less brightly. / But if it feels within / the sun's burning ray, / the discoloured petals outside display / the internal burning felt within the root. // Thus the young maiden / in love grows fairer / when love entices and does not offend her. / But if love's bright burning / penetrates her heart / her pale face shows / that the very root of life burns.

The dedication, dated Mantua, 27 June 1592 (and which contains, as we have seen, the first evidence of Monteverdi's service at the Gonzaga court), takes up both the images of this text (the plant which after flowering yields fruit) and its symbolism (Vincenzo = the sun) to function as mere courtly homage, leaving aside its eroticism:

> From that day, Most Serene Prince, when to my rare good fortune I came to serve Your Highness, I have had no greater thought, nor more anxious care,

than to act in such a way that you can in some way see that you have not proffered your grace to a useless and lazy servant, for just as any plant which is not barren produces fruit after flowers, so in my profession of music, although with the most noble practice of the *viola* which opened the fortunate gate of your service, I do not fail in offering my due servitude, nonetheless it does not seem to me to have provided in serving you anything but flowers, but these [madrigals], being more permanent, more resemble fruit. I now dedicate them to Your Most Serene Highness with all possible reverence, entreating you that you should deign to accept them kindly even if they are perhaps bitter and insipid to your most refined taste, but yet conceived and made for you and therefore not entirely unworthy of your grace. It pleases me to hope that just as the sun draws a plant's virtue from its roots into flowers, and from flowers into fruit, so Your Most Serene Highness, whom with great reason I should call my sun both for the effects which you produce in me and for the valour which shines in you, should be such that you grant me your customary kindness, for if my skill flowered for you in playing the *viola*, with its fruits now maturing it can more worthily and more perfectly serve you.

Ferrarese and Mantuan circles also have a clear influence on Monteverdi's choice of texts here, focusing primarily on Tasso and Guarini. Among the greatest poets of the time, they both had links with the Gonzaga court, where they had stayed at different times: Guarini from December 1591 to April 1592, and Tasso for little more than a year from July 1586 (it was Vincenzo Gonzaga himself who obtained from his cousin Alfonso II d'Este Tasso's release from the hospital of S. Anna), and again from February to November 1591 (the troubled poet published in 1591 an edition of his *Rime* in Mantua at the press of Francesco Osanna).

In place of the texts from [the] *Rime*, Tasso is now represented by two cycles taken from *Gerusalemme liberata*, two sequences of three madrigals each, corresponding to an equal number of stanzas in *ottava rima* from canto XII (*ottave* 77–79) and canto XVI (*ottave* 59–60 and 63). The first sequence, 'Vivrò fra i miei tormenti e le mie cure', describes Tancredi's grief following the duel in which he has killed Clorinda, and the second 'Vattene pur, crudel', Armida's outbursts of raging invective, alternating with bewildered languour, as she is abandoned by Rinaldo. Surrounding these are less intensely dramatic texts, but still tending toward pathetic or tender expression, mostly by Guarini. The different orientation indicates the readiness with which Monteverdi became a part of the musical tendencies that by the end of the century were to lead, on the one hand, to the expressionistic violence of Gesualdo and the bold expressive and harmonic intensity of Monteverdi himself and, on the other hand, to the monodic formulations of the Florentines and to opera. It is not hard to guess the road by which the invitations that found such a ready response in his temperament reached Monteverdi. In Mantua, Giaches de Wert, who had found dramatic inspiration in Ariosto's epic even before Tasso's, was still active. In nearby Ferrara, Luzzasco Luzzaschi, whose example even the arrogant Gesualdo later claimed to have followed, dominated the musical scene.[10]

The contents of the Third Book are:

1   'La giovinetta pianta' (madrigal)
2   'O come è gran martire' (Battista Guarini: madrigal)
3   'Sovra tenere erbette e bianchi fiori' (madrigal)
4   'O dolce anima mia, dunque è pur vero' (B. Guarini: madrigal)
5   'Stracciami pur il core' (B. Guarini: madrigal)
6   'O rossignuol che in queste verdi fronde' (Pietro Bembo: canzona stanza)
7   'Se per estremo ardore' (B. Guarini: madrigal)
8a   'Vattene pur, crudel, con quella pace' (Torquato Tasso: *ottave rime*)
 b   'Là tra 'l sangue e le morti egro giacente'
 c   'Poi ch'ella in sé tornò, deserto e muto'
9   'O primavera, gioventú dell'anno' (B. Guarini: *versi sciolti*)
10   'Perfidissimo volto' (B. Guarini: madrigal)
11   'Ch'io non t'ami, cor mio' (B. Guarini: madrigal)
12   'Occhi un tempo mia vita' (B. Guarini: madrigal)
13a 'Vivrò fra i miei tormenti e le mie cure' (T. Tasso: *ottave rime*)
 b   'Ma dove, o lasso me, dove restaro'
 c   'Io pur verrò là dove sete, e voi'
14   'Lumi, miei cari lumi' (B. Guarini: madrigal)
15a '"Rimanti in pace" a la dolente e bella' (Livio Celiano = Angelo Grillo: sonnet)
 b   'Ond'ei di morte la sua faccia impressa'

9 1594-1599

The success of Monteverdi's Third Book is revealed by the fact that it was soon reprinted (by Ricciardo Amadino in Venice in 1594 and 1600; other reprints would follow); it was the first of his collections to be so treated. This success was perhaps the chief factor contributing to the fame of the composer: two years after this edition, he was asked for the first time to take part in an anthology alongside 'various excellent musicians' (according to the title-page of the print). Titled *Il primo libro delle canzonette a tre voci* (Venice, Ricciardo Amadino, 1594), this anthology was the work of the Cremonese Antonio Morsolino, dedicated (Venice, 8 June 1594) to Count Bernardino da Porto. Morsolino included eight of his own compositions, plus four canzonettas by Omobono Morsolino, one by Orazio Vecchi, four by Monteverdi ('Io ardo sí, ma 'l fuoco è di tal sorte', 'Occhi miei, se mirar piú non debb'io', 'Quante son stelle in ciel e in mar arene', 'Se non mi date aita') and four of unknown origin. Monteverdi's inclusion was perhaps encouraged by the Cremonese connection, and perhaps by his friendship with Morsolino himself.

Monteverdi's four canzonettas have also survived – minus the second *canto* part – in a manuscript (Bologna, Civico Museo Bibliografico Musicale, Q.27) which includes the whole of Morsolino's anthology, but with spiritual texts (except for those poems which could already be read, albeit somewhat tenuously, as belonging to the genre of moral lyric poetry). In the case of Monteverdi's canzonettas, for example, 'Io ardo sí, ma 'l fuoco è di tal sorte' ('I burn, yet the fire is of such a kind') becomes 'Bella fiamma d'amor, dolce Signore' ('Beautiful flame of love, sweet Lord'), and 'Quante son stelle in ciel e in mar arene' ('How many are the stars in the sky, and grains of sand in the sea') becomes 'Quante son stell'intorn'a l'aureo crine' ('How many are the stars around the golden brow'), while the texts of the other two pieces remain unchanged. (The first part of this manuscript collection, the compiler of which remains anonymous, likewise contains spiritual reworkings of Amante Franzoni's *Nuovi fioretti*, published in 1605; this, too, contains a contribution from Monteverdi, 'Prima vedrò ch'in questi prati nascano', which is subjected to similar treatment.)

In Mantua, there was plenty of opportunity for Monteverdi to present himself to the attention of the duke. His various skills as a singer, string-player – 'a new Orpheus with the sound of his *viola*, in which he had no equals'[11] – and composer were first put to a significant test in 1595, when Vincenzo, alone among the Italian princes apart from the Pope, decided to respond to the call of Habsburg Emperor Rudolph II for a league against the Turks, who were posing an ever more serious threat to Europe from Hungary. On more than one occasion, Vincenzo had been on the point of realizing those chivalric ideals which he found idealized on an epic scale in *Gerusalemme liberata*: even if Lodovico Arrivabene, a court *letterato*, predicted in general terms that Vincenzo would become the champion of a new crusade in the Holy Land,[12] the duke might more conveniently and more immediately have practised his ideal of a holy war against the Huguenots in France (where he was summoned by his uncle, Ludovico Gonzaga di Nevers). But Duke Vincenzo responded to the call of Rudolph II, which was echoed by distressed appeals from the Pope, sending three companies of arquebusiers on horseback commanded by Count Carlo de' Rossi: the expedition, in which the duke decided to participate personally, left Mantua at the end of June 1595.[13]

While the cavalry went directly to the camp of the imperial troops at Gran, the duke made a more comfortable journey, passing through Trent, Innsbruck, Otting, Linz, Prague and Vienna, and enjoying the frequent celebrations prepared for him by his hosts. Vincenzo travelled in the company of a court that was reduced and yet complete: musical requirements were to be met by a small *cappella* comprising four musicians, at the head of which, perhaps precisely because of his many varied skills, was Monteverdi, who is specified in the papers of the expedition as 'maestro di cappella'[14] (the others were the castrato Teodoro Bacchino and the two basses Giovan Battista Marinoni and Serafino [?Terzi]).[15] Even after he had joined the camp of Archduke Matthias, Vincenzo did not deny himself a brilliant life, which was enlivened by the universally admired performances of his musical *cappella*.

This cannot have been used solely for sacred music as the official chronicler of the expedition, Fortunato Cardi, would have us believe, given his overriding concern to emphasize the Christian conduct of the Mantuans (a good number of Protestant forces were also present in the imperial camp).

> Here I should not fail to mention that in his pavilions, which were many and beautiful, the lord duke [Vincenzo] stayed and was served in the grand manner, for as well as the usual guard of arquebusiers which he kept around his person, he also had with him a most numerous and complete household, and in particular a large group of titled knights and gentlemen, wherefore he continually and to his great splendour maintained a most abundant table. Moreover, His Highness often sumptuously banqueted many lords and barons of the army, who for the better part of the day would come to pass the time in a friendly manner with His Highness, on whose order not just on feast days but every day four or five masses were said in his quarters, and he lived in a Catholic manner, but on the solemn [days] Vespers were sung with music by singers and an organ which he had brought with him, to the infinite pleasure not, I say, of those who were serving His Highness, but of other Catholics in the army, who gathered there, it also occurring many times that the Most Serene Archduke had music performed for his entertainment by the same singers.[16]

In November of that same year, 1595, the Mantuans, who took a leading role in the capture of Viszgrad in September, returned home after passing through Vienna, Styria, Karinthia and the Republic of Venice. Even laying aside the evident discomforts of the trip, it also placed financial burdens on Monteverdi (who then received a wage of 12½ scudi per month),[17] forcing on him unwanted extras in terms of expense. As he wrote to Annibale Chieppio some fifteen years later (L.6, Cremona, 2 December 1608): 'I tell Your Most Illustrious Lordship that the fortune I have known in Mantua for nineteen consecutive years has given me occasion to call it inimical to me, and not friendly; because if it has done me the favour of receiving from the Most Serene Lord Duke the honour of being able to serve him in Hungary, it has also done me the disfavour of saddling me with an extra burden of expense from that journey, which our poor household feels almost to this very day.'

Some time after the return of the expedition to Hungary, the *maestro di cappella*, Giaches de Wert, died (on 6 May 1596), and in his place was appointed the Cremonese Benedetto Pallavicino, who was senior to Monteverdi in terms both of his age and of his career (he had been in Mantua from 1582, and he had to his credit various collections of madrigals, plus contributions to anthologies). It was probably for this reason that Monteverdi enjoyed closer relations with Ferrarese circles in these years: perhaps he hoped to find in Ferrara that more prestigious and responsible post that seemed to be denied him at Mantua, for how long he could not tell. Even earlier, compositions by Monteverdi had been sent expressly to the court of Ferrara by Valeriano Cattaneo, who on 19 December 1594 had written from Mantua to Duchess Margherita Gonzaga, sister of Vincenzo and wife of Alfonso II d'Este:

'In conformity with the orders of Your Highness, I am sending four canzonettas by messer Claudio Monteverde, a musician here of the lord duke. The
pieces are similar to those already sent by Don Bassano [Cassola, a musician in
Mantuan service], as far as one can remember. However, in order to provide
for the greater satisfaction of the Lady Duchess of Urbino [Lucrezia d'Este], if
Her Highness will send texts, and also some indications of the style that would
be to her taste, she will be served to the limits of our abilities.'[18] Monteverdi
had also considered submitting some of his compositions to Duke Alfonso,
but the death of the duke (without heirs in 1597, which led to the annexation
of Ferrara to the Papal States in the next year) meant that his plan bore no
fruit: it also made him lose all hope of a new position there. 'Since in past years
I was unable to present some of my madrigals in manuscript to the Most
Serene Alfonso, Duke of Ferrara, because of the intervention of his death . . . ',
wrote the composer in the dedication of his *Quarto libro de madrigali a cinque
voci* (1603). However, this collection was offered to the members of the
Accademia degli Intrepidi of Ferrara, 'a most noble gathering of knights [and]
friends': 'and finding myself not only loving all of you with devotion but also
eternally obliged for the many favours received with diverse honourable
demonstrations towards me and towards my offspring such as they are, I have
thought it fitting not to depart from the same city, to which I am much
inclined, and to acknowledge the same knights my lords with all due gratitude, presenting and dedicating to you as I do with all the affection of my soul
both them and other new madrigals now printed'. Moreover, it was precisely
in Ferrara, in the last years of the century, that Giovanni Maria Artusi heard
those madrigals by Monteverdi which triggered his polemic against the
composer.

Another sign of Monteverdi's increasing fame is his first appearance in an
anthology printed outside Italy, the *Fiori del giardino di diversi eccellentissimi
autori* (Nuremberg, Paul Kaufmann, 1597). Monteverdi appears alongside
such musicians as Marenzio, Monte, Hassler, Vecchi, the Gabrielis, Wert,
Baccusi, Pallavicino, Rovigo and Gastoldi (the last five worked in Mantua).
Indeed he is among those best represented, equal with Marenzio and surpassed
only by Hassler: his contribution extends to six madrigals, five already
published – two from his Second Book ('Non si levav'ancor l'alba novella'
with its second *pars*, 'E dicea l'una sospirando allora', plus 'Dolcemente
dormiva la mia Clori') and three from the Third ('La giovinetta pianta',
'Sovra tenere erbette e bianchi fiori', 'Stracciami pur il core') – and one
apparently unpublished ('Ah dolente partita'), although it, too, could have
appeared in some now lost anthology, given that Kaufmann's anthology does
not generally contain unpublished works by Italian composers.

On 20 May 1599, in the Church of SS. Simone e Giuda in Mantua,
Monteverdi married Claudia Cattaneo, court singer and daughter of a colleague, the string-player Giacomo Cattaneo:

In the parish church of SS. Simone e Giuda of Mantua after having announced the banns three times and there not having emerged any impediment, was contracted the marriage of and between Signor Claudio Monteverdi and Signora Claudia Catteneo, whom I Girolamo Belledi, rector, joined in marriage, having first instructed them as required by the sacred Council of Trent: the witnesses were Signori Carlo Tommasi, Eugenio Cagnati [? = Cagnani] and Giuseppe Depretis.[19]

In two later letters referring to his marriage written after the death of his wife, Monteverdi's veiled language arouses suspicions that the duke – who enjoyed more than just the musical abilities of the female singers with whom he surrounded himself – had some special, perhaps not entirely honourable, interest in this court wedding between two of his servants. Speaking of his son Francesco, the composer calls him a 'most humble servant of Your Most Illustrious Lordship [probably Cardinal Ferdinando Gonzaga]; being (as he is) a vassal of the Most Serene House of Gonzaga, born of a father and mother who served Your Most Serene Highnesses for a long time, and of a marriage solemnized with the special consent of the Most Serene Lord Duke Vincenzo' (L.10, Cremona, 28 December 1610). Similarly, writing from Venice (to Annibale Iberti?) on 6 November 1615, he was to include among the other burdens placed upon him during his time at court 'the two sons born and bred in Mantua (for indeed Duke Vincenzo was responsible for my marriage)' (L.17).

Not 20 days after his wedding, Monteverdi was required to accompany the duke to Spa in Flanders, where Vincenzo went with his retinue to take the waters and for a pleasure-tour which would also allow him to demonstrate his pique against the Spanish after Madrid's indirect refusal to grant him the position of Governor of Flanders. They left Mantua on 7 June, heading for Trent; passing through Innsbruck, Basle and Nancy, they arrived at Spa on 10 July, where the duke and his court stayed for about a month before leaving for Lièges (11 August). They then went to Antwerp (21 August) and Brussels (29 August), leaving for Mantua on 20 September, where they arrived on 15 October 1599.[20]

From that trip, Monteverdi gained new artistic experiences (and Vincenzo perhaps his knowledge of the young Rubens, who was then in Mantua until 1608),[21] associated above all with the 'canto alla francese' ('song in the French style'). In the *Dichiaratione* which appeared as an appendix to the *Scherzi musicali* of 1607, his brother Giulio Cesare posed the rhetorical question: 'Who before him brought it [that type of song] back to Italy when he returned from the baths of Spa in the year 1599?' But in financial terms, and as usual, the composer had nothing but problems. Later, he again complained to Annibale Chieppio (L.6, Cremona, 2 December 1608): 'If fortune called me to His Most Serene Highness's service in Flanders, it also crossed me on that occasion by making my wife Claudia, living at Cremona, bring expense to our household with her maid and servant, she having at that time still only 47 lire a month from His Most Serene Highness, beyond the money my father gave me.' This echoed a request from his father to Duchess Leonora (Cremona, 27 November 1608) in which Baldassarre Monteverdi lamented of, among other things, 'having spent on the aforesaid Claudio on several occasions 500 ducats and more when he served His Most Serene Highness in Hungary, [and] in Flanders, when he came to Cremona with his wife, maid, servants, carriage and children'.[22]

10 The dispute over the 'seconda pratica'

A short while after his return from Flanders, Monteverdi became embroiled in a long and intricate controversy which although most heated in the first decade of the new century also had longer-range repercussions. It began in 1600 with the publication of *L'Artusi, overo Delle imperfettioni della moderna musica* (Venice, Giacomo Vincenti), a treatise by Giovanni Maria Artusi, canon regular of SS. Salvatore in Bologna and formerly a pupil of Zarlino in Venice. Artusi was vicar of S. Maria di Reno in Bologna from 1595 to 1598, he was then transferred to Ferrara in 1599 (as he himself says in passing in the course of the polemic, and see also his remark given below, p. 41), and he was at the Convent of Abano in 1600 when his text was printed.[23] *L'Artusi* is in the form of a dialogue between Vario, 'gentleman of Arezzo who is very skilled in music and very practised in all Italy', and the Austrian Luca 'from the city of Craic [? = Graz]' (fol. 1v): the material is divided into two 'ragionamenti' ('discussions'). The treatise seeks to demonstrate the corruptions within certain modern compositional tendencies which clearly contradict the traditional rules. In so doing, the Bolognese canon reproduces passages from madrigals (only the music, without the words) of an unnamed composer – Monteverdi – who significantly is taken as an example of the new tendencies that merit criticism: seven examples are drawn from 'Cruda Amarilli, che col nome ancora' (later published in the Fifth Book of 1605), one from 'Anima mia, perdona', and one more from 'Che se tu se' il cor mio', both likewise printed later, in the Fourth Book (1603). In the course of the dialogue, 'O Mirtillo, Mirtillo anima mia', another madrigal destined to appear in the Fifth Book, is also mentioned. According to the scenario presented by Artusi, the madrigals from which these examples were taken – all unpublished at the time – had been heard by Luca in Ferrara in a private gathering held at the house of the musician Antonio Goretti on 16 November 1598 (fol. 39r), during the period of festivities organized from 12 to 18 November for the wedding of Margherita d'Austria (we are to assume that the 'Austrian Luca' was among her retinue) and Philip III, King of Spain: this wedding took place by proxy in Ferrara Cathedral before Pope Clement VIII, who was present in the city having come to take possession of it following the death of Duke Alfonso II d'Este without heirs.

LUCA   Yesterday, sir, after I had left Your Lordship and was going towards the Piazza, I was invited by some gentlemen to hear certain new madrigals. Delighted by the amiability of my friends and by the novelty of the compositions, I accompanied them to the house of Signor Antonio Goretti, a nobleman of Ferrara, a young virtuoso and as great a lover of music as any man I have ever known. I found there Signor Luzzasco and Signor Hippolito Fiorini, distinguished men, with whom had assembled many noble spirits versed in music. The madrigals were sung and repeated, but without giving the name of the author. The texture was not unpleasing. But, as Your Lordship will see, in so far as it introduced new rules, new modes, and new turns of phrase, these were harsh and little pleasing to the ear, nor could they be otherwise; for so long as they violate the good rules − in part founded upon experience, the mother of all things, in part observed in nature, and in part proved by demonstration − we must believe them deformations of the nature and propriety of true harmony, far removed from the object of music, which, as Your Lordship said yesterday, is delectation. But in order that you may see the whole question and give me your judgement, here are the passages, scattered here and there through the above-mentioned madrigals, which I wrote out yesterday evening for my amusement.[24]

The 'passages' chosen by Artusi are the following (bar numbers follow the Malipiero edition of Monteverdi's works):

  1 'Cruda Amarilli, che col nome ancora', bars 13−14 ('ahi lasso')
2, 3 Ibid., bars 19−(20)-22 ('lasso, amaramente')[25]
4, 5 Ibid., bars 35−(36)-38 ('ma dell'aspido sordo')[26]
  6 Ibid., bars 41−42 ('e piú fera e piú fu[gace]')
  7 Ibid., bars 53−54 ('poi che col dir t'offen[do, / i' mi mor]rò tacen[do]')
  8 'Anima mia, perdona', from the fourth bar before the end to the penultimate bar ('proprio dolore')
  9 'Che se tu se' il cor mio', last three bars ('tuoi tormenti')

Artusi finds fault most of all (fol. 40v) with the dissonances − seconds and sevenths − produced between the bass and the upper parts, as in Nos. 1 (bar 13, with the soprano), 2 (bar 19, with the *quinto*), 4 (bar 36, with the alto) and 5 (bar 37, with the soprano); similarly, he later (fol. 44r) censures the sevenths in Nos. 2, 3, 4, 5, 6 and 7 for the reason that they should not be used 'in so absolute and exposed a manner'. Dissonance, then, is not itself a negative thing, but its improper use contrary to the rules is.

VARIO   I do not deny that discovering new things is not merely good but necessary. But pray tell me first why you wish to employ these dissonances as they employ them. If you do it in order to say, 'I wish them to be plainly heard, but so that the ear may not be offended', why do you not use them in the ordinary way, conforming to reason, in accordance with what Adriano [Willaert], Cipriano [de Rore], Palest[r]ina, Porta, Claudio [Merulo], [Andrea] Gabrielli, Gastoldi, Nanino, Giovanelli, and so many, many others in this academy have written? Have they perhaps failed to cause asperities to be heard? Look at Orlando Lasso, Filippo di Monte, and Giaches Vuert [Wert], and you will find full heaps of them.[27]

The diminished fifth formed by the tenor and bass in No. 3 (bar 21) is criticized because it is unprepared, after the rest in the bass: 'All composers have employed this interval, but in a different way. I say "in a different way", because although they employ it in the first and second parts of the bar, called *arsis* and *thesis*, they do not use it in either case after a "privation" of sound [i.e. a rest], but precede it with a sixth or some other consonance'.[28] On the whole, Artusi reaffirms Zarlino's principle of dissonance as a non-autonomous entity, which must necessarily arrive from a consonance and resolve to another.

LUCA   The truth is that all the arts and sciences have been brought under rules. But still, since dissonances are employed in harmonies as non-essentials, it seems that musicians are entitled to use them at their pleasure.

VARIO   I do not deny that dissonances are employed as non-essentials in compositions, but I say nonetheless that, being by nature contrary to consonance, they can by no means agree in the same way and should not be employed in the same way. Consonances are used freely in harmonies, by leap or by step, without distinction, but dissonances, being of another nature, must be considered in another way.[29]

Moreover, Luca continues, the moderns 'in modulating their parts, it seems to me that they use certain [descending] intervals that are inconvenient and far from good modulation',[30] such as the diminished fifth (C–F♯, G–C♯), the diminished fourth (C–G♯, F–C♯) and the minor seventh (D–E, C–D), prompting a deplorable confusion of *genera* between the diatonic and the chromatic:

LUCA   What do you think: should we believe that these compositions are indeed diatonic, or diatonic modulation, or rather should we say that this is a mixture of diatonic and chromatic modulation together?

VARIO   One is obliged to say that this is in fact a modulation mixing a chromatic note with a diatonic one, but that such a modulation is to be allowed or disallowed, I would say that it was disallowed.[31]

The use of accidentals, and of irregular cadences, further compromises modal structure, as occurs in 'O Mirtillo, Mirtillo anima mia':

LUCA   That is precisely what I had in mind to ask you, for in one of these madrigals there are more cadences on C than on G, and yet they make the madrigal out to be in the seventh mode.

VARIO   ... nor is it fitting to begin the song [*cantilena*] in the seventh mode and then have it in the middle assume that form of the twelfth or eighth mode, then make it end in the seventh, for this manner of composition is an impertinence.

LUCA   I heard a madrigal not many days ago which began on a note [*corda*] of the twelfth mode with B flat; then, if I remember it well, it was changed through B natural and became the first mode; and it seems to me that the words of the madrigal were 'O Mirtillo' by Guarini, taken from *Il pastor fido*. This gave me much to think about; nor do I know how one who makes a profession of being a worthy man can let himself fall into such imperfections

which are known to children from the moment when they begin to put their
lips to the fount of Helicon.[32]

Such blameworthy transgressions of the golden rules fixed by tradition
(and carved in stone in Zarlino's *Istitutioni harmoniche*, published in Venice in
1558) are justified by the 'moderns' by invoking the need for expression:

VARIO   Well said. But how can they excuse and palliate these imperfections, which
        could not possibly be more absurd?
LUCA   Absurd? I do not know how you can defend that opinion of yours. They call
        absurd the things composed in another style and would have it that theirs is
        the true method of composition, declaring that this novelty and new order
        of composition is about to produce many effects which ordinary music, full
        of so many and such sweet harmonies, cannot and never will produce. And
        they will have it that the sense, hearing such asperities, will be moved and
        will do marvellous things.
VARIO   Are you in earnest or are you mocking me?
LUCA   Am I in earnest? It is rather they who mock those who hold otherwise.[33]

It is significant that the 'moderns', in their search for expressiveness, should
have availed themselves of techniques specifically associated with vocal performance (this also applies to Luzzaschi) as regularly used by singers as
extemporized ornamentation of a given melodic line to underline a word, a
conceit or an interjection. In the examples cited by Artusi, Monteverdi uses (as
signifiers, associated with specific emotional effects, and not just as generally
decorative embellishments) figures proper to that 'affettuosa' ('affective')
performing practice which Ludovico Zacconi called 'cantar con gratia'
('singing with grace'): *accenti* ('accents'), rapid coloratura, *supposizioni* ('sup-
positions'; i.e. ascending or descending appoggiaturas) and *rotture* ('broken
passages'; i.e. avoided notes, *nota cambiata*) within the phrase:[34]

However, you have to know that the aforesaid figures [= notes] are
accompanied with some *accenti* caused by some delays and holdings of the
voice which are produced by taking one portion of a figure and attributing it
to another. And to begin to give you some insight into how these things
delight you, I say that when one has pronounced a figure, and when that
which one has to pronounce is distant from the first by a third, on the first
one should delay, which delay should not be longer than a semiminim,
whence not only should one take this semiminim from the second figure and
give it to the other, but also in holding it and ascending to its companion one
makes heard in the middle (fleetingly) something like a *semicroma* ... In this
matter, a singer should be warned that if he is singing some kind of fugue or
fantasy he should not delay on any note, so as not to break and spoil those
beautiful manners of imitation, but to sing them equally according to their
value without any ornament, so that those fugues have what they are due.
There are also other figures which because of the words have no need for any
accento, but [only] of their natural, lively force, such as when one has to sing
'Intonuit de celo Dominus' ['God called from heaven'], 'Clamavit' ['He
exclaimed'], 'Fuor fuori cavalieri uscite' ['Out, out, knights come out'], 'Al
arme al arme' ['To arms, to arms'], and many other such things, which the
prudent and judicious singer will need to judge. Thus, on the contrary, there
are also others which themselves prompt graces and pretty *accenti*, as would

be the case in singing 'dolorem meum' ['my grief'], 'misericordia mea' ['my mercy'], 'affanni e morte' ['torments and death'], which without the singer being taught them, themselves teach the manner in which they should be sung. Moreover, one is accustomed to break certain notes with some liveliness and force, which makes the greatest good effect in music, of which, wishing to give some notice, the following examples are formed.[35]

Artusi also discusses the *accento*:[36]

LUCA   Well said. But they say that all this is called grace and is an accented singing.

VARIO   I do not remember having read in any author – and countless excellent ones have written of music – that there is such a thing as accented music. I shall welcome it if you will tell me what it is, according to the pretension of these modern composers.

LUCA   They say that the *accenti* in composition have a remarkable effect and that these *accenti* occur only when a part ascends to a higher note; for example, that when four notes ascend by step, the *accento* is produced on the last note and not on the others, the voice beginning a third lower than the note on which the *accento* is to be produced and being carried gracefully to its level. But to produce good accord always, this demands the greatest discretion and judgement in the singer for its execution. Here is an example:

Examples of *accenti* are in Nos. 2, 7 and 8 of the Monteverdi extracts chosen by Artusi, and of *supposizioni* in all except No. 6, which instead presents *rotture* and *passaggi* (short scales, as in No. 7). Stripped of their embellishments (respectively *rotture* and short scales; *supposizioni*), Nos. 1 and 4–5 could emerge as given below.[37]

As regards the 'canto accentato' ('accented song') of No. 7, Artusi adds:

VARIO   And if you tell me that the effect which the tenor produces in the seventh bar tends to demonstrate this manner of accented singing, I will reply that the singer does not know at what point, in the opinion and intent of the composers, he should, with discretion, 'carry the voice'. For this reason there is necessarily an error in grammar. It would be better if, when they mean that the singer should, with judgement and discretion, 'carry the voice', they introduced at that point some sign indicating their wish, in order that, perceiving the need, he might produce better accord and more pleasing harmony than he produces by singing along at his own will.

LUCA   Such an indication would not be unprofitable if one could reasonably
         discover a universal sign to indicate this manner of 'carrying the voice' to the
         singer. But while these new inventors are exhausting themselves in new
         inventions to make this manifest, they go on scattering these passages
         through their compositions, which, when sung or sounded on different
         instruments by musicians accustomed to this kind of accented music, full of
         things left implicit, yield a not unpleasing harmony at which I marvel.

VARIO   This may result from two things. First, that the singers do not sing what is
         written, but 'carry the voice', sustaining it in such a way that, when they
         perceive that it is about to produce some bad effect, they divert it elsewhere,
         carrying it to a place where they think it will not offend the ear. Second, that
         which sounds good to the ear [*lo eccellente sensibile*] corrupts the sense,
         meaning simply that the ear is so taken up with the other parts that it does
         not fully perceive the offence committed against it (as it would if the
         composition were for two, three, or four voices), while reason, which knows
         and distinguishes the good from the bad, perceives right well that a decep-
         tion is wrought on the sense, which receives the material only in a certain
         confused way, even though it borders on truth. This manifestly is clearly
         seen when the organist adds to his other registers that of the twelfth; here it is
         reason and not the ear that discovers the many dissonances which occur
         among them.

LUCA   It is known that the ear is deceived, and to this these composers, or new inventors, apply themselves with enthusiasm. They seek only to satisfy the ear and with this aim toil night and day at their instruments to hear the effect which passages so made produce; the poor fellows do not perceive that what the instruments tell them is false and that it is one thing to search with voices and instruments for something pertaining to the harmonic faculty, another to arrive at the exact truth by means of reason seconded by the ear.[38]

Therefore, even in the *res facta* (the written musical text) Monteverdi, and with him the 'moderns', keep uppermost in the mind contemporary diminution practice – vocal and also instrumental – and thus matters which were usually relevant only to extemporized performance: this provides another source of disapproval for Artusi, who holds as good and proper not what appeals to the ear ('lo eccellente sensibile') but that which reason judges as conforming to traditional norms.

LUCA   They think only of satisfying the sense, caring little that reason should enter here to judge their compositions.

VARIO   If such as these had read the ninth chapter of the first book of Boethius and the first chapter of his fifth book, and the first chapter of the first book of Ptolemy, they would beyond doubt be of a different mind.

LUCA   They do not even think of looking at the volumes of Boethius. But if you would know what they say, they are content to know how to string their notes together after their fashion and to teach the singers to sing their compositions, accompanying themselves with many movements of the body, and in the end they let themselves go to such an extent that they seem to be actually dying – this is the perfection of their music.[39]

Artusi is equally critical – if somewhat more mildly – of another technique of improvised singing, *contrappunto alla mente*, according to which the various voices must take care primarily each to harmonize on its own account with the tenor part:

LUCA   These musicians observe the rule that the part forming the dissonance with the lowest part has a harmonic correspondence with the tenor, so that it accords with every other part while the lowest part also accords with every other part. Thus they make a mixture of their own.

VARIO   I see that this rule of theirs is observed in the first, fourth, fifth, sixth, and seventh bars. But in the sixth bar the quavers have no harmonic relation, either with the bass or with the tenor. With what sort of rule do you think they can save themselves?

LUCA   I do not know how they can help themselves here. I see the observance of no rule, although I believe that the quavers are the result of perceiving, with instruments, that they do not greatly offend the ear because of their rapid movement.[40]

In showering the page with all these techniques drawn from improvisatory practice (confusing, moreover, vocal and instrumental styles), according to Artusi composers should place a concern for not committing 'barbarisms' and for arranging parts which 'produce good accord' before expressive ends.[41]

Three years later, in 1603, the *Seconda parte dell'Artusi overo Delle imperfettioni della moderna musica* appeared, again from the press of Giacomo Vincenti in Venice. Here, the Bolognese canon (who had returned to his native city after having spent 1601–2 in monasteries in Piacenza and Ravenna)[42] reports his exchange of letters with one L'Ottuso Accademico (who remains unidentified), following it with more general theoretical remarks titled *Considerationi musicali*. The correspondence with L'Ottuso had taken place in Ferrara from 1599; it thus ran parallel with the preparation and publication of the first *Artusi*, with which it shares common material (the criticisms of modern tendencies), the targets under attack (passages from madrigals by Monteverdi, whose name is kept silent and replaced by the formula 'etc.') and the modes of argument. The madrigals involved here are 'Era l'anima mia' – the first twelve bars are given on p. 7[43] – and 'Ma se con la pietà non è in te spenta', the first eight bars of which are quoted in the *Considerationi* (p. 5; both madrigals were later published in Monteverdi's Fifth Book of 1605).

A statement made some years later by a person who hides behind the name of Antonio Braccino da Todi and who must have been very close to Artusi (if not Artusi himself) leads one to think that the correspondence with L'Ottuso was preceded by some letters from the Bolognese canon directly to Monteverdi, and that the latter had delegated his own response to the aforesaid academician:

> Artusi replies that it was Signor Claudio who was in the wrong, for when Artusi wrote him those letters, he wrote them full of amity and civility, and he, instead of replying in the same vein, made a response through a third person, with letters without a proper name, which then could only cause some indignation to arise in Artusi's breast, moved by which he wrote what everyone can see. And if on this occasion it were not to fill the page, indeed many pages, I would print the letters, copies of which are in my hands and which should also be in the hands of Signor Monteverde, only to clarify the truth, but on a better occasion I will do it. For now, suffice it to say that in the year 1600 Artusi exposed this composer who wished to bring into music things contrary to all others, and having been laid bare, he has never (although he has been invited and encouraged several times) said anything in response, but has always excused himself and avoided the issue, [and] having realized his error, thus he keeps his peace.[44]

For his part, Artusi had written:

> But first I say that finding myself in Ferrara in the year 1599, a letter without a proper name was given to me; however, there was a signature that said 'L'Ottuso Academico'. I then had it from reliable sources that this was a man of great authority, and because he was well versed as a musician, writing to me about some things pertaining to the songs of these modern destroyers of the good, established rules, he said in praise of that manner of composing: 'This modulation being new, for its finding with its novelty new sonorities [*concenti*] and new affects, without detaching itself from reason, even if it distances itself in a certain way from the ancient traditions of some excellent musicians'. At these words, which are still kept by me, I resolved, to give him satisfaction, to send him the following response, and my letter. However, it seems best to me before I proceed further to say that the ancient traditions were not left by the ancients without some foundation and reason

through demonstration, and argued through the very nature of the thing, and therefore I judge it problematic that this Signor Dottore says that it does not distance itself from reason, but from the ancient traditions of some excellent musicians.[45]

Of this first letter from L'Ottuso we know nothing other than the passage cited above by Artusi. As for his identity, as early as the beginning of the eighteenth century Zaccaria Tevo discounted the idea that L'Ottuso was Monteverdi himself.[46] But leaving aside the aforementioned statement by Braccino da Todi and the fact that in the exchange of letters Monteverdi is always styled as a third person (hidden behind a generic 'etc.'), in the preceding passage Artusi refers to the fact that L'Ottuso (also mentioned there as 'Sig. Dottore') practised music for pleasure and not professionally like Monteverdi. Also, on pp. 50–51 Artusi quotes fourteen examples taken from L'Ottuso's madrigals: these examples remain unidentified, but they are certainly not drawn from compositions by Monteverdi known today. Moreover, Monteverdi himself confirms, in his *Quinto libro de madrigali a cinque voci* (1605), that up to that point he had not made any public or official intervention in the polemic: 'Studious Readers, do not marvel that I am giving these madrigals to the press without first replying to the objections that *L'Artusi* has brought against some very minute details in them . . .'.[47] L'Ottuso therefore emerges not only as someone who understands music but also as a composer himself – for pleasure – and as the member of an academy (on the lines of the Ferrarese Accademia degli Intrepidi, to which Monteverdi dedicated his Fourth Book) which could, however, be a simple, non-institutional assembly of music-lovers such as gathered around Count Alfonso Fontanelli and was mentioned by Monteverdi himself. 'Now, given that he has composed many madrigals full of *fiori, fioretti, inganni, accenti, suppositi* and *artificii*, in order that they might be considered, I will present a selection sent to me from his academy',[48] says Artusi, who precisely because of the reactions from such circles could have been prompted to return to the polemic, making public his exchange of letters with L'Ottuso.

> When in the book already written by me and given to the press, the title of which is *The Artusi*, that is, on *The Art and Use of the Modern Musical Practice*, I said what seemed appropriate to me about some passages used by certain modern composers, without naming anyone, since it did not seem to me to be a civil thing to seek by name to offend those who do not offend nor give any occasion for offence, I said everything only so as to speculate on the truth, and so that the authors of similar mistakes, recognizing their error, should be satisfied, being reasonable if they could grasp and comprehend such reasons. But some of them guided by capricious humours not only have not changed their opinion, but going from bad to worse, as they say, they go about filling the pages with things that when they think, in the manner of an excellent painter, of discovering and making seen a well made figure and one proportioned in its parts, which is what those who are judicious do, they instead represent a monster similar to that which the poet of poets [Virgil] describes in the fifth book of the *Aeneid*. . . .[49]

Artusi's first reply to L'Ottuso, which cannot have been much delayed given that it is again dated 'From Ferrara, etc.', is quoted on pp. 6–11; L'Ottuso's reply, which similarly was not long awaited ('from the date of my letter to the receipt of the reply passed a month or a little more', says the Bolognese canon),[50] can be read on pp. 13–21; and Artusi's new refutation is on pp. 21–56.

As has been said, the matters under dispute are the same as before: the treatment of dissonances, incorrect intervals, the use of accidental alterations, modal ambiguity. Artusi now adds his intolerance of recitative-like declamation such as is used, for example, in the opening of 'Era l'anima mia' and 'Ma se con la pietà non è in te spenta'.

> Modulation is a movement which is made from one pitch [*suono*] to another through various intervals, but at the opening of the madrigal 'Era l'anima mia' the combined parts move now quickly and now slowly, but not through intervals, and they produce harmony [*concento*] because that fifth is divided by a middle note, which produces a minor third at the bottom and a major third at the top: therefore we have harmony without modulation of several parts joined together. We can say the same of that other madrigal 'Ma se con la pietà', where the parts stay each in the same position in terms of pitch and do not produce any interval, or do not move with an interval of voice [*o non si movono con intervallo di voce*]; thus it is necessary that here there is no modulation, and yet one hears and perceives harmony, which is that tempering of low and high as Plato said.[51]

'Era l'anima mia' begins in 'a certain amusing manner which induces men to laughter and to make fun of it, as with those *giustiniane* in the Venetian manner, to which it is very similar';[52] and at the beginning of 'Ma se con la pietà non è in te spenta', one does not know whether 'it is the beginning of a *giustiniana*, or else of a Mantuan *spifarata*'.[53]

Artusi then explains that correct vocal writing is one thing and correct instrumental writing another, in which specific irregularities can be permitted: 'It will indeed be true that in those pieces which are written for instruments, one can insert in them such intervals, for they are more suitable for use by players than by singers, for as regards having whatever interval one wants on instruments, they may be as inconvenient as can be, something which the natural voice cannot present so easily, readily and correctly'.[54] A certain interval can be 'false in voices and in modulation, but not false on the lute and the chitarrone, instruments from which these and many other intervals are drawn, and this is made apparent because in the same place where the player positions the fingers to make us hear a sixth, he places them also to make us hear this interval outside its natural notes, transposed into accidental notes'.[55] Other intervals will be 'useless to sing, with voices in ordinary songs, although they are and will be known by those who play the lute, chitarrone and other instruments so made'.[56]

L'Ottuso defends the novelties eagerly adopted by 'all the moderns, particularly those who have embraced this new second practice'.[57] Take, for example, the interval of a seventh:

> Who does not know that if we wish to take this interval in its simple and properly formed manner it will not have its real and true demonstration? But on the other hand, as an *accento* and an *inganno*, or rather, as a dissonance, yes, but sweetened by the accompaniment of the other parts, without doubt not only will it make a good effect, but as something new it will be of greater delight to the ear than would have been caused by the supposed octave.[58]

For L'Ottuso, one should not blame but should instead value and imitate the adoption of expressive embellishments written out in detail, such as 'the supposition of one note for another, and other such things ... However, if Your Lordship considers these madrigals by Signor etc. you will see them full of such *fiori*, and decorated with so terse a modulation, far from that of the crowd, and moreover full of judicious deceptions [*inganni*] ... hearing them [performed] by good singers, so that instead of blame, I am sure that you will give them praise'.[59]

For Artusi, all this belongs to a type of composition that is against nature, because it stands opposed to the traditional rules, founded on experience and on reason.

> It is indeed true that in this your new second practice, those who (to use your own words) act against nature and confound the matters and the rules of our forebears, these reputed as the better and as more elevated talents, and in this way you believe that both you and they are to become immortal, and you are greatly deceived. All artists seek to imitate nature, and however many philosophers there are and have been, they neither think of nor philosophize about anything other than the operations done by her. And do you offer praise to and consider more fully those who act against nature, and those things of theirs called *artificii, fiori, fioretti, suppositi, inganni* and *accenti*?[60]

On the one hand, according to Artusi, there is the natural style of good composers, and on the other, that artificial style of the 'moderns':

> The former use the accidental sharps and flats according to their nature, and the latter avail themselves of them against nature. The former use dissonances in the regular way, and the latter irregularly. The former in leaps adopt those intervals which are natural of a fifth and a fourth; the latter, entirely the opposite. The former do not suppose that a note is positioned in place of another, as do the latter. The former in the manner of uniting the consonances dispose order and progression in one manner; the latter, entirely the opposite. Thus it seems that from start to finish the latter are contrary to the former, and therefore if the former are desired for their charm, beauty, goodness and delightfulness, the latter, to be heard again, must needs not be desired for this end, but for the contrary; and it will be cause for laughter, joking and contempt considering the madness of these men of whimsy who, thinking that their songs produce new harmony and new affect give birth to new nausea and new contempt, because they bring in their train new confusion, given that they are full of things which confound the good and the beautiful of music. But what do I say, new nausea, new contempt? Rather, the nausea and contempt of the oldest, rancid, putrid merchandise

> held in whatever bizarre apothecary's shop you care to think of ... For now, I content myself with this *inganno*, this *accento*, *supposito*, *fiore*, *fioretto* and *artificio*, all things which with one single name L'Ottuso properly could and should explain with ease: confusion. This Ottuso wants it to be that as soon as the singer senses himself colliding in a seventh, he should rush with his voice to the octave, and thus the harmony arising from such an operation will stand very well, and will be done according to the rules. But tell me, will the singer have the time to be able to perform such shenanigans? Or does he want all the singers to pause until he himself can accommodate the voice and can turn and accommodate the seventh into an octave? Would it not be better without such flimflammery to give facility to the singer, thanks to the harmony that should be heard, accommodating each interval to its natural position, without so many *suppositi*, *fiori* and *inganni*?[61]

If the ear 'hears a seventh, or a second, it must through natural inclination and the effect of nature judge it so made, and not suppose another interval contrary to it'.[62]

Such techniques of artful composition, which for Artusi are 'tomfoolery' ('fatte alla Mingona'),[63] are for L'Ottuso justified by the aim of adhering better to emotional expression: 'so what will this be if not a new modulation full of new affect, to imitate thereby the nature of the verse, and justly to represent the true sense of the poet?'[64]

> However, it is not necessary that this music should perform the miracle of reviving the dead; it will well produce affect, that is, the desire with the novelty of its modulation to hear frequently such kinds of harmony, more apt to move our soul with its novelty in this new practice than in the past one, as that which more effectively strikes the sense.[65]

Here L'Ottuso touched on a key point of the entire debate, which basically identified him, together with certain other 'moderns', as the protector of a search for expressiveness in the context of which even established rules could eventually be sacrificed. When he needs to cite the authority of some composer, he calls Cipriano de Rore and Wert to his cause (on p. 15, for example), or else the 'petroso' ('severe', a term invoking Dante) Marenzio of the Ninth Book (on pp. 16–18). In another artistic field, it is significant that his poetic citations come from Tasso (p. 18) and Guarini (p. 17). All in all, the arguments are clearly placed in a Ferrarese–Mantuan context, and at the heart of those emotional tendencies served by a musical experimentation concerned to exalt poetic values over the rules of compositional craft, also because the audience for which these works were written were refined experts able to understand and justify deviations from the norm without committing the blunder of pedantically calling it an error.

This expressive tendency within 'modern' music is designated by L'Ottuso as a 'new second practice' (on p. 16), using a term which Artusi also adopts (on pp. 22 and 41). The term would appear to have been coined by Monteverdi: the composer claims paternity for it in the statement attached to his Fifth Book (1605: 'in order that the expression "Second Practice" may not be appropriated by anyone else'), and Giulio Cesare Monteverdi echoes him in the *Dichiaratione* published as an appendix to the *Scherzi musicali* (1607: 'My brother has made known to the world that this expression is assuredly his'). But even if it originated from Monteverdi, the auspicious term 'second practice' must have gained circulation in those Ferrarese circles around which both the composer and L'Ottuso gravitated.

In this 'practice', an important role was also given to the expressive capabilities of singers, on whom it was encumbent to display ('represent', says L'Ottuso) the 'affetti' ('affects') set to music: 'and remember that since the singer is the soul of music, and that which represents the true sense of the composer, in which representation according to the diversity of the subject the voice is sometimes strengthened, sometimes sweetened, for thus it is necessary to hear so spirited a manner of compositions done by extraordinary singers'.[66] Vincenzo Giustiniani, too, documents in his *Discorso sopra la musica de' suoi tempi* (c.1628) the practice of such an artful style, 'reservedly' (*reservatamente*) expressive, cultivated in the Ferrarese and Mantuan courts:

> But as the villanellas acquired greater perfection through more artful composition, so also every composer, in order that his compositions should satisfy the general taste, took care to advance in the style of composition for several voices, particularly Giaches Wert in Mantua and Luzzasco in Ferrara. They were the superintendents of all music for those dukes, who took the greatest delight in the art, especially in having many noble ladies and gentlemen learn to sing and play superbly, so that they spent entire days in some rooms designed especially for this purpose and beautifully decorated with paintings. The ladies of Mantua and Ferrara were highly competent, and vied with each other not only in regard to the timbre and training of their voices but also in the design of exquisite passages delivered at opportune points, but not in excess (Giovanni Luca [Conforto] of Rome, who served also in Ferrara, usually erred in this respect). Furthermore, they moderated or increased their voices, loud or soft, heavy or light, according to the demands of the piece they were singing; now slow, breaking off with sometimes a gentle sigh, now singing long passages legato or detached, now groups, now leaps, now with long trills, now with short, and again with sweet running passages sung softly, to which sometimes one heard an echo answer unexpectedly. They accompanied the music and the sentiment with appropriate facial expressions, glances and gestures, with no awkward movements of the mouth or hands or body which might not express the feeling of the song. They made the words clear in such a way that one could hear even the last syllable of every word, which was never interrupted or suppressed by passages and other embellishments. They used many other particular devices which will be known to persons more experienced than I. And under these favourable circumstances the above-mentioned musicians made every effort to win fame and the favour of the princes their patrons, who were their principal support.[67]

In the face of L'Ottuso's vindications of an expressive style, Artusi's arguments become vague and unsubtle, losing their efficacy and restricting themselves solely to defending tradition: 'And that music made by the ancients without these jokes produced marvellous effects, and this music produces tomfooleries.'[68]

> If the affect is a passion, or rather a movement of the soul, or, as Cicero says in the second book of *De inventione*, 'Est animi, aut corporis ex tempore aliqua de causa commutatio' ['it is a sudden change of the soul or the body from some cause'], as would be the case when the cheerful man for some reason should become melancholic and the meek one angry, or the healthy one should take on what belongs to the infirm body, and similar things, will it perhaps be true that the music of Signor etc. has produced or produces in the souls of men these effects and these changes? Is there some authentic proof? Has perhaps this kind of music produced some miracle as one reads that those ancient and excellent musicians did? It has not done so – and therefore it cannot make new affects, as Your Lordship says – even though, as I have said, it solicits the ear and roughly and harshly strikes it. And if it seems that these singers, for having it much in practice, present it with some little passage, and thus conceal such roughness in a manner that it does not cause offence, this occurs accidentally and not through the nature of those dissonances placed however one might wish, which always are and will be rough, crude, harsh and insupportable to the ear. And when this song is taken from the hands of such singers, it will inevitably be and appear thus, because in sum it is thus. And it is like that chimney-sweep who when sumptuously dressed in masquing costume seems good and beautiful, and pleases all the onlookers, but when in the end one takes off the costume and the garments accidentally placed upon him, the chimney-sweep remains in full ugliness ... But it is not for this that [the music of the 'protectors of this second practice'] produces those effects which L'Ottuso persuades himself to be given to understand, except for those which the singers themselves produce while they sing those songs, who slowly turn the head, arch their eyebrows, roll their eyes, twist their shoulders, let themselves go about in such a way that it seems that they wish to die, and they produce many other transformations which Ovid would never have dreamt of. And they produce these grimaces precisely when they arrive at those dissonances that offend the sense to demonstrate that that which they do, others should likewise do. But those who listen, instead of being moved, are ruffled by its roughness and its poor satisfaction, and going off their head they leave poorly satisfied.[69]

The revival of the debate following the publication of the *Seconda parte dell'Artusi* prompted Monteverdi to contemplate a direct response, and one containing a full theoretical justification: 'at which time [1603] my brother decided to begin writing his defence of himself against his opponent' says Giulio Cesare Monteverdi in the *Dichiaratione* in the *Scherzi musicali* (1607). The composer's reply was already drafted by July 1605, that is, the date of the dedication of his *Quinto libro de madrigali a cinque voci* as an appendix to which was published a statement to the 'Studious Readers' announcing the publication of his defence in a treatise to be called *Seconda pratica, overo Perfettione della moderna musica* ('Second practice, or Perfection of the modern music'), reversing the title of Artusi's treatise and, significantly, taking up again the auspicious term publicly put forward by L'Ottuso:

Do not marvel that I am giving these madrigals to the press without first replying to the objections that *L'Artusi* has brought against some very minute details in them, for being in the service of His Most Serene Highness of Mantua, I have not had at my disposal the time that would be required. Nevertheless, to show that I do not compose my works haphazardly, I have written a reply which will appear, as soon as I have revised it, bearing the title *Seconda pratica, overo Perfettione della moderna musica*. Some, not suspecting that there is any practice other than that taught by Zerlino [Zarlino], will wonder at this, but let them be assured that, with regard to the consonances and dissonances, there is still another way of considering them, different from the established way, which, with satisfaction to the reason and to the senses, defends the modern method of composing. I have wished to say this to you in order that the expression 'Second Practice' may not be appropriated by any one else, and further, that the ingenious may reflect meanwhile upon other secondary matters concerning harmony and believe that the modern composer builds upon the foundation of truth.

The revision of the treatise itself was to take up the rest of Monteverdi's life, for the composer cannot have been very familiar with theoretical problems and with the art of writing. Almost thirty years later, writing from Venice on 22 October 1633 (L.122 [123]), Monteverdi informed an unknown correspondent (but in all probability Giovan Battista Doni, as we shall see below):

Monsignor the Vicar of St Mark's, who was so kind as to tell me about Your Most Reverend Lordship's noble qualities and particular virtues, mentioned that you were writing a book on music; at which point I added that I too was writing one, though with fear that through my weakness I would fail to reach the desired conclusion. This gentleman being very devoted to the Most Illustrious Lord Bishop of Padua, I imagine that this is how His Most Illustrious Lordship may have heard of my writings, for I know of no other way, and I make no effort to let people know. But since His Most Illustrious Lordship has been kind enough to honour me so in Your Most Illustrious Lordship's favour, I beg you to consider the rest of what I have to say.

You should know, therefore, that I am indeed at work – but under compulsion, however, inasmuch as the event which years ago spurred me to begin, was of such a kind that it caused me unawares to promise the world something that (once I had become aware of it) my feeble forces could not manage. I promised, as I said before, in a printed work of mine to let a certain theoretician of the First Practice know that there was another way (unknown to him) of considering music, and this I called the Second Practice. The reason for this was that he had been pleased to criticize (in print!) one of my madrigals, as regards certain of its harmonic progressions, on the basis of tenets of the First Practice (that is to say, the ordinary rules, as if they were exercises written by a youth beginning to learn note-against-note counterpoint) and not according to a knowledge of *melodia*.

But on hearing of a certain exegesis published in my defence by my brother, he calmed down in such a way that from thenceforward not only did he stop overruling me but – turning his pen in my praise – he began to like and admire me. Since the promise was public, I could not neglect it, and for this reason I am compelled to pay the debt. I beg you therefore to consider me excused for my boldness.

The title of the book will be as follows, *Melodia, overo Seconda pratica musicale* ['*Melodia*, or Second musical practice']. I mean the second as regards numerical order, in modern style; first in order, in the old style. I am dividing the book into three parts corresponding to the three aspects of *Melodia*. In the first I discuss word-setting, in the second, harmony, and in the third, the rhythmic part.

Matteo Caberloti, tracing the composer's biography in his funeral oration, confirms that Monteverdi worked even to the end of his life on the long-suffered treatise, and notes how 'having given himself to philosophy he was about to complete a volume in which, explaining the most hidden secrets of his discipline, he was to ensure that never more in the centuries to come would there remain hidden to the studious the true paths to facilitate the acquisition of perfection in the art of music. But pitiless death hastened by a short illness has brought it about that it should remain imperfect, deprived of the light of the press'.[70] The few lines given as an appendix to the Fifth Book therefore remain the one and only public, direct intervention by Monteverdi in the polemic.

Another character – again hiding behind a pseudonym – became involved in the controversy between July 1605 (the date of the Fifth Book, where no mention is made of him) and July 1607 (the date of Giulio Cesare Monteverdi's *Dichiaratione*, which does refer to him): the aforementioned Antonio Braccino da Todi, who, because of his arguments and of his knowledge of particular pieces of information, seems to have been very close to Artusi. Indeed, he is traditionally identified as the Bolognese canon himself, although both Braccino and Giulio Cesare Monteverdi refer to Artusi always as if dealing with a third person; moreover, the letter of 1633 from Monteverdi to Doni (L.122 [123]) seems to suggest that Artusi had no further part to play in the polemic.

Braccino's first sortie is now lost: we know of it only from the *Dichiaratione della lettera stampata nel Quinto libro de suoi madregali* ('Statement on the letter printed in the Fifth Book of his madrigals') by Claudio's brother, which, placed as an appendix to the *Scherzi musicali* edited by Giulio Cesare Monteverdi (1607), constitutes the next stage in the polemic, with an authorized and systematic gloss on the brief comments offered by the composer in the Fifth Book.

> Some months ago a letter of my brother Claudio Monteverdi was printed and given to the public. A certain person, under the fictitious name of Antonio Braccini da Todi, has been at pains to make this seem to the world a chimera and a vanity. For this reason, impelled by the love I bear my brother and still more by the truth contained in his letter, and seeing that he pays attention to deeds and takes little notice of the words of others, and being unable to endure that his work should be so unjustly censured, I have determined to reply to the objections raised against them, declaring in fuller detail what my brother, in his letter, compressed into little space, to the end that this person and whoever follows him may learn that the truth that it contains is very different from what he represents in his discourse.

Now the arguments turned essentially on the points already identified by L'Ottuso, that breaking the rules was motivated by the need to search for expression: with a well-turned slogan, Giulio Cesare affirms that his brother's intention 'has been (in this kind of music) to make the oration [= the poetic text] the mistress of the harmony [= music] and not the servant'. 'If we take harmony absolutely, without adding to it anything else, it will have no power to produce any extrinsic effect', he then adds (quoting Zarlino), and continues:

> Artusi, like a good teacher, takes certain details, or, as he calls them, 'passages', from my brother's madrigal 'Cruda Amarilli', paying no attention to the oration, but neglecting it as though it had nothing to do with the music, later showing the said 'passages' deprived of their oration, of all their harmony, and of their rhythm. But if, in the 'passages' noted as false, he had shown the oration that went with them, then the world would have known without fail where his judgement had gone astray, and he would not have said that they were chimeras and castles in the air from their entire disregard of the rules of the First Practice. But it would truly have been a beautiful demonstration if he had also done the same with Cipriano's [Rore] madrigals 'Dalle belle contrade', 'Se ben il duol', 'Et se pur mi mantieni amor', 'Poiché m'invita amore', 'Crudel acerba', 'Un'altra volta', and, to conclude, with others whose harmony obeys their oration exactly and which would indeed be left bodies without soul if they were left without this most important and principal part of music, his opponent implying, by passing judgement on these 'passages' without the oration, that all excellence and beauty consist in the exact observance of the aforesaid rules of the First Practice, which makes the harmony mistress of the oration. This my brother will make apparent, knowing for certain that in a kind of composition such as this of his, his music turns on the perfection of the *melodia*, considered from which point of view the harmony, from being the mistress, becomes the servant of the oration, and the oration the mistress of the harmony, to which way of thinking the Second Practice, or modern usage, tends . . .
>
> By First Practice he understands the one that turns on the perfection of the harmony, that is, the one that considers the harmony not commanded but commanding, not the servant, but the mistress of the oration, and this was founded by those first men who composed in our notation music for more than one voice, was then followed and amplified by Occhegem, Iosquin de Pres, Pietro della Rue, Iovan Motton [Mouton], Crequillon, Clemens non papa, Gombert, and others of those times, and was finally perfected by Messer Adriano [Willaert] with actual compositions and by the most excellent Zerlino with most judicious rules.
>
> By Second Practice, which was first renewed in our notation by the divine Cipriano Rore (as my brother will make apparent), was followed and amplified, not only by the gentlemen already mentioned, but by Ingegneri, Marenz[i]o, Giaches Wert, Luzzasco, likewise by Giaccoppo Peri, Giulio Caccini, and finally by loftier spirits with a better understanding of true art, he understands the one that turns on the perfection of the *melodia*, that is, the one that considers harmony not commanding, but commanded, and makes the oration the mistress of the harmony.

Giulio Cesare Monteverdi concludes confirming that 'because of the command of the oration, modern composition does not and cannot observe the rules of the First Practice; and yet this method of composition is embraced by the world in such a way that it may justly be called a usage'. Having to cite the followers of the 'divine Cipriano Rore', he lists Ferrarese and Tuscan composers (significantly, noblemen and not musicians by profession) employed in the common, if variously construed, search – in the field of polyphony and/or monody – for a new expressive style: 'the Lord Prince of Venosa [Carlo Gesualdo], Emiglio del Cavagliere, Count Alfonso Fontanelli and the Count of Camerata [Geronimo Branchiforte],[71] Cavalier Turchi [Giovanni del Turco], [Tomaso] Pecci, and other gentlemen of this heroic school'. Once again, this list further clarifies the social and cultural contexts within which these issues were explored. Behind Monteverdi, who was active in cities that were courtly seats (above all Mantua, given his institutional affiliations, but also Ferrara), can be glimpsed those refined and exclusive cultural circles towards which he directed his work. On the other hand, Artusi was a cleric from a Bolognese monastery and therefore far removed – in terms of his education, experience and even location – from such a cultivated environment of connoisseurs. He ends up becoming the champion of tradition and of the norm, of an *aurea mediocritas* (golden mean) within the madrigal and thus of an art for wider circulation and not for a few select listeners who shun in aristocratic fashion the rules of common comportment.

It is not worth devoting too much time to Antonio Braccino da Todi's later intervention in the controversy (the *Discorso secondo musicale*, Venice, Giacomo Vincenti, 1608), which obviously favours Artusi: it reiterates the old arguments and refutes Monteverdi's motto of 'the oration [as] mistress and commanding lady'.[72] The warnings against Monteverdi's present degeneracy are founded upon calls to return to the good teaching of Ingegneri: 'the excellent Cipriano and Ingegnieri never dreamt of composing anything like what Monteverdi thinks':[73]

> Monteverdi knows that when he went to school under the excellent Signor Marc'Antonio Ingegnieri to learn *melopeia*, or the art of counterpoint as we would call it, he never availed himself in any way of oration, nor of rhythm, as an art which has its essence within itself; but he only applied himself to the accompaniment of the consonances and dissonances, but not in the way he uses them now.[74]

Some time later (two years after Artusi's death), Giovanni Battista Magone appointed himself conciliator in his *Ghirlanda mosicale* (Pavia, Giovanni Negri, 1615), seeking to marry the opposing arguments:

> On the part of Signor Artusi, there are adduced both in the first and in the second part profound reasons, solid and indubitable, being founded upon philosophical terms, learned speculations, geometrical and arithmetical considerations, even from the ancient founders [of music], first considered and then determined and distinguished in such a fine way that one cannot take any exception to his explanations. Nonetheless, begging the famous contradictor's pardon, one should not decry the works of Signor Claudio, both for the reasons considered by Signor Giulio Cesare his brother, which tend

towards the defence and honour of that Signor Claudio, and for the fact that I imagine that Signor Monteverdi directed his thought in composing to the delighting of the ear, the principal end of music . . .[75]

II 1601–1604

The period of the Artusi–Monteverdi controversy also saw a number of other important events that variously affected Monteverdi's life. His first son was born in the summer of 1601 – he was baptized on 27 August in the Church of SS. Simone e Giuda in Mantua with the names Francesco and Baldassarre (that of the Crown prince, one of the two godparents at the baptism, plus that of the paternal grandfather):

> Francesco Baldassarre, son of Signor Claudio Monteverdi and of Signora Claudia his wife was baptized by me, Girolamo Belledi, rector of the parish church of SS. Simone e Giuda: the godparents who raised him at the holy font were the most illustrious Signor Francesco Odini on behalf of the excellent Lord Prince of Mantua Francesco Gonzaga, and the most illustrious Signora Violante Caffino.[76]

Some months later the *maestro di cappella* to the court, Benedetto Palla-vicino, died: 'Monday 26 November, messer Benedeto Palavicini, in the district of Montenegro, died of a fever lasting one month, aged 50.'[77] In next to no time – only two days later – Monteverdi claimed the position for himself in a letter (L.1) sent to Duke Vincenzo: the duke was then involved in his third campaign against the Turks in Hungary (he had left Mantua on 18 July 1601) and was believed to be still at the siege of Kanisza, although in fact he had already begun his return journey, arriving home on 19 December 1601.[78]

> Most Serene Lord, My Most Respected Master.
>
> If I did not hasten to ask personally of Your Most Serene Highness's good grace, on this occasion of Pallavicino's death, for the musical appointment which Signor Giaches [de Wert] formerly had, perhaps envy in the designs of others might, to my detriment, use such obvious ploys – more akin to rhetoric than music – that tainting Your Most Serene Highness's good will towards me they could give you to believe that this arose from some fear of my incapacity, or from some excessive self-assurance; and therefore I was waiting ambitiously for what (unworthy servant that I am) I should have affectionately requested and sought out with special humility.
>
> Furthermore, if I did not also try to seize the chance of serving Your Most Serene Highness as often as an occasion presents itself, you would have particular reason to complain justly of my negligent service; and similarly my poor knowledge not seeking (to good ends) greater opportunity for showing itself to your most refined musical taste as of some worth in motets and masses too, you would have just cause to complain of me.
>
> And finally, the world – having seen me persevere in Your Most Serene Highness's service with much eagerness on my part and with good grace on

yours, after the death of the famous Signor Striggio, and after that of the excellent Signor Giaches, and again a third time after that of the excellent Signor Franceschino [Rovigo], and again (lastly) after this of the competent Messer Benedetto Pallavicino – could with reason murmur of my negligence if, not because of my skill but because of the loyal and singular devotion I have always maintained in regard to Your Most Serene Highness's service, I did not once more seek the position now vacant in this quarter of the church, and did not in all respects ask most eagerly and humbly for the afore-mentioned title.

For all the above reasons, then, and perhaps for those which – to my good fortune – your kindness could add (since you have never disdained to hear my humble compositions), I ask beseechingly to be *maestro* both of the chamber and of the church; which post, if your kindness and grace will so honour me, I shall receive with the humility that befits a feeble servant when he is encouraged and favoured by a great prince as is Your Most Serene Highness . . .

This letter would seem to suggest that Monteverdi was seeking the position of *maestro di cappella* 'both of the chamber and of the church', given that the first position was already more or less officially his (but from when?); and in fact, a little earlier in the letter, he asks that he might be also appreciated 'in motets and masses', perhaps implying, just as he had already been appreciated as a madrigalist. Whatever the case, it is clear that on the title-page of his *Quarto libro de madrigali a cinque voci* (the dedication is dated 1 March 1603) the composer could for the first time style himself 'master of the music of the Most Serene Lord Duke of Mantua'.

Monteverdi's responsibilities now extended over the whole musical activity of the court, even though Gastoldi remained *maestro di cappella* of S. Barbara (until 1609). His chief task was to maintain the effectiveness of, and renew, the ensemble, taking on good professionals. In the summer of 1609, while on his usual vacation in Cremona, Monteverdi explored the availability of some 'cornett and trombone players' who 'play together well and readily both dance and chamber music' (L.7, 24 August 1609), and he presented an extended report on 'a certain Galeazzo Sirena, composer and organist' (L.8, 10 September 1609). His criteria for judging aspiring court performers focus on their versatility so as to be sure that they would be capable of meeting the manifold demands of court service: a singer is tested in sacred and secular music in theatre and chamber styles ('I was entrusted by Messer Pandolfo (on behalf of Your Most Serene Highness) with hearing a certain contralto, come from Modena, desirous of serving Your Most Serene Highness, so I took him straightaway into S. Pietro and had him sing a motet in the organ-loft. I heard a fine voice, powerful and sustained, and when he sings on the stage he will make himself heard in every corner very well and without strain . . . I have not been able to hear him in madrigals, because he was all ready to set out' (L.9, 9 June 1610)). Similarly, when dealing with an instrumentalist, Monteverdi requires the ability to play on more than one instrument and the possession of various virtuoso techniques (L.11, 26 March 1611).

My Most Serene Lord and Most Respected Master.

Your Most Serene Highness left instruction with Messer Giulio Cesare the Cremonese [Bianchi] that if someone could be found who would play the recorder, cornett, trombone, flute and bassoon – for want of a fifth part in Your Most Serene Highness's wind band – you would be pleased to take him on. I therefore approach with this letter of mine to let Your Most Serene Highness know that there is a young man here of about 26 or 28 (I do not know whether he is passing through or has come on purpose) who can play on the aforementioned instruments very readily at least, and with assurance, because I have heard him play both recorder and cornett; moreover he says that he can also play the gamba and the *viola* . . .

As is my custom, I sounded him out and told him: 'If the Most Serene Lord Prince were pleased to take you on, this gentleman very much likes not only to hear a variety of wind instruments, he also likes to have the said musicians play in private, in church, in procession, and atop city walls; now madrigals, now French songs, now airs, and now dance-songs.'

Obviously, the duty of the *maestro della musica* was also to furnish new compositions, providing for the day-to-day and special needs of the court. Knowing Duke Vincenzo's passion for the theatre, such new music was certainly not lacking: 'for being in the service of His Most Serene Highness of Mantua, I have not at my disposal the time that would be required', writes Monteverdi in the statement to the 'Studious Readers' of the Fifth Book (1605). He is echoed by the gloss in the *Dichiaratione* appended to the *Scherzi musicali* of 1607: 'This my brother said, not only because of his responsibility for both church and chamber music, but also because of other extraordinary services, for, serving a great prince, he finds the greater part of his time taken up, now with tournaments, now with ballets, now with comedies and various *concerti*, and lastly with the playing of the two *viole bastarde*, a responsibility and study which is not so usual as his adversary would give us to understand.' Duke Vincenzo's most significant theatrical undertaking so far had been the staging of Guarini's *Pastor fido* in November 1598, embellished by sumptuous *intermedi* with stage machines. We do not know the composers of the many musical passages required therein in addition to those needed for the play itself (the 'ballo della cieca' and perhaps some choruses): with Wert and Rovigo dead – both had once been commissioned (at the beginning of the 1590s) to write some pieces for a performance (but one planned on a more modest scale) – it would seem logical to suggest that Monteverdi participated here not just as a performer but also, perhaps, as a composer.[79] However, if we can only guess at his involvement in the 1598 performance of *Il pastor fido*, it is clear that thereafter he was involved in similar, if less burdensome, entertainments.

Evidence of an excessively high workload in 1604 is provided by the letter (L.3) sent by Monteverdi to the duke in December of that year from Cremona, where he had gone to rest. This letter laments the decline of those physical powers

that I have enjoyed in the past. For they are still weakened from past exertions, and so feeble that neither through medicine, nor dieting, nor

giving up studies have they been restored to their initial strength, even
though partly so.

I hope nevertheless to recover them with the Lord's help, and when this
comes about (if it pleases His Divine Majesty) I shall then beseech Your Most
Serene Highness for the love of God never to burden me again either with so
much to do at once or in so short a time, for it is certain that my great desire
to serve you and the great exertion involved would inadvertently draw me
to my life's abridgement ...

In the same letter, Monteverdi discusses with the duke the music for a pastoral
ballet on the love of Diana and Endymion:

Ten days ago I received from the courier a letter from Your Most Serene
Highness commanding me to compose two *entrate*, one for the stars that
have to follow on the moon, the other for the shepherds who come on after
Endymion; and likewise two dances, one for the aforementioned stars alone,
and the other for the stars and shepherds together.

And so, with a most eager desire to obey and carry out Your Most Serene
Highness's commands as promptly as possible (which I have always possessed
and done, and will possess until I die and ever shall do), I set to work first on
the music for the stars. But not finding among the instructions how many
there must be to dance it, and wishing to compose it on an alternating plan,
as it would in my opinion have been novel, delightful and pleasing – that is,
having first of all a short and cheerful air played by all the instruments and
likewise danced by all the stars; then immediately the five *viole da braccio*
taking up a different air from the first one (the other instruments stopping)
and only two stars dancing to it (the others resting); and at the end of this
duo section, having the first air repeated with all the instruments and stars,
continuing this pattern until all the said stars have danced two by two – but
not having had the actual number, and this information being essential (if
indeed Your Most Serene Highness takes pleasure in this type of interspersed
arrangement as I mentioned), I have in consequence put off doing it until I
know; and in order to find out, I have written to Signor Giovan Battista the
dancer, so that he can give me the exact number through my brother.

Meanwhile I have composed this piece, which I am now sending off to
Your Most Serene Highness, for the shepherds and the stars ...

These *balli* probably had to serve as *intermedi* for the comedy staged in
Carnival 1605 (presented by the duke 'in his royal theatre') which the painter
Federico Zuccari described as 'most noble' and 'which turned out no less
beautiful, with many scene-changes, than the first', that is, the comedy of
Carnival 1604: 'a big, fine comedy ... which was indeed most noble and royal
for the decorations and everything else, with four or six changes of scene and
with most stupendous *intermedi*'.[80] Gabriele Zinano also refers to these performances in a letter from Naples of 17 February 1604: at the Gonzaga court,
there were performed 'comedies, music, *balli*, tournaments, to such an extent
that in foreign courts it was said that at Mantua they produced the most
impressive celebrations in Italy'.[81]

Later in Venice in 1615, Monteverdi (L.18; to Annibale Iberti?) recalled the
active role taken by the duke in organizing such undertakings, noting, for
example, that in the case of *balletti* he 'used to demand of me such productions

either in six, eight or nine movements, besides which he used to give me some account of the plot, and I used to try to fit to it the most apt and suitable music and metrical schemes that I knew'.

These years of intense work were also embittered by financial quarrels with the none-too-honest court treasurer Ottavio Benintendi (the painful twists and turns can be read, for example, in his letter (L.2) of 27 October 1604). Meanwhile, Monteverdi was granted Mantuan citizenship on 10 April 1602,[82] and two more children were born to him: Leonora (named after the Duchess of Mantua, and also Guglielmo Gonzaga's wife) at the beginning of 1603, and Massimiliano Giacomo (after the Archduke of Austria, Duke Vincenzo's uncle, and his maternal grandfather) in May 1604. Both were baptized in the cathedral of Mantua:[83]

> 20 February 1603: Leonora Camilla, daughter of Signor Claudio Monteverdi and of Signora Cattaneo, married, was baptized by me, the curate as written above: the godparents were the Lord Count Vincenzo Caffino, on behalf of the Most Illustrious Lord Count Giulio his father, and the Most Illustrious Lady Countess Polissena Gonzaga.

> 10 May 1604: at S. Pietro, Massimiliano Giacomo, son of Claudio Monteverdi and of Signora Claudia, married, was baptized by me, the curate as written above: the godparents were the Illustrious Lord Count Ottavio Massimiliano of Collalto, on behalf of the Most Serene Lord Archduke Maximilian Ernest, and also the Illustrious Lady Vittoria Nuvoloni on behalf of the Most Serene Lady Princess of Mantua, Margherita Gonzaga.

12 *Il quarto libro de madrigali a cinque voci* (1603)

Eleven years had passed since the Venetian printer Ricciardo Amadino printed Monteverdi's Third Book of madrigals. In the Fourth Book (likewise printed in Venice by Amadino), the composer included pieces dating back to the 1590s. In the dedication 'to my most illustrious lords and most respected patrons, the lord academicians of the [Accademia degli] Intrepidi of Ferrara' (dated Mantua, 1 March 1603), Monteverdi in fact recalls:

> Since in past years I was unable to present some of my madrigals in manuscript to the Most Serene Alfonso, Duke of Ferrara, because of the intervention of his death, now that there has arisen in that city a prince and head of a noble gathering of knights, friends and those who carry out virtuous actions gathered within a well-attended academy such as that of your most illustrious lordships; and finding myself not only loving all of you with devotion but also eternally obliged for the many favours received with diverse honourable demonstrations towards me and towards my offspring such as they are, I have thought it fitting not to depart from the same city, to which I am much inclined, and to acknowledge the same knights my lords with all due gratitude, presenting and dedicating to you as I do with all the affection of my soul both them and other new madrigals now printed.

Unfortunately, it is not possible to say which were the 'madrigals in manuscript' that Monteverdi intended to present to Alfonso II d'Este, who died on 27 October 1597 (Monteverdi must therefore have intended to present them before this date): nevertheless, the Fourth Book also contains those 'other new madrigals' written after 1597. One thing we can be sure of, however, is that at least 'Ah dolente partita' belongs to the earlier group, since, as we have seen, it was published in 1597 in the anthology *Fiori del giardino di diversi eccellentissimi autori* (Nuremberg, Paul Kaufmann). Moreover, 'Anima mia, perdona' and its second *pars* 'Che se tu se' il cor mio' were also attacked by Artusi in 1600: he claimed to have heard them in Ferrara at the end of 1598. Indeed, there seems to be an allusion to the Artusi–Monteverdi controversy (which was rekindled precisely in 1603, with the publication of the *Seconda parte dell'Artusi*) in the following passage in the dedication of the Fourth Book, when Monteverdi invites the Intrepidi to 'accept the gift, however small, with that greatness of mind which befits your virtue, birth and profession, bringing light to them with the brightness of your names and defending with your fortunate protection these my songs'.

The Accademia degli Intrepidi had been founded in Ferrara by Francesco Saracini in 1600: on 26 August 1601 Count Guidubaldo Bonarelli gave the inaugural address marking the beginning of its activities.[84] Soon it was endowed with a proper theatre commissioned from the architect Giovan Battista Aleotti (called 'L'Argenta'), who completed it in 1605.[85] Its distinguished members included the Duke of Mantua who, according to the later evidence of Saverio Bettinelli, was its leader: 'he wrote poetry and music, says Cagnani, whence he was appointed leader of the Accademia degl'Intrepidi of Ferrara'.[86] But even if some of these madrigals were conceived in connection with an attempt to approach the Este family, their publication (when Monteverdi was already *maestro della musica* at the Gonzaga court) is clearly related to Monteverdi's working environment at Mantua: the volume seems most likely intended, if only indirectly, as an act of homage to his own employer.

The texts and musical styles within the book also shift between Ferrara and Mantua: here we find the Tasso of the *Gerusalemme conquistata* ('Piagne e sospira, e quando i caldi raggi', VIII.6; compare *Gerusalemme liberata*, VII.19, 'Sovente, allor che su gli estivi ardori'), a good number of Guarini texts, and also verse by Ridolfo Arlotti, a poet friendly with Tasso and Guarini who towards the end of the 1580s had been counsellor and private secretary to the nephew of Duke Alfonso, Cardinal Alessandro d'Este.[87] However, the passages taken from *Il pastor fido* ('Ah dolente partita', III.3, lines 309–16; 'Anima mia, perdona' and 'Che se tu se' il cor mio', III.4, lines 34–42, 43–50; 'Quell'augellin che canta', I.1, lines 175–86 with some variants) should also be related to the various attempts by Vincenzo Gonzaga in the 1590s to stage Guarini's celebrated pastoral play, which were crowned by success only in November 1598, as we have seen; the Mantuan court must have retained a particularly vivid memory of this play, which met with considerable favour among madrigalists. If Monteverdi had already drawn on *Il pastor fido* at the time of the Third Book, setting to music lines 1–14 of Act III scene 1 ('O primavera, gioventú dell'anno'; with some variants), both Wert in 1595 and Pallavicino in 1600 also found in the play a number of emotional scenes to set to music. Even Marenzio often turned to it in that period (in his Seventh and Eighth Books of madrigals for five voices of 1595 and 1598 respectively), and likewise Philippe de Monte (in *La fiammetta* and the *Musica sopra Il pastor fido*, both published in Venice by Angelo Gardano respectively in 1599 and 1600), Giovan Pietro Flaccomio (*Il pastor fido: secondo libro de madrigali a cinque voci* (now lost)) and Luzzaschi (in 1601).

1	'Ah dolente partita' (Battista Guarini: *versi sciolti*)
2	'Cor mio, mentre vi miro' (B. Guarini: madrigal)
3	'Cor mio, non mori? E mori' (madrigal)
4	'Sfogava con le stelle' (Ottavio Rinuccini: madrigal)
5	'Volgea l'anima mia soavemente' (B. Guarini: madrigal)
6a	'Anima mia, perdona' (B. Guarini: *versi sciolti*)
b	'Che se tu se' il cor mio'
7	'Luci serene e chiare' (Ridolfo Arlotti: madrigal)
8	'La piaga c'ho nel core' (Aurelio Gatti: madrigal)
9	'Voi pur da me partite, anima dura' (B. Guarini: madrigal)
10	'A un giro sol de bell'occhi lucenti' (B. Guarini: madrigal)
11	'Ohimé, se tanto amate' (B. Guarini: madrigal)
12	'Io mi son giovinetta' (B. Guarini: madrigal)
13	'Quell'augellin che canta' (B. Guarini: *versi sciolti*)
14	'Non piú guerra, pietate' (B. Guarini: madrigal)
15	'Sí ch'io vorrei morire' (Maurizio Moro: madrigal)
16	'Anima dolorosa che vivendo' (B. Guarini: madrigal)
17	'Anima del cor mio' (madrigal)
18	'Longe da te, cor mio' (madrigal)
19	'Piagne e sospira, e quando i caldi raggi' (Torquato Tasso: *ottava rima*)

The unfolding of intense emotional expression characteristic of Monteverdi's output above all from the Third Book is emphasized and extended in the Fourth Book, basing itself on poetic situations that are no less strained and impassioned. If one excludes the graceful merriment of 'Quell'augellin che canta', all the other texts accumulate experiences that reflect the pain and suffering of the vicissitudes of love, on a scale moving from the decidedly sensual languors of 'Sí ch'io vorrei morire' to the more extended anguish of Nos. 2, 5, 7 and 11, from the spirited gallant skirmishing of 'Non piú guerra, pietate' to the emotional intensity of Nos. 3, 4, 6, 8, 10, 12, 16 and 19, which reaches a peak in various heart-rending moments of separation ('Longe da te, cor mio') or 'partenze' ('leave-taking'; see Nos. 1, 9 and 17). Indeed, the collection opens precisely with just such a 'partenza', as had already been the case with Wert (1595) and Gabucci (1598): 'Ah dolente partita' was also set to music by Belli (1593), Marenzio (1594), Wynant (1597), Artusini (1598), Bargnani (1599), Monte (1600), Apolloni (1600), Sartori (1600) and Dentice (1602), and it appears instead as a closing piece in Gian Antonio Cirullo's *Secondo libro de madrigali a cinque voci* (1598).[88]

Once again, it is in the poetry of Tasso that Monteverdi pits himself against the turbulent world of the most intense emotions, as had already occurred in the Third Book with the cycles concerning the abandoned Armida and Tancredi's lament. It is perhaps not without significance that the Fourth Book opens with the subtle emotionality of Guarini to end with the pained delirium of Erminia, which is scarcely inclined towards facile psychological games. Monteverdi's dramatic approach to Tasso would later become one of his most self-conscious proving grounds.

13   *Il quinto libro de madrigali a cinque voci* (1605)

In Venice in 1604, Ricciardo Amadino reprinted Monteverdi's Third Book (its fourth edition); in the following year there appeared an early reprint of the Fourth Book (scarcely two years after its first appearance) and a new collection, *Il quinto libro de madrigali*, dedicated directly to Duke Vincenzo Gonzaga:

> I come to present to Your Most Serene Lordship this my offspring of madrigals, entreating you that just as you have not scorned to hear them many times in your royal chambers while they were written in manuscript, and hearing them gave sign of welcoming them with singular favour, whence you honoured me with the task of heading your most noble music, so now may you welcome them in print, which, under the protection of so great a prince, will live an eternal life to the shame of those tongues which seek to bring death to the works of others.

The final reference is evidently to Artusi, first of all, and to those who associated themselves with his position. Monteverdi also makes specific reference to the Bolognese canon in the statement to the 'Studious readers' printed as an appendix here (and followed in the basso continuo partbook by the madrigal – just text – 'Chi l'armonia del ciel brama d'udire' by the preacher Fr. Cherubino Ferrari in praise of the composer), which has already been discussed.

We have seen that Artusi cited passages from 'Cruda Amarilli, che col nome ancora' and from 'O Mirtillo, Mirtillo anima mia' in his 1600 dialogue, and from 'Era l'anima mia' and from 'Ma se con la pietà non è in te spenta' in his treatise of 1603 (but still referring to 1598). Therefore if these madrigals seem clearly to date from before 1598, the dedication would seem to suggest that the others, too, are from before November 1601, when Monteverdi had sought to take the place of the deceased *maestro di cappella* Benedetto Pallavicino (after having heard and welcomed these madrigals, Vincenzo in fact 'honoured [Monteverdi] with the task of heading [his] most noble music').

1   'Cruda Amarilli, che col nome ancora' (Battista Guarini: *versi sciolti*)
2   'O Mirtillo, Mirtillo anima mia' (B. Guarini: *versi sciolti*)
3   'Era l'anima mia' (B. Guarini: madrigal)
4a 'Ecco, Silvio, colei che in odio hai tanto' (B. Guarini: *versi sciolti*)
  b 'Ma se con la pietà non è in te spenta'
  c 'Dorinda, ah dirò mia se mia non sei'
  d 'Ecco piegando le ginocchia a terra'
  e 'Ferir quel petto, Silvio?'
5a 'Ch'io t'ami, e t'ami piú della mia vita' (B. Guarini: *versi sciolti*)
  b 'Deh bella e cara e sí soave un tempo'
  c 'Ma tu, piú che mai dura'
6   'Che dar piú vi poss'io?' (madrigal)
7   'M'è piú dolce il penar per Amarilli' (B. Guarini: madrigal)
8   'Ahi come a un vago sol cortese giro' (B. Guarini: madrigal)
9   'Troppo ben può questo tiranno Amore' (B. Guarini: madrigal)
10 'Amor, se giusto sei' (madrigal)
11 ' "T'amo, mia vita" la mia cara vita' (B. Guarini: madrigal)
12 'E cosí a poco a poco' (B. Guarini: madrigal)
13 'Questi vaghi concenti' (madrigal)

Compared with the Fourth Book, the texts and styles of the Fifth Book show little change: Guarini clearly predominates, and with texts taken from *Il pastor fido*. Indeed, the Fifth Book turns still more than the Fourth to the situations and characters of Guarini's tragicomedy, drawing on various scenes: 1.2, lines 1–8 (No. 1); III.4, lines 1–13 (No. 2), already used in the Fourth Book ('Anima mia, perdona'); IV.9, lines 100–13 (No. 4a), 114–22 – with another line inserted (the fourth before the end) – (No. 4b), 123–30 (No. 4c), 138–48 (No. 4d), and 149–68 (No. 4e); III.3, lines 107–14 (No. 5a), 143–57 (No. 5b) and 158–73 – minus lines 167–9 – (No. 5c), a scene already exploited for 'Ah dolente partita' at the opening of the Fourth Book.

Well over half the volume is therefore dedicated to the sad fates of Guarini's characters: the lament of the unrequited lover, Mirtillo – which marks his first appearance in the play and which similarly gives to the opening of this new collection of madrigals a tone of painful anguish – and the parallel complaint of Amarilli, who cannot reciprocate his love; then the grieving reproaches of Dorinda to Silvio, who does not love her (with Silvio's emotional response), and of Mirtillo to Amarilli. From within *Il pastor fido*, Monteverdi – like Wert, Marenzio, Pallavicino and Luzzaschi before him – takes for the most part passages of lyric emotion from the sad tale of the couples Mirtillo and Amarilli, and Silvio and Dorinda, focusing above all on the more passionate moments of contemplation. As with Marenzio, however, Monteverdi's interest extends to the dialogue between Dorinda and Silvio, not just the speeches of a single character taken out of context to be enjoyed as an isolated madrigal.

The reference to a scenic and narrative framework becomes explicit: in effect, a dramatic entity is represented in a long chain of dialogues, with the first two madrigals entrusted to Dorinda, the next two to Silvio, and the final one again to Dorinda.

For the first time, Monteverdi also adopted in the Fifth Book a 'basso continuo for the harpsichord, chitarrone or other similar instrument, written particularly for the last six [madrigals] and for the others *ad libitum*', as the composer indicates on the title-page; he also emphasizes the indispensability of the continuo at the head of the basso continuo partbook ('which will necessarily be played for the requirement of the last six madrigals, and for the others *ad libitum*'). It was a common performing practice in the madrigal (and not only there) to add instruments to the voices both to double them and also to stand in their place: Caccini's preface to *Le nuove musiche* (1602) noted that listeners were 'accustomed then to hearing as solos madrigals published [originally] for multiple voices'.[89] The expressive experiments of the last decades of the sixteenth century had encouraged in some circles a particular interest in the practice of singing solo to instrumental accompaniment, a technique until then limited for the most part to improvisatory performing practices or else confined to minor genres (for example, the villanella). The turn towards a kind of monody with a very different character and emotional weight had prompted the parallel development of the accompanimental basso continuo (but conceived as another voice of a polyphonic ensemble) as was used at the same time by organists in the context of liturgical music.

> To these melodies for one voice one is accustomed to add the accompaniment of an instrumental part, commonly in the lower register, which, because it continues from the beginning to the end is usually called basso continuo; and it mostly consists of long notes that with the vocal line enclose the inner voices, which, for some few notes or more, are indicated with numbers as being less important; not acting as anything other than the filling [*il ripieno*] (as they say) they are left to the judgement of the player, given that it is not usual that he should depart significantly from the common and ordinary material, so to speak, of symphonizing . . .[90]

As we know, around 1600 these practices – either used on occasion or limited to exclusive élites – flourished extensively in music as much of the theatre as of the chamber and the church, being publicly and officially sanctioned by their diffusion through print: the Roman *Rappresentatione di Anima, et di Corpo* by Emilio del Cavaliere (1600) and the Florentine settings of *Euridice* by Caccini (1600) and Peri (1601); the first three books of madrigals by the Mantuan Jew Salomone Rossi (I, 1600 – 'with some of the said madrigals to sing with the chitarrone, with its tablature placed in the soprano partbook'; II, 1602 – 'with the basso continuo to play in concert placed in the soprano partbook'; III, 1603 – 'with its basso continuo to play on harmony instruments'); the *Madrigali* for 1–3 voices by Luzzaschi (1601); *Le nuove musiche* by Caccini (1602) and the two volumes of *Musiche* by Domenico Maria Melli (1602); Banchieri's *Concerti ecclesiastici* (1595); the half-dozen collections of masses, motets and psalms published by Orfeo Vecchi in Milan between 1597 and 1603; the reprint of the *Vespertina omnium solemnitatum psalmodia* by Giovanni Croce with the addition of the 'basso to play on the organ' (1601); Viadana's *Cento concerti ecclesiastici* (1602); the *Concerti ecclesiastici* by Pompeo Signorucci (1602) and Giacomo Moro (1604); and *Il secondo libro de mottetti* by Gabriele Fattorini (1602). Of all these works, Monteverdi must have been most aware of the collections by Viadana and above all (because they belong to the same genre, the madrigal) by Rossi – both composers were active at Mantua – and also the *Madrigali . . . per cantare et sonare a uno e doi e tre soprani* by Luzzasco Luzzaschi recently printed in 1601 in Rome by Simone Verovio.

14   1605–1607

In the same year as the Fifth Book, Ricciardo Amadino in Venice also published *I nuovi fioretti musicali a tre voci*, in which the Mantuan Amante Franzoni gathered together various compositions both by himself and by musicians associated with the Gonzaga court: Gastoldi, Giovanni Leite, Claudio and Giulio Cesare Monteverdi, and Giulio Cesare Bianchi (all represented by one piece each). Claudio Monteverdi's contribution to this anthology is 'Prima vedrò ch'in questi prati nascano', a strophic canzonetta on two *ottave* in eleven-syllable *versi sdruccioli* (i.e. twelve syllables per line, with the accent on the antepenultimate syllable) by an unknown poet (the first six lines are all in *rima baciata*) on a pastoral subject, as is almost inevitable with this type of verse (on the example of Sannazaro's *Arcadia*).

As the title-page makes clear, the collection has throughout a '*basso generale* for the harpsichord, chitarrone and other such instruments', providing evidence of the diffusion of a practice felt increasingly more indispensable. Monteverdi's canzonetta was reprinted in 1607 in the second edition of Franzoni's *Fioretti* (again printed by Ricciardo Amadino); it is impossible to date the spiritual version of this piece in the manuscript anthology (mentioned above) now in Bologna, Civico Museo Bibliografico Musicale, Q. 27. And continuing on the subject of reprints, some madrigals from Monteverdi's two most recent books were included by Melchior Borchgrevinck, 'organist of the Most Serene King of Denmark', in two volumes of his *Giardino novo bellissimo di varii fiori musicali scieltissimi* published in Copenhagen by Heinrich Waltkirch: in the first (1605), 'Io mi son giovinetta', 'Quell'augellin che canta', 'Non piú guerra, pietate' and 'Ah dolente partita'; and in the second (1606), 'Cruda Amarilli, che col nome ancora' and 'Cor mio, mentre vi miro'.

15 Orfeo (1607)

Yesterday was performed the comedy in the usual theatre and with the customary magnificence, and tomorrow evening the Most Serene Lord the Prince [Francesco Gonzaga] is to sponsor a performance in a room of the apartments which the Most Serene Madame of Ferrara used to occupy. It should be most unusual, as all the actors are to sing their parts; it is said on all sides that it will be a great success. No doubt I shall be driven to attend out of sheer curiosity, unless I am prevented from getting in by the lack of space.

Thus Carlo Magni, writing from Mantua on 23 February 1607, informed his brother Giovanni in Rome of the imminence of a unique – for Mantua – theatrical event in the current carnival.[91] On the same day, the Crown Prince, Francesco Gonzaga, promoter of the initiative, also wrote of the impending event to his brother Ferdinando – a passionate devotee of music and poetry – who was then a student at Pisa:

The musical play is to be performed in our academy tomorrow, since Giovan Gualberto has done very well in the short time he has been here. Not only has he thoroughly learnt the whole of his part by heart, but he delivers it with much grace and to great effect; I am most delighted with him. And since the play has been printed so that everyone in the audience can have a copy to follow while it is sung, I am sending Your Lordship a copy, just as I shall let you have, by another messenger, some placards just published for a tournament which may take place on Carnival day. If some similar entertainment has been held there, I beseech Your Lordship to favour me by sending me details.[92]

The première of Orfeo therefore took place on 24 February 1607 at the ducal palace in Mantua, in the apartments formerly occupied by Margherita Gonzaga, the widow of Alfonso II d'Este (the 'apartments which the Most Serene Madame of Ferrara used to occupy'), on the occasion of a meeting of the Accademia degli Invaghiti, founded in 1562 by Cesare Gonzaga, Duke of Guastalla.

However, this should not be cause for anyone's astonishment, it being typical of the lord academicians of the Invaghiti to perform miraculous tasks on every occasion, as more recently did the aforementioned most virtuous Lord Count Alessandro Striggio in defending his various conclusions on love which are still seen in print, with such readiness and fluency that everyone remained full of wonder. The same has also published, under the name of 'Ritenuto academico Invaghito', Orfeo, a stage play written in most graceful verses in the Tuscan tongue, which was then set to music by the virtuous Signor Claudio Monteverdi, and was staged in a great theatre with most noble scenery. In it sang Signor Francesco Rasio, so famous for his excellence in this profession that everyone holds that there can be few others in the world who can surpass him.[93]

Alessandro Striggio jr. was born in Mantua in about 1573, son of Alessandro Striggio and of the singer and lutenist Virginia Vagnoli: he studied law in his native city before entering a diplomatic career. Like his father, who was also a high-level functionary in the court bureaucracy, Alessandro cultivated interests in music and poetry for pleasure: he had the opportunity to display his talents on a court trip to Ferrara in 1584 as a singer (which gained him the appreciation of Alfonso II d'Este), and in Florence in 1589 as a viol-player in the course of the *intermedi* for Girolamo Bargagli's *La pellegrina*, performed for the celebrations of the wedding of Ferdinando de' Medici and Christine of Lorraine. In 1596, he edited his father's *Terzo libro di madrigali*, published posthumously in Venice by Angelo Gardano.[94]

The favourable reception granted *Orfeo* at its première encouraged the duke to have it repeated before a larger audience. As Prince Francesco wrote again to Ferdinando Gonzaga on 1 March 1607:

> The play was performed to the great satisfaction of all who heard it. The Lord Duke, not content to have been present at this performance, or to have heard it many times in rehearsal, has ordered it to be given again; and so it will be, today, in the presence of all the ladies resident in the city. For this reason Giovan Gualberto is to remain here at present; he has done very well, and given immense pleasure to all who have heard him sing, and particularly to Madame . . .[95]

Of the performers at the première, we know at least that they included Giovan Gualberto Magli, a castrato in the service of the Florentine court who had been lent to the Gonzagas for this occasion (he played Music in the prologue, and then Proserpina (Persephone) and another unspecified part, perhaps that of the messenger or Speranza (Hope)). There was also 'that little priest who played Eurydice' (Fr. Girolamo Bacchini?) and Francesco Rasi, a nobleman from Arezzo, singer (tenor) and composer active at the Mantuan court from 1598, who we can be sure took the part of Orpheus. Like Magli, Rasi was a pupil of Caccini and in the 1590s he was in Florence, close to the circles of the Camerata: in 1600 he was sent to the Medici court to take part in the theatrical spectacles staged to celebrate the wedding of Maria de' Medici and Henri IV of France, during which he sang in *Il rapimento di Cefalo* by Chiabrera and played the part of Aminta in Peri and Rinuccini's *Euridice*. Thus both Rasi and Magli came from Caccini's school of 'affective' solo singing; moreover, Rasi had been in contact with those Florentine circles interested in monody and in its applications on the stage, taking direct part in one of the first attempts at a totally sung stage work (*Euridice*).[96]

The Duke of Mantua had also attended the 1600 festivities in Florence: among other things, he was related to the Florentine court by marriage, having wedded a Medici. Moreover, his second-born, Ferdinando (who was a student at Pisa), was well informed of what was being done in Florence in the field of music. Also, from 1601 to 1607 the Medici court had taken up the habit of spending the months from January to Easter in Pisa, and before the court there, Ferdinando himself had had performed during carnival his own stage works composed in the new style: in 1606 the battle-piece *Dario e*

Alessandro, and in 1607 a 'comedy' in music.[97] The fact that Mantua followed Florentine theatrical endeavours, whether directly or no, is also witnessed by the request which concludes Francesco Gonzaga's letter of 23 February 1607. But whatever the case, as in Florence and Rome, in Mantua there was an élite circle of aristocratic intellectuals prepared to venture upon a form of entertainment as refined as it was fascinating, applying to the theatre the sophisticated erudition of solo song.

The unofficial character of the première of *Orfeo*, before a small audience, is due above all to the patronage granted it by the Crown prince and not by the duke in his official capacity, and also to the choice of location for the performance, not the ducal theatre but a 'room of the apartments which the Most Serene Madame of Ferrara used to occupy', according to Magni, who also hints at the scant room left for the audience: 'No doubt I shall be driven to attend out of sheer curiosity, unless I am prevented from getting in by the lack of space'. As for the composer, two years later, in the dedication of the printed score of *Orfeo* addressed to Prince Francesco Gonzaga – whose support for the composition and performance of the opera is duly acknowledged ('you, in the manner of a kind star, were propitious for it at its birth' says the composer, among other things) – Monteverdi recalls the limitations of the stage erected for the performance: 'the play of *Orfeo* which in the Accademia degli Invaghiti under the auspices of Your Highness was represented in music on a narrow stage ...' The success of the première and the admiring interest for this new theatrical genre must have encouraged a repeat performance: Prince Francesco's letter of 1 March proves that *Orfeo* was staged at least once more on that day.[98]

Striggio's text is based on the well-known story of the mythological singer of Thrace, Orpheus. After the prologue sung by Music, Act I opens with the celebrations made by nymphs and shepherds for the couple Orpheus and Eurydice, whose wedding is very near. In the act that follows, tragic news is delivered: while she was gathering flowers in a field, Eurydice was bitten by a snake and is dead; desperate, Orpheus decides to attempt an impossible task, to descend to the underworld to rescue his beloved. Thanks to the seductive power of his song, Orpheus overcomes the thousand obstacles of that hostile world, obtaining leave from the King of Hades, Pluto, to take Eurydice back to earth: but he must never turn towards her to see her until they have left the underworld. However, during their journey, Orpheus yields to the impulse to check whether Eurydice is in fact following him: at the moment when he sees his beloved, he loses her forever. Returning to earth alone, Orpheus abandons himself to despair, proclaiming that he will never again let himself be taken by love for a woman, but he is put to flight by a group of raving Bacchantes who set about punishing Orpheus for his new-found misogyny, causing him a terrible death.

The libretto was published in Mantua in 1607 by the ducal printer, Francesco Osanna (with the title *La favola d'Orfeo*, where 'favola' means 'scenic action'), 'so that everyone in the audience can have a copy to follow while it is sung', said Prince Francesco in the letter of 23 February given above. But the musical score was printed instead in Venice by Ricciardo Amadino only in 1609 (and reprinted in 1615) with a dedication to Francesco Gonzaga dated Mantua, 22 August 1609. Writing from Cremona on 24 August 1609, Monteverdi asked Striggio to present a copy fresh from the press to the dedicatee (L.7):

> I have nothing else to tell Your Most Illustrious Lordship except about *Orfeo*: I hope that tomorrow, which is the 25th, my brother will receive the finished publication from the printer, who will send it to him by the courier from Venice which arrives tomorrow, as it happens. And as soon as he receives it he will have one copy bound and will give it to His Most Serene Highness the Prince, and when he does so I beg Your Most Illustrious Lordship to put in a few words with His Most Serene Highness, conveying to him the great desire I have in my heart to prove what a very devoted and very humble servant I am, and explaining that I give little to His Most Serene Highness (who deserves much) really because of lack of opportunity rather than through any defect of spirit . . .

There are discrepancies between the libretto and the score. In addition to some minor differences[99] and cuts to the final choruses of the first three acts (set to music only until lines 116, 147 and 107 respectively), the most significant divergence is at the end of the opera. In Act v (after line 51), the libretto presents the onslaught of the Bacchantes who put Orpheus to flight and then abandon themselves to dionysiac celebrations before setting themselves to punishing with a horrible death the mythological singer, guilty of misogyny and their long-time enemy (but events on the stage end with the orgiastic dance; all the rest is left understood). Monteverdi's score omits the intervention of the Bacchantes, replacing it with the appearance *ex machina* of Apollo, who, after a dialogue with Orpheus, ascends with him to heaven while a chorus hymns the happy outcome.

This change has hitherto been explained by the limitations of the stage for the première ('the lack of space' mentioned in the letter by Carlo Magni given above; the 'narrow stage' mentioned by Monteverdi in the dedication of the score). It has been thought either that the Apollonian apotheosis was the original finale, which the composer had to abandon for technical reasons because of the restrictions of space, adopting the Bacchic ending but reviving his original intentions when preparing his score for the press;[100] or that the descent of Apollo on a machine was added 'for the enlarged staging of the repeat performance in the theatre'.[101] However, the details of the opera being transferred from the temporary stage of the première to a fixed court theatre are not confirmed clearly by the documents, and one can perhaps find other explanations for the substitution of the Apollonian finale transmitted by the score in place of the dionysiac ending now entirely lost to us (except perhaps for a passage drawn from the concluding *moresca*).

If one believes that the libretto – given its direct relevance to, and specific function for, the première – is a more accurate reflection of what happened at the first performance, then there is no doubt that one must regard the Bacchic finale as the original: above all, it also represents something more refined and exclusive compared with the explicit finality of the apotheosis in company with Apollo. The latter is not just a consolatory happy ending, but first and foremost it marks a clear end to the story. To conclude the performance with the dance of the Bacchantes signified entrusting to the cultural expectations of each spectator – the academicians at the first performance – the task of concluding the story in the mind, while to call up Apollo and to demonstrate the celestial triumph of Orpheus constituted a happy ending, one above all bringing the story to a definite close, while also fulfilling a didactic function entirely foreign to the other finale. The glorifying ascent of Orpheus with Apollo is in fact accompanied by a chorus that does not present a general moral (as had occurred in the preceding acts) but which instead tends to place the story that has just been represented clearly in the context of a specifically Christian religious experience – something alien to the text thus far – which from the earth, through the idea of *vanitas vanitatum*, necessarily leads to heaven. If we further consider that this final chorus is a brisk strophic song, as far removed as possible from the elaborate madrigalian style which distinguishes all the preceding choruses, we gain a still stronger impression that here is a finale that was perhaps added to apply retroactively (and in the spirit of the Counter-Reformation) didactic messages that were unnecessary in the case of a stage work destined for a highly select audience, but which became indispensable when it was enlarged for a wider public, whereupon it was felt necessary to justify the work by hasty recourse to the classical criterion of *juvare delectando*.

The fact that Striggio's text was originally destined for an academic audience has left perceptible traces, which can be reduced in essence to two complementary features: the search for a regularity of structure that perhaps penetrates every aspect of the work and which reveals the demands of models to be imitated or emulated; and the notable level of allusion in its components, which could be decoded by a culturally gifted gathering, such as that of an academy but that probably had scant significance for a wider and more heterogeneous audience.

The most obvious evidence of Striggio's need to structure his text according to the canons of the regular theatre of the sixteenth century is its division into the traditional five acts typical of all contemporary dramatic genres (tragedy, comedy, pastoral tragicomedy) but until now generally ignored in music theatre, with the exception of the Chiabrera–Caccini *Il rapimento di Cefalo*: in Florence, both *Dafne* and *Euridice* by Rinuccini and Peri had been divided into specific scenes, but not into acts (and similarly, probably the small pastoral plays produced by Laura Guidiccioni and Emilio del Cavaliere); and in Rome, Cavalieri's *La rappresentatione di Anima, et di Corpo* and Agostino Agazzari's *Eumelio* (1606) were each in three acts. With Striggio, the impression of regularity is emphasized by the systematic use of the chorus at the end of each act, contemplating and moralizing on the action according to the function it fulfilled in Classical Antiquity.

In the end, the canonic quality of the overall design carries the day even over the failure to observe the unities, especially that of place (Acts I, II and V are located 'on the plains of Thrace', and Acts III and IV in the underworld). The fact that the 'unity of place' is left unobserved also reveals that a fixed stage has been renounced in favour of one that changes, revealing opera's affinity with the spectacles typical of such 'rogue' genres as the *intermedio apparente*, which itself drew widely on mythology (indeed, the theme of Orpheus itself had been used to this end, for example, in Milan in 1599 and in Cremona in 1607).[102] But if the result of this was to attenuate the need for temporal compression, as had already occurred in Rinuccini's *Euridice*, the unity of action was, on the other hand, pursued thanks to the focus on what theorists would call a 'simple' plot (*intreccio semplice*), that is, limited to a single story (that of Orpheus and Eurydice) and avoiding digressions or subplots. In the end, this general sense of regularity mitigates the hybrid nature of the final product and confers an impression of homogeneity upon the mixture of classicizing echoes, *intermedio*-like scenic displays and pastoral traits that almost entirely characterized these first examples of fully sung theatrical works.

Like the majority of dramatic texts hitherto written to be set to music (all the Florentine ones, plus the Roman *Eumelio*), *Orfeo*, too, can be placed within the third genre established by sixteenth-century theatrical classifications, that is, as *boschereccio*, given that its pastoral features prevail over its other components. At root, this is because of the critical fortunes of the notion that the unrealistic nature of sung speech was most practicable when dealing with subjects that brought to the stage the legendary shepherds of Arcadia or the like, and mythological or allegorical characters (in the cast of *Orfeo*, Hope (Speranza) belongs to the latter category). This was made explicit some twenty years later within dramatic theory by, for example, Giovan Battista Doni and the anonymous author of *Il corago*.[103]

Doubtless it was the academic need for normative models that encouraged Striggio, because of this gravitation towards the pastoral, to place his work under the protection of the two most celebrated examples of the genre, Torquato Tasso's *Aminta*, and Battista Guarini's *Pastor fido* (which had received a memorable performance in Mantua not ten years before). These illustrious forebears produce in Striggio choices of phrases and images, the gelling of the emotions in climactic laments, and above all – because it is generalized and all-pervasive – the sense of rhetoric focusing on the sound of words and designed to constitute a linguistic pattern that is by itself 'musical'.[104] Thanks to these literary elements, Striggio's text becomes the bearer of cultural references and connotations according to a taste for cultivated allusion that is particularly evident in the two 'inferno' acts (III and IV), for which the pastoral tradition could not offer any assistance and which led the librettist to revive no less a poet than Dante, a truly remarkable source if one takes into account the present date and context.[105]

In fact, this discussion of Striggio's poetic models implicitly involves the complementary issue of the strong allusive quality of his text, one rich in literary resonances perhaps not identifiable to all but certainly very significant for Striggio and his academic colleagues. Indeed, only in this context can one fully understand the 'lieta canzon' ('happy song') sung by Orpheus in Act I ('Rosa del ciel, vita del mondo e degna'; 'Rose of the sky, life of the world and worthy . . .'); the meaning of this declaration to the sun is made clear only with reference to the device of the Accademia degli Invaghiti, an eagle with its eyes fixed on the sun, accompanied by the motto 'Nihil pulcherius' ('Nothing more beautiful').[106] Similarly, for Striggio's colleagues even the choice of subject must have been rich in references to a specifically local tradition: in Mantua the story had a distinguished history going back to Poliziano's *Favola d'Orfeo* and represented thereafter 'in its elaborations, *Orphei tragoedia* and the *Favola di Orfeo e Aristeo*, and its imitations. Nor do there lack other points of reference, like, for example, the short narrative cycle telling of Orpheus frescoed in an *atrium* of the Palazzo del Giardino in Sabbioneta, the icono-graphical design of which evokes Mantuan figurative traditions, specifically the Orpheus of Mantegna's Parnassus for the studio of Isabella d'Este Gonzaga, not to mention the figurative conventions of decorations for prints of favourite poets, and other iconographical issues.'[107]

However, the importance of these components, as with the question of the two finales, leads Striggio to distance himself from what must have been the most immediate predecessor of his literary endeavour, Rinuccini's *Euridice*. *Orfeo* is linked to *Euridice* by the subject-matter and perhaps by the reasons dictating its choice: for these first entirely sung stage-works, what better plot was there than such a paradigmatic *exemplum* of the power of music united with poetry as is celebrated by the final chorus of *Euridice* and the prologue of *Orfeo*? But the differences in the solutions adopted by the two authors are noteworthy. They begin with the title – even before the opera starts Striggio directs our attention to the real protagonist of the action (of whom Eurydice is more like a passive reflection) – and the prologue, to which Rinuccini had allocated a theoretical function, summarizing the intellectual debates of the Florentines. Also different is the design of the crucial scene in which the death of Eurydice is announced. In Rinuccini, the terrible news is given by the messenger (Dafne) only at the end of her narration, and it is followed immediately by a short lament by Orpheus – who then leaves the stage – and a general complaint. In Striggio, the news is given suddenly, and in his succeeding lament, Orpheus's decision to descend to the inferno visibly matures, without awaiting the external intervention and appearance – off-stage – of Venus (Venere) as is only narrated in Rinuccini. Then the inferno scenes – in particular, the exchange between Orpheus and Charon and later, the eventful return of Orpheus in company with Eurydice and his final loss – are all played out directly before the eyes of the audience, whereas in Rinuccini they are omitted or, again, just narrated.

Although Striggio was gifted with less literary knowledge and refinement than Rinuccini, he grasps the dramatic substance in a much more penetrating way to realize his expressive ends, for which he also invents long-breathed scenic devices which are effectively theatrical – such as those made up, for example, by the first two acts combined – which were to draw from the music a still greater capacity for communication.

16 The *Scherzi musicali a tre voci* (1607)

A few months after the performances of *Orfeo*, the *Scherzi musicali a tre voci* appeared in the summer of 1607: they were again published by Ricciardo Amadino in Venice, but edited by Monteverdi's brother, Giulio Cesare. This collection, like the later edition of *Orfeo*, was dedicated (Venice, 21 July 1607) to Prince Francesco Gonzaga, and it also contains as an appendix the aforementioned *Dichiaratione* of the 'Letter that is found printed in the Fifth Book' of Monteverdi's madrigals, as the title-page announces. In the collection, Giulio Cesare also included two of his own 'scherzi', 'Deh, chi tace il bel pensiero' and 'Dispiegate'. As for the texts, except for the *terze rime* by Sannazaro and the final 'balletto', they are all anacreontic canzonettas.

1 'I bei legami' (Gabriello Chiabrera)
2 'Amarilli onde m'assale' (G. Chiabrera)
3 'Fugge il verno dei dolori' (G. Chiabrera?)
4 'Quando l'alba in oriente' (G. Chiabrera)
5 'Non cosí tost'io miro' (G. Chiabrera)
6 'Damigella' (G. Chiabrera)
7 'La pastorella mia spietata e rigida' (Jacopo Sannazaro: *terze rime*)
8 'O rosetta che rossetta' (G. Chiabrera)
9 'Amorosa pupilletta' (Ansaldo Cebà)
10 'Vaghi rai di cigli ardenti' (G. Chiabrera)
11 'La vïoletta' (G. Chiabrera)
12 'Giovinetta' (A. Cebà)
13 'Dolci miei sospiri' (G. Chiabrera)
14 'Clori amorosa' (G. Chiabrera?)
15 'Lidia spina del mio core' (A. Cebà)
16 'Deh, chi tace il bel pensiero' (A. Cebà), by G. C. Monteverdi
17 'Dispiegate' (A. Cebà), by G. C. Monteverdi
18 'De la bellezza le dovute lodi' (Ferdinando Gonzaga?), 'balletto'

The *Dichiaratione* in the appendix also contains a (rather controversial) passage referring directly to the preceding *Scherzi* which prompts the suggestion that they were composed after 1599:

if the matter has to be considered in this light, my brother will have not a few arguments in his favour, in particular as regards the *canto alla francese* in this modern manner which has been a matter of marvel in publications of the last three or four years, now for motet texts, now madrigals, now canzonettas and arias. Who before him brought it back to Italy when he returned from the baths of Spa in the year 1599? Who before him began to apply it to Latin texts and to those in our vernacular tongue? Did he not then compose these *Scherzi*?

One should add that precisely in the first years of the new century, Chiabrera, the author of nearly all the texts set here, was associated with Vincenzo Gonzaga (in 1602 and 1603) and was in Mantua in person in 1602.[108]

But the question of the 'canto alla francese' brought back from the trip to Flanders in 1599 is a very thorny one. Scholars have variously linked the term with the *air de cour* and the *musique mesurée à l'antique* developed by Baïf's Académie de Poésie et de Musique (Prunières); the use of a rhythmic pattern – pairs of slurred quavers – which the theorist Wolfgang Schonsleder was to call the 'modus gallicanus' in 1631 (Osthoff); or more straightforwardly, the adoption of vocal performing practices typical of the north European school (Schrade).[109] This last hypothesis would seem to be the most likely, especially if one considers the instructions that accompany the use of this term in Monteverdi's later output.[110] In the *Madrigali guerrieri, et amorosi ... Libro ottavo* (1638), 'Dolcissimo uscignolo' and 'Chi vole aver felice e lieto il core' are each directed to be 'sung with full voice [*a voce piena*], in the French manner', and each alternates a solo voice (the soprano) and the 'tutti'. The third setting of 'Confitebor tibi Domine' in the *Selva morale e spirituale* (1640–41) is also marked 'alla francese': here we again find the use of a solo voice (the soprano) and the alternation of solo and *tutti*. Moreover, indirect evidence from 1600 is provided by Francesco Rasi concerning his pupil Sabina, who had been sent to the Duke of Mantua to 'learn to sing in the French manner', a manner in which Vincenzo evidently took delight; however, in a letter from Florence (where he was taking part in *Euridice*), Rasi objects that thus 'she will lose all the Italian style given her with such hard work over the past two years', adding that 'as much as the Spanish style helps the Italian one, so the French style detracts from it, filling it with many ugly actions such as movements of the mouth, of the shoulders and more'.[111]

Monteverdi's *Scherzi* are strophic *tricinia* framed by instrumental ritornellos similarly in three parts: it is the first example of the genre to appear in print. Michael Praetorius calls them 'Tricinia jocosa' (*Syntagma musicum*, 1619: III, *Termini musici*, p. 129) 'for two sopranos and one bass, with some texts [verses] to be sung, and immediately thereafter a ritornello without text to be played by instruments, two violins and a *violone* or bassoon (whenever a harpsichord or a chitarrone or theorbo are not available) and to be played at the beginning and at the end of the piece, or also between the various strophes of the text wherever it is written "repeat the ritornello"'. But the possibility of performance 'alla francese', that is, probably by alternating solo and *tutti*, is offered by the performing instructions set down at the head of the collection under the title 'Avvertimenti':

> Before beginning singing, the ritornello should be played twice.
>
> The ritornellos should be played at the end of every stanza, the soprano lines by two *violini da braccio* and the bass by a chitarrone, or harpsichord, or other such instrument.
>
> The first soprano, once the first stanza has been sung to three voices with the violins, can be sung solo or else an octave lower in the stanzas which follow, but resuming the last stanza with the same three voices and the same violins.
>
> Where one sees some lines in the position of the words, those notes which are placed above these lines should be played, but not sung.

This prescription is possible given the almost entirely homorhythmic writing, with the upper voice carrying the most significant melodic line (as often occurred in the minor lyric genres of the sixteenth century, as, for example, in the villanella and then the canzonetta) and the others in an ancillary position, the bass acting as a harmonic foundation and the second soprano as a filler. In general, the ritornellos (which have 'a subtle, fanciful coherence, and often explicit thematic connections' with the vocal part)[112] are also presented – excepting some cases in which the three parts are combined polyphonically (as for example in 'Fugge il verno dei dolori') – with two upper voices paired or in dialogue with the bass, according to schemes and structures that would be fully developed in the seventeenth-century trio sonata and which here can be regarded as something of an archetype.[113] Around the same time, Ricciardo Amadino also printed in Venice the first two books of Salomone Rossi's *Sinfonie et gagliarde* (1607, 1608), in which writing for two parts and basso continuo predominates. Therefore an essential contribution to the nascent sonata style of Lombardy and more generally of the Po valley is made by Mantuan composers, particularly with the three-part pieces by Monteverdi (for voices and instruments, including those in *Orfeo*), Rossi (for instruments alone) and a little later by their pupil Giovan Battista Buonamente (who was to inscribe to Monteverdi the 'Sonata prima' and the 'Sinfonia prima' of his *Settimo libro di sonate, sinfonie, gagliarde, corrente et brandi a tre*, Venice, Alessandro Vincenti, 1637).[114]

Metrical symmetry (and at the same time, strong rhythmic regularity) and diminutions in the melodic patterns are the equivalent of the diminutive words, the short verses, the polymetre and the numerous rhyme-schemes (*baciate, al mezzo, interne*) which are the basis of the anacreontic grace and lightness of Chiabrera's melic art, an art which – albeit with classicizing ambitions and taking account of French developments (Ronsard; the Pléiade) – sings of pastoral games, presenting in miniature the languors of love.[115] In his *Geri, dialogo della tessitura delle canzoni*, Chiabrera had made the chief interlocutor, Giovan Francesco Geri, say:

> in the vernacular, it is customary to compose verses from four syllables to twelve in length, so that one versifies in various ways, so that the main accent should fall on various syllables. And I will not speak of the art of construct-

ing such verses, because this is not what we have proposed ... Moreover, if Spanish and French, most noble languages, are rich in their variety of verses, it does not seem sound advice to have Tuscan stay with only two types of verse (for the great poets have until now not used any other but seven- and eleven-syllable lines). To be sure, it seems that the Greeks for some 600 years stayed with just the hexameter, but Archilochus, making new ones heard, encouraged the people to write them with infinite variety. And similarly, we see that the Romans wanted to do the same, in whose tracks it cannot be very dangerous to follow. One should also consider whether it is done well that for subjects of sweetness and tenderness there should be verse of a lesser quality than those which are adopted for sublime matters, and certainly it will not seem anything other than well done. And the example of the Greek and Roman poets persuades us of this, who in the works called lyric by them do not much encumber themselves with the hexameter, but leave it to one side to celebrate heroes, and the French today do the same ... Therefore if the Tuscan tongue has much variety of verses, and having them is the source of its dignity, and if one should not banish some of these verses for the little sound that they have, it should not seem strange, nor be a cause for criticism, that in writing canzonas the strophes should be provided with verses that differ among themselves. And indeed longer and shorter verses, halved and extended ones, should accompany each other and should mix their separate manners together. The example of the ancients advises us of this ... Today I see that composing canzonas in various verses does not cause boredom, and I see the people eagerly lending their ear to them, which is no small argument persuading us that it is a praiseworthy thing. And it is certain that singing masters willingly set such works to music, indeed they do it with great charm and readily confess that the variety of verses grants them the convenience of offering greater delight to the hearer with their notes; and widespread opinion is no vain proof, given that in every art the masters are to be honoured. Let all Italy, and especially Florence and Rome, bear witness that I do not tell lies.[116]

It seems clear that the metrical experiments in Chiabrera's lyric poetry were particularly appreciated by musicians around 1600, providing them with new ways of shaping minor musical genres. For pieces in this light and graceful vein, some composers adopted the name 'scherzo': for example, Gabriello Puliti in his *Scherzi, capricci et fantasie per cantar a due voci* of 1605; Domenico Brunetti in his *Euterpe* of 1606, which contains 'diverse madrigals, canzonettas, arias, stanzas and scherzos'; plus Monteverdi and, later, above all Cifra and Milanuzzi. The term has no formal implications and is taken from Chiabrera himself, who uses it in his *Geri*:

> I believe that you should read French poetry: recall their amorous charms, those flatterings, those tendernesses, which every woman and every man can and knows how to express, and everyone, when they are expressed, understands them easily; do you not take pleasure in seeing such pleasantries [*scherzi*] so lovingly represented, which require no effort, nor comment, nor gloss to be understood?[117]

The *Scherzi musicali* offer themselves as refined and delightful courtly pastimes 'da camera' – for the chamber – a destination to which Giulio Cesare Monteverdi also refers in the dedication, calling them 'flowers which in the beautiful garden of the royal chambers of Your Highness [Prince Francesco] were by my brother Claudio sown and cultivated'. Moreover, the piece which concludes the collection, 'De la bellezza le dovute lodi', is clearly located within courtly circles (even if the exact circumstances of its perform- ance are unclear). Called a 'balletto', it consists of an 'entrata' for instrumental trio (analogous to the ritornellos of the preceding pieces) and a sung 'balletto' – still *a3* – which is articulated in various sections to a text characterized by polymetre and strophic structures (this last formal characteristic, however, is not taken up in the musical setting). One passage, 'È la bellezza un raggio / de la celeste luce' seems modelled on Tasso's 'È la bellezza un raggio / di chiarissima luce', and also on Striggio, from the chorus which closes Act IV of *Orfeo* ('È la virtute un raggio / di celeste bellezza').

This text celebrates the beauty, and a victory, of Venus, probably resulting from the judgement of Paris. One can therefore suggest that it was used for a stage-work which drew on that subject. Indeed, in 1607 Ferdinando Gonzaga had asked Michelangelo Buonarroti 'il giovane' for his play *Il giudizio di Paride*, which was later given by him to the Medici court to celebrate the wedding of Prince Cosimo and Maria Magdalena of Austria. Writing from Florence on 31 July 1607, Buonarroti explained to Ferdinando that 'my play about Paris is already committed'; he also regrets this fact because Ferdinando had earlier sent him a letter 'in which you show yourself already to have designed some place [*luogo*] to honour it'.[118] A hypothetical 'place' conceived by Ferdinando could be precisely the *balletto* 'De la bellezza le dovute lodi', written by him and set to music by Monteverdi, which could have been used as a danced *intermedio*.

17 The summer of 1607 and the death of Claudia Cattaneo Monteverdi

During the summer of 1607, with Duke Vincenzo in Sampierdarena, Monte- verdi had permission to visit Cremona. Even in this holiday period, the demands of the court obliged him to work, since he had been commissioned to set two sonnets to music, as he himself states in a letter dated Cremona, 28 July 1607 (L.4), sent to the ducal counsellor Anibale Iberti in Genoa:

> As soon as His Most Serene Highness left Mantua, I too went away – to see my father in Cremona, where I still am – which is why I did not receive Your Most Illustrious Lordship's letter earlier than the 20th of this month, and so on seeing His Most Serene Highness's commission, I straightway began setting the sonnet to music, and was engaged in doing this for six days, then two more what with trying it out and rewriting it. I worked at it with the same devotion of mind that I have always had in regard to every other composition written by me in order the more to serve His Most Serene Highness's most delicate taste.

But I did not work with comparable physical strength, because I was a little indisposed. Nevertheless I hope that this madrigal is not going to displease His Most Serene Highness ...

Here then is the music I have composed; but you will be doing me a kindness by handing it over, before His Most Serene Highness hears it, to Signor Don Bassano [Cassola] so that he can rehearse it and get a firm grasp of the melody [aria] together with the other gentlemen singers, because it is very difficult for a singer to perform a part which he has not first practised, and greatly damaging to the composition itself, as it is not completely understood on being sung for the first time.

I shall send Your Most Illustrious Lordship the other sonnet, set to music, as soon as possible – since it is already clearly shaped in my mind.

It is not possible to identify the two compositions mentioned here; but it is worth noting that Monteverdi's *Sesto libro de madrigali a cinque voci* published in 1614 contains no less than seven pieces based on sonnets (Nos. 2, 3, 4, 6, 7, 8 and 9), two of which could well be the present settings.

In that same year, 1607, in Venice the printers Alessandro Raverii and Ricciardo Amadino reprinted all Monteverdi's books of madrigals before the Fifth (which had already reached its second edition) – Raverii the First and Second, and Amadino the Third and Fourth. In Cremona, Monteverdi also gained some manner of official recognition for his work, being admitted to the Accademia degli Animosi in its meeting on 10 August 1607: 'It was petitioned on behalf of Signor Claudio Monteverdi, musician and master of the music of the Most Serene Lord Duke of Mantua, that he be accepted in the academy; which he obtained so much the more because he had already made heard many times before the gentlemen academicians many of his most beautiful compositions.'[119]

A few days later, the composer was in Milan, a trip which is perhaps to be connected with the forthcoming publication of a selection of madrigals chiefly by him (from the Fifth Book) but also by other composers: Banchieri, Andrea Gabrieli, Giovanelli, Marenzio, Nanino, Vecchi. These madrigals had been turned into spiritual settings (with their secular texts in the vernacular replaced by others in Latin on sacred subjects) by Aquilino Coppini; they were dedicated to Cardinal Federico Borromeo, Bishop of Milan (the nephew of S. Carlo Borromeo), and published by Agostino Tradate in 1607 (the dedication is dated 'the nones [5th] of September'). The collection, which was reprinted four years later, was titled *Musica tolta dai madrigali di Claudio Monteverdi e d'altri autori, a cinque et a sei voci*. The settings by Monteverdi (whose name, we note, stands out alone on the title-page, providing clear evidence of his undoubted fame and his ability to act as a commercial draw) included therein were:

1 'Cruda Amarilli, che col nome ancora' as 'Felle amaro me potavit populus'
2 'Ecco, Silvio, colei che in odio hai tanto' as 'Qui pependit in cruce Deus meus'

3 'Ferir quel petto, Silvio?' as 'Pulchrae sunt genae tuae amica mea' (second *pars* of the preceding)

4 'Era l'anima mia' as 'Stabat Virgo Maria mestissimo dolore'

5 'Deh bella e cara e sí soave un tempo' as 'Sancta Maria quae Christum peperisti'

6 'Ma tu, piú che mai dura' as 'Spernit Deus cor durum' (second *pars* of the preceding)

7 'Dorinda, ah dirò mia se mia non sei' as 'Maria, quid ploras ad monumentum'

8 'Ecco piegando le ginocchia a terra' as 'Te Jesu Christe liberator meus'

9 'Troppo ben può questo tiranno Amore' as 'Ure me Domine amore tuo'

10 ' "T'amo, mia vita" la mia cara vita' as 'Gloria tua manet in aeternum'

11 'Ahi come a un vago sol cortese giro' as 'Vives in corde meo Deus meus'

During his stay in Milan, Monteverdi had the opportunity to show his recent *Orfeo* to his friend Cherubino Ferrari, theologian to the Gonzaga court, who wrote to the duke on 22 August 1607:

> Monteverdi has let me see the verses and hear the music of the comedy which Your Highness had done, and it is certain that the poet and the musician have so well represented the affects of the soul that [it] cannot be bettered. The poetry, as regards its invention, is beautiful, is even better as regards its disposition, and is excellent for its elocution, and in sum, one could not expect anything else from so fine an intellect as Signor Striggio's. Moreover, the music, in terms of its appropriateness [*decoro*] serves the poetry so well that one cannot hear better . . .[120]

At the end of summer 1607, on 10 September, Monteverdi's wife died in Cremona: 'Claudia Monteverdi Catanea, Mantuan, having confessed with the last rites, died on 10 September 1607 in the parish of S. Sepolcro, and as a foreigner, she was taken from the cathedral and buried in S. Nazaro.'[121] She had already been seriously ill from a year before, as we learn from the reference to the 'serious illness which I have had' in one of her letters to the ducal counsellor Annibale Chieppio written from Mantua on 14 November 1606, in which, as well as asking 'that our salaries should be paid from the taxes of Viadana' (the irregularity of the payments continued to distress the Monteverdi family, owing to the dishonesty of the ducal treasurer), she requested a dress ('which greatly worries me, seeing how cold it is becoming') and a skirt.[122] In the documents which have survived, Monteverdi mentions his wife only in a letter of one year later, written from Cremona on 2 December 1608 (L.6), concerning the usual complaints about money: 'His Most Serene Highness – after the death of my wife Claudia – made a resolution to leave me her allowance. However, on my arrival in Mantua he suddenly changed his mind.' A little earlier in the same letter, he laments his own misfortune, which had made him 'suffer from cold, lack of clothing, servitude, and very nearly lack of food through the stopping of my wife Claudia's allowance'.

18 The 1608 festivities: *Arianna*, the prologue for
L'Idropica, the *Ballo delle ingrate*

From Mantua a letter of 24 September 1607 came from Federico Follino to
recall Monteverdi: here Follino laments 'the loss of a woman so rare and gifted
with such virtue', exhorting the composer to return to service because he was
'on the point of gaining the summit of as much fame as a man can have on
earth'.[123]

In fact, the court was working hard to finalize the marriage of Prince
Francesco and Margherita of Savoy, daughter of the reigning duke, Carlo
Emanuele I: through this union, Mantuan diplomacy counted on smoothing
over the thorny question of Monferrato, of which the Gonzagas had recently
become dukes (in the time of Guglielmo) but which was also sought by
Savoy. Already they were establishing contacts to prepare in time the festivities to solemnize the wedding. These were the concern of Ferdinando
Gonzaga, Francesco's brother and a great art-lover, as we have seen, who had
been named cardinal at the end of 1607 (24 December). Both he and his
brother – among other things, sons of a Medici – had close links with
Florentine circles, from where Ferdinando planned to bring poets and musicians to be able to grace the wedding with the splendour of a pastoral play
entirely in music. Michelangelo Buonarroti 'il giovane' was summoned in
summer 1607: he was working on the text of the play *Il giudizio di Paride*
mentioned above and which was later used in Florence in 1608, again for
wedding festivities. Buonarroti's prior commitment of the play forced Ferdinando Gonzaga to turn to Francesco Cini, who had almost completed his *Le
nozze di Peleo e Tetide*, with music by Peri. As Cini wrote to Ferdinando:

> Most Illustrious and Most Excellent Lord Most Respected.
>
> Since I see how much Your Most Illustrious Excellency has to heart the
> comedy which you intend to have performed at the wedding of the most
> serene lord your brother, and since I desire both for your honour and for my
> pleasure that everything should turn out with honour and good fortune, I
> cannot fail to remind you of those things which I judge expedient for that
> end. And so I tell you, that although I know that you have around you men
> of great worth, however for those parts which Your Excellency intends to
> have recited in singing, and also for reciting his own part, our Iacopo Peri, or
> Zazzerino as we call him, seems to me that he could be of great use to this
> business, because, as you know very well, it is not enough that plays should
> be beautiful (I do not know if ours is) but they should also be well recited and
> staged, for it is from the diligence taken over some of the smallest things
> regarding the recitation, the actions, the costumes and a thousand other
> things to note, that some plays known by Your Excellency have gained such
> fame, and I can pledge that I have taken care of everything, just as our
> Zazzerino has taken care [of everything], who, I repeat to Your Excellency,
> would do well in this service. And I know that he would willingly serve,
> providing he had permission from the rulers here, which would be easy for
> Your Excellency to obtain, for I do not believe that the wedding here will be

celebrated before spring. I have spoken at very great length with Signor Rasi so that he can cast light on some matters to Your Most Illustrious Excellency, and where you should have any doubts, do me the favour of letting me know, so that you may remain satisfied.

I hear that Signor Ottavio Rinuccini is coming there, and that he will be used in these festivities. I do not want to fail to warn Your Excellency that while he may be very kind and polite in everything else, in matters of poetry, however, he is sometimes too partial towards himself, and he sometimes allows himself to be so carried away by self-interest that he does not mind disturbing and turning upside-down with most crafty cunning and wisdom the affairs of others.

I know that Your Excellency is most prudent and most shrewd, but it has seemed necessary to me that you should know the vice of our air which often gives us a rod with which to beat ourselves, as they say, and forgive me if I speak too freely.[124]

Cini's fears were not unfounded: Rinuccini arrived in Mantua on 23 October 1607 (certainly preceded by an exchange of letters), while *Le nozze di Peleo e Tetide* was rejected three days earlier.[125] But Cini did not stop there, and he returned to the fray, seeking also to involve in the business Mantuan musicians, above all Monteverdi:

I did not reply to Your Most Illustrious Excellency's letter last week because it was delivered to me two days after the departure of the post. I will say now that I have found so good a disposition and eagerness in our Signor Iacopo Peri that not only will he finish the play very soon, which is already nearly complete, and with the exquisiteness already written about to Your Excellency, but because of the desire which he has to give you complete satisfaction, he will come to Mantua when the time comes, if it will be done with the good favour of these rulers as he supposes, and also he will sing not only one part but two, and he will do in this that which no one else would have done for Your Most Illustrious Excellency. He has taken on the task of composing all the parts which are recited, and beyond that he will do the prologue and some ariettas among those of the nymphs or of the little Cupids, indeed he has it in mind to do all of them; whence there will not remain anything other than the full music of the choruses, that is the *intermedi*, and that of the gods who appear at the end, both those which are sung solo and those sung in chorus. I have thought concerning this music, if thus it will please Your Excellency, that you could have it done there by Monteverdi or some other of your musicians, both because they are worthy men and to save Your Excellency trouble and expense, and also because it is appropriate both so as not to attract jealousy and for the honour of Your Excellency's house, for just as there is no shame in using foreigners to help those of the house, as even we will do, having summoned the musicians of the Most Illustrious [Cardinal] Montalto, so there would be scant honour in not having also used one's own servants, and indeed I believe that if those belonging to Mantua are not made to join in, even if one did everything divinely, it would seem always badly done, and everything would be in shreds. And therefore I have considered that this principle should be maintained not only for the composers, but also as regards the singers. Wherefore, all things well considered, I have thought that five or at most six of these singers will suffice Your Excellency given that our Signor Peri can fittingly take the part of Proteus and that of Hymen, Giovannino the castrato the nymph Nuntia, Fabio the castrato Thetis, 'il Brandino' one of Peleus's companions, the most important one, [and] the boy Giovan Gualberto [Magli], who has been there before, Cupid and perhaps another nymph. Then Rasi who we assume will not be missing given that he is a servant of Your Excellency, can fittingly take the part of Peleus and that of Jove; a woman who I hear is there can do the Prologue. As for the other nymphs, or the chorus of little Cupids, or Peleus's other companions, I hear that there will be no shortage of boys or other tenors there, and thus Your Excellency will be served with less expense and less trouble, and in a more praiseworthy manner, if I am not mistaken. I emphasize, however, that our Signor Peri assumes that Rasi himself will sing, for if he does not, he does not intend do so himself unless there is someone well-born like him singing.

... May Your Excellency help us there, and guard himself from the wiles of that friend, which are more powerful than you believe, and keep me your servant, that Our Lord God grants you every good. I believe that it would be good if Rasi were given the order while he is staying here, so that he might come to our Signor Iacopo [Peri] or to me to consult and to practise concerning this service, because I hear that he is amazed that nothing has been written to him. And if Your Excellency wrote a line to your Messer Marco da Gagliano in case it should be necessary for him to help out, either with compositions or with other things, I know that he would receive it as a favour.

And if Your Excellency is resolved that the wedding should be celebrated at carnival, I emphasize that not an ounce of time should be lost and that all haste be sought, for things do not succeed and are not done well except with many rehearsals, and I bow to you with all due reverence. From Florence, 26 October 1607.[126]

However, Cini's attempts came to naught, and Rinuccini remained the poet destined to provide the play to be staged in music. Meanwhile, Monteverdi was being kept active, having been recalled to Mantua from his stay in Cremona by Follino. He offered his services to Prince Francesco, who on 10 October 1607 wrote to his father the duke:

Yesterday evening, Monteverdi came to me to speak, and showing himself desirous of serving Your Highness well in these wedding festivities, and particularly in the pastoral in music, he urged me to write to you that it would be necessary for him to have the words within seven or eight days so that he can begin working, for otherwise he has not the spirit in so little time as there is between now and carnival to do something good ...[127]

Certainly Monteverdi must have feared being relegated to the sidelines of so important an event, given that Marco da Gagliano had been summoned to Mantua in as early as October[128] – he was to set to music Rinuccini's old *Dafne* which had been revised for the occasion, and moreover on 3 December 1607 he promised Ferdinando some other theatrical work:

After Christmas, without any doubt I will move there to serve Your Most Illustrious Excellency, and I would come sooner if I saw any particular need, telling you how continually I go about putting myself in order with works suitable to the occasion and to your desire, and in particular I will have with me a little play [*favoletta*] to be recited in song, if Your Excellency would be pleased to use it, a work capable of being performed quickly and easily, and I inform you of this to make you see that I do not think of anything but serving you . . .[129]

With the wedding postponed to May 1608, it was decided to use that 'favoletta' together with *Dafne* in the course of the 1608 carnival festivities. As Gagliano says in the preface to *La Dafne . . . rappresentata in Mantova* (Florence, Cristofano Marescotti, 1608):[130]

Finding myself last carnival in Mantua, summoned by His Highness to honour myself by availing himself of me in the music to be done for the royal nuptials of the most serene prince his son and of the most serene infanta of Savoy, since they were postponed until May by the lord duke, so as not to let those days pass without some entertainment, he wished among other things that there should be performed *Dafne* by Signor Ottavio Rinuccini, on that occasion by him enlarged and made more beautiful, [and] I was engaged to set it to music, which I did in the manner which I now present to you.

Gagliano also informs us that Caterina Martinelli played Amor, Francesco Rasi Apollo and Antonio Brandi called 'Il Brandino' the Messenger,[131] while the staging was by Cosimo del Bianco and some of the music composed by Cardinal Ferdinando Gonzaga himself. As Jacopo Peri wrote to Ferdinando Gonzaga (Florence, 8 April 1608):[132]

The fame having universally flown around Florence of how joyfully and virtuously Their Most Serene Highnesses have passed the days of carnival with the two entertainments recited in music with the applause of all Mantua, and in particular *Dafne* staged by Your Most Illustrious Excellency enriched by the same Rinuccini with new inventions and composed by Signor Marco to the infinite delight to equal all others and more, since that manner of singing has been recognized as being more proper and closer to speaking than that of any other worthy man, as is my duty, I come to congratulate Your Most Illustrious Excellency, as I did Signor Marco, who in reply told me that Your Excellency composed some arias of the greatest excellence for that play, and so much has he commended them that the greatest desire has come upon me to see them.

Peri's ironic allusion to a 'worthy man' likely refers to Monteverdi: the only stage spectacles with music that the Mantuans could have heard were in fact his *Orfeo* and, earlier (and only for those present at the Florentine festivities of autumn 1600), Peri's own *Euridice*.

The plans for the Mantuan wedding festivities chiefly involved perform-ances of *L'Idropica*, a comedy by Battista Guarini with *intermedi* written by Gabriello Chiabrera, and *Arianna* by Rinuccini and Monteverdi, whose title-rôle was to be taken by Caterina Martinelli called 'La Romanina' (who had already been used in *Dafne*): she had been recruited at the age of thirteen in the summer of 1603 in Rome by the Mantuan bass Giovan Paolo Facone, papal singer in the Sistine Chapel, and sent to study in Monteverdi's house.[133] Rinuccini wrote to Striggio on 20 December 1607 concerning his libretto:

As for that which concerns the staging of *Arianna*, I do not see difficulties there, except that I had set great store by 'Il Brandino', by Settimia [Caccini] for Venus, and for the rest, by Giulio's [Caccini] women for the choruses, an ornament of great importance.

My play is growing in such a way that it needs great players, for its being I will not say the most beautiful, for my works do not deserve that title, but greater than the others. I would advise Your Most Illustrious Lordship to make every effort so that both Giulio's women and 'il Brandino' would come from here. I will bring Messer Marco [da Gagliano] with me: he has no need of permission to leave. Your Most Illustrious Lordship should reply, and should have the lord duke reply, saying that they will return within a few days of Lent. Twenty days' stay in Mantua will suffice: they are experienced people. These sung things are more difficult and more beautiful than people think: they require great exquisiteness, otherwise they do not succeed. As for the staging, it is necessary to have a care for the port and the beach by the sea, but time is not running out and I will be there very soon ...[134]

As for Monteverdi, his letters lead us to believe that *Arianna* was composed in large part in the last two months of 1607: the composer had returned to Mantua before 10 October, and Rinuccini arrived there on the 23rd. On 2 December 1608, Monteverdi was to write to Annibale Chieppio (L.6) noting 'If fortune favoured me last year by making the lord duke invite me to assist with the musical events for the marriage ...'; while many years later, on 9 January 1620 (L.38) he reminded Striggio that in the case of *Arianna* 'after it was finished and learned by heart, five months of strenuous rehearsal took place'. Given that *Arianna* was staged on 28 May 1608, this suggests that the music was already composed by the beginning of January. This is not far from the truth, given that on 2 February 1608 Cardinal Ferdinando, informing his brother Francesco of a serious type of smallpox which had struck down the lead singer, also noted the advanced state of the composition: '*Arianna* is doing badly, since it is not certain that La Romana will survive; in fact, she is in no little danger. As for the rest, Monteverdi is well under way with it, having finished almost all the music.'[135] Monteverdi's work must therefore have been done in great haste in the course of at most two or three months, and this all-consuming urgency would remain for him an unhappy memory never erased by time. Years later, on 6 November 1615 (L.17), he wrote from Venice (to Annibale Iberti?): 'I am not going to tell you about my past ailments, which I still feel in my head and body because of the great suffering I underwent with *Arianna*'; and again, writing from Venice on 1 May 1627 (L.91 [92]) to Striggio, he was to recall 'this lack of time being the reason why I almost killed myself when writing *Arianna*'.

While Caterina Martinelli's health underwent a noticeable improvement, on 26 February 1608 a meeting was held in the presence of the duchess of those who were involved in the preparation of the festivities: Rinuccini, Monteverdi, the architect Antonio Maria Viani, prefect of the ducal buildings, and Federico Follino, superintendent of the preparations. As Carlo Rossi wrote to the duke on 27 February:

> Rinuccini, Monteverdi, the prefect and Don Federico met yesterday morning, and as regards *Arianna* they were in conclusion. Here the [need for] haste was noted; of the rest I know nothing else. Madame has agreed with Signor Ottavio to enrich it with some action, since it is very dry. As for the comedy, in which I have things to do, Monteverdi has taken the prologue, Salomone [Rossi] the first intermedio, Don Giovanni Giacomo [Gastoldi] the second, messer Marco [da Gagliano] the third, Monteverdi's brother [Giulio Cesare] the fourth, and Paolo Birt [Virchi?] the *licenza*; and they fixed the names of those who sing and all the allocation of the musicians, so that all goes well.[136]

The most spectacular additions to *Arianna* were to be 'in the dialogue of Venus and Amor added in the first episode, and in the final intervention of the gods, with Venus rising from the water and Jove passing blessing from heaven – additions that alter the classical "regularity" of the drama. The original finale was to have concluded, after the arrival of Bacchus and Ariadne on stage, with the triumphal chorus "Spiega, omai, giocondo nume".'[137]

Moreover, to further enrich the festivities, perhaps it was on this occasion that the idea developed of commissioning from Rinuccini and Monteverdi a dance entertainment that became the *Ballo delle ingrate*.[138] The composer therefore found himself having to deal with two new texts (Rinuccini's *balletto* and Chiabrera's prologue) while he was coping with the none too easy rehearsals for *Arianna*, which were increasingly troubled by the worsening of Caterina Martinelli's physical condition: indeed, she died on 7 March 1608, seriously undermining the possibility of staging the opera, 'in which the death of Signora Caterina has brought so much turmoil that I don't know what will come of it. Certainly this young girl gained so much in the minds of everyone because of the performances which she gave at the end of Carnival, that if she isn't wept for, at least her death has caused universal pity' (Annibale Chieppio writing from Mantua on 8 March 1608 to a ducal counsellor in Turin).[139]

> 'La Romanina', an extraordinary singer, has died of smallpox; she was buried yesterday evening, with some pomp, in the Carmelite church. This loss is deplored by everyone in the entire city, on account of her having been so exceptionally gifted, and on account of the ineffable pleasure she gave [us] in the two plays performed during the recent Carnival. His Highness must be dismayed about her dying at the very time of these nuptials, considering the disruption of the new and regal plays that are being prepared (in one of which she played Ariadne wonderfully well); and these overseers are quite badly disconcerted. Another girl already has arrived, sent from Florence, but I understand she will not do, and negotiations are afoot to obtain a different one who is in the service of His Lordship Cardinal Montalto; but she cannot possibly prepare in time, as the moment for the nuptials here is drawing very close.[140]

The singer who had come from Florence was given the part of Venus, so the search for a possible substitute continued. 'Thus the comedy was in a good state, but now it is all confused, whenceforth Madame is sending to Bergamo ʾor that woman, since the Florentine will play Venus', wrote Carlo Rossi on ᵗMarch.[141] Eight days later, Antonio Costantini wrote:

Most Serene Madame is working frantically to ensure with all diligence that they work at and bring to an end everything for the arrival of the most serene bride. Her Highness is labouring particularly to put in order the sung comedy, and now she is most desperate after the death of the poor Signora Caterina because they cannot find someone who can appropriately take upon her shoulders the part of Arianna. They sent by post to Bergamo to see if they could have that young woman who had been suggested by Signor Monteverde as an excellent singer, but she has not wanted to come. Finally, the Lord inspired the trying out of La Florinda to see if she is suitable for playing this part, who in six days has it very well by heart, and she sings it with such grace and affect that it has made Madame, Signor Rinuccini and all the gentlemen who have heard her marvel ...[142]

Thus the title-rôle was entrusted to Virginia Ramponi, wife of the actor Giovan Battista Andreini (called 'La Florinda' because a few years earlier she had given a memorable performance in her husband's tragedy of the same name); Andreini and his acting company, the Fedeli, were in Mantua for the performance of *L'Idropica*. It was a fortuitous and fortunate solution to the problem, given that her acting abilities were evidently matched by her skills as a singer:[143] she displayed them further also in the *Ballo delle ingrate*. As the first Arianna, Ramponi earned the praise and admiration of, among others, Giovan Battista Marino, who says in his *Adone* (VII.88):

> E in tal guisa Florinda udisti, o Manto,
> là ne' teatri de' tuoi regi tetti,
> d'Arïanna spiegar gli aspri martiri
> e trar da mille cor mille sospiri.

> And in such a way you heard Florinda, o Manto, / there in the theatres of your royal roofs, / unfold the harsh torments of Arianna / and draw from a thousand hearts a thousand sighs.

Writing a few days earlier (on 14 March), Carlo Rossi refers to the now solved problem of the principal role of *Arianna* (note the 'she speaks' applied to Andreini, which is particularly fitting for a singer–actress). He also reports that by that date the music for the *intermedi* of the comedy was also ready and in rehearsal, including what had been entrusted to Monteverdi, who therefore had written it in little more than ten days, between 26 February (the day of the aforementioned organizing meeting) and 14 March:

> *Arianna*, which was dead because of the death of poor Caterina, is brought back to life, because with Madame having wished to hear La Florinda, who had learnt the most difficult part, she speaks [*dice*] it in such a way that she [Madame] has been astounded, such that it will be wondrous. And as for the hunchback [the young woman from Bergamo recommended by Monteverdi?], to whom Madame wrote by post and who did not want to come, let her go and stay there. As for the big comedy, this evening they have prepared a rehearsal of all the music, and in the coming week they will prepare the *papier-mâché* for the clouds, and the only things missing are *viole* and trombones, of which we have few, and two organs which they know where they are ...[144]

Rinuccini and Chiabrera were also in Mantua in April 1608 to supervise the staging of the entertainments for which they had provided the texts. From Turin, where he was for the wedding, Prince Francesco wrote to his brother on 28 April: 'Your Most Illustrious Lordship is wrapped up in poetry, being in company with Signor Rinuccini and Signor Chiabrera, but I am not without poets, for Marino is here, who is the most gallant man in the world.'[145] It is perhaps no coincidence that following on from this interest on the part of the Gonzagas in the Neapolitan *letterato* who had recently arrived at the court of Carlo Emanuele I in Turin, we find the first appearance of texts by Marino in a Monteverdi madrigal book: *Il sesto libro de madrigali a cinque voci* (1614) in fact includes five settings of his texts. Marino thus became involved in the festivities in Turin, but also in the Mantuan ones: he wrote the reply to the challenge (written by Chiabrera) of the tournament titled *Il trionfo dell'onore* ('The triumph of honour') and conceived by Prince Francesco in person, who had also invented the plot of a *balletto* for which the poetry was written by Striggio, *Il sacrificio di Ifigenia* ('The sacrifice of Iphigenia'). Striggio, informing the prince (in a letter dated 27 April) of the state of preparation of the festivities, reveals the climate of competition created between his *balletto* and the one by Rinuccini, who had enriched his text, adding the opening dialogue between Amor and Venus 'on a machine' and the emotional monologue of the Ingrate 'Ahi troppo, ahi troppo è duro': new verse which came to be added to that already set to music by Monteverdi, who, however, had finished his work by this date (26 April).

> Yesterday Your Highness's *balletto* was rehearsed. It was danced very well, but the Lord Count Canossa and Signora Anguissola were somewhat offended, whenceforth in their place Signor Carlo Cassini and Messer Giovan Battista did it. The music which is recited has been tried out, but it needs a performance if it is to turn out perfectly as is desired. Signor Rinuccini, in imitation of Your Highness's invention, has himself, too, added many things to the *ballo* of the *Ingrate*, and he has Amor and Venus in dialogue on a cloud and has La Florinda sing, who as the Ingrates return to the inferno will mingle with them and will appear as one of those who have danced, and will sing plaintively abhorring the cause of their suffering. And all this has been added secretly perhaps for fear that Your Highness's *balletto* would appear more beautiful than the other. I have been advised of everything by Messer Marco [da Gagliano], and I have some certain feeling about this, for I would not have wanted both the one and the other *balletto* to be done in the same manner. If there had been more time, and if it had been certain that the lord duke's *balletto* was to be designed as a recited play [*un'invenzione di favola recitata*], I would have been of a mind, with Your Highness's agreement, to change the invention: for what worries me is that Your Highness's *balletto* is to be the last entertainment that will be done. But whatever the case, I will not fail to ensure some change either in the *entrata* or in the instrumental music of the *ballo* that will be with the singing, even though I doubt that there will be the latter, because the design is taken from Signor Rinuccini, who, having heard it the day before yesterday praised it greatly to me. And I would also think it good that we should abandon the

cloud on which it was decided to have Diana appear above her temple, unless Your Highness commands the opposite, and that this deity should appear in the most noble part of the temple seated in majesty to receive the sacrifice. I have also discussed this my idea with the lord prefect [the architect Viani], who agrees with my opinion, so as not to do the same as will be done in the other *balletto*, where, as I have already said, Venus and Amor appear on a cloud. The costumes, both for the *balletto* and for the tournament, are being attended to with vigour, and I do not fail to urge them on . . .[146]

We have already seen that the period of preparation for these festivities remained for Monteverdi an unhappy experience which he would never forget, given the huge amount of work required all at once to set new parts to music and to rehearse them repeatedly. In December 1608 (L.6), the composer was to complain of having had '1500 lines to set to music': *Arianna*, the *Ballo delle ingrate* and the prologue to *L'Idropica* amount to about 1360 lines, so either the composer was exaggerating for the sake of dramatic effect or he had to perform some extra service in some other of the works staged (unless some of the sections already set to music were cut during the rehearsals).

The official account of the festivities was prepared by Federico Follino and published by the ducal printers Aurelio & Lodovico Osanna (Mantua, 1608) with the title *Compendio delle sontuose feste fatte l'anno MDCVIII nella città di Mantova, per le reali nozze del serenissimo prencipe d. Francesco Gonzaga con la serenissima infante Margherita di Savoia* ('Compendium of the sumptuous festivities done in the year 1608 in Mantua, for the royal wedding of the Most Serene Prince Don Francesco Gonzaga and the Most Serene Infanta Margherita of Savoy').[147] The bride arrived in Mantua on 24 May 1608 and the festivities began immediately. Follino presents the following accounts of those entertainments in which Monteverdi was involved:

The following Wednesday [28 May] there was performed in music in the theatre built for this purpose the tragedy *Arianna*, which Signor Ottavio Rinuccini had written for the occasion of this wedding, who was to this end summoned to Mantua with the greatest poets of our age.

There were present at this performance the princes, princesses, ambassadors, the ladies who were invited, and that greatest number of foreign gentlemen that the theatre could seat, which, although it has a capacity of six thousand and more persons and although the duke had prohibited entry therein to the knights themselves of his house and even to the other gentlemen of the city, was not able to contain all those foreigners who sought to enter, who gathered around the door in such number that neither the skill of Captain Camillo Strozzi, lieutenant of the guard of the ducal archers, nor the authority of Signor Carlo Rossi, general-at-arms, was sufficient to quieten such a crowd, so that it was also necessary for the duke himself several times to go and stand behind them.

This work was very beautiful in itself, and for the characters who took part, dressed in clothes no less appropriate than splendid, and for the scenery, which represented a wild rocky place in the midst of the waves, which in the furthest part of the prospect could be seen always in motion, giving a charming effect. But since to this was joined the force of the music by Signor Claudio Monteverde, *maestro di cappella* to the duke, a man whose worth is known to all the world, and who in this work proved to excel himself, combining with the union of the voices the harmony of the instruments disposed behind the scene which always accompanied the voices, and as the mood of the music changed, so was the sound of the instruments varied; and seeing that it was acted both by men and by women who were all excellent in the art of singing, every part succeeded more than wondrously, [and] in the lament which Ariadne sings on the rock when she has been abandoned by Theseus, which was acted with so much emotion and in so piteous a way that no one hearing it was left unmoved, there was not one lady who did not shed some little tear at her beautiful plaint . . .

It was Apollo who, representing the prologue, gave the introduction to so beautiful a play. He was sitting on a very beautiful cloud (which at the removal of the great curtain which covered the scene was seen in open air of brightest splendour), which, moving down little by little (while from within the stage was heard a sweet *concerto* of various instruments), reached in a short space of time the stage, and leaving Apollo on that part of the rock broaching the sea, it disappeared in a moment. Whence he, finding himself on foot on that mountainous rock, stepping forth majestically, placed himself forwards somewhat, and having finally stopped within view of the spectators, he began to sing with a very suave voice the verses that follow, with the said instruments accompanying throughout his beautiful song:

> Io, che ne l'alto a mio voler governo
> . . .
> l'antico onor ne novi canti ammiri.

> [I who on high rule to my wishes / . . . / see the ancient honour in new songs.]

When Apollo had brought an end to his song, he left the stage, and at the same time most beautiful Venus and her son Amor were seen to appear, who began the play in this manner:

> Ven[ere].   Non senz'alto consiglio
> . . .
> Nun[zio].   Ecco gli sposi, ecco i reali amanti.

> [*Venus*: Not without high advice / . . . / *Messenger*: Here is the bridal couple, here the royal lovers.]

There were seen to appear on the stage at the end of these words from the left-hand side of the scene Bacchus with the beautiful Ariadne, and Amor before them, surrounded in front and around by many pairs of soldiers girt with most beautiful arms, with proud crests on their heads, who, when they were on the stage, with the instruments that were within taking up the playing of a beautiful dance tune, one part of these soldiers performed a very delightful dance, weaving in and out in a thousand ways; and while these danced, another part of the soldiers began to accompany the sound and the dance with the following words:

> Spiega omai giocondo nume
> . . .
> destinaron del ciel gl'eterni fati.

> [Spread forth, happy god / . . . / [as] the eternal fates of heaven have destined.]

Venus, emerging from the sea:

Avventurosa sposa,

...

sanno gli dei del ciel tornar giocondo.

[Adventurous bride, / ... / the gods of heaven know to return happy.]

Jove, the heavens having opened:

Doppo trionfi e palme,

...

Bacco. Per celeste desio mortal bellezza.

[After triumphs and palms, / ... / *Bacchus*: ... mortal beauty through heavenly desire.]

The performance of this play lasted for 2½ hours, after which the princes went to rest.

On Monday [2 June], these princes enjoyed the performance of *L'Idropica*, a comedy by Cavalier Guarini, with so noble decoration of *intermedi* that the most judicious intellects were astounded. The invention of the *intermedi* was the work of Signor Gabriel Chiabrera, and they were composed by him under the supervision of the duke, who for this end had summoned him to Mantua. But the marvellous invention of the machines with which they were represented, imitating so well truth and nature, was all the labour of Signor Antonio Maria Vianini, prefect of the buildings of the state of Mantua and architect of that excellence which the world can appreciate from his works and from the particular esteem that the duke himself displays towards him ... When all the people which the theatre could hold were gathered together, care having always been taken by those ministers who had the responsibility for not granting entrance to other than foreign gentlemen, to whom were given for this end some copper medals, although the space (as at the other performance) could not hold everyone, wherefore many of them were forced to stay outside, the cardinals, the princes, the ambassadors and the invited ladies went to sit in their assigned places, and once the torches were lit in the theatre, the usual trumpet fanfare was given from behind the stage. At the third statement of the fanfare, the large curtain which concealed the stage disappeared with such speed, at the blink of an eye, that although it rose upwards few could see how it had been removed. With the stage revealed to the spectators, one saw on its sides many palaces and towers standing out, partitioned by loggias and porticos done with such realism that everyone quickly recognized the scene for the city of Mantua, which was illuminated in such a way that without seeing any light lit therein was revealed the splendour not of torches or other illumination but of the pure rays of the sun. Nor was anything lacking therein, so that the spectators would have believed that there it was day, and that the sun was then shining naturally (so well planned were the shadows and the light from those reflections), if they had not known that night had already fallen. This curtain had not disappeared before one saw in the air three most beautiful enclosed clouds, constructed with such artifice that they appeared no different from those made in the sky by the vapours of the earth, and with the stage-floor covered by pleasant waters it was so like real life that indeed it seemed that there lay a most placid lagoon. One saw the lagoon bubble in the middle and from it emerge the head of a lady who, rising little by little, revealed herself through her costume and attributes to be Manto, daughter of Teiresias and founder of Mantua, who was raised up in so measured a fashion that by the time the trumpets had finished sounding she stood on a little island bathed by those waters; and pausing among some reeds that were placed thereupon, to the sound of several instruments which were behind the stage she sang the following words, which enraptured the minds of all the audience:

> Ha cento lustri con etereo giro
>
> . . .
>
> e dolce fiume di gioir v'innondi.

> [It is a hundred *lustra* with the ethereal round / . . . / and engulf you in a sweet river of joy.]

When Manto began to sing the fourth stanza, the three clouds which were in the sky opened suddenly, and in the middle, one saw Hymen with torch in hand, who, for his garments rich in gold which he had around him and for the reflections of some lights which with much artifice had been hidden within that cloud, was so resplendent that he resembled a heavenly god. In the cloud which was on the right, the Three Graces were seen, so well placed and so beautiful that they seduced the sight of the onlookers; and in the left [cloud] were Fecundity and Peace, both with lit torches in their hands and adorned with flowers and gold, who breathed most suave perfumes.

Manto had finished singing the aforesaid stanza, she began to sink into the same waters from whence she had risen, and at the same time the clouds began to move downwards very slowly, the deities therein singing the words that follow to the greatest delight of the audience:

> Pronte scendiamo a volo,
>
> . . .
>
> amato in pace, e paventato in guerra.

> [Let us ascend quickly in flight / . . . / loved in peace, and feared in war.]

This song was composed with such measure that at the end of its final strains the clouds found themselves on the stage, leaving behind them the buildings which represented the city and covering all sight of them, whence Hymen, placing his foot on the little island, sang the verses written below:

> Coppia real, che di sua mano insieme
>
> . . .
>
> udite i canti, e rimirate i giochi.

> [Royal couple, who together with his hand / . . . / hear the songs, admire the games.]

While Hymen sang the second quatrain, the Graces, having left the cloud and walking slowly along the little island, seated themselves on his right, with Fecundity and Peace doing the same on the left, whence the three clouds, remaining empty, wondrously dissolved in the blink of an eye; and of the three that there were there was made one, but of another shape, for it seemed a dense fog which engulfed all the view of the stage behind the little island. Once Hymen had finished singing, he approached Fecundity and Peace, and no sooner was he placed seated at their side than the island split apart, dividing itself into two equal parts, one of which moved towards one part of the stage, and the other towards the other, carrying those deities off-stage through the waves, and at that same point the waters and the cloud disappeared, and the scene representing the city of Padua remained clear for the play to come.[148]

... The duke had decided to perform on the evening of that Wednesday [4 June] in the theatre of the comedy a *balletto* of very beautiful invention, the work of Signor Ottavio Rinuccini, in which participated the duke and the prince–groom, with six other knights and with eight ladies from the principal ones of the city in terms as much of nobility as of beauty and of grace in dancing, so that in all they reached the number sixteen. Whence-forth, the princes and princesses, the ambassadors and those members of the nobility that the place could hold having gathered there, they positioned themselves on the steps which, forming a semicircle in the part of the theatre opposite its side, rose from the floor to its ceiling, leaving empty that space in the middle which is between the stage and the aforesaid steps for the performance of the *balletto*. In that part of the wall which on the right side of the theatre is within the confines of the steps and the stage, there was a large platform where the lord ambassadors were placed, and facing it was seen another of equal shape, in which stood a large number of musicians with various string and wind instruments.

Now when all were comfortably seated, the sign having been given with a frightening banging of discordant drums under the stage, the curtain was raised with that wondrous speed with which it was raised in the comedy, and in the middle of the stage one saw the large mouth of a wide and deep cavern, which, stretching beyond the confines of the scene, seemed that it went so far beyond it that the human eye could not reach to discern its end. That cavern was surrounded within and around by burning fire, and in its darkest depths, in a part very deep and distant from its mouth, one saw a great abyss behind which there rotated balls of flames burning most brightly and within which there were countless monsters of the inferno so horrible and frightening that many did not have the courage to look upon it. It seemed a horrifying and monstrous thing to see that infernal abyss full of such fire and so monstrous images, but it caused the people to wonder all the more to see in front of that fiery mouth from the outside part, where some small misty and gloomy light shone, beautiful Venus who held her beautiful son Amor by the hand, who, to the sound of sweetest instruments which were behind the stage, sang with a very suave voice the verses written below in dialogue with Amor:

> Am[ore]. De l'implacabil dio
> ...
> Ven[ere]. Discreto pargoletto.
>
> [*Amor*: Of the implacable god / ... / *Venus*: ... discreet youth.]

When Venus had finished these last words, Amor entered that deep abyss with all courage, passing through the fires and flames without suffering any injury; and meanwhile, Venus, turning to the spectators and looking at the ladies who were before her, sang in this manner:

> Udite donne, udite, e i saggi detti
> ...
> di lisci e d'acque a la fallace aita.
>
> [Listen, ladies, listen, and the wise sayings / ... / of pools and waters to the false assistance.]

At the end of her beautiful song, one saw exit from the right-hand side of that horrible cavern Pluto, formidable and awesome in sight, with garments

as are given him by poets, but burdened with gold and jewels, who, coming
with Amor before Venus, spoke in song in this manner, replying and
repeating the one after the other as follows:

>   Plut[one].   Bella madre d'Amor, che col bel ciglio
>   . . .
>   feri ministri, udite.

>   [*Pluto*: Beautiful mother of Love, who with the fair brow / . . . /
>   harsh ministers, listen.]

At Pluto's call, there appeared from the cavern many horrible and monstrous
shades who poured forth flames from various parts, to the great terror of
all, and presenting themselves before him, they said with horrendous yet
harmonious voice:

>   Omb[re].   Che vuoi, che imperi?

>   [*Shades*: What is your wish, what is your command?]

And Pluto added:

>   Aprite
>   . . .
>   traete qui la condennata schiera.

>   [Open / . . . / drag forth the condemned band.]

While those cruel shades went to carry out Pluto's intention and to lead
forward the condemned band of ungrateful women who were to do the
balletto, Venus, having turned towards Pluto, sang the following verses:

>   Non senz'alto diletto
>   . . .
>   scorno del Tebro e de la dotta Atene.

>   [Not without great delight / . . . / the scorn of Tiber and of learned
>   Athene.]

Scarcely had Venus delivered these words than Amor ran into that cavern to
lead out those unfortunates, whence, turning to his mother, as if he were
disturbed by that wretched sight, he pointed to them, hurrying her departure, with the singing of the following words:

>   Ecco ver noi l'addolorate squadre
>   . . .
>   non ritardar Pluton vezosa madre.

>   [Here towards us the grieving band / . . . / do not delay Pluto,
>   beautiful mother.]

At Amor's words, Venus turned towards the burning cavern, and having
seen those unfortunates in so unhappy a state, with a pitying voice she took
up the song:

>   Ahi vista troppo oscura, o miserelle,
>   . . .
>   men fere e crude, o men leggiadre e belle.

>   [Ah sight too dark, o wretched ones / . . . / less harsh and cruel, or
>   less graceful and beautiful.]

Whenceforth, Pluto, seeing Venus and Cupid so disturbed, exhorted them to leave from there, then hurrying the steps of those unhappy ones with a sonorous and threatening voice:

> Tornate al bel seren celesti numi:
> movete meco voi d'amor ribelle.

[Turn to the beauty of the serene, heavenly deities: / move with me, you rebels of love.]

While Pluto spoke thus, Venus, having taken Amor by the hand, left those tear-filled shores, and the condemned band, passing through that abyss and between the flames and fire, came out of the cave, looking at the air and the light with much grief and with actions worthy of great compassion.

These condemned souls were dressed with garments in a very extravagant and beautiful style, which draped to the ground, made up of a rich cloth that was woven precisely for this effect. It was grey in colour, mixed with most subtle threads of silver and gold with such artifice that to look upon it it seemed to be ashes mixed with flashing sparks; and thus one saw the dresses, and likewise the cloaks (which hung from their shoulders in a very bizarre manner), embroidered with many flames made of silk and gold, so well arranged that everyone judged that they were burning; and between the said flames, there could be seen scattered in most beautiful order garnets, rubies and other jewels which resembled glowing coals. Their hair was also seen to be woven with these jewels, which part cut short and part spread around with wondrous art, seemed destroyed and burned; and although it was all covered with ashes, nonetheless it showed between the ash and the smoke a certain splendour, from which one could well recognize that at another time they were blondest of blondes like gold thread; and their faces, showing signs of a former beauty, were changed and palled in such a way that they brought terror and compassion together on looking upon them.

They moved (but with great grief indicated by gestures) two by two in a pleasing descent from the stage, accompanying their steps with the sound of a great number of instruments which played a melancholic and plaintive dance tune; and having reached the floor of the theatre, they did a *balletto* so beautiful and delightful, with steps, movements and actions now of grief and now of desperation, and now with gestures of pity and now of scorn, sometimes embracing each other as if they had tears of tenderness in their eyes, now striking each other swollen with rage and fury. They were seen from time to time to abhor each other's sight and to flee each other in frightened manners, and then to follow each other with threatening looks, coming to blows with each other, asking pardon and a thousand other movements, represented with such affect and with such naturalness that the hearts of the onlookers were left so impressed that there was no one in that theatre who did not feel his heart move and be disturbed in a thousand ways at the changing of their passions.

After these Ingrates had danced so much, that weaving among themselves in various ways they found themselves occupying the whole space of the floor, they stood still at a sign from Pluto (who was standing before the stage) in a group along it, eight on each side, and he, moving among them towards the princesses with great gravity, who were in view facing the stage, once he had approached them, full of horrid majesty he began to sing, accompanied by instruments, in a very courteous manner the following verses:

Dal tenebroso orror del mio gran regno

. . .

tornate a lagrimar nel regno inferno.

[From the dark horror of my great kingdom / . . . / return to weep in the infernal kingdom.]

At the end of these words, with the instruments taking up a new dance tune more plaintive than the other, those Ingrates began another *balletto* with gestures full of greater desperation and of greater grief, and with a thousand interweavings and a thousand changes of affect they came approaching little by little the stage, and mounting it in the same order that they descended, when they were all on it, Pluto, with a voice of horror and of fear, said singing:

Tornate al negro chiostro

. . .

tornate ove si sferza il fallir vostro.

[Return to the black cloister / . . . / return where your fault forces you.]

Scarcely had Pluto spoken than one of the Ingrates, who had stayed on the stage when the others descended to dance, burst forth in such tear-filled accents accompanied by sighs and sobs, that there was no woman's heart in that theatre which did not let loose from their eyes some pitying tear. The words which she said in her beautiful plaint were the following:

Ahi troppo, ahi troppo è duro

. . .

apprendete pietà, donne e donzelle.

[Ah too, ah too harsh / . . . / learn pity, ladies and maidens.]

At the end of so beautiful a plaint they again entered the cave, but in such a manner that they seemed pushed by a lively force; no sooner were they swallowed up by it than, closing its great mouth, the scene remained with a beautiful and delightful view.

As well as the official description of the festivities, other accounts were sent to their respective governments by the foreign ambassadors present in Mantua. With reference to *Arianna*, the Venetian envoy wrote on 28 May that 'only today do the festivities begin, which start with a comedy in music which will be sung this evening',[149] while the next day the Estense ambassador wrote:

There was then done a comedy in music, which began before the Ave Maria and lasted until three hours of night, and all the performers, well costumed, did their parts very well, but best of all was the actress Ariadne; and it was the play of Ariadne and Theseus, who in her lament in music accompanied by viols and violins, made many weep at her disgrace. There was one Rasi, musician, who sang divinely; but the part of Ariadne surpassed him, and the castratos and others seemed as nothing.

There appeared a cloud from the heavens with Jove who blessed the wedding of Ariadne and Bacchus; nor was the scene changed, and it was all mountains, rocks and sand.[150]

Of the *Ballo delle ingrate*, the Estense ambassador wrote:

> The *balletti* were done ... which turned out lovely. First there was an
> ordinary large entertainment with *passi e mezzo* and galliards with positions
> [*con piantoni*]; then on the stage of the large comedy, one saw the inferno
> burning, and from there came Pluto, but first Venus and Cupid appeared,
> who sang many verses and with Pluto made a scene in song, which when
> they concluded, the souls who were ungrateful women in life came little by
> little to see the world again; whence there appeared eight ladies and eight
> knights all dressed as women and as damned souls of the inferno, with pallid
> masks; and having descended from the stage, they did a *balletto* in the room
> where the entertainment was, which is the same as the comedy. That done,
> Pluto returned them to the inferno, and in leaving many souls cried in music:
> 'O Dio! Prendete pietà donne et donzeli' ['O God! Take pity ladies and
> maidens'], and the entertainment, which began at the Ave Maria, was
> concluded at three hours of night.[151]

But the spectacular climax of the festivities was the *intermedi* for *L'Idropica*,
which were discussed fully by all those who produced written accounts of
these entertainments. Federico Zuccari, in his *Passaggio per l'Italia, con la dimora
in Parma* (Bologna, Bartolomeo Cocchi, 1608), said concerning this comedy
that 'although *L'Idropica* by Lord Cavalier Guarini was beautiful and well
performed, yet it acted as an *intermedio* to the *intermedi*'.[152]

Arianna, which the Estense ambassador calls a 'comedy in music', was
certainly a unique and important theatrical event, but it was not the most
significant entertainment of the festivities (the same had applied to the
Florentine *Euridice* compared with *Il rapimento di Cefalo*), given that such
importance was assigned to the stage-work richest in 'machines', which was
normally the prerogative of the *intermedi*. Monteverdi himself was to confirm
this situation precisely with reference to *Arianna* in a letter from Venice (L.24,
6 January 1617) to Striggio concerning a text to be set to music sent him from
Mantua:

> I admit, Most Illustrious Lord, that when I wrote my first letter in reply to
> your first, the story which you sent me having no title on it other than this –
> *Le nozze di Tetide*, a maritime fable – I must admit that it could have been
> something to be sung and staged with music as was *Arianna*. But, after
> gathering from Your Most Illustrious Lordship's last letter that it has to serve
> as *intermedi* for the main play, just as I believed at first that it was something
> of little importance, so on my second impression I consider it, on the
> contrary, a worthy and most noble work ...

Of all the music for *Arianna*, today we know only the lament 'Lasciatemi
morire', which Monteverdi later called 'the most essential part of the work'
(L.50 [51], Venice, 20 or 21 March 1620) and which was also the only part to
be published – in 1623 both in Venice by Bartolomeo Magni of the Gardano
press (with the title *Lamento d'Arianna*) and in Orvieto by Michelangelo Fei &
Rinaldo Ruuli (in the collection *Il maggio fiorito*, edited by Giovan Battista
Rocchigiani). By that date, however, Monteverdi had already published the

greater part of the lament in a version for five voices in his *Sesto libro de madrigali a cinque voci* (Venice, Ricciardo Amadino, 1614), while copies of the original must certainly have circulated in manuscript. One such copy could well have been the one now in Florence (Biblioteca Nazionale Centrale, Magliabechiano XIX.114, pp. 18–34): compared with the printed version, although it similarly omits the four choral interventions commenting on Arianna's despair, it also gives the exchanges between her and Dorilla (but without the latter's replies) up to the final chorus (omitted). The version contained in this manuscript, an anthology of arias and madrigals (the latter, further laments) for solo voice (tenor or soprano) and basso continuo, perhaps descends from the copy of the 'lament of Ariadne' remaining in Florence 'in the house of Your Most Illustrious Lordship [Cardinal Ferdinando Gonzaga]', to which reference is made in a letter from Florence dated 1 July 1608 to the Cardinal sent from Marco da Gagliano.[153] Finally, Monteverdi was later to publish a solo-voice *contrafactum* of this lament (in the *Selva morale e spirituale*, Venice, Bartolomeo Magni, 1640–41), with a sacred Latin text, entitled *Pianto della Madonna sopra il Lamento d'Arianna* ('Iam moriar, mi fili'), providing evidence of his personal interest, and that of music lovers, in this piece.[154] Rinuccini's text itself received four editions in 1608 alone: two Mantuan ones from the press of the ducal printers, Aurelio and Lodovico Osanna (one inserted in Follino's *Compendio* and one on its own, which was probably distributed at the première); one from the Giunti press in Florence; and the fourth printed in Venice by Bernardo Giunti and Giovan Battista Ciotti.

The story represented here has a double prologue: the first by Apollo, the second by Venus who prefigures the story to come to Amor in a dialogue situated on a desolate beach. A short distance from there, as she has described, Theseus and Ariadne disembark on that island, having come from Crete where the hero killed the horrible Minotaur and succeeded in escaping from the labyrinth thanks to her help. During the night, for reasons of political expediency, Theseus is advised not to return to Athens together with Ariadne, and he leaves in secret, abandoning her. Having awoken and realizing his shameful action, the desperate woman is prepared to kill herself, but the signals announcing the arrival of a new fleet divert her from her intention. However, it is not Theseus who is returning to her, but Bacchus, who, thanks to the intervention of Amor, feels pity for Ariadne and is immediately attracted to her. They soon celebrate their wedding, while all rejoice. Although the libretto is not divided into acts or scenes, it can in effect be divided into eight sections; all except the first (the dialogue between Venus and Amor, which seems like an additional pleonastic prologue perhaps added at a later stage) end classically with a chorus.

What the Gonzaga court offered him must have been felt by Rinuccini as an opportunity to realize his own theatrical ideals even more fully than in the case of the 1600 Florentine festivities. Thus in the prologue we find taken up again – albeit diluted by the predominant need for celebration – the ideological justifications for the new genre, rejecting the poetics of epic and tragedy ('Ma gli alti pregi tuoi, le glorie e l'armi / non udrai risuonar corde guerriere'; 'But your high worth, the glories and arms / you will not hear resound, warlike notes') and adopting the theme of love ('Pieghino al dolce suon l'orecchie altere / su cetera d'amor teneri carmi'; 'Let elevated ears bend to the sweet sound, / tender songs on love's lyre'). We also discover here that the essential ingredient of the play is the pathetic (anticipating the principal scene of the opera, the lament of the abandoned Ariadne: 'Odi, sposa real, come sospiri / tradita amante in solitaria riva' – 'Listen, royal bride, how sighs / a betrayed lover on the solitary bank'), through which the mythical Greek theatre might be revived ('Forse avverrà che della scena argiva / l'antico onor ne' novi canti ammiri'; 'Perhaps it will happen that of the Argive stage / the ancient honour you may admire in new songs').

Such self-consciousness of intent is also revealed in the title of the work, called a 'tragedy', for example, in the title-page of its libretto, a label that stands out in terms of the typography: 'The right to be called tragedy comes, as in the tradition of the genre, from the royal birth and political motivations of its characters. Unlike comedy or pastoral, it does not untangle the personal vicissitudes of private persons, but rather the actions of public personages, which also affect the life and happiness of a state and its citizens.'[155] The tragic impulse must have made Rinuccini conceive a somewhat bare dramatic action, little inclined towards the delights – above all the scenographic delights – usual in such festive contexts. Not for nothing did the Duchess of Mantua find Rinuccini's work 'very dry' in the meeting discussed above, recommending – nay, insisting upon – less severity and more spectacle.

Compared with the first operas, *Arianna* presents some differences worthy of note. It is true that the pastoral world does not appear here, but nevertheless its place is taken by the world of fishermen that is entirely equivalent to it. Its novelty, then, lies not so much here as in the existence of two clearly different levels within its range of characters: on the one hand, we have the humble fishermen, and on the other, Ariadne, Theseus and the court. The entirely pastoral melodiousness of the fishermen's dialogues contrasts markedly with the sustained eloquence of Theseus and Ariadne, and similarly the themes which these two worlds present are handled from opposite angles. In contrast to the 'elevated' dialogues of the royal couple – the military undertakings, the noble summons of the counsellor to Theseus and the consequent dispute over the need (on the part of one with royal responsibilities of government) to sacrifice love and pleasure for honour and duty respectively – stand the humble work of the fishermen (the activities inherent in their occupation, the musical pastimes) and the absence of those cares and of those troublesome thoughts that do not give respite to men of state, needing obedience only to the laws of love. The chorus 'Avventurose genti' is emblematic: here we find celebrated the wisdom of renouncing 'città superbe' ('proud cities') and ambition in favour of a more self-conscious – because reconquered – age of gold: a theme which since the Tasso of *Aminta* and *Gerusalemme liberata* (the episode of Erminia among the shepherds) had become a topos in pastoral literature.

The aspirations to tragedy running through *Arianna* are intermingled with some of the characteristics fundamentally typical of this repertory, so that the work's climax, the emotional highpoint of the lament of Ariadne abandoned by her beloved, sits squarely in this context. Rinuccini probably recast echoes of Virgil (the episode of the abandoned Dido), Ovid (the tenth book of the *Heroides*) and Catullus (lines 52–264 of *Carmen* LXIV), onto which are grafted the stories of Olimpia abandoned by Bireno (*Orlando furioso*, X.19–34), and Armida by Rinaldo (*Gerusalemme liberata*, XVI.36–62). But the most influential source seems to have been the long passage referring to the abandoned Ariadne in Giovanni Andrea dell'Anguillara's translation (printed in 1561) of the *Metamorfosi di Ovidio* (VIII.92–150), which constitutes an extensive interpolation compared with the original (in the eighth book of the *Metamorphoses*, Ariadne is given only lines 176–9).[156]

Although *Arianna* tends only partly towards tragedy – the genre is diluted by contact with the elements of the piscatorial eclogue and with more extrinsic demands for spectacle (the opening dialogue and the happy ending, both focused on stage machines) – its ambitions were certainly transmitted by Rinuccini to Monteverdi, if only through the close collaboration between the two as described by Giovan Battista Doni in his *Trattato della musica scenica*: 'and likewise Monteverdi received the greatest assistance from Rinuccini in *Arianna*, even though he knew nothing about music (making up for this with his most fine judgement and with the most exacting ear that he had; as one can further see from the quality and texture of his poetry)'.[157] For his part, Monteverdi clearly fell under the ideological influence of such classicizing tendencies, and while later remembering *Arianna* (in L.122 [123], Venice, 22 October 1633), he felt obliged to summon in his support the authority of Plato:

> I found out in practice that when I was about to compose the *Lamento d'Arianna* – finding no book that could show me the natural way of imitation, not even one that would explain how I ought to be an imitator (other than Plato, in one of his shafts of wisdom, but so hidden that I could hardly discern from afar with my feeble sight what little he showed me) – I found out (let me tell you) what hard work I had to do in order to achieve the little I did do in the way of imitation ...

Earlier (L.21, Venice, 9 December 1616), Monteverdi had taken the opportunity to justify the need for a single-minded approach to the composition of such theatrical works, seeking a focused and coherent expression of the emotions as was made possible by a monothematic subject (as had already been the case with *Orfeo*, which centred on a single character). It was not necessary to imitate 'the Lord Cardinal Montalto, who put on a play in which every character who appeared made up his own part. Because if this were something that led to a single climax, like *Arianna* and *Orfeo*, you would certainly require a single hand – that is, if it led to singing speech, and not (as this does) to spoken song'. This is another way of emphasizing the slogan of the *seconda pratica*, in which one must do things so as 'to make the oration the mistress of the harmony and not the servant' (from the *Dichiaratione* of the *Scherzi musicali*).

In a preceding passage, this same letter identifies in the famous lament the natural emotional and dramatic climax of such a poetic framework. Rejecting a text that was being suggested to him, Monteverdi asserts: 'And as to the story as a whole – as far as my no little ignorance is concerned – I do not feel that it moves me at all (moreover I find it hard to understand), nor do I feel that it carries me in a natural manner to an end that moves me. *Arianna* led me to a just lament, and *Orfeo* to a righteous prayer, but this fable leads me I don't know to what end. So what does Your Most Illustrious Lordship want the music to be able to do?' And a few lines earlier, he had written: 'I have noticed that the interlocutors are winds, Cupids, little Zephyrs and Sirens: consequently many sopranos will be needed, and it can also be stated that the winds have to sing – that is, the Zephyrs and the Boreals. How, dear Sir, can I imitate the speech of the winds, if they do not speak? And how can I, by such means, move the passions? Ariadne moved us because she was a woman, and similarly Orpheus because he was a man, not a wind.' Such an ability to move the listener by way of solo singing on stage was considered an achievement worthy of the mythical music of antiquity, as Marco da Gagliano confirms in the preface of his *Dafne* (1608):

> among the many admirable entertainments that were ordered by His Highness for the splendid nuptials of the most serene prince his son and the most serene infanta of Savoy, he wanted there to be performed a play in music, and this was *Arianna*, written for that occasion by Signor Ottavio Rinuccini, whom the lord duke made come to Mantua for this end. Signor Claudio Monteverdi, most celebrated musician and head of the music of His Highness, composed the arias in so exquisite a way that one can truly affirm that the excellence of ancient music was revived, since he visibly moved the whole theatre to tears.

As with some of the madrigal output of the late sixteenth and early seventeenth centuries, so too in the nascent musical theatre the lament tended to become an expressive *locus* of high degree and with the status of a topos. Examples had already been provided by 'Dunque ruvida scorza' in *Dafne* and 'Funeste piagge' in Peri's *Euridice* – thus from the very beginning of opera's history. Because of its extreme expressive and communicative power, the *Lamento d'Arianna* would soon take on mythical proportions:

> Likewise, *Arianna* by the same Rinuccini received great applause, which was clothed in suitable melody by Signor Claudio Monteverde, today *maestro di cappella* of the Republic of Venice, who has published the most principal part of it, which is the lament of Ariadne herself, which is perhaps the most

beautiful composition that has been written in our times in this [recitative] genre.[158]

Similarly, the Florentine Severo Bonini, in his *Prima parte de' discorsi e regole sovra la musica* (c.1650), was to document the success and wide diffusion of this lament:

> Among foreigners, first it was Signor Claudio Monteverdi who enriched this style with rare ornaments and new ideas in the play entitled *Arianna*, the work of Signor Ottavio Rinuccini, gentleman from Florence: it was so appreciated that there has been no house which, having harpsichords or theorbos therein, did not have its lament.[159]

Elaborated and modified from the start by its composer himself (the version for five voices and the sacred *contrafactum* discussed earlier), this lament was to be the object of imitation and/or emulation as much in polyphonic contexts (note the later versions by Claudio Pari and Antonio il Verso of 1619, and one in manuscript by Giulio Cesare Antonelli)[160] as in monody: witness the laments of Armida (1609) and Olimpia (1623) published by Sigismondo d'India; the two settings of the *Lamento d'Arianna* – on the same text by Rinuccini – by the Florentine Severo Bonini (1613) and Francesco Costa from Liguria (1626); the *Lamento della Madonna* in Claudio Saracini's *Seconde musiche* (1620; the collection opens with a madrigal for solo voice, 'Udite, lagrimosi', dedicated specifically to Monteverdi); and, in a theatrical context, the many laments in the Roman *Aretusa* by Filippo Vitali (1620) or those contained in the Florentine *La regina Sant'Orsola* (1624) and *La Flora* (1628) by the poet Andrea Salvadori ('Toglietemi di vita' and 'Lasciatemi, ch'io mora' respectively), which are explicitly related to Rinuccini's model given their echoes of his text.

With Olimpia's lament 'Voglio, voglio morir, voglio morire', given by the Roman (by adoption) musician Luigi Rossi (1598–1653) in a manuscript which also contains the *Lamento d'Arianna* (London, British Library, Add. MS 30491), Monteverdi seems to have imitated himself, given that 'Olimpia's lament shows itself in terms of its text to be almost a plagiarized version of that famous lament of Arianna'.[161] The situation is identical, and also the images and the development of the speech are the same: Olimpia goes step by step through the same poetic topoi used by Arianna in the first three sections of her monologue. The music, too, suggests a clear relationship, starting with the opening refrain strictly repeated at the conclusion of the first group of verses; and several passages are modelled on parallel places in *Arianna*, albeit with less expressive force and with frequent recourse to declamatory clichés. It is the pale, slavish character of this imitation that casts doubts on whether this lament is in fact correctly attributed to Monteverdi.

Monteverdi's music for the prologue for *L'Idropica* has not survived; while the *Ballo delle ingrate* was published only much later, in the *Madrigali guerrieri, et amorosi* (1638). The *Ballo* is made up of some dance sections held together by sung interventions (dialogues and monologues), according to the structure of the courtly *balletto* which at the end of the sixteenth century was being most elaborately developed above all in France (in the *ballet de cour*): we should not forget that the librettist, Rinuccini, had from 1600 been several times at the court of Maria de' Medici in Paris. In the printed version, the *Ballo delle ingrate*, said to be 'in the representative genre', is preceded by a list of the 'Characters' ('Amor, Venus and Pluto, four shades of the inferno, eight ungrateful souls who dance'), of the instruments to be used ('five *viole da brazzo*, harpsichord and chitarrone, which instruments are doubled according to the need of the size of the place in which it is to be performed'), and by scenery and stage directions which can usefully be compared with Follino's description given above:

> First a stage is made the scene of which forms a mouth of the inferno with four entrances on each side, which throw forth flames, from which appear two by two the ungrateful souls with lamenting gestures at the sound of the *entrata* which marks the beginning of the *ballo*, which is repeated by the players as many times as needed until they [the dancers] find themselves in the middle of the space in which the *ballo* is to be begun. Pluto stands in the middle, leading them forward with solemn steps, then, he having retired somewhat, after the *entrata* is finished they begin the *ballo*. Then Pluto, stopping them in the middle of it, speaks to the princes and ladies who will be present in the manner written. As regards the ungrateful souls, their costume will be ash-coloured, adorned with feigned tears. The *ballo* ended, they return to the inferno in the same way as they left it and to the same lamenting sound, one of them staying at the end on-stage, performing the lament which is written, then she enters the inferno. At the rise of the curtain, a *sinfonia* will be done as required.

The narrative framework of the *Ballo* is very simple. With Amor's arrows rendered ineffectual, Venus decides to descend to the inferno to beg Pluto to free the souls of those who in the past were insensible to his power and who now languish in the deepest parts of the abyss for that former harshness. The sight of such a horrid *exemplum* is intended to persuade the ladies present no longer to be so severe in dealing with their lovers. Therefore the text is a gallant warning, an erotic 'morality' summed up by the *ottava* sung by Venus, 'Udite, donne, udite e i saggi detti' ('Listen, ladies, listen, and the wise sayings . . .'). The message would have appealed to the tastes of the libertine duke, and elsewhere the text is closely linked to the life and even the small-time gossip of the court: see, for example, the passage 'Donne, che di beltade . . .' ('Ladies, who of beauty . . .') and that which follows, particularly the verses 'O barbara fierezza, / una io ne vidi (e potrei dirne il nome . . .)' ('O barbarous pride, / I saw one (and I could say her name)'), perhaps alluding to Barbara Sanseverino, Countess of Sala. Nor should one forget that Vincenzo and Francesco Gonzaga, according to the custom of the time, took an active part in the dance sections with, according to Follino, 'six other knights and with eight ladies from the principal ones of the city'.

19 1608–1609

'At the return of these gentlemen I heard with great joy the news of your most happy festivities which succeeded so admirably and with so great pomp that they are not yet sated with praising them', wrote Jacopo Peri to Ferdinando Gonzaga on 28 July 1608. Similarly, on 24 June 1610 Rinuccini noted that 'The fame of the entertainments done in Mantua is very great, and certainly with reason when I think on it.'[162] The heavy duties imposed on Monteverdi first because of the urgency of the festivities and then because of their scale laid low his delicate health, for his phlegmatic temperament was ill-suited to any haste or confusion: 'speed and quality do not go well together', he asserted in a letter (L.26) of 1617, repeating the same proverb ten years later (L.91 [92]); and on 4 February 1617 (L.27) he declared that 'I hold nothing more inimical to my nature than shortness of time in my undertakings.'

In Cremona, where he had gone in the first days of July for his usual summer vacation, Monteverdi this time stayed longer than usual, but he was not inactive. In a letter of 26 November 1608 (L.5; to Cardinal Ferdinando Gonzaga?), as well as speaking of 'my indisposition (from which I have not yet recovered) due to the heavy tasks undertaken yonder in recent days', he refers to the sending of an unidentified composition: 'I began – as soon as the footman arrived – to carry out your commission for the piece of music I am sending you.' The following day, the composer had his father the doctor write to the duchess:

> Most Serene Lady.
>
> As soon as the most solemn festivities in Mantua were ended, Claudio Monteverde, my son, came to Cremona seriously ill, with debts, poorly clothed and without the salary of Signora Claudia, with two poor little sons thus left on his shoulders after her death, having nothing but the usual 20 *scudi* per month, all of which I consider having been caused by the Mantuan air, which by its nature is harmful, and by the great tasks he has carried out and will continue carrying out if he stays in service, and by his bad fortune which has persecuted him for the nineteen years in which he has found himself in the service of the Most Serene Lord Duke of Mantua. In the past few days, I resolved to write to His Most Serene Highness on bended knee that for the love of God he should grant him a dismissal with his good grace, because it is certain, Most Serene Lady, that if he returns to Mantua under those heavy duties and the air, his life will soon leave him, and those poor children will rest on my shoulders, which are most weak because of age and expense, having a wife, children, maids and servants [to support], and for having spent on the aforesaid Claudio on several occasions 500 ducats and more when he served His Most Serene Highness in Hungary, in Flanders, when he came to Cremona with his wife, maid, servants, carriage and children, and for other occurrences which for the sake of brevity I will omit. Since, Most Serene Madame, I have not had a reply from His Most Serene Highness, I have taken this course of beseeching Your Most Serene Highness that you might, for the love of God, beg the most serene lord your consort

that he might grace me with this so just request, so that all which will result to the benefit of the said Claudio from this favour he will deem it to have come from the generosity and kindness which is Your Most Serene Highness's. For certainly I say again to Your Most Serene Highness that if he returns there under that air and to those duties, it will be the death of him and my ruin, therefore do not fail through your infinite generosity and compassion to grant the present favour to me, a poor old man. Unable to do anything else, I here will make a most humble bow to Your Most Serene Highness, praying always to the blessed Lord for the happy health of all the most serene house of Your Most Serene Highness.

From Cremona, 27 November 1608.

Your Most Serene Highness's most humble and most obliged servant.[163]

Some three weeks earlier (on 9 November), Baldassarre Monteverdi had in fact written in vain to the duke in person, begging him to agree to dismiss his son, providing him with a testimonial that would bear witness to his professional merits and would perhaps facilitate an appointment at some other court: otherwise he asked at least that he might be exempted from such heavy duties, requesting that he be assigned only those concerning sacred music (Gastoldi, *maestro* in S. Barbara, was very ill; in fact, he died two months later).

Most Serene Lord.

Claudio Monteverde, most humble servant of Your Most Serene Highness and my dearest son, loved tenderly by me because from him I have always received obedience and the greatest desire to have himself honoured through his virtues, four months ago came to me in Cremona with his two sons, seriously ill because of the Mantuan air which has always been harmful to him, and of the many and great duties he has performed, and of the further burden of debts to the Jews because he is lacking the salary of the wretched Signora Claudia, his wife, and with the loss of his dowry and without the land, not having anything other than his usual salary which suffices only to feed himself and scarcely his sons. Thus moved by fatherly compassion, thinking of his so bad fortune received continually and now more greatly, and thinking that if he returns to Mantua to work certainly he would soon end his life, leaving the sons on my shoulders, and most poor, just as poor Signora Claudia their mother left them on his shoulders, so I am reduced to coming to Your Most Serene Highness's feet to beg you by God's heart to grant him an honourable discharge together with your good favour so that he can find other air for his health and less trouble, and another fortune for the well-being of his poor sons. This honourable discharge will equally benefit me his father, for if I add further expense to that of the past so that he can do himself honour, without doubt it would be my final ruin, for I still feel the noteworthy losses of the earlier expenses, from when he first came to serve Your Most Serene Highness and from when he came to serve you in Hungary and in Flanders, leaving with me in Cremona his wife and a servant, and from when last year I carried out the funeral of his said wife, and the payments to a servant, sons and for a carriage, and finally that which has now been spent for four months and more on him and his sons, and all these expenses I know have taken over 500 *ducatoni* from my purse, above and beyond the small amounts sent to him in Mantua. Thus, Most Serene Lord, finding myself old with two other sons, wife, maid- and man-servant, I know that if this spending continued it would be the final ruin of my house. Whenceforth I turn yet again to beseech you that by Christ's heart you permit him the requested discharge, assuring Your Most Serene Highness that all his well-being he will always recognize as coming from your generosity, for if from the favour of your generous dismissal it happens that he serves a prince, I know that in this respect he will be viewed favourably. If Your Most Serene Highness commands only that he serves in the church, that he will do, for even from this source he will draw 400 *scudi* as a fixed income and 150 as extras, from which he will be able to advance something for his sons, availing himself also of me if the need arises. If further Your Most Serene Highness wishes so to add favours that as well as the free dismissal you wish, I say, to give him the pension that you promised him through the most serene lord prince and Signor Chieppio, he will accept it from Your Most Serene Highness's generous hand to give it to his sons, assuring you that as poor as my son finds himself to be, you could summon him through having made a large donation to him and to me and to all our poor house, for which I will always be obliged, praying to God for Your Most Serene Highness's health, to whom in conclusion I make a most humble bow

From Cremona, 9 November 1608

Your Most Serene Highness's   Most humble and most obliged servant.[164]

Not only did the duke not consent to dismiss his own *maestro di cappella*, but in reply the responsibility for the sacred music in S. Barbara was entrusted first as an *interim* measure to Antonio Taroni, and then to Stefano Nascimbeni; and on the last day of November the order reached Monteverdi to return to court to apply himself to new theatrical music, perhaps for the carnival of 1609. On 2 December 1608, still writing from Cremona (L.6), the composer vented his feelings to Annibale Chieppio over his situation and his scant fortune at Mantua notwithstanding his heavy workload, comparing them with the successes, including financial successes, of other more prosperous colleagues still active or who had recently died leaving significant inheritances to their heirs.

> Today, which is the last day of November, I received from Your Most Illustrious Lordship a letter from which I learned of His Most Serene Highness's command: that I come as soon as possible to Mantua. Most Illustrious Signor Chieppio, if he orders me to come and wear myself out again, I assure you that unless I take a rest from toiling away at music for the theatre, my life will indeed be a short one, for as a result of my labours (so recent and of such magnitude) I have had a frightful pain in my head and so terrible and violent an itching around my waist, that neither by cauteries which I have had applied to myself, nor by purges taken orally, nor by blood-letting and other potent remedies has it thus far been possible to get better − only partly so. My father attributes the cause of the headache to mental strain, and the itching to Mantua's air (which does not agree with me), and he fears that the air alone could be the death of me before long. . . .
>
> If fortune favoured me last year by making the Lord Duke invite me to

assist with the musical events for the marriage, it also did me a bad turn on that occasion by making me perform an almost impossible task, and further-more, it caused me to suffer from cold, lack of clothing, servitude, and very nearly lack of food (through the stopping of my wife Claudia's allowance and the onset of a serious illness), without my being in the slightest degree favoured by His Most Serene Highness with any public mark of esteem, though Your Most Illustrious Lordship knows very well that the favours of great princes help servants both in regard to honour and in what is useful to them, particularly on an occasion when there are visitors.

If fortune granted me a livery from His Most Serene Highness, to wear at the time of the marriage, it also let me down badly by making me have it of cloth which was woven from silk and floss-silk, with no overcoat, no stockings and garters, and no silk lining for the cloak, wherefore I spent out of my own pocket 20 *scudi* in Mantuan currency.

If fortune has done me a favour by letting me have so very many opportunities of being commissioned by His Most Serene Highness, it has also caused me this loss, that the Lord Duke has always spoken to me about hard work, and never about bringing me the pleasure of something useful.

If lastly (to go on no longer) fortune has looked kindly upon me by making me think I had a pension from His Most Serene Highness of 100 *scudi* in Mantuan currency from the captaincy of the piazza, it showed its black side even then because when the marriage ceremonies were over there were not 100 *scudi* but only 70 (along with the loss of my extra fee and loss of money from the previous months), as if perhaps it were amazed by the 100 *scudi* being too much; and those added to the 20 I am getting made about 22 *ducatoni* a month. If I had received them, what would I then have set aside for the use of my poor sons?

Oratio della Viola would have had to work very hard to get an income of 500 *scudi* a year, without the usual perquisites, if he had nothing but the aforementioned every month. Similarly Luca Marenz[i]o would have had to work quite hard to become as rich, and likewise Filippo di Monte and Palest[r]ina, who left his sons an income worth more than 1,000 *scudi*. Luzzasco and Fiorini would have had to work quite hard to get an income of 300 *scudi* each, which was then left to their sons; and lastly (to say no more) Franceschino Rovighi [Rovigo] would have had to toil away to save 7,000 *scudi*, as he did, if he had nothing but the aforementioned wages, which hardly suffice to pay the expenses of a master and servant and clothe him; for I don't know about his having two sons as well, which is the case with me . . .

What clearer proof do you want, Your Most Illustrious Lordship? To give 200 *scudi* to Messer Marco de Galiani [da Gagliano] who can hardly be said to have done anything, and to give me nothing, who did what I did . . . Signor Federico Follini promised in one of his letters, inviting me from Cremona last year to Mantua for the wedding preparations – I tell you he promised me what Your Most Illustrious Lordship can see in this letter of his that I am sending you; and then at the end of it all nothing happened, or if indeed I had something, it was 1,500 lines to set to music.

Dear Sir, help me to obtain an honourable dismissal, for it seems to me that this is the best possible thing, because I shall have a change of air, work, and fortune; and who knows, if the worst comes to the worst what else can I do but remain as poor as I am?

Monteverdi was therefore persisting in his intention to abandon the Gonzaga court, or perhaps he was only threatening it so as to obtain better treatment. But whatever the case, on 19 January 1609 the duke confirmed by decree the pension of 100 *scudi*:

> Given that we have decided to reward with some sign of our liberality the service that for many years past Messer Claudio Monteverdi has performed for us as *maestro* of the music of our chapel, giving at the same time evidence to the world of the esteem which we have placed and do place on his virtue, worthiness and merit, with this decree, certain knowledge and well deliberated mind, we grant a free, perpetual and inviolable gift to the said Monteverdi, for him, his heirs and successors of whatever kind, of an annual pension or allowance [*risponsione*] of 100 *scudi* at 6 *lire* per scudo in our Mantuan currency . . .[165]

As for his musical output, in 1608 Monteverdi also published two new madrigals ('Pensier aspro e crudele' and 'Sdegno la fiamma estinse', the last on a text by Orsina Cavaletta) in Giaches de Wert's *Duodecimo libro de madrigali*, a posthumous work that also included compositions by other musicians in Mantuan circles: Gastoldi, Virchi and Taroni. Of these pieces, however, only the bass part has survived.[166]

In 1608 and 1609, Ricciardo Amadino reprinted in Venice the Fifth Book of madrigals and the *Scherzi musicali* respectively, while in Milan (where Borromeo's counter-reforming ideals were still in force) the press of the heirs of Agostino Tradate issued two more collections of spiritual *contrafacta* prepared by Aquilino Coppini: *Il secondo libro della musica di Claudio Monteverde e d'altri autori a cinque voci* (1608) includes versions of madrigals from the Third, Fourth and Fifth Books (together with pieces by Cima, Croce, Flaccomio, Giovanelli, Marenzio, Merulo and Tresti); and *Il terzo libro della musica di Claudio Monteverde a cinque voci* (1609), madrigals from the Fourth and Fifth Books, and one unpublished piece ('Una donna fra l'altre onesta e bella') later included in the Sixth Book:

1 'O come è gran martire' as 'O dies infelices'
2 'La giovinetta pianta' as 'Florea serta laeti contexite'
3 'Ch'io t'ami, e t'ami piú della mia vita' as 'Te sequar, Jesu mea vita'
4 'Che dar piú vi poss'io?' as 'Qui regnas super alta poli'
5 'M'è piú dolce il penar per Amarilli' as 'Animas eruit e domo'
6 'O Mirtillo, Mirtillo anima mia' as 'O mi fili, mea vita Jesu'
7 'O primavera, gioventú dell'anno' as 'Praecipitantur e torrente nives'
8 'Ah dolente partita' as 'O infelix recessus'

1 'Una donna fra l'altre onesta e bella' as 'Una es o Maria'
2 'Amor, se giusto sei' as 'Amem te domine spes mea'
3 'Ma se con la pietà non è in te spenta' as 'Qui pietate tua'
4 'Cor mio, mentre vi miro' as 'Jesu, dum te contemplor'
5 'Cor mio, non mori? E mori' as 'Jesu, tu obis'
6 'Luci serene e chiare' as 'Luce serena lucent animae'
7 'La piaga c'ho nel core' as 'Plagas tuas adoro Christe'

 8 'Voi pur da me partite, anima dura' as 'Tu vis a me abire'
 9 'A un giro sol de bell'occhi lucenti' as 'Cantemus laeti quae Deus effecit'
10 'Piagne e sospira, e quando i caldi raggi' as 'Plorat amare'
11 'Anima del cor mio' as 'Anima quam dilexi'
12 'Longe da te, cor mio' as 'Longe a te, mi Jesu'
13 'Sí ch'io vorrei morire' as 'O Jesu, mea vita'
14 'Anima dolorosa che vivendo' as 'Anima miseranda quae offendis Deum tuum'
15 'Sfogava con le stelle' as 'O stellae coruscantes'
16 'Volgea l'anima mia soavemente' as 'Ardebat igne puro'
17 'Anima mia, perdona' as 'Domine Deus meus peccavi'
18 'Che se tu se' il cor mio' as 'O gloriose martyr' (second *pars* of the preceding)
19 'Io mi son giovinetta' as 'Rutilante in nocte exultant'
20 'Quell'augellin che canta' as 'Qui laudes tuas cantat'

Certain parts of Coppini's dedications are also significant. In the *Secondo libro*, he insists on the expressiveness of Monteverdi's music, labelled 'rappresentativa' ('representative') not because it is destined for the stage but in terms of its capacity to give a vivid representation of the world of the 'affections':

> The representative music of Signor Claudio Monteverdi's Fifth Book of madrigals, governed by the natural expression of the human voice in moving the affections, stealing into the ear in sweetest manner and thereby making itself the most pleasant tyrant of souls, is indeed worthy of being sung and heard not (as some say out of spite) in the pastures and among the sheep, but in the retreats of most noble spirits and in royal courts. And it can also serve many as an infallible norm and idea of composing harmonically conforming to the best rules madrigals and canzonas ... Given that the first book was received by the most principal cities of Italy with pleasure and great applause, I have sought to be able to publish also the second ... I dare promise you a similar offspring every year.

When sending the three collections to his friend Hendrik van der Putten in Louvain in July 1609, Coppini returned to the strongly expressive character of Monteverdi's compositions, requiring an appropriate performance paying attention to 'affective' values even from the point of view of rhythm and tempo: 'I send you a threefold offspring. It concerns musical *concerti* ... Those by Monteverdi require, during their performance, more flexible rests [*respiri*] and bars that are not strictly regular, now pressing forward or abandoning themselves to slowings down, now also hurrying. You yourself will fix the tempo. In them there is a truly wondrous capacity for moving the affections.'[167] And in presenting the *Terzo libro* to Prince Francesco Gonzaga, Coppini invoked the performance of *Arianna* (appropriately, since it was prepared for his wedding) and Monteverdi's capacity to apply an emotional style even to the theatre:

> The most ancient and most beautiful city of Mantua was at all times ... the fecund mother and kindly nurse of the most elevated intellects, among which today Claudio Monteverde, dedicated to the service of Your Highness's most serene house, has reached in music such excellence that those musical effects which we read with great wonder in ancient books should no longer appear strange. Of this, among many other works, clear evidence is given by *Arianna*, a work which, staged at the most happy wedding of Your Highness and the Most Serene Infanta of Savoy, with Monteverdi's new and suave notes, not to speak of the expression of the other affections, was able to draw with living force from the eyes of the famous audience and of whomsoever later heard it, thousand upon thousand pitying tears.

In these same years, the Bolognese Adriano Banchieri also praised the expressive power and the 'artful' style of Monteverdi, directed towards empowering to the greatest possible extent the 'oration'. His comments closely resemble – in the terminology, the arguments and the composers cited, as also in the allusions to circles of aristocratic music-lovers ('honoured salons and heroic academies') – the writings associated with Monteverdi in the controversy with Banchieri's fellow Bolognese, Artusi:

> There is no doubt that music, as regards harmony, should be subject to the words, given that the words are that which express the conceit, wherefore if the word seeks out grief, passion, sighs, questioning error or some other such phenomenon, these words should be clothed with equivalent harmony ... And if the intelligent modern composer (*sapienti pauca*) sometimes here and there throughout the song departs from the mode and uses foreign cadences, one should not therefore say that he hits now the hoop and now the cask, and that this is done without consideration, but rather it is practised industriously [for example, by Tommaso Pecci and Gabriele Fattorini] ... And here so as not to leave a rich feast deprived of salt, I must not fail to name the most suave composer of music, Claudio Monteverde, head of the music of the Most Serene Lord Don Vincenzo Gonzaga, Duke of Mantua (although his worth is known universally to professors of music), in matters of modern composition, for his artful sentiments are truly worthy of total commend-ation, uncovering therein every affective part of perfect oration, industrious-ly laid out and imitated by equivalent harmony: just as thus and likewise have had and have practised the Lord Prince of Venosa, the Lord Count Alfonso Fontanelli, Signor Emilio Cavallieri, Benedetto Pallavicino and other modern and elevated intellects, whose worth is known within honoured salons and heroic academies.[168]

1609 (the year of the publication of *Orfeo*) also saw an unidentified com-positional project mentioned in the letters (L.7, from Cremona, 24 August 1609, to Striggio):

> I received a letter from Your Most Illustrious Lordship together with certain words to be set to music, as a commission from His Most Serene Highness, and they arrived yesterday which was the 23rd of this month. I shall start to

work on them as soon as possible, and when they are all done I shall inform Your Most Illustrious Lordship or bring them myself to Mantua, because I want to be back in service shortly. I thought first of setting these words for a solo voice, but if later on His Highness orders me to re-arrange the air for five voices, this I shall do.

In the same year, during his customary summer stay in Cremona, Monteverdi also attended – on 27 September – a meeting of the Accademia degli Animosi, into which he had been admitted two years earlier.[169] Meanwhile, on behalf of the Gonzaga court and directly following a request from Striggio, he had explored the inclination of some 'suonatori da fiato' (wind players) in service at Cremona Castle to move to Mantua (L.8, 10 September 1609; see also the extract from L.7 given on p. 53). Monteverdi reports in detail his own cautious approaches and their responses: ' "If the lord commander or governor of the castle knew that you wanted to leave, would he give you permission?" They replied that not only would he not give permission, but he would hinder them in every way so that they could not leave. "And if the need should arise, how would you leave?" They answered: "We would go without saying anything." I did not discuss the matter further' (L.8). He also compiled a detailed report on 'a certain Galeazzo Sirena, composer and organist': this had been requested by Prince Francesco Gonzaga, who wanted to know whether he 'would come and serve ... and what salary he would like', as well as seeking information on 'his capability and intelligence' (L.8). Sirena was well known personally to Monteverdi, given that the former visited his house almost daily ('I am very well acquainted with the said Galeazzo – indeed he comes daily to see me at home'), and therefore the composer could offer a full, professional and perceptive report alive to Sirena's strengths and weaknesses (L.8). He had great ability above all in 'handmade things' – as a result of which he successfully ventured upon making instruments – and as a composer he demonstrated a good training, if tied to rather idiosyncratic views: 'In music he is certainly intelligent, but self-opinionated; and he insists that whatever comes out of his head is the most beautiful of its kind, and if others are not quick to say so, he himself is the first.' A composer of 'canzonas to be played on string or wind instruments, these being very practical, technically well worked out, and of a certain novel invention', Sirena had in sacred music written works 'in a style that is certainly opulent but difficult to sing, because he keeps chasing certain voice-parts and rests, which greatly tires and worries the singers'. He was totally ignorant of the theatrical style, while as an organist he was not gifted with great 'elegance of hand, since he has not the touch to bring off runs, trills, appoggiaturas, or other ornaments, and he himself admits to not making a profession of it'. In addition to his professional judgements, Monteverdi added some notes on Sirena's character, not failing to underline his scant affability ('he has ample conviction but no idea of making himself liked by the singers, for those in

Cremona are not happy singing under him, although they respect him, and he readily speaks ill of a third party') and to emphasize with some ill-feeling his presumption (he is 'very well endowed both as regards the poverty and the conviction of his thought'). For the rest, it was clear right from his opening remarks that Monteverdi's account was not designed to inspire enthusiasm. Here he said that Sirena had no intention of seeking a court position, hoping to assay the path of professional semi-independence tied to stable ecclesiastical service: Sirena 'replied that he had no mind to go and serve princes, but was keen to go and live in Milan as *maestro di cappella* at the church of La Scala [Santa Maria della Scala] (especially since certain Milanese singers promised to make that post available to him), because with a chance like that he says he could earn his living by teaching, making music for the city, composing for the nuns, and having chitarrones and harpsichords made for sale; and so by this means he would hope to become rich in a short time'. The reason for such diplomatic caution on Monteverdi's part becomes clear in the closing section of the letter, where he openly reveals his fears to his friend Striggio:

> So, Signor Striggio, I thought I would write to Your Most Illustrious Lordship a few words about the things that make me uneasy, because I mean the prince is entitled to do just what seems right and pleasing to His Most Serene Highness, but by taking either him or others as Director of Music (indeed, if he wants to give him such a title, and that I don't know), on the death of the most serene duke; and should Almighty God allow me to survive – the prince having a *maestro di cappella* – what would you wish me to do: go away from Mantua then?

In short, Monteverdi had been obliged to obey the prince's request, but his fear of encouraging the rise of a possible future rival had dictated to him an account as analytical as it was skilled in toning down the positive elements.

One can also assign to the period 1607–10 the spiritual canzonettas surviving (only the soprano part) in the Biblioteca Queriniana in Brescia in a manuscript titled *Canzonette e madrigaletti spirituali a 2 e 3 voci d'auttori diversi. Libro VIII* ('Spiritual canzonettas and madrigals for two and three voices by various composers. Book VIII'; with the shelf-mark MS L.IV.99), which bears the inscription: 'Mich. Parius scribebat Parmae anno 1610' ('Michele Pario in Parma wrote [this] in the year 1610'). Alongside compositions by Pario himself, plus Bertani, Ghizzolo, Vecchi, Scaletta, Franzoni, Salomone Rossi, Pecci, Gesualdo, Nenna and others, appear five pieces by Monteverdi, three of which – 'Su fanciullo', 'O rosetta che rossetta' and 'Dolce spina del mio core' (headed 'D'una spina del Signore insanguinata'; 'On a blood-stained thorn of Our Lord') – are spiritual versions of *scherzi* drawn from the 1607 collection (respectively 'Damigella', 'O rosetta che rossetta' and 'Lidia spina del mio core'), while the other two – 'Se d'un angel il bel viso' (headed 'Quam dilecta tabernacula, etc.'; 'How delightful the tabernacles, etc.') and 'Fuggi, fuggi, cor, fuggi a tutte l'or') have no relationship with any earlier works now known in Monteverdi's output.[170]

20   The 'Mass and Vespers of the Blessed Virgin' (1610)

The projects on which Monteverdi worked in the summer of 1610 – in both sacred and secular spheres – were not unambitious. The singer and vice-*maestro di cappella*, Bassano Cassola, satisfied Ferdinando Gonzaga's curiosity on 26 July thus:

> Monteverdi is having printed an *a cappella* Mass for six voices of great studiousness and labour, having obliged himself to handle for every note and in every way, always reinforcing the eight points of imitation that are in the motet 'In illo tempore' by Gomberti [Gombert], and together he is having printed also psalms for Vespers of the Madonna, with various and diverse manners of invention and of harmony, and all on the *cantus firmus*, with the idea of coming to Rome this autumn to dedicate them to His Holiness [the Pope]. He is also preparing a collection of five-part madrigals, which will contain three laments: that one of Ariadne, with the usual melody throughout; the plaint of Leander and Hero by Marini; and the third, given to him by His Most Serene Highness, of a shepherd whose nymph is dead, to words by the son of the Lord Count Lepido Agnelli on the death of Signora Romanina . . . [171]

Already in the autumn of 1608 (see, for example, L.6 of 2 December 1608) Monteverdi had raised the idea of leaving Mantuan service. The publication of this Mass and Vespers (in Venice, at the press of Ricciardo Amadino in 1610), dedicated to Pope Paul V, constitutes the most concrete attempt initiated by the composer to obtain this end.[172] Wishing to see to things personally, Monteverdi also went to Rome, where he hoped to achieve two results: an audience with the Pope to enable him to offer his sacred collection in person, and a free place for his son Francesco 'in the Roman seminary with a benefice from the church to pay his board and lodging, I being a poor man. But without this favour I could not hope for anything from Rome to help Franceschino, who has already become a seminarian in order to live and die in this calling' (L.10, Cremona, 28 December 1610). Once in Rome, he could also have explored the possibility of a new position. However, none of these objectives was achieved, even though Monteverdi had had himself preceded by recommendations from Duke Vincenzo to Cardinal Montalto and Cardinal Borghese.[173]

The composer referred to his trip to Rome in his letter – presumably to Cardinal Ferdinando Gonzaga – from Cremona of 28 December 1610 (L.10: 'Before I left Rome . . . '), in which he shows that he had not lost all hope of placing his son:

> For if Rome, even with Your Most Illustrious Lordship's favour, were not to help him, he and another brother of his would remain poor, so that they would hardly be able to start the New Year with bread and wine, which I lack. I shall look out for some simple benefice or other that can bring in a stipend sufficient to obtain the satisfaction of this need from His Holiness, if

Your Most Illustrious Lordship will be so kind as to try and assist both him and me at the same time (as I hope from your infinite virtue), both with His Holiness and with Monsignor the Datary; otherwise, fearing that I troubled him too much when I was in Rome, I would not dare to ask him again for any favour.

In full, the title-page of Monteverdi's new work reads: *Sanctissimae Virgini missa senis vocibus ad ecclesiarum choros ac vespere pluribus decantanda cum nonnullis sacris concentibus, ad sacella sive principum cubicula accommodata, opera a Claudio Monteverde nuper effecta ac beatiss. Paulo V pont. max. consecrata* ('To the Most Holy Virgin Mass for six voices for church choirs and Vespers to be sung by many with some sacred concertos, suited to the chapels or apartments of princes, a work newly done by Claudio Monteverde and dedicated to the Most Blessed Paul V *pontifex maximus*'). The long title makes explicit, if not uncontroversially, the contents and function of the collection. As for the contents, it is easy to distinguish a Mass for six voices and the Vespers for six and more (seven, eight and ten, to which are added up to eight instrumental parts), with some sacred 'concertos', the whole in honour of the Virgin and thus presumably to be used chiefly on the occasion of the feasts dedicated to her, the most important of which were her birth (8 September), the annunciation (25 March) and her assumption (15 August). In terms of function, the Mass is said to be appropriate for church *cappelle*; the rest, instead – it seems – is for oratories and court chapels.

The upsurge in the cult of the Blessed Virgin – anti-Protestant in function – was a widespread phenomenon in the Catholic world after the Council of Trent, extending even through the seventeenth century. In music, whole collections of motets and spiritual madrigals were dedicated to her: Jacob Regnart's *Mariale* (Innsbruck, 1588), Philippe de Monte's *Eccellenze di Maria Vergine* (Venice, 1593), Palestrina's two books of spiritual madrigals (the first, published in 1581, ends with Petrarch's canzona to the Virgin, and the other, of 1594, is subtitled 'Priego alla Vergine' ('Prayer to the Virgin')), the anthology *Rosetum marianum* edited in 1604 by Bernhard Klingenstein, and Francesco Soriano's *Canoni et oblighi di cento e dieci sorte sopra l'Ave maris stella* (Rome, 1610).

No less connected to the cult of the Virgin is the motet 'In illo tempore' by the Flemish Nicolas Gombert (c.1500–c.1556) which gives its name to the Mass with which Monteverdi's collection opens. Within the volume, it is called 'Missa da capella a sei voci fatta sopra il mottetto "In illo tempore" del Gomberti le fughe del quale sono queste' ('Mass *a cappella* [that is, written in vocal polyphony, supported by the organ] for six voices [plus the basso continuo, in effect a *basso seguente*, for the organ] composed on the motet "In illo tempore" by Gombert, the fugues of which are these') – here follow ten musical ideas taken from Gombert's motet, changing only certain note values and in two cases (the seventh and tenth 'fugue') simplifying the melodic line. In the original motet, Monteverdi's 'fugues' are sometimes complete subjects (the first and third), but more often segments cut at a certain point for reasons of mode (in an attempt to produce musical material that is homogeneously Ionian), isolated and detached from their context.

These 'fugues' correspond to the following passages in Gombert's motet:[174]

1 'In illo tempore', bars 3–7, *basso*
2 'loquente Iesu ad tur[bas]', bars 14–17, *sesto*
3 'Beatus venter qui te portavit', bars 36–39, *basso*
4 'et custodiunt', bars 81–82, *basso*
5 'At ille dixit', bars 56–58, *canto*
6 'extollens vo[cem]', bars 21–23, *alto*
7 '[custo]diunt illud, bars 95–97, *sesto*
8 'quaedam mu[lier]', bars 29–30, *alto*
9 'et ubera', bars 48–49, *sesto*
10 'Quin im[mo]', bars 62–64, *basso*

The practice of composing Masses on pre-existing musical material, formerly adopted by the Flemish school, was now very common in sacred music, as used, for example, by Morales, Palestrina, Lasso, Monte, Andrea Gabrieli, Victoria and Gian Francesco Anerio. Such reworking through paraphrase or parody techniques is closely related to the Renaissance poetics of imitation: 'aesthetic appreciation is directed towards the *bravura* effect of re-telling, recomposing and variation'.[175] In the letter cited above, Cassola himself spoke concerning this Mass of the 'great studiousness and labour, [Monteverdi] having obliged himself to handle for every note and in every way, always reinforcing the eight [*recte* ten] points of imitation that are in the motet "In illo tempore" by Gomberti'. The compositional artifice imposed on Monteverdi by the need to adhere closely to the *prius factus* material of Gombert, the notable dimensions in terms of a larger than usual scoring (for six voices, moving to seven in the final section of the *Agnus Dei*; the texture is reduced – traditionally so – to four voices only in the 'Crucifixus' of the *Credo*) and the continuously contrapuntal style (except the usual homophony at the 'Et incarnatus' again in the *Credo*) are all features which encourage the notion that Monteverdi, already established in the fields of the madrigal and of theatre music, was now seeking to establish himself in the sacred style at the highest and most complex level to make an impression also in this repertory, to which Roman circles were obviously more sensitive than others.

The Mass is followed by the *Vespro della B[eata] V[ergine] da concerto, composto sopra canti fermi* ('Vespers of the Blessed Virgin in *concerto* [i.e., for voices together with instruments], composed on *cantus firmi*', as the title within the volume, in the basso continuo partbook, states (the general title-page has just *Vespere*, 'Vespers'). The 'Vespers' is made up of a respond, five psalms, a hymn ('Ave maris stella') and the Magnificat (which are the elements common to all the most important feasts of the Virgin), intermingled with motets for voices and instruments and with a 'sonata': in fact, the general title-page had announced 'cum nonnullis sacris concentibus' ('with some sacred concertos'). The two settings of the Magnificat could be intended to offer a choice between larger- and smaller-scale versions, or else, and more probably, could relate to the two services of Vespers, the first of the vigil and the second celebrated on the day of the feast.

As for the use of instruments side by side with voices (with functions not limited to the basso continuo) in settings of texts from the psalms or for Vespers services, sporadic experiments with such combinations had recently been made in the *Concerti* of the Paduan Giulio Radino (Venice, Angelo Gardano, 1607), the *Concerti ecclesiastici* by the Ferrarese Arcangelo Crotti (Venice, Giacomo Vincenti, 1608), Agostino Agazzari's *Psalmi sex* (Venice, Ricciardo Amadino, 1609) and, naturally, in the Venetian compositions of Giovanni Gabrieli and Giovanni Croce which were, however, printed only later (Gabrieli's *Sacrae symphoniae* in 1615).[176]

'Domine ad adiuvandum'	respond	'sex vocibus [SSATTB] et sex instrumentis' (2 cornetts and/or 2 *violini da braccio*, 1 *viola da braccio*, 2 *viole da braccio* and/or 2 trombones, 1 trombone and/or 1 *viola da braccio* and/or 1 *viola contrabassa da gamba*) plus basso continuo
'Dixit Dominus'	psalm	'sex vocibus [SSATTB] et sex instrumentis' (*idem*) plus continuo
'Nigra sum'	motet	solo voice (tenor) and continuo

'Laudate pueri'	psalm	'a 8 voci [SSAATTBB] sole nel organo' ('for 8 solo voices with organ'); the continuo is written largely in three parts
'Pulchra es'	motet	2 voices (sopranos) and continuo; the continuo is written largely in three parts
'Laetatus sum'	psalm	6 voices (SSATTB) and continuo
'Duo seraphim'	motet	3 voices (tenors) and continuo; the continuo is written largely in three parts
'Nisi Dominus'	psalm	10 voices (divided into two choirs: SATTB and SATTB) and continuo
'Audi coelum verba mea'	motet	'prima ad una voce sola' ('first for one voice [tenor]') and continuo – some passages with 'echo' effects – then for 6 voices (SSATTB) and continuo
'Lauda Jerusalem'	psalm	7 voices (SSAATBB) and continuo
Sonata sopra 'Sancta Maria, ora pro nobis'	sonata	soprano ('Parte che canta sopra la sonata a 8' ['The part which sings above the sonata *a8*']) and 8 instrumental parts (2 *violini da braccio*, 2 cornetts, 1 trombone, 1 trombone or 1 *viola da braccio*, 1 *viola da braccio*, 1 *trombone doppio*) plus continuo
'Ave maris stella'	hymn	8 voices divided into two choirs (SATB, SATB) and continuo, with instrumental ritornellos in five parts (SSATB) and continuo
Magnificat I	canticle	'septem vocibus [SSATTBB] et sex instrumentis' (2 violins, 3 cornetts and 1 *viola da braccio*) – there are also parts for 2 flutes, 2 *fifare* and 2 trombones – plus continuo (with indications of registration for the organ)
Magnificat II	canticle	6 voices (SSATTB) and continuo (with indications of registration for the organ)

Scholarly views of Monteverdi's 1610 'Vespers' differ according to whether the collection is seen as being liturgically heterogeneous and incomplete (Redlich, Stevens, Biella) or, on the contrary, governed by a unifying logic

(Schrade, Osthoff, Bonta, Kurtzman, Gallico).[177] Those who have most recently re-examined the question from the point of view of liturgical function (Bonta and Kurtzman) have been able to validate the hypothesis already put forward by Schrade: that the *sacri concentus* should be viewed as antiphon-substitutes.[178] In effect, such a solution fulfils the requirements of utility: since the antiphons belong to the Proper, they change for each feast, so to substitute for them motets – plus the *Sonata* – relevant to the Virgin but more generic in scope meant making the collection valid for almost all Marian feasts, if not, indeed, for a devotional celebration that did not specifically require close conformance to the liturgical canon. To have set to music the texts of the antiphons would have meant either tying this work to a specific feast or else increasing its size beyond all bounds if there was to be an attempt to provide the antiphons proper to each Marian service.

Although Monteverdi's collection shares similarities in terms of its contents with prints by Francesco Terriera (1601), Serafino Patta (1606), Giovanni Righi (1606) and Pompeo Signorucci (1608), it is distinguished by the fact that, apart from the Mass, it uniquely contains material relevant to Vespers and moreover places the *sacri concentus* not at the end but between the psalms, in the position expected of the antiphons which they replace.[179] The work therefore presents even in terms of its typographical layout a progression, a binding constructional logic: dedicated to one single ceremonial category (Marian devotions), it is articulated variously but compactly, in a unified manner, according to a fully preordained and canonic plan. Such rigidity without doubt renders the collection somewhat unmanageable, to the extent of giving the impression that its practicality was of little importance to Monteverdi. In sum, it was not a question of throwing together a handbook of liturgical music for widespread use (and marketability), and one good, with appropriate adaptations, for ecclesiastical musical establishments of all sizes: Monteverdi was not a *maestro* at some church of greater or lesser importance, nor was he writing for unknown colleagues in *cappelle* with greater or lesser financial resources. His collection was above all a presentation volume which the musical director of a great princely court was dedicating to the Pope in the hope of drawing from it some professional advantage, therefore lavishing on it all the resources of his own compositional technique and with an unequivocal inventiveness. In so doing, Monteverdi organized the volume as a grandiose rite as suitable as possible for the glorification of the Virgin, and so, for that very reason, somewhat general and imprecise in terms of its liturgical make-up.

There is yet another unique feature: even within their diversity, the various movements have a common point of reference in Gregorian chant, in homage to a compositional orthodoxy displayed in the title ('composed on *cantus firmi*') and indicated in the aforementioned letter from Cassola, who noted the 'various and diverse manners of invention and of harmony, and all on the *cantus firmus*'. This was not at all common in contemporary psalm-settings, which tended to use the *cantus firmus* either in *falsobordone* or only as material for polyphonic openings (exceptions are provided, before and around the time of Monteverdi, by two examples by Giovanni Croce ('Domine, probasti me', published in 1603) and Gian Francesco Capello ('Benedictus Dominus Deus Israel', 1612), each using the chant for an entire movement). This is even more the case with the two Magnificats: in the early seventeenth century, the links between polyphonic settings and the Magnificat's Gregorian setting were very brittle.[180] In Monteverdi's case, however, everything (respond, hymn, psalms, Magnificat) is based on the *cantus firmus*, which runs through the collection from beginning to end, constituting its skeleton, its point of reference, the axis around which all else revolves.

This respectful adherence to the ancient patrimony of the traditional ecclesiastical chant certainly contributes to the unity of the work, cementing it together and acting as its centre of gravity. However, from the point of view of the composer, it is also equivalent to the 'fugues' by Gombert used in the Mass. Given that the constant and uninterrupted recourse to Gregorian psalm melodies in compositions of such length could in fact generate a sense of repetitiveness and of tedium, the obligation to adhere to it was for Monteverdi certainly a further *tour de force*, a demonstration of compositional skill beyond the norm, according to a plan of action summed up – perhaps in the composer's own words – in Cassola's account: to produce 'various and diverse manners of invention and of harmony'.

Within the collection, we also find a piece in which the voices are silent to leave room for instrumental polyphony. The *Sonata sopra 'Sancta Maria, ora pro nobis'*, the last in the series of *sacri concentus*, is the one movement of all the Vespers where the true protagonists are the instruments. The soprano is in fact limited to eleven intermittent and irregular intonations of the invocation 'Sancta Maria, ora pro nobis' ('Holy Mary, pray for us'), set to the melody used for the Litany of the Saints: Monteverdi used it again, and once more as an ostinato, in a motet for two voices and continuo ('Santa Maria, succurre miseris') printed in Giovan Battista Ala's *Primo libro di concerti ecclesiastici* (Milan, Filippo Lomazzo, 1618) and then reprinted in the third volume of Johannes Donfried's *Promptuarium musicum* (Strasbourg, Ledertz, 1627). The same subject had also been used, and similarly with ostinato repetitions, in one of the *Motecta* by Antonio Gualtieri (Venice, Giacomo Vincenti, 1604: 'Beatissimus Marcus'), and it was to reappear in Ignazio Donati's *Sacri concentus* (Venice, Giacomo Vincenti, 1612).[181] Monteverdi's *Sonata* merges the tradition of the motet based on an ostinato subject with that of the sonata for instruments and single voice, examples of which are in the aforementioned *Concerti ecclesiastici* by Arcangelo Crotti, in Giovanni Gabrieli's motet 'Dulcis Jesu, patris imago', and, after Monteverdi, in the *Apparato musicale* by the Mantuan Amante Franzoni (Venice, Ricciardo Amadino, 1613).[182] Other examples were to be provided by Frescobaldi in his *Primo libro di capricci* (Rome, Luca Antonio Soldi, 1624: the tenth *capriccio* has the 'Obligo di cantare la quinta parte senza toccarla, sempre di obligo del sogetto scritto' – 'Requirement to sing the fifth part without playing it, always according to the subject written') and in his *Fiori musicali* (Venice, Alessandro Vincenti, 1635: *Recercar* 'con obligo di cantare la quinta parte senza toccarla' – 'with the requirement to sing the fifth part without playing it'). Although Monteverdi's *Sonata* prompts one to think of the instrumental compositions of Giovanni Gabrieli, in fact it distances itself significantly from them as regards its style, the melodic material used, and the way of handling this material and of placing it within the various sections, if not for the extensive recourse to writing for two parts and continuo, given that pairs of high instruments (i.e. cornetts and violins) predominate over everything else.[183]

Therefore the 'Vespers' presents in a near-systematic way a survey of the techniques proper to the style then called 'modern' – combining voices and instruments, the use of the basso continuo, the adoption of styles of writing for solo voice, the recourse to polyphonic textures for small forces (duets, trios), and new rhythmic/melodic patterns deriving for the most part from 'chromatic' writing *a note nere* and therefore on average using note values smaller than those generally appearing in *a cappella* music – yet always interwoven with traditional elements (polyphony in *a cappella* style, divided choirs, *falsobordone*). All this was then made to gravitate constantly around the central axis of the Gregorian *cantus firmus*. Moreover, on the uniform compositional flow derived from the Franco-Flemish style are in general imprinted the signs of an *ars aedificatoria*, of a clear desire for structure, and one that is analogous to the same desire that had emerged in Monteverdi's most recent secular works for both theatre and chamber. As much as the *Missa 'In illo tempore'*, in which Monteverdi had ventured upon the most complex and artful practices of traditional sacred music, the 'Vespers' bears the hallmarks of a monumental and illustrative *summa*, and it acts as a solid and highly compact – even in its stylistic variety – celebration of the inventive and professional resources at the composer's command. If in terms of Monteverdi's career this collection was to remain without results (he did not obtain the Roman position that he perhaps desired), nevertheless in the history of early seventeenth-century sacred music it represents without doubt a focal point, where orientations and experiments which until then had only been explored here and there and by fits and starts are reassembled within a formal plan of the utmost unifying logic.

21 1610–1613: the death of Vincenzo I Gonzaga, Monteverdi's dismissal from Mantua, his move to Venice

Monteverdi's trip to Rome, with a stay in Florence, gave him the opportunity to come into personal contact with some of the circles which defined the musical life of those cities (in Rome, the circle around Cardinal Montalto), to hear some celebrated virtuosos working there (Ippolita Recupito Marotta, Francesca Caccini) and to compare their abilities with those of Adriana Basile, the famous singer newly arrived in Mantua in June 1610:[184]

> Before I left Rome I heard Signora Ippolita sing quite well; at Florence I heard the daughter of Signor Giulio Romano [Francesca Caccini] sing quite well and play on the theorbo-lute and harpsichord, but at Mantua I heard Signora Adriana sing, play and speak extremely well. Even when she is silent and tunes up, she has qualities to be admired and worthily praised.

In the same letter (L.10, from Mantua, 28 December 1610), most likely addressed to Cardinal Ferdinando Gonzaga and therefore obviously biased in favour of the recent recruit to the Mantuan court, Monteverdi also recalls the musical gatherings that were held under his direction on 'Friday evening[s] in the Hall of Mirrors'. More extended mention of them is made in another letter to Ferdinando of 22 June (?January) 1611 (L.12), which exalts the 'dramatic' virtues of Adriana Basile's performances:

> Every Friday evening music is performed in the Hall of Mirrors. Signora Andriana comes to sing in concert, and lends the music such power and so special a grace, bringing such delight to the senses that the place becomes almost like a new theatre. And I think that the carnival of concerts will not end without the Most Serene Lord Duke having to post guards at the entrance, for I swear to Your Most Illustrious Lordship that in the audience this last Friday there were not only the Most Serene Lord Duke and Most Serene Lady Duchess, the Lady Isabella of San Martino, the Lord Marquis and Lady Marchioness of Solferino, ladies and knights from the entire court, but also more than a hundred other gentlemen from the city too.
>
> On a similar splendid occasion I shall have the theorbos played by the musicians from Casale [Giovan Battista and Orazio Rubini, violinists], to the accompaniment of the wooden organ (which is extremely suave), and in this way Signor Andriana and Don Giovanni Battista [Sacchi] will sing the extremely beautiful madrigal 'Ahi, che morire mi sento' and the other madrigal to the organ alone. Tomorrow I shall take the aforesaid compositions and present them to Signora Andriana, and I know how precious they will be to her, yet I do not want to tell her the composer's name until she has sung them. I shall then send a report to Your Most Illustrious Lordship of the entire outcome.

The mysterious composer of the two madrigals was clearly the very same Cardinal Ferdinando Gonzaga, whose activity as an amateur poet and musician has already been mentioned, including theatrical productions in Pisa for the Medici court (1606–7) and perhaps the *balletto* 'De la bellezza le dovute lodi' given to Monteverdi to be set to music and then included by him in the *Scherzi musicali*. The 'cantata with accompaniment for two chitarrones' which Monteverdi requested in the last few days of 1610 must have been another composition by Cardinal Ferdinando: Monteverdi wanted it 'so that I can let His Most Serene Highness hear it one Friday evening in the Hall of Mirrors' for the forthcoming carnival celebrations of 1611 (L.10). It should be noted that this letter from Monteverdi provides the first evidence – to the best of our knowledge – of the use of the term 'cantata', which was to reappear in his letters some years later (for example, the 'cantata in praise of His Serenity' the doge of Venice mentioned in L.29 dated 21 April 1618) and which in the course of the century was destined to achieve widespread ascendancy.

The arrival of Adriana Basile at Mantua also allows us to narrow down significantly the date of a 'sacro madrigale' ('sacred madrigal') written by Monteverdi to a text by the Benedictine friar Angelo Grillo. In congratulating Monteverdi, Grillo says that he imagines it superbly performed by some prominent virtuoso at that moment in service among the court musicians (are we therefore dealing with a piece for solo voice?), such as the famous Adriana, or else Francesco Campagnolo, who was also at the Gonzaga court in summer 1610 after a long stay in England.[185] Given that Grillo addresses his letter (published without a date) 'Al sig. Claudio Monteverde. Mantova', it must be dated sometime between June 1610 and July 1612, when the composer was dismissed.

> To Signor Claudio Monteverde. Mantua.
>
> Argument: in favour of the music written on a madrigal by him.
>
> And how well the divine subject of my sacred madrigal corresponds to Your Lordship's divine music, and how it is made entirely heavenly by your heavenly harmony. And what a *concerto*. If only I had the words to praise it as it merits as I have the ears to know it as it should be known, especially when sung by Signor Campagnolo or his equal. For the composition is for none other than a sublime singer and an angelic voice, as precisely is that of Signora Adriana, who, marrying the voice with the instrument, and with gesture giving soul and speech to the strings, brings forth the sweet tyranny of our souls, while leaving them in our bodies on earth, takes them with the hearing to heaven. And this my purple rose of the bleeding eyes of the dead Christ, in its sweetest accents, as if among tenderly pricking dear thorns, will call forth (so I well believe) lively tears of tenderness from the ears of the listeners, and from their mouths a thousand blessings of Your Lordship, who while you compose do not write notes for the words and the affections, but form sceptres demonstrating the power that they have through your virtue over hearts and minds, not to say arrows which wound with joy and wonder. But these praises are perhaps too poetic, and yet they are not unsuited to you, who lives among the muses, and who not poetically but truly deserves them. And may God our Lord, the creator of your merit and reward, grant Your Lordship every happiest and desired recompense.
>
> From Venice.[186]

As well as praising the affective power of Monteverdi's style, Grillo hints at the poetic content of this mysterious 'sacred madrigal'. Among the poems printed in his *Pietosi affetti* (Venice, Bernardo Giunti & Giovan Battista Ciotti, 1608) appear a pair of madrigals either one of which, on the basis of the references here, could plausibly be the one described by the poet: No. LXIII on p. 38 (headed 'Rosa a Cristo sanguinolente'; 'Rose to the bleeding Christ') and No. CCXVII on p. 194 ('Maria all'istesso'; 'Mary to the same [the crucifix]').

O vermiglietta rosa,
al purpureo colore
tu mi somigli il sanguinoso amore,
ed a la spina che ti cinge intorno,
l'error mio che lo punge e gli fa scorno.
O bel fior de' fior nostri,
che la sua pena e la mia colpa mostri.

O crimson rose / with your deep-red colour / you represent to me the
bleeding love, / and with the thorn that surrounds you, / my error which
stabs and scorns it. / O beautiful flower of our flowers, / who shows his
suffering and my fault.

O purpurea mia rosa,
che su la spina di quest'empia croce
languisci a morte atroce;
al tronco tuo ben io
spargo per ravvivarti un largo rio.
Ma il mio doglioso umore
mi torni in sangue e mi trapassi il core.

O my crimson rose, / who on the thorn of this wicked cross / languishes in
terrible death; / on your stem I do indeed / spread a wide river [of tears] to
revive you. / But my grieving mood / comes back to me in blood, and
overwhelms my heart.

But whatever the case, neither of these two madrigals figures among the texts
of Monteverdi's surviving works.

From the letters of these years, we also learn that Monteverdi's eldest child,
Francesco – a novice in an unknown seminary – was also showing distinct
promise as a singer: 'until now it seems to me that he manages both *trillo* and
ornaments quite well' (L.12, 22 June (?January) 1611). As for his own
compositional activity, the letter to Prince Francesco Gonzaga of 26 March
(L.11) cites various sacred and secular works coming from that year:

> At this point in my letter I am also praying that Our Lord grant you a happy
> Easter, and I beseech you to be so kind as to accept the *Dixit* for eight
> voices[187] which Your Most Serene Highness ordered me to send, together
> with which I am also sending you a little motet for two voices to be sung at
> the Elevation of Our Lord, and another for five voices for the Blessed
> Virgin. Once Holy Week is over I shall send a couple of madrigals, and
> anything else that I understand may be to Your Most Serene Highness's taste.
>
> You will do me a special kindness by letting my brother see these
> compositions a little before Your Most Serene Highness may condescend to
> hear them, so that my brother, the singers, and the players can – as a group –
> get acquainted with the melody of the said songs, for Your Most Serene
> Highness will then be less offended by this feeble music of mine.

Unfortunately, it is hard to identify these pieces. The list of Monteverdi's
works includes four settings of 'Dixit Dominus' for eight voices, two each in
the *Selva morale e spirituale* and the 1650 *Messa ... et salmi*. As for the other
items, at least two perhaps match up with known works by Monteverdi: for

example, the 'little motet for two voices to be sung at the Elevation [? = Ascension] of Our Lord' could be the 'Et resurrexit' later printed in the *Selva morale e spirituale*,[188] while 'another [little motet] for five voices for the Blessed Virgin' could be 'Exultent coeli' published by Lorenzo Calvi in 1629 (in the *Quarta raccolta de sacri canti*). But 'Exultent coeli' was clearly destined for the Feast of the Immaculate Conception (8 December): if in Monteverdi's letter 'of the Blessed Virgin' is to be understood instead as following on from 'Elevation' (i.e., the Assumption of the Blessed Virgin), then the case for even such a tentative identification collapses. For the rest, it is totally impossible to identify the 'couple of madrigals'. But whatever the case, this 'Dixit Dominus' and the two small motets, together with the 1610 collection, remain the only traces of Monteverdi's activity in sacred music in Mantua, which must have been significantly lower in terms of quantity than his secular compositions, given the existence of a ducal church with its own *maestri di cappella*. And it is probably among this 'Dixit Dominus' and the five psalms of the 1610 'Vespers' that one should look for the compositions by Monteverdi performed in Modena in the cathedral at Christmas 1611, evidently, if we are to believe a local chronicler, to the significant disappointment and even distaste of those present: 'Geminiano Capilupi also called "Lovetto", *maestro di cappella*, had sung certain psalms by Monteverdo, *maestro di cappella* of the Duke of Mantua, which were to everyone's disgust.'[189]

Finally, this period also saw new Venetian editions (still issued by Ricciardo Amadino) of Monteverdi's most frequently reprinted books of madrigals: the Third (1611), Fourth (1611) and Fifth (1610 and 1611). And as witness to his wide fame, Monteverdi was ever more frequently honoured with public recognition by his colleagues and also by *letterati*, proving how his name was circulating well beyond specialist circles. Already Tommaso Stigliani, a Neapolitan but present in Parma from 1603 to 1621, had dedicated 'to Signor Claudio Monte Verde' the madrigal 'O sirene de' fiumi, adorni cigni' included in his *Rime* printed in Venice by Giovan Battista Ciotti in 1605.[190] In 1611, the composer was included by Giovanni Soranzo in his survey of the most illustrious artists of Lombardy in an *ottava rima* stanza of his poem *Lo Armidoro* (Milan, Giovan Giacomo Como, 1611, XLII.36): 'Odo 'l Lambrugo, il Monteverde io sento: / ambi nel canto han d'angiolo talento' ('I hear [Giovanni Battista] Lambrugo, I listen to Monteverdi: / in song both have an angelic talent').[191] And in the same year, as we have seen (see note 114), the organist of the ducal church of S. Barbara, Ottavio Bargnani, published in his *Secondo libro delle canzoni da suonare* the first of the series of instrumental pieces titled to Monteverdi in this decade by musicians from Lombardy such as Melii, Merula, Lappi and Marini, a series later completed by Buonamente (1637).

On 18 February 1612, Duke Vincenzo died in Mantua (Duchess Eleonora had herself died shortly before, on 8 December 1611). He was succeeded by his son, Prince Francesco, who thus became the fifth duke of Mantua and the third of Monferrato. As the Venetian ambassador Pietro Gritti informed the senate:

> In these states, Duke Francesco has now succeeded to the throne. He is very young in age, not having yet completed twenty-six years. He is a prince abundantly endowed with the gifts of nature, having a most well proportioned body and such beauty and grace both in his face and in his eyes and in all the rest that grant him no less affection than a certain respect and esteem from everyone at first sight. He gives indications that he will turn out to be just and tempered in his pleasures, grave and tenacious in nature, measured in spending, and circumspect in his every deed. In government, he displays a grand manner and so great diligence, meeting with all his Counsellors of State and listening readily to each one, such that his subjects marvel greatly, being used to his father, who left all the weight of affairs of state to his wife and bothered himself with nothing. He deals with his subjects in a reserved and serious manner; nor does he let himself reveal anger or affection towards one more than another of his servants and ministers. His first actions, when he entered into the state, were to restrain under stricter conditions and subject to harsher laws the Jews, who are many and rich in Mantua and who in the time of Duke Vincenzo enjoyed all freedom. He also lifted monopolies and such things designed to provoke poverty made by men who, paying a fixed price to the Treasury, placed an excessive burden on that commerce, through which they alone were able to sell, and now things are sold freely by all to the common good. However, it seems that in general his subjects remain more satisfied with the rule of Duke Vincenzo, even if some of his actions instead merited blame and caused harm to those same subjects. And it is believed that this is caused in some by the fact that they reaped rewards from his disorder and were supported by his copious expenses; in others because in the course of time they became accustomed to love and hold dear the same defects of their ruler; and in many because the liberal, affable and pleasant nature of the former duke was more in conformance with and accommodated to the natural manners of these people than seems to be the serious and reserved manner held by the present duke.[192]

A little earlier in his report, Gritti also noted the first provisions made by the new duke to strip the court of the many parasites who lived there:

> The expenses used to be great in the times of the former duke, since he spent much in maintaining a large court, which amounted to 800 people, a great deal on his tastes and private pleasures, and much on his travel, which very often he made more out of delight than for necessity. Now [these expenses] have been greatly reduced, for all the alchemists have been dismissed, and many superfluous salaries paid to important ladies of the city and to men who had no other duty than to serve the tastes of the duke have been lifted.[193]

Francesco Gonzaga had been the dedicatee of the *Scherzi musicali*, collected by Giulio Cesare Monteverdi, and of *Orfeo*, which had been born under his patronage. Proof of his good will towards Monteverdi is offered by a letter of recommendation dated 16 March 1612 to Monsignor Ricordati in Rome seeking to obtain for the composer's son that place at the Roman Seminary which Monteverdi had already solicited some two years earlier.

You will see from the enclosed memorandum what Monteverdi has requested from us, and since for the honourable service which he does us and for the merit of his presence we wish him every convenience, we desire that with this letter of recommendation, written with true affection, which is sent to you with the present one you should carry out the task as appropriate with the Lord Cardinal of S. Cecilia, procuring the successful outcome of the favour requested.[194]

But a few months later, both Claudio and Giulio Cesare Monteverdi were dismissed from the Gonzaga court for reasons which still remain unclear. This must have occurred towards the end of July 1612, given that on the 31st of that month Monsignor Vincenzo Agnelli Suardi wrote: ' . . . since His Highness has dismissed Monteverdi . . . '.[195] In his capacity as *maestro di cappella* the composer was temporarily replaced by Sante Orlandi, presently in private service to Cardinal Ferdinando in the same position. Orlandi himself, on 3 August, informed the cardinal of what had happened: 'On Monday, after dinner, His Highness summoned the entire musical academy, where there were, as well as His Highness, princes and very many knights, and after having sung and played a great deal, the lord duke allocated many positions, above all of which he made me the head, giving me the title of his *maestro di cappella*, since he had the day before dismissed Signor Claudio and his brother.'[196]

Leaving Mantua, where he had been in service for more than twenty years, Monteverdi returned to Cremona: in November 1615, by now in Venice, he was to lament having 'left that most serene court in so sorry a plight – by God! – as to take away no more than 25 scudi' (L.17). Meanwhile, the news having spread, other musicians set to offering themselves as candidates for the vacant position, including the Sicilian Pietro Maria Marsolo, *maestro di cappella* of Ferrara Cathedral, who on 2 September 1612 wrote to the duke: 'It has been heard as most certain that Signor Monteverde has absented himself from Your Most Serene Highness's service; if this is true, I offer myself to you for such service.'[197]

In Mantua, there was no lack of malicious gossip about the former *maestro*. Taking a cue from Monteverdi's trip to Milan (perhaps to see in person what possibilities the city offered for employment), the rumour spread that the composer was aspiring to the post of *maestro di cappella* of the cathedral there and that he had badly failed the audition. Through the singer Francesco Campagnolo, on 26 September 1612, the duke sought information on the matter in Milan from Alessandro Striggio, who was there as ducal ambassador.

His Most Serene Highness our lord, having heard that in recent days Signor Claudio Monteverde has been in Milan seeking the post of master of the music at the cathedral there, and that while carrying out that task one morning produced such disorder in the music that he was not sufficiently able to put it back in order, whenceforth to his scant honour he was obliged to return to Cremona, has commanded me, having received this story from an insecure source and perhaps from people not wishing well for the same Monteverde, that I should write to Your Most Illustrious Lordship . . .[198]

The story was scarcely true. Above all, this position was not vacant, given that it had been held for less than a year by Vincenzo Pellegrini. But not even the rest had any foundation, as Striggio had the opportunity to confirm on 10 October 1612: 'So far from the truth is it that Monteverdi left this city with little honour, that indeed he was honoured in the extreme by knights, and as well regarded and cherished as possible, and his works are sung here with great praise in the most distinguished salons. Nor is it true that it has fallen on him to perform the duties of *maestro di cappella* of the cathedral here, which position Monteverdi has not wanted to seek so as not to do wrong to him who is in it, the post not being vacant.'[199]

Towards the end of 1612, an epidemic of smallpox which had broken out in Mantua caused the death first of Federico Gonzaga (the Crown-prince, not yet two years of age) and then Duke Francesco himself (on 22 December). As a result, Cardinal Ferdinando returned to join his sister-in-law Margherita of Savoy in a regency; he was to be crowned duke with full powers a few months later, when Monferrato was invaded by the troops of Carlo Emanuele I of Savoy. As for Monteverdi, the prospect of a new permanent position appeared in the summer of 1613. In Venice, Giulio Cesare Martinengo, *maestro di cappella* in St Mark's, had died, and a replacement was being sought even outside the city and the territorial confines of the republic. Monteverdi's name was put forward, and the *Procuratori de supra*, who superintended the ducal basilica, gave the order to the Venetian resident in Milan (given that then the composer was in Cremona, in Milanese territory) to gather information about him:

> Since the reverend *maestro di cappella* of our Church of St Mark has died, several individuals have been proposed, among whom is Signor Claudio Monteverde, *maestro di cappella* of His Highness. Therefore may it content you to collect information about his worth and competence and to report on it, and if some other individual should come to mind, we would receive it as a favour to be particularly advised of their condition . . .
>
> Antonio Landi   16 July 1613
>
> [in the margin] Written to Rome, Padua, Vicenza, Brescia, Bergamo, Milan and Mantua to the residents.[200]

Monteverdi was summoned and interviewed in Venice, where he was subjected to a practical audition: in St Mark's on 1 August 1613 a Mass by him was sung, which he was able to rehearse in S. Giorgio in the preceding days, as is witnessed by payments to the porters 'who took and brought back two organs to S. Zorgi [Giorgio] for preparing the audition of Signor Claudio Monteverde, *maestro di cappella*', and (on 10 September) to the '20 ordinary instrumentalists for having played at S. Zorzi to prepare the audition of the Mass by our *maestro di cappella*, and on the day of the said audition in the church of St Mark'.[201] Judging the performance favourably, on 19 August the procurators unanimously approved the appointment of Monteverdi as the new *maestro di cappella* of St Mark's:

19 August in the Sacristy of St Mark's

The Most Illustrious Lords Federico Con[tari]ni, Nicolò Sagredo, Zuan [Giovanni] Corner and Ant[oni]o Lando, Procurators, have determined by ballots as follows:

The Most Illustrious Lord Procurators wishing to arrive at the appointment of a *maestro di cappella* of the Church of St Mark in place of the deceased reverend *maestro* Giulio Cesare Martinengo, and it having been written on the order of Their Most Illustrious Lordships to the Most Illustrious Lord Ambassador in Rome, to all the most illustrious rectors of the [Venetian] mainland and to the residents of the Most Serene Signory in Milan and Mantua to have information of individuals qualified in this profession for the said service, having understood from the replies that the person of Lord Claudio Monteverde, formerly *maestro di cappella* of the Lord Duke Vincenzo and Duke Francesco of Mantua, is commended as a most outstanding individual, Their Most Illustrious Lordships are further confirmed in this opinion of his quality and virtue both by his works which are found in print and by those which today Their Most Illustrious Lordships have sought to hear to their complete satisfaction in the Church of St Mark with its musicians. Therefore they have balloted and voted in unanimous agreement that the aforesaid Lord Claudio Monteverde should be appointed *maestro di cappella* of the Church of St Mark with a salary of 300 ducats per year, and with the usual and accustomed perquisites, with a house in the chancellery according to custom which should be provided as soon as posssible with the fittings which are necessary, and moreover he should be given 50 ducats as a gift, both for the expenses of his journey as for the time which he has stayed in this city on the order of Their Most Illustrious Lordships, which appointment is willingly made according to custom with the voting Yes – 4 and No – 0.[202]

Monteverdi began service in his new post only around 10 October 1613. He had reached Venice at the beginning of the month after a few day's journey completed together with his son Francesco (called 'prettino'; 'seminarian') and his maid from Mantua to Este on the post-carriage and from Este to Venice by boat via Padua and Fusina. In the first part of the journey, near Sanguinetto, the carriage was attacked by three highway robbers who stole from the composer 'more than a hundred Venetian ducats in goods and money', as Monteverdi himself recounted perhaps to Alessandro Striggio or to Annibale Iberti (L.13, Venice, 12 October 1613):

I am writing to let Your Most Illustrious Lordship know how, being in the company of the Mantuan courier and leaving with him for Venice, we were robbed at Sanguinetto (not in the actual place, but rather two miles away from it) by three ruffians – bandits – in this manner. Suddenly from a field adjoining the main road there came two men of a brownish complexion, not much beard, and of medium height, with a long musket apiece (the flint-wheel type) and its firing-pin down. Then, one of these approaching on my side to frighten me with the musket, and the other holding on to the bridle of the horses – which went along quietly – they drew us aside into that field without saying a word.

And making me kneel down as soon as I had alighted, one of the two who had the muskets demanded my purse, and the other demanded the cases from the courier. They were pulled down from the carriage by the courier, who opened them for him one by one, that assassin taking what he liked, and having everything given to him promptly by the courier. I was still on my knees all the while, guarded by the other one who had a gun, and in this manner they took whatever they wanted, as the third of the three assassins, who had a spike in his hand and had acted as lookout, was continuing to do this, making sure that nobody should enter from the road.

When they had well and truly turned over all the goods, the one who was looking into the things obtained from the courier came up to me and told me to undress myself because he wanted to see whether I had any other money. On being assured that I did not, he went over to my maidservant for the same purpose, but she – helping her cause with all manner of prayers, entreaties, and lamentations – made him leave her alone. Then, turning to the things and the cases, he made a bundle of the best and finest, and while looking for something to cover himself with he found my cloak – a long one of serge, brand new – which I had just had made for me in Cremona.

He said to the courier, 'Put this cloak on me'; but when the assassin saw that it was too long for him, he said: 'Give me another one.' So he took my son's, but finding it too short, the courier then said, 'Look, master, it belongs to that poor seminarian – give it to him'; and he complied. The courier also found the said boy's suit and did the same, and then when he asked with many entreaties for the maidservant's things as a gift, the ruffian handed them over to him. They made a huge bundle of the remainder, took it on their shoulders, and carried it away. Then we picked up the things that were left and went off to the inn.

On the following morning we filed a charge at Sanguinetto, then we left (I being much upset) and reached Este. We took a boat for Padua, which held us up all Thursday night and nearly the whole of Friday in silt, nobody worrying about the fact that we finally got away at the twentieth hour, in heavy wind and rain, on an uncovered barge, and with none other rowing in the stern but our courier, who made a really hard job of it. We arrived at Padua, but it was as much as we could do to get in by one hour of night.

After rising early on Saturday morning to leave for Venice, we waited more than two hours after sunrise to get under way, and during the time we were in Padua, the courier put his arm in a sling saying that this happened because of that business about the cloaks, when he was robbed. I, knowing that nothing of the coachman's was touched or even looked at, was beside myself to say the least. This act of the courier aroused suspicion among all who were with us, because they had previously seen him without any injury at all.

And there was someone in the Padua boat who said to the courier, 'What kind of tale is this, brother?', and being about to add further words (I would say, perhaps, as a jest) the courier dropped out of the conversation. So we reached Venice at the twenty-fourth hour on Saturday, while he was joking and laughing . . .

III

Venice

22 Venice

In the early seventeenth century, Venice was no longer what it had been in the past, an expanding power and a dynamic player in the Italian and European political scene. Now almost every sphere of its activities was marked by that retrenchment which would characterize the decades to come in an attempt to limit the damage of changing international circumstances. The progressive relocation of the trade routes to the orient and the opening up of new sea routes, the increasingly aggressive competition from other European merchant navies (particularly the English and Dutch) and also qualitative changes in commerce began to weigh heavily on the Venetian economy, which in the first years of the seventeenth century entered a phase of recession – after the great boom of the last decades of the preceding century – rendered all the worse by the more general stagnation which affected Europe and also the Ottoman Empire around 1620. Moreover, in terms of politics, the strengthening of the absolute monarchies and the activities of the papacy – with the Spanish and Austrian Habsburgs in support – posed ever more pressing threats to the very existence of the Most Serene Republic, above and beyond the traditional menace of the Turks.

Venice proudly resisted even the Pope (Paul V) from 1605 to 1609 in the course of a jurisdictional dispute during which Rome went so far as to resort to the weapon of interdiction. As for the Spanish, their presence was particularly worrying for the Republic: they bounded Venice on the west by Milan, and on the north and partly on the east, by the Tyrol and the Archduchy of Austria – moreover the Kingdom of Naples, which extended through Puglia, was in a position to control the lower reaches of the Adriatic. Venetian foreign policy, taking realistic account of the European royal powers, relied on adopting a neutral line, but without hiding understandable sympathies for the French. Nevertheless, this did not prevent the opening up of more or less direct anti-Spanish hostilities when the need arose. Thus, in 1615 the two-year-old war against the Uscocchi (Adriatic pirates from the Balkans, with bases on the Dalmatian coast) shifted onto the mainland along the Isonzo, against the troops of Habsburg Archduke Ferdinand, their protector. Peace was reached in 1617, but in that same year Venice had to face on the Adriatic the warmongering of the fleet of the Duke of Osuna, Viceroy of Naples, which in 1618 was forced to beat a retreat, while in Venice (in May 1618) the palace of the Spanish ambassador, the Marquis of Bedmar, was attacked (he was suspected of being the instigator of a conspiracy against the Republic).

But in the following decade, these successes were to be reversed, revealing full well the decline and the progressive marginalization of Venetian power: on 6 March 1626 the Treaty of Monson, bringing an end to the war in Valtellina, was signed by France and Spain without Venice's knowledge (even though she was France's ally), while the help offered by Venice during the siege of Mantua (1629–30) was of little use, given that the army sent there was quickly routed – thus the peace negotiations once again saw Venice subordinated to the wishes of her French allies.

It is perhaps no coincidence that the world of culture and of art also displays signs of retrenchment and self-glorification. Compared with the great heights of the sixteenth century, painting in the new century shows signs of generational decline as regards painters trained locally (Jacopo Palma il Giovane, Sante Peranda, Francesco Maffei, Pietro Vecchia, Pietro Liberi): significantly, the most interesting developments were fostered by foreigners such as Domenico Fetti, Jan Liss, Carlo Saraceni and Bernardo Strozzi, who all lived for a greater or lesser time in Venice.

However, the remarkable experience of Paolo Sarpi as a jurist and historian – primarily in the fight against the papacy in the period of the interdict – was to mark a peak of high intellectual and moral tension in a cultural context that although not particularly incisive in terms of its originality was nevertheless varied and lively enough. Proof of this is offered by the many academies which flourished in Venice, each dedicated to the usual literary exercises both in Italian – with a polemical adherence to the new Marinist poetic – and in dialect (the Cacciatori, the Filoponi, the Immaturi, the Laboriosi, the Peripatetici, the Provveduti, the Sollevati), to eloquence and philosophy (the Discordanti), and to the devising of *imprese* (the Assicurati), but also focusing on more technical and even more practical matters, such as politics (the Fileleuteri, the Informi) and nautical sciences (the Marittimi). Nor should we forget the meetings founded around 1630 by Gian Francesco Loredano, such as the Difesi, the Inoltrati, and first and foremost the Incogniti, with its decidedly 'libertine' intellectual stance.

The social circumstances of the city of Venice, so typically polycentric, were not to be without influence on Monteverdi's career. In fact, the composer, in addition to his duties as an employee of the Republic's administration, was able to take significant advantage of free-lance work thanks to the patronage of private bodies – as well as foreign courts – such as religious orders, civic institutions (the Scuole – i.e. confraternities – and foreign communities in Venice), academies and noble families. But Monteverdi also entertained working-relations with the entrepreneurial circles of music-publishing and – later – of the public opera houses, the new theatrical genre on which were concentrated the interests of the prosperous business of carnival entertainment. To this was joined a tendency in favour of investment in real-estate that was characteristic of this phase of the Venetian economy and apparent since the preceding century in the purchasing of farm-holdings on the mainland and in the building as much of 'pleasure' villas on country estates as of palaces in the city (for the seventeenth century, take the example of the buildings planned by Baldassare Longhena, who was given the public commission of the votive church for the end of the plague, S. Maria della Salute).

As *maestro di cappella* of St Mark's, Monteverdi occupied the position which in the preceding century had been held by Adriano Willaert and then by his pupils Cipriano de Rore and Gioseffo Zarlino. Between the sixteenth and seventeenth centuries, with *maestri* such as Baldassare Donati, Giovanni Croce and finally Giulio Cesare Martinengo, the effectiveness of the *cappella* had diminished considerably, owing to the poor discipline and scant control of those in authority.[1] When Monteverdi assumed his new duties, the *cappella* was made up of some 30 singers and six instrumentalists:[2] the vice-*maestro* was Marcantonio Negri (from 22 December 1612), while the two organists – in positions formerly held by Gerolamo Parabosco, Annibale Padovano, Claudio Merulo, Giuseppe Guami and the Gabrielis – were Giovan Paolo Savi (first organist from 26 July 1610) and Paolo Giusti (second organist from 15 September 1591).[3] For particular celebrations, the *cappella* was augmented to a significant degree, and above all in terms of instrumentalists, as is documented by the following decision taken by the procurators on 7 December 1614 at the request of those involved:[4]

> It having been requested to Their Most Illustrious and Most Excellent Lordships by the instrumentalists who serve extraordinarily in the Church of St Mark, who, although they are paid from time to time at a rate of one half scudo per service, entreat that for their greater honour they should be included in the roll of paid musicians of the Church of St Mark with that salary which seems more appropriate and pleases Their Most Excellent Lordships, and the information having been taken that these at present number sixteen non-salaried musicians, and that throughout the year general music in which the aforesaid instrumentalists take part is made on twenty-six occasions, including Ascension Day if, because of bad weather, His Serenity [the Doge] stays in the Church of St Mark for Mass, which amounts to the cost of 91 lire per person per year, which cost should not be withdrawn but rather should be increased as necessary for the honour and splendour of the Church of St Mark, they have determined by ballots that the persons listed below should be taken onto the rolls as salaried instrumentalists with the consideration of 15 ducats per year per person, with the duty of serving in person at all the services and musical performances which are usually done, and also at rehearsals and at all those other performances that might occur extraordinarily, having always to hold themselves ready for the entrance of the Most Serene Signory [into the church] so as to be able to serve in the organ lofts and in any other place that they shall be ordered by the *maestro di cappella* and by the *capo de concerti* on all those instruments which they know how to play, with the condition that he or they who might be lacking in

their duty should be marked by the Marker Ordinary elected by Their Most
Excellent Lordships one mark per service, and should they miss any of the
more solemn days, such as the evening before or day of Christmas, the days
of Easter, the vigil or day of St Mark and the vigil of Ascension, they should
be given two marks per service, which marks cannot be remitted or excused
except with all the votes of Their Most Excellent Lordships, and thus so that
they should have cause to do their duty, and not to default because they are
salaried, which election is made at the will of Their Most Excellent
Lordships. The musicians are the following:

Pasqualin Savioni	Zuane Chilese
Ant[oni]o Padovan	Piero Loschi
Franc[esc]o [player] of the violin	Alvise Grani
called Bonfante	Francesco Venier
Ant[oni]o Chilese	Zuane de Giac[om]o
Zaneto Sanson	Ger[ola]mo Coltrer
Bastian Menegazo	Zuane de Ventura [player] of the
Tonio Menegazo	violon contrabasso
Batt[ist]a Fabri	Ant[oni]o Leoni [player] of the
	violin

Giovanni Rovetta also speaks of such (sometimes flamboyant) uses of
instruments with the vocal *cappella*: in the preface to his 'Kind Readers' in his
Salmi concertati a cinque et sei voci et altri con doi violini, con motetti a doi e tre voci
printed in Venice by Bartolomeo Magni in 1626 (and composed seeking 'to
follow the steps of a newly living Apollo, on whose Green Mountain [*Verde
Monte*] the Muses themselves seek shelter to learn the tones of exquisite
concerti', says the dedication), Rovetta claims that 'there are in this most serene
service [in St Mark's] not only thirty and more singers, but also twenty and
more wind and string players'.[5] Similarly, Bellerofonte Castaldi, in a *capitolo*
written in Naples in May 1638 and dedicated to Monteverdi, said of Venice:

> Spero nulla di meno che concesso
> mi fia dal ciel di ritornarci presto,
> e venire a godervi piú da presso,
>   sol per quei concertoni in die festo
> tanto ordinati e con tant'armonia,
> che fan che l'uom tal or esca di sesto.[6]

I hope nonetheless that it will be granted / to me by heaven that I might soon
return there / and come to enjoy you in closer quarters, / if only for those
great *concerti* on festal days, / so ordered and with such harmony / that they
make any man sometimes transported.

Monteverdi's chief task in St Mark's was to train and maintain the efficiency of the *cappella*. He was also concerned with recruiting new members:[7]

The Most Illustrious and Most Excellent Lord Procurators Barbon
Mor[osi]ni, Zuane Corner and Ant[oni]o Barbuo wishing to appoint two
tenor singers, and having auditioned this day six voices, which have been
heard in the Church of St Mark, and having received a written report sworn
by the *maestro di cappella* and by other singers of that chapel, their Most

Illustrious Lordships having given mature consideration they have determined by ballots to appoint Don Vincenzo Mantoano and Z[uane] p[ie]ro
[?] with the salary of sixty ducats per year per person as it pleases Their Most
Illustrious Lordships. [Votes:] 3–0

The Most Illustrious and Most Excellent Lord Procurators named above
having received a report from the said Claudio Monteverde, *maestro di
cappella*, have ballotted to take in as singer in the Church of St Mark Don
Ant[oni]o Vicentini, Mantuan, with the salary of fifty ducats per year as it
pleases Their Most Illustrious Lordships and their successors. [Votes:] 3–0

Their Most Illustrious and Most Excellent Lordships having received notice
from the *maestro di cappella* and from the aforesaid Don Gio[vanni] Paulo
Savii that M[esser] Gio[vanni] Batt[ist]a Grilo, organist, is a leading figure in
this profession, as is known to the city, therefore they have determined by
ballots that the aforesaid M[esser] Zuan Batt[ist]a Grilo should be appointed
organist in St Mark's in place of the aforesaid Don Gio[vanni] Paulo Savii
with the salary of 120 ducats per year as it pleases Their Most Illustrious and
Most Excellent Lordships. [Votes:] 3–0

On other occasions, we find Monteverdi occupied with running the com-
petitions for the post of second organist, such as led to the appointment of
Giovan Piero Berti in 1624, and Francesco Cavalli in 1639, both of whom
were formerly in St Mark's as singers (the other organist was, from May 1623,
Carlo Fillago):[8]

The Most Illustrious Lord Procurators having met in the Church of St Mark
to hear the audition for organists on the small organ in place of the deceased
Paulo de Savii, they had presented to themselves by the lord *maestro di cappella*
a few extracts [*sonate*] of plainchant drawn from a book which had been sent
for from the sacristy, and having made the lots of the candidates and having
drawn them by chance, each played in the following order:

M[e]s[ser] Z[uane] Piero Berti
M[e]s[ser] Fr. Francesco Usper
M[e]s[ser] Z[uane] Battista Loccadello
M[e]s[ser] Zuane Picchi.

And all four having been heard, Their Most Illustrious Lordships withdrew
to the sacristy and held a secret ballot, and there was elected by all three votes
in favour the aforesaid
M[e]s[ser] Z[uane] Piero Berti
with the salary of 140 ducats per year. [Votes:] 3–0[9]

The Most Excellent Lord Procurators having met in the Church of St Mark
to hear the audition for organists on the small organ in place of the deceased
G[iovan] Piero Berti, they had presented to themselves by the lord *maestro di
cappella* a few extracts of plainchant drawn from a book which had been sent
for from the sacristy, and having made the lots of the candidates and having
drawn them by chance, each played in the following order:

Fr. Niccolò Fontei
Francesco Caletto called Cavalli
Fr. Nadal Monferato
Giacomo Arigoni.

And all four having been heard, Their Most Excellent Lordships withdrew
to the *loggietta* and held a secret ballot, and there was elected by all three votes
in favour the aforesaid M[e]s[ser] Francesco Caletto called Cavalli with the
salary of 140 ducats per year.[10]

The high opinion held of the *maestro di cappella* plus his good salary and its
associated privileges (including an apartment in the presbytery of St Mark's)
made Monteverdi fully appreciate his new position. All this, together with the
fact that he found himself dependent on a state institution that was not subject
to the fickle whims of a prince, made Venetian service very different from his
experiences at the Gonzaga court. The composer himself was anxious to
emphasize the point to Striggio in 1620 (L.48 [49], 13 March 1620), rejecting
an invitation to return to Mantua:

> I shall therefore submit for Your Most Illustrious Lordship's consideration
> the fact that this Most Serene Republic has never before given to any of my
> predecessors – whether it were Adriano or Cipriano, or Zarlino, or anyone
> else – but 200 ducats in salary, whereas to me they give 400; a favour that
> ought not to be so lightly set aside by me without some consideration, since
> (Most Illustrious Lord) this Most Serene Signory does not make an innova-
> tion without very careful thought.
>
> Wherefore – I repeat – this particular favour ought to command my
> utmost respect. Nor, having done this for me, have they ever regretted it: on
> the contrary they have honoured me, and honour me continually in such
> manner, that no singer is accepted into the choir until they ask the opinion of
> the *maestro di cappella*; nor do they want any report about the affairs of singers
> other than that of the *maestro di cappella*; nor do they take on organists or a
> vice-*maestro* unless they have the opinion and the report of that same *maestro
> di cappella*; nor is there any gentleman who does not esteem and honour me,
> and when I am about to perform either chamber or church music, I swear to
> Your Most Illustrious Lordship that the entire city comes running.
>
> Next, the duties are very light since the whole choir is subject to the
> register except the *maestro di cappella* – in fact, it is in his hands, having a
> singer's absence marked or not, and giving leave or not; and if he does not go
> into chapel nobody says anything. Moreover his allowance is assured until
> his death: neither the death of a procurator nor that of a doge interferes with
> it, and by always serving faithfully and with reverence he has greater
> expectations, not the opposite; and as regards his salary money, if he does not
> go at the appointed time to pick it up, it is brought round to his house.

Even later, in 1627, and again to Striggio (L.104 [106], 10 September 1627),
Monteverdi emphasized the stability of his present economic position, under-
lining how his work was made easier by the presence of another *maestro* with
similar vicarial duties (after Negri, Alessandro Grandi from 17 November
1620 and Giovanni Rovetta from 22 November 1627)[11] and by not having to
undertake any teaching:

> I am certainly not rich, but neither am I poor; moreover I lead a life with a
> certain security of income until my death, and furthermore I am absolutely
> sure of always having it on the appointed pay-days, which come every two
> months without fail. Indeed, if it is the least bit late, they send it to my house.

> Then as regards the *cappella* I do as I wish, since there is the sub-director, called vice-*maestro di cappella*; and there is no obligation to teach . . .

That Monteverdi applied himself assiduously – thanks also to his own professional authority – to bringing to peak efficiency the *cappella* of St Mark's is made clear by Matteo Caberloti, who (for all his tortuous prose) perhaps reveals how the composer also renewed the performance practices of the *cappella* as regards the new techniques offered by the *stile moderno*:

> Whenceforth, the Ducal [Church] of St Mark lacking at that time a *maestro di cappella*, judging this [post] a prize proportionate to his virtue when by those Most Knowledgeable Fathers he was appointed to this position having assayed every demanding test, he elected to apply himself to the service of the Most Serene Republic of Venice, in whose service he judged himself to be selecting his own centre of action. He drew not by lot but by his own merits the charge of this most celebrated choir of Italy; he was unanimously raised to this desired position, in which, not excusing fatigue, he opened with facility the way to the no longer used manner of singing, and distanced himself from the ancient rite, obliging himself, however, with the gentleness of his manners to secure the support of the worthy singers, who with goodwill devoted themselves to embracing the manners of singing no longer practised by them. And although he was foreign, and from a different homeland, nonetheless I do not know whether through the constancy of God in favouring him, or rather through that of the heavens and of the stars in giving him to the world so full of the true cognition of this excellent discipline, they [the singers] all conspired together in his favour always to love and revere him. Since they studied with all spirit to correspond to the command of his instructions, he, not ungrateful for such homage, sought to enrich them with a marvellous abundance of harmonic modes which because of the corruption of the art were formerly hidden. He served this Most Serene Dominion with happy spirit, being accustomed to say that to arrive at the true and entire perfection of the discipline of music heaven could not put him in a place where things were more harmonious, considering that this aristocratic government of this Most Serene Republic represents precisely that harmony which those schools of philosophy deem caused by the unceasing movement of those celestial rotations which – their intelligence has it – perpetually rotating with incomplete harmony encircle this inferior globe, the place of us mortals.[12]

To this end, in as early as 1614 Monteverdi had taken steps to procure printed and manuscript works largely by Flemish and Roman composers, that is, those who were most distinguished in the *a cappella* style.[13]

> The *maestro di cappella* of our Church of St Mark having noted that there are only a few books to sing mass in chapel for four, five and six voices in ferial days throughout the year, as is the custom for the sake of brevity, and that it would be good for the dignity of the Church to have others, so as to change and not always sing the same ones, hence considering that to have written in manuscript either his own compositions or others' would be very expensive, and that since volumes printed in Rome by various famous composers can be found, he would judge it better for now to procure six books of these masses for four, five, six and eight voices, all of this heard and considered by Their

Most Illustrious and Most Excellent Lordships, and they having had brought into their presence these printed books, and an agreement having been reached with Gardano, bookseller, they have concluded the purchase of the Second and Fifth Books of Masses by Palestrina *a4, 5* and *6*, of the First Book *a4* by Franc[esc]o Soriano, of the Masses *a6* and *8* by Orlando Lasso, of Ger[ola]mo Lambardi *a4*, and of the First Book of Paulo Paisoti *a4* and *5*, all bound in heavy, firm cardboard with a blue parchment cover as the sample given to him, with its blue ties, for 44 ducats, and so they have determined by ballots: in favour 2–0

Let there be paid 39 lire to the father of S. Salv[ado]r for having given a manuscript of music for the Church of St Mark in royal folio and bound, on the advice of the *maestro di cappella* and seen by Their Most Illustrious Lordships: 2–0

But side by side with the thus restored *a cappella* style also appeared the 'modern' style (for solo voices and continuo, and later other instruments), as is shown, for example, by the following entries:[14]

That Don Ger[ola]mo Marinoni be recruited as a tenor in the Church of St Mark, to whom should be given the salary of 80 ducats per year, given the good service rendered by him and which he still renders both in singing in the *cappella* and in the *concerti* to the organ, as much with his voice as with instruments, the present payment beginning in September–October and this as it pleases Their Most Illustrious Lordships: 3–0

That Flaminio Coradi be enlisted as a singer in the Church of St Mark with the salary of 80 ducats per year as it pleases Their Most Illustrious Lordships, and [that] he be obliged to serve both in the *cappella* and in the *concerti* to the organ with the theorbo, as he may be commanded by the *maestro di cappella*, he not being subject to any condition, but having carried out his duties in St Mark's he will be free to go and sing and serve where it will seem appropriate and will please him: 2–0

Don Girardo Biancosi, singer and musician, having requested some increase, given that at present he has only 60 ducats per year, which was the salary on his initial appointment, and given that he serves not only as a singer but also with the theorbo in the *concerti*, Their Most Illustrious Lordships, having heard and considered everything, have appointed anew the said Girardo with a salary of 80 ducats per year as it pleases Their Most Illustrious Lordships: 3–0

As well as appointing qualified personnel, establishing a broader repertory and seeking out useful colleagues, with the agreement of the procurators Monteverdi also worked towards establishing a greater degree of discipline for the singers, the lack of which would have impeded any attempt to revive the musical fortunes of the *cappella*. Indeed, the 'disciplines to be observed in the ducal *cappella*' established directly by Monteverdi 'were extensively maintained in exact observance by the procurators'.[15]

Their Most Illustrious Lordships, seeing that the singers of the Church and *cappella* of St Mark do not do their duty as is fitting, and that from the meagreness of the marks [for absence] which are given them conforming to the practice hitherto observed they do not lend the required service that they have held, have determined by ballots that in the days of the evening and morning of Christmas, Easter day, [the feast of] St Mark in the month of April – both the vigil at Vespers and the following morning at mass – [and] the vigil of the Ascension of Our Lord at Vespers, those who do not come to work at the required time should be fined [*apontati*] two *scudi* for each mark, and in the other days when the Most Serene Signory will come to church two ducats per mark. In the other feasts or days in which the Most Serene Signory does not come to church, and when the Pala d'oro is opened, and one sings in two choirs, and also in the days of processions, they should be fined one ducat per mark. On the other truly ferial days should be observed the marks given up to now, that is of one *soldo* per ducat of the salary paid to each singer, and moreover it is decided with the present resolution that every year at the beginning of the month of July, beginning in the present year, all the singers should be voted on again, so that those who are scandalous or who do not do their duty as according to their contract might be dismissed, in the understanding that those who do not gain a majority vote should be dismissed: 2–0

[in the margin] On the said day [14 April 1615] the said resolution was read to the singers summoned to the presence of Their Most Illustrious Lordships, absent only Fr. Gio[vanni] Batt[ist]a Catabeni and Don Ger[ola]mo.[16]

Similarly, since many of the singers salaried for the service of the *cappella* of St Mark's are permitted not to come and be present as according to their contract in that *cappella*, Their Most Illustrious Lordships resolving have resolved that the same marker should keep particular note of each one's failed appearances, with our treasurers having to withold from their wages for each missed feast day two *soldi* and for the other ordinary days 1 *soldo* 4 *denari* conforming to the note of their absence kept by the aforesaid marker, none of those singers being permitted to leave the city without the written permission of the most illustrious paymaster, a copy of the present decision being given to the *maestro di cappella* so as to have it read for the clear understanding of everyone: 3–0[17]

Monteverdi's letters also reveal the major feasts for which the *maestro di cappella* of St Mark's was officially required to provide his own music, above all Christmas Eve, which 'is the greatest [feast] that the *maestro di cappella* has in the entire year' (L.112 [113], 30 October 1627) and for which he had to write a new and highly demanding mass. On 2 February 1634 (L.123 [124]), Monteverdi in fact mentions a letter received 'before Christmas – at a time when I was entirely taken up with writing the Mass for Christmas Eve (a new mass being expected of the *maestro di cappella* according to a custom of this city)'; while on 29 December 1616 (L.22) he complained to Striggio of 'the hard work that had to be done on the Mass for Christmas Eve, for what with composing it and copying it out I had to give up the entire month of December almost without a break'. The letter then continues: 'Now that by the grace of God I am free of it, and everything went off respectably, I turn once again to Your Most Illustrious Lordship with this letter asking that you honour me by letting me know what His Most Serene Highness wishes me to do; because being unoccupied, and through with the labours of Christmas Eve and Christmas Day, I shall have nothing to do in St Mark's for some little time.'[18]

Similarly, on 28 January 1615 (L.14), the composer wrote (to Annibale Iberti?) 'at present there is nothing going on at St Mark's'. In fact, the next set of important liturgical commitments following Christmas were those of Holy Week (from Palm Sunday to Holy Saturday), 'at which time many functions take place in the presence of the Most Serene Signory, who comes to church in that week' (L.15, 11 February 1615); these commitments 'are by no means few – for the *maestro di cappella* – in times like this' (L.32, 7 March 1619), for 'throughout Holy Week I am at St Mark's, and the three feast-days likewise', i.e. Easter Sunday, the following Monday and the Octave of Easter (*Domenica in albis*; L.33, 22 March 1619).[19]

In spring there was the feast of St Mark (25 April): Monteverdi's letter of 1 May 1627 (L.91 [92]) speaks of 'the Vigil of St Mark, a day which kept me extremely busy looking after the music'. This feast, together with that of the Holy Cross (3 May), stood side by side with that of the Ascension, a great religious and also political ceremony given that on that day was celebrated the so-called 'wedding of the sea'. These last two feasts are mentioned by Monteverdi in a letter of 21 April 1618 (L.29):

> on Thursday week (which is Holy Cross Day) the Most Holy Blood will be displayed, and I shall have to be ready with a concerted Mass, and motets for the entire day, inasmuch as it will also be displayed throughout that day on an altar in the middle of St Mark's, set up high especially.
>
> Then after that I shall have to rehearse a certain cantata in praise of His Serenity, which is designed to be sung every year in the Bucintoro when, with all the Signory, he attends the wedding of the sea on Ascension Day. And I must also rehearse a Mass and solemn Vespers, which is sung in St Mark's on such an occasion ...

The feast of the Redeemer (the third Sunday in July) also had political resonances as 'a day celebrated by the Most Serene Republic in memory of a favour received from the hand of God, which was the liberation of the city from a terrible plague' (L.57 [58], 19 July 1620), as, still more, did the anniversary of the battle of Lepanto on 7 October: 'on that day the Most Serene Doge goes in procession to S. Giustina to give thanks to God our Saviour for the joyous naval victory. He is accompanied by the entire Senate, and solemn music is sung' (L.110 [111], 25 September 1627; see also L.108 [109], 18 September 1627). Finally there was All Saints' Day, on 1 November, mentioned by Monteverdi on 11 July 1620 (L.56 [57]). To these traditional feasts, which Venice celebrated annually, would be added occasional celebrations, for example – as we shall see – for the appearance in Venice of distinguished visitors arriving in a more, or less, official capacity.

Above and beyond these duties required of Monteverdi as an employee of the Republic, Monteverdi was also able to enjoy a busy professional career thanks to his associations with foreign courts (in particular, with the Gonzagas) and especially with institutions and private citizens of Venice. 'As for the city of Venice?' the composer asked himself in the letter of 13 March 1620 (L.48 [49]), explaining in a slightly earlier passage:

> then there is occasional income, which consists of whatever extra I can easily earn outside St Mark's of about 200 ducats a year (invited as I am again and again by the wardens of the guilds) because whoever can engage the *maestro di cappella* to look after their music – not to mention the payment of thirty ducats, and even forty, and up to fifty for two vespers and a mass – does not fail to take him on, and they also thank him afterwards with well-chosen words.

Monteverdi's claim is repeated some years later, on 10 September 1627 (L.104 [106]): 'also the city is most beautiful, and if I want to put myself to minimal trouble I come up with a further 200 good ducats'.

An extremely useful summary of the duties of the *maestro di cappella* of St Mark's, and also of the possibilities for free-lance work, was provided many years later by a musician from Rome, Giacomo Razzi, writing to Giacomo Carissimi just after Monteverdi's death and inviting him to apply as his successor to the now vacant post.[20]

> Very Illustrious and Very Reverend Lord, Most Esteemed Patron.
>
> I believe Your Lordship already knows that, arriving here during the past years to take back Monello, who had come here to recite with Rabacchio in one of these theatres, I was constrained by the kindness of these most excellent patrons (on account of the good opinion and report they had about me) to remain for the service of this Church of St Mark, without any trial, [and] with the greatest provision that may be given, where, in order not to abuse and refuse their favours, I fixed my inconstancy in the immobile waves; and I find myself every day more satisfied, and enjoy in good health this miraculous city, in which there are all those favours which God has created and which one can desire. And the music is [held] in such regard that I have never seen anything like it. Moved by the extraordinary affection I have always had [for you], and influenced no less by our friendship than by your merit, now that these most excellent [gentlemen] are about to provide themselves with a *maestro di cappella* (on account of the death of Monte Verde), [and] since they are accustomed to wish to choose the best subjects that may be found, I have, in order to give you the chance of showing your worth, and because your fame is spread about in this city (which is [the] port of the whole world), justly submitted your person for such consideration; [and] I surely think you will be asked for. And in order that you may be partly informed about this office, so that you may be able, at your convenience, to come to a decision with some basis [for deciding], I tell you that the office is perpetual, and has 400 ducats as provision, with a good residence in the presbytery of St Mark's. And I think you will also have 100 [ducats] as a gift, which they were finally giving to Monte Verde. It is a simple advantage that the *maestro* comes when it is convenient for him, [and] that he has the vice-*maestro* who always assists; and ordinarily they sing from the large book, and in the *cantus firmi* the counterpoint is improvised. On the solemn feasts, since the Most Serene [Doge] comes, with all the Senate, great music is made for four, five and six choirs, with different groups [*concerti*] for

voices and instruments, at the disposition of the *maestro*. There are two large, most perfect organs, adjusted to perfection, with two most talented organists. There are about 40 ordinary singers for the church, and about twelve instruments, among violins, *violoni*, trombones and cornetts; and others outside the church are also called at the pleasure of the *maestro*. And here one has the chance of bringing about [all kinds of] interplay, and spirited and gay inventions, with [instrumental] symphonies which compete among themselves in imitating and answering the lively suggestions of the voices. I almost hear these things, and almost see you at work. And here the hearts of this numerous nobility are enraptured, and every least nobleman here can [do] more by far than a cardinal there. And they are so enamoured of music, especially of novelties, that it is impossible to believe it. And no attention is paid to the expense of making music outside the church; truly, there are many who strive to make it on account of the great profit there is. One earns a great deal, since [such performances] are almost continual. And there is no music, however small it may be, that does not come to 50 ducats. There are [some that make] 100, 200, and 300; and the coins march along. Every year, you will earn some hundred *scudi* for the music of some theatre; and if you will wish to present some musical evening, you will see how great a concourse [of people] and how much profit you will have. In fact, it is incredible to speak of the profit those make who strike the [popular] taste, as I am sure you would do. And here you have the convenience of these good [music-]presses, which will be immortalized under a name so glorious [as yours]. Not to say anything else, I conclude [by saying] that that delicacy of your works ([which are] stupendous in every class) would be as revered and loved by all, as your playing and your good manners. And I exhort you, as a true servant, that you urge us, and seize fortune when it shows you the mane, since there are other subjects of much merit who are contending [for the position]. Confer secretly with Monsignor Ottoboni, since he is very powerful, and affectionate towards virtuosos; and he has here his brother, who can [do] what he wishes, and obtains every favour, especially this, which is to the liking of the whole city. Come by writing; go to the mail of Venice; and, [if] I can serve you further in whatever you judge to be more useful to you, I will serve you with all affection. And in closing I kiss your hands dearly.

Venice, 5 December 1643

Your Most Illustrious and Most Reverend Lordship's

Most affectionate servant and true

Iacomo Razzi

For their part, the procurators did not fail to give the new *maestro di cappella* tangible signs of their complete satisfaction with his work and with his first public performances (in the course of which Monteverdi's first-born, the fourteen-year-old Francesco, also showed himself as a singer with some success):[21]

Their Most Illustrious and Most Excellent Lordships being fully satisfied with the good and diligent service proffered by messer Claudio Monte Verde, *maestro di cappella* of their Church of St Mark, who in past musical performances has given proof of his worth in composition and in the *concerti* done with great satisfaction both to the public and to individuals, and wishing in some part to recognize so good and affectionate a servant, and to give him the spirit to go from good to better, and to place all his efforts in the service and honour that he should offer to our Lord God, with the satisfaction of the Most Serene Signory, and also to recognize the service proffered by Franceschin his son, who on various occasions has served in church in the matter of the said music with universal applause, have decided that to the person of the aforesaid *maestro* should be given 50 ducats as a gift, and for his said son, 10 ducats. [Votes:] 2–0

Their Most Illustrious Lordships, recognizing the worth and competence of the said Claudio Monteverde, *maestro di cappella* of St Mark's, and wishing to retain him and to give him the incentive to attend with greatest spirit to the service of the Church for the honour of God, and so that he might have the opportunity to resolve to live and die in this service, have determined by ballots that he be retained for ten years, with a salary of 400 ducats per year with the usual and accustomed perquisites, etc.

23 *Il sesto libro de madrigali a cinque voci* (1614)

In the same year that Monteverdi took up his position in St Mark's, Amadino reprinted his Fifth Book of madrigals, while in 1614 portions of the *cantus* part of 'Non piú guerra, pietate' (from the Fourth Book) appeared in Adriano Banchieri's treatise *Cartella musicale* (Venice, Giacomo Vincenti, pp. 103–4), with the addition, for instructional purposes, of a second contrapuntal part (for alto).

1614 also saw a new collection by Monteverdi, *Il sesto libro de madrigali a cinque voci*, likewise published in Venice by Ricciardo Amadino and the first printed work in which the title-page calls the composer '*maestro di cappella* of the Most Serene Signory of Venice in St Mark's'. This volume also contains, at the end of the 'partitura' for the basso continuo, a sonnet headed 'D'incerto' ('Anonymous'), beginning 'Per queste meraviglie tue chi sale', celebrating, among other things, Monteverdi's welcome 'nel sen d'Adria' ('in Adria's bosom'). But for the first time there is no dedication, which seems to suggest that the volume arose from an entrepreneurial initiative involving only the composer and the printer, without patronage or other support.[22]

All the madrigals of the Sixth Book have a 'Basso continuo per poterli concertare nel clavacembano ed altri stromenti' ('Basso continuo so that they may be concerted with the harpsichord and other instruments', according to the title-page) in the manner already used in the Fifth Book. The music in the volume that can be securely dated all goes back to Monteverdi's Mantuan period. 'Una donna fra l'altre onesta e bella' had already been published, in a spiritual version, by Aquilino Coppini in his *Terzo libro* of 1609, while the *Lamento d'Arianna* and the *Sestina* must date back at least to 1610: witness the letter from Bassano Cassola of 26 July 1610 given above, according to which Monteverdi was also 'preparing a collection of madrigals for five voices, which will contain three laments: that of Ariadne with the usual melody [*canto*] throughout; the plaint of Leander and Hero by Marini; and the third, given to him by His Most Serene Highness, of a shepherd whose nymph is dead, to words by the son of the Lord Count Lepido Agnelli on the death of Signora Romanina'.[23] The suggestion made earlier (pp. 74–5) that one should associate with this volume the two sonnets cited in the letter that Monteverdi sent to Genoa to Annibale Iberti on 28 July 1607 (L.4) – the *Sesto libro* has seven sonnet settings (Nos. 2, 3, 4, 6, 7, 8 and 9) – is nothing more than a hypothesis. But if this were correct, and if it were similarly true that Monteverdi's interest in Marino dated only from 1608 (the year in which Prince Francesco Gonzaga, betrothed to Margherita of Savoy, encountered the Neapolitan poet at court in Turin),[24] then the two works in question could be among those set to texts not by Marino ('Zefiro torna e 'l bel tempo rimena', 'Una donna fra l'altre onesta e bella' and 'Ohimé il bel viso, ohimé il soave sguardo').[25]

1a	'Lasciatemi morire' (Ottavio Rinuccini: *versi sciolti*)
b	'O Teseo, o Teseo mio'
c	'Dove, dov'è la fede'
d	'Ahi che non pur risponde'
2	'Zefiro torna e 'l bel tempo rimena' (Francesco Petrarca: sonnet)
3	'Una donna fra l'altre onesta e bella' (sonnet), 'concertato nel clavicimbalo'
4	'A Dio, Florida bella, il cor piagato' (Giovan Battista Marino: sonnet), 'concertato nel clavacembano'
5	*Sestina: Lagrime d'amante al sepolcro dell'amata* (Scipione Agnelli)
a	'Incenerite spoglie, avara tomba'
b	'Ditelo, o fiumi, e voi ch'udiste Glauco'
c	'Darà la notte il sol lume alla terra'
d	'Ma te raccoglie, o ninfa, in grembo il cielo'
e	'O chiome d'or, neve gentil del seno'
f	'Dunque, amate reliquie, un mar di pianto'
6	'Ohimé il bel viso, ohimé il soave sguardo' (F. Petrarca: sonnet)
7	'Qui rise, o Tirsi, e qui ver me rivolse' (G. B. Marino: sonnet), 'concertato nel clavacimbano'
8	'Misero Alceo, dal caro albergo fore' (G. B. Marino: sonnet), 'concertato nel clauacimbano'
9	'"Batto" qui pianse Ergasto, "ecco la riva"' (G. B. Marino: sonnet), 'concertato nel clavicembano'
10	'Presso a un fiume tranquillo' (G. B. Marino: canzonetta), 'dialogo a 7 concertato'

We have seen that according to Cassola the new volume was to be based on three 'laments', of the abandoned Ariadne, of a shepherd on the death of his beloved nymph (Duke Vincenzo Gonzaga hid himself behind the guise of the shepherd Glauco, while the nymph Corinna whom he laments is Caterina Martinelli, the court singer who died at the age of 18 at the time of *Arianna*), and of Hero on the death of Leander. This last lament, on a text by Marino (from his *Lira*, II.9 – to be compared with the painting of the same subject by Rubens done in Mantua in 1604–5 and also mentioned by Marino in his *Galleria*?), is therefore missing from the volume: nor can one say whether this is because Monteverdi decided to omit it or because of a change to his original plan.

The texts set in the *Sesto libro* include several by Giovan Battista Marino, a poet perhaps discovered by Monteverdi in 1608 or at the latest in 1610 (i.e. the association was fostered either by the links between Francesco Gonzaga and the Savoy court, or by the arrival in Mantua of the Neapolitans Giovan Battista and Adriana Basile),[26] but scarcely close on the heels of the poet's phenomenal popularity in the musical world on the publication of the *Rime* in 1602.[27] Moreover, Monteverdi's choice of texts reveals his somewhat individual adherence to Marino, given that he prefers not the witty syntheses and conceits of the madrigals appreciated and adopted by nearly all composers, but rather four sonnets and a canzonetta, confirming the composer's interest at this stage 'in the large-scale articulation of musical form'.[28] Unlike the continual pairing of poetic and musical images which had characterized, for example, Monteverdi's encounter with Tasso in the Second Book, here the variety of the episodes found an orderly disposition within large formal pillars which, with clear design, add a sense of discipline to their flow and effectiveness.

The volume is structured 'in two analogous sections, each having a polyphonic cycle [a lament] and an unaccompanied madrigal [on verse by Petrarch]'[29] with a basso continuo (*seguente*) but not called 'concertato'. In each section, these pieces precede madrigals (often dialogues) which are instead explicitly so labelled (the harpsichord is required to do the 'concerting'). The former in fact use the full five-voice ensemble almost continuously, whereas the latter have passages – sometimes long ones – for one, two or three voices, needing the harmonic support of the continuo, which becomes a *basso seguente* when the number of parts increases, as had already occurred in the Fifth Book.

With the *Lamento d'Arianna*, Monteverdi printed for the first time, albeit in a polyphonic setting, the 'usual melody' (as Cassola said) of the abandoned Ariadne, which had already gained such favour and had spread through manuscripts. According to Giovan Battista Doni, the polyphonic arrangement was done at the request of a Venetian gentleman,[30] who evidently judged the more artful and learned frame of counterpoint better suited to that famous melody. Like the monodic version, this five-part setting also became established as a model, an object for emulation on the part of composers such as the Mantuan Giulio Cesare Antonelli or the Sicilians Claudio Pari and

Antonio il Verso: Pari and Il Verso set only the opening of Rinuccini's celebrated text (which in Pari's case is followed by his paraphrases) in, respectively, the *Lamento d'Arianna: quarto libro de madrigali a cinque voci* and the *Decimoquinto libro de madrigali a cinque voci*, both printed in Palermo by Giovan Battista Maringo in 1619.[31]

Conceived for the most part in Monteverdi's last years in Mantua, this new volume of madrigals therefore took up again themes and characteristics of the preceding books, while at the same time pursuing with clear determination fresher ideas and experiments. As with those collections, so this book was to have its high points in large-scale emotional madrigal-cycles (the two long laments of the abandoned Ariadne and of the shepherd at the tomb of his beloved nymph), followed by single pieces in the same (or at least a sentimental) vein, but gradually decreasing in emotional intensity as they distance themselves from those extended concentrations of expressiveness taken to extremes. Just as the Mass and Vespers of 1610, Monteverdi's Fifth and (still more) Sixth Books display now in the field of secular music a wealth of compositional approaches both used separately and above all integrated in effective and highly imaginative ways. Similarly, and again following the Mass and Vespers, here in Monteverdi's secular output one can distinguish two clearly contrasted stylistic poles, one which can be called *antico* as regards its being close to traditional writing, and the other instead *moderno* because of its profound innovations to the madrigalian tradition. Not for nothing did Monteverdi reserve the former for the archaic classicism of Petrarch's sonnets, while experimenting with the latter in more recent examples of this poetic form just as the contemporary Marino was promoting a quixotic revival of the form itself.

24 1614–1619

A timely eulogy of Monteverdi's latest highly but refinedly expressive style, the product of a *musica reservata* geared towards a select audience, comes from the pen of Angelo Grillo in August 1614, to whom the composer had sent in homage his newly printed collection.

> To Signor Claudio Monteverde. Venice.
>
> Argument: With an abundance of graceful praises, the author comes to thank Signor Claudio Monteverdi of the gift made him of music, in which in this age he has none who goes before him.
>
> It was indeed right that the Sixth Book of your madrigals lately published came to me from the kind hand of Your Lordship and not from another, for there is no one who esteems and honours the clear worth of your virtues and the rare kindness of your manners more than I. And as for your harmonious gift, I can indeed affirm, if I consider it in all its excellence, that not so much,

as I receive it, does it come to me from the earth, as, as I hear it, it seems to me to come to me from heaven. These my monks, having considered them at length, given that the work requires forethought and preparation, made me hear part of it, whenceforth just as my heart was seized by the sweetness of the harmony, so my intellect was diverted by the novelty of the artifice. This is not music for a popular ear or a popular intellect, because the manner is not popular, and the composer is not popular, but lifted above the ordinary ways and beyond the common populace of musicians. May Your Lordship's modesty so permit me, and permit me willingly, [to say] that if your music, by moving the emotions wondrously, has been able greatly to seize power over my soul, it is no marvel if your merit almost at the same moment has been able eagerly to snatch my pen and make me write to you about you that which I would write at greater length to others about you if I had the opportunity. I say the same of the pieces in manuscript, in which Your Lordship shows himself to be so much the greater master so much the lesser is the assistance of the words: but under a great knight even a hag will seem a Bucephalus. And my words are too much honoured both by your praises and by your harmony, which will make them fly on as many wings as there are notes with which you have marvellously enlivened and adorned them, and they will sing sweetly in your music where they resound badly in our poetry. For all of which be praised God, our Lord, our praise and our worth, and may He grant Your Lordship true and endless rewards.

From Capo d'Istria.[32]

Thus together with his Sixth Book, Monteverdi had sent Grillo 'pieces in manuscript' to his texts, a clearer identification of which is provided by other references in Grillo's letters. Indeed, again in 1614 (the mentions of the Sixth Book make it seem very recent), Don Giovanni Battista Magnavacca, a cleric living in Venice, had submitted to Monteverdi some of the poems of Grillo's *Pietosi affetti* so that he might draw from them something to set to music. On more than one occasion, Grillo sought to thank him for his generous initiative.

To Father D[on] Gio[vanni] Battista Magnavacca of the Regular Clerics. Venice.

Argument: under the guise of praise he thanks him for the honour which he does to his *Pietosi affetti*.

Well, Your Fathership does not judge yourself to be kind with me unless you are extremely kind. Already those my rough stones refined in the artifice of your efficacious eloquence and bound in the gold of your fine praises have been turned into precious jewels, nay finest rings worthy indeed to be married to the harmony of Signor Monte Verde and to be kept by me as a token of his singular kindness and of my particular obligation. The which I confess and profess, consigning Your Fathership to the purse of divine reward, which makes all rich of His holy grace.

From Venice.[33]

To Father D[on] Gio[vanni] Battista Magnavacca of the Regular Clerics. Venice.

Argument: He explains why he cannot satisfy him; says that he has heard of the death of a priest; speaks in praise of Signor Claudio Monteverde and shows himself grateful for his offerings.

... And to our Signor Claudio, truly the emperor of music, be it granted to build on his green mountain [*monte verde*] an harmonic tower so high as to touch the sky. And if he will make use of these my sacred and poetic stones, such as they may be, then he could with some justice make me be what Your Reverend Fathership makes me seem through excessive kindness. For which I would say that I remain obliged to you, and so too for your most generous offerings, if I did not know that you know how much I love you and how much I desire to serve you out of duty and out of nature.[34]

And in another letter, Grillo tells Magnavacca of the kindness recently shown him by Monteverdi in sending him his Sixth Book together with some compositions on his own texts, which he now specifies as two spiritual madrigals.

To Father D[on] Gio[vanni] Battista Magnavacca of the Regular Clerics. Venice.

Argument: he also offers implied thanks to this father, who had some of the sacred madrigals of our reverend father set to music by the famous Monteverde, and he praises his worth.

The miracles of love are well known through fame, but Your Fathership wishes that I should know them through proof while you act for my consolation, and thus by your own action, so that one well sees that you are not guided by anything other than by the loving intelligence to make me enjoy your favours, and those of your great friends and great virtuosos, as is Signor Claudio Monteverde, of whom all the parts of his truly harmonic and sovereign skill are to our ears parts of human blessedness and a likeness of the heavenly. The Sixth Book of his madrigals newly published by him and sent to me confirms it, and our two spiritual madrigals and other of our sacred poetry honoured by his angelic harmony confirm it, in such manner that his green mountain will be as a capitol of an always verdant triumph of our poetry over time and death. My one regret is not to be so backwards in years and advanced with the muses that my verses should be worthy material for the heavenly form of his famous numbers and of his celebrated measures. Certainly with the help of so pious and health-giving tyranny, I would draw not just a sad lament from eyes still wanton in the objects of the sense, but deep sighs from the frozen and petrified hearts under the chill and under the power of perverse custom. Father Don Gio[vanni] Battista, the works of this genius move wondrously the affect of pity where they seek to move, since he has, in my opinion, invented the final perfection, and especially in these his latest madrigals, all [presenting] sadness and powerful eloquence even to the most hardened ears and most severe minds, while they have the favour of voices and of secure singing, for the music has something of the unusual. So much is said for the glory of His Divine Majesty, which now through the eyes and now through the ears and through all ways seeks to draw us to heaven, whither He leads us in the end for His mercy.

From S. Nicolò d'Oltra.[35]

However, it is now very difficult to attempt a further identification of these two spiritual madrigals, and likewise the 'other ... sacred poetry' by Grillo set to music by Monteverdi: indeed, the latter could be only a vague reference to the fact that this was not the first time that the composer had availed himself of his texts (for example, the sonnet at the end of the Third Book and the 'sacred madrigal' of 1610–12). However, a spiritual madrigal drawn from the *Pietosi affetti* accompanied by Monteverdi's music survives in the *Selva morale e spirituale* ('È questa vita un lampo'): it is very likely that this was one of the two sent separately by Monteverdi to the poet in the summer of 1614, unless the composer's interest in setting this text to music arose following Magna-vacca's initiative in 1614. Whatever the case, this letter is also significant for what it says about the Sixth Book, emphasizing its expressiveness and that style beyond the ordinary already praised in a preceding letter, this last a feature that must have posed no few problems for, and indeed perhaps perplexed, the honest monks before whom Grillo had placed the volume to have some part of it sung.

Also in 1614, Francesco de' Medici wrote from Florence requesting from the Gonzagas the score of *Arianna*, we do not know whether with the intention of staging it: 'Having the most ardent desire to have the music by Claudio Monteverdi on Signor Ottavio Rinuccini's *Arianna*, performed at the wedding of Lord Duke Francesco, then prince, of glorious memory, I come with this letter to entreat Your Highness most efficaciously to do me the favour of it, and the more promptly it is done and it will please you to send it to me quickly, the more will I singularly oblige myself to your kindness.'[36]

1615 saw the reprinting in Venice by Amadino of the *Scherzi musicali* and of the madrigals of the Fourth, Fifth and Sixth Books, while in Antwerp Pierre Phalèse similarly reissued the Third, Fourth and Fifth Books (the first two with the addition of a continuo). Monteverdi also contributed a setting for two voices ('2 sopranos or tenors') and continuo, 'Cantate Domino canticum novum' (the text is drawn from Psalm 97; *AV* 98), to an anthology edited by Giovan Battista Bonometti, *Parnassus musicus ferdinandaeus* (Venice, Giacomo Vincenti, 1615): the title derives from the dedication to Archduke Ferdinand of Austria, who some years later was crowned emperor as Ferdinand II. Bonometti collected in five partbooks pieces by various composers, some of whom were active at the archducal court in Graz where he himself in that same year entered service as a singer.[37] Previously he had worked in the choir of Milan Cathedral (from 1608 to 1613), and it is likely that it was here that he had known Monteverdi personally: the composer's presence in Milan is documented, for example, in Autumn 1612.

From 1615 also dates Monteverdi's documented resumption of professional contacts with the Mantuan court, where Ferdinando Gonzaga requested his urgent presence in January of that year (see L.14, which is Monteverdi's reply, dated 28 January 1615). Ferdinando (then regent) probably intended to make use of the composer for the forthcoming carnival, having him set to music a 'favola' by himself, as it seems from Monteverdi's next letter (L.15, 11 February 1615). Here he promised that once he had received the text he would 'toil away at it harder than you can imagine, sending you by the courier from week to week what I would keep doing from day to day'. But it was already late and nothing was done, perhaps also because of the worrying political situation as hostilities with Savoy over Monferrato turned into open warfare.

The pressure of events forced Ferdinando to assume the full title of duke, and thus in January 1616 he was crowned sixth duke of Mantua and fourth of Monferrato. It was perhaps with this event and its associated festivities in mind that in November 1615 the Gonzaga resident in Venice officially asked Monteverdi, with a letter from Ferdinando, to prepare, the composer said, 'a ballet to music; but the commission did not go into any other detail, unlike those of the Most Serene Lord Duke Vincenzo – may he be in glory!' (L.18, 21 November 1615). In the same letter, Monteverdi proposed that he should produce a pastoral ballet 'of six movements' (that is, in six sections whose changes of metre were to be matched by similar changes in the choreography), preceded by a dialogue between a shepherd, Thyrsis (Tirsi; tenor), and his nymph, Chloris (Clori; soprano). This had been begun before the summer in the light of the composer's plans for a trip to Mantua (which was never made), but it was completed only in November following Ferdinando's commission. The text is usually attributed to Striggio, but the relevant letters, to an unidentified addressee (who was clearly unfamiliar with the work), offer no support for this. The letter including the ballet also contains some interesting instructions by the composer:

> However, believing that a ballet of six movements should turn out to be to His Most Serene Highness's liking, I straightway tried to finish the enclosed, of which two movements were lacking; and this in fact I began in recent months in order to present it to His Most Serene Highness, thinking that I would be in Mantua this past summer for certain business affairs of mine.
>
> While I am sending it off by the hand of the Resident to Your Most Illustrious Lordship, to present to His Most Serene Highness, I also thought it a good idea to accompany it with a letter of mine addressed to Your Most Illustrious Lordship, to tell you at the same time that if His Most Serene Highness should want either a change of tune in this ballet, or additions to the enclosed movements of a slow or grave nature, or fuller and without imitative passages (His Most Serene Highness taking no notice of the present words which can easily be changed, though at least these words help by the nature of their metre and by the imitation of the melody), or if he should want everything altered I beg you to act on my behalf so that His Most Serene Highness may be so kind as to reword the commission, since, as a most devoted servant, and most desirous of acquiring His Most Serene Highness's favour, I shall not fail to carry it out in such a way that His Most Serene Highness will be satisfied with me.
>
> But if by good fortune the enclosed should be to his liking, I would think it proper to perform it in a half-moon, at whose corners should be placed a chitarrone and a harpsichord, one each side, one playing the bass for Chloris and the other for Thyrsis, each of them holding a chitarrone, and playing and singing themselves to their own instruments and to the aforementioned. If there could be a harp instead of a chitarrone for Chloris, that would be even better.
>
> Then having reached the ballet movement after they have sung a dialogue, there could be added to the ballet six more voices in order to make eight

voices in all, eight *viole da braccio*, a contrabass, a *spineta arpata*, and if there were also two small lutes, that would be fine. And directed with a beat suitable to the character of the melodies, avoiding overexcitement among the singers and players, and with the understanding of the ballet-master, I hope that – sung in this way – it will not displease His Most Serene Highness.

Also, if you could let the singers and players see it for an hour before His Most Serene Highness hears it, it would be a very good thing indeed . . .

Monteverdi learnt from Striggio(?) a few days later how pleased Ferdinando was with this work on hearing some parts of it performed: 'I have at hand Your Most Illustrious Lordship's advice as to how you not only received the ballet, but also presented it to His Most Serene Highness; and as it is reported that what little His Most Serene Highness has deigned to hear gave him pleasure, I am greatly comforted by this news' (L.19, 28 November 1615).

The music for this ballet was printed by Monteverdi a few years later, in his *Concerto: settimo libro de madrigali* (1619), with the title *Tirsi e Clori* and with some modifications. The ballet proper (in 'six sections', coinciding with the six six-line stanzas in seven-syllable lines which make up its text, concluded by a brief 'Riverenza') is 'for five parts for instruments and voices, concerted' (so says the basso continuo partbook), while the instructions in Monteverdi's letter of 21 November 1615 (L.18) refer to eight voices (to the two voices who sing the parts of Thyrsis and Chloris 'there could be added . . . six more voices in order to make eight voices in all' doubled by 'eight *viole da braccio*', while 'a contrabass, [and] a *spineta arpata*' were to realize the basso continuo ('and if there were also two small lutes, that would be fine'). It is curious that the *entrée* of the *ballo* is constructed on the threefold presentation of a bass line (G–C–D–G) which also appears in the motet 'Cantate Domino canticum novum' printed in the *Parnassus musicus ferdinandaeus* of 1615.

Monteverdi's continuing relations with Mantua concerned personal as well as professional matters: he was still a Mantuan citizen and a number of relatives on his wife's side still lived there (his father-in-law Giacomo Cattaneo, his brothers-in-law Cesare Cattaneo, a Capuchin monk – mentioned in letters of 1615–16 (L.17, 20) and 1622 (L.70 [71]) – and Ippolito Belli, with whom Monteverdi was involved in litigation in 1624–5 over the estate of his father-in-law). The most pressing matter concerned the pension awarded him by Duke Vincenzo on 19 January 1609, the collection of which – owing to the irregularity of its payments – was to be a problem for the composer throughout his life: his attempts to convert it into a fund that would guarantee an equivalent annual return were in vain. To keep in hand his Mantuan dealings, Monteverdi repeatedly had recourse to the high-placed connections he had in the city (Striggio; the ducal secretary Count Ercole Marigliani, to whom he sent a gift of 'beverages' in 1625 – L.82 [83]), each of whom were always willing to offer their friendly assistance. Not for nothing did Monteverdi write on 18 April 1620 perhaps to Striggio: 'As for the future, Most Illustrious Lord, do not bother yourself further about setting to rights the troubles of the likes of me, for they are numerous because of the constant necessity that besets me, and if one of them is taken care of today, another comes up tomorrow' (L.54 [55]). The letters which refer to these matters (L.16, 17, 20, 40 [41], 41 [42], 44 [45], 45 [46], 48 [49], 54 [55], 59 [60], 60 [61] and 124 [126]) cover the period 1615–43, in other words, almost the whole time that Monteverdi was in Venice: indeed, the very last letter from Monteverdi known to us, written a short time before his death, concerns precisely this very pension.

But Monteverdi's contacts with Mantua were primarily to do with work, particularly in the case of a duke such as Ferdinando Gonzaga, who was devoted to poetry and music.

> Ferdinando Gonzaga, present duke of Mantua, is now about twenty-six years of age of middling height, sparing and dry in manner – more than is usual in his family – and of delicate complexion, graceful appearance and with likeable looks full of charm. He is suitably healthy, and would perhaps be still more so if, leaving aside the advice of one of his personal doctors, he did not make such frequent use of medicines as he does, but cared for his health through the vigour of his years, the exercise he does and the natural propensity he has to eat and drink very little, which certainly cannot be any more frugally and with more sobriety than is the case with His Highness. He suffers a little from attacks of catarrh, particularly when the seasons change, but it is nothing important, and as I have said, the parsimony of the way of living which is customary and one might say natural to His Highness would be enough to keep him well. But from what I have heard, when he feels himself I will not say indisposed but in some way disturbed, altered or a little chilled, he quickly turns to some medication; and so that it is less harmful to him, he takes it reduced to an essence in a little sweetmeat, whence in this manner it turns out more active [*spiritoso*] and powerful, not to say violent both to his stomach and to his complexion. In common opinion, it brings more harm than good. This prince has a very lively and very acute intellect, a good wit and a very wide concern for all matters. But it is in academic studies in particular that he has made considerable progress, having been placed by Duke Vincenzo his father for much of his youth in study in Germany and in Pisa, having always had the idea of applying it at the court in Rome and that he would be a cardinal. He has a remarkable memory and claims never to forget anything that he has once seen or read, which also serves him very well. As well as our ordinary vernacular tongue, he has a good command of Latin, German, French and Spanish, and he also reads Hebrew and Greek well, even if he does not speak these languages and is not as assured in them as in the others; but in Spanish and Latin he puts things together with as much facility as in Italian. He has written extensively on philosophy and theology, but above all on legal matters, and he says openly that he has little need of the opinions of other scholars. In his dealings with Savoy, so as not to demonstrate so much self-reliance, he does not rest from taking the opinion of those who understand these matters as appropriate. He takes extraordinary delight in poetry: he always has to hand, as they say, all the good ancient and modern poets, in the vernacular as in Greek and Latin, and he writes gracefully and enjoys speaking of what he has written and of how his works are praised. He has the greatest taste for music and is very well versed in it, setting to music with great facility various of his poems, which

he then has sung; and they succeed wondrously, since he maintains, as well as a very large choir of singers for his chapel at S. Barbara, three women singers as well, truly singular, who play and sing excellently. And although this pastime of music costs the lord duke as much as I have already said, nevertheless he savours and enjoys it to the extent that I do not believe that he feels the expense; and he has told me many times that he has no other comfort and solace in these recent most weighty troubles than that of music, and that he would now be dead were it not for this comfort. And truly his natural inclination carries him to an incredible degree towards a taste for music and poetry. And because he sleeps but very briefly, it is believed that through the night he forms in his mind some brief verse; and in the morning on leaving his bedroom he always has something graceful to say and to communicate to some *letterato*. This does not please the rest of his gentlemen of the chamber and the court, who were accustomed to being treated more familiarly by Duke Francesco and Duke Vincenzo, since it seems to them that the present duke does not esteem anyone save those for whom letters is a profession.[38]

The wedding of Ferdinando with Caterina de' Medici in 1617 prompted as usual the preparation of solemn festivities, for which contact was also made with Monteverdi. Towards the end of 1616, the composer was asked for his opinion on a libretto (*Le nozze di Tetide*; the subject was typical for a wedding) by a poet whose name was not revealed to him (Count Scipione Agnelli, the author of the sestina set in 1610 and printed in the Sixth Book). Monteverdi's initial assessment was given in an important letter of 9 December 1616 (L.21), in which he criticized the uniformity of the scenes and of the characters (for the most part mythological and unreal), then the versification and the length of the dialogues, the absence of lyrical passages and more generally of 'affects', all aspects which, looked at from the other side, provide important evidence for outlining a Monteverdian poetics of the theatre:

> I received Your Most Illustrious Lordship's letter from Signor Carlo de' Torri with most hearty rejoicing, also the little book containing the *favola marittima, Le nozze di Tetide*. Your Most Illustrious Lordship writes that you are sending it to me so that I may look at it carefully and then give you my opinion, as it has to be set to music for use at the forthcoming wedding of His Most Serene Highness. I, who long for nothing so much as to be of some worth in His Most Serene Highness's service, shall say no more in my initial reply than this, Your Most Illustrious Lordship – that I offer myself readily for whatever His Highness may at any time deign to command me, and always without question honour and revere all that His Most Serene Highness commands.
>
> So, if His Most Serene Highness approves of this play it ought therefore to be very beautiful and much to my taste. But if you add that I may speak my mind, I am bound to obey Your Most Illustrious Lordship's instructions with all respect and promptness, realizing that whatever I may say is a mere trifle, being a person worth little in all things, and a person who always honours every virtuoso, in particular the present Signor Poet (whose name I know not), and so much the more because this profession of poetry is not mine.
>
> I shall say, then, with all due respect – and in order to obey you since you

so command – I shall say first of all in general that music wishes to be mistress of the air, not only of the water; I mean (in my terminology) that the ensembles described in that play are all low-pitched and near to the earth, an enormous drawback to beautiful harmony since the continuo instruments will be placed among the bigger creatures at the back of the set – difficult for everyone to hear, and difficult to perform within the set.

And so I leave the decision about this matter to your most refined and most intelligent taste, for because of that defect you will need three chitarrones instead of one, and you would want three harps instead of one, and so on and so forth: and instead of a delicate singing voice you would have a forced one. Besides this, in my opinion, the proper imitation of the words should be dependent upon wind instruments rather than upon strings and delicate instruments, for I think that the music of the Tritons and the other sea-gods should be assigned to trombones and cornetts, not to citterns or harpsichords and harps, since the action (being maritime) properly takes place outside the city; and Plato teaches us that 'the cithara should be in the city, and the tibia in the country' – so either the delicate will be unsuitable, or the suitable not delicate.

In addition, I have noticed that the interlocutors are winds, Cupids, little Zephyrs and Sirens: consequently many sopranos will be needed, and it can also be stated that the winds have to sing – that is, the Zephyrs and the Boreals. How, dear Sir, can I imitate the speech of the winds, if they do not speak? And how can I, by such means, move the passions? Ariadne moved us because she was a woman, and similarly Orpheus because he was a man, not a wind. Music can suggest, without any words, the noise of winds and the bleating of sheep, the neighing of horses and so on and so forth; but it cannot imitate the speech of winds because no such thing exists.

Next, the dances which are scattered throughout the play do not have dance measures. And as to the story as a whole – as far as my no little ignorance is concerned – I do not feel that it moves me at all (moreover I find it hard to understand), nor do I feel that it carries me in a natural manner to an end that moves me. *Arianna* led me to a just lament, and *Orfeo* to a righteous prayer, but this play leads me I don't know to what end. So what does Your Lordship want the music to be able to do? Nevertheless I shall always accept everything with due reverence and honour if by chance His Most Serene Highness should so command and desire it, since he is my master without question.

And so, if His Most Serene Highness should order it to be set to music, I would say that – since deities have more dialogue than anyone else in this play, and I like to hear these deities singing gracefully – as regards the Sirens, the three sisters (that is, Signora Adriana and the others) would be able to sing them and also compose the music, and similarly Signor [Francesco] Rasi with his part, and Signor Don Francesco [Dognazzi] as well, and so on with the other gentlemen; in this way copying Cardinal Montalto, who put on a play in which every character who appeared made up his own part. Because if this were something that led to a single climax, like *Arianna* and *Orfeo*, you would certainly require a single hand – that is, if it led to singing speech [*parlar cantando*], and not (as this does) to spoken song [*cantar parlando*].

I also consider it, in this respect, much too long as regards each of the speaking parts, from the Sirens onwards (and some other little discourse). Forgive me, dear Sir, if I have said too much; it was not to disparage anything, but through a desire to obey your orders, so that if it has to be set to music (and were I so commanded), Your Most Illustrious Lordship might take my thoughts into consideration . . .

The name of the author of the libretto submitted to Monteverdi had been kept from the composer so as not to influence his judgement. Although Monteverdi declared himself open to the duke's wishes, manoeuvring with cautious circumspection – the text could have been the work of some court functionary, if not the duke himself – the composer raises so many and such substantial objections as to reveal his entirely negative opinion of the work. As has been said, his statements offer much insight into Monteverdi's craft, with his poetics of variety and of characterization obtained even by timbre, his theory of imitation and his slender Platonism, the search for 'affective' equivalences and for the human qualities of a text or of a scenic situation usable for musical ends, the need for a direct dramatic effectiveness, the exaltation of words over music and the ideal of 'parlar cantando' opposed to 'cantar parlando' which, as we have seen (p. 97), is a formulation entirely equivalent to that of 'the oration [as] the mistress of the harmony and not the servant'.

Striggio himself had also raised doubts about whether this text could be set to music in a letter to the duke of 22 November 1616:

> The poetic agility of Lord Count Scipione Agnelli has not been able to wait for the impulses of Your Highness's command as regards whether [the idea of] representing the play [*favola*] of Peleus and Thetis pleased you, for with the quickest of speeds he has put it into verse, as I send Your Highness in the enclosed. The Count says that he will place himself under your most prudent judgement ... As for my opinion, it seems very noble, and I hope that it will succeed set to music; I see the need only to cut the soliloquies of Peleus and of Neptune, and the first dialogue that Thetis has with Proteus, which, having to be sung, could perhaps turn out too long.
>
> If Your Highness will be pleased to accept this play, let the Lord Prefect [of the ducal buildings, Viani] say that it will be necessary for this to be the first to be done; for since it will be the most difficult to put on stage because of the waves and of the ship and other things, it needs more time to be prepared. For the second [entertainment], now a *veglia*, so as to give an opportunity to the prefect to display an inferno we are thinking of the play of *Ati e Cibele* arranged by Signor Rasi ... For the third entertainment, we are reserving as a condiment the most beautiful play of *Endimione*, which I am expecting from Your Highness given that it was not returned here on your departure. I have not let Signor Monteverdi know anything else since I will go to Venice ...[39]

On 19 December, Striggio passed Monteverdi's assessment on to the duke:

> It seems that Signor Monteverdi does not know how to get down to setting to music the little play [*favoletta*] by the Lord Count Scipion Agnelli of *Le nozze di Peleo et di Teti*, having written me a long letter in which he tells me that it is without affect, [that] he does not know how with it he can move and delight, as well as that the dialogues and especially the soliloquies turn out too long. As a result, I have had some discussion with the aforesaid count, and he, at my request, has interrupted the scene of Thetis and Proteus with a number of exchanges, so that with a frequent change of song it will be less tedious. And since he had already conceived the idea of another play which has more of the pathetic, in a short time he has given it birth, and it is the

Congiunta d'Alceste et d'A[d]meto, which is sent to Your Highness to see whether your most noble taste will be satisfied with it. For if this one pleases you more than the other, it could quickly be sent to Monteverdi, who would apply his spirit to it more willingly. And in such a case, if it was to be put on stage, I would say some things to the author concerning its representation, which I judge it necessary to note. Signor Rasi's *Cibele* is in good order, and I will send it to Your Highness in seven or eight days, still awaiting from you your *Endimione*, another matter, at least on your return, which is greatly desired by the people here. The prefect is not working on the staging because he wants money first ...[40]

Although he was scarcely convinced by the project, on 29 December Monteverdi sent a plan of action (L.22), again promising to begin applying himself to it once his duties for Christmas in St Mark's had ended:

I shall therefore start to work a little on that play if you so command, but more than that I shall not do until Your Most Illustrious Lordship's further orders.

I have gone back to look more closely and carefully at it, and as I see it, many sopranos will be needed, and many tenors. There are very few dialogues, and those few being in recitative do not call for attractive ensembles. There are no songs for chorus other than the Argonauts in their ship, but this will be most attractive and appealing and will be worked out eventually for six voices and six instruments. There are of course the Zephyrs and Boreals, but I do not know how these have to sing, though I do know that they blow and whistle; and it so happens that Virgil, speaking of winds, uses the word 'sibilare' which exactly imitates in its pronunciation the effect of the wind.

There are two more choruses, one of Nereids and the other of Tritons, but it seems to me that these ought to be doubled by wind instruments, so that if they were performed in this way, what pleasure – I ask Your Lordship – would they bring to the senses! And in order that Your Most Illustrious Lordship may carefully perceive this truth for himself, I am sending Your Most Illustrious Lordship on this enclosed sheet the plan for the scenes as they occur in this play, so that you may favour me by telling me your opinion.

Nevertheless everything will turn out very well, as it depends on the intelligence of His Most Serene Highness, to whom I readily bow and show myself to be a most humble servant.

This letter crossed with one from Striggio which told the composer of the duke's intention to have the music of *Le nozze di Tetide*. Declaring himself ready to obey (L.23, 31 December 1616), Monteverdi requested the names of 'those who will have to play the parts as written, so that I can supply the music appropriate to the subjects', and he offered his excuses in advance if 'there should be any deficiency, as I know very well there will be, I being a most feeble subject, and also for my having been somewhat removed from this type of singing'. The next letter (L.24, 6 January 1617), as well as documenting the progress of Monteverdi's work (he had already set to music some 150 lines of verse), shows that the composer had been made aware of the fact that he was not dealing with a play 'to be sung and staged with music as was *Arianna*' but '*intermedi* for the main play' (and we have already seen the greater dignity of this dramatic genre):

> Your Most Illustrious Lordship's most precious letter, which I have now received along with the sheet that lists the singers who are to perform in the play about Thetis, has considerably enlightened me as regards contriving something that may be suitable to Your Most Illustrious Lordship's taste, for I know also that it will similarly be to the taste of His Most Serene Highness, for whom I earnestly desire to do something that may prove agreeable.
>
> I admit, Most Illustrious Lord, that when I wrote my first letter in reply to your first, the story which you sent me having no title on it other than this – *Le nozze di Tetide*, a *favola marittima* – I must admit that it could have been something to be sung and staged with music as was *Arianna*. But, after gathering from Your Most Illustrious Lordship's last letter that it has to serve as *intermedi* for the main play, just as I believed at first that it was something of little importance, so on my second impression I consider it, on the contrary, a worthy and most noble work.
>
> However in my opinion it does lack – at the very end after the last line which runs:
>
> > Torni sereno il ciel tranquillo il mare
> > [Let heaven regain its serenity, and the sea its calm]
>
> – it lacks, I would say, a canzonetta in praise of the most serene princely bridal pair, the music of which could be heard in the heaven and earth of the stage, and to which the noble dancers can dance, since a noble ending of this kind seems to me suitable to a noble scene such as I have proposed. And if at the same time you could accommodate to a dance measure the lines which the Nereids have to sing (to the tempo of which you could make expert dancers dance gracefully), it seems to me that it would be a much more suitable thing.
>
> I have a slight objection to the three songs of the three Sirens, and it is this: if all three have to sing separately I am afraid the work will turn out to be too long for the listeners, and with little contrast; for what with one thing and another there will be need of a *sinfonia* to come between them, runs that can support the declamation, and *trilli* – and so in general a certain similarity will emerge. So for this reason, and for overall variety, I would consider having the first two madrigals sung alternately, now by one voice, now by two together, and the third by all three voices.
>
> As for the role of Venus (the first part, which comes after the plaint of Peleus, and the first to be heard in the florid style of singing – that is, with runs and *trilli*) I would have thought it a good idea if it could perhaps be sung also by Signora Adriana [Basile], in a loud voice, and by her two other sisters, so that she is answered by an echo, in consideration of the fact that her speech has in it this line:
>
> > E sfavillin d'amor gli scogli e l'onde
> > [And let the rocks and waves tell of love]
>
> first of all preparing the minds of the audience with a *sinfonia*, played by instruments placed in mid-scene if possible, because after Peleus has sung his plaint these two lines appear:
>
> > Ma qual per l'aria sento
> > celeste soavissimo concerto?
> > [But what most sweet celestial concert do I hear in the air?]

and I believe Signora Adriana would even have time to make herself up as one of the other three ladies.

Until now I am thinking that there must be about 150 lines, possibly more, and I believe that before next week is over (if it pleases the Lord) all the soliloquies will have been finished – that is, the ones in recitative. Afterwards I shall get down to those in florid style. Please to God that just as I have a most eager mind to do something to satisfy that Most Serene Lord's taste, so also the outcome for me may be that the results serve as true witnesses in His Most Serene Highness's favour . . .

But not ten days later, Monteverdi received the order to stop work, since the duke (L.25, 14 January 1617)

has decided that for the time being nothing further is to be done with regard to the play about Thetis, preferring that another one should be worked on.

What I regret is that virtually all of this was nearly finished – the soliloquies, moreover, had already been completed – still, he is master and I look upon myself as his most obedient servant in obeying whatever His Most Serene Highness may deign to command me, pointing out to Your Most Illustrious Lordship that for setting to music a complete play, to be sung throughout, there is little enough time from now to Easter; and for the *intermedi* in the main play one should not lose time if anything elaborate is to be done.

Given that the news of the fast approaching Gonzaga-Medici wedding was now public, Monteverdi, disillusioned by the poor outcome of *Le nozze di Tetide* – a good part of which was finished – and perhaps fearful of being supplanted by some colleague, made a none too veiled reproach to Striggio (who had vaguely announced a 'new play to set to music'), reminding him that he in turn had refused an offer from Florence made via Rinuccini precisely because of the work he had accepted for Mantua (L.26, 20 January 1617):

Your Most Illustrious Lordship tells me about the definite arrangement of the marriage of His Most Serene Highness with Tuscany, concerning which I shall now have to make a firm resolution to write some music in time for Easter, and for this purpose you will be sending me a new play to set to music. If this regard for serving His Most Serene Highness (the son of the Duke of Mantua, my former master) did not keep me in Venice, I would certainly move to Florence, having received an invitation in a very warm-hearted letter from Signor Ottavio Rinuccini who advises me, on this great occasion of the Duke of Mantua's, to try and move to Florence.

For indeed I shall be seen not only by all the nobility, but also by the Most Serene Grand Duke himself, and besides the Mantuan wedding we are speaking of, others too are expected, so I would therefore enjoy going; and he more or less indicated that I would be employed on some musical task, and tells me that the marriage arrangements with His Highness of Mantua were concluded to the very great satisfaction of the entire city of Florence.

But Monteverdi was still awaiting the new text on 4 February (L.27): 'if His Most Serene Highness wants me to set something to music, do not be tardy in letting me have the words, because I hold nothing more inimical to my nature than shortness of time in my undertakings'. In mid-February, the composer was informed that the duke no longer intended to make use of him for such work: in his reply (L.28, 18 February 1617), Monteverdi alludes to 'troubles and disappointments' perhaps felt on his part, probably on account of the drawn-out dealings over *Le nozze di Tetide*: 'Just as I looked forward to going over to Mantua and becoming involved in this joyful occasion of His Highness's, so will it be extremely disagreeable for me to stay behind, even if it is due to the troubles and disappointments of that Most Serene Lord.'

Sante Orlandi's *La Galatea* of 1612 was staged instead, with a new prologue appropriate for the occasion.[41] The Fedeli then performed Giovan Battista Andreini's *La Maddalena*, a *sacra rappresentazione* with musical episodes commissioned from Monteverdi, Muzio Effrem, Salomone Rossi and Alessandro Guivizzani.[42] This music was published by Bartolomeo Magni of the Gardano press in Venice in the same year, 1617, with the title *Musiche de alcuni eccellentissimi musici composte per La Maddalena sacra rappresentazione di Gio. Battista Andreini fiorentino* ('Music by some most excellent musicians composed for *La Maddalena*, a *sacra rappresentazione* by Giovan Battista Andreini, Florentine'). Monteverdi's participation in this compilation was limited to the prologue, for which he provided an instrumental ritornello in five parts and a setting – using standard recitative formulas – of a quatrain of eleven-syllable lines sung by Divine Favour (Favor Divino; 'Su le penne de' venti il ciel varcando'): this setting was evidently to serve also for the other strophes of the prologue, between which the ritornello was to be inserted.

Around this time, Monteverdi also contributed a motet for two sopranos and continuo ('Sancta Maria, succurre miseris') to Giovan Battista Ala's *Primo libro di concerti ecclesiastici* (Milan, Filippo Lomazzo, 1618). As with Bonometti's *Parnassus musicus ferdinandaeus*, the volume's composer (Ala, born in Lombardy, was active in Milan) and Monteverdi may have known each other personally: a decade later, this motet was reprinted in Strasbourg (by Paul Ledertz in 1627) in the third volume of Johannes Donfried's *Promptuarium musicum*. The text is the litany of the saints which had already been used by Monteverdi in the *Sonata* in the 1610 'Vespers'.

In spring 1618, Monteverdi received from Mantua another text to set to music: *Andromeda* by Count Ercole Marigliani, chancellor, ambassador and ducal counsellor, who had already provided Giulio Cesare Monteverdi with the libretto of *Il rapimento di Proserpina*, staged at Casale in 1611.[43] The first of Monteverdi's letters relating to *Andromeda* (perhaps to Marigliani; although Denis Stevens suggests Prince Vincenzo Gonzaga) is dated 21 April 1618 (L.29): as well as requesting preliminary information on the singers, this letter reveals that the composer had already begun work. Marigliani was sending him from time to time new parts of the text, concerning which there was still some doubt about how it was to be set to music, for it had not been decided whether music was to be used throughout or alternating with sections that were simply spoken:

The daily round at St Mark's throughout Holy Week and Easter has kept me so busy that I have been unable before now to send Your Most Illustrious Lordship the music for the *Andromeda* libretto. I do not know whether it will be to your liking, but I do know that it has been composed by me with a singular desire to serve Your Most Illustrious Lordship with all affection ...

I have moreover received by the present post yet more verses on the same subject of *Andromeda* ... It would be a great favour if I could find out who will be singing the part of the Messenger, so that I can give some thought to the appropriate natural voice, and whether it will be one or two who are to declaim the music, seeing that there are actually two messengers, one sad and the other bringing happiness; and to know how many there are going to be in that chorus of ladies, so that I can set it for four or more, or fewer voices.

On 21 July 1618, Monteverdi sent other sections of the 'favola':

I am sending off to Your Most Illustrious Lordship by this post the remainder of the song for the Messenger of Joy, which was lacking in the other letter already despatched. I could wish that it were as fully effective as my mind's desire would have it – a mind bent on serving Your Most Illustrious Lordship's pleasure, that would have worked harder had it not been for a slight headache caused by the heat which suddenly occurred after the recent rains, and which kept it well away from study.

I would have delayed sending it to Your Most Illustrious Lordship until the next post, so as to have had time to improve it, but fearing that lateness would in your eyes be a worse evil than some deficiency in the music, I wanted for this reason to send it by the present post, being content to receive praise rather for a mediocre but rapid service, than for a good but slow one, because I know to what extent rehearsal time matters to the singer.

I shall keep on setting to music those other lines I have in my possession which are not provided with notes, so that you may hear everything at an early stage, and have time to order from me – according to your wishes – whatever is not to your taste. I shall send Your Most Illustrious Lordship the canzonetta sung by the chorus of fishermen which begins 'Se valor di forti braccia' ['If the virtue of strong arms'] by the next post, but you will be doing me a favour by letting me know for how many voices, and how it has to be performed, and whether any instrumental symphony will be heard beforehand, and of what kind, so that I can make it all fit together.

Similarly you will be doing me a favour by letting me know whether the canzonetta that begins 'Il fulgore onde risplendono' ['The radiance with which they shine'] (sung by the chorus of damsels) will be sung and danced – and on what instruments it will be played, and also by how many voices it will be sung – so that I can write appropriate music also for that. The Messenger of Sadness, who begins with 'Sarà mai ver che veggia' ['Will it never be true that I see ... '] will also, I hope, be with Your Most Illustrious Lordship soon ...

The impossibility of having this work ready for Carnival 1619 had forced Striggio to ask Monteverdi for a 'ballo' (no other details are given) to be used as a substitute on this occasion: 'But since Your Most Illustrious Lordship is pleased to have the *ballo* for this Easter, you may be sure of receiving it', wrote Monteverdi on 9 February 1619 (L.31). Meanwhile, the composition of *Andromeda* was becoming tediously drawn out, as on 22 March the composer felt it necessary to justify himself, perhaps to Striggio (L.33; Stevens suggests Vincenzo Gonzaga):

> It is true that Signor Marigliani, whom I very much honour and like, has not one reason to complain but rather a thousand, because in view of both my affection for His Lordship and the countless obligations I have towards him, I ought some time ago to have finished the music for those very beautiful words of his. For this failure I really blush, and (by Heaven!) there is not a day, Most Illustrious Lord, when I do not rise from my bed with the firm intention of sending them to His Lordship, set to music, seeing that I am already well ahead.

Marigliani (Stevens suggests Striggio) had already in March 1619 given Monteverdi 'the boon of a little time to write the music to [these] very beautiful words' (L.32) – although this may refer to Striggio's eclogue, *Apollo* (see below) – but the setting was not even finished in the following year. To bring it to conclusion, matters went so far as to involve the intervention of the duke's brother, which provoked some resentment on Monteverdi's part (L.38, 9 January 1620):

> Signor Marigliani (in a letter addressed to me) has passed on a formidable request from Signor Don Vincenzo: that I finish the *Andromeda* – already begun – a play by the aforementioned Signor Marigliani, so that it can be performed for His Most Serene Highness this carnival time, on his return from Casale. But just as I am having to do a bad job through being obliged to finish it in a hurry, so too I am thinking that it will be badly sung and badly played because of the acute shortage of time. I am also greatly surprised that Signor Marigliani wishes to involve himself in such a dubious enterprise, since even if it had been begun before Christmas, there would hardly be time to rehearse it, let alone learn it.
>
> Now consider, Your Most Illustrious Lordship: what do you think can be done when more than four hundred lines, which have to be set to music, are still lacking? I can envisage no other result than bad singing of the poetry, bad playing of the instruments, and bad musical ensemble. These are not things to be done hastily ...

In the same letter, Monteverdi also used as an excuse for his slowness the fact that 'my ecclesiastical service has somewhat alienated me from the musical style of the theatre', but the order of the duke's brother obliged him to finish the opera as soon as possible. Monteverdi told Striggio on 16 January 1620 (L.39) that 'the new commission which the Prince has given me – that I send him the music for *Andromeda* as soon as possible – dictates my inability to attend to anything else'. The last reference (it seems) to *Andromeda* is in the letter of 15 February 1620 (L.43 [44]), in which Monteverdi tells Marigliani that he is on the point of sending him 'the eight-part song, and as Your Lordship gives me no further orders I shall continue to believe that with the enclosed compositions I am sending you, there will be no other commands'. But the composer's scant intention of completing this work is revealed by a preceding letter of 1 February 1620 (L.40 [41]), in which, given that the duke had decided to stage another theatrical work by Monteverdi (the danced eclogue *Apollo*), the composer could calmly confess to Striggio that some time before he had in fact decided not to make a journey to Mantua (where he intended to go to take care personally of the annoying business of the pension) for fear of being forced to finish this very libretto:

> But remembering that Signor Marigliani's play would have fallen entirely on my shoulders – and knowing that with the passage of time a feeble branch can bear a huge fruit, so that in no time at all the ability to hold up without breaking would be out of the question – in order not to break myself (in my feeble state of health) I did not want to come at such short notice to sustain this impossible weight, because something other than haste is needed to do justice to such a project, and it is no small matter to make a success of it even with plenty of time.
>
> Wherefore I have resolved to stay, and I am sorry about it because of my own interests, but in order to avoid dying I would give up whatever worldly interests you like.

Because of the turn taken by these affairs, so as to stage the work it was necessary to be satisfied with what Monteverdi had done until then, turning to others to finish it. A recently discovered printed libretto in fact provides evidence that 'the *favola* of Andromeda' was 'brought to the stage in music by the most excellent prince Don Vincenzo Gonzaga, Carnival 1620'.[44]

At the beginning of 1619, Monteverdi had to deal with a delicate family matter concerning his eldest son, Francesco, then not yet eighteen. Francesco was in Padua studying jurisprudence, but he instead showed more interest in music and particularly in singing (he had already performed as a singer in St Mark's in 1615 and 1618 with notable success). Because of his skill, he was often invited to take part in private academies (in particular, that of the canon Gian Francesco Morosini), which distracted him from his studies and could introduce a dangerous worldliness into the upbringing of the youth. Even when he had both his sons together with him in his house in Venice, Monteverdi had shown himself preoccupied over 'the dangerous liberty here in Venice' which made him 'bound to maintain a tutor' (L.20, 27 July 1616) at considerable expense. Similarly, he wrote (to Annibale Iberti?) a few months earlier (L.17, 6 November 1615):

> Impelled by the heavy expenses that I am obliged to meet in bringing up my sons – desiring that they learn to read, write, grow up in the fear of God and become a credit to society, on account of which most necessary considerations I have always had to maintain them and their tutor in my own lodgings, so that they and he have been costing me more than two hundred ducats a year ...

As a result of the situation created in Padua, where the musical salons threatened to lead Francesco astray, Monteverdi decided to move him to another university, Bologna, boarding him at the monastery of S. Maria dei Servi, as he wrote to Striggio on 9 February 1619 (L.31):

I went with my elder son Francesco to Bologna (as the first feast-days of Christmas were over) and had the chance to remove him from Padua – to remove him from the splendid time which the Most Illustrious Lord Abbot Morosini was kindly giving him so as to enjoy a little of the boy's singing. And in the long run he would have turned out to be a good singer with all the other additions (as one would say – although it is better to keep quiet about that), rather than an average doctor; and yet my way of thinking would prefer him to be good in the second profession and mediocre in the first, as if it were an ornament.

So, for the sake of helping the boy (as indeed I have done) and for my own satisfaction, I went – as I said – to settle him in Bologna as a boarder with the Servite fathers, in which priory they read and debate every day. And I was there for this purpose for about fifteen days ...

Monteverdi had already arranged the education of his two sons and their future professions: 'one is aiming at a doctorate in law, and the other in medicine' he wrote to Striggio on 8 February 1620 (L.41 [42]). Profiting from the opportunity provided by Francesco, the composer had at the same time also placed Massimiliano (then some 15 years old) in the seminary at Bologna in January–February 1619: Monteverdi's letter of 22 March 1619 (L.33) in fact makes explicit reference to his journey 'all the way to Bologna' for 'my sons', in the plural. Later, on 7 August 1621 (L.66 [67]), Monteverdi was able to inform the Duchess of Mantua that by that date Massimiliano had 'left the seminary at Bologna, having completed there the course in humanistic studies and rhetoric'. Having made such a decision also for his younger son, Monteverdi must have hoped to have dealt both with the need to provide him with an education and with the many problems clearly caused by his difficult character, or so one can gather from what he writes to Striggio on 11 July 1620 (L.56 [57]) concerning an abandoned trip to Mantua, not made in the end at the insistence of his father-in-law who dissuaded him from taking a 'journey these hot days. So tending to think that my father-in-law had said this because he knows that Massimiliano is here with me (and I fear he bears him little love, for the boy knows his own mind) and because he is worried that I might bring my son along, causing him displeasure.'

25   *Concerto: settimo libro de madrigali* (1619)

Monteverdi's Seventh Book of madrigals was the first not issued by the press of Ricciardo Amadino, who up to this point had printed all Monteverdi's output from the Mantuan years and also the Sixth Book; it appeared instead in Venice in 1619 from the press of Bartolomeo Magni, who six years before had taken over the printing firm of his father-in-law, Angelo Gardano (in fact, the title-page bears the usual formula 'Stampa del Gardano'). This volume, too – this time at its head – contains a poem in homage to the composer, the anonymous sonnet 'Sul Monte che da terra al cielo asceso'.

The Seventh Book also marks a more substantial first in the composer's career, concerning its contents, which according to the subtitle consists of 'madrigali a 1, 2, 3, 4 e sei voci, con altri generi de canti' ('madrigals for one, two, three, four and six voices, with other kinds of songs'). Above all, then, this volume contains a heterogeneous mixture of madrigals and pieces that cannot be so classified, following a fashion that is for the most part foreign to the madrigalian tradition and which instead from the first years of the century was adopted frequently by composers and publishers of music for solo voices, following the prototype of this repertory (Caccini's *Le nuove musiche* of 1602) and now spread also through more usual channels (for example, Tommaso Cecchino's *Madrigali et arie* for five voices, published in Venice by Alessandro Vincenti again in 1619).

However, the Seventh Book is more closely related to the former rather than the latter type of collection, containing above all madrigals concerted with basso continuo – and sometimes also with upper instrumental parts – especially for two voices (14 settings; Nos. 2, 4–16), plus four for three voices (Nos. 17–20) and three for various scorings, i.e. one each for one (No. 23), four (No. 23) and six voices (No. 3); it is significant that there is not one setting for the customary combination of five voices. In addition, there are the 'other kinds of songs' announced on the title-page: arias (Nos. 1, 24) and canzonettas (Nos. 27, 28), pieces in the *stile rappresentativo* (Nos. 25, 26) and a *balletto* (No. 29). The title *Concerto* is partly justified by the regular use of the concerted style with basso continuo, but more relevant is the collection's appearance of being intended as something of a miscellany:[45] this title prefaces the Seventh Book in conformity with the fashion – already noticeable in the last years of the sixteenth century and spreading wider with the diversification of styles and genres exploding in the new century and with the 'modern' music – for heading printed collections with whimsical and fanciful titles. The fact that the term is intended to designate a varied collection of different types of music brought together is confirmed by the similarly named collection by Filippo Vitali printed by Bartolomeo Magni ten years later, with the title *Concerto di . . . madrigali et altri generi di canti.*

1 'Tempro la cetra, e per cantar gli onori' (Giovan Battista Marino: sonnet), 'voce sola [tenor]'
2 'Non è di gentil core' (?Francesca degli Atti: madrigal), 'a doi soprani'
3 'A quest'olmo, a quest'ombre et a quest'onde (G. B. Marino: sonnet), 'a sei voci [SSATTB] et istromenti', 'concertato'
4 'O come sei gentile' (Battista Guarini: madrigal), 'a doi soprani'
5 'Io son pur vezzosetta pastorella' (Incolto accademico Immaturo: sonnet), 'a doi soprani'
6 'O viva fiamma, o miei sospiri ardenti' (sonnet), 'a doi soprani'
7 'Vorrei baciarti, o Filli' (G. B. Marino: madrigal), 'a doi contralti'
8 'Dice la mia bellissima Licori' (B. Guarini: madrigal), 'a doi tenori'
9 'Ah che non si conviene' (madrigal), 'a doi tenori'

10   'Non vedrò mai le stelle' (madrigal), 'a doi tenori'

11   'Ecco vicine, o bella tigre, l'ore' (Claudio Achillini: sonnet), 'a doi tenori'

12   'Perché fuggi tra' salci, ritrosetta' (G. B. Marino: madrigal), 'a doi tenori'

13   'Tornate, o cari baci' (G. B. Marino: madrigal), 'a doi tenori'

14   'Soave libertate' (Gabriello Chiabrera: madrigal), 'a doi tenori'

15   'Se 'l vostro cor, madonna' (B. Guarini: madrigal), 'a doi, tenor e basso'

16   'Interrotte speranze, eterna fede' (B. Guarini: sonnet), 'a doi tenori'

17   'Augellin che la voce al canto spieghi' (madrigal), 'a 3: doi tenori e basso'

18   'Vaga su spina ascosa' (G. Chiabrera: madrigal), 'a 3: doi tenori e basso'

19   'Eccomi pronta ai baci' (G. B. Marino: madrigal), 'a 3: doi tenori e basso'

20   'Parlo, miser, o taccio?' (B. Guarini: madrigal), 'a 3: doi soprani e basso'

21   'Tu dormi, ah crudo core!' (madrigal), 'a 4: soprano, alto, tenore e basso'

22   'Al lume delle stelle' (Torquato Tasso: madrigal), 'a 4 voci: doi soprani, tenor e basso'

23   'Con che soavità, labbra adorate' (B. Guarini: madrigal), 'concertato a una voce e 9 istrumenti'

24a   'Ohimé, dov'è il mio ben, dov'è il mio core?' (Bernardo Tasso: *ottava rima*), 'romanesca a 2'

  b   'Dunque ha potuto sol desio d'onore'

  c   'Dunque ha potuto in me piú che 'l mio amore'

  d   'Ahi sciocco mondo e cieco, ahi cruda sorte'

25   'Se i languidi miei sguardi' (C. Achillini), 'lettera amorosa [in *versi sciolti*] a voce sola [soprano] in genere rapresentativo e si canta senza batuta' ['love-letter for solo voice in the representative style, and one sings without a beat']

26   *Partenza amorosa* ('Se pur destina e vole': *versi sciolti*), 'in genere rapresentativo voce sola [tenor] et si canta senza battuda'

27   'Chiome d'oro', '[anacreontic] canzonetta a due voci concertata da duoi violini, chitarone o spinetta'

28   'Amor, che deggio far?', 'canzonetta a 4: concertata come di sopra'

29   *Tirsi e Clori* ('Per monti e per valli', ?Alessandro Striggio), 'ballo concert[ato] con voci et istrumenti a 5'

The Seventh Book opens with a sonnet that is introductory in function, which is therefore set in a manner not unlike a theatrical prologue.[46] Preceded by a *sinfonia* – almost an *entrata* – in five parts, this piece has a programmatic significance entirely similar to the theatrical monologues as prologues but in fact unusual in the madrigal literature. Settings with the characteristics of an *exordium* appear here and there in the solo song repertory: invocations to a personal muse ('Cara mia cetra, andianne' in the 1609 *Le musiche* by Sigismondo d'India mentioned above; 'Novelli accenti dettami', called 'proemio', in Giulio Santo Pietro del Negro's *Secondo libro delle grazie et affetti di musica moderna*, Venice, Giacomo Vincenti, 1614), and addresses to the reader–listener (the duet 'Voi ch'ascoltate in rime sparse il suono' again by d'India, in his *Musiche . . . Libro terzo*, Milan, Filippo Lomazzo, 1618). However, Monteverdi's setting announces intentions and poetic orientations unknown to these predecessors, and related perhaps to the madrigal 'Così nel mio parlar voglio esser aspro' which introduces Marenzio's Ninth Book for five voices (Venice, Angelo Gardano, 1599):

> Tempro la cetra, e per cantar gli onori
> di Marte alzo talor lo stile e i carmi
> ma invan la tento et impossibil parmi
> ch'ella già mai risoni altro che amore.
>   Così pur tra l'arene e pur tra fiori
> note amorose Amor torna a dettarmi
> né vol ch'io prenda ancor a cantar d'armi
> se non di quelle ond'egli impiaga i cori.
>   Or l'umil plettro e i rozzi accenti indegni,
> Musa, qual dianci accorda infin ch'al canto
> de la tromba sublime il ciel ti degni.
>   Riede ai teneri scherzi e dolce intanto
> lo dio guerrier temprando i feri segni
> in grembo a Citerea dorma al tuo canto.

I tune my lute, and to sing the honours / of Mars I now raise my style and songs / but vain is my attempt, and it seems impossible to me / that it should ever resound aught but love. // Thus even in arenas and even among flowers, / Love turns to dictate to me amorous notes; / nor will it let me again take up songs of arms / save of those with which he attacks hearts. // Now may the humble plectrum and the rough, unworthy accents, / o Muse, unite us until with the song / of the sublime trumpet heaven honours you. // Meanwhile, there returns at the tender jokes and sweetness / the god of war, tempering his harsh features / let him sleep in Cytherea's bosom to your song.

The notion of a simple style, of a lyrical and erotic *mediocritas* as an alternative to the elevated epic, is anticipated – it can be read between the lines of the usual protestations of courtly devotion – in the dedication of the book to the Duchess of Mantua, Caterina de' Medici, wife of Ferdinando Gonzaga:

Most Serene Lady and Most Respected Patron.

I would not burn to present this my new Concerto of madrigals to Your Most Serene Highness if I were not certain that you, although you are accustomed to musical concertos sounded by Apollo himself, would not yet disdain hearing now and again some rough sound from the lowly pipe, for in your cradle you learnt from your great parents to prize rare things and not to scorn lowly ones ... Thus the words of this my feebleness were so many fecund tongues, and the notes so many eloquent pens, to celebrate in some part the heroic virtues of Your Most Serene Highnesses; but since I know that they are more worthy of being admired in silence than celebrated with words, here I will be silent, and with as great a spirit as I can, I pray for you from heaven the fulfilment of all true happiness ...

To borrow the terminology of Monteverdi's next madrigal book, the Seventh Book presents itself as a collection just of 'madrigali amorosi' ('madrigals of love'). If the Third to the Sixth Books had shown a clear emphasis on the pathetic, heart-rending aspects of the experience of love – and similarly the development of a style that went beyond the norm, and which was artfully expressive – the Seventh exalts that variety of approaches already seen in the Sixth, where the strained atmosphere of the two great laments is progressively tempered by more serene texts.

If one can again follow a hint from the title, the choice of texts here – which 'essentially is Marinian or pre-Marinian (especially with Guarini)'[47] – provides a 'concerto' of very diverse elements related to the dominant theme of love. In general, the section containing madrigals is ordered according to the increasing number of voices, an organizing principle which enjoyed some favour among composers in Roman circles, as can be seen in collections by Gian Francesco Anerio (1611 and 1617), Antonio Cifra (1613, 1614, 1617 and 1619) and Raffaello Rontani (1614, 1618 and 1619), but which is also adopted elsewhere (Brunetti, 1606; Brunelli, Cecchino and Cesana each in 1613; Ugoni, 1616; Falconieri, 1618). Here we also find the precedents for that type of concerted madrigal of the second decade of the century using from one to four solo voices, which is also practised by Florentine composers (Severo Bonini, *Lamento d'Arianna*, Venice, Gardano [Bartolomeo Magni], 1613; Marco da Gagliano, *Musiche*, Venice, Ricciardo Amadino, 1615; Claudio Saracini, *Le musiche*, Venice, Giacomo Vincenti, 1614) and also by Mantuans (Francesco Dognazzi, *Il primo libro de varii concenti*, Venice, Gardano [Bartolomeo Magni], 1614) and Venetians (Alessandro Grandi, *Madrigali concertati*, Venice, Giacomo Vincenti, 1615; Biagio Marini, *Madrigali et symfonie*, Venice, Gardano [Bartolomeo Magni], 1618). Some collections also focus specifically and exclusively on the music for two voices and continuo that plays so big a part in Monteverdi's book: the first four books of *Canzonette, madrigali et arie alla romana* by Enrico Radesca da Foggia (I, Milan, Heirs of Simon Tini and Filippo Lomazzo, 1605; II, ibid., 1606; III, before 1610; IV, Venice, Giacomo Vincenti, 1610), all reprinted several times; plus Nicolò Rubini's *Madrigali e pazzarelle* (Venice, Ricciardo Amadino, 1610), Severo Bonini's *Affetti spirituali* (Venice, Gardano [Bartolomeo Magni], 1615) and Sigismondo d'India's *Le musiche* (Venice, Ricciardo Amadino, 1615).

Although Monteverdi's chamber music for solo voices and basso continuo was published only towards the end of the second decade of the seventeenth century in this Seventh Book, his rapprochement with this medium (especially the duet) can already be documented in the last years of his service at the Gonzaga court in Mantua. In fact, on 24 June 1610, Rinuccini wrote to Cardinal Ferdinando: 'Those few things which appeared by Monteverdi, such as the duet and other arias, are admired universally by all, and by Zazzerino [Jacopo Peri] beyond bounds; a reaction which causes me no surprise.'[48] We should also note that Monteverdi was among the very first to experiment in the field of the printed madrigal with joining voices and upper instruments: the technical solutions adopted in the relevant settings in the Seventh Book grant him a position of absolute priority given that whoever had preceded him had adhered strictly to the plan of alternating, and not integrating, the instrumental sections and the vocal ones. Thus both Alessandro Scialla's *Primo libro de madrigali* for five voices (Naples, Giovan Giacomo Carlino & Costantino Vitale, 1610) and Angelo Notari's *Prime musiche nuove* for one to three voices (London, Guglielmo Hole, 1613) each contain a madrigal 'con sinfonia'; while the madrigal set as a dialogue by Marcantonio Negri subtitled 'Baci affettuosi et iscambievoli' in his *Affetti amorosi* (Venice, Ricciardo Amadino, 1611) links sections for one, two and five voices with 'sonate' and 'sinfonie' for two violins. Similarly, in the *Madrigali et symfonie* of Biagio Marini, 'musico della serenissima Signoria di Venetia' ('musician of the most serene Signory of Venice'), we find one for solo voice 'con ritornello per il bassetto e chitarrone con 2 violini' ('with [a] ritornello for the *bassetto* and chitarrone with two violins'), and one for five voices which 'comprende un a solo di violin' ('includes a part for solo violin'). In the same year as Monteverdi's Seventh Book, Stefano Bernardi, *maestro di cappella* of the cathedral in Verona, published in his *Terzo libro de madrigali a cinque voci* (Venice, Giacomo Vincenti, 1619) some pieces with 'sinfonie' for violin and cornett (one for solo cornett) and basso continuo. Nor, for the rest, should we forget that Monteverdi himself had already given examples of 'sinfonie' interleaved with the voices in the closing madrigal of his Fifth Book ('Questi vaghi concenti'), but which perhaps stands apart from the other pieces cited here because it may have been intended for the theatre (so the text suggests) and not for the chamber.

The 'other kinds of songs' included in the Seventh Book (in effect, the settings that are not madrigals) appear – in addition to the opening sonnet set as strophic variations – from No. 24 onwards; with the exception of that distant prologue, they are therefore gathered together in a compact section that concludes the book, in a manner similar to the aforementioned collections of solo songs by Caccini and of polyphonic settings by Cecchino. At the head of this series is placed a 'romanesca', that is, an *ottava rima* by Bernardo Tasso ('Ohimé, dov'è il mio ben, dov'è il mio core?') set to music couplet by couplet – and with the traditional repetition of the even-numbered verses – for two sopranos over a bass that is identical in each of the four strophes and which is based on the so-called 'aria della romanesca', a melodic–harmonic scheme already used in improvised solo song and recovered for art music above all by the Roman and Florentine monodists, beginning with Caccini in the preface to *Le nuove musiche* (1602). The Romanesca was also used for polyphonic 'arias' (Giovanni Ghizzolo included one for six voices in his *Secondo libro de madrigali*, Venice, Ricciardo Amadino, 1614) and as an ostinato in various instrumental compositions (for example, by Frescobaldi in the first book of his *Toccate e partite d'intavolatura di cimbalo*, Rome, Nicolò Borboni, 1615; and later by Biagio Marini in 1620, Salomone Rossi in 1622 and Adriano Banchieri in 1626). A decade before Monteverdi introduced it into his own collection, it had begun to appear in the printed volumes of composers active in northern Italy (Sigismondo d'India's *Le musiche* of 1609; Francesco Dognazzi's *Il primo libro de varii concenti*, Venice, Gardano [Bartolomeo Magni], 1614; the aforementioned volume by Ghizzolo of 1619) and even in Venetian circles (see the anthology *Affetti amorosi* edited by Giovanni Stefani in 1618). It was in Venice, too, that the Romanesca received a mention in an *ottava rima* stanza of Giulio Strozzi's poem *La Venetia edificata*, which sanctions its literary fame:

> Leggiadre canzonette, arie novelle
> s'odono uscir con gran diletto ogn'ora:
> ma fra quante s'udian vezzose e belle,
> una d'ogn'altra piú grata innamora,
> né cantan mai le lascivette ancelle,
> che quella pur non si ricanti ancora.
> Romana ha l'aria e in otto versi è stretta,
> e dal numero illustre ottava è detta.[49]

> Charming canzonettas, new arias / are heard abroad with great delight today: / but among the many delightful and beautiful ones that are heard, / one above all others charms more gratefully, / nor do wanton handmaidens ever sing / if it is not sung again and again. / The aria is called 'Romana', and is constrained within eight verses, / and from that distinguished number, *ottava* it is called.

Two *lettere amorose* ('love-letters') follow the Romanesca, 'Se i languidi miei sguardi' and the *Partenza amorosa* ('Amorous parting'). In fact, in the Seventh Book only the first is explicitly labelled *lettera amorosa*; but when they were reprinted in 1623 (Venice, Gardano [Bartolomeo Magni]), in a small collection which sees them linked to the *Lamento d'Arianna*, both were so called. A 'letter' ('Io sono in basso stato') had already opened Innocenzo Alberti's *Terzo libro de' madrigali* for four voices (Venice, Giacomo Vincenti, 1607), and a *lettera amorosa* for two voices, on a poem by Giovan Battista Marino ('Foglio, de' miei pensieri'), appears in Enrico Radesca da Foggia's *Quarto libro delle canzonette, madrigali et arie alla romana* (Venice, Giacomo Vincenti, 1610). On the other hand, Biagio Marini's 'Le carte in ch'io primier scrissi e mostrai' (in the aforementioned *Madrigali et symfonie* of 1618) is for solo voice and 'in stile recitativo' ('in the recitative style'); however, it is not explicitly identified as belonging to the epistolary genre. After Monteverdi's two examples, there appeared in the monody repertory 'O carta avventurosa' by Claudio Saracini (*Le terze musiche*, Venice, Alessandro Vincenti, 1620), a text earlier set for five voices by Amadio Freddi (*Il quarto libro de madrigali*, Venice, Ricciardo Amadino, 1614); 'Torna dunque, deh torna', a 'lettera amorosa del cavalier Marini' in Sigismondo d'India's *Le musiche ... Libro quarto* (Venice, Alessandro Vincenti, 1621); 'Misero, e pur convien, occhi crudeli', a 'lettera amorosa in genere rappresentativo a voce sola e si canta senza battuta' ('*lettera amorosa* in the representative style for solo voice, and it is sung without a beat') – a precise echo of Monteverdi's specifications for his own two pieces in the Seventh Book – in Filippo Vitali's 1629 *Concerto*; 'Vanne, o carta amorosa', a text by Girolamo Preti already set for two voices by Giovanni Valentini (*Musiche*, Venice, Alessandro Vincenti, 1622; Preti is also the poet of 'Questa candida carta' for three voices in Valentini's *Quinto libro de madrigali*, ibid., 1625), in Frescobaldi's *Secondo libro d'arie musicali* (Florence, Giovanni Battista Landini, 1630); and finally Orazio Tarditi's 'Queste carte ch'io sparsi', a 'lettera amorosa in stile recitativo a voce sola' (*Madrigali a doi, tre e quattro voci in concerto. Libro secondo*, Venice, Alessandro Vincenti, 1633).

In words exactly echoed by Vitali, as we have seen, Monteverdi prescribes for his two *lettere amorose* performance 'for solo voice in the representative style, and it is sung without a beat'. This last instruction does not present any particular problems, since it clearly refers to the need for a declamatory style that avoids all rhythmic rigidity in favour of free recitative governed only by the flow of the *oratione* and of the emotion. As for the description 'in genere rappresentativo', this term had come into musical use some years before: there are examples from the first decade of the seventeenth century. Monteverdi himself, in a letter of 1607 (L.4), had written that it was something 'very difficult for a singer to represent [*rappresentare*] a part which he has not first practised', here perhaps using the verb simply as a synonym for 'perform'. However, one of the composer's friends, Cherubino Ferrari, not one month later, praised in his *Orfeo* 'that the poet and the musician' had 'so well represented the affections of the soul' (see p. 76), while in a letter to the Duke of Modena of March 1608, he spoke of 'good singers to sing solo, and to represent the affections of the soul'.[50] 'Rappresentativo', then, was an attribute closely linked to the solo song, and one characteristic of the highly expressive performances practised in a few exclusive musical circles in the late sixteenth and early seventeenth centuries. Similarly, another Milanese admirer of Monteverdi, Aquilino Coppini, in presenting his second book of spiritual madrigals (1608) was able to note: 'The representative music [*musica rappresentativa*] of Signor Claudio Monteverdi's Fifth Book of madrigals, governed by the natural expression of the human voice in moving the affections, stealing into the ear in sweetest manner and thereby making itself the most pleasant tyrant of souls, is indeed worthy of being sung and heard' (see p. 105).

The equivalence of this term with 'stile recitativo' and with what Doni would later call, in Greek manner, 'monodia', is demonstrated by Pietro de' Bardi (writing in 1634), who says that Vincenzo Galilei was 'the first to make heard the song in representative style', and that Jacopo Peri was the perfector 'of the representative style'. In his *Trattato della musica scenica*, Doni himself deplored the customary interchangeability of these terms and instead proposed distinguishing them (the relevant chapter, Chapter 11, in fact bears the title 'A response is made to some objections and it is shown how the *stile recitativo* differs from the *[stili] rappresentativo* and *espressivo*'. But he offers the best evidence of their substantially similar functions:[51]

> But I first wish to note that the *stile recitativo, rappresentativo* and *espressivo* are not entirely the same, even though ordinarily no difference is made between them. For the style called *recitativo*, today we mean that kind of melody in which one can recite appropriately and with taste, that is, solo singing in a manner such that the words are understood, or to do that on theatrical stages, or in churches or oratories in the manner of dialogues, or else in private chambers or elsewhere. And lastly, with this term we understand all kinds of music which one sings solo to the sound of some instrument, with scant drawing out of the notes and in such a way that it approaches common, yet affective speech. In this style are accepted all kinds of graces or *accenti*, even very long *passaggi*, not that they are apt to express the affections (for, as Giulio Romano [Caccini] says, there is nothing in music more contrary to them), but to please those who listen less carefully, or else because singers themselves wish to demonstrate their disposition and, as one says, to go over the top. Similarly, here are admitted many repetitions for the propriety of our language, but however much more sparsely and with decorum than in the style of madrigals and motets, for these are not usually done except on full cadences and in a complete sentiment, whereas in madrigals and motets things are said over and over again, and in a disjointed manner, almost without caring for the sentiment of the words and for connecting the verses, an invention born in a very barbaric time and of men ignorant of all science and perfection, and which has lasted until now because of the artifice of counterpoint and the sweet composition of the consonances, which gives the greatest content to the ears, even though the intellect does not receive its due. But some want *stile espressivo* to be understood as that which better expresses the sense of the words and the human affections, with which, however, they do not show any particular observance about how to form an appropriate manner of melody, wherefore one should rather consider it a quality and particular perfection of singing, rather than a different species, as is the madrigal style compared with the recitative, given that every kind of music (intending here perfect music, which contains signifying words) which does not have something of the expressive must be judged defective; and let this be as it seems, although not every kind of expression is to be used indifferently, as we shall see below. But for 'representative', we should understand that kind of melody which is truly proportionate to the stage, that is, for every kind of dramatic action that one wishes to represent (the Greeks say μιμεῖδαι, imitate) with song, which is almost the same as today's *stile recitativo*, but not entirely, because some things should be removed to bring it to perfection, and others added, as will be shown below. Therefore it pleases me better to call this style accommodated to the stage *rappresentativo* or *scenico*, rather than *recitativo*, because the actors called in Greek ὑποκριταί and in Latin *histriones* do not recite but represent, imitating the actions and human manners, and also because as I have demonstrated in my *Discorsi musicali*, this style would be excellently adapted to reciting in public to the sound of some

instrument, conforming to ancient practice, some heroic poem, as for example Preti's *Oronta*, with those precautions that I noted there.

Thus expressive singing for solo voice and basso continuo was called equally *recitativo* or *rappresentativo* (but the former term was until then more widely used, and thereafter had greater fortune),[52] as for the rest is shown by the lexical oscillation seen in the preceding list of *lettere amorose* (see Marini, Vitali and Tarditi). In this sense, the term could be used equally in all kinds of music adopting the new style; and thus as much music for the church (in 1609 Bernardino Borlasca could say that his *Scherzi ecclesiastici sopra la cantica* for three voices (Venice, Alessandro Raverii) were 'appropriate to be sung among serious *concerti* in the *stile rappresentativo*', that is, alternating with accompanied monodies on sacred subjects), as for the chamber (the *lettere amorose* by Monteverdi and Vitali) or for the theatre (in 1620, Monteverdi would describe his *Arianna* as being in the 'genere di canto rappresentativo' – 'the theatrical style of song'; L.53).

It was precisely the multiple functions of the solo song that made it a genre with wide-ranging powers, granted theatrical potential even when deprived of a scenic context. Francesco Rasi's *Dialoghi rappresentativi* (Venice, Alessandro Vincenti, 1620) are balanced between the chamber and the theatre, and the same applies in essence to Monteverdi's two *lettere*, which were reprinted a few years later together with an explicitly theatrical (and famously so) piece, the *Lamento d'Arianna*. One must also not forget that this style of expressive song was accompanied and underlined by gestures, as singers of emotional madrigals had already started to do in the late sixteenth century, which was, as we have seen, an object of ridicule for Artusi; and in fact, Monteverdi's *Madrigali guerrieri, et amorosi* of 1638 contains, according to its title-page, 'some little works in the representative genre that will serve as brief episodes among the songs without action'.

Claudio Achillini, the poet of the first *lettera*, gave it the title *L'amorosa ambasciatrice* ('The ambassador of love') and added the rubric 'cavaliere impaziente delle tardate nozze scrive alla sua bellissima sposa questa lettera' ('a cavalier impatient over his delayed wedding writes to his most beautiful bride this letter').[53] One should not be deceived by the soprano range: the sender of the 'letter' is indeed an 'impatient cavalier', and the voice which gives it body certainly does not aim for verisimilitude.[54] It was precisely the requirement of realism (a correspondence between voice and character) that prompted the censure of Giovan Battista Doni when faced with Monteverdi's two works: 'The invention of the *Lettere* has more of the capricious than the reasonable: for although both are recounted, as we are to believe, to some lady who knows how to sing and play, however it does not seem good that that which the lover should say or sing should be sung by the woman.'[55]

For Doni, both these *lettere* well exemplify that type of *stile recitativo* 'with simple and plain music' which in his opinion was to be avoided in favour of a more elaborate setting and one 'modulated with more artificial and varied song':

> And although all [musicians] call this *recitativo*, meaning every melody which is sung by a solo voice, it is, however, very different where one sings in a well formed way almost in the manner of madrigals, and where reigns that simple, current style that one sees in two *lettere amorose* published by Monteverdi with his *Lamento d'Arianna*, and the account of the death of Orpheus [*recte* Eurydice] in *Euridice* [= *Orfeo*]. And if all dramatic actions were made up of this style, there is no doubt that they would delight less than the aforesaid pieces, for although it is a style of singing halfway between reciting and artful singing, not for this do halfway things always please more, for otherwise the otter, which is half fish and half meat, would please more than capon meat or sturgeon fish . . .[56]

In the Seventh Book, the *lettere amorose* are followed by two 'canzonette', 'Chiome d'oro' and 'Amor, che deggio far?'. In terms of the text, they share in the anacreontic lightness broached by Monteverdi chiefly in his encounter with Chiabrera in the 1607 *Scherzi musicali* (these styles are most readily apparent in No. 27). The two canzonettas obviously share a light tone, but also the use of instrumental ritornellos which in its time had been a novelty and which now Monteverdi – as we have seen – was tending to transfer from lesser repertories to the madrigal itself. These pieces have fewer pretensions than the 'arias' (which in the Seventh Book are for good reason based on the distinguished forms of the sonnet and *ottava rima*), but like them they present that variant of strophic structure which has only the bass line remain the same, even in the case of the ritornellos (and in 'Chiome d'oro' the bass line of the ritornellos is the same as that of the vocal sections): thus both the vocal sections and the instrumental ones appear as strophic variations on their own basses, according to a structural procedure that for the moment Monteverdi seemed to prefer over literal strophic repetition.

The Seventh Book concludes with the 'ballo concertato' *Tirsi e Clori* of 1615 which has already been discussed; this crowns the collection of 'altri generi de canti', broadening its purview and setting a seal with choreographic festivity on an anthology of chamber music which had opened with an almost theatrical prologue. It is a worthy conclusion to a volume which had taken as its programme the 'concerting' of multiple genres and various stylistic orientations.

26   1619–1624

The Seventh Book has a dedication (dated Venice, 13 December 1619) to Caterina de' Medici, Duchess of Mantua, who two years earlier had married Ferdinando Gonzaga. One piece in the collection ('Io son pur vezzosetta pastorella') seems to refer to a Florentine lady-in-waiting in Caterina's retinue, since one part of the text reads:

> Di Flora non vi è qui nobil donzella
> o schiera di pomposi cittadini
> che quando in lor m'incontro, faccia inchini,
> il titol non mi dian de la piú bella.

There is here no maiden of Flora [= Florence] / or group of proud citizens / who do not bow to me when I meet them / [and] do not give me the title of fairest of all.

As for Monteverdi, he must have hoped above all that the dedication would encourage the resolution of the old question of his pension: it was precisely to seek help over it that the composer decided to present the book in person to the duchess. As Monteverdi wrote to Striggio on 19 October 1619 (L.34):

> If the printer, as indeed he promised, had handed over to me my little publication, I would already have presented it to the Most Serene Lady (to whom it is dedicated) so as to be able to obtain through her infinite kindness and humanity that favour which was also granted to me by the Most Serene Lady Eleonora – may she be in glory! – that is, her kindness in counting me among the number of her humblest, indeed, but also devoted and faithful servants: a favour which guaranteed me certain help (and genuine, too, through being really deserved for once) from that small endowment or property from which I have been able to draw the income that I greatly need – little though it is – of 100 scudi given to me by the Most Serene Lord Duke Vincenzo of glorious memory.
>
> But the tardiness of that printer has been and is even now the reason why I am not in Mantua, and have not gone. I hope however it will be ready by the 8th or 10th of next month.

Two months later, on 13 December (L.36) – the same day as he signed the dedication – he told Striggio: 'I have in readiness a little publication of mine to present to the Most Serene Lady, and I am waiting for her return for this carnival; for if she were not to return, I would decide to send it rather than bring it, as indeed I shall do if she comes to Mantua.' The idea of presenting the Seventh Book personally to the duchess is confirmed also on 16 January 1620 (L.39), but at the beginning of February Monteverdi wrote to Striggio that he had temporarily postponed the trip to Mantua so that he would not be forced, on his arrival, to rush to complete Marigliani's *Andromeda* (L.40 [41], 1 February 1620):

> I was thinking of travelling to Mantua to present my books – which I have now had printed – dedicated to the Most Serene Lady (to take an advantageous road that may lead me to the goal I so much desired and worked for) so as to be able, once and for all, to get possession of that small donation which the Most Serene Lord Duke Vincenzo, of beloved memory, was kind enough to grant me.
>
> But remembering that Signor Marigliani's play would have fallen entirely on my shoulders . . . I did not want to come at such short notice to sustain this impossible weight . . .

A few days later, Monteverdi gave up the idea for good, and he sent the Seventh Book to Striggio by way of his father-in-law, asking him 'to present, in my name, to the Most Serene Lady, those madrigals dedicated to Her Highness, which I thought of presenting in person had I been able to come to Mantua; but the obvious impediments prevent me from doing so' (L.41 [42], 8 February 1620). For this favour (which is mentioned in L.42 [43] and 44 [45] of 15 and 22 February respectively), Monteverdi reveals his gratitude to Striggio on 13 March 1620 (L.48 [49]). From the duchess, as a sign of her appreciation, he had received a 'beautiful necklace as a gift' (L.53, 4 April 1620), for which he thanks her in a letter of the same date (L.52 [54]).

In fact, Monteverdi also had to abandon the trip to Mantua in an attempt to clear up a somewhat difficult situation that had been created with the procurators of St Mark's. Sante Orlandi, *maestro di cappella* of the Gonzaga court, had died in July 1619: Monteverdi, who had maintained connections with the court since his first years in Venice, was then in Mantua 'staying at the house of ... Signor [Francesco] Campagnolo' (L.48 [49], 13 March 1620). Not surprisingly, he was soon asked to return to the duke's service. This trip had not failed to arouse suspicions in Venice, as Monteverdi related to Striggio on 22 February 1620 (L.44 [45]), declining an invitation to come to Mantua as quickly as possible: 'I would have brought back (as I also did last time) a suspicion of changing masters, since the doge here was given to think that I had gone to Mantua in order to change employment, and I had no small difficulty in removing the aforesaid suspicion.' Offers from Mantua were renewed in November 1619 by way of Francesco Dognazzi, who had gone to Venice and had indiscreetly leaked the reasons for his visit, which further fed rumours of Monteverdi leaving St Mark's. Monteverdi himself recounted the whole affair to Striggio on 8 March 1620 (L.47 [48]), who yet again had made the composer an offer from the duke:

> I implore you however that this proposal, made to me by His Most Serene Highness's infinite goodness, may in no wise (whether the outcome is successful or not) be guessed at by any singer, player, or other of His Most Serene Highness's musicians whatever, for you can be sure that no sooner would they hear about it than they would straightway noise it abroad in Venice, and everything would turn out to my ruin.
>
> And this was one of the main reasons why I did not try in any way to discuss the said business with Signor Don Francesco Dognazzi, when he was here in Venice this past November to do me this outstanding favour on behalf of His Most Serene Highness, which was likewise the matter of offering me employment. But he, through being in the profession, was in consequence capable of getting excited about it, and did not keep it to himself, so that not long after his departure I heard it rumoured that I was returning to Mantua.
>
> And what is more, a month ago, when I let it be known that as soon as Their Highnesses returned from Casale I wanted to bring and present to them those books of mine, the Most Illustrious Primicerius, son of the Most Excellent Lord Procurator, My Lord of the House of Cornaro, said to me:

'This business of your going to Mantua – they say you are going there for good!'

And this, perhaps, was one of the main reasons that kept me from bringing those books in person, because (dear Sir) the substance is bound to be dearer to me than the accident.

Monteverdi's response to Striggio's proposal came a few days later, on 13 March 1620 (L.48 [49]): the composer could not return to Mantuan service on the terms offered, in part because the rewards he gained from St Mark's and from other private sources were greater, but above all because of the certainty of his income, independent of the bureaucracy unlike his experience in Mantua. However, the letter suggests that had the terms been different he might have been able to accept. And in fact the suspicions on his behalf were not quenched, as Monteverdi wrote to Striggio on 17 March 1620 (L.49 [50]): 'whenever I say a word about wanting to come to Mantua, there is not a soul who refrains from putting sinister thoughts into the heads of these Most Excellent Lords, and all to my disadvantage through the suspicions which they put into their minds'. In such circumstances, the dedication of the Seventh Book to Duchess Caterina, in December 1619, certainly represented the most public display on Monteverdi's part of his availability to return to Mantua, but the composer's tactics did not pay off, and he therefore remained in Venice.

Between December 1619 and February 1620, Monteverdi was requested by the Duke of Bracciano, Paolo Giordano Orsini, to negotiate with the Venetian printer Alessandro Vincenti over the publication of a volume dedicated to the duke by the Cremonese musician Francesco Petratti (his *Primo libro d'arie a una et due voci con un dialogo in fine*, printed by Vincenti in 1620).[57] Having taken charge of the matter, Monteverdi told the duke on 25 January 1620 that 'the printer is sending to Signor Cavaliere Fei, by the present messenger, four copies of the finished work', also asking him 'kindly to accept that copy of my little madrigals (now published) which I sent directly to the Signor Cavaliere by the previous post, so that he could present it to Your Excellency in my name': this refers to a copy of the Seventh Book fresh from the press, whose 'low style' and reduced dimensions (pieces primarily for two voices) are once more emphasized by the composer by calling it a collection of 'madrigaletti'.

At more or less the same time, the composer received from Mantua a commission to set to music a new text by Striggio, which seems to be mentioned for the first time in his letter of 19 October 1619 (L.34) – but see p. 155 – and is called an 'egloga' (eclogue); by then 'the greater part (if not all)' was composed and he promised it complete by Christmas. On 13 December 1619 (L.35) Monteverdi confirmed that 'half of it is already composed', and he promised to finish the task 'once the feast of Christmas Eve is over'. In his letter of 9 January 1620, this eclogue is also called a 'ballo': therefore we seem to be dealing with a pastoral *balletto* with sung narrative, on the model of *Tirsi e Clori*. This same letter in fact begins with a reference to two of the characters

involved, Apollo and Amor, and insists on the search for a musical characterization of the affections, especially contrasting ones:

> I am sending Your Most Illustrious Lordship the 'Lament of Apollo'. By the
> next post I shall send you the beginning, up to this point, since it is already
> almost finished; a little revision in passing still remains to be done. At the
> place where Amor begins to sing, I would think it a good idea if Your Most
> Illustrious Lordship were to add three more short verses of like metre and
> similar sentiment, so that the same tune could be repeated (hoping that this
> touch of gladness will not produce a bad effect when it follows – by way of
> contrast – Apollo's previous doleful mood), and so go on to demonstrate
> how music can constantly vary its manner of expression, just as speech itself
> does.

That this eclogue was a *ballo* is confirmed beyond shadow of a doubt in the
letter of 16 January 1620 (L.39), from which we learn Striggio's satisfaction
over the lament for Apollo, probably on the lines of the celebrated *Lamento
d'Arianna*: 'I am sending Your Most Illustrious Lordship the beginning of the
ballo: please to God that this may impress you favourably as did the Lament
already dispatched to you, since in your very kind letter you point out that it
was very welcome.' Monteverdi himself was evidently pleased with it, too: he
had also had it performed before some Venetian gentlemen, who had thought
to use it for a carnival entertainment in the Bembo palace (L.40 [41], 1
February 1620):

> The 'Lament of Apollo' has been heard by certain gentlemen here, and since
> it pleased them in the manner of its invention, poetry, and music they think –
> after an hour of concerted music which usually takes place these days at the
> house of a certain gentleman of the Bembo family, where the most impor-
> tant ladies and gentlemen come to listen – they think (as I said) of having
> afterwards this fine idea of Your Most Illustrious Lordship's put on a small
> stage. If I have to compose the *ballo* for this, would Your Most Illustrious
> Lordship send me the verses as soon as possible? But if not, I shall add
> something of my own invention so that such a fine work of Your Most
> Illustrious Lordship's can be enjoyed.

From this same letter we learn that in Mantua, alongside the staging of the
aforementioned *Andromeda* to a text by Marigliani, it had been decided to
perform Striggio's *ballo*, which Monteverdi was accordingly ordered to finish
as quickly as possible:

> I have received Your Most Illustrious Lordship's very kind letter and
> understood the reason for the delay, and what you wish from me. I reply to
> Your Most Illustrious Lordship that, believing you did not want to do
> anything else, I gave up work for the time being. Now that you tell me you
> are about to have it performed, I assure you that if you do not receive from
> me, by the next post, everything that is outstanding, little will remain in my
> hands to finish.
>   You have only to let me know – once the verses are finished – what more I
> have to do, because if you wanted the *ballo* to be sung as well, let Your Most
> Illustrious Lordship send me the words, for which I shall try (in setting them)

to invent something in the metre that you give me; but should there be one metre in all the verses, I shall certainly change the tempo from time to time.

A week later (L.41 [42], 8 February 1620), the composer sent

> the other remaining pieces of music for Your Most Illustrious Lordship's very fine and beautiful eclogue. The part of the River [Peneius] is still to be done, and this – now that I know Signor Arigoni [Amigoni?] will be singing it – I shall despatch by the next post: and perhaps to my greater satisfaction too, since I shall compose it more to the mark now that I know who is going to sing it.
>
> I further understand that you will be glad, up to this point, to give me an opportunity to serve you further at present since he has finished learning the aria already written.

Sadly, the pre-existing composition ('the aria already written') that they were planning to use cannot be identified. However, Monteverdi sent by the next post (L.42 [43], 15 February 1620)

> the song of Peneius and the three little verses for Apollo which had slipped my mind. This song of Peneius I have composed in such a manner – like a hybrid style [*alla bastarda*] – because I know how effective such a style is when Signor Arigoni sings it. It will also serve to provide a change from the other songs, and the distinction will appear greater if such a deity sings only once. Please to God that it may be to Your Most Illustrious Lordship's liking ... By the next post I will send the little symphonies.

In fact, on 22 February (L.44 [45]), the composer, while complaining that 'I have been burdened with no little toil this carnival time', sent 'the symphony for Amor, and another for the Entry' of the *ballo* proper.

It is significant that in the letter of 15 February (L.42 [43]) Monteverdi, when referring to the part of the third character – the river Peneius (since Peneius was the mythological father of the nymph Daphne, it is likely that the subject of the eclogue concerned the love of Apollo and Daphne) – emphasizes his poetics of contrast, also using the term singing 'alla bastarda'. This term is found in the soprano partbook of Adriano Banchieri's *Virtuoso ridotto* (Milan, Heirs of Simon Tini & Filippo Lomazzo, 1607: 'parte superiore alla bastarda', 'upper part *alla bastarda*'); in Bartolomeo Barbarino's solo-voice setting of Cesare Rinaldi's sonnet 'Sciogli, ardito nocchier, vela d'argento' included in his *Terzo libro de madrigali* (Venice, Ricciardo Amadino, 1610: 'basso alla bastarda'); and finally in the *ottava rima* again for solo bass, 'Pasciti pur del core e de' suoi danni', in Giulio Santo Pietro del Negro's *Grazie ed affetti di musica moderna* (Milan, Filippo Lomazzo, 1613: 'basso alla bastarda sopra l'aria di Ruggiero di Napoli', 'bass *alla bastarda* on the *Aria di Ruggiero* of Naples'). Then some years later (and in the field of instrumental music), Carlo Milanuzzi's *Armonia sacra* (Venice, Alessandro Vincenti, 1622) included a 'Canzon a 2 alla bastarda per il trombone e violino' ('Canzona *a2 alla bastarda* for the trombone and violin'), called *La Guaralda*, by one P. A. Mariani. Barbarino's setting is nothing more than a normal madrigal rich with *passaggi* – like del

Negro's piece (four variations on the same bass) its range only exceptionally covers or exceeds two octaves – and there is nothing particularly distinctive about Banchieri's composition. Therefore one is led to assume that the term 'alla bastarda' is a manner of singing characterized by something to do with performance (for example, the use of the falsetto voice)[58] and not so much a distinctive compositional style.

The successful outcome of the performance of the eclogue is clear from the satisfaction revealed by Monteverdi to Striggio on 8 March 1620 (L.47 [48]): 'I have heard about the success that my feeble music has won – helped, protected, and raised up as it was by the great and infinite merit of Your Most Illustrious Lordship's most beautiful words, no less admired and honoured by those illustrious gentlemen for what is now affirmed by me (and I say this with a true and sincere heart).'

In March 1620, Monteverdi reveals how Striggio asked him by way of Antonio Calligari (called 'Il Bergamaschino') 'in the name of His Most Serene Highness to have *Arianna* recopied as soon as possible, and then send it without delay to Your Most Illustrious Lordship. I straightway gave it out to a copyist, so I hope that within a week or ten days Your Most Illustrious Lordship will have it without fail' (L.49 [50], 17 March 1620). In the rest of this letter, the composer says that for the moment he is unable to come to Mantua: in fact, the court was thinking of a repeat performance of the famous *Arianna* to be done in May 1620 for the duchess's birthday celebrations, and Monteverdi was summoned to take personal charge of the musical preparations, as is clear from his letter of 21 March (L.50 [51]):

> In order to show you that as soon as I received Your Most Illustrious Lordship's command (in the name of His Most Serene Highness) I did not fail to act upon it, here I am already sending you four quires, recopied. I could have sent five of them, but I wanted to keep the last one by me so as to improve on it. This quire, along with the others, I shall send off to Your Most Illustrious Lordship by the next post. I would even have held on to the ones enclosed, had I not persuaded myself that every bit of time gained is to the good, inasmuch as a month (or a little more) for rehearsal is by no means too long. In the meantime, however, this opening section can be learnt.
>
> I am also sending the first part of the 'Lament', which I had already copied at home on a different sheet of paper, so you will also gain time with this item, being as it is the most essential part of the work. Signor Bergamaschino, bearer of this letter, will be able to certify to Your Most Illustrious Lordship how busy I am at the moment; and at the same time he will also render the service of begging Your Most Illustrious Lordship on my behalf to secure for me an extension of time until Low Sunday is past, for then I shall be able to come over to Mantua and have the pleasure of directing *Arianna* and anything else that might be required.

Monteverdi also told Striggio about the copying and revision of *Arianna* in his letters of 28 March (L.51 [52]) and 4 April 1620 (L.53):

> I am sending Your Most Illustrious Lordship the enclosed quires of *Arianna*. I was thinking of sending you everything, but the man who is copying it for

me lags behind – not indeed because he does not work hard, but because it is turning out to be longer than was believed. I shall however send it to you for sure, all complete, by the next post; nay, even sooner if I had someone to give it to for special delivery, since the music is finished – all that is lacking is part of the words. Had I been warned, or (to put it better) informed, before now, I would have sent it considerably more improved; because I know what I am talking about.

Your Most Illustrious Lordship will do me a favour by making my excuses to His Most Serene Highness should he perhaps in some way not be satisfied with me; but believe me, Your Most Illustrious Lordship, time is the good and the bad element in works such as this.

I am sending off to Your Most Illustrious Lordship the remainder of *Arianna*. If I had had more time, I would have revised it more thoroughly, and even perhaps greatly improved it. I shall not let a day go by without composing something in this theatrical style of song – and all the more willingly if you will make me worthy of it to a greater extent with your beautiful verses . . .

However, doubts already seem to have been cast on the projected performance according to Monteverdi's letter of 18 April 1620 (L.54 [55]), when he told Striggio 'whenever you may be so good as to give me the slightest hint about my helping with *Arianna* or anything else, you will see and know from the results my genuine willingness, and the great desire I have, to show myself no less a very humble servant of His Most Serene Highness than I desire to be an affectionate and grateful servant to Your Most Illustrious Lordship'. About a month later, Monteverdi learnt that neither *Arianna* nor Jacopo Peri's *Adone* (Peri is called by his nickname, Zazzerino) had been staged, and that the court had contented itself with staging only a *balletto* with music by Peri (L.55 [56], 10 May 1620):

It was a good decision that the Most Serene Lord Duke made, in not letting *Arianna* (and also that other composition by Signor Zazzerino) be put on the stage at such short notice, because really and truly haste is far too harmful to such projects, inasmuch as the sense of hearing is too general and too delicate – all the more so in company where the presence of great princes such as himself has to be taken into account. And the Most Serene Lady has shown great prudence by deciding on the *balletto*, for the presence of great subject-matter is enough to provide what is needful for festivals like this, but in others it does not work out in this way.

For then Signor Zazzerino may be given a chance to show that he too is a servant worthy of Her Most Serene Highness's favour. Not only does he possess all the qualities about which you write to me, but the gentle and healthy rivalry will give the others a better chance to do something else in order to gain favour for themselves; for without knowledge of the way one cannot arrive at the place decided upon.

From the letter of 24 July 1620 (L.58 [59]), we learn that *Apollo* (already performed in carnival that year) received a further performance in early summer 1620: 'Your Most Illustrious Lordship adds new information about a new favour; namely that my poor music – which served with great courage, it is true, but little strength, for Your Most Illustrious Lordship's beautiful eclogue – has once more been doubly honoured and praised: by His Most Serene Highness and by Your Most Illustrious Lordship.' Meanwhile, Monteverdi's eldest son, Francesco, had decided to abandon the law studies he was undertaking in Bologna to take orders and enter the order of the Discalced Carmelites. The composer told all this to Striggio on 11 July (L.56 [57]): 'my son Francesco (aged twenty and thinking of becoming a Doctor of Law in a year or just over) unexpectedly decided in Bologna to become a friar of the reformed order of Discalced Carmelite Fathers, wherefore what with the journey (going to Milan) and the friar's habit, he has saddled me with a debt of more than 50 scudi'. It is likely that Francesco – a good singer and doubtless employed as such no less than when he was in Padua (or indeed even earlier, in St Mark's) – took this decision because he wanted to dedicate himself professionally to music, which he could do much more easily as an ecclesiastic than as a doctor of law. Certainly Francesco had had an opportunity to make himself appreciated as a singer in Bologna: witness his recruitment for the important civic ceremonials in S. Petronio in October 1619.[59] As a result of his son's decision, Monteverdi was required to go to Bologna: this must have occurred in June 1620, given that on the 13th of that month, the feast of St Anthony, the composer was present at S. Michele in Bosco for a meeting in his honour held by the Accademia dei Floridi. Years later, Adriano Banchieri was to invoke the 'memorable recollection of St Anthony's Day in the year 1620 when Your Lordship honoured with his presence in a public gathering the Florid Academy of S. Michele in Bosco, accompanied by Signor Don Girolamo Giacobbi and a most virtuous company of Bolognese musicians, where speeches were said and concertos were harmonized in praise and honour of Your Lordship.'[60] In addition to his journey to Bologna, Monteverdi also visited Mantua (L.59 [60] and 60 [61], 22 September and 9 October 1620), where he was in September 1620; on that occasion he also went to Goito, where the duke was, obviously to petition that he might 'be so good as to give me an order that the sums due should be paid to me, since I have in my hand vouchers from my donation' (L.59 [60]).

Monteverdi's printed output in the 1620s is largely devoted to pieces in anthologies of sacred music, three of which appeared in or around 1620. One, edited by Don Lorenzo Calvi (*maestro di cappella* of Pavia Cathedral) and published in Venice by Alessandro Vincenti (1620–21), bears the title *Symbolae diversorum musicorum* ('for two, three, four and five voices' and continuo). It contains two motets by Monteverdi, 'Fuge anima mea mundum' and 'O beatae viae', the first of which (for soprano, alto, violin and continuo) perhaps relates to the feast of St John the Baptist (24 June). Indeed, again in 1620 the Flemish diplomat Constantin Huygens, visiting Venice, was able to be present at Vespers for that feast in S. Giovanni Elemosinario, near the Rialto (Huygens writes 'Saint Jean et Lucie'), where he heard music by Monteverdi directed by the composer himself:

On 24 June, the feast of St John the Baptist, I was taken to vespers in the church of St John and Lucy where I heard the most perfect music I had ever heard in my life. It was directed by the most famous Claudio Monteverdi, *maestro di cappella* of St Mark's, who was also the composer, and was on this occasion accompanied by four theorboes, two cornetts, two bassoons, one *basso di viola* of huge size, organs and other instruments, all equally well handled and played, not to speak of ten or twelve voices. I was delighted with it.[61]

The second motet (for two sopranos and continuo) is an antiphon for the feast of St Rock (16 August). Both represent the sacred, motet-orientated version of the style of writing for two voices and continuo seen in the recent Seventh Book.

The two other printed collections of 1620 both contain motets by the Cremonese Giulio Cesare Bianchi (who was active in Milanese circles after having been a cornett player at the Mantuan court, where he had begun his studies in composition under Monteverdi): the *Libro primo de motetti in lode d'Iddio nostro signore* (Venice, Bartolomeo Magni ['stampa del Gardano'], 1620) and the *Libro secondo de motetti in lode della gloriosissima Vergine Maria nostra signora* (Venice, Alessandro Vincenti, 1620). The title-page of the *Libro primo* announces, as well as Bianchi's motets, 'un altro a cinque, e tre a sei del sig. Claudio Monteverde' ('one other for five, and three for six [voices] by Signor Claudio Monteverde'), respectively 'Christe, adoramus te' and 'Cantate Domino', 'Domine, ne in furore tuo' and 'Adoramus te, Christe', all *a cappella* with a *basso seguente*. On the other hand, Bianchi's *Libro secondo* contains (according to the title-page) 'le letanie a sei voci del sig. Claudio Monteverde' ('the litanies for six voices by Signor Claudio Monteverde'), which were to be reprinted twice, in the *Rosarium litaniarum beatae V. Mariae*, edited by Don Lorenzo Calvi (1626), and in the posthumous collection of Monteverdi's works called *Messa a quattro voci, et salmi*, printed and edited by Alessandro Vincenti (1650).

The two motets by Monteverdi in Calvi's *Symbolae diversorum musicorum* provide concrete musical evidence of the composer's connections with Venetian ecclesiastical institutions outside of St Mark's: 'Fuge, anima mea, mundum' can perhaps be associated with the aforementioned ceremony in S. Giovanni Elemosinario, while 'O beatae viae' was surely commissioned by the Scuola di S. Rocco (with which the composer was to be associated at least in 1623 and 1627). Monteverdi's letters often speak of such connections with the institutions and churches of the city, as for example the letter to Striggio of 13 March 1620 (L.48 [49]), which mentions his earnings

outside St Mark's of about 200 ducats a year (invited as I am again and again by the wardens of the guilds) because whoever can engage the director to look after their music – not to mention the payment of thirty ducats, and even forty, and up to fifty for two vespers and a mass – does not fail to take him on, and they also thank him afterwards with well-chosen words.

Indeed, a few days later, on 17 March (L.49 [50]), Monteverdi told Striggio that he was almost permanently employed to provide sacred (but not liturgical) music for the private oratory of Marc'Antonio Cornaro, primicerius in St Mark's, 'for whom – every Wednesday, Friday, and Sunday – I make music in a certain oratory of his, to which half the nobility come'.

For 4 November 1620, the feast of St Carlo Borromeo, Monteverdi was employed by the Milanese community resident in Venice (which had its own chapel in the Basilica dei Frari) to take charge of the music. It was for this that the composer had asked the Mantuan court in October to be able to make use of Francesco Dognazzi, who had succeeded to the post of court *maestro di cappella* (L.61 [62], 21 October 1620):

> The Milanese gentlemen very much want to engage Signor Don Francesco Dognazzi, the better to celebrate their Feast of San Carlo which will take place on the 4th of next month, but I want him more than they do because they have asked me to be in charge; and so, desiring to do ample justice to this, over and above the request of these gentlemen I add mine most affectionately, begging Your Lordship (should the opportunity arise in His Most Serene Highness's presence for an earnest request of that sort to allow him to come) to try and oblige me also – if I can be even more grateful for the infinite favours received from Your Most Illustrious Lordship – in this matter of smoothing the way so that this Signor Don Francesco can come to Venice for a week, not more, and lodge in my house.

Dognazzi's negative response arrived a short while after: it was impossible for him 'to get leave because of his responsibility for personally supervising His Most Serene Highness's music; and since he has to perform music on All Saints' Day and All Souls' Day it was (I repeat) impossible for him to leave such duty' (L.62 [63], 31 October 1620).

Some months later, it was the turn of the Florentine community in Venice to commission from Monteverdi a mass for the service in memory of the deceased Grand Duke Cosimo II de' Medici: on 17 April 1621, the composer told Ercole Marigliani (L.65 [66]) of 'the pressure I am now under because of the Requiem Mass for the Most Serene Grand Duke, which has to take place soon for the colony of Florentine gentlemen in Venice, who are preparing worthy and well-thought-out ceremonies'. The service was held on 25 May 1621 in the church of SS. Giovanni e Paolo; its official chronicler was Giulio Strozzi, who was to have an important working relationship with Monteverdi (with whom he began his noteworthy activity as a librettist). While Monteverdi's son, Francesco, appeared with success as a singer, Monteverdi directed the music, part of which (the introit ['O vos omnes' plus perhaps the 'Requiem aeternam'], 'Dies irae', 'De profundis' and the five responds ['Subvenite, sancti Dei', 'Qui Lazarum', 'Domine, quando veneris', 'Ne recorderis', 'Libera me, Domine']) was composed by him, while the rest was written by Giovan Battista Grillo and Francesco Usper, both organists in St Mark's (first and temporary second organist respectively). The description of the event by Strozzi (who underlined the expressiveness of the Monteverdi style, capable of reviving the mythical power of Greek music) was printed in Venice by Giovan Battista Ciotti in 1621 with the title *Esequie fatte in Venetia dalla natione fiorentina al serenissimo d. Cosimo II quarto gran duca di Toscana il dí 25 di maggio 1621* ('Obsequies celebrated in Venice by the Florentine nation for the Most Serene Don Cosimo II, Grand Duke of Tuscany, on 25 May 1621'). Strozzi wrote of Monteverdi's music (pp. 19–20):

> The music of the Mass and of the Responds was newly either concerted or composed by Signor Claudio Monteverde, *maestro di cappella* of St Mark's, and from the glorious name of the composer one can excellently comprehend the quality of the work, since he committed himself with particular conviction to these compositions because of the devotion which seized him to honour with his virtue our most serene patrons.
>
> First, the grieving solemnities were begun with a most plaintive *sinfonia* apt to draw forth tears, nay excite grief, imitating the ancient Mixolydian mode formerly rediscovered by Sappho. At the end of the *sinfonia*, Signor Don Francesco Monteverde, son of Signor Claudio, intoned these lamenting words most sweetly: 'O vos omnes attendite, et videte dolorem nostrum [. . .] et lucem perpetuam luceat ei', with the remainder of the Introit. These words, often interspersed with the aforementioned *sinfonia*, were heard with great delight and attention.
>
> Once the Introit had been sung with singular sadness, we came to the Kyrie [by Grillo; the Gradual and Tract were by Usper]. The *Dies irae*, the work of the aforesaid Signor Claudio, and a most suave *De profundis* at the Elevation of the Host, by the same, sung as a dialogue as if by souls standing in the torments of Purgatory and visited by angels, produced admiration for the novelty and excellence of the art. [The 'Domine Jesu' and the Post Communion verse were by Grillo.] In sum, so for the rest of the mass as for the five Responds by Signor Monteverde, which followed, it was the judgement of all that Signor Claudio and the other composers of this sacred task had not shown themselves any different from those many others who go about with such glory through the hands of men, and in truth, that the music corresponded to the rest of the setting [apparato], as the world will be able to see from the printed version of it that will be published.

However, it is not known if the announced publication appeared: there is no trace of it now.

Meanwhile, Monteverdi maintained close ties with Mantua, for which he often provided compositions to be used for the usual requirements of court life. At the beginning of 1621, he had sent a work which could serve as a *mascherata* for carnival time, as we gather from the letter to Striggio of 26 February 1621 (L.63 [64]): 'I have taken note of what Your Most Illustrious Lordship asked me to do in this matter; that much I shall do. Your Most Illustrious Lordship knows that I wrote the piece for carnival time so that you could, at your pleasure, have the whole thing in masks; for I intended nothing other than what arose from Your Most Illustrious Lordship's considerable prudence and will.' This unspecified 'matter' must have been very important, if on 5 March 1621 (L.64 [65]) Monteverdi felt it necessary to write to the duchess in the following terms:

> I received Your Most Serene Highness's command with such solace that I admit to not having words capable of expressing the happiness within me, being the recipient of so remarkable a favour. I come in all humility to offer Your Most Serene Highness the greatest thanks I can utter, praying God that He make me as worthy of the undertaking in Your Most Serene Highness's estimation, as He has made me worthy of the command.
>
> I shall be sending the music to Signor Marigliani, Your Most Serene Highness's most worthy secretary, from whom also I shall continue to hear what Your Most Serene Highness will command.

Thus the texts for this work were to be provided by Ercole Marigliani, with whom Monteverdi had also worked some years before on the complex affair of *Andromeda*. Given this important task – on which the composer maintained his reserve – Monteverdi was dispensed from having to provide music for carnival, as he himself told Marigliani on 17 April 1621 (L.65 [66]):

> I had a communication from Your Very Illustrious Lordship to the effect that it would be sufficient if I worked only on certain scenic arias, since with regard to certain others (which ought to have a definite order and duration for as long as the machines are operating) you have been pleased to give this task to those gentlemen composers who are on hand; besides which you also told me that you felt that I could have until September of this year.
>
> Because of this I sent nothing by the last post, nor indeed (on account of there being such pressure on my time) am I sending anything at the moment, as I am holding over the special tasks until twenty or more days from now ...

Thus the 'matter' starts to become clearer. It was a question of 'certain scenic arias' – 'canti rappresentativi' – which, on 10 September 1621 (L.67 [68]) and again to Marigliani, Monteverdi clarified as *intermedi*: 'By the present post I am sending off to you part of the third musical *intermedio*. The remainder (if it please God) I hope to send you by the next post.' At the end of November, the work was finished and the composer informed the duchess accordingly (L.68 [69], 27 November 1621): 'By the previous post I sent off to Signor Marigliani the musical *licenza* for the *intermedi* which Your Most Serene Highness was good enough to commission from me.' In the same letter, Monteverdi offered to take charge personally of the performance at the appropriate time, and he said that he also had available 'a solemn Mass set to music':

> However I come with this letter of mine to Your Most Serene Highness's feet, to thank you from the bottom of my heart for the honour received from this Your Most Serene Highness's commission, offering myself to you as a most humble servant were it to happen that these *intermedi* might be performed for you, both in the matter of scoring for the instruments in symphonies and in the various vocal dispositions.
>
> Nor should I neglect to offer at the same time to Your Most Serene Highness's infinite humanity a solemn Mass set to music, if perhaps it might please you to accept it.

The special occasion for which such solemn festivities were being put in train must surely have been the proposed marriage of Eleonora Gonzaga, sister of Duke Ferdinando, and the Habsburg Emperor Ferdinand II.[62] With the negotiations successfully completed, in January 1622 a sumptuous welcome for the Emperor was organized as he entered Mantua to meet his bride. The climax of the many entertainments was the performance of *Le tre costanti*, a comedy by Ercole Marigliani (printed in Mantua by Aurelio & Lodovico Osanna, 1622) with grand *intermedi* to texts also by Marigliani and machines designed by Antonio Maria Viani (prefect of the ducal buildings): it was surely these *intermedi* that Monteverdi had composed by the November of the preceding year. In the absence of the music, there remains the description by Gabriele Bertazzolo (*Breve relatione dello sposalitio fatto della serenissima principessa Eleonora Gonzaga con la sacra cesarea maestà di Ferdinando II imperatore*, Mantua, Aurelio & Lodovico Osanna, 1622), who, as well as being involved in the preparations for the event, was also its official chronicler:

> That same Tuesday [18 January] the order was given to perform the most noble comedy titled *Le constanti*, for in it were seen signs of most noble constancy on the part of three women before their beloveds. The *intermedi* concerned the contests of the two loves, one heavenly and the other earthly, representing Reason and Feeling, which, together with the comedy, were written by Signor Ercole Marigliani, most worthy secretary to His Highness, and they were staged at the hands of Signor Antonio Maria Vianini, prefect of the ducal buildings and most singular in this profession. For their account, we will give only the plot of each one, with a description of the stage and of the machines, leaving out for the sake of brevity the texts, especially given that they will soon be published by the same author . . .
>
> The threefold trumpet call for beginning having been given, and all having fallen into a most pleasant silence, one saw the great curtain which hid the stage disappear like a lightning bolt, and with universal admiration the superb scenery of the stage was displayed before the eyes of the spectators. This scene was set to play the prologue, the subject of which was to demonstrate whence derives honest love, Jove and heavenly Venus being its progenitors. As the father of Cupid, representing lascivious love, was represented Erebus, and as mother, Night. All the above-named deities were seen little by little as the occasion required, some placed in very resplendent clouds, and others situated in dark grottoes.
>
> One saw the violence done by Cupid because Love did not descend to earth, and on the contrary, the force with which the latter resisted to prevent him ascending to heaven. Cupid boasted of making insuperable displays of his strength to shame Love, and with Love promising that nothing could turn out well without his help, the prologue ended, leaving everyone curious to see what was to follow.
>
> At the end of Act I of the comedy, the scene changed to most delightful gardens, with fountains and pergolas admirable to see. Cupid, to prove the power of his torch, wanted to show that Alcides, representing heroic virtue, would have been so powerfully in love with Omphale, representing lascivious emotion, that he would have forgotten his virtues. Love, to show Cupid wrong, sent Mars from heaven, representing Intellect, who made Alcides realize the errors into which he had fallen over Omphale, and having mounted a cloud rising from the earth, he took him to heaven, leaving Cupid scorned, and Omphale abandoned; and thus finished the first *intermedio*.
>
> After the end of Act II of the comedy, the scene changed entirely into the

sea and rough mountains. There one saw ships sailing, whales, orcs, dolphins and other fish. Cupid arose from the waves, signifying the instability of earthly things, accompanied by four Sirens. The love of Neptune for Amphitrite was represented, but because it was not directed to an honest end, heavenly Love, with the help of Aeolus, made the sea moved by the winds in such a way that the gods of the waves found themselves greatly troubled. Neptune, having turned back with prayers to Juno that she might chase the winds from the air and calm the sea, received her favour. It was made clear to him, however, that this had occurred because he was besieging the soul of Amphitrite with an unworthy flame. Neptune agreeing to this, he returned Amphitrite, tritons rose from the waves, and the other celebrating gods accompanied them with joy, and the *intermedio* ended.

The third *intermedio* was staged among rocky mountains, from which there seemed to appear thick clouds. In their middle was imitated with so artful a manner a torrent, which left the onlookers doubting whether it was feigned or no. The story which served for this *intermedio* was the love of Boreas for Oreithyia. But because he raped her through the wiles of Cupid, he could not reach his end until an honest betrothal between them was fixed by Hymen on the order of heavenly Love. One saw in this *intermedio* a dance of flying winds, during which it snowed endlessly. And once the winds had left, Apollo calmed the air, who on a chariot drawn by four steeds brought a most beautiful splendour; and thus the *intermedio* ended.

The fourth *intermedio* was marvellous, with its representation of the loves of Pluto and Proserpina, for the scene was half the middle of a horrid inferno, and the other half represented the Elysian fields. Proud Cupid, accompanied by his brothers, vaunted his ability to brighten the inferno with his torch; but heavenly Love, so as not to leave him enjoying his glories, sent Mercury to free Proserpina. This was done while a darkest night descended, which had no other light than that of the stars and the moon. This disappearing, one saw a most beautiful dawn arise, and meanwhile Proserpina, guided by Mercury, trod the path that led her from these horrors. And to the song of various birds and of Aurora, the fourth *intermedio* ended happily.

The *licenza* after the last act of the comedy represented a triumph of Cupid accompanied by a multitude of lovers, who made a most beautiful dance. Meanwhile, the triumphal Love appeared from heaven accompanied by the Graces, Mars, Apollo, Mercury and Venus, all in their machines in due proportion and in their separate places. Love called on Jove to revenge the outrage and arrogance of Cupid, whence he, appearing in majesty in a large heaven, with a large following of gods and carried forward by a large eagle, cast a lightning bolt at Cupid, who suddenly disappeared beneath the stage, and with Jove, the Graces and all the other deities singing the praises of heavenly Love, Cupid's followers repeated the same praise, and the *licenza* ended.

At a further signal from the trumpets, there descended from heaven a large coat of arms of the most august house of Austria, surrounded by four eagles, the sign of the most serene house of Gonzaga, and by six orbs entwined with them, representing the arms of the most serene house of Tuscany. There also arose from the earth a large tablet, on which was a motto 'Aeterno stabunt tempore' ['They will stand for eternal time'], and the entertainment was ended, leaving all most comforted by the admirable spectacle.

More or less contemporary with the composition of the *intermedi* for Mantua, Monteverdi took advantage of the occasion to ask the duchess for a recommendation to have his other son, Massimiliano, admitted to Cardinal Montalto's college in Bologna, where according to his father's plans, he was to study medicine (L.66 [67], 7 August 1621):

> Most Serene Lady, I have a son aged sixteen-and-a-half years – a subject and most humble servant of Your Most Serene Highness – who has now left the seminary at Bologna, having completed there the course in humanist studies and rhetoric. I would like him to go on to the other sciences in order to obtain a Doctorate in Medicine. He has always been under the discipline of tutors who have kept him in the fear of God and on the right lines of study.
>
> Considering his liveliness and the licentious freedom of students (because of which fact they fall oftentimes into bad company, which diverts them from the rightful path, causing great sorrow to their fathers and tremendous loss to themselves), and in order to ward off the great harm that could come about, I thought that a place in the college of the Most Illustrious Lord Cardinal Montalto – which he has in Bologna – would be a real boon to me, and the salvation of my son; but without a royal hand to aid me in so great a need it would not be possible for me to obtain such an outstanding favour.

The duchess's intercession had its effect, and on 10 September 1621 (L.67 [68]) Monteverdi could announce to Marigliani: 'I heard from Bologna that Cardinal Montalto has already received Her Most Serene Highness's request with especial pleasure, and I am told that they regard it as certain that I shall be granted this favour. The reply, it is thought, will be received either by this post, or by the next, without fail.' In the end, on 26 February 1622 (L.69 [70]) Monteverdi thanked the duchess directly: 'I have finally received ... the certificate allowing Massimiliano, my son and Your Most Serene Highness's most humble subject, to enter the college of the Most Illustrious Lord Cardinal Montalto in Bologna.' Perhaps as a sign of gratitude for her involvement, in spring 1622 Monteverdi sent her a small exotic gift (L.70 [71], 15 April 1622): 'The Reverend Father Friar Cesare (my brother-in-law) having given me – on his return from Alexandria in Egypt – a small young monkey which has been praised by gentlemen for the unusual appearance of its fur, I have therefore been encouraged to come to Your Most Serene Highness's feet with all reverent affection, begging you that you may deign to be so kind as to accept it.'

Monteverdi contributed the motet 'O bone Jesu, o piissime Jesu', for two sopranos and continuo, to the *Promptuarii musici ... pars prima*, printed in 1622 in Strasbourg by Paul Ledertz; here Johannes Donfried, rector of the Latin School of Rottenburg, had collected motets by various composers for two, three and four voices. As for secular music, and to emphasize Monteverdi's success also in that sphere, the years 1620–22 saw the reprinting (by Bartolomeo Magni in Venice) of all his books of madrigals, including the earliest ones which had not been published for over a decade: the Fifth and Sixth books appeared in 1620, the First, Second and Third in 1621, and finally the Fourth and Seventh in 1622.

From this period also dates the composer's inclusion in the survey of illustrious artists given by Alvira, a character in Guidubaldo Benamati's poem *La vittoria navale* (Bologna, Giacomo Monti, 1646), canto XII, stanza 95:

> De l'armonia venìano i mastri, e d'essi
> con profuso parlar contogli i merti.
> Di Claudio fè, tra questi, i pregi espressi,
> che spiega in Monte Verde i suoi concerti.
> Ad Alessandro Grandi ancor concessi
> fur grandi onor, tra i piú ne l'arte esperti:
> e Sigismondo D'India entro le sue
> lodi piú belle indi raccolto fue.[63]

> The masters of harmony came, and of them / with lengthy speech she [Alvira] expounded the merits. / Among these, she made express praise of Claudio, / who spreads his *concerti* on a Green Mountain. / To Alessandro Grandi were also granted / great honours, as being among the most expert in the art: / and Sigismondo d'India was also / accepted within her finest praises.

Moreover, in the dedication of his *Canora sampogna* (Venice, Bartolomeo Magni, 1623), Pellegrino Possenti noted the 'so beautiful compositions of such distinguished men, and in particular those of Signor Monte Verde, which, since he through his height has reached heaven and has learnt harmonious song from the angels, fill the world with heavenly harmony'.

Because of his association with the Gonzagas, Monteverdi was required more than once to act as an agent between Venice and Mantua as regards engaging musicians, and also actors. In Autumn 1622, Lorenzo Giustiniani – currently in negotiation with Giovan Battista Andreini (called 'Lelio'), who was then in Mantua – asked the composer to act to secure that the celebrated actor and his company (which included La Florinda, i.e. Virginia Andreini, who had been the first Arianna) might come to perform in Venice in the public theatre owned by the Giustiniani family (perhaps the Teatro S. Moisè, where the Andreini in fact were in 1623):[64]

> Three days ago the Most Illustrious Signor Giustiniani, a gentleman of great authority in this Most Serene Republic and a very good patron of mine, paid a special visit to my house in company with many other very distinguished gentlemen, to tell me how only a few days previously he arranged for an invitation to be written to Signor Lelio Andreini the actor, so that he might make himself available – together with Signora Florinda and all his company – to come to Venice and produce plays for the general public; provided however that the most serene [duke] was not opposed to it, for in such a case he would in no wise wish to negotiate.
>
> He received a reply to the effect that Andreini was as ready as could be; all the more so because the Lord Duke had already let it be known that he would not be against it. The only thing lacking was for Arlecchino to say yes, for without this – to avoid loss of reputation through having to act in the place where Fritellino was also acting (even though in another hall) – he

could not agree to come. So, this most illustrious gentleman had a letter sent to the said Arlecchino, and received a reply saying that if His Most Serene Highness were not making use of him, and would grant him official leave also, he would come on the understanding that a certain Doctor Gratiano, who is now in Savoy, were to come.

But while this gentleman is trying by negotiation to set everything straight, lo and behold Signor Lelio writes him a letter, saying that as far as he is concerned personally he stands in complete readiness to be of service, and that he offers himself as a most humble servant, but nevertheless makes it known to his Most Illustrious Lordship that Signora Florinda does not wish to act, and that she has put it into his head to perform as a buffoon on his own (even in other companies) for two years, and no longer as head of a company, in view of the fact that so many unpleasant things happen and there are so many problems in trying to run a company.

This most illustrious gentleman, having gathered from the letter that the negotiation had almost collapsed, and knowing how very humble a servant I am of His Most Serene Highness and of Your Most Illustrious Lordship, begged me (as also did those other gentlemen who were with him) that I try with a letter of mine – still assuming His Most Serene Highness is not against it – to ask Your Most Illustrious Lordship most urgently to persuade this Signor Lelio to oblige the gentleman, and if Signor Lelio should insist on making excuses because of the shortage of actors in his company, this gentleman offers him Gratiano and Zanni and Doctor, and any other part that might be lacking.

I am therefore writing to beg Your Most Illustrious Lordship, or rather (to put it better) I am writing to entreat Your Most Illustrious Lordship's infinite kindness to honour me by asking Your Most Illustrious Lordship to try and be so kind as to perform this service of requesting the said Signor Lelio to place himself at the disposal of this most illustrious gentleman, for he will show himself full of kindness towards Signor Lelio's person, both with gifts and with payment of travel costs and so on; and also to bring Signora Florinda, and others of whom he approves.

But if he does not want to, would you ask Signor Lelio to consider that as a result of the expectations already raised by his letters, Signor Giustiniani will not only be hindered in his search for another company, but his theatre will be prevented (because of Lelio) from giving performances – a disappointment which he can well imagine.

Your Most Illustrious Lordship's authority will, I know, be such as can take care of everything perfectly . . .[65]

In the reverse direction, Monteverdi served Duke Ferdinando, seeking out singers and instrumentalists in Venice to be recruited to Mantua:

His Most Serene Lordship the Duke, my particular lord, has kindly informed me verbally – through Signor Bergamaschino who has now returned from Mantua to Venice – that he would like me to be in Mantua by the next courier and to bring with me two sopranos and two chitarrone players . . . As for the sopranos, believe me, Your Most Illustrious Lordship, there is nobody suitable, nor is there anyone who can play continuo on the chitarrone other than moderately well, therefore in my opinion it would not be worth the expense of getting ordinary players from here. But there are certainly good wind instrumentalists, and if Your Most Illustrious Lordship will let me know about these, I would hope to send you someone reasonably good.

Regarding the need for rank and file chitarrone players, I believe His Most Serene Highness would find satisfactory ones at Verona, and much less expensive.[66]

In the handling of these near permanent personal contacts between a dependent individual, as Monteverdi was, and a foreign court, it is worth noting the diplomatic caution and correctness then shown by the composer. Thus in summer 1627, concerning the eventual recruitment of a Bolognese 'light bass' who had arrived in Venice (L.96 [97], 97 [98], 99 [100] and 100 [101]), he asked whether the imperial resident Nicolò Rossi could handle the matter 'for then these singers [of St Mark's] could not say that I was turning other singers away' (L.97 [98]). And on the contrary, the official invitation to the Duke of Mantua's organist, Ottavio Bargnani, to have an audition in Venice made by Monteverdi at the request of the procurators (St Mark's had recently lost Giovan Battista Grillo) was accompanied, and indeed preceded, by a private letter to his friend Striggio (L.75 [76], 31 December 1622) so that he might show the duke that this was not done on his own initiative: his reticence in this matter was to be a source of some friction between the composer and Bargnani.

Towards the end of April 1623, Ferdinando Gonzaga was in Venice 'to fulfil a vow and to visit the body of St Lucy, whose intercession he believed had brought about the recovery of sight in one eye which he had totally lost'.[67] At the beginning of May, Valerio Crova, the Mantuan resident in Venice, informed a ducal secretary that Ferdinando was 'most cheerful and in the best of health, having decided to wait for the Most Serene Madame, then Ascension, for which these gentlemen are preparing most beautiful celebrations'.[68] In fact, an anonymous Venetian chronicle reports for the date 27 May 1623: 'Thursday, Ascension Day, the Most Serene Duchess of Mantua was on the galley Gradeniga to see the ceremony of the wedding to the sea, and after lunch she went to Murano, and on her late return she stopped in that canal to hear some musical *concerti*, with very sweet playing and singing also by her ladies-in-waiting.'[69] And on 3 June: 'This day after lunch a most beautiful ball was held for Their Highnesses in the Palazzo Cà Foscari with the participation of over 100 of these gentlewomen dressed sumptuously and adorned with richest pearls, who at the end were given a splendid feast of sweetmeats.'[70] In all probability, Monteverdi met (and perhaps served) the duke on this occasion, given that the latter turned to the composer to have Adriana Basile and Muzio Baroni – who had formed part of his retinue in Venice and had obtained a triumphal welcome – return to Mantua as soon as possible: 'Your Most Serene Highness's letter having been shown to Signor Donati, he at once – without demur – offered to obey your commands, and so he is coming together with Signora Adriana and Signor Mutio, who is bringing him without his having to spend any money' (L.79 [80], 4 June 1623).[71]

1623 was also the year in which Francesco Monteverdi entered (in July) the *cappella* of St Mark's as a tenor (his appointment was reconfirmed in January

1630);[72] as for publishing, this year saw the Seventh Book reprinted, and the appearance of a spiritual contrafactum of 'Vaga su spina ascosa', given the text 'Ave regina mundi' by Fr. Pietro Lappi (*maestro di cappella* of S. Maria delle Grazie in Brescia and in 1616 the composer of an instrumental *canzona* dedicated to Monteverdi) and included in his *Concerti sacri*. Most important, there appeared in 1623 the first edition of the *Lamento d'Arianna* for soprano and continuo, combined with the 'due lettere amorose in genere rappresentativo' (according to the title-page) of the Seventh Book to produce a collection of monodies of the kind that was ever more in demand according to contemporary taste (all these publications were published in Venice by Bartolomeo Magni at the 'stampa del Gardano'); for example, in the same year, Alessandro Vincenti printed the *Musiche del cavalier Sigismondo D'India a una et due voci da cantarsi nel chitarrone, clavicembalo, arpa doppia et altri stromenti da corpo … libro quinto*, containing, among other songs, the laments of Dido, Jason and Olimpia.

In the winter of 1622–23, Monteverdi, whose health was never very stable, suffered from physical ailments which dragged on for some months, as he himself told Striggio on 10 February 1623 (L.77 [78]):

> I am writing this letter to beg you to try and be so kind as to let His Most Serene Highness know that really I am so badly affected by an illness which (as a result of a purge I gave myself at the beginning of October last year) has made its way down from my head to my shoulders and the whole of my waist, that it is necessary for me to have myself dressed, for I am hardly able to help myself because of the pain in my hands, arms and feet.
>
> It is true that there seems to be some indication of the beginnings of a recovery, but I am nevertheless more on the bad side than the good, apart from which I have experienced for about the past three days a weakening of the body which does not allow me any repose.

On 11 March (L.78 [79]), Monteverdi again told Striggio: 'actually I am still rather ill – much more so just recently – yet at present (thank God) I feel better and hope for further improvement at the first purge'. The illness also hindered his fulfilling a commission from the Duke of Modena, Cesare d'Este, who in the last months of 1622 and the beginning of 1623 had begun to obtain music from Venice, whether printed or in manuscript, with a particular focus on Monteverdi's works. Indeed, to that end he had requested two madrigals from the composer, which were sent to him one in March 1623 and the other in July 1624. It is as yet impossible to identify these pieces; the same should be said for the two later madrigals commissioned from the composer in 1624 (we cannot even be sure that they were actually composed).

At one point in his correspondence with the Este court, Monteverdi offered his 'canzonette a tre voci', examples of which have survived in the posthumous collection of 1651 (*Madrigali e canzonette a due e tre voci*) and also in a manuscript actually in Modena (Biblioteca Estense, α.κ.6.31). This manuscript bears the title *Libro di villanelle*, and on fols. 16v-17r it has 'Ahi che si parte il mio bel sol'adorno', for three voices (two sopranos, tenor and continuo) in four stanzas, which appears besides pieces by Vincenzo Pellegrini, Quagliati, Pace and Giovanelli. On the flyleaf, we find the note 'Hic liber est Monaldi Brancaleonis et suorum amicorum' ('This book belongs to Monaldo Brancaleone and his friends'). Given that this is the only source to transmit this piece, one can suggest that Monaldo Brancaleone's anthology had collected at least one of these canzonettas by Monteverdi.[73]

27 The *Combattimento di Tancredi et Clorinda* (1624)

While Monteverdi was establishing professional contacts with a new Italian court, he continued to cultivate his usual connections with Venetian circles outside St Mark's. On 15–16 August 1623 he was working in the Scuola di S. Rocco for their patronal feast,[74] and in carnival 1624 one of his compositions 'in genere rappresentativo' (perhaps preceded by others 'senza gesto', 'without action'), with the title *Combattimento di Tancredi et Clorinda*, was performed at the Palazzo Mocenigo 'as a carnival pastime', just as four years earlier the eclogue *Apollo* had perhaps been given in Bembo's palace. The *Combattimento* was later printed in Monteverdi's Eighth Book of madrigals (1638) – included among the 'opuscoli in genere rappresentativo che saranno per brevi episodii fra i canti senza gesto' ('little works in the representative genre that will serve as brief episodes among the songs without action'), so the title-page says – preceded by instructions that reflect the 1624 première:

> *Combatimento di Tancredi et Clorinda* in music, as described by Tasso, in which, since it is intended to be done in the representative genre, one will have enter unexpectedly (after some madrigals without action have been sung) from the side of the room in which the music is performed, Clorinda armed and on foot, followed by Tancredi armed on a Marian horse [*cavallo Mariano*], and the Testo [Narrator] will then begin the singing. They will perform steps and gestures in the way expressed by the oration, and nothing more or less, observing diligently those measures, blows and steps, and the instrumentalists sounds excited or soft, and the Testo delivering the words in measure, in such a way that they create a unified imitation. Clorinda will speak when appropriate, the Testo silent; and similarly Tancredi. The instruments – that is, four *viole da braccio*, soprano, alto, tenor and bass, and a *contrabasso da gamba* which continues with the harpsichord – should be played in imitation of passions of the oration. The voice of the Testo should be clear, firm and with good delivery, somewhat distanced from the instruments, so that the oration may be better understood. He should not make *gorghe* or *trilli* anywhere other than in the song of the stanza which begins 'Notte'. For the rest, he will deliver the words according to the passions of the oration.
>
> In this manner ... it was performed in the palace of the most illustrious and most excellent Signor Girolamo Mozzenigo [Mocenigo], my particular lord, with all refinement, given that he is a knight of excellent and delicate taste, and in carnival time as an evening pastime [*passatempo di veglia*], in the presence of all the nobility, which remained moved by the emotion of

compassion in such a way as almost to let forth tears; and [the audience] applauded it for being a song of a kind no longer seen nor heard.[75]

So the plot and the work's literary foundations were provided by Tasso's *Gerusalemme liberata*, 'with more than moderate licence, as in the change made in the first two lines and the frequent, deliberate contamination of the version of the *Liberata* (canto XI [*ottave* 52–62 and 64–68]) with that of the *Conquistata* [*Tasso's Gerusalemme conquistata*] (canto XV)'.[76] Around that time, other composers had also shown an interest in characters of Tasso's great epic poem: in his *Musiche . . . Libro quarto* (Venice, Alessandro Vincenti, 1621) Sigismondo d'India had already set for solo voice the episode concerning the death of Clorinda (XII.66–68), and Biagio Marini had availed himself of various paraphrases of Tasso by Guido Casone for his *Le lagrime d'Erminia* (Parma, Anteo Viotti, 1623) 'in stile recitativo'. A few years later, Francesco Eredi from Ravenna set for five voices (but with frequent sections for solo voice) *L'Armida del Tasso* (Venice, Alessandro Vincenti, 1629), i.e. *Gerusalemme liberata*, XVI.56–66 and XX.123–24.

In the preface to his Eighth Book, Monteverdi was himself to explain the reasons behind his choice of text: 'I took the divine Tasso, as a poet who expresses with the greatest propriety and naturalness the qualities which he wishes to describe, and selected his description of the combat of Tancredi and Clorinda as an opportunity of describing in music contrary passions, namely, warfare and entreaty and death. In the year 1624 I caused this composition to be performed in the noble house of my especial patron and indulgent protector the Most Illustrious and Excellent Signor Girolamo Mozzenigo, an eminent dignitary in the service of the Most Serene Republic, and it was received by the best citizens of the noble city of Venice with much applause and praise.'[77]

Even if Monteverdi should have failed on several occasions to clarify whether the *Combattimento* is music 'with action', its musical characteristics make it absolutely clear. The work – for soprano (Clorinda), two tenors (Tancredi and the Testo) and four instrumental parts ('four *viole da braccio*, soprano, alto, tenor and bass, and a *contrabasso da gamba* which continues with the harpsichord') – is in fact entirely interwoven with episodes which, even if closely linked to the expressive manners of the madrigal – are here directed resolutely towards action, implying and indeed requiring explicit dramatic realization.

For more than fifteen years there had begun to appear even in prints (for example, by Sigismondo d'India, Saracini, Marini and Rontani) chamber compositions based on that type of emotional and expressive solo song which many had called 'recitative', and others (above all, Monteverdi) 'representative'. Monteverdi himself had recently provided examples with the two *lettere amorose* included in the Seventh Book of 1619 and recently reprinted in the small collection of 1623 together with the *Lamento d'Arianna*. Compared with all its predecessors – for the rest, lyrical monologues – the *Combattimento* stands apart chiefly for its narrative and strongly dramatic nature, combining episodes that are explanatory, in dialogue, active, epic, meditative and lyrical, and also for the fact that it uses more than one voice/character. Among these characters, however, appears one which, having to link the none-too-frequent speeches of Tancredi and Clorinda, ends up by taking a dominant role in the piece. Based on a part of a text which was not designed for the stage, the *Combattimento* has all the characteristics of a hybrid – it is for the chamber yet with an allusive theatricality – combining protagonists involved in the action (Tancredi, Clorinda) and observers outside it (the Testo), plus direct dialogue and mediated action, a drama experienced in the first person, and a visualized account that tempers its passion and immediacy. Moreover, and again differently from preceding compositions in a similar genre, in the *Combattimento* Monteverdi employs for the first time instruments on upper parts (the group of *viole da braccio*) which play variously with the voices.

From the instructions given above, it would seem that at the Palazzo Mocenigo the musicians were placed in a room apart from that which contained the gentlemen invited to the *veglia*. In fact, 'Clorinda armed and on foot, followed by Tancredi armed on a Marian horse' enter 'from the side of the room in which the music is performed': with the instrumentalists hidden from the audience, only Tancredi and Clorinda offered themselves to view, plus the Testo, whose voice was kept 'somewhat distanced from the instruments, so that the oration may be better understood'. And the entrance of these characters 'unexpectedly (after some madrigals without action have been sung)' must have had a significant effect on the guests, who were certainly not expecting the surprise that 'the Testo will then begin the singing'.

The instrumental elements of the *Combattimento* seem associated with a taste for sound and timbre which is certainly connected with Monteverdi's long involvement with the technique of bowed string instruments. Indeed, the opening section of the *Combattimento* closes with the juxtaposition of two instrumental passages – that is, in long note-values to represent the 'passi tardi e lenti' ('slow, lingering steps') of the two warriors who 'vansi incontro' ('go to meet each other') and in fast repeated notes ('e d'ira ardenti', 'and burning with anger') with tremolo effects, this latter precisely a development of the vocal style which had been transferred to instrumental music already in the 1610s in the printed works of Venetian composers such as Francesco Usper, Biagio Marini (whose sonata *La Foscarina* in his *Affetti musicali* (Venice, Gardano, 1617) has the instruction 'tremolo con l'arco', 'tremolo with the bow') and Giovan Battista Riccio, who in his *Terzo libro delle divine lodi* (Venice, Gardano [Bartolomeo Magni], 1620) includes two three-part canzonas (*La Pichi, La Grimaneta*) 'con il tremolo'. But above and beyond mere technical effect, it should be noted that in the *Combattimento* Monteverdi uses the tremolo for refinedly expressive ends.

Similarly, to represent the succeeding savage fight between Tancredi and

Clorinda, the composer seeks out sonorities hitherto unexploited in print, some close to noise, such as the use of the pizzicato ('Qui si lascia l'arco, e si strappano le corde con duoi diti' – 'Here one puts aside the bow and the strings are struck with two fingers' – is the instruction for the string instruments in the passage in question) at the most agitated moment, significantly when the duel degenerates into a brawl. This is the first known appearance of this instrumental effect, at least in Italy: it had already appeared in *The Souldiers Song*, the first of *Captaine Humes musicall Humors* published by Tobias Hume in *The first Part of Ayres, French, Pollish and others together* (London, John Windet, 1605), where it is used in the same way as a characterizing and descriptive effect in a military context.

28   1624–1627

1624 also saw the publication of works by Monteverdi in secular and sacred anthologies. In the *Madrigali del signor cavaliere Anselmi ... posti in musica da diversi* (Venice, Bartolomeo Magni ['Stampa del Gardano']) appeared 'O come vaghi, o come' (for 'doi tenori' and continuo) and 'Taci, Armelin, deh taci' ('*a3*, alto tenore e basso' plus continuo), both light fripperies flavoured by some emotional touches for the cruelty and the wounds of Love. In 'Taci, Armelin, deh taci', Giovan Battista Anselmi's text seems to hark back to the fourteenth-century poetic madrigal, moreover with, in the second tercet, a *ripresa* of the first two lines appropriately underlined by the return of the same musical material as at the opening.

In the case of the *Quarto scherzo delle ariose vaghezze* by Carlo Milanuzzi, organist at S. Stefano in Venice, the edition issued in 1624 by the Venetian printer Alessandro Vincenti was a reprint (we do not know the date of the first edition, which could also have been 1624, given that the *Terzo scherzo* was published in 1623). The title-page announces also a 'cantata' ('O come vezzosetta') by Milanuzzi 'and other arias by Signor Monteverde, and by Signor Francesco, his son, with some by Signor Gio[van] Pietro Berti and by Guglielmo Miniscalchi'; Berti was a singer in St Mark's who had been appointed organist that same year, and Miniscalchi was *maestro di cappella* in S. Stefano and therefore Milanuzzi's superior. Monteverdi's 'arie' are 'Ohimé ch'io cado, ohimé', 'La mia turca che d'amor' and 'Sí dolce è 'l tormento'; 'Ahi che morir mi sento, e tu che sei' and 'Ama pur, ninfa gradita' are by his son (they mark his debut as a composer, under the auspices of his father but with no further outcome, as far as we know). All are for soprano and continuo, even if the title-page claims that they are 'appropriate to be sung by solo voice to the harpsichord, chitarrone, double harp and other such instrument, with the alphabet letters tablature ... for the Spanish guitar'. They represent the two types of 'aria' most typical of the period: strophic variation on a repeated bass (in 'Ohimé ch'io cado, ohimé', each strophe is preceded by a ritornello for the continuo alone) and strophic setting pure and simple (all the others). It should be noted, however, that from the layout of the print it would seem that it contains four, not three, pieces by Monteverdi: to the three cited above, one could add 'Prendi l'arco, invitto Amor'. In terms of music and text, this would seem to be just the last stanza of 'La mia turca che d'amor' (and it is published as such in volume IX of Malipiero's edition), but in the print itself, it is set off by its own decorated initial, and moreover the list of contents gives it as a separate work.[78] If the madrigals for two and three voices on Anselmi's texts were entirely similar to those collected by Monteverdi in his Seventh Book, the pieces which the composer contributed to this latest volume of Milanuzzi's successful series dedicated to light music for popular consumption offer examples of his rapprochement with the genre of the chamber aria already seen, again, in the Seventh Book, but not in the uncomplicated, facile format of the last two canzonettas here.

As for sacred music, three motets by Monteverdi appeared in 1624 in the *Seconda raccolta de sacri canti ... de diversi eccellentissimi autori* (Venice, Alessandro Vincenti) edited by Don Lorenzo Calvi, the above-mentioned *maestro di cappella* of Pavia Cathedral for whom Monteverdi had provided two pieces in his 1620 volume: the new motets are 'Ego flos campi' (from the *Song of Songs*, 2) for 'voce sola [alto] e b.c.'; 'Venite sitientes ad aquas', 'a 2' (two sopranos) and continuo; and 'Salve o Regina', 'a voce sola [tenor] e b.c.'.

In summer 1624, Monteverdi was also involved in legal action with Ippolito Belli concerning the estate of his father-in-law, Giacomo Cattaneo, who had died on 24 April of that year. The dispute, which particularly concerned Cattaneo's house in Mantua, dragged on to the end of December 1625 (it was resolved in Monteverdi's favour), even obliging the composer to appear before a Mantuan judge on 15 July 1624.[79]

The private visit to Venice in March 1625 of the heir to the Polish throne, Władisław Sigismund, gave Monteverdi the opportunity to earn the appreciation of the prince, who later, on his return to Poland, was to increase the already significant flow of Italian musicians there, also importing the novelty of plays performed entirely in music which he had seen in the Italian courts. The solemn concerted mass heard by Władisław in St Mark's on 9 March was by Monteverdi:

> The little patience which he [Władisław] has in all things which require punctiliousness, gravity and decorum − since he is rather of a cheerful, free nature, dedicated to pleasure − could have been the cause of him not wanting to visit [the doge], and whether or not this is true, this prince moves very quickly, and he gets fed up with things, and very quickly; even at mass, when it goes on for too long, he dislikes being there. If the music of the solemn mass in St Mark's had lasted a little longer, he would not have enjoyed it, but since it was reasonably short, he took great delight in it, never ceasing to praise the intelligence of Monteverde, *maestro di cappella*, the exquisiteness of the instruments, and in particular that of the organs of St Mark's.[80]

In a letter of 15 March 1625 (L.81 [82]), Monteverdi himself refers to 'the multitude of tasks I have had, and still have to do, in serving this Polish prince both in his chapel and at his court'. And one can assume that Władisław was indeed satisfied by Monteverdi's service, given the offer made to the composer to move to the Polish court (made sometime between 1625 and 1638), 'but being old, he did not want to move away'.[81]

We have a group of letters from August 1625 to March 1626 (L.82 [83], 83 [84], 85 [86], 86 [87] and 88 [89]) all addressed to Ercole Marigliani in which Monteverdi reveals his interest and abilities in alchemy: in the first letter he enlarges upon an explanation of the method 'for calcinating gold with lead', furnishing his instructions with a sketch showing the necessary receptacle; while in the other letters he says that he had ordered a vessel from Murano (L.83 [84]) and had sent to Mantua some pure mercury (L.85 [86], 86 [87] and 88 [89]). In Venice, Monteverdi was in contact with local experts such as 'Signor Piscina and Signor de Santi the doctor, both great men in this field'. Monteverdi himself withdrew behind alchemical experiments on more than one occasion: 'I must then tell you how I shall be able to make mercury from unrefined matter which changes into clear water, and although it will be in water it will not however lose its identity as mercury, or its weight; because I have tested it by taking a drop, and have put it on a brass spoon and rubbed it, and it became all tinged with silver colour. From this purified water I shall hope to make something worth while, inasmuch as it is a powerful solvent of silver.' Thus he writes to Marigliani on 23 August 1625 (L.82 [83]); while on 28 March 1626 (L.88 [89]) he reveals that 'I am at present engaged in making a fire under a glass beaker, with its cover on, to extract something from it and then make something of it, so that (please God) I may then cheerfully explain this something to My Lord Marigliani.'

In 1625–6, Monteverdi was enrolled in the Accademia dei Filomusi, Bologna, founded in 1625 by Girolamo Giacobbi. This association is twice confirmed by Adriano Banchieri.[82] First, we have the dialogue between Ottavio Arzellati (from Bologna – he speaks in dialect) and Vespasiano del Testa (from Siena) contained in the *Discorso* published by Banchieri (Bologna, Girolamo Mascheroni, 1626) under the pseudonym Camillo Scaligeri Dalla Fratta (the passage given below is on pp. 107–110):

OTTAVIO As for music [in Bologna], the house of the Reverend Signor Don
    Girolamo Giacobbi, the author of much esteemed prints and works in
    manuscript, stands out, which one can appositely call an earthly Parnassus,
    where recently there has been established a very well esteemed academy
    under the protection of the Lord Count Romeo Pepoli, a gentleman of the
    senate chamber. The vice-protector is another gentleman again of the senate
    chamber, that is Signor Alfonso Fantuzzi, and the leader at the moment is the
    Reverend Father Adriano Banchieri, the celebrated composer of musical
    works in print.

VESPASIANO How does this academy work? We, too, have a similar one in Siena
    called the Armonici Intronati: its device is a ripe pumpkin with two apoth-
    ecary's pestles, and a motto, *Meliora latent* ['The better things are hidden'].

OTTAVIO My dear sir, this [academy] is worthy of a visit. The musicians who take part are all composers, and as a whole not only singers but also instrumentalists playing harpsichords, lutes, chitarrones, pandoras, trombones, cornetts, *pifferi*, flutes, *violoni*, viols and violins: in sum, as one says, *de omni genere musicorum* ['of all kinds of musicians'] Although all are skilled, there are, however, two who are indeed excellent: one is called Alessandro Piccinini, who was a musician of Duke Alfonso d'Este, unique in playing the lute, and the other Alfonso Pagani, who was in service at the Polish court, extraordinary in playing the violin. The room in which this academy meets is entirely decorated with gold leather, with a structure for the academicians, adorned with pictures by Reni, Carracci, Centino and others; similarly, within one sees the devices painted in oil in gold frames not only of the local academicians but also of foreigners ...

VESPASIANO ... Can you recall the names of the academicians?

OTTAVIO They are called the Filomusi.

VESPASIANO ... How do they proceed with their public academic meetings?

OTTAVIO They perform various *concerti* for one and more voices accompanied by the above-mentioned instruments, sometimes *in concerto* [one to a part] and sometimes *con ripieni* [with parts doubled]. Halfway through the entertainment, a virtuoso ascends the rostrum, who delivers an oration or discourse on some matter of curiosity, and then they turn again to performing ...

VESPASIANO You have told me that around the room are the devices of local and foreign academicians; are foreigners still being enrolled?

OTTAVIO Up to today, in the course of one year, two have been enrolled: Claudio Mont'verd, *maestro di cappella* of St Mark's in Venice, and Augustin Facco, organist of Vicenza Cathedral.

Second, Banchieri's *Lettere armoniche* (Bologna, Girolamo Mascheroni, 1628, contains (pp. 141–42) a congratulatory note (undated) from him sent directly to the composer:

> To Signor Claudio Monteverde, head of the music of the most illustrious signory in St Mark's, Venice.
>
> In congratulation.
>
> It seems appropriate for me to convey a word of congratulation to Your Lordship, together with the great delight that we felt in our Accademia Filomusa for our having gained a person so eminent as Signor Claudio Monteverde.

When Giacobbi died in February 1629, it was Banchieri who told the composer in a letter later included in his *Lettere*.[83]

Monteverdi's 'Ego dormio et cor meum vigilat' (from the *Song of Songs*, 5) for soprano, bass and continuo was included in the *Sacri affetti* compiled by Francesco Sammaruco (Rome, Luca Antonio Soldi, 1625). As with the publication of the *Lamento d'Arianna* in *Il maggio fiorito: arie, sonetti, e madrigali, à 1.2.3. de diversi autori* (Orvieto, Michel'Angelo Fei & Rinaldo Ruuli, 1623), Monteverdi's music was now reaching Roman circles: it seems that the composer's reputation in print – hitherto largely focused on the north (the Po valley but also beyond the alps towards Austria and Germany) extending southwards at most to Florence – was now spreading as far as Rome, where the composer had unsuccessfully sought to establish himself with the 1610 *Missa ... ac vespere*. But on the other hand, the other anthology published in 1625 containing music by Monteverdi was due to a singer in St Mark's, Leonardo Simonetti, whose *Ghirlanda sacra* was printed by Bartolomeo Magni (at the 'Stampa del Gardano'; it was reprinted in 1636). This includes four motets by Monteverdi for tenor and continuo: 'O quam pulchra es, anima mea' (from the *Song of Songs*, 4), 'Currite, populi, psallite timpanis' (for the feasts of saints), 'Ecce sacrum paratum convivium' and 'Salve Regina'.

We also find evidence of a lost composition by Monteverdi performed on 15 June 1626 during an official banquet in honour of the senate and foreign diplomats. This is described in the dispatch of the Medici resident, Nicolò Sacchetti, who underlines the anti-French allusions of the texts sung (particularly significant given the Republic's political situation following the Treaty of Monson):

> Last Monday, the feast of St Vitus, in which according to ancient custom the most serene doge gives a solemn banquet to the ambassadors of princes and to the senate, Monteverdi, *maestro di cappella* of St Mark's, had sung, while the banquet was being held, some of his songs as usual, in the trios of which was repeated: *Non se li può piú credere, perché non vi è piú fede* ['One cannot believe them, because there is no faith there']. These words were noticed by all, and in particular by the French ambassador, and thus were the cause of him, for all the time that he stayed in the palace, displaying a very disturbed and mortified countenance.[84]

Monteverdi may well have had some sympathy with such sentiments, given the undated denunciation delivered anonymously to the Venetian State Inquisitors, accusing the composer of pro-Habsburg and pro-Spanish sympathies, as well as of blasphemy (note, too, the reference to music for the feast of St Vitus in 1623):

> Most Illustrious and Most Excellent Lords.
>
> The zeal that I have for the preservation of my country and of Your Serenities forces me to notify you that there is in this city one Claudio Monteverde of Cremona, at present serving as *maestro di cappella* in St Mark's, who has said that he still hopes to see an eagle rule this piazza in place of the emblem of St Mark. And at this [occasion] were present Ottavio Vicentino and Francesco dal'Orso, barbers in the Piazza San Marco at the sign of the Bear.
>
> Item, [he said] that he would like to see this Most Serene Republic, for the health of its souls, subjugated to the King of Spain. At this [occasion] were present Antonio Padoan, Giovan Batista, scaleter [= confectioner] at Santa Marina, and Pietro Furlan, who plays the cornett.
>
> Item, on the day of St Vitus in 1623, the Signoria was present in the church of S. Vito, and the doge's Cavalier brought, in his name, four singers for the music for the banquet. Complaining that he had not been given due recognition by asking his permission, Monteverdi said: 'And I serve these fools and dotards! They don't know my service, my worth!' This he said in the presence of all the singers.

Item, at the time of the feast of the Ascension, at Vespers, when the *cappella* was in the pergola, he made a most notable error. When he was reproved for this error, he said: 'I despise the clergy, and I do not care how many priests are here; to hell with them – I am Claudio.' At this all the singers were present.

Item, his mouth is so used to swearing in the names of Our Lord and of the Blessed Virgin that it is a marvel to behold.

Of Your Most Illustrious Excellencies,

most faithful subject,

N.

As far as we know, the denunciation had no outcome: it was probably treated merely as malicious rumour on the part of some scandalmonger.

Meanwhile, Monteverdi's younger son, Massimiliano, had graduated in medicine at Bologna (in the first months of 1626),[85] and the composer was seeking to find him work in Mantua using his own acquaintances. On 19 March 1626, he wrote to Striggio (L.87 [88]): 'The bearer of this letter is a son of mine, who as many as four years ago (thanks to the Most Serene Lady) gained a place in Montalto College at Bologna, in order to study. Now, with a Doctorate in Medicine, he has come to Mantua purposely to express those very great thanks that he owes to his Most Serene Patrons, and at the same time to make himself known as their most humble servant and vassal.' A few days later (on 26 March, L.88 [89]), he recounted to Marigliani what his son had told him of his first dealings in Mantua: 'He writes to me in his letters that he is now asking admission to study-circles, and is attending the astrology lectures of a certain Jesuit father, as well as applying himself to consultations. He still continues to work for the Most Excellent Signor Bertoletti, and at the same time works for Count Bruschi, my lord.' But a year and a half later, Massimiliano was to be the cause of very serious concern for his father, since he was imprisoned by the Holy Office for having read a prohibited book, as Monteverdi told Striggio on 18 December 1627 (L.114 [115]):

> About my coming to Mantua, I shall also have to be excused at present, for because of my reputation I am not allowed to go there since my son Massimiliano is in the prisons of the Holy Office. He has been there for three months, the reason being that he read a book which he did not know was prohibited. He was accused by the owner of the book, who got himself imprisoned, and was deceived by the owner who said that the book dealt only with medicine and astrology. As soon as Massimiliano was in prison, the Father Inquisitor wrote to me saying that if I gave him a pledge of 100 ducats for being legally represented until the case was dispatched, he would release him at once.
>
> In one of his letters, Signor Ercole Marigliani, the counsellor, offered of his own accord to protect my son, and because of this known partiality of his, I begged him to pass on the task of arranging for my security payment to the Father Inquisitor to come out of the annual income paid to me by that Most Serene Prince my master, but since two months have gone by without my receiving an answer either from the Father Inquisitor or from Signor

Marigliani, I am turning (with the greatest possible reverence) to Your Most Illustrious Lordship's protection in delegating this particular matter to Signor Marigliani, in Massimiliano's favour and in accordance with his interests.

If he does not wish to undertake this security settlement, I shall always be ready to deposit 100 ducats so that my son can be released ...

Monteverdi was unable to obtain the necessary sum of money for bail from the pension granted him by Duke Vincenzo (which was never paid regularly) and so was forced to sell a necklace, presumably the one given him by the duchess at the time of the dedication of the Seventh Book (L.115 [116], to Striggio, 1 January 1628):

The favour which I now beg of Your Most Illustrious Lordship's great authority, with all due affection, is this: only that you may be so kind as to influence the Father Inquisitor so that he lets Massimiliano go back home, by virtue of the pledge which he himself requested of me. I desire nothing else of Your Most Illustrious Lordship's grace, since I have handed over a necklace worth 100 ducats to Signor Barbieri (a rich dealer in precious stones who is here in Venice, both a countryman of mine, and a close friend for many years) so that he may write by this post asking Signor Zavarella, who looks after the customs-duties of His Most Serene Highness of Mantua and is a very close friend of the aforesaid Signor Barbieri, to come to Your Most Illustrious Lordship and offer to look after the said pledge personally.

I do not intend to inconvenience you, or beg for anything, otherwise than to induce the Father Inquisitor to let Massimiliano go back home.

However, in July 1628 Monteverdi was still afraid that his son would be imprisoned again, and hence he sought permission to have him brought to the composer in Venice (L.118 [119] to Striggio, 1 July 1628; L.119 [120] of 8 July says similar things):

The misfortune is that I thought my son Massimiliano was in fact freed from his wretched plight, and in consequence from the pledge and all other problems.

But as long as two weeks ago he wrote to me that, because the case of the rogue who brought the prohibited book for him to read has not yet come up, he fears that he may have to return to prison again. I do not know why, since he already let it be seen that he was not to blame. Now because of this fear I begged Signor Marigliani the counsellor, my master, to try and arrange for my son to come and stay with me. Having obtained this favour, he kindly informed me of the fact, and discussed it with the Father Inquisitor at Padua, [and] they have assured me that my son is not guilty and did not deserve to be in prison at all.

Now, anxious that he should not return to prison (although confirmed by Signor Counsellor Marigliani), I am writing again to beg Your Most Illustrious Lordship to deign to arrange this business with Signor Counsellor Marigliani, and ask him for the love of God to try and help me in this, further considering that my son has not only not erred, but that he is a Mantuan who entered the College of Physicians, and is very much a servant of Your Most Illustrious Lordship's.

Thereafter, Massimiliano gained some fame also as a *letterato*, for Arisi mentions him in his list of Cremonese writers: 'Massimiliano Monteverdi, son of the most celebrated musician Claudio, doctor of philosophy and of medicine, published a *Tyrocinium medicum*, printed I cannot remember where, for it slipped my mind on the burning of the third volume of my *Cremona literata*, where I dealt with it.'[86] Massimiliano died on 14 October 1661 and was buried in the church of S. Nazaro.[87]

While Johannes Donfried reprinted 'Sancta Maria succurre miseris' and 'O bone Jesu, o piissime Jesu' in the *Promptuarii musici . . . pars tertia* (Strasbourg, Paul Ledertz, 1627), Don Giovanni Maria Sabino, *maestro di cappella* of S. Barbara in Castelnuovo at Naples, included in his *Psalmi de vespere* (Naples, Ambrosio Magnetta, 1627) Monteverdi's psalm-setting for four voices and organ, 'Confitebor tibi Domine'. Sabino, who had joined Monteverdi with four motets in Simonetti's *Ghirlanda sacra* two years before, was from 1630 to 1634 organist at the Neapolitan Chiesa dei Filippini. To quote Giuseppe Vecchi:

> It therefore seems very likely that in addition to the publication of this 'Confitebor', it was on his initiative that two other compositions by Monteverdi in manuscript ('Voglio di vita uscir, voglio che cadano' and a *Gloria* for eight voices) survive in the Filippini archives in Naples. Perhaps one can also link to Sabino a chapter in the fortunes of Monteverdi's music in Naples, in a period still some time away, of the posthumous performance of *L'incoronazione di Poppea* (1651).[88]

Whatever the case, further evidence of the spread of Monteverdi's fame in central and southern Italy in the mid-1620s – already noted above – is also provided by the publication in Rome of the *Madrigali a 4 di Jahnes Archadelt di nuovo ristampato e corretto in Venetia da Claudio Monteverde* (Rome, Paolo Masotti, 1627) printed 'ad istanza di Gioseppe Cesareo all'insegna dell'Arpa al Colleggio Romano' ('at the request of Gioseppe Cesareo [bookseller] at the sign of the harp in the Roman College'). This edition continued the trend of using this near century-old collection by the Flemish Arcadelt as a pedagogic tool; it still continued to enjoy a wide dissemination in the first half of the seventeenth century, being reprinted some twenty times (in the dedication, Masotti refers to 'these madrigals which to the young are wont to be their first introduction to this science').

In the first months of 1627, the exchange of letters between Monteverdi and the Mantuan court increased due to an unidentified commission first mentioned in a letter of 2 January 1627 (L.89[90]): 'Signor Cavalier Campagnolo, having arrived in Venice, came expressly to visit me and tell me of the continual and special affection which Your Most Illustrious Lordship deigns to bestow upon me, and he added that you have in mind the desire to honour me with a commission to set to music some poetry which you would be so kind as to send me.' From what Monteverdi writes a few months later (L.91 [92], 1 May 1627), it appears that the occasion prompting this commission was rather important, certainly something to do with the ascent to the ducal throne of Vincenzo II, the brother of Ferdinando, who had died on 29 October 1626.

> I would wish, however, to pray and beseech Your Most Illustrious Lordship that His Most Serene Highness, graciously allowing me to set to music the play which you mention, might deign to take two points into consideration: one, that I should have ample time to compose it; the other, that it should be written in an excellent style. For I would no less have to put up with considerable worry and little peace of mind (indeed very great distress) by setting tawdry verses to music, than I would if I had to compose in a hurry – this lack of time being the reason why I almost killed myself when writing *Arianna*.
>
> I know that it could be done quickly, but speed and quality do not go together. So, if there were time, and again if I were to have the work of production from your most noble intellect, you may be very sure that my joy would be boundless, because I know what facility and propriety Your Most Illustrious Lordship would bring to it. If the project related to *intermedi* for a full-length play, its birth would be neither so tiring nor so long drawn out, but a sung play, which says as much as an epic poem, to be set in a short time – believe me, Your Most Illustrious Lordship, it cannot be done without falling into one of two dangers: either doing it badly or making oneself ill.
>
> However, I happen to have set many stanzas of Tasso – where Armida begins 'O tu, che porte parte teco di me, parte ne lassi' ['O thou who takest part of me with you, leave part of me here'], continuing with all her lament and anger, with Ruggiero's reply; and these perhaps would not be displeasing. I also happen to have set to music the fight between Tancredi and Clorinda. Again, I have carefully considered a little play by Signor Giulio Strozzi, very beautiful and unusual, which runs to some 400 lines, called *Licori finta pazza innamorata d'Aminta* ['Licoris, the feigned madwoman, in love with Amyntas'], and this – after a thousand comical situations – ends up with a wedding, by a nice touch of stratagem.
>
> Both these and similar things can serve as short episodes between other pieces of music. They do not come off too badly, and I know they would not displease Your Most Illustrious Lordship. Then, if church music were needed, either for Vespers or for Mass, I rather think I might have something of this kind that would be to His Most Serene Highness's liking.

Instead of becoming involved in a new enterprise, Monteverdi therefore sought to have accepted earlier works either already finished, such as the *Combattimento* of 1624, or near completion, such as the similar work based on Tasso concerning Armida abandoned by Rinaldo (not Ruggiero, as Monteverdi wrote in error). The latter, which must have been very like the *Combattimento* and created on the impulse of the favour with which the latter had been received, began with the speech of Armida 'O tu che porte / parte teco di me, parte ne lassi' (*Gerusalemme liberata*, XVI.40), 'continuing with all her lament and anger, with Ruggiero's [Rinaldo's] reply', i.e. probably through to stanza 60, with suitable cuts. Monteverdi had already turned to this episode for a madrigal cycle which appeared in the Third Book; now he was inspired by it again, perhaps finding therein that poetics of 'opposites' noted in

Tasso's epic and experimented with in the *Combattimento*, for whose opposition of 'warfare' and 'entreaty and death' was now substituted 'lament and
anger', probably with new applications of the *concitato* style.

The reply from Mantua may have been that something new in terms of an
entirely sung play was required, for which Monteverdi sent two librettos for
consideration: an *azione scenica* by Giulio Strozzi, *La finta pazza Licori*, and an
old pastoral by Rinuccini, *Il Narciso* (L.92 [93], 7 May 1627):

> I am sending off to Your Most Illustrious Lordship *La finta pazza Licori* by
> Signor Strozzi (as you stipulated in your very kind letter), so far neither set
> to music, nor printed, nor ever acted on the stage; for as soon as the author
> had completed it he himself straightway gave me, with his own hands, a
> copy of it, which was in fact this one.
>
> If the aforementioned Signor Giulio gets to know that it might be to His
> Most Serene Highness's taste, I am quite sure that with extreme promptness
> of thought and deed he will put it in order – divided into three acts, or
> however His Most Serene Highness wishes – desiring beyond all measure to
> see it set to music by me, and rejoicing to see his most honoured literary
> works clothed with my modest music. For truly both in the beauty of its
> verse, and in its ideas, I have found it indeed a most worthy subject,
> absolutely ready for setting, so that if such a story were to Your Most
> Illustrious Lordship's taste, you need pay no attention to its present form,
> because I know for sure that the author will arrange it to your complete
> satisfaction in a very short space of time.
>
> In my opinion, the story is not bad, nor indeed is the way it unfolds;
> nevertheless the part of Licoris, because of its variety of moods, must not fall
> into the hands of a woman who cannot play first a man and then a woman,
> with lively gestures and different emotions. Therefore the imitation of this
> feigned madness must take into consideration only the present, not the past
> or the future, and consequently it must emphasize the word, not the sense of
> the phrase. So when she speaks of war she will have to imitate war; and when
> of peace, peace; when of death, death, and so forth.
>
> And since the transformations take place in the shortest possible time, and
> the imitations as well – then whoever has to play this leading role, which
> moves us to laughter and to compassion, must be a woman capable of
> leaving aside all other imitations except the immediate one, which the word
> she utters will suggest to her. All the same, I believe that Signora Margherita
> will be best of all.
>
> But to give further proof of my heartfelt affection (even though I know
> for sure that the task would be more difficult for me) I am sending you the
> enclosed *Narciso*, a play by Signor Ottavio Rinuccini, which has never been
> set to music, or actually produced. This gentleman, when he was alive (how
> fervently I pray that he is now in heaven!) did me the favour not only of
> giving me a copy but also of asking me to take it on, for he liked the work
> very much, and hoped that I might have to set it to music.
>
> I have had a go at it several times, and turned it over to some extent in my
> mind, but to tell Your Most Illustrious Lordship the truth it would not, in
> my opinion, succeed so powerfully as I would wish for, because of the
> numerous sopranos we would have to employ for so many nymphs, and the
> numerous tenors for so many shepherds, and nothing else by way of variety.
> And then a sad and tragic ending! However, I did not want to neglect
> sending it so that Your Most Illustrious Lordship could look it over and give
> it the benefit of your fine judgement.

I have no copy of either work other than the present ones I am sending off to Your Most Illustrious Lordship. When you have read everything please do me the favour of sending back the aforementioned originals so that I can make use of them should some occasion arouse my interest, for as you may know they are very precious to me.

Towards the end of May 1627, the choice was made in favour of Strozzi's text, to which Monteverdi had tried to steer things, finding there opportunities not only for a variety of emotions – including comic ones, paralleling the mad scenes practised by actors of the *commedia dell'arte* (for example, Andreini's *La pazzia di Isabella* (1589) or Francesco Gabrielli's *La pazzia di Scappino* (1618)) – but also for new techniques (Monteverdi speaks of 'a new kind of music' below) and for the possibility of realizing that poetics of 'opposites' which was sparked off in these very same years (L.93 [94], 22 May 1627):

> I have received from the courier not only Your Most Illustrious Lordship's most welcome letter, but also both *Narciso* and *La finta pazza*. I have also received Your Most Illustrious Lordship's opinion and instructions regarding *La finta pazza*, and I truly agree with Your Most Illustrious Lordship's verdict that a supposedly crazy girl like that will – on stage – turn out to be even more novel, versatile and amusing. But now that I have come to know your mind, I have no intention of failing, when Signor Strozzi arrives from Florence in three or four days' time – I repeat, I have no intention of failing – to confer with him and (as is my habit) to see that this gentleman enriches it to an even greater extent with varied, novel and diverse scenes.
>
> This I shall explain according to my judgement, in order to see whether he can improve it with other novelties, such as additional characters, so that the crazy girl is not seen so frequently in action. In this way, each time she comes on stage she can always produce new moods and fresh changes of music, as indeed of gestures, and I shall give a most detailed report of all this to Your Most Illustrious Lordship.
>
> In my opinion she has very good speeches in two or three places, but in two others it seems to me that she could have better material – not so much on account of the poetry, as of the originality. And I must also insist on his rearranging the discourse of Amyntas, when the girl is fast asleep, for I would like him to speak as if he had not enough voice to be able to wake her up. This consideration – the need to speak in a low voice – will give me a chance to introduce to the senses a new kind of music, different from what has gone before. And likewise I shall insist that he decides, with special reason and consideration, on the ballet inserted in the middle; and then, as I have said, I shall give Your Most Illustrious Lordship a detailed account of it all . . .
>
> I shall not fail to consider doing what Your Most Illustrious Lordship has commanded me, for up till now I have already assimilated the ideas fairly well, and soon hope to send something to Signora Margherita, as principal singer; but I would like to know about the actual range of her voice, as regards her highest and lowest notes.

With the choice made for *La finta pazza Licori*, Monteverdi undertook to have it modified: since it was conceived as an 'entertainment at a musical evening which a certain Most Illustrious Signor Mozenigo . . . had arranged to give' (Mocenigo had provided for the *Combattimento* in similar circumstances), it was too limited and focused too much on a single character, and therefore was unsuitable 'for the entertainment of great princes':

> As yet, Signor Giulio Strozzi has not returned from Florence, but I keep looking out for him anxiously because of the great longing in my heart to do what Your Most Illustrious Lordship has ordered with regard to *La finta pazza*. I would have written about it already, at some length, had I not been waiting for the author to improve it to a very considerable extent; for according to letters received from him recently he ought surely to be in Venice within two or three days (God willing), and I hope it will then be rearranged in such a state of acceptability to Your Most Illustrious Lordship that you will be well and truly satisfied.
>
> I have already assimilated it so that the entire work is in such shape that I know I could set it to music in a very short while; but my aim is that whenever she is about to come on stage, she has to introduce fresh delights and new inventions. In three places I certainly think the effects will come off well: first, when the camp is being set up, the sounds and noises heard behind the scenes and exactly echoing her words should (it seems to me) prove quite successful; secondly, when she pretends to be dead; and thirdly, when she pretends to be asleep, for here it is necessary to bring in music suggesting sleep. In some other places, however, because the words cannot mimic either gestures or noises or any other kind of imitative idea that might suggest itself, I am afraid the previous and following passages might seem weak.[89]

> Three days ago Signor Giulio Strozzi arrived in Venice, and having been urged by me very insistently to do me the honour of adapting *La finta pazza Licori* to my way of thinking, so that I could make use of it for the entertainment of great princes, he willingly offered his services, confessing that in writing this play he did not achieve the degree of perfection he had in mind, but wrote it in dialogue to provide entertainment at a musical evening which a certain Most Illustrious Signor Mozenigo, my lord, had arranged to give. I, visualizing its presentation with some by no means straightforward rearrangement, did not want to set it to music.
>
> I told him that I would like to make use of it to present to His Most Serene Highness of Mantua on some occasion, and he (knowing that besides Signora Margherita there are also two other very fine lady singers) told me that he would take care of each one as regards letting them be heard, as likewise with the other virtuoso singers in His Most Serene Highness's service. He also admits that as far as the part of Licoris is concerned, he will make her come in later, and not in almost every scene, yet he will see to it that she always expresses new ideas and actions . . .
>
> [P.S.] I heard from the aforementioned Signor Giulio Strozzi, on his arrival from Florence, that His Most Serene Highness there wanted to send me something of a theatrical nature (as it so happens) for setting to music, but since Signor Gagliano has worked hard on his own account, it seems that His Most Serene Highness is well content. Signor Giulio adds that they are preparing beautiful things without knowing the whys and wherefores.[90]

Although a Venetian, Giulio Strozzi had grown up in Florentine circles. His first contact with Monteverdi was at the latest in 1621, the time of the requiem for Cosimo II of which Strozzi had been the official chronicler. He had also reserved for the composer – plus his pupil and vice-*maestro* Alessandro Grandi, as had already been the case with Benamati – a specific mention in his poem *La Venetia edificata* (Venice, Girolamo Piuti, 1626: XII.74), in the description of the delightful palace of the sorceress Irene:

> S'il Grandi allor, s'il Monteverde a gara
> in vestir sacri o lascivetti carmi
> con dolce canto e sinfonia sí rara
> stati in quella stagion fossero in armi,
> qual dalle lor discordie illustre e cara
> consonanza nascea dentro a que' marmi
> dove la maga in quelle fiamme estive
> s'ingegna d'allettar l'alme piú schive.

> If Grandi, then, if Monteverdi competing / to clothe sacred or lascivious songs / with sweet song and such rare symphony / were to have stood armed in that season, / from their discords what distinguished and precious / consonance would have been born within those statues / where the sorceress in those summer flames / sought to delight those more bashful souls.

On 20 June 1627 (L.97 [98]), Monteverdi told Striggio that Strozzi had 'returned from Padua, but even though he was absent, he has not on that account forgotten to improve *La finta pazza Licori*, which he has rearranged in five acts. Within four days he will either give it to me completely finished, or give me about two or three completed acts by way of a beginning, so that by Saturday week at the latest I hope to send some of it to Your Most Illustrious Lordship with the music added.' A few days later, in fact, he began composing (L.98 [99], 3 July 1627):

> As long as a week ago I had the first act of *La finta pazza* from Signor Giulio Strozzi, and spent a day working at it, when suddenly three evenings ago I began to feel a catarrh coming on – with much pain – by the side of the right eye, together with a swelling and a weakening of the body, which I thought would make no little progress. But, God be praised, it has already begun to give way somewhat, and now permits me to write this to Your Most Illustrious Lordship, which it would not have done yesterday or the day before yesterday.
>
> By the next post I hope to send Your Most Illustrious Lordship a good piece of the said act set to music, and at the same time I shall send the text of the entire act so that you can enjoy reading it.

But on 10 July 1627 (L.99 [100]) he seems to have sent only the text:

> I am sending off to Your Most Illustrious Lordship the first act of *La finta pazza* by Signor Giulio Strozzi, as you ordered. I wanted to send his original copy so that Your Most Illustrious Lordship could look not so much at the verses as at the plot of the play and the characters in the author's own hand. Two of the middle acts, which the author will give me tomorrow or the day after, have been completed; and he says that the feigned madness will begin in the third act, which I shall also send off to you as soon as I have received it. There will be a ballet in every act, each one different from the other, and in a fantastical style.

I beg Your Most Illustrious Lordship, as soon as you have read each act, to try and be so kind as to send it back to me, as I have not been able to finish making a copy because of my eye trouble, which I told Your Most Illustrious Lordship about in my last letter; which illness (God be praised) has almost entirely gone away. And Signor Giulio has told me that each act will present a new subject, so I rather think that nothing bad can possibly come of it.

It will now be up to Signora Margherita to become a brave soldier, timid and bold by turns, mastering perfectly the appropriate gestures herself, without fear or favour, because I am constantly aiming to have lively imitations of the music, gestures and tempos take place behind the scene. And I believe it will not displease Your Most Illustrious Lordship because the changes between the vigorous, noisy harmonies and the gentle, suave ones will take place suddenly so that the words will really come through well.

Towards the end of the month Strozzi had completed the text in verse (L.100 [101], 24 July 1607):

I now have it all in my hands, given me by the same Signor Giulio, and full of many beautiful variations. At present I am having it written out at home, so that no copies, either partial or complete, can be taken.

I have already completed practically all the first act, and would be even further ahead if I had not had that little trouble with my eyes that I told Your Most Illustrious Lordship about, and if I had not had some church music to write. From now on I shall work harder at it . . .

On 10 September, Monteverdi finally sent the complete text in five acts.[91] However, in Mantua ideas about what was to be done were far from clear; indeed, a few days later, Monteverdi, writing to Striggio (L.108, 18 September), reveals that *La finta pazza Licori* had been put aside (which is why the composer probably left off at the first act): 'In truth, what Your Most Illustrious Lordship thinks about *La finta pazza*, I had likewise thought, although everything could be kept going with some variation of the vocal line. I have not completely finished *Aminta* [*Armida*] – it would take at least two months because I no longer enjoy those youthful powers of composition – but I have done a good part of it.' Therefore the *Armida* project was being revived,[92] and it was completed three months later (L.114 [115], 18 December 1627): 'I received at Parma two of Your Most Illustrious Lordship's letters: in the one you instructed me to let you have *Armida*, which was so much to the liking of the Most Serene Lord Duke my master, and likewise that I should come to Mantua. . . . On my return to Venice three days ago, I at once handed over *Armida* for recopying: I shall be sending this to Your Most Illustrious Lordship by the next post.' But the death of Duke Vincenzo II, at the end of December 1627, had put an end to all plans. Nevertheless, on 4 February 1628 (L.117 [118]), Monteverdi replied to Striggio's request for a copy of *Armida*:

How distressing it was, then, for me to receive Your Most Illustrious Lordship's renewed instructions that I send *Armida*, because of my being (as I am) in Parma, and having *Armida* in Venice – may God be my witness! I refrained from sending it to Your Most Illustrious Lordship this Christmas, because of the death of the Most Serene Lord Duke Vincenzo (may he be in glory!) as I would never have thought that you might wish to enjoy it at carnival time. This failure on my part, if Your Most Illustrious Lordship could see into my heart, upsets me very much, believe me truly. *Armida* is however in the hands of the Most Illustrious Signor Mozenigo, my very affectionate and special master.

Now by this post, which leaves today for Venice, I am writing very urgently to the said gentleman, that he honour me with a copy of it . . .

It is possible that Striggio had requested *Armida* for the celebrations for the coronation of the new duke, but, as is well known, this was a very complicated matter, and one causing bloodshed as it developed into the war that in 1630 laid Mantua under seige and led to its sack by the Imperial troops.

The letter which Monteverdi sent to Striggio on 10 September 1627 (L.104 [106]) contained a general reference to 'the kind and special affection of the Most Serene Lord Duke, my special master': even if it is not made explicit, that 'affection' seems to have involved an offer to return to the Gonzaga court. In turning down the invitation, the composer asked the duke, however, to use his influence with his sister the Empress (Eleonora, wife of Habsburg Emperor Ferdinand II) concerning his request for a canonry in Cremona so as to grant some stability to his impending old age (Monteverdi was then 60):

Nothing could give my soul peace with satisfaction except to have a canonry at Cremona, in addition to my lands, without anything of benefit from the Treasury; and I could have that canonry at once by means of an order from Her Majesty the Empress to the Governor of Milan, or to the Cardinal of Cremona himself. The canonry would provide me with about 300 *scudi* in that currency. Thus feeling secure on this firm basis, and with the addition of my estate, I could be sure – after serving as long as I were able – of then having somewhere to retire, honourably and in godly manner, for the last days of my life.

Otherwise, as I told Your Most Illustrious Lordship, I would always be in fear of some colossal trick that my ill-fortune might play on me, and I could certainly expect it because I am no longer young. With this end in mind – of the said canonry – before the prelacy was allowed to lapse by His Majesty, I was on the point of passing through Mantua to ask for letters of recommendation from His Most Serene Highness to Her Majesty the Empress (since I was about to present her with some of my compositions, expressly in order to be favoured with that canonry), since the Lord Prince of Poland became very involved in the matter; but ill-luck called on me, because I did not wish to present his letters for a certain reason.

On 18 September 1627 (L.108), Monteverdi told Striggio 'I leave the matter of the canonry in Your Most Illustrious Lordship's care, reserving a fuller discussion for the time when I can come to Mantua'; this is the last mention of the issue in his letters, although it is doubtless to be associated with subsequent events discussed below.

Meanwhile, special commissions were also occupying Monteverdi in Venice. In July 1627, the Elector of Brandenburg, Georg Wilhelm,[93] was visiting incognito, and Monteverdi was required to provide music to entertain him. This is described in a letter to Striggio dated 24 July 1627 (L.100 [101]), which also mentions further duties at the Carmine:

> I beg you to forgive me for missing the previous post, not having replied to Your Most Illustrious Lordship's most kind and courteous letter; because the many tasks I had last Saturday (the post-day) were the reason for my failure. There were two tasks: one was having to provide chamber music from the seventeenth until the twentieth hour for the Most Serene Prince of Neuburg, who is staying incognito in the house of the English ambassador; and this music being over, I then had to go – pressed by the entreaties of many friends – to the Carmelite Church, as it was the day of First Vespers of the Most Holy Madonna of that Order, and stayed there fully occupied until almost one hour of night.

And on 25 September 1627 (L.110 [111]), Monteverdi told Marquis Enzo Bentivoglio of another undertaking, this time in Chioggia: 'the Most Excellent Lord Procurator Foscarini, my particular master, has a son who is mayor of Chioggia, and since this gentleman wanted to avail himself of my services in some musical function, I stayed on in Chioggia a day more than I intended'.

29 Festivities in Parma, 1628

Monteverdi was in contact with Bentivoglio in this period concerning a commission of considerable importance for the Farnese in Parma, the wedding of Duke Odoardo and Margherita de' Medici.[94] Parma was planning appropriate entertainments, the responsibility for which was given to Marquis Enzo Bentivoglio of Ferrara. (As an aside, these were the 'whys and where-fores' of the 'beautiful things' which, according to Strozzi's gossip – see L.95 [96] – were being prepared in the summer of 1627.)

> The Marquis Bentivoglio, very much my master for many years past, wrote to me as long as a month ago asking if I would set to music some words of his, made by His Excellency for use in a certain very important play that would be written for performance at a princely wedding. These would be *intermedi*, not a play sung throughout. As he was very much my special master I replied that I would do everything possible to carry out His Excellency's orders. He answered with particular appreciation and told me it was going to be used at the wedding of the Duke of Parma. I replied that I would do whatever he would be so kind as to ask of me.
> He at once informed Their Most Serene Highnesses of this, and I received a reply saying that I should start work on the assignment, so he at once sent me the first *intermedio*. I have already half finished it, and shall compose it easily because they are almost all soliloquies. Their Highnesses do me great honour with such a commission, for I have heard that about six or seven applied for the appointment, but of their own accord these gentlemen were so kind as to elect myself . . .

This letter to Striggio, dated 10 September 1627 (L.104 [106]) recalls Monteverdi's long acquaintance with Bentivoglio, the leader of the Ferrarese Accademia degli Intrepidi, to which Monteverdi had dedicated his Fourth Book of madrigals (1603); by then, Monteverdi had already set one of Bentivoglio's texts, the madrigal 'La bocca onde l'asprissime parole' in the Second Book. As for the 'six or seven [who] applied for the appointment' in Parma, one can identify some active in the Po valley: Domenico Mazzocchi, Giovan Battista Crivelli, Sigismondo d'India and Antonio Goretti. And it was indeed the latter, in whose musical *ridotto* – it will be recalled – Artusi had placed the performances of Monteverdi's music which became the pretext for the famous long polemic, who was appointed Monteverdi's assistant to act as copyist to help him in the mammoth undertaking. This involved first and foremost the *intermedi* for Tasso's *Aminta* arranged by Ascanio Pio di Savoia on the following subjects: Atlante's enchanted castle, Dido and Aeneas, Diana and Endymion, the Argonauts, and the four continents. Monteverdi set to work around the middle of September 1627, studying the first texts sent to him and planning out the 'kinds of music' to be used, taking particular account of the need for variety and for the juxtaposition of different affects:

> Yesterday, which was the 9th of this month, I received from the courier Your Most Illustrious Lordship's [Enzo Bentivoglio] package in which there was an *intermedio* and a letter from Your Most Illustrious Excellency, doing me infinite kindness and honour, together with a copy of a paragraph from a letter of the Most Serene Duchess of Parma, written to Your Most Illustrious Excellency, in which she deigns to honour me by commanding me (through Your Most Illustrious Excellency) to set to music what will be ordered by Your Most Illustrious Excellency. I have hardly been able to read the said *intermedio* twice before having a chance to write – this being the day when the courier leaves – yet I have seen so much beauty in it that, truth to tell, I was deeply moved and captivated by so fine a work.
>
> Although time has been short, I have not been entirely useless in this respect, for I have already begun work, the modest results of which Your Most Illustrious Excellency will see by next Wednesday. I have already taken into account the four kinds of music that will be used to adorn the said *intermedio*: the first, which starts at the beginning and goes so far as the onset of the quarrel between Venus and Diana, and between their arguments; the second, from the beginning of the quarrel until the arguments are over; the third, when Pluto comes in to establish order and calm, lasting until Diana starts to fall in love with Endymion; and the fourth and last, from the beginning of the said falling in love until the end.[95]

I am hoping, without more ado, to send Your Most Illustrious Excellency by the next post, Saturday, the *intermedio* of *Dido* in its entirety. I thought that I might even send it by the present post, but a misfortune came upon me and has prevented me from composing for two days. I do hope this *intermedio* will not displease Your Most Illustrious Excellency, for not much has to be done to complete the first one. I further acknowledge receipt from Your Most Illustrious Excellency, by courier, of the verses sent to me for the use of the tournament. These I have not read thoroughly as yet because of insufficient time, and because of my concentration on writing the said *intermedio* of *Dido*.

I have, however, taken a quick glance at the Months and how they speak, and I have also looked at Discord. I have also thought a little about the representation of the aforementioned Discord, and it seems to me that it will be a little difficult. The reason is this: since the Months have to sing together in mellow harmony – and I shall seek out the kind that will provide the most plausible representation of each – I am going to assign the opposite kind of music to Discord (I mean opposite to that which is suitable for the Months). I cannot for the moment think of anything else but to have her declaim in speech and not in music.

This however is a first thought, which I wanted to let Your Most Illustrious Excellency know about, so that with your most refined judgement you can assist my ability the better to serve Your Most Illustrious Excellency's pleasure, which I desire with all my heart. Yet I would not deny that those speeches of the aforementioned Discord might be intensified by music; that is, she would have to speak just as if she were actually singing, but this singing of hers would not however be based on any instrumental harmony, and this (it seems to me) would be the way to represent Discord.[96]

Aminta – for which Claudio Achillini (then in Odoardo Farnese's service) had specially written the prologue *Teti e Flora* which was to be added to the texts to be set to music – was to be performed in an open-air theatre erected for the occasion in the courtyard of S. Pietro Martire, in the ducal palace, to plans made by Francesco Guitti and Francesco Mazzi. Accordingly, on 25 September (L.110 [111]) Monteverdi warned Bentivoglio:

It will be a prudent move to come and see the theatre in Parma, in order to be able to adapt (as far as possible) the music that is right and fitting for the vast area. It will not be such an easy task, in my opinion, to perform the many and varied soliloquies that I see in these very beautiful *intermedi*. In the meantime I shall go on composing and writing, to be able to show Your Most Illustrious Excellency something more, and the best that I can do.

This last remark would seem to suggest that Monteverdi had the intention of presenting to Bentivoglio an important composition (better, he implies, than the *intermedi*) that was already ready (*La finta pazza Licori* or *Armida*?). But the plans for the festivities were already settled, including, besides *Aminta* adorned with those spectacular *intermedi*, a tournament (*Mercurio e Marte*) to be performed in a theatre built in a hall of the ducal palace by Duke Ranuccio I Farnese ten years before and never opened; its architect was the Ferrarese Giovan Battista Aleotti called 'L'Argenta', who had already been the designer of the Teatro degli Intrepidi in Ferrara (it is significant that Marquis Bentivoglio was also involved in both these enterprises).

At the end of September 1627, Monteverdi had to hand the texts of the first four *intermedi*, sent to him by Goretti, as the latter wrote to the marquis: 'I inform Your Most Illustrious Lordship that I received the *intermedi* and the libretto: I have sent the *intermedi* to Venice to Signor Monteverde as Your Most Illustrious Lordship ordered.'[97] Towards the end of October, both Goretti and Monteverdi were together in Parma, after having passed through Modena and having perhaps received some fine welcome at the court there, with which the *maestro di cappella* of St Mark's had been in professional contact for some years: 'I must also tell Your Most Illustrious Excellency about the beautiful entry that we made, the most courteous Signor Goretti and I, in Modena. This having obtained the approval of all, the journey was undertaken joyfully. Now we are working cheerfully and with determination to obtain the result that this gentleman and I warmly desire', wrote Monteverdi to Bentivoglio from Parma on 30 October 1627 (L.112 [113]). The two musicians soon met Count Fabio Scotti, Enzo Bentivoglio's agent in Parma, and they made their first contact with the singers – Goretti himself was to complain to the marquis about their pretensions and about the lack of female voices (only Settimia Caccini was at present engaged):[98]

> We arrived here in Parma last Tuesday evening, and I soon took Signor Claudio to Lord Count Fabio, whom we found to be beset with gout ... I gave him the letter of Your Most Illustrious Lordship and we talked somewhat, and then he sent for a carriage to go to court, and he had us driven there in what I think was a very regal manner. We returned to Lord Count Fabio and told him that we had a letter for the Most Serene Madame from Your Most Illustrious Lordship, which Signor Claudio was ordered by Your Most Illustrious Lordship to present to her and to pay reverence to her ... We have looked over the musicians who are to come, and as regards women there is none other than Signora Settimia, who, to tell Your Most Illustrious Lordship the truth, I doubt will do as well as one thinks, and Signor Claudio thinks the same. For the rest, these singers are a pretentious bunch, to the extent that we were amazed. And I promise Your Most Illustrious Lordship that Signor Claudio wants no one else but me, such do I say and do, and all is said to Your Most Illustrious Lordship in all sincerity ... Signor Claudio pays reverence to Your Most Illustrious Lordship.

Together, Monteverdi and Goretti paid the obligatory homage to the Duke and Duchess of Parma and then went to visit the theatre which was being built in the courtyard of S. Pietro for the performance of *Aminta* and its *intermedi*, remaining astounded by the edifices and the machines there in profusion, but also worried by the acoustic created by such a space. Goretti wrote:

> Then at three hours of night, the Most Serene Madame and the Lord Duke summoned Signor Monteverdi and myself, and so both of us paid reverence to them and from these rulers we received a most grateful and courteous audience, and we were as slaves, and to Your Most Illustrious Lordship [Bentivoglio] we are much obliged ... From now on something will be begun, although I do not fail to encourage Signor Claudio ... I was amazed by the theatre and the new stage, and we went there with Signor Claudio, and all will go well. Providing that the courtyard will be covered and enclosed as appropriate, for any other way the voices will have no effect, and the instruments with difficulty. I am sure that Your Most Illustrious Lordship will have satisfied your longing for making machines and for putting timber to work. We will wait for you so as to be able to turn homewards for Christmas – which Signor Claudio still insists on doing – so as to return straight after the Christmas celebrations, which will still give us time ...[99]

The meeting with the duke and duchess and the kindness with which they were treated was also reported to Bentivoglio by Monteverdi, who was rather pleased with this reception (L.112 [113]): 'I come to do reverence to Your Most Illustrious Excellency, and at the same time to give you the greatest thanks I know and am capable of, for the particular and extraordinary honours received from the Most Serene Duchess and Duke, who have not only issued instructions to the Lords Ministers that every comfort be given me, but have assured me personally of this singular favour.' A little later in the same letter, dated Parma, 30 October 1627, the composer also informed the marquis of the state of work: 'I find that I have finished the first *intermedio*, which is about Melissa and Bradamante, but not that of *Dido*; this will be the second. I am busy with the third, and when that is done, I shall start rehearsing something. During the period of these first rehearsals I shall also (please God) finish the fourth. As yet I have not had the fifth, but I think it will be given to me as soon as possible. Nor have I so far neglected to do some work on the tourney ... [of which] at any rate the greater part – if not all of it – is planned ...'.

A few days later, the text of the fifth *intermedio* was also ready: therefore three were fully set to music, and the fourth was in progress while rehearsals were commencing, and meanwhile the matter of recruiting new singers was not forgotten:

> Now once more I tell you that we have had the fifth *intermedio*, and also the words sent by Signor Don Ascanio to Signor Monteverdi to adjust an *intermedio* ... However, we have selected ... a boy for [the role of] Amor who is in Ravenna with the Lord Cardinal Caponi, and so says the said Lord Count, who will have letters written for the one [a bass from Ancona] and the other ... For my part, I am not failing to do as much as is humanly possible to urge on Signor Claudio, who has completed three *intermedi* and who is working on a fourth. He pays reverence to Your Most Illustrious Lordship and wants to go to Venice for Christmas, and as soon as that is done, he will return on the first day of the [new] year, showing and saying that to serve that republic he cannot do anything less; in this time, however, he will finish all five *intermedi*. He has also done part of the tournament, and he will never stand idle and will also press ahead to finish the rest in time. The Lord Count has it in mind to allow him, and the said Signor Claudio pays reverence to Your Most Illustrious Lordship ... Today we were in the *salone* with Lord Count Fabio: in truth, it is a marvellous thing. Signor Claudio was entirely amazed, and they tried out the three Furies, which is certainly a thing of great wonder.[100]

Monteverdi's plan was to finish composing the *intermedi* in November 1627 and to take up his pen again in the New Year for the music of the tournament, since his presence in St Mark's in Venice for the Christmas celebrations was indispensable:

> Now I inform you that Signor Claudio pays reverence to Your Most Illustrious Lordship [Bentivoglio] and I am urging him on, and at the end of the present month he will have finished the five *intermedi* very well, and in

good taste, and as soon as they are finished he wants to present himself to the
lord duke and then to come to Venice to do the Christmas celebrations, and
as soon as they are done, on the first day of the [new] year he will return and
meanwhile he will press ahead with the tournament, and thus one could have
the musicians come for after Christmas to stage these entertainments, as they
say, at the end of carnival.[101]

However, first it was necessary to firm up arrangements for the tournament,
and Count Scotti thought it best to request the actual presence of Marquis
Bentivoglio, given his renowned skill in such chivalric exercises:

> But since I am still lacking any skilled person to rehearse them, it will be
> necessary for Your Most Illustrious Lordship to be willing to come here to
> direct them and also to glance over that which is being done in the theatres,
> and to manage and adjust that which must be done with Signor Monteverdi,
> the which Signor Monteverde is working on his compositions, and this is
> indeed a very considerate idea of his.[102]

The marquis's arrival was also requested by Goretti, who hoped thereby that
he, by a show of power, would take control of those thorny questions of
rivalry and jealousy created by the distribution of the parts among the singers
– as if the problems caused by the mountain of work and the haste were not
enough (indeed, these ended up causing problems over the legibility of what
Monteverdi was writing, of which Goretti was then required to make a fair
copy). Bentivoglio was also expected to solve a no less serious technical
problem concerning the position of the orchestra in the large permanent ducal
theatre built by Aleotti, which was arranged on noble classical lines but which
therefore lacked an effective solution to the recurring problem in contemporary theatres of where to put the instrumentalists.[103]

> We are still waiting for Your Most Illustrious Lordship for many things, and
> in particular as regards our own affairs, since Signor Claudio and I have
> decided that Your Most Illustrious Lordship should be the one to distribute
> the parts to these singers, nor will any part be given out before your arrival. I
> wish to know what has emerged as regards Angiola [Zanibelli?]. Signor
> Claudio pays reverence to Your Most Illustrious Lordship and remembers
> himself as your servant.[104]

> Here there is the Lord Duke Sforza, who has two brothers – castratos – who
> have already been in Ferrara at the [Accademia dello] Spirito Santo, one of
> whom pleases me, so that to hand out the parts, and given that neither Signor
> Claudio nor I wish to become embroiled in this task of handing them out
> given the blessed tiffs that exist between the singers on this matter ... We
> have been several times to the *salone* to begin to organize the places for the
> musicians both for accompanying the singers and as decoration where it is
> needed, and we have repeatedly found many difficulties because of the
> narrowness of the place for this blessed music, which is an essential part, and
> they never think at the right time about how it is to be done, and yet it is so
> very necessary. We were hoping that in this new theatre there would have
> been more space, but it is entirely the opposite and worse than the *salone*, so
> that it will be up to Your Most Illustrious Lordship to find space for it – for

we have not got the spirit to do it – so that the music can have that outcome which we desire. Signor Claudio pays reverence to Your Most Illustrious Lordship and thanks you for the welcome news that he can go to Venice for Christmas ...[105]

Taking advantage of the fact that Guiti is coming to you, I come with the present letter to pay reverence and to give you the news that the four *intermedi* are finished, and of the tournament the duke's first invention is done, and it was proposed to shorten the part of Mercury and of Mars, but Madame seemed to have no inclination to shorten it, or else it was the result of pressure from Signor Achilino, and so both parts have been done as they are. There remains the handing out of parts, and I have already written a good deal of the work done by Signor Claudio, which as it comes into my hands is so intricate and involved and confused that I promise Your Lordship that it makes me rack my brains, yet we're getting on. I have also written some parts to be handed out, but as regards handing them out, one never finds an end to giving them out: I would not tell you the reason, [but] it is necessary that it should be someone other than us, given that there is some unknown tiff between these singers which we do not want to get involved in, since the proof will make everything clear ... Meanwhile, I pay you reverence, as also does Signor Claudio ...[106]

Francesco Mazzi also referred to the problems connected with positioning the musicians on 16 November 1627: 'Signor Monteverde has been to see the place for the music, and there is a considerable difficulty to satisfy him according to his ideas, and at the very first, he began to say that he could not understand it, but we will not fail in every way to seek to satisfy him.'[107] The huge amount of work and these logistical problems led Monteverdi to ask – and to have the duke ask – the procurators of St Mark's to extend his leave (L.113 [114], 8 November 1627). But as Christmas gradually approached, Monteverdi grew increasingly anxious to return to Venice, better still, taking with him some virtuoso singers to be used in the celebrations in St Mark's, thereby showing the procurators that the absence of their *maestro* was not damaging the *cappella* and indeed might benefit it. However, those in charge of the ducal establishment seem to have been little inclined towards this idea of lending musicians, and they held on to the composers's coat-tails to have him stay in the city for as long as possible.

Today we have begun to hand out the parts for the rehearsals. I am certain that nothing will be done before Christmas, since it is very close and Signor Claudio greatly insists on going to Venice as soon as possible, since he has to produce a service before Christmas, for which he is being urged by letters, and they are services which will earn up to 40 ducats, and for this he is also insisting – very much so – that I should go, and when he goes, he wants four of these singers to come with us and with him to Venice, who are one Signor Gregorio [Lazzarini], Signor [Antonio] Grimani [both castratos], a bass from the *cappella* and a good tenor also from the *cappella*. I mentioned this to Lord Count Fabio, as I was requested to by them, who did not seem very happy with the idea, but he reserved himself to speak about it with Madame, and he has said that concerning Signor Claudio he does not want him to leave until directly before Christmas, something which does not please him although Signor Claudio does not know this since I am keeping it to myself, and I keep him in good hope, so that he presses ahead with the work, which certainly needs to go on with much speed, for often he laments and complains about the long work and the multitude of verses [to be set] in short time. Before we leave, four *intermedi* will be finished, and the invention of the lord duke is now finished but not perfected, since there are many things to adjust, which will be finished as I have said; and I promise both from him and from me to unburden him as much as possible, and I attempt with all diligence to help him in everything as much as I can.[108]

Overwhelmed by the amount of work and by the organizational problems, in a moment of nervousness Goretti sent Marquis Bentivoglio an outburst which provides a fair sketch of Monteverdi's character. In his usual phlegmatic way – and even in the midst of these difficulties – the composer did not intend to deprive himself of certain creature-comforts (a post-prandial nap) or of the pleasure of conversation, however much the zealous Goretti imposed on him a rigid order of silence and avoided letting him go out:

Madame has had removed from the third *intermedio* the part for Diana, whence it is necessary to do this again as well. Signor Claudio will do it, but he wants to go to Venice at the end of the coming week, so that we shall go there and then return after Christmas if, that is, it is convenient and things are to be done for carnival. I shall do what I can about hurrying the workmen along, as Your Most Illustrious Lordship bids me, but understand that I have so much to do that I do not have time to breathe. We never go out of doors, and I alone go, with effort, to Mass. Signor Claudio composes only in the morning and the evening: during the afternoon he does not wish to do anything at all. I urge him, and I relieve him of such labour – which means taking the work from under his hands, after having discussed and arranged it together; and I find it so intricate and tangled that I give Your Most Illustrious Lordship my word that I labour more than if I were to compose it all by myself; and that if it had to be left to him to write it, it would take time and plenty of it (and if I were not at his heels so much, he would not have done half of what he has done). It is true that the labour is great, and tedious; but still, he is a man who likes to talk things over in company at great length (and about this, I make it a rule to take the opportunity away from him during working hours) – so that I wish to say that my job is no small one, and I say this to Your Most Illustrious Lordship in all calmness and truth.[109]

While letters were being sent from Venice ordering Monteverdi to return to his post,[110] at Parma, his departure was repeatedly being delayed both for the desire to see the composition finished – or at least as far on as possible – and also for the delight which the duke and duchess took in attending rehearsals, which were until then held in the chamber of the two musicians but which now also took place in the ducal rooms.

We held it for certain that we should leave if not yesterday at least today, and to show the work in good shape to these rulers, we have laboured and worked all day without ever leaving our chamber and until seven or eight hours of night to finish four *intermedi*, and the entire invention of the lord duke, and to make a master-copy which is the original of the work, and I promise Your Most Illustrious Lordship that we are tired and need to breathe a little. These rulers having seen this diligence and this lively push forward (if indeed they know of it) have taken it in mind not to be happy that the rehearsals are done in our chamber, but that they should be repeated in the chamber of Madame and the lord duke, and they have shown themselves – to put it badly – to gain such delight from this to the extent that they have delayed our departure until next Sunday, and please God that it should not go beyond then, since I have gathered that they want to hear something in the *salone*, something which, if this were the case, could not be done but poorly, but it needs a few more days, for it is one thing to rehearse in a room and another to rehearse on the stage, for it is necessary first to concert it well with the instruments in the chamber and then on the stage, and now there are no suitable instrumentalists in Parma. So they go on retaining Signor Claudio to his displeasure, for since the celebrations which must be done for Christmas in Venice are pressing such that it could be a reason for forcing him to leave that service, since never has a letter come from the Signory saying that they are happy that he is here ... Signor Claudio and I pay reverence to Your Most Illustrious Lordship and we remember ourselves as always yours ... I doubt that Madame will want to give permission to these gentlemen to go to Venice with Signor Claudio, and they are mortified.[111]

Finally, it was decided to release Monteverdi for the moment. At the same time as his return to Venice, Odoardo Farnese wrote in person to the doge (on 9 December) asking for new permission on the composer's behalf so that 'the said celebrations having passed, he can return here, where his person is necessary for the execution of that which with such good grace he with his skills has put in train for the entertainments to be done for my wedding'.[112] On 9 January, from Venice, the composer wrote (to Striggio?) in Mantua (L.116 [117]):

I hope that, within two days, I shall return to Parma to prepare for Their Most Serene Highnesses the music for the tournament and the *intermedi* of the play that is going to be produced. From there, if it please you, I shall send news of the outcome of these events. From Venice, through the Most Excellent Lord Procurator Contarino, my master (as he is procurator of St Mark's), I heard yesterday by word of mouth that His Excellency not only believes, but fears, that the wedding will not take place this carnival time, nor this May – letters from Ferrara say it will take place then – and perhaps not even at all. Anyway I shall go and prepare the music that I have been given, for more than this I cannot, nor must I do.

Some ten days later, Monteverdi and Goretti were again in Parma. The latter wrote to Bentivoglio on 21 January 1628 that 'Signor Claudio pays reverence to Your Most Illustrious Lordship and he, too, wishes you here',[113] while the composer told Striggio on 4 February (L.117 [118]):

Here in Parma the music is being rehearsed, having been written by me in haste – Their Most Serene Highnesses believing that the noble wedding might have to take place some time before the appointed date – and these rehearsals are being held because in Parma there are Roman and Modenese singers, instrumentalists from Piacenza, and others. Since Their Most Serene

Highnesses have seen how these musicians fulfil their needs, and the success they are having, and their confident outlook upon the event that they are preparing in a very few days, it is considered that we – all of us – could go home, until firm news of the outcome, which they say could be this May, though others favour this September.

There will be two most beautiful entertainments – one a complete spoken play with the *intermedi apparenti* in music (there is no *intermedio* that is not at least 300 lines in length, and each has a different character, the words having been written by the Most Illustrious Don Ascanio Pio, son-in-law of the Marquis Enzo Bentivoglio, and a most worthy and gifted nobleman); the other will be a tournament, in which four squadrons of knights will take part, and the master of ceremonies will be the duke himself. Signor Achillini has written the words for the tournament, and there are more than a thousand lines, which is very nice for the tournament but very long drawn out as regards the music. They have given me a great deal to do.

Just now they are rehearsing the music for this tournament. Whenever I could not find enough emotional variety, I tried to change the instrumentation, and I hope this will give pleasure.

While the work was proceeding, a solution was found for one of the greatest problems that had worried Monteverdi and Goretti from the outset, that of positioning the musicians in the large ducal theatre, and particularly of the special acoustic requirements imposed on them by so big a space. Guitti, the architect, informed the marquis on 18 February 1628 of the successful resolution of so serious a problem:

> Signor Monteverde has finally found harmony, for I have provided him with a place to suit him – which much pleases him – which is on the level of the lower stairway in this way: area A is a pit and goes to the level of the *salone*, and it will be behind a balustrade which surrounds it, and the instruments will not be seen, yet it goes very well with the stage and permits the opportunity to light also the balustrades C and advances level B so that there remains a very large space for His Most Serene Highness to ascend the stage. The steps can be within, and when needed, they can be pushed forward to good effect, and the semicircle C will be provided with a wall to protect the musicians from the water. But the sketch is not to scale: suffice it that Your Most Illustrious Lordship understands it, and that it truly serves well both for the sight-lines and for the music, and the rehearsal has shown this solution to be good.[114]

Instead of putting the musicians behind the stage or hidden in balconies, as was most often the case, it had therefore been decided to place the instrumentalists in the space beneath the proscenium between the two flights of movable stairs which connected the floor of the theatre with the stage, protected and rendered invisible by balustrades reinforced by a watertight covering to prevent the proposed flooding of the hall (in fact, there were plans for a *naumachia*) from harming the musicians. A similar solution had been adopted in Florence in 1622 for the performance of *Il martirio di sant'Agata*, a *sacra rappresentazione* by Jacopo Cicognini prepared by the Accademia degl'Infiammati with scenery by Alfonso Parigi and music by Giovan Battista da

Gagliano and Francesca Caccini; here, too, the musicians were placed at the foot of the proscenium, behind a palisade.[115] In 1638, Guitti was to repeat this arrangement of the musicians for the tournament *L'Andromeda* in the Ferrarese theatre of the Sala Grande: clearly he was convinced of the effectiveness of what had been done ten years before in Parma in collaboration with Monteverdi.[116] In fact, this solution was both practical and very effective; the singers and the instrumentalists were perfectly visible one to the other, facilitating their joint need for performing together, and the sound was significantly brought forward to the extent of being able to spread to the centre of the room. For all these reasons, such a solution soon imposed itself on theatre design of the mid-seventeenth century, rendering systematic an innovation which up to this time had been adopted only sporadically.

On his part, Goretti wrote to Marquis Enzo to tell him of the technical expedient now adopted, and at the same time to reveal to him that they were thinking of using more sonorous instruments such as, for example, the claviorgano (a harpsichord plus an organ controlled by the same keyboard), and also to reinforce the harpsichords, for example, with resonating chests. The rest of this letter is also very interesting, referring to Venice and to the entertainments which the local nobility were organizing for carnival, in which Monteverdi was hoping to take part just as he had done in the past (remember that such circumstances produced the pastoral *balletto* of 1620, the *Combattimento* of 1624 and also the first version of the projected *La finta pazza Licori*). The composer counted on being able to profit from the temporary halting of work for Parma, and perhaps to succeed in taking with him one or more virtuosos engaged for those entertainments, but those in charge of the organization did not seem very disposed to favour him: Monteverdi was left only to complain of good money going up in smoke.

> We have been working hard both to finish the work for the *salone* and to produce four books to play from, as has now been all done, and also in the case of the comedy, four books have been produced to play from for the first and the second *intermedio*. One cannot go ahead any further because of the problems which Your Most Illustrious Lordship must know. We have also adjusted the sound appropriate for the theatre by having had made some pipes to help the harpsichords, and we have also added them to the front of the stage, in the space between the arms of the stairways, where the machinery of the stairs stands, and this, too, for the music, so that it will be in the same manner as we did for Your Most Illustrious Lordship, so that the sound will be adjusted. Guitti says that all this will provide decoration for the stage-front. There remains only a small difficulty, and that is over the water, for which it will be necessary to build part of a wall in the said place of the stairways to save the instruments and the claviorgano which we propose should be placed there. Guiti highly praises the enterprise, and so does Tamera, but the Lord Count is not inclined towards it, so that I do not know how it will turn out.
>
> All this goes well, but we do not have anything more to do at present, and they do not want to give us permission to leave, and Lord Count Fabio is reluctant to grant permission for Signor Gregorio [Lazzarini] with those

other two singers to come with us to Venice, for which Signor Gregorio is displeased and he holds it certain that an order must be coming from Rome that he should return, so that if Your Most Illustrious Lordship does not help us, and quickly, with a letter so that we might go, we will stay here gazing at the moon . . .

Signor Claudio has nothing to say, but I realize the serious loss he suffers by being absent from Venice given the many entertainments that are done, for which he receives twenty plus twenty ducats apiece.[117]

Perhaps to calm down ill-feelings – but also so as not to keep those involved inactive and to profit from such an extraordinary gathering of architects, costume-makers, singers, instrumentalists and composers at carnival time – an attempt to prepare something, if only a *mascherata* with floats, could not be resisted, even if it was to the detriment of the preparations for the wedding which were so laborious on their own account. For the occasion, Monteverdi provided a 'madrigal . . . sung for three voices' on a float in the form of the 'ship of the Argonauts', for which Achillini had prepared the text: but this perhaps was nothing more than a foretaste of the fourth *intermedio* of *Aminta*, which had as its subject the golden fleece.

From the last time I wrote to Your Most Illustrious Lordship until now, little work has been done, and almost nothing, because we are waiting to serve the Lord Prince Francesco Maria for *mascherate*, for which a float with musicians is being made, and now a ship is being made for Sunday, which should move by itself and be of a good size, and it must carry twenty men, which I have sketched here, but very ornate with gold trimmings. On this, the Lord Prince must go, pretending to be on the ship of the Argonauts who search for the golden fleece, meaning glory. Signor Achillini had written a madrigal to this effect which has been set to music by Signor Monteverde, and it is sung in three parts by Signor Grimani, Signor Gregorio and that bass from Rome, with the instruments from Piacenza.[118]

On the other hand, the preparations for the wedding entertainments were proceeding far from quickly:

After the things which I have already written to Your Most Illustrious Lordship, it remains for me to give you a report on the rehearsals, since the musicians' parts have been changed, and they are inexpert and also frightened, and these harmonies of Signor Monteverde do not work at all, and I have seen the Most Serene Lord Duke somewhat less than pleased with the music, which is organized more in terms of speeches than of actions, and when they are ordered to be rehearsed, they do not give time to move and stop the machines, so that it is almost no rehearsal at all, and one works in vain, because nothing significant is ever done; and the machines break down more than anything else.[119]

The rehearsals were still continuing in November 1628. At the beginning of the month, Goretti told Marquis Bentivoglio: 'With this opportunity of someone being sent by the post to get another pandora . . . we are in order for the tournament, and there has been a general rehearsal which turned out very well for the first one. This evening we return to do it again, and there will be gains without losses, so that I hope that things will go much better than what was hoped. The task is large, and the urgency ... is very pressing.'[120] On 28 November, Goretti again wrote with some concern:

> We are at the end of the month and we are also at the time to stage these entertainments. We have rehearsed them and for our part the music turns out very well indeed. The machines are beautiful and wondrous, but they still do not move in time; however, all are hoping that the machines and the music will go together, [and] it is necessary for the two to go well, so that we carry on working, and I do not see when I shall see the end of it so as to be able to come.[121]

Marcello Buttigli, the chronicler of the entertainments, has left us a *Descritione dell'apparato fatto per onorare la prima et solenne entrata in Parma della serenissima d. Margherita di Toscana duchessa di Parma e Piacenza* ('Description of the pomp made to honour the first and solemn entrance into Parma of the Most Serene Lady Margherita of Tuscany, Duchess of Parma and Piacenza'; Parma, Seth & Erasmo Viotti, 1629).[122] In his account, however, the references to the music are all somewhat incidental. As regards the *intermedi* for *Aminta*, performed on 13 December 1628 in the theatre built in the courtyard of S. Pietro Martire, Buttigli writes:

> [Prologue, p. 154]
> ... they sat in their places and suddenly one heard a very sweet *sinfonia* of instruments, both played by hand and wind instruments, at the end of which in the blink of an eye the curtain disappeared ...

> [First *intermedio*, p. 166]
> The first act having been performed, and a well-concerted *sinfonia*, the woodland scene disappeared ...

> [Second *intermedio*, pp. 181, 190 and 197]
> The second act having been performed, while a very sweet harmony of angelic voices and of musical instruments delighted the ears of the spectators, the unexpected disappearance of the woodland scene tricked the eye ... hearing a very sweet *sinfonia*, [Juno] appeared with a chorus of fourteen nymphs, all dressed in gold cloth, changing into peacock blue. These, playing various wind instruments, were carried on a large cloud ... [and the *intermedio* was ended by] musical *concerti* of angelic voices ...

> [Fourth *intermedio*, p. 251]
> Orpheus having now arisen in the middle of the ship, and placing on his left shoulder the curved and hollow wood, and with an ivory and gilded plectrum suavely touching the strings of the heavenly lyre, with superhuman harmony sang the following verses: 'Numi del cielo e mar, s'a vostra lode' ['Gods of the heaven and sea, if to your praise'] ...

> [Fifth *intermedio*, p. 244]
> The *sinfonia* lasted so long that from heaven to earth descended the

[heavenly] city described above, with its knights, who on leaving the cloud, were aroused by the heavenly chorus singing ...

Buttigli grants more space to the appearance of Aurora (Dawn) in the introduction of the tournament *Mercurio e Marte*, held in the Teatro Farnese on 21 December 1628, given that the singer who gave voice to this character was the celebrated Settimia Caccini:

> Now while the horse [Pegasus], gently beating its wings, drew the chariot from the waves, and as the sea and the rocks were illuminated little by little at its ascent, a distinguished singer, singing the following verses with super-human grace and an angelic voice, made the air resound and filled the entire theatre with sweetest accents:
>
> > Lascia Titon, deh lascia ...
> > [Leave, Titon, ah leave ...]
>
> As soon as Signor Settimia, representing Aurora, began to sing, all conver-sation among the spectators ceased on account of the amazing illumination of the scene produced by Aurora's rays, and of the representation of the aforesaid sea, and all eyes were amazed by the divinity manifest in the countenance and garments of the goddess, in the chariot and in the skilful motion of Pegasus. Similarly, all ears were so consoled by the sweetness of the voice and the divine quality of the song, that among the 10,000 people seated in the theatre, there was no one, however feeble of judgement, who did not grow tender at the trills, sigh at the sighs, become ecstatic at the ornaments, and who were not stupified and transfixed by the miraculous beauty and song of a heavenly siren ... As long as the ascent of the chariot from the bottom to the topmost part of the scene, guided with imperceptible motion through a quarter-circle, lasted, so long was the silence retained and did the ecstatic vision of the spectators last, who, while a new *sinfonia* accompanied other admirable things as regards aerial motions which pre-ceded the appearance of the zodiac, while the ear enjoyed to an incredible extent the harmony produced by those most well concerted instruments, nonetheless the enjoyment of an earlier greater pleasure diminished some-what the taste for a lesser one following, and everyone's tongue was loosened in sincere commendation of the no less graceful and beautiful as learned and excellent singer, of whom the honoured memory was revived of that lady having performed well and excellently singing in the smaller theatre [of S. Pietro Martire] the vehement passions of the betrayed Dido, and they imagined with greater expectation what she would be like in the forth-coming vice-regency of the goddess Juno ... Aurora having left, while the five choruses with suave *concerti* of voices and instruments entertained the audience, large-scale aerial changes began ... [pp. 270–72]

Monteverdi was also in Parma for the period of the entertainments to take charge of the performance of the music. Here he received first a letter from his pupil and vice-*maestro di cappella*, Giovanni Rovetta, and then a notice from the procurators (dated 13 December 1628), both of which requested him to return as soon as possible to St Mark's, given that the Christmas celebrations were fast approaching.[123]

30   1628–1632

1628 saw the reprinting (in Venice, by Bartolomeo Magni) of the Seventh
Book and the *Scherzi musicali a tre voci*, and also the setting of *I cinque fratelli*,
'sonnets by Giulio Strozzi honoured with music by Signor Claudio Monteverde and sung in the royal banquet held by the Most Serene Republic of
Venice in its famous arsenal for the most serene princes Don Ferdinando II,
Fifth Grand Duke of Tuscany, and Don Carlo de' Medici his brother'
(according to the title-page).[124] The music has been lost, and only the text
survives ('La Garda impoverir di pesci egregi', 'Pasceran gli occhi i due
bramosi erranti', 'L'ingegno diede alle grandezze uguale', 'S'uniran queste
prore alla tua prora' and [?]'Si fa, ch'a rivoltar dotti volumi') printed in Venice
by Evangelista Deuchino in 1628.[125]

In 1629, Monteverdi contributed three motets to Don Lorenzo Calvi's
Quarta raccolta de sacri canti (Venice, Alessandro Vincenti); as we have seen,
Calvi was *maestro di cappella* of Pavia Cathedral, and he had published his own
sacred compositions on several previous occasions. In the dedication (dated 28
September 1629), Calvi said that he had been able to collect those 'musical
concerti ... by distinguished authors ... thanks to their favour'. In Monteverdi's case, he included two Marian motets (the three-voice 'Salve o Regina'
– for alto, tenor, bass and continuo – later included in the *Selva morale e
spirituale*,[126] and the five-voice 'Exultent coeli et gaudeant angeli', for two
sopranos, alto, tenor, bass and continuo, for the feast of the Annunciation [25
March]), plus a Christmas antiphon ('Exulta filia Sion'), 'a voce sola e
continuo' ('for solo voice [soprano] and continuo').[127]

For Carnival 1630, Monteverdi was commissioned to write a canzonetta by
an unknown correspondent who, because of the references to Parma and of
the fact that Goretti is brought into the matter, can perhaps be identified as
Marquis Bentivoglio.[128] On 23 February (L.120 [121]), Monteverdi informed
him (Stevens suggests Don Ascanio Pio di Savoia) that he had not been able

> immediately to write music for the very beautiful words sent to me, because
> I was a little taken up with certain ecclesiastical compositions for some of the
> nuns of S. Lorenzo who insisted no little on my doing it.
>   I shall certainly hope to send Your Most Illustrious Lordship, by the next
> post, the canzonetta which you requested of me.

The words, then, seem to have been by Bentivoglio (if my identification of
the addressee of this letter is correct), and Monteverdi sent the piece off on
9 March:[129]

> Illmo et ecc.^{mo} mio sig.^r et p.ron coll.^{mo}

> Mi perdonerà se tardi son statto un poco a mandar a V. Ecc.^{za} Illma la
> canzonetta che si è degnata comandarmi, poiché per mia molta disgratia mi è
> convenuto per una ganba starmene in letto quattro giorni, et è ancora la
> ganba alla quale a Parma mi feci un poco di male come bene il sig.^r Goretti

potrà certificarne V.E.Illma Piacia a Dio che io abbi incontrato nel suo finiss.^{mo} gusto: quando che no, si pagherà ch'io non ho saputo la propria aplicatione che forsi averei scritto piú apropriato, et l'animo mio con cui desidero servirla integriss.^{te} in tutto sarà quello che intrerà a congiovarmi, con il quale anco calda.^{te} prego a V.E.Illma ogni maggior felicità et contento, mentre con il piú vivo del core gli faccio umill.^{ma} riverenza et gli bacio la mano.

da Venetia gli 9 marzo 1630

di V.Ecc.^{za} Illma

Umill.^{mo} et obblig.^{mo} se.^{re}
Claudio Monteverdi

My Most Illustrious and Most Excellent Lord and Most Respected Master.

You will forgive me if I have been a little slow in sending Your Most Illustrious Excellency the canzonetta which you have deigned to commission from me, for (much to my displeasure) it was advisable for me – because of my leg – to stay in bed for four days; and again it is the leg which gave me some trouble in Parma, as Signor Goretti can well testify to Your Most Illustrious Excellency. Please God that I have met your very fine taste; and if not, it will suffice that I have not known the proper application with which I would perhaps have written more appropriately, and my spirit – with which I desire to serve you most fully in all things – will be that which enters to support me. With which I also pray fervently for Your Most Illustrious Excellency's greater happiness and pleasure, while with all my heart I pay you most humble reverence and kiss your hand.

From Venice, 9 March 1630,

Your Most Illustrious Excellency's

Most humble and most grateful servant
Claudio Monteverdi

In this same period, Monteverdi was involved in writing the music for *Proserpina rapita*, an 'anatopismo' (the meaning of the term is unclear) by Giulio Strozzi written for the wedding of Giustiniana Mocenigo and Lorenzo Giustiniani, which took place in spring 1630. To celebrate the event in a princely way, Count Girolamo Mocenigo wished to have performed in his palace (where the *Combattimento di Tancredi et Clorinda* had been given in 1624), some theatrical work with music. In dedicating to the Count the libretto (dated 16 April 1630), Evangelista Deuchino wrote:

> This graceful composition should have no other protecting power than Your Most Illustrious Lordship. With your most prudent advice, it was constructed by Signor Strozzi, and with your great authority you had it adorned with music, and divinely concerted with proportioned harmonies, by Signor Claudio Monteverde. Having then entrusted the dances and the choreography to Signor Girolamo Scolari, and the scenery and the machines to the most ingenious Signor Giuseppe Schioppi, today with your usual munificence you wish to have it performed at the most happy wedding of your most illustrious daughter.

The libretto contains a number of references to the music:

[p. 6] Paranetic Acclamation

With Phrygian harmony, enthusiastic, that is aroused and vehement, sung in the theatre by two full choruses before the curtain fell.

> Scenda omai la cortina: e che si tarda? ...
> [Let the curtain descend, and why the delay? ...]

[p. 7] Prologue

Sung by Hymen and partitioned by a most lively *sinfonia* in choreographic rhythm, that is, in a dance-style; and Hymen descends from the sky on a golden eagle full of roses, alluding to the arms of the wedding couple, Giustiniani and Mozzenigo:

> Dall'alta, augusta, adamantina rocca ...
> [From the high, majestic, adamantine rock ...]

[p. 12] Parthenian canzonetta sung by the three nymphs with Lydian harmony, that is soft in sound and suitable for young girls:

> Come dolce oggi l'auretta ...
> [How sweet the breeze today ...]

[pp. 15–16] Pachinos and Anapos come from afar singing together this beginning of a hymn to Love, which the Greeks called *prosodio*, and it was delivered by them while walking to the sound of an aulos, that is of a pipe or other wind instrument:

> La pargoletta acerba ...
> [The harsh girl ...]

[p. 22] Pachinos with Mixolydian harmony accompanied only by the lyre players unfolds his lament called threnody by the ancient Greeks:

> Misero esempio di schernito amante ...
> [Wretched example of a scorned lover ...]

[p. 29] *Ballo* of Cruelty danced by four shepherds and sung by three nymphs to the full lyre:

> Il valor d'ogni beltà ...
> [The power of all beauty ...]

[p. 34] Chorus of infernal deities – Minos, Aeacus and Rhadamanthys, Clotho, Lachesis and Atropos with six other spirits – who dance to their song an infernal dance sounded by the aulos players, or wind instrumentalists:

> Chi mai costei sarà ...
> [Who will ever be she ...]

The entertainment, which seems to have been not fully in music, concluded with a *ballo* before which Strozzi, through the character of Pachinos, introduces a short eulogy of the celebrated composer: 'Quanto nel chiaro mondo / su VERDI arcadi MONTI / di te si cantarà?' ('How much in the clear world / on GREEN Arcadian MOUNTAINS / will be sung of you?') [p. 42].

An account of the event has also survived in the diary of Girolamo Priuli, who for the same 16 April 1630 noted:

> With the occasion of the marriage of D... his daughter to Ser Lorenzo Giustiniani, [son] of the deceased Ser Girolamo, Ser Girolamo Mocenigo, [son] of the deceased Ser Andrea, held a most solemn and extraordinary banquet for the relatives and friends, with truly royal trappings, giving them in the meal that was prepared meat and fish, and cold and hot dishes – all that could be offered – with four or five servings of confections, both regaling the dishes and as *intermedi* between one and the other courses. After this meal there was dancing until the twenty-fourth hour, and then in the evening with torches there was recited and represented in music (something the like of which had never been seen) the Rape of Proserpina with most perfect voices and instruments, with aerial apparitions, scene changes and other things, to the astonishment and wonder of all those present. The banquet was held in the house where he lives and which he owns on the Calle delle Rasse on the lower floor, and on the upper floor owned by Messer Gritto there was represented the play which was invented by Signor Giulio Strozzi, Florentine, a virtuous person living in this city, and the music was the work of Monteverde, famous *maestro di cappella* of the ducal chapel, and the French Dukes of Roan and Candales were there with singular satisfaction and also equal admiration.[130]

Only a fragment of this music survives, the 'Parthenian canzonetta' 'Come dolce oggi l'auretta' later published in the posthumous Ninth Book of *Madrigali e canzonette* (1651).[131] However, it can be seen that in the librettist's description, the search for a fitting musical realization of the *affetti* was steeped in classicism: an instrumental *ballo* becomes a '*sinfonia* in choreographic rhythm', the viol-players 'lirodi' and the 'pipe', an 'aulos'. The colouring of the infernal instruments which appeared in the sung *ballo* 'Chi mai costei sarà' – with its emphasis on 'aulos players, or wind instrumentalists' – was traditional (we have already seen it in *Orfeo*). No less typical, but above all Monteverdian, was the *topos* of Pachinos's lament (a 'threnody', obviously), 'Misero esempio di schernito amante', among other things accompanied 'only by the lyre players', i.e. just as the celebrated *Lamento d'Arianna* had been accompanied by '*viole* and violins'.[132] And the reference to the 'Phrygian harmony, enthusiastic, that is aroused and vehement' makes one think of Monteverdi's experiments of the 1620s concerning the *genere concitato* which climaxed in the *Combattimento* but which received its theoretical justification only later, in the preface to the Eighth Book (1638). This may have been influenced by that veneer of Greek culture which was widespread earlier and which in the case of Monteverdi in these years (he was soon to exchange letters with so erudite a person as Giovan Battista Doni) was revived perhaps because of his contacts with Strozzi.

The complicated dynastic dealings concerning the succession of the duchy of Mantua after the death of the last son of Vincenzo Gonzaga, Duke Vincenzo II (d. 1627), led to war; the most disastrous of its consequences was certainly the spreading to northern Italy of the plague introduced by the

Imperial troops who, among other things, besieged, conquered and sacked Mantua (18–21 July 1630). The epidemic spread slowly and even into the Veneto, and it was perhaps brought to Venice by Alessandro Striggio himself, who went there as ambassador to seek help against the army encircling the capital of the duchy and who instead died there – he was already ill – on 8 June 1630.[133] As the plague spread in Venice (it raged from summer 1630 to autumn 1631, with a peak in autumn 1630, causing almost 50,000 deaths, about a third of the city's population),[134] Monteverdi made a vow to the Virgin that, if he escaped, he would make a pilgrimage to Loreto. In the first months of 1634 – the danger was now some time past – this vow had not yet been fulfilled (L.123 [124], 2 February 1634): 'Because of a special favour received of the Most Holy Virgin's consummate goodness in the year of the plague at Venice, I am bound by a vow to visit the Most Holy House of Loreto. I hope soon, with the Lord's help to fulfil it ...'. But we have no further mention of the matter.

During the plague itself, public vows were soon joined to private ones; the former included (as over fifty years before with the Chiesa del Redentore) the building of a church in honour of the Virgin so that she might intercede to obtain the freedom of the city from contagion.[135] On 26 October 1630 in St Mark's were held the solemn ceremonies proclaiming the vow (agreed by the Senate two months earlier) in which the musicians of the *cappella* (and so certainly Monteverdi) took part: 'the litanies of the Most Blessed Virgin for two choirs were begun'.[136] After the procession in St Mark's square, they returned into the church: 'The oration [votive, recited by the doge] finished, which was heard by all most attentively, the Low Mass of the Blessed Virgin was recited by the primicerius, with His Serenity and the cardinal responding to the Introit. At the Secret were sung two motets to the organs.'[137] The first stone of the church was solemnly laid on 1 April 1631, during a service in St Mark's which also involved a procession to the Dogana, the place destined as the site of the new Chiesa della Salute:

> The Mass completed, the litanies of the Blessed Virgin were begun by singers, and at the invocation 'Santa Maria, ora pro nobis', the procession set off through the great door of the church ... After the benedictions, having returned to the church [the new one, temporarily erected in wood], the same patriarch, having taken off his mitre and cope, put on a white chasuble and recited a Low Mass of the Blessed Virgin, with the Most Serene Doge responding to the Introit as usual. All stood there with great devotion. At the Secret was sung in music the psalm 'Deus misereatur nostri etc.', and this lasted until the Elevation; and after was similarly sung the psalm 'Laudate'. At the end of the Mass, the patriarch having dismissed himself, they returned in procession to St Mark's in the same order, singing the same litanies.[138]

In the last months of 1631, the plague was finally defeated, and the event was marked by public displays proclaiming the passing of danger. As usual, the ceremonies held in St Mark's (on 21 November) included a procession to the quarter of the votive church, which had been provided with temporary decorations and the like to guarantee its presentability: 'The Minister of Health arrived, before whom were the trumpets and drums which in the church itself gave the sign of rejoicing. They remained in the church, and the Minister took his place ... A most solemn Mass was sung, with the trumpets sounding on some occasions in the *Gloria in excelsis* and in the *Credo*.'[139] Then the procession left St Mark's along the square:

> After the congregations [of clerics] came the canons of [S. Pietro in] Castello, who stopping before the church sang the *Te Deum*, and last were the clergy of St Mark's with the musicians, and the most holy image of the Blessed Virgin was carried by four clerics with the customary robes, and the umbrella was carried by the same Minister of Health, with beside him four priests who helped him. The trumpets and drums preceded, then the canons with copes and Monsignor Primicerius with the mitre on his head and the crook in hand. Once the most holy image was placed on the altar, and when His Serenity arrived, the *Te Deum* was sung by musicians.[140]

According to Marco Ginammi, the music of these ceremonies was directed – and perhaps composed – by Monteverdi himself: 'a most solemn Mass was sung, and during the *Gloria* and *Credo*, Signor Claudio Monteverdi, the *maestro di cappella* and the glory of our age, had the singing unite [*facendo ... unir il canto*] with the *trombe squarciate* with exquisite and marvellous harmony'.[141]

In summer 1632, Monteverdi made a trip to Mantua 'for a business matter which greatly concerns me', as he explained in a request for leave to Doge Francesco Erizzo (L.121 [122]), which was granted him on 7 March 1632.[142] Because of illness, he stayed in Mantua at least until 20 August 1632, for on that date the procurators were forced to request his return to Venice:

> To Signor Don Claudio Monteverde, *maestro di cappella* to the Most Serene Signory of Venice.
>
> Most Illustrious and Reverend Sir,
>
> We have received yours of the 7th instant, but have received no other letter, and we sympathize with your past illness and with the nuisance of the litigations which have kept [you] in those parts, but we rejoice, however, that you are recovered and that you are at the end and conclusion of your disputes, wherefore we will be expecting you as soon as possible so that you can return to the service of the church and to your post as soon as you are able, and this is the desire of their most excellent lords here and ours, with which we commend ourselves to you.[143]

It will be noted here how Monteverdi is given the title 'Don', one reserved for clerics or, according to Spanish custom, for high-placed people (but the latter is clearly not to be considered here). An earlier example is also provided by the *Scherzi musicali*, printed in 1632 and headed by a dedication dated 20 June: here the title-page registers the new ecclesiastical position of the composer, since they are styled works 'del m.^to ill.^re e m.^to r.^do sig.^r Claudio Monteverde maestro di capella della Sereniss. Repub. di Venetia' ('of the Very

Illustrious and Very Reverend Signor Claudio Monteverde, *maestro di cappella* of the Most Serene Republic of Venice'). After the failure of his attempt (in 1627) to obtain a canonry in Cremona (see above, p. 205), it is likely that Monteverdi, now close to seventy years in age, had thought to guarantee himself a tranquil old age by becoming a priest and enjoying the economic benefits tied to the institution of canonries.

> In this city, in the service of the ducal chapel of St Mark's, our Claudio decided to stay; I call him 'our', since he renounced any other homeland, knowing as a truly wise man that where one lives well, there is one's home. A good four *lustra* passed as Monteverdi, with his spirit fixed on the sole study of his art, emulating all new invention through the exquisiteness of his skill, was publicly acclaimed the first composer known in our centuries. He did not grow proud at such glory, but just as with harmonic number he had found the more than perfect art of musical composition, so he sought with his advancing studies to advance himself still more in his virtues, not having given in the long space of full twenty years any sign of being other than prudent and wise and above all religious, considering that if he had gratefully gained so noble an acquisition as to be glorious in the world, he wanted equally by way of advancing steps to gain the glory of heaven. And since through his art he was already called divine, he wished by way of sacred orders to sanctify himself. For which end, having laid aside his secular habit, he clothed himself with the ecclesiastical one, and he made himself a priest. Let another pen come to describe the integrity of his life, the exemplariness of his manners, for it remains for me only to say that by divine action he always corresponded to his divine vocation, and having to all his greater praise overcome the ordinary envy persecuting those who journey to the height of skill, heaven granted two further *lustra* so that Claudio, a priest, practising all religious duties, but above all else to benefit the future, having given himself to philosophy was in the process of writing a volume in which, noting the most hidden secrets of his art, he sought to prevent that never more in centuries to come would be hidden from students the true paths to facilitate the gaining of perfection in the art of music.[144]

According to Caberloti, Monteverdi passed 'a good four *lustra*' ('full twenty years' he says elsewhere) in the laity, and 'two more *lustra*' as an ecclesiastic. Recent archival discoveries allow us to document precisely the composer's path to this new status.[145] The process was set in motion in the first months of 1629: the dismissory letter from the see of Cremona, whose clergy Monteverdi wished to join, is dated 8 May. He took the tonsure and was admitted to the four Minor Orders on 9 March 1631 in Venice in the chapel of the patriarch's palace in S. Pietro di Castello by the patriarch, Giovanni Tiepolo. Two singers from St Mark's bore witness to his good morals, Don Giovanni de Blasiis da Arzignano and Fra Stefano Rinieri da Ferrara. Holy Orders were conferred again in Venice: subdeacon and deacon respectively on 10 April (in S. Maurizio) and 13 April 1632 (in S. Maria del Giglio), and then the priesthood on 16 April in S. Maria Zobenigo. He most probably celebrated his first High Mass in Cremona, of whose clergy he was now a member and which provided the endowment guaranteeing the annual income associated with his new position (perhaps the country property in Pusichello, near Cremona, which Monteverdi rented out for three years to one Giovanni Battista Rimondi on 11 November 1633).

31 The *Scherzi musicali* (1632)

Just about a decade after the slim collection of solo songs titled *Lamento d'Arianna*, there appeared from the press another volume of works by Monteverdi (Venice, Bartolomeo Magni ['Stampa del Gardano'] 1632); again, this collection is scarcely distinguished either by its complexity or by the compositional effort involved in the pieces included therein. Indeed, everything points to this volume being of somewhat minor importance: the less than significant size (only some ten pieces), the 'light' tone of the genre (the 'scherzo'). It was perhaps for these reasons, rather than because of his new status as a priest, that Monteverdi did not take a personal hand in publishing the *Scherzi*. Among other things, he was not even in Venice when they were about to appear: the dedication bears the date 20 June 1632, and we know that at that time the composer was in Mantua for some months on family business. Moreover, the title-page itself explains that these pieces were 'raccolti da Bartolomeo Magni e novamente stampati' ('collected by Bartolomeo Magni and newly printed').

The impulse for this initiative was almost certainly Magni's desire to offer a small collection of vocal pieces containing those kinds of compositions reflecting the simple, and also anacreontic, styles (in so-called *ariette*) which had come into fashion in the preceding years and were so liked by the public, to judge by the large number of such publications that had appeared in the meantime (take, for example, the many collections of such songs by Cifra, Milanuzzi, Stefani and Kapsberger). Perhaps Magni counted to no small extent on Monteverdi's fame and on the success which a similar volume by one of the most celebrated composers of the age might achieve with the musical public.

The catastrophic plague epidemic which had scarce ended was the grimmest of blows for Venice in a period already beleaguered by a general economic crisis. The effects of all this were also serious for music-printing: reduced to very low levels, and despite a recovery in 1633–4, Venetian output entered from that moment on a period of irreversible decline.[146] Monteverdi's volume appeared at a critical point, and was one of only four titles printed in Venice in 1632 (not even one had appeared in the preceding year), and perhaps its small dimensions reflect the difficulties of the times. By associating himself with one of the most famous composers of the period, a genial contrapuntalist and *maestro* in St Mark's, Bartolomeo Magni evidently requested some works ready for use to put together a thin (and thus not very expensive) volume

capable of arousing the interest of a dormant market which he hoped to
revive.

1   'Maledetto' (anacreontic canzonetta), 'a voce sola', soprano
2   'Quel sguardo sdegnosetto' (canzonetta), soprano
3   'Eri già tutta mia' (canzonetta), soprano
4a 'Ecco di dolci raggi il sol armato' (*ottava rima*), tenor
5   'Et è pur dunque vero' (canzonetta), for soprano 'con sinfonia' for
     unspecified instrument (in treble clef) and basso continuo
4b 'Io che armato sinor d'un duro gelo' (*ottava rima*), tenor
6   'Zefiro torna e di soavi accenti' (Ottavio Rinuccini: sonnet), 'ciac-
     cona a 2 voci', 2 tenors
7   'Armato il cor d'adamantina fede' (madrigal), 2 tenors

The collection's title-page calls these *scherzi musicali* ('a 1 et 2 voci'), 'arias
and madrigals in the recitative style, with a *ciaccona*'. The *ciaccona* is No. 6,
where a two-bar bass pattern is strictly repeated sixty times under the two
tenor parts. This melodic/harmonic scheme had been used intermittently in
vocal music for some fifteen years: it was first taken up by composers in
Roman circles – Domenico Visconti (1616), Alessandro Capece (1625), Domenico Crivellati (1628), Francesco Manelli (1629) and Girolamo Frescobaldi
(1630) – or from southern Italy (the Neapolitan Andrea Falconieri in 1616),
but the fashion then spread to musicians in northern Italy: thus a *ciaccona*
appears in the *Affetti amorosi* edited by the Venetian Giovanni Stefani in 1618.

The rest of the volume – if we believe the title-page – would therefore seem
to contain 'arias and madrigals in the recitative style' (i.e. for one voice) which,
in the dedication to Pietro Capello ('most worthy mayor and captain of Capo
d'Istria'), Bartolomeo Magni generically calls 'ariette'. In fact, the greater part
of the settings here exploit strophic organization involving both voice and
bass (in 'Maledetto' and in 'Eri già tutta mia', where for the most part there are
repetitions of small rhythmic patterns and a final recurrence of the opening),
or else only in the continuo, producing strophic bass variations (as in 'Quel
sguardo sdegnosetto' – in which identical phrases are assigned to the first two
pairs of verses – and 'Et è pur dunque vero').

If the 'arias' are to be distinguished, as was customary in the period, by their
use of strophic organization (either partial, in the bass, or total), the 'madrigals' must be those pieces in which such organization is not present: this means
that one can place in this category only 'Ecco di dolci raggi il sol armato' and
above all 'Armato il cor d'adamantina fede'. It should be noted that although
'Io che armato sinor d'un duro gelo' is not next to 'Ecco di dolci raggi il sol
armato', everything suggests that it is its second *pars* (and in fact they were
printed together in Giovan Battista Camarella's *Madrigali et arie*, Venice,
Alessandro Vincenti, 1633): they have the same metre (alternating *endecasillabi
piani* and *sdruccioli* – the latter consistently concluded by dotted rhythms in the
music – and organized as two *ottave*), the same vocal scoring (which is

different from all the other settings in the volume), and the same refrain ('arda dunque d'amor, arda ogni core'). Nor do their differences in style militate against this conclusion, given that they are to be considered in terms of the characteristics of the text: the declamatory *sprezzatura* of the second part in fact returns to the regular rhythmic patterns in the bass of the first *ottava* when the text changes person ('*Io che armato sinor*'), as in the following *ciaccona*.

32 1633–1638

As well as composing, in the 1630s Monteverdi also devoted himself to preparing a musical treatise, to which he turned his hand more or less at the same time as when he became a priest (or at least, so Caberloti says):

> heaven granted two further *lustra* for Claudio, a priest, practising all religious duties, but above all else to care for the future, having given himself to philosophy was in the process of writing a volume in which, noting the most hidden secrets of his art, he sought to prevent that never more in centuries to come would be hidden from students the true paths to facilitate the gaining of perfection in the art of music.[147]

Monteverdi had had the idea of writing a treatise at the time of his controversy with Artusi some thirty years before; now the project was taken up again, even if Monteverdi's duties and his scant familiarity with theoretical matters and with the discipline of writing scarcely made the task any easier. The composer had the opportunity to talk of the treatise, to be called *Seconda pratica* – 'Second practice' – (just as announced in the Fifth Book), and of the issues associated with it in two letters of 1633–4 (L.122 [123] and 123 [124]) to an unknown correspondent in Rome. The latter can almost certainly be identified as Giovan Battista Doni, both because certain remarks are entirely appropriate to him (the correspondent is a scholar involved in theoretical works, and also the inventor of 'a new instrument' – the 'lyra Barberina' – with which to revive ancient music),[148] and because when writing to the French scholar and music-theorist Marin Mersenne then or shortly after, Doni referred to Monteverdi's treatise and to his correspondence with the composer.

Monteverdi's first letter to Doni, replying to a letter from him that had initiated the correspondence, dates from 22 October 1633 (L.122 [123]): 'Enclosed with a most kind letter from the Most Illustrious Lord Bishop Cornaro, my particular lord and most revered master, sent to me from Padua, there was one from Your Most Reverend Lordship addressed to me, so abundantly fruitful in honour and praise for my feeble self that I was almost lost in wonder at it.' In the rest of the letter (given above on pp. 48–49), the composer reported the reasons which had encouraged him to write the treatise and noted the plan of the work, adding:

I keep telling myself that it will not be unacceptable to the world, for I found out in practice that when I was about to compose the *Lamento d'Arianna* – finding no book that could show me the natural way of imitation, not even one that would explain how I ought to be an imitator (other than Plato, in one of his shafts of wisdom, but so hidden that I could hardly discern from afar with my feeble sight what little he showed me) – I found out (let me tell you) what hard work I had to do in order to achieve the little I did do in the way of imitation, and I therefore hope it is not going to be displeasing, but – let it come out as it will in the end – I shall be happier to be moderately praised in the new style, than greatly praised in the ordinary; and for this further presumption I ask fresh pardon.

Well, what pleasure I felt on learning that in our own times a new instrument had been invented! May God be my witness – whom I pray with all my heart to maintain and bless the most virtuous person of the inventor, who was none other than Your Most Reverend Lordship – I have indeed often thought about the reason for its discovery, on which (I mean to say, where) the ancients based their ideas in order to find so many differences in it (as they did), because not only are there many that we use, but many that have been lost. Nor has there been even one theorist of our times (yet they have professed to know all about the art) who has shown even one to the world. I hope, however, in my book, to say something about this point that perhaps will not be displeasing.

From the pleasure I have told you about, Your Most Reverend Lordship can decide for sure whether it will be precious to me – the favour promised me in due course through your kindness – that is, in being favoured with a copy of such a worthy treatise, containing such new and recondite things.

Monteverdi's other letter to Doni is dated 2 February 1634 (L.123 [124]):

I have received two letters from Your Most Reverend Lordship: one before Christmas – at a time when I was entirely taken up with writing the Mass for Christmas Eve (a new mass being expected of the Director of Music according to a custom of this city) – and the other one two weeks ago from the courier, which found me not properly recovered from a catarrhal descent which started to appear over my left eye just after Christmas, and this kept me far not only from writing but also from reading, for many a long day. Nor am I yet free from it, in fact, for it still keeps troubling me to some extent, and because of these two real impediments I am writing to beg Your Most Reverend Lordship to forgive this fault of mine in replying so tardily.

Only two weeks ago I read Your Most Reverend Lordship's first letter, most courteous and most helpful, from which I gathered the most kindly advice, all of it worthy of my careful consideration; and for this I am sending you my infinite thanks. I have however seen the Galilei – not just now, but rather twenty years ago – the part where he mentions that scant practice of ancient times. I valued seeing it then, perceiving in that same part how the ancients used their practical signs in a different way from ours, but I did not try to go any further in understanding them, being sure that they would have come out as very obscure ciphers, or worse, since that ancient practical manner is completely lost.

Whereupon I turned my studies in another direction, basing them on the principles of the best philosophers to have investigated nature. And because, in accordance with my reading, I notice that the results agree with those reasonings (and with the requirements of nature) when I write down practical things with the aid of those observations, and really feel that our present rules have nothing to do with those requirements, I have for this basic reason given my book the title of *Seconda pratica*; and I hope to make this so clear that it will not be censured by the world, but rather taken seriously.

I keep well away, in my writings, from that method upheld by the Greeks with their words and signs, employing instead the voices and characters that we use in our practice, because my intention is to show by means of our practice what I have been able to extract from the mind of those philosophers for the benefit of good art, and not for the principles of the First Practice, which was only harmonic.

Would to God that I might find myself near to Your Most Reverend Lordship's singular affection and singular prudence and advice, for I would tell you all, by word of mouth – begging you to hear me out, I mean in everything – as much about the plan, as about the principles and the divisions of the parts of my book; but my being far away prevents it. Because of a special favour received of the Most Holy Virgin's consummate goodness in the year of the plague at Venice, I am bound by a vow to visit the Most Holy House of Loreto. I hope soon, with the Lord's help, to fulfil it; on which occasion I would come on to Rome (if it please the Lord to grant me the favour) in order to be able to present my service personally to Your Most Reverend Lordship, and enjoy both the sight and the most beautiful sound of your most noble instrument, and be honoured by your most brilliant conversation.

I have seen a drawing of the instrument on the piece of paper you sent me, which – far from diminishing my eagerness – has on the contrary made it grow.

With his interests in questions of organology, Doni had asked Monteverdi to procure sketches of the many extravagant instruments invented and used by the celebrated Francesco Gabrielli, called 'Scapino': in promising them (Gabrielli was then in Modena, not in Venice), Monteverdi included one of an Arab instrument – perhaps a *rebāb* – seen by him thirty years before at the Mantuan court.

A few months later, in a letter (8 April 1634, in French) from Rome to Mersenne – who had requested information on music treatises published in Italy – Doni was able to give advance notice of Monteverdi's own treatise: 'As regards works on music, to my knowledge for a long time there have not been any published in Italy worth reading. I believe that for questions of musical practice, very useful will be the work titled *Nuova seconda pratica di musica* promised by Signor Claudio Monteverde, who is, as you well know, a very great composer, and in the event of its publication, I will procure a copy for you.'[149]

Despite the somewhat elevated tone of his two letters to Doni (a further reflection of this is the many corrections made in the course of their preparation), Monteverdi had freely admitted that scholarly research was not for him, and that he had instead directed his attention to illustrate the new 'second practice' – that is, concerning the musical realization of the poetic *affetti* – discovered empirically, drawing inspiration from 'the best philosophers to have investigated nature'. With the passing of time, however, relationships between Monteverdi and Doni deteriorated (the composer must have taken issue with some parts of Doni's *Compendio del trattato de' generi e de' modi della musica* (Rome, Andrea Fei, 1635), which the theorist had sent him without receiving any thanks, not even for the honourable mention he receives therein). It is doubtless for this reason that when corresponding again with Mersenne from Rome, on 7 July 1638 (again, in French), Doni wrote with tangible ill-will towards Monteverdi, who was still much valued as a composer but less as a man of culture:

> Moving on to the fact that you (on p. 61 [*recte* 65] of the *Livre 7 Des Instrumens de percussion* [*De l'harmonie universelle*, II (Paris, Pierre Ballard, 1637)]) place Frescobaldi on the level of the most esteemed musicians of Italy, together with Lucas Marenzio and Monteverde, you should not be misled in this. For today in Rome there are a dozen musicians who are more esteemed than him.... As for Claudio Monteverde, he is not a man of many letters – no more than other modern musicians – but he excels in writing emotional melodies, thanks to the long experience he had in Florence with those fine intellects of the academies, such as Signor Rinuccini, who was gentleman of the chamber to the deceased King Henri [IV] the Great and an excellent poet, who (from what I know from a good source), although he understood nothing about music, contributed more than Monteverdi to the beauty of this *Complainte d'Ariadne* written by him. I am assured that he [Monteverdi] has been working for many years on a great work concerning music, where he deals with the songs of all peoples, where he contradicts me over many things. That does not greatly trouble me, indeed I would like to see these curiosities soon, for I fear that his death might prevent it. I am somewhat upset that he has never written since I sent him my book, nor even acknowledged my letter, whereas before he wrote to me a few times. And you know if in this book I spoke to his disadvantage.[150]

More or less the same ideas had been expressed a year before by the Flemish theorist Johann Albert Ban, writing from Harlem ('18 kal. Jan. 1637'; in Latin) to the English ambassador in Belgium, William Boswell:

> The end of music is to educate, delight and move. It is common both to the musician and to the orator, even if the musician is allowed to use different means. And although this end has been at least to some extent the objective of almost all musicians (or μουσουργοῖς [*mousourgois*]), up till now as far as I know it has been discussed by no one. All the attempts to date seem to concern only delight, to the point that at the end of the sixteenth century, music had only the capacity to produce pleasure, without any theatrical doctrine. The Italians, first, have begun to adapt the words to the sounds in madrigals, but their approach [*ratio*] has not been sufficiently accurate and clear. The French have improved all this in a more elevated manner in their *modulis aulicis* [*airs de cour*].
> But all this music has been up to now deprived of the capacity to move the soul, however much it delights us. In no way is it παθητική [*pathètikè*], even if some judge it ἠθικήν [*èthikèn*]. Claudio Monteverdi, in his Fourth, Fifth, Sixth and Seventh Books of madrigals has first attempted and let flower the affects of the soul, without entirely succeeding. In fact, he did this more by

chance and according to his natural industry than on the basis of some acknowledged theory (or μουσικοσοφία [*mousicosofia*]). And there is nothing sadder than to see something divine like music present itself without theoretical support and a capacity of moving, with only delight provided by the harmony of the voices, with the total confusion of the words. For this reason, scholars have been given no little opportunity to consider somewhat Greek music, as praised by writers contemporary with it for its superhuman power (even if the Greeks are renowned in history as liars), and the fact that, in the inferiority of these our times, this art itself has been contemptuously relegated to the lowest level.[151]

As for composing, in 1634 Monteverdi contributed two pieces for soprano and continuo ('Piú lieto il guardo' and 'Perché, se m'odiavi') to the *Arie de diversi* (Venice, Alessandro Vincenti), edited by the printer himself and, according to the title-page, 'convenient to be sung to the harpsichord, chitarrone and other like instrument, with the alphabet letters for the Spanish guitar' – the last instrument was much in vogue in this period.

His advanced age notwithstanding – he was approaching seventy – Monteverdi continued his intense activity in St Mark's and in other institutions of the city. On 3 and 4 November 1635, he again directed the music for the Feast of S. Carlo at the Frari, commissioned as usual by the Milanese community in Venice. The occasion is described by Gian Vincenzo Imperiale in the 'Giornata sesta' ('Sixth day') of his *Viaggi*: 'On the evening [of 3 November] we went to hear first vespers at the Frari, the church of S. Carlo. We were privy to a music perfect in all exquisiteness, being directed by Monteverde, a man of great spirit.'[152]

Some pieces later destined to be brought together in the Eighth Book hint at a much more prestigious task. Here we can see compositions which make reference to Habsburg Emperor Ferdinand III ('Ogni amante è guerrier: nel suo gran regno' in *versi sciolti*; the *ballo* 'Volgendo il ciel per l'immortal sentiero') or else to the kingdom on the Danube (the printed version of the old *Ballo delle ingrate*) and which could have been commissioned from Monteverdi on the occasion of the celebrations in honour of Ferdinand III's coronation as Holy Roman Emperor held towards the end of 1636 (there is no evidence for a performance of the *Ballo delle ingrate* in Vienna in 1628). In fact, the first two texts had been written by Ottavio Rinuccini for Henri IV, King of France, some thirty years before; much the same can be said of the third, which was produced for the Gonzaga court, as we have seen. In the versions of the text set by Monteverdi in the Eighth Book, we lose the references both to Henri (replaced by Ferdinand) and to Mantua (replaced by the Habsburg capital). Such changes lead one to suspect that these compositions were indeed sent to Vienna for the enthronment of the new emperor. Things could have happened thus. Given that the unexpected death of Emperor Ferdinand II suddenly created the need to provide for the proclamation of his successor, the Austrian court must have had to move very quickly to get to grips with all the requirements of the ceremonies. As regards music, they turned to Monteverdi, who must have had some relationship with the deceased emperor in terms of patronage, given that he was considering dedicating his new madrigal book to him. Given the urgency, Monteverdi decided either to turn to things already written, removing the most obvious discrepancies (as is the case in the *Ballo delle ingrate*), or to write pieces anew, taking second-hand texts (the remainder) already in his possession – again adjusted – to save time. But as we shall see, only in the case of the *ballo* 'Volgendo il ciel per l'immortal sentiero' can we suggest a performance in Vienna, perhaps on 30 December 1636.

A later *Ballo del Monte Verde*, no better identified and reduced to the skeleton-like format of the intabulations typical of the instrument in question, can be found in the hugely successful collection by Pietro Milioni and Lodovico Monte, *Vero e facil modo d'imparare a sonare et accordare da se medesimo la chitarra spagnuola* ('True and easy way of learning to play and tune by oneself the Spanish guitar'), first printed in Rome by Salvioni and Grisei in 1637, and then given numerous subsequent editions.[153]

In an entirely different area, in June 1637 Monteverdi was involved in a somewhat unpleasant episode caused by a grave gesture of disobedience by one of his subordinates. The singer Domenico Aldegati had allowed himself to get carried away with serious verbal insults in public concerning his *maestro di cappella*, who immediately and with clear resolve denounced the fact to the procurators.

Most Illustrious and Most Excellent Lords and Most Respected Masters.

I, Claudio Monteverdi, Director of Music at St Mark's, most humble servant of Your Excellencies and of the Most Serene Republic, come humbly unto your presence to set forth to you how Domenico Aldegati, a singer at St Mark's, a bass – yesterday morning which was the 8th of the present month of June 1637, before the great door of that church, at the time of the greatest concourse of people, among whom there was a large number of singers and players (and there was also a certain Bonivento Boniventi, a musician who was handing out to the singers and players certain moneys given to him by the Most Illustrious Nuns of S. Daniele for the Vespers service they held before the processional raising of the body of St John Duke of Alexandria), whether the reason for this was perhaps because he did not get the said moneys, or because his share was less in comparison with the other shares, I do not know, because I never interfere with the money affairs of singers – beyond all reason and justification, and having respect neither for the office that I hold from the Most Serene Republic nor for my age and my priesthood, nor for the honour of my family and of my virtue, but spurred on by a wild fury and with a loud raucous voice, after a few minutes of first insulting my person (and having brought together in a semicircle more than fifty people, part of whom were strangers, among whom those present were:
– Signor Giovanni Battista, called the Bolognese, singer of the chapel
– Signor Gasparo Zorina, a Brescian, who plays the double-bass
– Signor Alovisi Lipomani
– Signor Don Anibale Romano, singer of the chapel
– Signor Giovan Battista Padovano, who plays trombones
and the said Signor Bonivento Boniventi who was handing out the said

moneys) spoke these exact words, as indeed some of the said witnesses reported to me:

'The Director of Music belongs to a whoreson race, a thieving, cheating he-goat', with many other wicked insults, and then he added: 'And I call him and whoever protects him an ass, and so that each one of you can hear me, I say that Claudio Monteverdi is a thieving he-goat, and I am telling you, Bonivento, so that you can go and report it as coming from me.'

I come therefore to Your Excellencies' feet not as Claudio Monteverdi the priest, for as such I shall forgive him all and pray that God may do the same; but as Director of Music, whose authority deriving from the royal hand of the Most Serene Republic I would not allow to be ill-used and insulted in such a way, nor my virtue nor the honour of my family, which is protected by the most serene hand of this Most Serene Republic; and with a mind to this man, that the other singers may take care to limit themselves to honourable terms regarding anyone, especially him who holds the name of Director of Music. Otherwise for the sake of my honour, I would be forced to avoid a second occasion of hearing him or the likes of him, and ask for an honourable discharge, to go away under the protection of my freeholds, left to me by my ancestors, which are few but nevertheless sufficient to support me far from such evils and licentious occasions. Hoping this to be a just cause I here bow to the ground before you.

I, Claudio Monteverdi, have written this and beg that this man's life may not be harmed.[154]

Monteverdi was scarcely litigious or vindictive. Indeed, what few insights we have into his private life show him perhaps too much a lover of the quiet life, disliking excessive effort or bother of any kind, inclined to the small pleasures of his own habits, with a taste for disinterested chat, happily intent on domestic pastimes (for example, his passion for alchemy), and perennially and perhaps excessively troubled by financial worries. At least, all this seems to be deducible from the few remarks in his letters, from the account by Goretti given above, and finally by a later anecdote which depicts him involved with less gifted colleagues or with aspiring and importunate musicians: 'That great man, to whomever forcibly showed him such [musical] compositions without the necessary condiments (something to be abhorred by a man of good part), and so as not to embitter him with correction, since *veritas odium parit* ["truth breeds hatred"], he used to rid himself of it quickly with these words: "Well, well, it's all sol-fa, it's all sol-fa." '[155]

The matter over Aldegati, however, was something entirely different. Without prompt punishment, such insubordination threatened both the prestige and honour of Monteverdi, *maestro di cappella* of the Republic of Venice, and the future efficiency of the musical establishment of the basilica. Thus just as Monteverdi's normal behaviour scarcely betrayed the extraordinary inventiveness and industry of the artist, the composer, so accommodating in private, showed himself to be firm and fully cognisant of his own professional public responsibilities, to the extent of threatening resignation if serious measures were not taken against someone who had so unreasonably offended him.

The proceedings against Aldegati began on 12 June 1637 and dragged on until the next month.[156] In a memorandum presented on 18 June, the singer under investigation claimed that the insults were directed at Bonivento, 'who is not a musician but who serves the said Signor *maestro* in carrying the books',[157] and certainly not at Monteverdi:

> indeed that very evening I found the said Signor *maestro* in Marzaria and I saluted him, removing my hat, and Father Fra Francesco di S. Stefano, who sings tenor, can be a good witness of what I did, for he was with the Signor *maestro* himself, and the said Signor *maestro* responded by raising his hat as well. Moreover, when I was in the square, coming from Prestaria with a singer of St Mark's called Father Oratio and a Servite father, who is *maestro*, the Signor *maestro* passed by, and we all saluted him together by raising our hats, and so did he in return, and I never intend in all my imagination to go against him, and I have always obeyed and revered him as merits a virtuoso of his like, and for the good order that he maintains.[158]

But Giovan Battista Padoan, for example – when summoned to testify by Monteverdi himself – instead confirmed the accusations:

> I know that [Domenico Aldegati] shouted at Bonivento, to whom he said that he should tell the Signor *maestro* that he is a whoreson, a thief, a disgrace and a damned he-goat, 'and tell him that I say this for this reason, that you can tell him', and then he called Bonivento from the square because he was defending the Signor *maestro*, and the said Dominico withdrew to Spadaria, and Bonivento went there too, to which Bonivento Dominico said: 'Come on, you damned he-goat and he who protects you', but thinking that he was speaking to me, I went and asked him whether he was speaking of me, but he replied that he was speaking of that damned he-goat of a *maestro*, and Bonivento. And this is what I know. *Et sic iuravit* etc.[159]

In the end, the inquiry ended with Aldegati being given a severe reprimand and Monteverdi satisfaction.

In 1637, the composer acted as an agent for the purchase of a Cremonese violin to be used by Alberto Galilei, nephew of Galileo and then an instrumentalist in the service of the Duke of Bavaria. Between 1637 (the year of its foundation) and 1638, Monteverdi also provided music for the Accademia degli Unisoni, the creation of his friend and collaborator Giulio Strozzi, who had involved, among others, Gian Francesco Loredano, Paolo Vendramin and Ferrante Pallavicino. This can be gleaned from the anonymous satirical dialogue *Dei sentimenti giocosi in Parnaso per l'accademia degli Unisoni* included in a manuscript of *Satire contro gli Unisoni*; these satires rudely attack Strozzi, accusing him of poetic ineptitude, venality and even pimping for his adopted daughter, the singer and composer Barbara Strozzi.[160]

In the course of this dialogue, however, Monteverdi is accorded particularly respectful treatment: he receives commiseration for having become involved in such an enterprise, and moreover for being forced to set to music Strozzi's poetic extravagances (including 'Gira il nemico insidïoso Amore' later published in the Eighth Book?). The author also hopes that the composer would have the wisdom to distance himself from an imminent theatrical enterprise planned by the academy (sadly, unidentified) even if earlier events were no cause for optimism. And in this matter, another sign of the respect paid the composer is that there is no explicit mention of his name in a much criticized revival of the *intermedio* of the Argonauts written ten years earlier for the festivities in Parma. In fact, the Unisoni had arranged a performance of this *intermedio* (judged a crude antique), shortened with a few cuts, for their meeting on 5 January 1638. The evening was later described in the *Veglia terza de' signori accademici Unisoni avuta in Venetia in casa del signor Giulio Strozzi. Alla molto illustre signora la sig. Barbara Strozzi* ('Third evening of the Signor Academicians of the Unisoni held in Venice in the house of Signor Giulio Strozzi. [Dedicated] to the Very Illustrious Lady, Signora Barbara Strozzi'), published in Venice in 1638 by Sarzina, which includes only general references to the music.

MOMO   This virtuoso [from Bologna] completed his dangerous and stormy oration without any other mishap except that he received less applause than that widower, either because many were asleep, or because they cared little for those vanities. But however they were reawoken by some new music, although it was itself older than the modern notes with which it was sung.

VENIERO   And what was this?

MOMO   A dialogue from the play of Jason and Medea with the ship of the Argonauts who were going to Colchis to gain the golden fleece.

VENIERO   Strozzi would have gladly embarked on it.

MOMO   No, because it was something that had been sung many times, and many years ago at the wedding of Their Highnesses of Parma, they did their part well, and they were sung securely.

BERNIA   And yet it was not successful?

ARISTOTILE   It could not succeed because it was something so decayed, since in all times it is new things that please the human spirit.

    ...

MOMO   When in the end the whole audience was well and truly tired, they put an end to this croaking, not singing, with Strozzi declaring that the end of the dialogue had been cut for the sake of brevity.

BERNIA   Woe for us, Momo, if it had been sung complete.

MOMO   Other things are sung [in this academy], as I have said, but [Strozzi] enjoys always troubling Monteverdi in musical compositions, which arouses my sympathy, since one often does not know what to think about his bizarre, fantastic poetry.

APOLLO   Monteverdi also appears in that place?

MOMO   He is brought there for I do not know what reason, and God willing that he does not also go on to the stage, where all the others are to produce one of these evenings a comic and musical performance.

ARISTOTILE   If he is not there in deed, he could be there in thought, since he will perhaps have advised the whole business.[161]

33 The *Madrigali guerrieri, et amorosi* ... *Libro ottavo* (1638)

In the mid-1630s, Monteverdi was preparing one of his most demanding collections, indeed, his largest in terms of his secular output. The Eighth Book of madrigals, with the title *Madrigali guerrieri, et amorosi*, was printed in Venice by Alessandro Vincenti in 1638 – almost twenty years after the Seventh Book – and was dedicated 'to the sacred, Caesarean majesty of Emperor Ferdinand III' with the date Venice, 1 September 1638. The dedication explains that originally the Eighth Book was to have been dedicated to Habsburg Emperor Ferdinand II, who in 1622 had taken as his second wife Eleonora Gonzaga:

> I present to the feet of Your Majesty, as the protecting power of virtue, these my musical compositions.
> Ferdinando, Your Majesty's great father, deigning, through his innate goodness, to accept and honour them in manuscript, granted me an as it were authoritative passport to entrust them to the press.
> And lo I eagerly publish them, consecrating them to the most revered name of Your Majesty, heir no less of kingdoms and of the empire than of his valour and kindness.

Since Ferdinando II died in 1636 – which forced Monteverdi to switch dedicatees – the collection must have largely been ready by that year: for that matter, it contains a good deal of older music, including 'Armato il cor d'adamantina fede' (first printed in the 1632 *Scherzi musicali*), the *Combattimento di Tancredi et Clorinda*, written in 1624, and also the *Ballo delle ingrate*, which goes back to 1608. Further evidence of this is perhaps offered by a discrepancy over the dating of the *Combattimento*, which the preface to the Eighth Book says was performed at the Palazzo Mocenigo in 1624, while the brief note at the head of the work itself places the performance a surprising 'twelve years' before, thus 1626. If the collection, at least in terms of its basic outline, was ready to be presented to Ferdinand II in 1636, this note was right about the date of the *Combattimento*; the fact that it was not corrected may have been due just to an oversight.

'Altri canti d'amor, tenero arciero' alludes in general terms to a 'gran Fernando' ('great Ferdinando'), while Ferdinand III – 'sempre invitto' ('always unbeaten') and 're novo del romano impero' ('the new king of the Roman empire') – receives more specific mentions in 'Ogni amante è guerrier: nel suo gran regno' (especially in the second part, 'Io che nell'otio nacqui e d'otio vissi ...') and in the *ballo* 'Volgendo il ciel per l'immortal sentiero', both texts by Rinuccini from the beginning of the seventeenth century and dedicated to the king of France, Henri IV, and therefore adapted as appropriate for the new addressee.[162] It has been suggested that they, and also the *Ballo delle ingrate*, were used for the festivities for the coronation of the new emperor. In particular, 'Volgendo il ciel per l'immortal sentiero' may have been staged on 30 December 1636 when, after the performance of a pastoral play by Valeriano Bonvicino, *Il vaticinio di Silvano*, the various parts of the empire paying homage to the new sovereign were represented in an allegorical *balletto*.[163] The text of the *Ballo delle ingrate*, too, underwent some changes compared with the 1608 version (for a revival on the same occasion?). The lines 'Donne, che di beltade / tolgono a l'alba in ciel la gloria e 'l vanto, / là ne la nobil Manto' ('Ladies, who in beauty / take the glory and prize from dawn in the sky, / there in noble Mantua') and 'Vegga su 'l Mincio ogn'anima superba' ('See on the Mincio each proud spirit') were changed respectively to 'Donne, che di beltate e di valore / tolgono alle piú degne il nome altero / là nel germano impero' ('Ladies, who in beauty and in worth / take the proud name from all worthies / there in the German empire') and 'Vegga su l'Istro ogni anima superba' ('See on the Istro [= Danube] each proud spirit'). The following lines, however, were cut entirely, given their too obvious reference to some uncaring 'beauty' of the Mantuan court: 'Una io ne vidi (e potrei dirne il nome), / per non far lieto altrui di sua bellezza, / tutto il volto velar, non pur le chiome' ('One I saw of them (and I could tell her name), / who so as not to make another happy of her beauty / veiled her entire countenance, nay even her hair').

Monteverdi matches the importance of his dedicatee with a more elevated endeavour in both practical and theoretical terms: the Eighth Book is in fact preceded by an ambitious – if not always clear and straightforward – preface. This is headed 'Claudio Monteverde a chi legge' ('Claudio Monteverde to him who reads [this]'), and here we find the theoretical framework and the classical sources justifying the new 'concitato genere' ('agitated genus'), the first examples of which were now in print. In this preface, which is the longest theoretical text that we have from Monteverdi (it may have been influenced somewhat by his association with Giulio Strozzi), there come together various theoretical interests being cultivated in those years by the composer, evidence of which is also offered by the two letters to Doni of 1633–4 and by the attempted treatise on the *Seconda pratica*.

> I have reflected that the principal passions or affections of our mind are three, namely, anger, moderation, and humility or supplication; so the best philosophers declare, and the very nature of our voice indicates this in having high, low, and middle registers. The art of music also points clearly to these three in its terms 'agitated', 'soft' and 'moderate' [*concitato, molle, temperato*]. In all the works of the former composers I have indeed found examples of the 'soft' and the 'moderate', but never of the 'agitated', a genus nevertheless described by Plato in the third book of his *Rhetoric* [*Republic*] in these words: 'Take that harmony that would fittingly imitate the utterances and the accents of a brave man who is engaged in warfare.' And since I was aware that it is contraries which greatly move our mind, and that this is the purpose which all good music should have – as Boethius asserts, saying, 'Musicam nobis esse coniunctam, mores, vel honestare, vel evertere' ['Music is related to us, and either ennobles or corrupts the character'] – for this reason I have applied myself with no small diligence and toil to rediscover this genus.

After reflecting that according to all the best philosophers the fast pyrrhic measure was used for lively and warlike dances, and the slow spondaic measure for their opposites, I considered the semibreve, and proposed that a single semibreve should correspond to one spondaic beat; when this was reduced to sixteen semiquavers, struck one after the other, and combined with words expressing anger and disdain, I recognized in this brief sample a resemblance to the passion which I sought, although the words did not follow metrically the rapidity of the instrument.

To obtain a better proof, I took the divine Tasso, as a poet who expresses with the greatest propriety and naturalness the qualities which he wishes to describe, and selected his description of the combat of Tancredi and Clorinda as an opportunity of describing in music contrary passions, namely, warfare and entreaty and death. In the year 1624 I caused this composition to be performed in the noble house of my especial patron and indulgent protector the Most Illustrious and Excellent Gerolamo Mozzenigo, an eminent dignitary in the service of the Most Serene Republic, and it was received by the best citizens of the noble city of Venice with much applause and praise.

After the apparent success of my first attempt to depict anger, I proceeded with greater zeal to make a fuller investigation, and composed other works in that kind, both ecclesiastical and for chamber performance. Further, this genus found such favour with the composers of music that they not only praised it by word of mouth, but, to my great pleasure and honour, they showed this by written work in imitation of mine. For this reason I have thought it best to make known that the investigation and the first essay of this genus, so necessary to the art of music, came from me. It may be said with reason that until the present, music has been imperfect, having had only the two genera – 'soft' and 'moderate'.

It seemed at first to the musicians, especially to those who were called on to play the basso continuo, more ridiculous than praiseworthy to strum on a single string sixteen times in one measure, and for that reason they reduced this multiplicity to one stroke in the measure, sounding the spondee instead of the pyrrhic foot, and destroying the resemblance to agitated speech. Take notice, therefore, that in this genus the basso continuo must be played, along with its accompanying parts, in the form and manner as written. Similarly, in the other compositions, of different kind, all the other directions necessary for performance are set forth. For the manners of performance must take account of three things: oratory, harmony, and rhythm.

My rediscovery of this warlike genus has given me occasion to write certain madrigals which I have called *Guerrieri*. And since the music played before great princes at their courts to please their delicate taste is of three kinds, according to the method of performance – theatre music, chamber music, and dance music – I have indicated these in my present work with the titles *Guerriera*, *Amorosa*, and *Rapresentativa*.

I know that this work will be imperfect, for I have but little skill, particularly in the warlike genus, because it is new and *omne principium est debile* ['every beginning is weak']. I therefore pray the benevolent reader to accept my good will, which will await from his learned pen a greater perfection in the said style, because *inventis facile est addere* ['it is easy to add to what has been discovered']. Farewell.

So the new 'agitated genus' (now called the *stile concitato*) is defined as the fast repetition of notes of the same pitch and length (very short, in semiquavers, and therefore analogous to the short syllables of classical pyrrhic metre), 'combined with words expressing anger and disdain', as Monteverdi theorized after having used it with success in the *Combattimento* of 1624. This latter work was written 'to obtain a better proof' after a period of experimentation (including the anticipations of the technique in some parts of *Orfeo* and *Arianna*?). It was then used in both sacred and secular settings, and was also imitated by other composers, thus becoming fashionable, which is why the preface makes so clear a statement of Monteverdi's precedence in investigating such novelties.

The significance of Monteverdi's theoretical and practical invention was quickly recognized by contemporary musicians (notwithstanding the problems of circulation concerning printed music, as the passage below also reveals), and it received an immediate and wide diffusion – also in geographical terms – which well reveals the fame and international esteem enjoyed by the seventy-year-old composer. André Maugars, the French man of letters and viol-player, could write in a summary of the state of music in Italy prepared in Rome in October 1639:

> I was on the point of ending here, but I realize an error that my memory was about to make me commit, forgetting that great Monteverde, *maestro* composer of the Church of St Mark's, who has discovered a most wondrous new manner of composing suitable as much for instruments as for voices, which prompts me to place him as one of the foremost composers of the world; [and] I will send you some of his most recent works when, if it please God, I shall pass through Venice.[164]

Similarly, in his *Zangh-Bloemzel* printed in Amsterdam (by Louys Elzevier) in 1642, Johann Albert Ban lays out the principles of the *stile concitato* and the resulting expressive effects, paraphrasing the preface of the Eighth Book, which had come into his possession a year before. He also adds some remarks on Monteverdi's earlier output, considering him as following Marenzio (who in his turn is described as a follower of Wert) in the first two books of madrigals, as gaining a personal style in his middle period (from the Third to the Fifth Books), and then developing still further in this third phase (the Eighth Book). Ban concludes by complaining that Monteverdi had not devoted the same attention to the exploration of the expressive qualities of melody, and by hoping that for the good of music, this great man will so apply himself at this very time.

> However, among all the others, I hold in great esteem above all Signor Claudio Monteverde, Pomponio Menna [Nenna] and the Prince of Venosa; in their works I have found things corresponding particularly to that which I illustrated earlier. And last year, 1641, I had the opportunity to read a preface by Signor Monteverde in which he has observed and described the differences of speed and the proportions, illustrating the metres of Greek vocal music, that is, the spondee which has two long syllables, and the pyrrhic which has two short ones. He renders the first (which is appropriate for temperate and majestic words) with a whole measure called semibreve; and

the second, that is the pyrrhic, with sixteen semiquavers delineating the vocal line, adapted to the expression of agitated subjects. According to his opinion, by these means the ancients knew how to express all various situations. This man has indeed done much, albeit concerning only a part of the desired moving of the heart and of the senses, that which strikes us only externally, limiting himself to the simple auditory impression, as do all those military instruments of fixed sound (drums, wood and metal percussion instruments and the like). Certainly, Monteverdi composed his first two books of madrigals in the style of Luca Marenzio (in his turn, a follower of Giaches de Wert, a Dutchman from Antwerp, so far as I have known), less personal than the second style of his Third, Fourth and Fifth books. These books in turn have been surpassed by his latest work, which according to this preface was first performed publicly in Venice in 1624, [which style appears] later adopted with greater complexities in various books of vocal music for church and chamber, according to what he himself says. No one else in the art of vocal music has ever done as much as this man, who is worthy of the greatest praise. However, if he had gone further into the expressive power of sounds – for example, intervals by step or leap – he would have gone much further in doing wondrous things. And perhaps his able mind is attending to that now, which I hope from the bottom of my heart. In fact, for one who is a sincere friend of knowledge and for a spirit which tends towards art, nothing is more welcome than to find many colleagues working in one's own field of enquiry.[165]

Monteverdi's invention also found an echo in the music of Heinrich Schütz, who came to know the composer directly during his second stay in Venice in 1629.[166] As well as mentioning this circumstance, the address *Ad benevolum lectorem* prefacing his *Symphoniarum sacrarum secunda pars* printed in Dresden in 1647 notes 'the Italian manner now for the greater part still unknown ... (for which, however, according to the opinion of the able Signor Claudio Monteverdi in the preface to the Eighth Book of his madrigals, music has now reached its final perfection'. And a little later: 'If I, too, in the *concerto* 'Es steh[t] Gott auff, etc.' have tried somewhat to follow a madrigal by Signor Claudio Monteverdi ('Armato il cuor, etc.') and also a *Ciaccona* by him for two tenors, I will leave judgement to those who know the aforesaid composition of how much I have held to it.'[167] It is true that, as Schütz himself warns us, his 'Es steht Gott auf' is a 'parody' of two works by Monteverdi in the 1632 *Scherzi musicali*, 'Armato il cor d'adamantina fede' and 'Zefiro torna e di soavi accenti' (the first also reprinted in the Eighth Book). But Schütz also uses the *stile concitato* to signify the 'new song' in the concertato motet 'Singet dem Herrn ein neues Lied' ('Sing unto the Lord a new song'). And in the *Cantate, ariette e duetti* (1651) by Barbara Strozzi – who in the dedication to the Habsburg Emperor Ferdinand III (the same dedicatee as of the Eighth Book) calls herself a pupil of a pupil of Monteverdi (i.e. Francesco Cavalli) – the *stile concitato* is used (at least in the continuo) for the line 'tremò Parigi e torbidossi Senna' ('Paris shook, and the Seine grew rough') in the lament 'Su 'l Rodano severo'.

As the title itself suggests, Monteverdi's Eighth Book falls into two parts, 'songs of war' and 'songs of love', with each part corresponding to the other owing to their clear symmetries.

Canti guerrieri

0   *Sinfonia*, 'for two violins and one *viola da braccio*', 'which goes before the madrigal which follows'

1   'Altri canti d'Amor, tenero arciero', 'for six voices [SSATTB] with four *viole* and two violins'

2a 'Or che 'l cielo e la terra e 'l vento tace' (Francesco Petrarca: sonnet), 'for six voices [SSATTB] with two violins'

 b 'Cosí sol d'una chiara fonte viva', 'for six voices [SSATTB] with two violins'

3a 'Gira il nemico insidïoso Amore' (Giulio Strozzi: canzonetta), 'for three voices: alto, tenor and bass'

 b 'Nol lasciamo accostar, ch'egli non saglia'

 c 'Armi false non son, ch'ei s'avvicina'

 d 'Vuol degli occhi attaccar il baloardo'

 e 'Non è piú tempo oimé, ch'egli ad un tratto'

 f 'Cor mio, non val fuggir: sei morto o servo'

4   'Se vittorie sí belle' (Fulvio Testi: madrigal), 'for two tenors'

5   'Armato il cor d'adamantina fede' (madrigal), 'for two tenors'

6a 'Ogni amante è guerrier: nel suo gran regno' (Ottavio Rinuccini: *versi sciolti*), 'for two tenors'

 b 'Io che nell'otio nacqui e d'otio vissi', 'bass solo'

 c 'Ma per quel ampio Egeo spieghi le vele', 'tenor solo'   .

 d 'Riedi, ch'al nostro ardor, ch'al nostro canto', '*a3*: two tenors and bass'

7   'Ardo, avvampo, mi struggo, ardo: accorrete' (sonnet), 'for eight voices [SSAATTBB] with two violins'

8   *Combattimento di Tancredi et Clorinda* (Torquato Tasso: *ottave rime*), soprano, two tenors, 'four *viole da braccio*' (SATB) and basso continuo

9a *Introdutione al ballo* 'Volgendo il ciel per l'immortal sentiero' (O. Rinuccini: sonnet [*sonetto caudato*]), for tenor 'with two violins'

 b *Ballo* 'Movete al mio bel suon le piante snelle' (O. Rinuccini: sonnet), 'for five voices [SSATB] with two violins'

Canti amorosi

10a 'Altri canti di Marte e di sua schiera' (Giovan Battista Marino: sonnet), 'for six voices [SSATTB] and two violins'

 b 'Due belli occhi fur l'armi onde trafitto', 'for six voices [SSATTB] and two violins'

11 'Vago augelletto che cantando vai' (Francesco Petrarca: sonnet quatrains), 'for six [SSATTB] and seven voices [a third tenor is added]

with two violins and a *contrabasso*' (instead of the last, the contents-page gives a *viola*)

12   'Mentre vaga angioletta' (Battista Guarini: madrigal [*madrigalessa*]), 'for two tenors'

13   'Ardo e scoprir, ahi lasso, io non ardisco' (*ottave*), 'for two tenors'

14   'O sia tranquillo il mare, o pien d'orgoglio' (sonnet), 'for two tenors'

15a 'Ninfa che, scalza il piede e sciolto il crine' (anacreontic canzonetta), 'tenor solo'

  b 'Qui deh meco t'arresta, ove di fiori', 'for two tenors'

  c 'De l'usate mie corde al suon potrai', 'for three voices: two tenors and bass'

16   'Dolcissimo uscignolo' (B. Guarini: madrigal), 'for five voices [SSATB] sung in full voice [*cantato a voce piena*], in the French style'

17   'Chi vole aver felice e lieto il core' (B. Guarini: madrigal), 'for five voices [SSATB] sung in full voice', 'in the French style'

18a 'Non avea Febo ancora' (O. Rinuccini: canzonetta), '*a3*: two tenors and bass'

  b *Lamento della ninfa* ' "Amor", dicea, e 'l piè', 'for four voices: soprano, two tenors and bass. *Rapresentativo*'

  c 'Sí tra sdegnosi pianti', '*a3*: two tenors and bass'

19   'Perché te 'n fuggi, o Fillide?' (madrigal in *versi sdruccioli*), '*a3*: alto, tenor and bass'

20   'Non partir, ritrosetta' (canzonetta), '*a3*: two altos and bass'

21   'Su, su, su, pastorelli vezzosi' (anacreontic canzonetta), '*a3*: two sopranos and alto'

22   *Ballo delle Ingrate* (O. Rinuccini: *versi sciolti*, with an *ottava rima* and a quatrain), '*in genere rapresentativo*'

The parallels between the two halves of the collection are apparent in the two sonnets that each act as a prologue to their respective parts ('Altri canti d'Amor, tenero arciero' and 'Altri canti di Marte e di sua schiera'); in the fact that both halves close with pieces 'in genere rappresentativo', the last of which is in both cases a *ballo* (Nos. 8–9, 18 and 22; the title-page had announced 'with some little works *in genere rappresentativo* which will be as brief episodes between the songs without action'); and also in the organization of the central body of each half, made up of concerted madrigals for two voices (Nos. 4, 5 and 6a; 12, 13, 14 and 15b) framed by other settings for larger vocal and instrumental groupings (Nos. 2, 3, and 7; 11, 16 and 17). In both halves, too, the second text set is a sonnet by Petrarch.[168] However, the bipartite division of the volume should not mislead us: the 'wars' described in the first part are always the gallant wars of love, and the epic, martial quality of the musical gestures – at times almost excessively pretentious – is exploited here not without some humorous intent in the context of the erotic poetry.

In the dedication to Cardinal Barberini of his *Partitura de' madrigali a cinque*

voci e d'altri varii concerti (Rome, Francesco Zannetti, 1638), Domenico Mazzocchi said: 'The most ingenious study that music has, most eminent prince, is
that of madrigals, but today few are composed, and fewer are sung, since to
their misfortune they have been more or less banned from the academies.' A
couple of years later, Pietro della Valle echoed him in his discourse *Della
musica dell'età nostra che non è punto inferiore, anzi è migliore di quella dell'età
passata* ('On the music of our times, which is in no way inferior to, and indeed
is better than, that of former times'): 'Today, not so many are composed
because the singing of madrigals is in little use, nor is there any opportunity
for them to be sung, because people now like better to hear free singing from
memory with instruments in hand than to see four or five companions singing
around a table with the book in hand, which seems too scholarly and
academic.'[169] In more or less the same period, Severo Bonini, too, complained:

> Do you not see that today one is only concerned with composing little arias
> for one and two voices concerted with harpsichords or similar instruments?
> Madrigals to be sung at the table without instruments have been sent to
> oblivion, as is church music, all of which are too composed, and so little by
> little one will carry on losing this art, because today hard work seems
> somewhat unhealthy, having given the boot to the rules of Zarlino and to
> however many books one finds by rule-givers.[170]

Therefore, it is significant that on the threshold of the 1640s Monteverdi gave
to the press his most demanding and largest collection of madrigals, when for
almost twenty years the genre had fallen into irreversible decline, supplanted
by arias and canzonettas; this seems a clear sign of the composer's unassailable
trust in his pre-eminence in the field of secular music. While Venetian
music-printing was in deep recession, and while the vogue for anthologies of
solo songs – moreover, with a skeleton accompaniment for the Spanish guitar
– increased, Monteverdi reaffirmed and creatively updated the ideals of the
polyphonic tradition (and even its poets – witness Petrarch), albeit in very
different formats from those of the late sixteenth century, and thus in the
modern style, for the most part not in madrigals for two or three voices (as in
the Seventh Book) but instead in settings for larger vocal forces and also
concerted with upper instruments.

Monteverdi's inventiveness and capacity for renewing his stylistic vocabu-
lary in fulfilling this project is clear from the variety of styles and techniques
used here. A further reflection of this is the varied treatment of the formal
structures themselves, and the fact that Monteverdi avoids as much as possible
simple musical repetition in the case of strophic texts such as canzonettas. It
was with good reason that his friend and unconditional admirer Bellerofonte
Castaldi, in a *capitolo* written in Naples in May 1638 (thus a few months before
the Eighth Book appeared), could praise the great stylistic variety and powerful affective capacity of Monteverdi's music,

che fan che l'uom tal or esca di sesto
    sí che non sa in qual mondo egli si sia,
tanto il vostro compor muove l'affetto
col gir per nuova, inusitata via.
    Siate voi mille volte benedetto,
e benedetta la carta e l'inchiostro
che scuopre i frutti del vostro intelletto,
    che fan ch'unico sete al secol nostro,
e dican quanto vogliano i pedanti
col mordere e abbaiare al nome vostro,
    che stitico è lo stil di tutti quanti.
Ho sentito di Roma il smusicare,
che sopr'ogn'altro par si glorii e vanti;
    i cantanti per certo non han pare,
ch'il terren li produce a millïoni
e cantano con gratia singolare;
    ma se i compositori non son buoni
per quel suo stil ch'è sempre fatto a un modo
che mi stracca le orecchie, son minchioni.
    Non c'è un proceder varïato e sodo,
non un piccante, un garbo, una eccellenza,
com'è nel vostro far ch'ammiro e lodo.
    Qua in Napoli or mi trovo di voi senza,
predico il vostro nome glorïoso
ch'in bocca mia fa la sua residenza.[171]

which makes man now so beside himself / that he does not know in which
world he is, / so does your composing move the emotion / by turning into
new and unaccustomed paths. / May you be a thousand times blessed, / and
blessed the paper and ink / that reveal the fruits of your intellect, / which
make you unique in our century; / and let the pedants say what they like /
with their biting and barking at your name, / for the style of all of them is
constipated. / I have heard the noise-making in Rome, / which prides and
lauds itself above all others; / certainly the singers have no equals, / for that
place produces them by the millions / and they sing with singular grace; / but
if the composers are not good / in terms of their style, which is always done
in just one way / which tires my ears, they are dunces. / There is no style,
varied and well-grounded / no piquancy, no taste, no excellence / as in your
writing that I admire and praise. / Here in Naples, now I find myself without
you, / [but] I proclaim your glorious name / which finds its home in my
mouth.

Castaldi also echoed these revealing comments on Monteverdi's style in a
sonetto caudato, which says, among other things: 'Però nel inventioni ardito e
prattico, / nobile, vario e bello e sempre verde / si mostra e senza pari sotto il
sole' ('However, eager and practised in inventions, / noble, varied and
beautiful and always green / you show yourself to be without equals under the
sun').[172]

34 The *Selva morale e spirituale* (1640–1641)

Just as the Eighth Book prompts admiration as a remarkable climax of Monteverdi's career as a madrigalist, the *Selva morale e spirituale* is a worthy crown to his continuing exploration of invention and experimentation for expressive ends within the sphere of sacred music. Monteverdi must have been preparing it around the same time as the Eighth Book, and it represents his biggest sacred collection – a compendium of almost thirty years of experience as a church *maestro di cappella*. It is also the last volume published during his lifetime. The *Selva morale* was printed in Venice by Bartolomeo Magni in 1640–41: the title-page (at least in some partbooks) in fact has the date 'MDCXXXX', whereas the dedication is signed 'From Venice, 1 May 1641'. However, the latter date seems more likely, given that the date on the title-page could reflect a dating *more veneto* which was not corrected for the actual appearance of the volume.

Quite apart from their chronological proximity, the impression that the *Madrigali guerrieri et amorosi* and the *Selva morale* form a pair is enhanced by the relationship between their respective dedicatees. If the Eighth Book was to have been offered originally to Habsburg Emperor Ferdinand II, the *Selva morale* was actually dedicated to his second wife, Eleonora Gonzaga, daughter of Duke Vincenzo I Gonzaga whom Monteverdi had served 'for a period of 22 continuous years', as the composer himself noted in the dedicatory letter.

1 'O ciechi, il tanto affaticar che giova?' (Francesco Petrarca: *capitolo*), 'moral madrigal', 'for five voices [SSATB] and two violins'

2 'Voi ch'ascoltate in rime sparse il suono' (F. Petrarca: sonnet), 'moral madrigal', 'for five voices [STTTB] and two violins'

3 'È questa vita un lampo' (Angelo Grillo: madrigal), 'for five voices [SSATB]'

4 'Spuntava il dí quando la rosa sovra', 'moral canzonetta for three voices [ATB]'

5 'Chi vol che m'innamori', 'moral canzonetta *a3* [ATB] with two violins'

6 *Messa a 4* [SATB] *da capella*
  a Kyrie
  b [Gloria . . .] Et in terra pax
  c [Credo . . .] Patrem omnipotentem
  d Sanctus
  e Benedictus
  f Agnus Dei

7 Gloria, 'for seven voices [SSATTBB] concerted with two violins and four *viole da braccio* or four trombones, which can also be omitted if necessary'

8 'Crucifixus', 'for four voices: bass, tenor, *quinto* [tenor] and alto'

9 'Et resurrexit', 'for two sopranos or tenors with two violins'

10 'Et iterum venturus est', 'for three voices: bass and two contraltos concerted with four trombones or *viole da braccio*, which can be omitted, which "Crucifixus" will serve as a variation of the *Messa* for four [voices] taking this passage in place of the one marked there between the two signs'

11 'Ab aeterno ordinata sum', 'motet for solo voice, a bass'

12 'Dixit Dominus' I, 'for eight voices [SSAATTBB] concerted with two violins and four *viole* or trombones which should the need arise can also be omitted'

13 'Dixit Dominus' II, 'for eight voices [SSAATTBB] concerted with the same instruments as the first and in the same way'

14 'Confitebor tibi Domine' I, 'for three voices [ATB] with five other voices [SSATB] in the choruses [*repieni*]'

15 'Confitebor tibi Domine' II, 'for three voices [CTB] concerted with two violins'

16 'Confitebor tibi Domine' III, 'in the French style [*alla francese*] for five voices [SSATB] which can be concerted if one wishes with four *viole da braccio* leaving the soprano part to the solo voice'

17 'Beatus vir' I, 'for six voices [SSATTB] concerted with two violins and three *viole da braccio* or three trombones which can also be omitted

18 'Beatus vir' II, 'for five voices [SATTB], which can be sung doubled and loud or as one wishes'

19 'Laudate pueri Dominum' I, '*a5* [SSTTB] concerted with two violins'

20 'Laudate pueri Dominum' II, 'for five voices [SATTB]'

21 'Laudate Dominum omnes gentes' I, 'for five voices [SSTTB] concerted with two violins and a chorus for four voices [ATB; the fourth part is not specified] which can be sung and played with four *viole* or trombones, which can also be omitted if necessary'

22 'Laudate Dominum omnes gentes' II, 'for eight voices [SSAATTBB] and two violins'

23 'Laudate Dominum omnes gentes' III, 'for eight voices [SSAATTBB]'

24 'Credidi propter quod locutus sum', 'for eight voices [in two choirs: SATB, ATTB] *a cappella*'

25 '[Memento Domine David] et omnis mansuetudinis', 'for eight voices [in two choirs: SATB, ATTB] *a cappella*'

26 'Sanctorum meritis' I, 'for solo voice [S] and two violins on the which melody can also be sung other hymns provided they have the same metre'

27 'Sanctorum meritis' II, 'concerted for solo voice [T] with two violins

on the which melody can also be sung other hymns in the same metre'

28 'Deus tuorum militum', for solo voice (T) and two violins (same music as No. 27)

29 'Iste confessor', for solo voice (T) and two violins (same music as No. 27)

30 'Iste confessor', 'for solo voice [*recte* SS] and two violins on the which melody one can equally sing "Ut queant laxis" for St John the Baptist and the like'

31 'Ut queant laxis', for two voices (SS) and two violins (same music as No. 30)

32 'Deus tuorum militum', for three voices (TTB) and two violins, 'on the same melody can also be sung "Jesu corona Virginum", "Christe Redemptor omnium" and other [hymns] in the same metre'

33 Magnificat I, 'for eight voices [in two choirs: SATB, SATB] and two violins and four *viole* or four trombones which if necessary can be omitted'

34 Magnificat II, 'for four voices [SATB] in *a cappella* style'

35 'Salve Regina [Audi coelum]', for solo voice (T) 'with within an echo [for] solo voice [T] replying as echo and two violins'

36 'Salve Regina', 'for two voices: two tenors or two sopranos'

37 'Salve [o] Regina', 'for three voices: alto, bass and tenor or soprano

38 'Jubilet tota civitas', 'for solo voice[s] [SS] in dialogue'

39 'Laudate Dominum in sanctis eius', 'for solo voice: soprano or tenor'

40 *Pianto della Madonna* ('Iam moriar mi fili'), 'for solo voice [S] on the *Lamento d'Arianna*'

The *Madrigali guerrieri, et amorosi* had already presented a remarkable mixture of different forms, genres and styles, but compared to that volume the *Selva morale* gives a still greater impression of heterogeneity, of spontaneous and verdant natural growth, as indeed the title itself seeks to suggest. In fact, this 'forest' of musical compositions is certainly very varied, but it is less forest-like than we are led to believe. The volume clearly falls into five distinct sections: a preamble with spiritual settings (Nos. 1–5), a complete Mass with substitute sections (6–10), a series of psalms (12–25), various hymns (26–32), music for use in Marian feasts (33–37) and one recitative setting in Latin (40). But although the *Selva morale* is almost entirely focused on liturgical music, it is introduced and ended by pieces which are sacred in content but which stand apart from liturgical requirements, first in the vernacular and last in Latin. The first two of the five spiritual madrigals that open the collection are to texts by Petrarch: No. 1 combines two *terzine* from the *Trionfo della morte* (lines 88–100 and 82–85), and No. 2 sets the celebrated opening of the *Canzoniere*. Chosen for their aphoristic qualities (and their sense of constituting an introduction), these texts – a *capitolo* and a sonnet – are also set in the recitative style of contemporary operatic prologues.

35 Opera in Venice

In this period, *Arianna* also returned to the forefront of Monteverdi's activities in the arena most proper to it, the theatre: in Carnival 1640, *Arianna* inaugurated the conversion of the Venetian Teatro S. Moisè to opera.[173] Until now, this public theatre had been home to the usual repertory of spoken plays, but now it too turned to the new fashion for opera that had spread to Venice a few years before, in Carnival 1637, with the performance at the Teatro S. Cassiano of Francesco Manelli's *Andromeda* (to a libretto by Benedetto Ferrari). After a somewhat patchy existence in Florence, Rome and various northern cities, the new theatrical genre was brought to Venice – where it took on the characteristics of a public entertainment with a paying, not just invited, audience – by a predominantly 'Roman' troupe which, the year before, had performed in Padua in the introduction of a tournament called *L'Ermiona* (in Spring 1636).[174] On that occasion, the troupe had been supplemented by local musicians, among whom are listed four singers from the *cappella* of St Mark's: the Mantuan baritone Giacomo Rapallino (who played Jupiter), the Roman soprano castrato Girolamo Medici (Mercury), the other Roman soprano castrato Anselmo Marconi (Victory) and Monteverdi's son, Francesco (in the double role of Apollo and Hymen).[175] The Ferrari–Manelli partnership also supplied the 1638 season at the Teatro S. Cassiano, presenting *La maga fulminata*. In 1639, Manelli moved to open the Teatro SS. Giovanni e Paolo (with *La Delia*, to a libretto by Giulio Strozzi), where Ferrari also presented *Armida* (he wrote the text and perhaps the music), and in 1640, Manelli staged *Adone* (to a libretto by the Venetian Paolo Vendramin), which for a long time was wrongly attributed to Monteverdi.[176] Meanwhile, Manelli and Ferrari were replaced at the Teatro S. Cassiano by a Venetian (by adoption and training) composer and a pupil of Monteverdi, Francesco Cavalli, who produced works for the three carnival seasons of 1639–41 (*Le nozze di Teti e Peleo* to a libretto by Orazio Persiani, 1639; *Gli amori di Apollo e Dafne*, Gian Francesco Busenello, 1640; *La Didone*, Busenello, 1641). As was the case with *L'Ermiona* in Padua, these performances in Venice also involved the participation of singers from St Mark's: indeed, five of them (Francesco Angeletti, Annibale Grasselli, Giovan Battista Bisucci, Girolamo Medici and Anselmo Marconi – the last two had also sung in Padua in 1636) joined Manelli and his wife in the partnership that sponsored the performance of *Andromeda*, as well as then taking part in it as performers. Two of them, Angeletti and Bisucci, also appear among the cast of *La maga fulminata* in 1638.[177]

Monteverdi turned again to this new genre – new for Venice but not for him, since he had been involved in opera in his Mantuan period – which involved musicians of his *cappella*, his pupils and even his son, first by reviving his old and famous opera, *Arianna*: its revival opened the series of opera seasons in the third Venetian public theatre dedicated to opera, the Teatro S. Moisè.

For the occasion, the libretto was also reprinted: there were two editions in 1640 from the presses of Salvadori and Bariletti – the second includes a sonnet by Benedetto Ferrari 'dalla tiorba' headed 'To Signor Claudio Monteverdi, oracle of music'. These librettos reveal some changes from the version staged in Mantua in 1608, with cuts, and alterations to passages too closely linked to the first performance.[178]

36 *Il ritorno di Ulisse in patria* (1640)

At the same time as the revival of *Arianna* at the Teatro S. Moisè, Monteverdi prepared a new work for the same carnival season at the Teatro S. Cassiano, *Il ritorno di Ulisse in patria*. The libretto was by the noble Venetian Giacomo Badoaro, who after this successful debut was to continue his career as an amateur theatre-poet, turning again to Homer's epic and to events related to the Trojan Wars with *Ulisse errante*, set to music by Francesco Sacrati in 1644, and *Elena rapita da Teseo* set in 1653 by an unknown composer traditionally but wrongly identified as Cavalli. It is the dedication introducing the libretto of *Ulisse errante* (Venice, Giovan Pietro Pinelli, 1644) that provides one of the earliest pieces of direct evidence for the collaboration between Badoaro and Monteverdi: 'The *Ritorno d'Ulisse in patria* was adorned with the music of Signor Claudio Monteverde, subject of all fame and of long-lasting name . . .'.

For his text, Badoaro drew his plot from the *Odyssey* (specifically, Books XIII–XXIII). These well-known events are preceded by a moralizing prologue in which Human Frailty declares herself subject to the tyrannies of Time, Fortune and Love: the events that follow will provide – even if it seems something of a pretext – an illustration of this pessimistic conclusion.

> ACT I. The Trojan War has long ended. But Ulysses has not yet returned to Ithaca, where his wife still awaits him, refusing to believe him dead and resisting the offers of marriage made her by the Suitors (the Proci), who have established themselves in the leaderless kingdom. Even if her hopes of embracing her husband again are but few, she remains stubbornly faithful to him. Meanwhile, the Phæacians, whom Ulysses had most recently reached in the course of his wanderings, have brought the hero to Ithaca, leaving him sleeping on the beach; they will pay for this with death, given that Neptune, who is opposed to Ulysses's return to his homeland, transforms them and their ship into a rock as punishment for having gone against his will. Waking, Ulysses believes that he has been abandoned and betrayed, but on meeting a shepherd by chance he learns that the island on which he finds himself is his native Ithaca. In reality, this youth is none other than Minerva – Ulysses's protectress – in disguise; after she has revealed herself to him, she advises him for his protection to assume the appearance of an old man so as to enter the court unrecognized and better to prepare his revenge against the usurping Suitors. Under this disguise, he meets the faithful shepherd Eumæus (Eumete), telling him of the forthcoming return of his king.
> ACT II. While he is staying with Eumæus, Ulysses meets his son, Tele-

machus, returned from Sparta, where he had gone to seek news of his father: he reveals himself to him and together, having recovered from the shock and unexpected joy, they plan their return to the palace. Penelope is there constantly besieged by the exhortations to marriage from the maid Melantho and, with some degree of self interest, from the Suitors. The arrival of Eumæus with his happy news of Ulysses's imminent return encourages the Suitors to act with decision; above all, they will kill Telemachus on his arrival, removing thereby an obstacle from their path, and they will persuade Penelope to marry one of them. Ulysses arrives at the palace in the guise of an old beggar and is poorly treated by the Suitors, who provoke him against one of their followers, the parasite Irus (Iro); the two fight and Ulysses quickly defeats his lazy adversary, thus gaining a welcome at court. With precious gifts, the Suitors attempt to gain the favour of Penelope, who proclaims that she will marry whoever succeeds in stringing the mighty bow that once belonged to Ulysses. One after the other, the Suitors take the test in vain. The beggar, too, asks to be admitted to the trial: Penelope permits him, and to general amazement he succeeds in the task, loosing forth arrows against the Suitors who die, all slaughtered.

ACT III. While those who were among the followers of the Suitors are left in dismay, Ulysses's supporters exult, recognizing him in the avenging beggar. Only Penelope resists, believing herself to be victim of a new trick, and she refuses to believe what Eumæus, her nurse Euryclea (Ericlea) and Telemachus say. She is convinced only when Ulysses, who in the meanwhile has resumed his true appearance, is able to offer an exact description of the nuptial quilt which she herself had made and which has never been seen by anyone save her husband.

The opera survives in an anonymous manuscript (Vienna, Nationalbibliothek, MS 18763), the authenticity of which in the past was sometimes called into question.[179] However, it is now generally agreed that the score is by Monteverdi. It transmits only the vocal parts and the basso continuo: only sinfonias and ritornellos are – in almost all cases – written in five parts. Also missing is any indication of the instrumentation, such as those prescriptions and scorings that appear, for example, in the printed score of *Orfeo*; but in the latter case, we are dealing with an edition commemorating an event linked to court life the memory of which was intended to be preserved, whereas here we are concerned with a working copy, a text to be used for a performance.

A letter from Badoaro headed 'To the very illustrious and very reverend Signor Claudio Monte Verde, great *maestro* of music' prefacing one copy of the libretto of *Il ritorno di Ulisse in patria* underlines the character of his work as both pastime and 'academic' exercise, and also informs us of the opera's success, which up to that point had been 'seen performed ... ten full times with an equal gathering of the city'. Badoaro also praises Monteverdi 'who has indeed made known to the world what is the true spirit of theatrical music not well understood by modern composers', and who has shown to the city of Venice 'that in the warmth of the emotions there is a great difference between a true sun and a painted one'.[180]

Further evidence of the success of *Il ritorno* is provided by the fact that it was one of the two operas (the other was *La Delia*, with a libretto by Giulio Strozzi and music by Francesco Manelli) to be performed at the Teatro Guastavillani in Bologna during the tour of a company coming from Venice (the same as of the première?), consisting at least of Maddalena Manelli (Minerva in *Il ritorno*), Giulia Paolelli (Penelope), the singer Costantino Manelli and the theorbo player Benedetto Ferrari. These musicians were in fact the recipients of poetic tributes collected in the *Glorie della Musica celebrate dalla sorella Poesia* (Bologna, Giovan Battista Ferroni, 1640), which also includes a sonnet by 'Ber. Mar.' (perhaps Bernardino Mariscotti) headed 'For *Ulisse*, musical work by Signor Claudio Monteverdi' – beginning 'Scioglie vela al gioir, se spiega un foglio' ('Loose sail to joy, if paper reveals') – and another by 'Clotildo Artemii' (a pseudonym?) headed 'For *Ulisse*, drama by the most illustrious Signor Giacomo Badoero, and music by Signor Claudio Monteverdi', beginning 'De l'itaco guerriero il bel ritorno' ('Of the Ithacan warrior, the fine return').[181]

Perhaps connected with some theatrical enterprise involving Monteverdi is the autograph document (now lost) by the composer dated 19 July 1640: he seems to have been engaging a singer called Leonida Donati. Some two years later, on 14 February 1642, she in fact summoned the composer before the primicerius of St Mark's (as a priest Monteverdi could not be tried before any other tribunal), producing this document in support of her claims. Given that the legal records are now lost, we know few details about this case: it was concluded in the summer of 1643 with Monteverdi being ordered to compensate Donati to the sum of 210 lire.[182]

37 1641–1642

The printing initiatives of the *Madrigali guerrieri et amorosi* and the *Selva morale* were completed in 1641 with a Venetian reprint of the Seventh Book by Bartolomeo Magni. We have already seen how Monteverdi's printed output in the 1620s and 1630s diminished significantly, limiting itself to isolated contributions to sacred or secular anthologies or to two small individual volumes (the 1623 collection including the *Lamento d'Arianna*, and the *Scherzi musicali* of 1632): the most consistent endeavour was the reprinting of all his books of madrigals, from the First to the Seventh, in 1620–22 (and of the 1607 *Scherzi musicali* in 1628). From then on, only the Seventh Book continued to be reprinted in Italy (in 1623 and 1628); neither the Eighth Book nor the *Selva morale* was ever reprinted.

The reasons for all this are various and interlinked: the uniqueness of these last two volumes, which are also out of the ordinary in terms of their format and size; the decline of the traditional madrigal and the rise of a new taste which rendered obsolete the early madrigal books and more fashionable the Seventh Book; the more general economic crisis of the 1620s and in particular the ups and downs of the Venetian printing industry, linked to the scant activity of the bookselling trade and to the increasing difficulty of finding patrons and consumers of any secular material that a given composer wished to give to the press. Outside Italy, on the other hand, the situation was more dynamic. It is revealing that apart from the reprint of the Seventh Book by Bartolomeo Magni in 1641, only in Antwerp at the press run by the heirs of Pierre Phalèse in their shop 'at the sign of King David' – which in 1615 had reprinted the Third, Fourth and Fifth Books (and in 1616, 'Lumi, miei cari lumi' from the Third Book in the anthology *Il Helicone: madrigali de diversi eccellentissimi musici*) – did reprints of Monteverdi's madrigals appear in the 1630s and 1640s (the Sixth Book in 1639 and the Fourth in 1644). It is also significant that it was to the Habsburg court that Monteverdi turned to find dedicatees for his most demanding, and therefore expensive, volumes.

In 1641, Monteverdi – now well over seventy – again received a new commission from outside Venice: a *balletto* with sung narrations ordered by Duke Odoardo Farnese (the same as was involved in the 1628 Parma festivities) to celebrate in Piacenza the birth of his seventh child, Ottavio. This *balletto* had a text by Bernardo Morando and was titled *Vittoria d'Amore*; it was performed on Thursday 7 February 'in the citadel of Piacenza in the carnival of this year 1641 decorated with machines, with music and with invention', as we are told by the title-page of the description left us by Morando himself and printed in Piacenza by Giovanni Antonio Ardizzoni (the print is undated but certainly comes from 1641):[183]

> And lo, while in the usual room of court destined for the entertainments, in the presence of Their Most Serene Highnesses they are directing the usual dances, a sweetest *sinfonia* sounds unexpectedly to the ear, produced by twenty-five well-concerted *viole* and by various other musical instruments. And suddenly the eye is drawn to the great vault of that room (which to give space for the machines was split and open), where one sees appear, as if from heaven, a great cloud, except that in the sky there is no trace of an opening. Within the cloud, which, with a hole in the middle, is all around resplendent, appears a goddess, who, dressed in silver crêpe and shoed with besilvered buskins, with a quiver at her side, a bow in hand and a half moon on her forehead, is recognized as Diana.
>
> The cloud first descends slowly in a perpendicular motion so that it seems that it will fall on the heads of the spectators. Then, it advances moving directly towards the front of the theatre, and then, turning on itself, advancing and descending at the same time, with three different movements, to the back of the room and towards its centre, it comes to a halt.
>
> On reaching the ground, Diana, proud of her achievements and happy at her followers, sweetly singing, flatters herself and commands the cloud to open and to return to heaven, with these verses:
>
> > O cieli, o terra, o numi,
> > . . .
> > tornino i monti al suol, le nubi al cielo.
>
> [O heavens, o earth, o gods / . . . / let the mountains return to the sun, and the clouds to the heavens.]

At the delivery of these last notes, the cloud obediently opens and at the same time ascends very quickly to heaven. And the mountain, which was enclosed in it, stops on the ground, to the marvel of the theatre, which does not know how to understand how within a cloud, which was all open in the middle, could be hidden a rocky mountain, larger than the cloud itself and filled with eleven people whom at the removal of the cloud all saw with different movements and with wondrous speed ordered in their places. Diana remains in the highest part between two nymphs, who, a little beneath her, they too armed with quiver and bow, wear, apart from the half-mooned brow, the same apparel. Beneath them stand arranged the latest followers of the goddess, dressed in most delightful fashion, with rich devices and superb ornaments all of silver, and they too armed with bow and arrows. With the mountain halted and arranged in the manner almost of a theatre, Diana turns to the shepherds – escorted by the two nymphs – emphasizes her own merits and flashes forth a thousand curses against Cupid; she invites them to put him to flight, and not only to impress within hearts this motto FUGGIAMO AMORE ['Let us flee Love'] but also to form a *balletto* in which through dancing they express the same words AMOR FUGGIAMO. To this end, now Diana, now the nymphs turning to the shepherds, thus sweetly singing, are made heard:

> Là nei zaffiri eterni
>
> . . .
>
> *Fuggiam, fuggiamo Amor* nei balli istessi.
>
> [There among the eternal zephyrs / . . . / *Let us flee, let us flee Love* in dances themselves.]

That ended, with the mountain moving forward somewhat, it leaves room for the shepherds to descend to the place destined for the *balletto*. And no sooner have they descended than the mountain itself turns to its side and with rapid movement goes to the great door of the room, and then it leaves with Diana and with the nymphs.

At the first step which the shepherds, having descended from the machine, take on the ground, they begin to the sound of the same many instruments the majestic *entrata* of the *balletto*, moving on without a break to the *balletto* itself, which with a most graceful air invented anew by Provost Aschieri, invites them to direct gracefully the regular motions of the foot with the harmonious law of the sound. Within it, with various interweaving and turning mutations, they go with proficiency and skill so arranging themselves that they themselves form, one by one, the letters with which the following words are expressed: AMOR FUGGIAMO . . .

Towards the end of the *balletto*, while the eight dancers find themselves arranged in a perfect circle in the shape of the last letter O, the theatre suddenly goes dark and one hears a rumbling and noisy sound of thunder, accompanied by lightning, which with fleeting flashes of light now and again rend asunder the darkness which had arrived, and there is added an impetuous wind from which the air all around becomes agitated and moved. At the unexpected arrival of the imperious storm, the shepherds, astounded, leaving off the dance and moving some to one side and some to the other, stand astonished to watch the outcome. Meanwhile the wind is followed by a fine rainfall, or rather a showering of most perfumed waters which orange and cedar trees are able to distil from their most pleasant flowers.

And lo, the darkness and the rain not having entirely ceased, one begins to see a heavenly rainbow in the sky, at the appearance of which the theatre remains lit anew, and Iris, descending little by little, marvellously reveals the splendour of her colours. On the raised part of the rainbow sits Cupid, a winged boy with quiver at his side and bow on his back, whom eight little Cupids crown, they too winged and armed with bow and quiver. He, all furious, carries in his right hand the lightning bolt of Jove and shows on his brow the lightning bolt of scorn. Aroused by the outrages of Diana and of the *balletto* done to the detriment of him and his followers, having sent ahead almost as his precursors the Winds, Thunder and Storms, he comes armed for revenge. Iris's machine descends halfway through the air, while Cupid, all vexed and quivering with rage, accompanies with song and with gestures these words:

> Non piú d'orride nubi in ciel s'accampi
>
> . . .
>
> de l'offeso onor mio l'alta vendetta.

> [No more may horrid clouds stay in the heavens / . . . / of my offended honour the great revenge.]

Speaking thus, Iris lowers herself little by little and the eight little Cupids, preparing themselves for the act of wounding, jump to the ground. Suddenly the machine raises itself again and in its first position, halfway in the sky, it stops, with Cupid staying on it as spectator of the deeds of his ministers. Among these and the followers of Cynthia is begun, in the manner of a skirmish, a new and most graceful dance. They are equal in number; their arms are not different, but the defenders have the advantage in size, the attackers in outlandishness. The ones and the others practising to the same guidance of the music their feet and their bows, they direct the warring dance with wondrous delight. But who does not know that Love wins all? Cynthia's champions, while brave and unconquerable elsewhere, yet remain at the end defeated and bound in the presence of Cupid. He, applauding the victorious Cupids and welcoming the subjugated champions, refuting the injuries of Diana and exaggerating his own pleasantness, with a sweeter style, he takes up his song again in this manner:

> O de le forze mie, de' pregi miei
>
> . . .
>
> fioccare in seno al verno i fior d'aprile.

> [O of my strength, of my merits / . . . / to shower forth in the depths of winter the flowers of April.]

That scarcely said, lo there descends from the heavens by virtue of the power of Love, an unaccustomed and delightful shower or storm of freshest and perfumed flowers, which falling on the head and lap of the ladies and from all around on the spectators, fills the theatre with a surprising and most pleasant spring. Cupid, as soon as he sees that the noise caused by collecting the flowers of this shower had died down, having turned again all courteously to the shepherds, thus he sings pleasantly as follows:

> Già nel seren de' volti io scorgo espresso
>
> . . .
>
> ch'oggi è per lor vittorïoso Amore.

> [Now I see expressed in the serenity of their countenances / . . . / that today for them Love is victorious.]

That finished, the little Cupids, with slow steps as of victors, lead as prisoners the followers no longer of Cynthia but of Cupid. And all together in a long and most grateful line, in order alternating a shepherd and a little Cupid, they dance the *retirata* of the *balletto*, making deep bows to Their Most Serene [Highnesses], then bowing to the ladies, while triumphant Love on the heavenly rainbow, in the melody of sounds, returns to heaven and leaves the entertainment ended.

In that same carnival of 1641 at the Venetian Teatro SS. Giovanni e Paolo, Monteverdi presented another new opera, *Le nozze d'Enea in Lavinia*, to an anonymous libretto often wrongly attributed to Badoaro.[184] At the time of the première, only an *Argomento et scenario* (Venice, n.p., 1640) was published, which is introduced by a *Lettera dell'autore ad alcuni suoi amici* ('Letter of the author to some of his friends'). This *Lettera*, as well as proving the error of the traditional attribution to Badoaro,[185] refers to a revival – in carnival 1641 – of *Il ritorno di Ulisse in patria*, to its success on its première in 1640, and to its subsequent diffusion also outside Venice (perhaps a reference to the Manelli tour to Bologna):

> Now approaches the end of the year [1640] in which was performed for the first time the most beautiful tragedy of *Il ritorno d'Ulisse in patria* by our most illustrious and most virtuous friend. With this occasion, you know how as a pastime [*per scherzo*] I formed the argument of *Le nozze d'Enea in Lavinia*, which you showed yourself to welcome such that you wanted me to build on it some scenes, and then should carry on with the rest, so that set to music it might serve us for entertainment in the present year ... But whatever the state of this my monster of a few months, nevertheless you wanted it set to music by Signor Monteverde without caring that to that great man was due another composition, so that there would not be an infinite disproportion between the music and poetry. Add to that the fact that my work was to be staged after a new performance of that of our friend; and who does not know of his most deserved plaudits from the whole city and from foreigners? – as a sign of which, very eminent persons have sought it out to see and hear it elsewhere.[186]

In particular, reference is made to the comic role of Irus, which encouraged the author to imitate Badoaro and to introduce a similar ridiculous character: 'I have made use of him [Numano] as a comic character, not finding in the author [Virgil] anyone else more appropriate, and knowing the disposition of many onlookers, to whom please jokes like this more than serious things, just as we see the Iro of our friend having caused wondrous delight, to which kind of character I truly would not have given a place in any other tragedy.'[187]

Le nozze d'Enea in Lavinia, called a 'tragedia di lieto fine' (a tragedy with a happy ending) in the *Argomento*, inaugurated a series of operas based on Trojan–Roman subjects – the theme had already been hinted at in *Le nozze di Teti e di Peleo* by Persiani and Cavalli (Teatro S. Cassiano, 1639) – which were to assume particular importance on the Venetian stage.[188] 'From this marriage [of Aeneas and Lavinia], the same Hymen takes the opportunity to touch again upon the origin and greatness of Rome, mentioned first by Virtue in the prologue, and then the birth of our Venice, certainly not too far away and by forced extension, given that this most noble city began when Rome was seen to fall under the yoke of the barbarians.'[189]

Behind this *Lettera* one can see a small group of *letterati* – perhaps amateurs – a group to which the author turns out of preference and with which he shares ideas and common cultural values, and under whose encouragement and applause the work was undertaken: 'Now since you have asked me for the argument of the opera to communicate it to other friends, with this I first intend to pass through some justifications – not with you, who know my intention – so that where I am not in a position to receive praise, at least I can distance myself as much as I can from criticisms.'[190] For the rest, this suggests the academic context of early opera in Venice, even if it developed in paying theatres.[191]

The anonymous poet goes further to underline Monteverdi's interest in the expression of the emotions, and consequently his own preoccupation with providing a text which would encourage him in that direction:

> Thus as a result of that unexpected news ['of approaching danger'], Aeneas awakes disturbed, and complaining of the continuation of such wicked fortune he discourses on [p. 15] his past mishaps, which at least in part must be known to the onlookers. Then as a brave man he regains his strength, thus passing from calm to trouble, and then to joy at the appearance of his mother. These changes of emotions, which always appear good in such poems, also greatly please our Signor Monteverde since he has the opportunity with emotional variety to show the wonders of his art ... Beyond which, if music requires lightness, it also seeks clarity since, using its divisions and partitions, with many metaphors and other figures one comes to render the sentiment obscure; for which reason I have avoided thoughts and conceits taken from the abstruse, and I have rather aimed for the emotions, as Signor Monteverde wishes, to please whom I have also changed and left aside many things from what I first wrote ... Now you, my lords, tolerating the imperfection of my poetry, enjoy cheerfully the sweetness of the music of the never enough praised Monteverde, born to the world so as to rule over the emotions of others, there being no harsh spirit that he does not turn and move according to his talent, adapting in such a way the musical notes to the words and to the passions that he who sings must laugh, weep, grow angry and grow pitying, and do all the rest that they command, with the listener no less led to the same impulse in the variety and force of the same perturbations. To this truly great man, this most noble art of music – and particularly theatrical music – knows itself to be so much in debt that it can confess that it is thanks to him that it has been brought to new life in the world more efficacious and perfect than it was in ancient Greece or wherever else it has ever been that the fine arts have been held in esteem. That this Signor Monteverde, known in far-flung parts and wherever music is known, will be sighed for in future ages, at least as far as they can be consoled by his most noble compositions, which are set to last as long as can resist the ravages of time any more esteemed and estimable fruit of one who is a wondrous talent in his profession.[192]

To emphasize the extent to which Monteverdi's fame truly extended 'to far-flung parts', in 1641–42 the Leipzig printer Henning Kölern issued three collections of 'concertos and spiritual harmonies', edited by Ambrosius Profe, organist of St Elisabeth, Breslau (Wrocław), which include spiritual *contrafacta* of works taken from Monteverdi's latest printed collections.

Erster Theil geistlicher Concerten und Harmonien (1641)

'Vaga su spina ascosa' (Seventh Book) as 'Jesum viri senesque'

Ander Theil geistlicher Concerten und Harmonien (1641)

'Altri canti di Marte e di sua schiera' (Eighth Book) as 'Pascha concelebranda'
'Due belli occhi fur l'armi onde trafitto' (Eighth Book) as 'Ergo gaude laetare' (also texted 'Lauda anima mea')

Dritter Theil geistlicher Concerten und Harmonien (1642)

'Io che armato sinor d'un duro gelo' (1632 *Scherzi musicali*) as 'Spera in domino'
'Armato il cor d'adamantina fede' (1632 *Scherzi musicali* and Eighth Book) as 'Heus bone vir'
'Voi ch'ascoltate in rime sparse il suono' (*Selva morale*) as 'Haec dicit Dominus'

(Also includes 'Laudate Dominum in sanctis eius' and 'Iam moriar mi fili' (*Pianto della Madonna*) from the *Selva morale*)

38 *La coronatione di Poppea* (1643)

Monteverdi soon had the opportunity to broach opera again in the season of carnival 1643,[193] setting to music a text by the Venetian lawyer Gian Francesco Busenello, who had already written for Cavalli (*Gli amori di Apollo e Dafne* and *La Didone*). This new opera was staged at the Teatro Grimani in SS. Giovanni e Paolo, with the famous Anna Renzi in the role of Octavia.[194] The première saw the publication not of the libretto but only of a *Scenario dell'opera reggia intitolata La coronatione di Poppea che si rappresenta in musica nel teatro dell'illustr. sig. Giovanni Grimani* ('Scenario of the royal opera called *La coronatione di Poppea* which is represented in music in the theatre of the most illustrious Signor Giovanni Grimani'; Venice, Giovan Pietro Pinelli, 1643). The complete text, with the title *L'incoronazione di Poppea*, appeared only some years later in the literary edition of Busenello's librettos, brought together in the volume titled *Delle ore ociose* (Venice, Giuliani, 1656).

Two scores of the opera have survived, both untitled and anonymous, descending from the same source which is now missing:[195] one in Venice (Biblioteca Nazionale Marciana, It. IV.439[= 9963]) and perhaps prepared under the supervision of Francesco Cavalli, who owned it; and the other in Naples (Conservatorio di Musica S. Pietro a Majella, Rari 6.4.1), which can be connected with the above-mentioned performance in Naples in 1651 (see p. 1). Both scores transmit only the vocal lines plus basso continuo: the *sinfonie* and ritornellos are given in three parts in the Venice manuscript, and for the most part in four in the Naples score (in both cases minus indications of instrumentation).

It is worth noting that with one possible exception – a recently discovered copy of the libretto – no contemporary source known today gives details of the composer of the music set to Busenello's text, in accordance with the usual practice of considering the poet, more than the musician, as essentially the creator of a sung drama. Monteverdi's name begins to be associated with *La coronatione* in the second half of the seventeenth century, not least on the Venetian score formerly owned by Cavalli which then passed into the collection of the noble music-lover Marco Contarini. The attribution was officially sanctioned, as it were, in the first published catalogue of operas, inserted by Cristoforo Ivanovich in his *Minerva al tavolino* (Venice, Nicolò Pezzana, 1681; a bibliography of librettos had already appeared in Leone Allacci's *Drammaturgia* of 1666), and since then no one has cast doubt upon it.

However, most recently some concern has grown over the final duet for Nero and Poppæa, 'Pur ti miro—Pur ti godo', which is present in the scores and in the manuscript librettos, but not in those printed (all after the première; the *Scenario*, which was published at the time of the first performance, seems not to refer to the duet). This text had already appeared in the Bolognese revival of *Il pastor regio* (1641) by Benedetto Ferrari (he wrote the words and music), which was originally written for Venice and performed for the first time in 1640 (but without the duet in question). The duet was present in all the performances of Ferrari's opera after 1641 (in Milan and Piacenza), and it was also included in the collection of Ferrari's *Poesie drammatiche* which he himself published in Milan in 1644. Thus the text certainly seems to be by him. If at this point one might be tempted to suggest that Ferrari also wrote the music, the situation is complicated by *Il trionfo della fatica* (Rome, G. Barberi, 1647; a copy survives in Rome, Biblioteca Apostolica Vaticana, Miscell. G.8), called a 'carro musicale del Poeta Inesperto posto in musica da Filiberto Laurentii e rappresentato in Roma nel carnevale dell'anno 1647' ('Musical *carro* by the Inexpert Poet set to music by Filiberto Laurenzi and performed in Rome in the carnival of the year 1647'), which concludes with the duet in question sung by Ricchezza and Valoriano. Since only the text has survived, it is impossible to say whether the music was the same as in the score of *La coronatione* (in which case it might appear to have been composed by Laurenzi). Similarly, Monteverdi's younger contemporary in Venice, Francesco Sacrati has recently been suggested as the composer of the final scene of the opera. So as well as Monteverdi, the candidates for having composed this duet (the text of which should be attributed to Ferrari) are at present Laurenzi,

Ferrari, Sacrati, and also perhaps Cavalli, who was probably the editor of the Venice score.[196]

The question thus remains open, today unanswerable: 'the modern listener has no certainties beyond those of the pervasive vocal and erotic delights of the music itself'. In sum, as Lorenzo Bianconi continues with customary acumen, the duet is distinctive not just for its musical qualities, but also for its position, not within the opera itself – an obvious place in the context of what is essentially a love-story – but at the very end, and in the manner of a final summary providing an ardent epitaph to the events just staged, which overrules a generic finale in some triumphal manner to go right to the heart of the dramatic substance of the work. 'The identity of the composer, in fact, is of little importance; what really matters is that *this* piece at *this* very moment of *this* drama is nothing short of a true *coup de théâtre* – even if due, maybe, to the wayward whims of some anonymous "Feboarmonico".'[197]

PROLOGUE. While Fortune and Virtue discuss which of them has most influence on men, Amor arrives to affirm his own primacy; even the others end up acknowledging it, and Amor proposes to show it yet one more time. ACT I. Returning from the fields of Lusitania, Otho (Ottone) comes to discover that his adored Poppæa has in the meantime become the lover of Nero, with the secret ambition of placing herself at his side on the throne. Meanwhile Octavia, the legitimate and unfortunate empress, spurns with scorn the encouragements of her Nurse (Nutrice) to repay her traitorous husband in the same coin, and she incites the imperial counsellor, Seneca, to follow his fine words of consolation with some concrete act to prevent Nero repudiating her. Meeting the emperor, the philosopher succeeds only in making him angry and in having himself dismissed. Considering him an impediment to the repudiation of Octavia and thus to her own marriage to the emperor, Poppæa succeeds in extracting from Nero the order to rid himself of Seneca. In vain, Otho begs his beloved Poppæa not to abandon him: now her sights are set higher. To assuage his own grief, Otho turns his affection to the young Drusilla. ACT II. First Mercury and then Pallas Athene announce to Seneca that his death is imminent, and in fact shortly thereafter arrives a freedman (Liberto) bringing him Nero's order that forces him to kill himself: the philosopher obeys, stoically consoling his friends who try to prevent him from making this final act. Otho gives way to the idea of revenge, and indeed of killing Poppæa; in this he is encouraged also by Octavia, who suggests that he should approach her dressed in women's clothes so as not to be recognized and as to have easier access. Drusilla, informed by Otho of his plans, herself provides the clothing, with which Otho, armed, enters Poppæa's apartments while she sleeps. But Amor rushes to arouse her, thus succeeding in preventing the violent act. While Poppæa cries for help, Otho, mistaken for Drusilla, flees. ACT III. Drusilla is captured and tried but, despite torture, does not reveal the truth so as to save her beloved Otho. Moved by such love, he confesses all and is sent to exile with Drusilla. Octavia, implicated in the plot, is conveniently repudiated and sent herself, too, into exile. Nero can thus finally marry Poppæa, who in the triumphal finale is crowned empress.

More than in the case of *Il ritorno*, the action brought to the stage in *La coronatione* presents itself as a demonstration of the argument presented in the prologue, almost in the manner of a *quaestio* – with an academic flavour and in a classical format – of who has most influence over the affairs of mankind, whether Fortune or Virtue. However, the reply that emerges is unexpected and unusual, standing somewhat apart from this traditional opposition, given that victory is claimed and won by Amor: 'Oggi in un sol certame / l'una e l'altra di voi da me abbattuta, / dirà che 'l mondo a' cenni miei si muta' ('Today in a single contest, / both the one and the other of you conquered by me / will say that the world turns on my instructions'), affirms Amor at the end of the prologue, preparing to give a theatrical *exemplum* of this pessimistic conclusion according to which history emerges not from the active capacities of men nor from the blind will of chance, but rather from the irrational impulse of the emotions.

Unique in Busenello's significant output is the choice here of the subject through which to give body to this abstract, general idea: an event from classical Rome for which the poet could find material both from the best-known histories (chiefly Tacitus) and perhaps from the *Octavia* attributed to Seneca.[198] Already in Florentine and Roman circles, librettists had made use of ideas drawn from literary works to find good plots for opera, and the practice quickly took root in Venice: take, for example, Monteverdi's two immediately preceding works (*Il ritorno di Ulisse in patria* and *Le nozze d'Enea in Lavinia*), which stage parts of the most celebrated epic narratives. Busenello, however, turned not to myths or to romance, but to real history with real characters, albeit obviously taking the liberty to treat things at his convenience. Even if the hagiographic operas performed in Florence and above all Rome had staged real and not imaginary events, nevertheless they surrounded them with such legendary haloes that they appeared not too much unlike mythological plots.

One should add, however, that Busenello's choice (which he himself attempted to repeat with his *La prosperità infelice di Giulio Cesare dittatore*, which may never have been staged) must be considered exceptional. In fact, *La coronatione* does not provide the prototype of that historical–Roman thread that is so important in the Venetian libretto of the second half of the seventeenth century, destined to burst forth only some twenty years later and under very different ideological constraints. At that later period, these subjects served the cause of a patriotism tied to the support of Austria against the common enemy, the Ottoman empire, while in Busenello's case – in an entirely different political and cultural context – we are dealing with an explicit polemic against the court and against monarchy (apparent in Act I scene 2) which must have found particular favour in republican Venice and which, for example, is also found in *Il ritorno* – albeit only in passing and much more on the margins – in the character of Eumæus (I.11 and II.12; a variant of the traditional theme of 'Erminia among the shepherds') and also in some speeches from Melantho (III.2: 'Cosí all'ombra de scettri anco pur sono / mal

sicure le vite: / vicine alle corone / son le destre esecrande anco piú ardite';
'Thus in the shadow of sceptres are still also / insecure our lives; / close to
crowns / desecrating hands are still more eager'). In *La coronatione*, imperial
Rome is represented in terms of palace intrigues in which are mixed unbridled
ambitions and power-seeking, where all feeling is trodden underfoot, no
appeal is made to the emotions, and one can resort even to murder. Compared
with Seneca, who invokes an authority voluntarily subordinate to law and
reason (1.9: 'consiglier scellerato è il sentimento / ch'odia le leggi e la ragion
disprezza', 'a wicked counsellor is sentiment / which hates laws and scorns
reason'), or at least reason of State ('Siano innocenti i regi / o s'aggravino sol di
colpe illustri'; 'Let kings be innocent, / or aggravate matters only with
illustrious crimes'), Nero is the tyrant who rules by caprice, obeying only base
instincts.

It should not be forgotten that both Badoaro and Busenello were members
of the Venetian Accademia degli Incogniti (the first with the name 'L'Assicu-
rato', the 'Assured One'), an esoteric gathering that cultivated an intellectual
libertinism which also reveals itself in the clear preference 'for all public
literature – for entertainment and widely disseminated – falling between the
sceptical and the licentious, which can be very clearly documented, for
example, in their massive output of novellas and romances'.[199] Both Badoaro
and Busenello clearly reflect themes, tastes and cultural debates of those circles.
As well as its anti-monarchical gibes, the text of *Il ritorno* perhaps draws from
them the facile epicureanism of Melantho and the cynicism of the Suitors,
which are even capable of infecting Penelope and causing her mythical fidelity
to falter (II.12). To the anti-conformist thought and open-mindedness of the
Incogniti can perhaps be imputed certain situations represented in *La coronatione*, such as the insolent and even violent derision of the venerable
philosopher Seneca on the part of the Valet (Valletto; 1.6). More tangentially,
this context and Busenello's professed faith in Marinism lead to certain of his
stylistic tendencies in the direction of an openness to the use of different
expressive levels: from lowly and day-to-day locutions to more exalted and
imaginative metaphors, from lyric charm to the specificity of specialist
(technical, scientific, legal, philosophical) vocabularies.[200]

But on a more general level, *La coronatione* reveals themes common to the
prose narratives of other members of the Incogniti. Fictionalized events drawn
from the history of imperial Rome stand at the centre of *Agrippina, madre di
Nerone* (1642) and *Agrippina, moglie di Britannico* (1642) by Ferrante Pallavicino; and Francesco Pona's *La Messalina* (1627) and Federico Malipiero's
L'imperatrice ambiziosa (1640) have protagonists who revel in sensuous luxury.
Outside the context of ancient Rome, political intrigue is also the focus of
Maiolino Bisaccioni's *Demetrio moscovita* (1643), and sensuality – which for the
rest is spread through many works by the Incogniti – as the expression of the
irrational licentiousness of a despot is described particularly in Giovan Battista
Moroni's *Lussi del genio esecrabile di Clearco* (1640).

Given such a multi-faceted text, Monteverdi found an abundance of opportunities to practise his preferred depiction of the emotions, here all the more varied given that the characters present themselves with changing slants and are focused differently as the story develops. Confronted with the many psychological situations presented to him by Busenello, Monteverdi enhanced the pliability of his style, responding flexibly to its stream of emotions but more often manipulating the text to extract from it above all musical segments which he can privilege with a communicative function.

Monteverdi's encounter with Busenello allowed the composer to conclude in the best of ways a compositional career that had been entirely devoted to giving life, with always renewed technical and stylistic means, to the changing world of the emotions. In this last phase, this world was controlled by his very great and secure musical skill, and above all by his capacity – right until the end – to expand and render ever more effective and complex the expressive powers of his own techniques. This was a gift recognized unanimously by his contemporaries and was noted in the funeral eulogy written for him by Caberloti.

> In this [musical] art favoured by Apollo, our Claudio appeared at the most serene courts of Mantua and Parma, and there having found poetic compositions by most noble intellects who mute in their metric numbers did not produce in the spirits of princes those emotions they desired, Claudio with harmonious number or musical measure achieved what more than could ever be granted to any other mortal professing music. Finding himself at the aforesaid most serene courts at the time of wedding festivities, and while the spirits of all were preparing for celebration, it would scarcely have suited them if this highest intellect had not with various modes of music partitioned their delight, since as a most perfect possessor of harmonic number, with the Dorian he urged prudence and caused in their breasts desires of chaste thoughts; with the Phrygian he provoked to battle those lively princes and enflamed their hearts with angry vows; with the Aeolian he calmed the internal tempests and storms of their souls and bestowed sleep and rest on their pacified wills; and finally, with the Lydian he revived the intellects, and relieving them of the desire for earthly things, he aroused their yearning for heavenly ones, and so acting most distinguishedly he produced a thousand good things ... But it is worth speaking the truth. Among the infinite number of celebrated singers from the first centuries until our own days, such as the likes of Orpheus, Amphion, Philammon, Ardalus, Tritaeus and others, who will be left aside because of their great number, they received from heaven some singular musical way of moving some particular emotion in the breasts of men. Only Claudio (I believe that it was fate that gave him this name, since he enclosed in himself so much worth) enjoyed the community of the emotions and produced at will in human minds the dispositions and moved the feelings to the selection of that delight which he offered them. His many compositions do not let me lie, in which having partitioned the above-mentioned modes, there is no one who can bend his ear to them without surrendering himself. Who has the strength to hold back tears while he stops to hear the just lament of the unfortunate Ariadne? What joy does he not feel at the song of his madrigals and musical *scherzi*? Can they perhaps not yield to true devotion on hearing his sacred compositions? Do they not

dispose themselves to all modest a form of life who stop to enjoy with their ear his moral compositions? And in the variety of his compositions written for princely weddings or staged in the theatres of this most serene city, do they not vary their emotions from moment to moment? For now they invite you to laughter, from which in a moment you are forced to change to weeping, and when you think of taking up arms in revenge, precisely then with the harmony changing itself in a miraculous metamorphosis your heart is disposed to clemency; and in a flash you feel yourself filled with fear, when with no less speed you gain all confidence. Say it and believe it, my lords, that Apollo and all the Muses have gathered to increase the excellency of Claudio's skill; for Clio taught him to sing of victories, Melpomene of tragic happenings, Thalia of lascivious loves, Euterpe to accompany song with the sweetness of flutes, Terpsichore to enlarge and move the emotions, Erato to handle the plectrum, Calliope to write heroic songs, Urania to emulate the heavenly motions, Polyhymnia to measure the times, and finally Apollo as if as *maestro* taught him to partake with infallible order in such a variety of tasks.[201]

39 1643: Monteverdi's death

From May 1643 – if we are to believe Caberloti – and although he was 76 years old, Monteverdi, 'with full permission from the most illustrious and most excellent procurators of the Church of St Mark set to touring Lombardy, where for six months he revisited and favoured with his presence his favourite cities, which, anxious to see him again, awaited opportunities to indicate with happy encounters how much they esteemed his virtue'.[202] In Mantua in summer 1643, he once again had the opportunity to reclaim the pension granted him by Duke Vincenzo, also bearing a letter of recommendation to the regent Maria Gonzaga which he had requested (L.124 [126]) and obtained from the doge, Francesco Erizzo.

But this trip in Lombardy (a term that in the period referred generically to the central part of the Po valley, including part of present Emilia Romagna) to receive honours but also to arrange important business affairs, greatly tired the old composer:

> But now old and in decline, given the excess of such very honoured receptions overcome by an extravagant weakening in his strength, while greatly improving in spirit he brought upon himself in such old age the final accident, and just as a swan, who reaching the final hour of his days approaches the waters and there forms sweetest passages with a harmony suaver than normal, passes as a gentle musician to another life, so Claudio returned, flying not to the waters of Meander but to his more favoured waters of the bosom of the Adriatic, where, wonder residing, who approaches is forced to admire the excesses of nature and art. He returned flying to Venice, queen of the waters and daughter of Neptune, where, as well as the Brenta, Adige, Sil [Sile], Livenza, flows as tributary to revere it with golden sand the most vast Eridano [Po]. Arriving at the desired waters,

the human swan delighted with the usual delicacy of harmonious compositions his regained homeland, overburdened, however, in his 75th year with a brief illness and scant for having little of the earthly, armed with the sacred sacraments and desirous to go among the seraphim, he left his mortal flesh and united himself with God.[203]

Death took Monteverdi in Venice on 29 November 1643 after nine days' illness: 'the very illustrious and reverend Don Claudio Monte Verde, *maestro di cappella* of the Church of St Mark aged 73 [*recte* 76], days [of illness] 9: doctor – Rotta' was recorded on that date in the *Libro dei morti* of the Provveditori alla Sanità.[204] He was buried in the Frari, in the Lombard Chapel – to which nationality he belonged – dedicated to S. Ambrogio, as Don Giustiniano Martinioni notes in the continuation of Francesco Sansovino's *Venetia città nobilissima et singolare* (Venice, Steffano Curti, 1663, p. 195): 'In the chapel and tomb of the Milanesi is buried Claudio Monteverdi, *maestro di cappella* of St Mark's, great theorist of song and sounds. Famous for his worth and for his compositions, which are a great part in print. This great man died in the year 1643, on 1 December.'

> The news of so great a loss disturbed and turned all the city to sadness and mourning, and it was accompanied by the choir of singers not with song but with tears and weeping, these singers being more than usually devoted to his name and obedient to his instructions. But considering that changed from an earthly to a heavenly swan he must be happily forming among the cherubim harmonious and divine melodies, having laid aside all sadness, they unanimously decided to honour him with one of the most solemn funerals that our homeland has seen and heard, directed by the most illustrious Signor Giovanni Rovetta, who, recognized as more worthy than any other, as an emulator of the deceased works in the post left vacant by him, and having with great steps with the nobility of his compositions arrived at the greatest perfection, he knows himself how to form conceits with miraculous effect. But not content with this honour – even though it was very great – the spirit of the most illustrious and most reverend Don Giovan Battista Marinoni, called Giove, as fecund with the greatest display of gratitude for the benefits received from a man of such merit, having a few days later with truly regal pomp erected a catafalque in the church of the lesser friars of the Frari, [the church] decorated all in mourning but resembling a very bright night rich in an infinite number of stars thanks to the large number of lit lights, decided to celebrate another funeral directed by him with such display of his worth, that in directing the largest choir that the city could bring together, he earned the name of most expert *maestro*.[205]

The search for Monteverdi's successor in St Mark's involved the usual consultations with the city's ambassadors and residents, in the course of which proposals were received from Padua for Antonio della Tavola, from Mantua for Francesco Turini, from Milan for Buzatti (Cherubino Busatti?) and from Bergamo for Giovan Battista Crivelli, while from Rome Romano Micheli nominated himself, although he later reversed his decision and let the matter drop.[206] In the end, the choice fell on Monteverdi's own vice-*maestro di cappella* and pupil, Giovanni Rovetta, who gained the new appointment on 21 February 1644.

> The Most Illustrious and Most Excellent Lord Procurators wishing to come to the election of a *maestro di cappella* in the Church of St Mark in place of the deceased Don Claudio Monteverde, who has recently died, and since it has already been written according to the usual practice on the order of Their Most Excellent Lordships to Rome to the Most Illustrious and Most Reverend Ottobon, *auditore* of the Sacra Rota, to Vienna, to all the rectors of the Venetian mainland and to the Venetian residents to have information of individuals qualified in this profession who might be inclined towards the aforesaid position, from whose replies they have understood that there is no one of quality and ability who is interested, nor have others appeared except Giovanni Rovetta, vice-*maestro di cappella*, whose abilities and worthy condition having been well considered by Their Most Illustrious and Excellent Lordships, they have by ballots elected him to the said position, with him having the appropriate house in the presbytery as usual, to be consigned to him with the necessary appurtenances. For: 2 – Against: 0.[207]

Still in 1644, the Venetian printer Francesco Miloco issued a miscellaneous volume titled *Fiori poetici raccolti nel funerale del molto illustre e molto reverendo signor Claudio Monteverde* ('Poetic flowers gathered for the funeral of the very illustrious and very reverend Signor Claudio Monteverde'), in which the composer's former colleague, Giovan Battista Marinoni (1596–1657), gathered together poems on the death of Monteverdi. Marinoni (not the same Marinoni who went with Monteverdi to Hungary in 1595) had been a tenor at St Mark's from 1623 and was now *maestro di cappella* at Padua Cathedral. These poems were preceded by a funeral oration written by Matteo Caberloti – curate of the Venetian church of S. Tomà – called *Laconismo delle alte qualità di Claudio Monteverde* ('Laconism on the high qualities of Claudio Monteverde'). The authors of these poems – in Latin and Italian, and some arranged as acrostics – were Caberloti himself, Paolo Piazza, Pietro Quadrario, 'fra Maur. Monc. Fer. min. con.', Alfonso Grilotti, Antonio de' Vescovi, Ambrosio Rossi, Simon Olmo, Ottavio Ragucci, Antonio Adami, 'G. A. N. A.', Guerino Rodiseo, Pietro Maurici, Giacomo Pighetti, Francesco Bolani, Lodovico Battaglia, Francesco Rodiseo, Baldassare Bonifacio, Marcantonio Romito and Bernardo Moscatelo. (A sonnet *In morte di Claudio Monteverdi musico famoso* – 'Mille e mille nel sen Claudio chiudea' – is also included in Giuliano Bezzi's *Il torneo et altre rime* printed in Bologna by Giacomo Monti in 1645, the second quatrain of which praises in the usual manner the affective powers of Monteverdi's music: 'O quante volte e quante egli struggea / d'indurato macigno ogn'alma in pianto! / E quante poi con dupplicato vanto / da le lagrime al riso ei la spingea' – 'O how many, how many times did he force / every soul of harsh stone to tears! / And how with double vantage / did he move them from tears to laughter'.) On the title-page of the *Fiori poetici*, one can also see, framed within an oval, the composer's head: this was probably engraved from the portrait of Monteverdi done by Bernardo

Strozzi, a Genoese painter active in Venice from 1631–44 (the reversed pose is a result of the shift from the engraving to the print), and which was kept in the gallery of Paolo del Sera, a noble Florentine living in Venice, next to Giorgione's *La Tempesta*, as Marco Boschini records:

> Se vede in prima de Zorzon un quadro
> dove se osserva alcuni religiosi
> con diversi istrumenti armonïosi
> far un concerto musico legiadro.
> Ghé 'l retrato vesin del Monteverde,
> de man del Strozza, pitor genoese,
> penel che ha fate memorande imprese,
> sí che Fama per lú mai no se perde.
> Par giusto che sia là, per ascoltar
> quei madrigali aponto e quei moteti.
> L'è là tuto atention. Piú vivi afeti
> nò se podeva veramente far.
> O che 'l componimento elo g'ha fato,
> o che Zorzon ghe insegna quel tenor!
> Par vivo in su quel quadro ogni cantor,
> e, per reflesso, vivo anche el retrato.[208]

One first sees a painting by Giorgione / where one observes some clerics / with various harmonious instruments / perform a graceful musical concert. / Next to it is the portrait of Monteverdi, / by Strozzi's hand, a Genoese painter, / whose brush has performed memorable tasks / so that fame will never be lost to him. / It seems right for it to be there, to hear / just those madrigals and those motets. / All attention is on there. More lively *affetti* / could not in truth ever be achieved. / O, either he himself has written the music / or Giorgione teaches him that tenor! Every singer seems alive on that picture, / and, in return, the picture seems alive too.

This portrait of Monteverdi (oil on wood; the composer is shown in half-bust with an open book in his hands) is now in the Gesellschaft der Musikfreunde, Vienna (it reached there via its former owner, the private collector Oskar Strakosch).[209] It served as the model for a similar portrait owned by Ludwig V. Vieser which in 1880 passed to the Tiroler Landesmuseum Ferdinandeum, Innsbruck (a reworking more than a copy)[210] and perhaps for the Parisian one bought by André Meyer:[211] Giovanni Grevenbroch clearly made use of it, as he himself reveals, for his *Abiti dei veneziani di quasi ogni età con diligenza raccolti e dipinti nel secolo XVIII* ('Clothes of Venetians of almost every era diligently collected and painted in the eighteenth century'; a manuscript in Venice, Museo Correr, 49/II, see f. 39).[212] The larger size of the Viennese painting compared with the Innsbruck one (the former is 96 cm. high, the latter 84 cm.; their widths are more or less the same) allows us to see clearly what was omitted in the replica: the right-hand page of the music-book which Monteverdi holds open in his hands, and above all the cippus on which he leans, bearing an important inscription (somewhat difficult to read) written by Giulio Strozzi which clearly attests to the source of the painting and the name of the person represented therein:[213]

BERNARDI EGREGIA
STROZZ[AE] DEPICTU[S]
AB A[RT]E CLAUDIUS
VIRIDI MONTE RE[...]
  VOCOR
SERA CUPIS RE..O
SENES SECERNERE ...
O MEDEA TUUM
SPERNERET ARS ...
  IULII STROZZAE

Giulio Strozzi had collaborated several times with Monteverdi in the 1620s and 1630s, and his own portrait was painted by Bernardo Strozzi in 1635.[214] A portion of the inscription conceived by him ('SERA CUPIS ...') seems to contain a veiled reference to Del Sera, who commissioned the picture for his collection (and in fact the cippus was tacitly omitted, also with the inscription, in the replica of the painting intended for elsewhere).

This portrait, which can be placed 'in the late phase of the Venetian period' of Strozzi,[215] is today the only secure image of Monteverdi alive. The identification of Domenico Fetti's *Ritratto di comico* as a portrait of Monteverdi is not at all convincing,[216] since it is very hard to believe that in 1622–23 (the period from which the painting dates, coming from the time of Fetti's stay in Venice) the *maestro di cappella* of St Mark's would have had himself painted without any attribute that would indicate his musical profession, and indeed with a comic's masque in his hands. To interpret this masque as a symbol of his release from service to the Gonzagas is pure fantasy; nor for that matter is there any likelihood in another suggestion that it should be associated with the role played by the composer in the birth of opera, since in those years opera was entirely linked to the occasions of court life, and its institutionalization in Venice was still to come.

40 The posthumous publications

Monteverdi's death left incomplete a project the details of which had perhaps reached Venice in the days immediately after his death, when the news had not yet spread abroad: the composer had been offered a new commission from Piacenza on behalf of Odoardo Farnese, to set to music another text by Bernardo Morando – as in 1641 – to be staged for carnival 1644.[217]

It seems, too, that another more significant theatrical enterprise was abandoned on his death, the aforementioned *Ulisse errante* by Badoaro, in which the librettist perhaps intended to profit from the Homeric vein inaugurated with *Il ritorno di Ulisse in patria*, and possibly to revive its success. This text was then in fact set to music by Sacrati, but a passage in the dedication of the libretto gives the impression of this being a makeshift solution caused by the recent death of the composer, for whom the libretto was originally designed: 'The *Ritorno d'Ulisse in patria* was adorned with the music of Signor Claudio Monteverde, a subject of all fame and perpetuity of name; now it will lack this condiment, since the great *maestro* has gone to perform the music of the angels before God.'

Although the already rich list of Monteverdi's works is deprived of these items, it was however destined to be increased later thanks to the music which the composer kept back and which was therefore to pass to his heirs and friends, continuing to foster the memory of his life's work. In fact, on his death Monteverdi left a number of pieces in manuscript that were to provide material for posthumous publications. A large mass in folio by him was later listed in the *Inventario de' libri musicali inservienti all'uso della cappella di S. Marco* ('Inventory of the musical books serving for the use of the *cappella* of St Mark's') dated 25 September 1720,[218] and there has also survived in manuscript a *Gloria* for eight voices – in two choirs – preserved in the Archivio dei Filippini in Naples, in which, as often happens in similar works, episodes for small solo groupings variously alternate with *tutti* passages.

As for printed editions, in 1644 the Phalèse press reissued in Antwerp the Fourth Book of madrigals with the addition of a basso continuo, while in the first book of *Motetti a voce sola de diversi eccelentissimi autori* (Venice, 'Stampa del Gardano', 1645) appeared the antiphon 'Venite, videte', for the feast of an unspecified martyr, for soprano and continuo (multisectional and in aria style throughout, with an opening idea that is used as a refrain). In 1649, Ambrosius Profe offered new spiritual versions of madrigals from Monteverdi's last two books in another of his collections this time called *Corollarium geistlicher collectaneorum*, published again in Leipzig but now by the printer Timotheus Ritzsch, including:

1   'Parlo, miser, o taccio?' (Seventh Book) as 'Longe, mi Jesu'
2   'Tu dormi, ah crudo core' (Seventh Book) as 'O Jesu lindere meinen Schmertzen'
3   'Al lume delle stelle' (Seventh Book) as 'O rex supreme Deus'
4a   'Or che 'l cielo e la terra e 'l vento tace' (Eighth Book) as 'O du mächtiger Herr'
  b 'Cosí sol d'una chiara fonte viva' (Eighth Book) as 'Dein allein ist ja großer Gott'
5   'Vago augelletto che cantando vai' (Eighth Book) as 'Resurrexit de sepulchro' (also texted 'Veni soror mea')
6   'Ardo, avvampo, mi struggo, ardo: accorrete' (Eighth Book) as 'Alleluja, kommet jauchzet' (also texted 'Freude kommet, lasset uns gehen')

Of all these posthumous publications – which provide concrete evidence of the lasting fame of the composer in the decade following his death and of the interest of printers and the public in his music – the most significant are obviously those entirely devoted to Monteverdi's works which appeared shortly thereafter. The first was the *Messa a quattro voci et salmi* printed in Venice by Alessandro Vincenti in 1650 and dedicated to the Camaldolese monk Odoardo Baranardi, abbot of the Paduan monastery of S. Maria delle Carceri. In the dedication (dated Venice, 11 December 1649), Vincenti, who edited the volume personally, explains the reasons behind his undertaking: 'These sacred remains of the works of the most excellent Monteverde, which not without a miracle after his death I was able piously to collect, are now published by me to satisfy common devotion.' In truth, not everything that appears here was unpublished: Vincenti himself had issued in 1620 and in 1626 the Litanies that conclude the present volume (in Bianchi's *Libro secondo de motetti in lode della gloriosissima Vergine Maria nostra signora* and in Calvi's *Rosarium litaniarum beatae V. Mariae*), while a large part of No. 2 (from 'Virgam virtutis tuae' to 'De torrente') is none other than an adaptation of the first 'Dixit Dominus' in the *Selva morale*.

Perhaps this use of second-hand pieces was motivated by an attempt to enhance the usefulness of the collection: as is clear from the title-page, as well as an *a cappella* Mass for four voices and the final Litanies of the Blessed Virgin, it contains 'psalms for one, two, three, four, five, six, seven and eight voices, concerted, and some *a cappella*'. These fulfil the requirements of both the male and the female *cursus* ('Dixit Dominus', 'Laudate pueri', 'Laetatus sum', 'Nisi Dominus', 'Lauda Jerusalem'), which, as well as for the feasts of Virgins of the Common of Saints, also serves for Marian celebrations. To satisfy fully the liturgical requirements of the latter, it was necessary to dust off the old litanies mentioned above and to turn to the promising second organist of St Mark's, Francesco Cavalli, for the missing but indispensable Magnificat.

1 *Messa a 4 da capella* [SATB, bc]
   a Kyrie
   b [Gloria ...] Et in terra pax
   c [Credo ...] Patrem omnipotentem
   d Sanctus
   e Benedictus
   f Agnus Dei
2 'Dixit Dominus', '*a8* [SATB, SATB]'
3 'Dixit Dominus', 'for eight voices [SATB, ATTB], *alla breve*'
4 'Confitebor tibi Domine', 'for solo voice [S] with violins'
5 'Confitebor tibi Domine', 'for two voices [ST] with two violins'
6 'Beatus vir', 'for seven voices [SSSA, TTB] with two violins'
7 'Laudate pueri Dominum', 'for five voices [SATTB] *a cappella*'
8 'Laudate Dominum omnes gentes', 'for solo bass'
9 'Laetatus sum', 'for five instruments [2 violins, 2 trombones and bassoon] and six voices [SS, TT, BB]'

10 'Laetatus sum', '*a5* [SATTB]'
11 'Nisi Dominus', '*a3* [STB] and two violins'
12 'Nisi Dominus', '*a6* [SSATTB]'
13 'Lauda Jerusalem', '*a3* [ATB]'
14 'Lauda Jerusalem', '*a5* [SATTB]'
15 Magnificat, 'for seven voices ['six' in the basso continuo part] and two violins by Signor Francesco Cavalli organist of St Mark's'
16 Laetaniae della Beata Vergine, 'for six voices [SSATTB]'

However, the list of Monteverdi's sacred works was brought to a definite end only one year later, in 1651, with the inclusion in the *Raccolta di motetti a 1, 2, 3 voci di Gasparo Casati e de diversi altri* (Venice, Bartolomeo Magni) of the strophic hymn 'En gratulemur hodie' for tenor, two violins and continuo (the volume also includes the psalm 'Laudate Dominum' for bass and continuo first published in the *Messa ... et salmi* of 1650).

Finally, a last book of *Madrigali e canzonette a due e tre voci ... Libro nono* was published in 1651 in Venice again by Alessandro Vincenti, who in this case, too, was the editor of the volume. According to Vincenti's dedication to Gerolamo Orologio (dated 27 June 1651), 'Signor Claudio Monteverde, one of the chief lights of our century in music, honoured me while he lived with some of his musical *concerti*, of which, since I have enriched my press, I have thought it good to fulfil my ambitious desire for your favour to offer them to you freely as a gift.'

1 'Bel pastor dal cui bel sguardo' (Ottavio Rinuccini: anacreontic canzonetta), '*a2*, soprano or tenor'
2 'Zefiro torna e di soavi accenti' (O. Rinuccini: sonnet), 'for two tenors', *ciaccona*
3 'Se vittorie sí belle' (Fulvio Testi: madrigal), 'for two tenors'
4 'Armato il cor d'adamantina fede' (madrigal), 'for two tenors'
5 'Ardo e scoprir, ahi lasso, io non ardisco' (*ottave rime*), 'for two tenors'
6 'O sia tranquillo il mare o pien d'orgoglio' (sonnet), 'for two tenors'
7 'Alcun non mi consigli' (canzonetta), '*a3* [ATB]'
8 'Di far sempre gioire' (anacreontic canzonetta), '*a3* [ATB]'
9 'Quando dentro al tuo seno' (anacreontic canzonetta), '*a3* [TTB]'
10 'Non voglio amare' (anacreontic canzonetta), '*a3* [TTB]'
11 'Come dolce oggi l'auretta' (Giulio Strozzi: anacreontic canzonetta), '*a3* [SSS]'
12 'Alle danze, alle gioie, ai diletti' (anacreontic canzonetta), '*a3* [TTB]'
13 'Perché, se m'odiavi' (anacreontic canzonetta), '*a3* [TTB]'
14 'Sí, sí, ch'io v'amo' (anacreontic canzonetta), '*a3* [TTT]'
15 'Su, su, su, pastorelli vezzosi' (anacreontic canzonetta), '*a3* [TTB]'
16 'O mio bene, o mia vita' (anacreontic canzonetta), '*a3* [TTB]'

In this Ninth Book, Alessandro Vincenti, also the printer of Monteverdi's preceding book of madrigals, included some pieces already printed by him in the *Madrigali guerrieri, et amorosi*: Nos. 3, 4 (also in the *Scherzi musicali* of 1632), 5 and 6 (No. 2 had also appeared in the 1632 *Scherzi musicali*). Nos. 13 and 15 involve two texts already broached by Monteverdi in settings also published by Vincenti (respectively, in the *Arie de diversi* of 1634 and among the 'madrigali amorosi' of the Eighth Book); if No. 15 shares only the text with the preceding setting, in No. 13 the first tenor and the continuo of the three-voice version published in 1651 closely resemble – apart from the final section – the monodic setting of 1634.

Vincenti probably unearthed these pieces to flesh out a volume that otherwise would have been too thin, although in the preface to the 'Courteous Reader' he appealed to practical requirements: 'Do not be surprised if in this work you will find some madrigals already printed in the Eighth Book: I have only printed them in this work for the greater convenience of virtuosos: soon, if it pleases God, you will have other new works.' But Vincenti's promise was destined to remain unfulfilled, even if he did not seem to be lacking material by Monteverdi: the canzonetta 'Come dolce oggi l'auretta' was extracted from *Proserpina rapita* of 1630,[219] and the following 'Alle danze, alle gioie, ai diletti' also seems to come from some similar theatrical context.

The title-page divides the contents of the volume into 'madrigals and canzonettas', and in fact Nos. 3–6 fall into the first category and Nos. 7 to the end in the second; Nos. 1 (a canzonetta whose strophic structure, however, is somewhat obscured) and 2 (the *ciaccona*) stand apart. From No. 7 on, strophic structures prevail, either in full or limited just to the bass (in Nos. 7 and 8, which alternate – *alla francese?* – solo strophes and a *tutti* refrain, and also in No. 12; Nos. 7 and 12 contain sections in the recitative style – respectively at the beginning and in the middle of each strophe – which contrast with the regular aria style of the rest).[220]

Taking an overview of this volume, one cannot but note that all the more elaborate settings (the *ciaccona*, the small group of madrigals) do not involve new works, Monteverdi having already published them elsewhere. As a result, the only original material presented by Vincenti was the series of *ariette*, for the most part in anacreontic metres, which take up the larger part of the volume. The relative unimportance of this posthumous volume becomes all the clearer if one compares it with the stylistic and even theoretical weight of the Eighth Book, which the composer put together himself. Precisely for this reason, the Ninth Book (which not by chance takes only the less complex items from its predecessor) – more than the Eighth – ends up reflecting the musical taste of its period, inclined to facility and to the simplification of polyphonic structures rather than to a learned and renewed contrapuntal practice. Significantly, if the erudite *Madrigali guerrieri, et amorosi* attracted (and still attracts) the admiration of music-lovers and composers, these pieces from the Ninth Book enjoyed instead the favour of singers and audiences: 'and such were they that Anna Renzi, celebrated among singers ... used always to choose them to delight the noble academies of music, by which she was continually called to be the honour'.[221] At root, this last volume of music entirely by the composer presents clear signs of how a musical world as complex as that introduced and developed by Monteverdi was fast on the way to obsolescence.

Notes

Introduction

1 See Chiarelli, 'L'incoronazione di Poppea o Il Nerone', pp. 123, 151.

2 Jonckbloet & Land (eds.), Musique et musiciens au XVIIe siècle, p. ccxiv.

3 Müller-Blattau (ed.), Die Kompositionslehre Heinrich Schützens in der Fassung seines Schülers Christoph Bernhard, p. 90. Important evidence of the spread of Monteverdi's music to England is provided by the manuscript London, British Library, Add. MS 31440, which contains numerous settings taken from the Fourth, Fifth and Seventh Books of madrigals, sometimes in versions reduced for two voices and basso continuo (like those, again from the Fourth and Fifth Books, in the final section of the manuscript Oxford, Christ Church, 878 and 880, significantly in perhaps the same hand as that of Add. MS 31440), plus one of his settings in the Madrigali del signor cavaliere Anselmi published in 1624 and the lament 'Voglio, voglio morir, voglio morire', here lacking the heading Lamento d'Olimpia and moreover unattributed. As for the identity of the compiler of Add. MS 31440, one suggested candidate is Walter Porter, who was in Venice (perhaps between 1613 and 1616) as a pupil of Monteverdi: in the preface of the copy of his Mottets of 2 Voyces (London, William Godbid, 1657) in Oxford, Christ Church, at the printed reference to 'that unparallel'd master of musick, my good friend and maestro' there is added in a seventeenth-century hand – probably Porter's – 'Monteverde'; see Arkwright, 'An English Pupil of Monteverdi'; Hughes, 'Porter, Pupil of Monteverdi'; Willetts, 'A Neglected Source of Monody and Madrigal'.

4 Doni, De praestantia musicae veteris libri tres (1647), pp. 57, 67.

5 Kircher, Musurgia universalis, i (1650), p. 594. Kircher mentions Monteverdi also on pp. 310 and 313, respectively as a theatre composer and a madrigalist. In the classifications of styles proposed by Angelo Berardi in his Ragionamenti musicali (1681), pp. 133–7, and following the example of his teacher Marco Scacchi's Cribrum musicum (1643), Monteverdi is cited in the fields both of 'music ... of the chamber [among the composers of 'concerted madrigals with the basso continuo'] and of the theatre'.

6 Menestrier, Des representations en musique anciennes et modernes (1681), pp. 164–5.

7 A somewhat general mention (and one prompted mainly by civic pride) is made of Monteverdi by the Jesuit priest Ansaldo Cotta in his oration Omnia Cremonae summa delivered on 16 December 1653 in the Church of S. Marcellino in Cremona (given in Monterosso et al. (eds.), Mostra bibliografica dei musicisti cremonesi, p. 3):

But until when, o my speech, will I go speaking at length of others forgetting you, o Claudio, who takes his name from the green mountain? Most wise craftsman of musical suavities, exalted builder of singing sweetness, memorable architect of melic pleasure, no one who has experienced an example of your art or has applied the ear to your notes can restrain from swearing that in you alone are gathered all the Venuses and the Graces, admiring in your sonorities something that transcends human art. Witness to the extraordinary worth of this most famous man was Vincenzo, Most Serene Duke of Mantua, to whose ears the singing sweetness of Claudio was more welcome than the honey-filled song embellished in the throats of the swans in the marshes of the Mincio. Witness to it was the city, queen of the Adriatic, who perhaps saw its waves troubled by impetuous winds grow calm at the song of this new Arion, and the proudness of the waves diminish. Witness to it was the most august king of Poland, who would have considered his happiness complete if he could have eagerly heard more frequently the notes of Claudio, called to his court. O man to be inscribed in heaven with celestial letters, so that he lives in eternity among the musical plaudits of the spheres, given that in life he had certainly emulated on earth the music of the skies.

8 In fact, their surviving output includes a few madrigals, in print (Dal Pane) or more often in manuscript. As for Abbatini, in whose private academy were sung regularly 'con gran diletto / al tavolin i persi madrigali' ('with great delight / at table the now lost madrigals'), see his autobiographical *capitolo* in *terza rima* addressed to Sebastiano Baldini (given in Bianconi, *Il Seicento*, p. 286, trans. Bryant as *Music in the Seventeenth Century*, p. 291). The point is confirmed by Arcangelo Spagna in his *Oratorii overo melodrammi sacri con un discorso dogmatico intorno l'istessa materia*, i (Rome, Buagni, 1706; the relevant passage is transcribed in Becker (ed.), *Quellentexte zur Konzeption der europäischen Oper im 17. Jahrhundert*, p. 65):

> in a virtuous academy which met once a month in the house of Signor Antonio Maria Abbatini, famous contrapuntalist of the last century, where I found myself many times, among the other matters discussed and aired there it was recognized that our recitatives had succeeded those madrigals which were set to music by the Prince of Venosa [Gesualdo] and by Monteverdi, a characteristic of which is the total observance of the aforesaid verses.

9 Pitoni, *Guida armonica … Libro primo* (c.1690), p. 96; see Durante, 'La "Guida armonica" di Giuseppe Ottavio Pitoni'.

10 Tevo, *Il musico testore* (1706), pp. 175–8.

11 Arisi, *Cremona literata*, iii (1741), pp. 38–39.

12 Quadrio, *Della storia e della ragione d'ogni poesia*, v (1744), p. 509; vii (1752), p. 176.

13 Arteaga, *Le rivoluzioni del teatro musicale italiana dalla sua origine fino al presente*, i (1783), pp. 195–6.

14 Martini, *Storia della musica*, ii (1770), p. 338.

15 Martini, *Esemplare o sia saggio fondamentale pratico di contrappunto sopra il canto fermo*, ii (1774), pp. 180–98, 242–50.

16 Hawkins, *A General History of the Science and Practice of Music* (1776, repr. 1853), ii, pp. 524–9, 589–90; Burney, *A General History of Music*, iii (1789), pp. 233–6, 239–40; iv (1789), pp. 27–30, 32–34.

17 Medici & Conati (eds.), *Carteggio Verdi–Boito*, i, p. 129 (letter of 5 October 1887).

18 Gerber, *Historisch-biographisches Lexicon der Tonkünstler*, i (1790), cols. 965–7.

19 Id., *Neues historisch-biographisches Lexicon der Tonkünstler*, iii (1813), cols. 452–4.

Cremona

1 The baptismal record is given in Italian translation in Sommi Picenardi, 'D'alcuni documenti concernenti Claudio Monteverde', p. 155 (and see also id., 'Claudio Monteverdi a Cremona', p. 474); and in German translation in Vogel, 'Claudio Monteverdi', p. 317. As well as these studies, further contributions to Monteverdi's biography in his Cremonese period are offered – directly or indirectly – by Monterosso *et al.* (eds.), *Mostra bibliografica dei musicisti cremonesi*; Pontiroli, 'Notizie di musicisti cremonesi nel secoli XVI e XVII'; id., 'Notizie sui Monteverdi, su personaggi ed artisti del loro ambiente e la casa natale di Claudio'; id., 'Casa natale de Claudio Monteverdi e ampliamento dell'albero genealogico della famiglia Monteverdi'; Santoro, *La famiglia e la formazione di Claudio Monteverdi*; id., 'La casa natale dei Monteverdi nel quartiere Piazano'; Pontiroli, 'Nuove ricerche sui Monteverdi'; id., 'Della famiglia di Claudio Monteverdi'.

2 This tempers somewhat the presumed frostiness adopted by Ingegneri towards his pupil suggested by Nino Pirrotta in 'Scelte poetiche di Monteverdi', p. 10 ('Monteverdi's Poetic Choices', p. 271).

3 See Engel, 'Marc Antonio Ingegneri'.

4 See Cesari (ed.), *La musica in Cremona nella seconda metà del secolo XVI e i primordi dell'arte monteverdiana*, p. xii, and *Vita religiosa a Cremona nel Cinquecento*, pp. 46–48.

5 Cesari (ed.), *La musica in Cremona nella seconda metà del secolo XVI e i primordi dell'arte monteverdiana*, pp. xii, xv.

6 Ibid., p. xvi.

7 To flesh out this brief survey, see Fabbri, 'I Campi e la Cremona musicale del Cinquecento', and the bibliography cited therein.

8 Sommi Picenardi, 'Claudio Monteverdi a Cremona', p. 491.

9 Cerone, *El melopeo y maestro* (1613), p. 89.

10 Cerone, *El melopeo y maestro* (1613), p. 89.

11 See Pirrotta, 'Scelte poetiche di Monteverdi', p. 10 ('Monteverdi's Poetic Choices', pp. 271–2).

12 Fabbri, 'I Campi e la Cremona musicale del Cinquecento', p. 21.

13 *Vita religiosa a Cremona nel Cinquecento*, p. 26.

14 Chabod, *Lo stato e la vita religiosa a Milano nell'epoca di Carlo V*, p. 359.

15 *Vita religiosa a Cremona nel Cinquecento*, p. 58.

16 That *sacra cantio* has the same meaning as motet is clear, for example, from the title of Orlando di Lasso's *Sacrae cantiones vulgo motecta appellatae* ('*Sacrae cantiones* called in the vernacular motets') published in Venice by Antonio Gardane in 1566. Compare also Philippe de Monte's *Sacrarum cantionum ... quae vulgo motecta nuncupantur liber primus* (Venice, Scotto, 1572), Cipriano de Rore's *Sacrae cantiones seu moteta (ut vocant)* (Louvain, Phalèse & Bellère, 1573) and *Sacrae cantiones quae dicuntur motecta* (Venice, Angelo Gardano, 1595).

17 See the discussion in Ferrari Barassi, 'Il madrigale spirituale nel Cinquecento e la raccolta monteverdiana del 1583'.

18 Ibid., pp. 234–5 (and see p. 236).

19 Bianconi, 'Claudio Monteverdi', p. 771.

20 De' Paoli (ed.), *Claudio Monteverdi: lettere, dediche e prefazioni*, p. 376. De' Paoli corroborates his statement with reference to G. Bresciani, *Libro delle famiglie nobili della città di Cremona*, a manuscript surviving in Cremona, Libreria Civica.

21 Nevertheless, see Ferrari Barassi, 'Il madrigale spirituale nel Cinquecento e la raccolta monteverdiana del 1583'.

22 Ibid., p. 236 (and see pp. 247–51).

23 De' Paoli (ed.), *Claudio Monteverdi: lettere, dediche e prefazioni*, p. 378.

24 Pirrotta, 'Scelte poetiche di Monteverdi', p. 12 ('Monteverdi's Poetic Choices', p. 272). In De' Paoli, *Monteverdi* (1979), p. 32, it is stated that the texts are 'all by unknown authors – with the exception of a canzonetta by Livio Celiano and another by G. B. Guarini', without however giving a source for such a statement.

25 See Pirrotta, 'Scelte poetiche di Monteverdi', p. 12 ('Monteverdi's Poetic Choices', pp. 272–3).

26 Ibid., p. 12 ('Monteverdi's Poetic Choices', p. 272, presents a slightly different version).

27 See ibid., pp. 14–15 ('Monteverdi's Poetic Choices', p. 430 n. 9).

28 In this context, see for example the following remark from the anonymous author of the *Rime dell'Acuto in lode dell'onoratissimo ridotto dell'illustre signor conte Mario Bevilacqua* (Verona, G. Discepolo, 1587), given in Paganuzzi, 'Medioevo e Rinascimento', p. 80:

> From when I found myself in the delightful city of Naples I heard praised the most honoured *ridotto* of virtuosos headed by Your Lordship, then I was so inspired by you that I could never forget the name MARIO BEVILACQUA, as you encouraged me, saying I [IO] am the SEA [MAR], DRINK THE WATER [BEVI L'ACQUA] of the sea, thus giving me a peg on which to hang the memory. And my inflamed desire increased still more when I was in Cremona, for the honoured company of Signor Marc'Antonio Ingegneri, *maestro di cappella* in the cathedral there (as Your Lordship knows), revived my memory of you, whence I was forced, encouraged by a too ardent desire, to come so as to hear that of which I had heard other mouths speak fully.

29 See Pirrotta, 'Scelte poetiche di Monteverdi', p. 13 ('Monteverdi's Poetic Choices', pp. 273–4); and Einstein, *The Italian Madrigal*, ii, p. 721.

30 See Pirrotta, 'Scelte poetiche di Monteverdi', p. 14 ('Monteverdi's Poetic Choices', pp. 274–5); and Einstein, *The Italian Madrigal*, ii, p. 719.

31 Bianconi, 'Claudio Monteverdi', p. 771.

32 See Pirrotta, 'Scelte poetiche di Monteverdi', pp. 12–13 ('Monteverdi's Poetic Choices', p. 273 (adapted)).

33 G. B. Strozzi 'il giovane', *Orazioni et altre prose* (Rome, Grignani, 1635), p. 174, given in G. B. Strozzi 'il vecchio', *Madrigali inediti*, ed. Ariani, p. lviii.

34 Pirrotta, 'Scelte poetiche di Monteverdi', p. 14 ('Monteverdi's Poetic Choices', p. 274). This must be the Femia mentioned by Vincenzo Giustiniani in his *Discorso sopra la musica* of c.1628; see Solerti, *Le origini del melodramma*, p. 107 (in MacClintock (trans.), *Hercole Bottrigari, 'Il Desiderio . . .'; Vincenzo Giustiniani, 'Discorso sopra la musica'*, p. 69). Anthony Newcomb (*The Madrigal at Ferrara, 1579–1597*, i, p. 17) suggests that this Femia is Eufemia Jozola.

35 See Solerti (ed.), *Le rime di Torquato Tasso*, ii, pp. 389–446.

36 Pirrotta, 'Scelte poetiche di Monteverdi', p. 17 ('Monteverdi's Poetic Choices', p. 276). The correct arrangement of Nos. 12–15 is restored in Monteverdi, *Madrigali a 5 voci: libro secondo*, ed. Monterosso Vacchelli, p. 14.

37 De' Paoli (ed.), *Claudio Monteverdi: lettere, dediche e prefazioni*, p. 382. The claim made in the mid-seventeenth century by the generally imprecise Luigi Rossi that Monteverdi was enrolled in the Congregazione di S. Cecilia, Rome, in 1590 (see Giazotto, *Quattro secoli di storia dell'Accademia Nazionale di Santa Cecilia*, i, pp. 121, 129) seems most unlikely: the twenty-three-year-old composer was scarcely known in local circles.

Mantua

1 De' Paoli (ed.), *Claudio Monteverdi: lettere, dediche e prefazioni*, p. 34. Subsequent references to this edition are made within the text (L.1, L.2, etc.). Letters not given in De' Paoli were discovered subsequently and published in Stevens, 'Monteverdi, Petratti, and the Duke of Bracciano'; Fabbri, 'Inediti monteverdiani'; and Vitali, 'Una lettera vivaldiana perduta e ritrovata, un inedito monteverdiano del 1630 e altri carteggi di musicisti celebri'. Given that De' Paoli's edition is not entirely trustworthy, I have checked and corrected the readings of at least the letters by Monteverdi in the Archivio di Stato, Mantua (Raccolta d'autografi, Busta 6: Claudio Monteverdi), which constitute the great majority of his correspondence (111 out of 127 known letters). The first edition of Stevens (trans.), *The Letters of Claudio Monteverdi*, adopts a similar sequence; where Stevens's numbering differs from De' Paoli, both numbers are given here (Stevens's in square brackets). The projected second edition of Stevens's translation alters his sequence as follows: 11 = 12, 12 = 11, 14 = 25, 15 = 27, 16–26 = 14–24, 27 = 26, 122–6 = 123–7.

2 Vasari, *Le vite de' più eccellenti pittori, scultori ed architettori*, ed. Milanesi, vi, p. 490.

3 This account of Mantua can be read complete in Segarizzi (ed.), *Relazioni degli ambasciatori veneti al senato*; the passages cited here are taken from pp. 78–82. For the cultural history of Mantua in the sixteenth and seventeenth centuries, see the following volumes in the series published by the Istituto Carlo d'Arco per la Storia di Mantova: Faccioli (ed.), *Mantova: le lettere*, ii; Mazzoldi, Giusti & Salvatori (eds.), *Mantova: la storia*, iii; Marani & Perina (eds.), *Mantova: le arti*, iii.

4 The point is made in Gallico, 'Guglielmo Gonzaga signore della musica'. To the material there can be added the following account given in Bettinelli, *Delle lettere e delle arti mantovane* (1774), p. 86: 'Curzio Gonzaga is the author of two volumes of poems printed in Mantua in 1588 and of the *Fido amante*, or *Fidamante*, an heroic poem, for which the music was written by Duke Guglielmo himself, according to Cagnani. This poem was first published in Mantua in 1582, then printed in Vicenza in 1585 and in Venice in 1591. It has 36 cantos in *ottava rima* and was praised by Torquato Tasso, just as Ippolito Capilupi honoured it with two epigrams.' See also Gallico, *Damon pastor gentil*.

5 Sartori, 'Mantua'; Tagmann, *Archivalische Studien zur Musikpflege am Dom von Mantua (1500–1627)*; id., 'La cappella dei maestri cantori della basilica palatina di Santa Barbara a Mantova (1565–1630)'; id., 'The Palace Church of Santa Barbara in Mantua, and Monteverdi's Relationship to its Liturgy'.

6 See Canal, *Della musica in Mantova*, pp. 49–64, and MacClintock, *Giaches de Wert*

(1535–1596), p. 49. The most recent, and best, study of musicians at the Gonzaga court is Parisi, *Ducal Patronage of Music in Mantua, 1587–1627*, which appeared too late for me to be able to take account of its findings here.

7 Canal, *Della musica in Mantova*, p. 87.

8 De' Paoli (ed.), *Claudio Monteverdi: lettere, dediche e prefazioni*, p. 385. The letter was first cited in Davari, 'Notizie biografiche del distinto maestro di musica Claudio Monteverdi', p. 81.

9 Pirrotta, 'Scelte poetiche di Monteverdi', p. 25 ('Monteverdi's Poetic Choices', p. 283).

10 Ibid., p. 21 ('Monteverdi's Poetic Choices', pp. 279–80). On the trends of the poetic madrigal at the turn of the century, see also A. Martini, 'Ritratto del madrigale poetico fra Cinque e Seicento'.

11 Caberloti, *Laconismo delle alte qualità di Claudio Monteverde* (1644), p. 8.

12 This is the subject of five sonnets printed as an appendix to Arrivabene, *Della origine de' cavaglieri del Tosone e di altri ordini* (1589).

13 On Vincenzo's three expeditions to Hungary, see Errante, 'Forse che sí, forse che no'; the 1595 expedition is described on pp. 29–33.

14 Ibid., p. 31.

15 Canal, *Della musica in Mantova*, pp. 89, 92.

16 F. Cardi, *Relatione del primo viaggio che il ser.mo sig. duca di Mantova fece alla guerra d'Ongheria l'anno 1595 et di tutto quello che successe mentre S.A. si fermò in corte cesarea et in campo*, MS in Mantua, Archivio di Stato, Archivio Gonzaga, Busta 388, fol. 11 (cited in Errante, 'Forse che sí, forse che no', pp. 31–2).

17 De' Paoli (ed.), *Claudio Monteverdi: lettere, dediche e prefazioni*, p. 34 (L.6).

18 Newcomb, 'Alfonso Fontanelli and the Ancestry of the Seconda Pratica Madrigal', p. 60 (see also Fabbri, 'Inediti monteverdiani', p. 71). I do not believe that these four canzonettas are to be linked with those printed by Morsolino in the same year.

19 Gallico, 'Newly Discovered Documents Concerning Monteverdi', p. 71. See also id., 'Dimore mantovane di Claudio Monteverdi', p. 29:

> The young Cremonese musician married in his adopted city a fellow professional; naturally, the ceremony was celebrated in the bride's parish church (the wedding took place in S. Simone); and perhaps the pair agreed to live with the bride's father (the baptism of their first-born son took place in S. Simone). One cannot exclude the possibility that Monteverdi was Cattaneo's guest or tenant right from the start of his stay in Mantua, something which would have been natural for a foreign artist, who at first maintains relationships only with the musicians, whom he knows and frequents for his own duties.

20 Prunières, 'Monteverdi and French Music', pp. 98–9; id., 'Monteverdi e la musica francese del suo tempo', p. 487.

21 Marani & Perina (eds.), *Mantova: le arti*, p. 437.

22 Vogel, 'Claudio Monteverdi', p. 428.

23 Mischiati, *La prassi musicale presso i Canonici regolari del Ss. Salvatore nei secoli XVI e XVII*, pp. 15, 19–20.

24 Artusi, *L'Artusi, overo Delle imperfettioni della moderna musica* (1600), fol. 39,

translated in Strunk, *Source Readings in Music History*, p. 394. On the circumstances surrounding the meeting at Goretti's house, see also Cavicchi, 'Per far piú grande la meraviglia dell'arte', pp. 23–4.

25 A slight variant in the version printed by Monteverdi changes bar 19 of the *quinto*, adding an *accento* not present in the reading given by Artusi. This is noted in Vogel, 'Claudio Monteverdi', where the polemic is extensively discussed on pp. 325–39.

26 Bars 37–38 in Monteverdi compared with Artusi involve swapping the parts between tenor and *quinto*.

27 Artusi, *L'Artusi, overo Delle imperfettioni della moderna musica* (1600), fol. 42r, translated in Strunk, *Source Readings in Music History*, p. 400. See also the analysis of 'Cruda Amarilli che col nome ancora' given in G. B. Martini, *Esemplare o sia saggio fondamentale pratico di contrappunto sopra il canto fermo*, ii (1774), pp. 191–4:

> From the use of the dissonances, and particularly of the seventh in a free manner and entirely foreign to the rules of the first *maestri*, which the author has made in this madrigal of his, it will be clear why so many opponents were aroused against him, as we have mentioned in connection with the previous example. The zealots, unable to suffer silently such practice against the ancient rules, were alarmed at him, reproaching him for having used false intervals and dissonances without any preparation. However, to the shame of all their rebukes, he had the fine pleasure of seeing the practice he had introduced so well accepted and embraced by composers that until our day its credit has been entirely maintained. The young composer can easily understand from this example how and when dissonances foreign to the rules can be used in a praiseworthy manner, with the warning, however, that the said dissonances were introduced and are permitted in the concerted styles of church music, of madrigals, and of secular, dramatic and instrumental music, but they have never been practised up to our day in the *a cappella* style, because they are alien and repugnant to such a style, which sadly, and I say it with great displeasure, in our day is almost entirely lost, and there are few who have the capacity to write precisely *a cappella* and who have a full understanding of the true and legitimate character of this style. Let us now turn to the analysis of this madrigal. At the words 'Cruda Amarilli' ['Cruel Amaryllis'] the author twice introduces a beautiful contrapuntal web, and similarly at the words 'Che col nome ancora d'amor' ['Who again with the name of love']. As proof of what we have said above of his use of dissonances, let the young composer note the music for the words 'ahi lasso' ['ah, alas'], and how the soprano at No. 1 [bar 13 of Malipiero's edition] enters on a ninth, or second, and immediately proceeds by leap to the seventh without any preparation, or without proceeding by step between two consonances, as is prescribed in the *Regola della nota buona e cattiva* ['Rule for the good and bad note'] shown in the first part of this *Esemplare* at p. xxv. Observe, too, at No. 2 [bar 19] the seventh without any preparation, which seventh serves as preparation to tie to the fourth. This progression, while rare and not practised at the time of the author, is however frequently used in our day. A graceful attack presented by the tenor I is seen at No. 3 [bar 34] on the words 'Ma del aspido sordo' ['But of the deaf asp'], to which all the parts respond, including the contralto at No. 4 [bar 36], and so that the answer is real it forms a seventh by leap, while at No. 5 [bar 36] the tenor at the same time passes by step to the second, which is repeated at Nos. 6 [bar 37] and 7 [bar 38]. These accompaniments of the major seventh on its own, or of the second accompanied by the fourth and the minor seventh are often practised in our day. Then on the words 'e piú sorda' ['and more deaf'] there is a short contrapuntal passage, which is repeated on the words 'e piú fera' ['and more harsh'] at the fourth above with the addition of a seventh in the soprano at No. 8 [bar 41]. An unusual cadence is seen at No. 9 [bar 46], which were it to have its fundamental bass, which is *E la mi*, it would come to resemble a perfect cadence, which has been discussed in the first part of this *Esemplare* in various places, and particularly at p. 186. That this passage is a perfect cadence becomes clear at No. 10 [bar 49], in which there are all those elements usually used in cadences, with the only difference that a seventh is added, indicated at No. 11 [bar 49]. This passage is repeated at Nos. 12 [bar 54] and 13 [bar 57], and since the parts find

themselves in a different position, thus in some manner it comes to appear different, although it is substantially the same. At No. 14 [bar 63] the soprano enters on a second, and similarly the contralto at No. 15 [bar 63] enters on a fourth, at the same time as the tenor II finds itself on a fifth, so that these two parts come to clash with a second. On the last two lines 'Poiché col dir t'offendo, I' mi morrò tacendo' ['Since by speaking I offend you, I will die in silence'], we find written by the composer music with various subjects brought together with all art and naturalness. Let the young composer reflect on the fact that the author does not use dissonances alien to the rules except in cases where the expression of the words requires it, and only in madrigals. And since by common agreement the more grateful consonances are to the ear, the more unpleasant are dissonances, this is the reason why the latter should not be used except where appropriate, but either with a tie or in passing, so that they should not appear annoying and displeasing. These [dissonances] are used in madrigals because, being sung by only the parts of which they are composed and without the accompaniment of any instrument, they could be intoned perfectly by few singers more easily than is the case in church compositions, in which the whole crowd of singers sings, who, as experience teaches us, are not all disposed towards a just and perfect intonation.

There is seen at this sign + [bar 21] the diminished fifth without preparation, and that which should most be noted is that the bass enters on a dissonance without it having been earlier tied. However, the expression of the words 'amara morte' ['bitter death'; *recte* 'amaramente', 'bitterly'], shows how the author has used such a licence in a praiseworthy manner.)

28 Artusi, *L'Artusi, overo Delle imperfettioni della moderna musica* (1600), fol. 43v, translated in Strunk, *Source Readings in Music History*, p. 403.

29 Ibid., fol. 42v, translated in Strunk, *Source Readings in Music History*, p. 401.

30 Ibid., fol. 48r.

31 Ibid., fol. 48r.

32 Ibid., fol. 48v.

33 Ibid., fol. 40, translated in Strunk, *Source Readings in Music History*, p. 396. The title-page of Monteverdi's copy of Zarlino's famous treatise (now in Yale University Library) is reproduced as Plate IV in Reese, *Music in the Renaissance*.

34 These points are clearly brought out in Palisca, 'The Artusi–Monteverdi Controversy'; a somewhat similar discussion appears in Gianturco, *Claudio Monteverdi*, pp. 119–29; and see also Carter, 'Artusi, Monteverdi, and the Poetics of Modern Music'.

35 Zacconi, *Prattica di musica*, i (1592), fol. 56. Later (in the second part of the *Prattica di musica* printed in Venice by Alessandro Vincenti in 1622), Zacconi was to make explicit reference to Monteverdi, taking him as an example of transgressing a specific rule (the use and position of dissonances) for expressive ends (p. 63):

arranging the aforesaid dissonances among the consonances, and moving from one to the other with excellent disposition, they make their presence felt always in the second part of the tactus, and never the first, unless for some affects, in all not singable to be sung, but to become more grateful compositions [*melodie*], of which the works of Signor Claudio Monte Verde can be seen to be full, where in this manner he wants to have it so that the singer, in moving quickly away from the delivery of the said bad interval, then gives greater pleasure in making the good interval heard, as can be seen in this example:

MONTEVERDI

And to whomever should ask me where he took this from, I would say that he drew it from the second part of the motet by Cipriano Bora [= Rore] 'O altitudo divitiarum', which uses there this arrangement of notes

DE RORE

wanting that the first minim, sounding bad for the purpose of an *affetto*, should make the second appear so much the better, as the composition requires. Or let us say that although he could have taken it from the aforesaid [Rore], however he was not entirely inspired by him, but by that daily practice which singers of today have to sing their things with such grateful *affetti* as they can to make them more pleasant to the listeners. . . .

36 Artusi, *L'Artusi, overo Delle imperfettioni della moderna musica* (1600), fol. 41r, translated in Strunk, *Source Readings in Music History*, pp. 397–8.

37 Palisca, 'The Artusi–Monteverdi Controversy', pp. 131–2.

38 Artusi, *L'Artusi, overo Delle imperfettioni della moderna musica* (1600), fol. 41v–42r, translated in Strunk, *Source Readings in Music History*, pp. 398–9.

39 Ibid., fol. 43r, translated in Strunk, *Source Readings in Music History*, p. 402.

40 Ibid., fol. 43r, translated in Strunk, *Source Readings in Music History*, p. 401.

41 See ibid., fol. 41v (Strunk, *Source Readings in Music History*, p. 398).

42 Mischiati, *La prassi musicale presso i Canonici regolari del Ss. Salvatore nei secoli XVI e XVII*, p. 20.

43 With a small variant in the tenor (bar 9) and omitting some accidentals.

44 Braccino da Todi [? = Artusi], *Discorso secondo musicale* (1608), p. 6.

45 Artusi, *Seconda parte dell'Artusi overo Delle imperfettioni della moderna musica* (1603), p. 5.

46 Tevo, *Il musico testore* (1706), p. 175, cited in Vogel, 'Claudio Monteverdi', p. 332.

47 The address to the 'Studiosi Lettori' in the Fifth Book (1605) and the *Dichiaratione* in the *Scherzi musicali* (1607) are given in De' Paoli, *Claudio Monteverdi: lettere, dediche e prefazioni*, pp. 390–407. Here and below the translation follows Strunk, *Source Readings in Music History*, pp. 405–12, with minor adaptations as appropriate.

48 Artusi, *Seconda parte dell'Artusi overo Delle imperfettioni della moderna musica* (1603), p. 47.

49 Ibid., *Considerationi*, p. 29.

50 Ibid., p. 11.

51 Ibid., pp. 25–6.

52 Ibid., p. 26.

53 Ibid., *Considerationi*, p. 5. Another figure objecting to Monteverdi's practices, with specific reference to 'Sfogava con le stelle', is the 'Maestro . . . ignorantone' ('Master . . . Ignorant') who appears towards the end of Severo Bonini's *Discorsi e regole sovra la musica* (probably written between 1640 and 1663) in Florence,

Biblioteca Riccardiana, MS 2218 (fol. 96v; see p. 168 of the modern edition edited by M. A. Bonino):

> although [his pieces] are full of unusual ideas, nonetheless there are some madrigals, such as in particular 'Sfogava con le stelle', where it occurs to me to note that this author, while he composed it, confused the good rules of counterpoint, since there are many perfect consonances of the same species which descend and rise together. But in my [works] such errors are not found, even though they are decked with a thousand ornaments with the observance of the strict rules.

However, when not satirizing such critics of modern music, Bonini takes several opportunities to praise Monteverdi as a representative of modern tendencies: see, for example, fols. 34v, 96v and 101v (pp. 56, 169, 178), where he mentions in general the composer's 'concerti'. Similarly, Bonini sees in the opening madrigal of the Fourth Book a typical example of the contemporary emotional style (fols. 95v, 101v; pp. 166, 177):

> Monteverdi can be called a composer singular for the affective style of the third order [the modern] in his madrigals for five voices, 'Ahi dolente partita', [and] in his concertos, where there are the words 'Non è di gentil core' [in the Seventh Book], of the same third order. This most eminent *maestro* with his unusual inventions has aroused sleepy spirits to invent new caprices ... But in the style of the third order, you will imitate in the said madrigals ... Monteverdi in that specific collection that begins [with] 'Ahi dolente partita' ...

54 Artusi, *Seconda parte dell'Artusi overo Delle imperfettioni della moderna musica* (1603), p. 32.

55 Ibid., *Considerationi*, p. 31.

56 Ibid., *Considerationi*, p. 32.

57 Ibid., p. 16.

58 Ibid., p. 16.

59 Ibid., p. 19. See also p. 45: '"supposed" (because they say that they suppose one note for another)'.

60 Ibid., p. 22.

61 Ibid., pp. 27, 38.

62 Ibid., p. 45.

63 Ibid., p. 42.

64 Ibid., p. 14.

65 Ibid., p. 17.

66 Ibid., pp. 19–20.

67 Solerti, *Le origini del melodramma*, pp. 107–8, translated in MacClintock (trans.), *Hercole Bottrigari, 'Il Desiderio ...'; Vincenzo Giustiniani, 'Discorso sopra la musica'*, pp. 69–70.

68 Artusi, *Seconda parte dell'Artusi overo Delle imperfettioni della moderna musica* (1603), p. 44.

69 Ibid., pp. 10, 41.

70 Caberloti, *Laconismo delle alte qualità di Claudio Monteverde* (1644), p. 10.

71 See Cerone, *El melopeo y maestro* (1613), p. 150: 'Similarly, to many professors [of music] it is clear how meritorious are the works of Don Geronimo Branchiforte, Count of Camerata.' This contrasts with the usual identification of the 'Count of Camerata' as Giovanni de' Bardi.

72 Braccino da Todi [? = Artusi], *Discorso secondo musicale* (1608), p. 7.

73 Ibid., p. 11.

74 Ibid., p. 8.

75 Magone, *Ghirlanda mosicale* (1615), p. 23.

76 Gallico, 'Newly Discovered Documents Concerning Monteverdi', p. 71.

77 Given in Prunière's, *La vie et l'oeuvre de Claudio Monteverdi*, p. 294 (*Monteverdi, his Life and Work*, p. 208 n. 13).

78 Errante, 'Forse che sí, forse che no', pp. 45, 77.

79 A description of the event survives in G. B. Grillo, *Breve trattato di quanto successe alla maestà della regina d. Margherita d'Austria* (1604), transcribed in Neri, 'Gli "Intermezzi" del "Pastor Fido"'.

80 Given in Fabbri, *Gusto scenico a Mantova nel tardo rinascimento*, pp. 53–4.

81 Given in Davari, 'Notizie biografiche del distinto maestro di musica Claudio Monteverdi', p. 80.

82 Ibid., p. 84.

83 See Gallico, 'Newly Discovered Documents Concerning Monteverdi', p. 68:

> Claudia gave him three children: Francesco, baptized in the church of SS. Simone e Giuda on 27 August 1601; Leonora, baptized in the cathedral church of S. Pietro on 20 February 1603; Massimiliano, baptized in the same cathedral church on 10 May 1604. The two different parishes suggest that between the birth of Francesco (1601) and Leonora (1603) the Monteverdi family had moved from one place of residence on the outskirts of Mantua to another in the centre within the parish of S. Pietro, Mantua's cathedral. This move, which occurred in 1602, was probably the result of an important change of rank on the part of the artist in the Mantuan musical hierarchy, and of his increased responsibilities and duties. In fact, from 10 April 1602 Monteverdi had been granted Mantuan citizenship, and in 1603 he could style himself on the title-page of his Fourth Book of madrigals 'Maestro della Musica del Ser.mo Sig. Duca di Mantova' ['Master of the Music of the Most Serene Duke of Mantua']. As a result of so great a progression in his career, he therefore went to live in the ducal palace (in the parish of S. Pietro) or in its immediate vicinity, perhaps in one of those elegant buildings which still today surround the royal palace, extending its exuberant architectural construction, as it were, with more restrained elegance and with singular decorum.

84 Vogel, 'Claudio Monteverdi', p. 339. See also Maylender, *Storia delle accademie d'Italia*, iii, pp. 342–4; Reiner, 'Preparations in Parma', p. 289.

85 Povoledo, 'Ferrara', col. 182. Here the foundation of the academy is dated 1602, 'under the auspices of Cardinal Legate Bevilacqua and of Duke Vincenzo Gonzaga. The initiative of building a permanent theatre came from Enzo Bentivoglio, leader of the Academy.'

86 Bettinelli, *Delle lettere e delle arti mantovane* (1774), pp. 79–80. On the contacts between Vincenzo and the Intrepidi, see also the preceding note.

87 See Newcomb, 'Alfonso Fontanelli and the Ancestry of the Seconda Pratica Madrigal', p. 50.

88 Some of these settings are compared in Petrobelli, '"Ah, dolente partita"'; Szweykowski, '"Ah, dolente partita"' (see also Palisca, 'Marco Scacchi's Defense of Modern Music (1649)'); Bianconi, '*Ah dolente partita*'.

89 Solerti, *Le origini del melodramma*, p. 58, translated in Caccini, *Le nuove musiche (1602)*, ed. Hitchcock, pp. 45–6.

90 Ibid., p. 225, from Doni, *Compendio del trattato de' generi e de' modi della musica* (1635), p. 101. Evidence of Monteverdi's knowledge of, and indeed excellence in, accompanied solo singing is provided by a letter sent by Arcangiolo Manara from Verona on 9 January 1603 to the duke of Mantua (given in Bertolotti, *Musici alla corte dei Gonzaga in Mantova dal secolo XV al XVIII*, p. 81) recommending a musician able, among other things,

> to play and sing to the theorbo, I will not say more than any other who is of this profession, with certain canzonettas composed by him that Your Highness will remain entirely astonished in hearing him, if this you will deign to do. We know that in your service you have a Rasi, a Monteverdi whose worth is so renowned, especially as regards the theorbo, however if Your Highness will hear this one, if you will not judge him superior to them, at least you will not hold him inferior.

Of Monteverdi's familiarity with the theorbo – his favoured instrument for composition and which he therefore held 'always to his breast' – later evidence is provided by his friend Bellerofonte Castaldi; see Fabbri, 'Inediti monteverdiani', p. 81. Monteverdi's expertise in singing is mentioned specifically, among other examples, in his letters L.80 [81], 96 [97], 97 [98], 99 [100], 100 [101], 114 [115].

91 Solerti, *Gli albori del melodramma*, i, p. 69. The translation is adapted from Fenlon, 'Monteverdi's Mantuan *Orfeo*', p. 170.

92 Bertolotti, *Musici alla corte dei Gonzaga in Mantova dal secolo XV al XVIII*, p. 86, translated in Fenlon, 'Monteverdi's Mantuan *Orfeo*', p. 165 (adapted). Fenlon also gives additional information on requests for castratos made to the Medici court on the part of Francesco Gonzaga once he had decided, in January 1607, to stage an opera, and on the hoped for arrival of Magli. He further suggests (ibid., p. 165) an identification of the anonymous singer whom the Mantuan architect Gabriele Bertazzolo mentions in a letter from Florence, 28 October 1608, to the Duchess of Mantua describing the banquet held in Florence on the evening of 19 October on the occasion of the wedding of Cosimo de' Medici and Maria Magdalena of Austria: 'In two stages appeared two small triumphal chariots, on one of which, which was the first and which appeared from the right side, sang the Roman girl in the service of the most illustrious Cardinal Montalto, and on the other, which appeared from the left-hand side, sang that little priest who took the part of Eurydice in the most serene lord prince's *Orfeo*' (given in Solerti, *Musica, ballo e drammatica alla corte medicea dal 1600 al 1637*, p. 55). According to Fenlon, this 'little priest' is Fr. Girolamo Bacchini.

93 E. Cagnani, *Lettere cronologica* (from Mantua, 19 February 1612), given in Faccioli (ed.), *Mantova: le lettere*, p. 621. Four years after *Orfeo*, we find Rasi appearing as Neptune 'playing a double-harp' – as had occurred in the prayer scene in Act III of *Orfeo*, 'Possente spirto e formidabil nume' – in the final *balletto* of *Psiche*, performed at Casale on 30 April 1611; see the *Breve descrittione delle feste fatte dal serenissimo sig. prencipe di Mantova nel giorno natale della serenissima infanta Margherita* (1611), fol. 11, cited in Solerti, *Gli albori del melodramma*, i, p. 139.

94 See Hanning, 'Alessandro Striggio'.

95 Bertolotti, *Musici alla corte dei Gonzaga in Mantova dal secolo XV al XVIII*, p. 87, translated in Fenlon, 'Monteverdi's Mantuan *Orfeo*', p. 168.

96 See Kirkendale, 'Zur Biographie des ersten Orfeo, Francesco Rasi'.

97 See Solerti, *Musica, ballo e drammatica alla corte medicea dal 1600 al 1637*, pp. 37–39.

98 From the fact that Magli stayed in Mantua until Spring 1607, Fenlon ('Monteverdi's Mantuan *Orfeo*', pp. 168–9) argues that a third performance was in preparation for the projected state visit of Carlo Emanuele, Duke of Savoy, to Mantua,

which then did not take place, vitiating these preliminary plans. In the carnival of 1610, Prince Francesco Gonzaga, temporarily in Turin, requested in great haste the score of *Orfeo* from Striggio: together with it, he was expecting the arrival of performers and theatrical materials. This has given rise to the idea of a projected performance of *Orfeo* somewhere in Turin, or perhaps Casale: see Bertolotti, *Musici alla corte dei Gonzaga in Mantova dal secolo XV al XVIII*, p. 92; Solerti, *Gli albori del melodramma*, i, pp. 70, 138–9. The notion of a performance in Salzburg in 1614 – see Antonicek, 'Claudio Monteverdi und Österreich', p. 267 – remains hypothetical (but see Seifert, 'Marcus Sitticus von Hohenems und Mantua'). However, secure documentation survives of a performance before 1646 in Genoa, in the theatre attached to the Osteria del Falcone owned by the Adorno family. In that year, Giacinto Adorno wrote to the notary Tommaso Oncia: 'it is my desire that the musicians' and actors' companies should be lodged outside the theatre and not in the aforesaid theatre as was the case on the occasion when Signor Monteverde's *Orfeo* was performed, much to the scandal of the magnificent Fathers of the Comune, and that to this end a suitable place should be provided' (given in Giazotto, *La musica a Genova nella vita pubblica e privata dal XIII al XVIII secolo*, p. 195). In addition to this, Girolamo Pinello states in the *Avvertimento* to the reader prefacing the edition of his *favola boschereccia, La ninfa ribelle* (Genoa, Casamara, 1653; see Giazotto, *La musica a Genova*, p. 204):

> Many turned themselves and many still turn themselves now and at all times to the musical setting of more or less tragic plays of ancient Greece. Such was the example of the *Orfeo* by Monteverde which in all parts of Italy received and still receives universal applause. Signor Monteverde showed how much the exercise of music could do in the tragic style, and, as the Genoese were able to hear, he makes himself the messenger of this revived music.

The 1653 edition is the second of Pinello's play: if we knew the date of the first edition, we could perhaps come closer to a *terminus ad quem* for the Genoa performance of *Orfeo*. However, the date of 1630 suggested by Giazotto (*La musica a Genova*, p. 207) is entirely arbitrary, as has rightly been pointed out by others (for example, Ivaldi, 'Gli Adorno e l'hostaria–teatro del Falcone di Genova (1600–1680)', pp. 118–19). In the 1681–2 season, the Teatro del Falcone staged a revival of *La coronatione di Poppea*; see Giazotto, *La musica a Genova*, p. 323.

99 See Gallico, *Monteverdi*, pp. 63–64.

100 Pirrotta, 'Teatro, scene e musica nelle opere di Monteverdi', p. 51 ('Theater, Sets, and Music in Monteverdi's Operas', p. 259).

101 Gallico, *Monteverdi*, p. 64. The following arguments have been anticipated in a different context in Fabbri, 'Striggio e l'*Orfeo*'.

102 See respectively Solerti, 'Precedenti del melodramma', pp. 225–30 (see also Fabbri, *Gusto scenico a Mantova nel tardo rinascimento*, pp. 49–51), and Sommi Picenardi, 'Claudio Monteverdi a Cremona', p. 502. The latter suggests that *Orfeo* was previewed in Cremona before the première in Mantua, but the surviving documentation (the manuscript by Giovan Battista Assandri cited in Chapter II, n. 119) offers absolutely no support for this hypothesis.

103 For Doni, see the extracts from his *Trattato della musica scenica* (1633–5) included in Solerti, *Le origini del melodramma*, pp. 203–5. As for the other anonymous treatise, see *Il corago, o vero alcune osservazioni per metter bene in scena le composizioni drammatiche*, ed. Fabbri & Pompilio. For these issues, see Nino Pirrotta's fundamental *Li due Orfei*, pp. 302–5 (*Music and Theatre from Poliziano to Monteverdi*, pp. 262–5).

104 Fabbri, 'Tasso, Guarini e il "divino Claudio"', pp. 238–42.

105 Ibid., pp. 242–4.

106 See Chapter II, n. 100.

107 Gallico, *Monteverdi*, p. 62. See also Bettinelli, *Delle lettere e delle arti mantovane* (1774), p. 87: 'Another old and most beautiful *bas relief* like this one is in the room next [to that with the chimney] under a window, in which [there is] Pluto, with Cerberus at his feet, sitting and with on one side a woman standing with her face covered by a veil, facing a young man with a wind instrument on his shoulder, in such a manner that it would seem to be Orpheus who requests and awaits Eurydice.'

108 Neri, 'Gabriello Chiabrera e la corte di Mantova', pp. 318–19.

109 For more detailed information, see Gallico, 'Emblemi strumentali negli "Scherzi" di Monteverdi', especially pp. 56–59.

110 See Schrade, *Monteverdi*, pp. 175–8. For the madrigals of the Eighth Book, see also Pirrotta, 'Scelte poetiche di Monteverdi', p. 37 ('Monteverdi's Poetic Choices', pp. 292–3, p. 438 n. 53).

111 Given in Canal, *Della musica in Mantova*, p. 86.

112 Gallico, 'Emblemi strumentali negli "Scherzi" di Monteverdi', p. 64.

113 Gallico, 'Emblemi strumentali negli "Scherzi" di Monteverdi', p. 64.

114 The same thing was done by Tarquinio Merula (*Il primo libro delle canzoni a quattro voci per sonare con ogni sorte de strumenti musicali*, Venice, Bartolomeo Magni, 1615; the 'Canzon nona' is titled *La Monteverde*) and by Pietro Lappi (*Canzoni da suonare ... Libro primo*, Venice, Gardano, 1616; the 'Canzona vigesima terza' *a13* bears the same title). To these composers, already noted in Vogel, 'Claudio Monteverdi', p. 398, should be added: Ottavio Bargnani, organist of the Duke of Mantua, who in his *Secondo libro delle canzoni da suonare* (Milan, Heirs of Tini & Filippo Lomazzo, 1611) includes the 'canzone settima' *a4* titled *La Monteverde*; Pietro Paolo Melii, composer of a 'Gagliarda' called *La Claudiana* 'Entitled to the very illustrious Signor Claudio Monte Verde, most worthy *maestro di cappella* of the most serene signory of Venice in St Mark's' in his *Intavolatura di liuto attiorbato. Libro secondo* (Venice, Giacomo Vincenti, 1614); Biagio Marini, whose *Affetti musicali* (Venice, Bartolomeo Magni ['Stampa dal Gardano'], 1617) contains *Il Monteverde*, 'German *balletto a2*, violin and bass'; and again Tarquinio Merula, who in his *Quarto libro delle canzoni da suonare* (Venice, Alessandro Vincenti, 1651) includes *La Monteverda* '*a2*, violin and bass'.

115 'The texts used by Monteverdi come from the *Rime* of 1599' (Pirrotta, 'Scelte poetiche di Monteverdi', p. 37; 'Monteverdi's Poetic Choices', pp. 437–8 n. 50). 'Amarilli onde m'assale', 'Quando l'alba in oriente' and 'Non così tosto io miro' all make reference to the same woman, called Alba.

116 Chiabrera, *Canzonette, rime varie, dialoghi*, ed. Negri, pp. 561, 563, 566, 568.

117 Ibid., p. 564.

118 Given in Solerti, *Gli albori del melodramma*, i, p. 75. That this play was initially written for Ferdinando is made clear in the following letter, from Florence, 10 November 1608, with which Buonarroti sends him a copy of the print (given in ibid., p. 76): 'There is no one else who should protect my play *Il giudizio di Paride* more than Your Most Illustrious Lordship, since it was first intended by me for

you, before Their Highnesses [in Florence] were pleased to want to make use of it in these most happy wedding celebrations.' For this whole affair, see also Carter, 'A Florentine Wedding of 1608'.

119 Assandri, *Gli atti della nobiliss.ᵃ academia di Cremona*, fols. 9v-10r (cited in Sommi Picenardi, 'Claudio Monteverdi a Cremona', p. 502).

120 Davari, 'Notizie biografiche del distinto maestro di musica Claudio Monteverdi', p. 86.

121 Sommi Picenardi, 'Claudio Monteverdi a Cremona', p. 502.

122 See Gallico, 'Monteverdi e i dazi di Viadana', pp. 242–3.

123 Davari, 'Notizie biografiche del distinto maestro di musica Claudio Monteverdi', p. 88.

124 Solerti, *Gli albori del melodramma*, i, pp. 78–79. The documents concerning Buonarotti 'il giovane' and Cini are given in ibid., pp. 75–85 (some had already been cited in Davari, 'Notizie biografiche del distinto maestro di musica Claudio Monteverdi', pp. 173–83). See also Carter, 'A Florentine Wedding of 1608'.

125 Solerti, *Gli albori del melodramma*, i, p. 80.

126 Ibid., pp. 82–84.

127 Ibid., p. 82 (and Davari, 'Notizie biografiche del distinto maestro di musica Claudio Monteverdi', p. 88).

128 Vogel, 'Marco da Gagliano', pp. 551–2.

129 Ibid., p. 552.

130 The preface is given in Solerti, *Le origini del melodramma*, pp. 78–89.

131 A letter from Pandolfo Stufa to Cardinal Ferdinando Gonzaga, dated 22 January 1608, speaks of the imminent arrival in Mantua of 'messer Santi [Orlandi?] and the boy', who were perhaps also used in *Dafne*; see Solerti, *Gli albori del melodramma*, i, p. 91.

132 In ibid., p. 88.

133 See Ademollo, *La bell'Adriana ed altre virtuose del suo tempo alla corte di Mantova*, pp. 36–47. Ibid., p. 38, gives a letter from Mantua of 26 July 1603 in which one can read Duke Vincenzo's instructions concerning Martinelli: 'for the time necessary for learning, instead of studying with Giulio Romano, she will stay in the home of Claudio Monteverdi, our *maestro di cappella*, who has a wife and other family, and where she will remain, one might say, under our eyes, with every necessary convenience until, having been taught as planned, she may then come at once to stay in the palace in the service of our duchess' (translated in Strainchamps, 'The Life and Death of Caterina Martinelli', pp. 159–60).

134 Solerti, *Gli albori del melodramma*, i, pp. 89–90.

135 Ibid., p. 91 (translated in Strainchamps, 'The Life and Death of Caterina Martinelli', p. 167). The affair is also discussed in Reiner, 'La vag'Angioletta (and others)', pp. 82–83. Reiner also gives other details of the recruiting of singers for these festivities.

136 Solerti, *Gli albori del melodramma*, i, p. 92.

137 See Pirrotta, *Li due Orfei*, pp. 330–31 (*Music and Theatre from Poliziano to Monteverdi*, p. 270 n. 105).

138 This has already been suggested in Solerti, *Gli albori del melodramma*, i, p. 92.

139 Ibid., p. 94 (translated in Strainchamps, 'The Life and Death of Caterina Martinelli', p. 169).

140 Reiner, 'La vag'Angioletta (and others)', p. 55: dispatch from Mantua to Rome wrongly dated 8 March 1608.

141 Solerti, *Gli albori del melodramma*, i, p. 94. The Florentine singer was not Settimia Caccini, as was once believed (and as hoped for in Rinuccini's letter of 20 December 1607, see above, p. 81); see Carter, 'A Florentine Wedding of 1608', p. 100.

142 Solerti, *Gli albori del melodramma*, i, p. 95.

143 In a manuscript in Milan, Biblioteca Nazionale Braidense, Fondo Morbio, can be found among other things verse in praise of Virginia Andreini headed 'Pe 'l suo meraviglioso modo di cantare e di suonare' ('For her wonderous manner of singing and playing'), see Zanetti, 'Virginia A[ndreini] Ramponi', col. 565. See also Bevilacqua, 'Giambattista Andreini e la Compagnia dei "Fedeli"', pp. 160–64.

144 Solerti, *Gli albori del melodramma*, i, p. 95.

145 Ibid., pp. 95–96 (but Marino had already sent poetry to Vincenzo Gonzaga in 1604 and 1607; see Schizzerotto, *Rubens a Mantova fra gesuiti, principi e pittori*, pp. 64, 68).

146 Striggio to Francesco Gonzaga, in Solerti, *Gli albori del melodramma*, i, pp. 96–97.

147 Extracts are given in ibid., iii, pp. 207–34. Other sources, some hitherto unknown (Pablo Gumiel, Giovanni Matteo Cavalchini, the libretto of the *Mascherata dell'Ingrate*) are cited in Schizzerotto, *Rubens a Mantova fra gesuiti, principi e pittori*, pp. 78–79.

148 We know for sure that the prologue was sung by Angela Zanibelli, according to a letter sent by her to Marquis Bentivoglio from Mantua, 11 April 1608, in Reiner, 'La vag'Angioletta (and others)', p. 60:

> As to learning, I am learning. My role is the prologue, whom I represent as being Mantua [i.e. Manto, the mythical founder of Mantua] coming from underneath the ground; and I am to say (singing) that she built the aforesaid city, and to end by praising to the skies all those sovereigns. My other part is the ending, [in] which they present me as the goddess of joy, in a cloud; and I dismiss them [saying] that they should go with 'lartenuta fra lor del ben guire' ['the art, unfamiliar to them, of rejoicing well']. I regret only that Your Most Illustrious Lordship, Her Ladyship the Marchesa, and Signora Caterina are not going to hear whether I perform my part[s] well: for I already know them and have rehearsed them on the stage.

Zanibelli's 'lartenuta fra lor del ben guire' ('L'arte ignota fra voi del ben gioire') is indeed Laetitia's last line in the *licenza* of the comedy, set to music by Birt and similarly sung by Zanibelli. Fétis (*Biographie universelle des musiciens et bibliographie générale de la musique*, i, p. 107) also notes a Jean-Vincent d'Angelo, 'celebrated singer in Italy' who died at the beginning of the seventeenth century. Fétis claims that he was attached to the Mantuan court and sang Monteverdi's works; and that he was also the recipient of a sonnet by Marino beginning 'Angelo, or tu fra gli

Angeli ten' vai'. This vague information is rendered somewhat useless by the fact that this sonnet was really written on the death of the *letterato*, Angelo Grillo.

149 Solerti, *Gli albori del melodramma*, i, p. 98 (and in Tiepolo, 'Minima monteverdiana', p. 135).

150 Solerti, *Gli albori del melodramma*, i, p. 99.

151 Ibid., pp. 101–2.

152 Ibid., iii, p. 240.

153 This letter, which survives in the Archivio di Stato in Mantua, is transcribed in Rossetti, 'Una corrispondenza inedita di Marco da Gagliano'. The Florentine version of the *Lamento d'Arianna* is edited in Vogel, 'Claudio Monteverdi', pp. 443–50, and in Solerti, *Gli albori del melodramma*, i, after p. 96.

154 In Sommi Picenardi, 'Claudio Monteverdi a Cremona', p. 501, we read of Francesco Monteverdi that 'Ten years after the death of his father, he adapted the music of *Arianna*, composed by the same Claudio, to the verses of the *Stabat mater*, honourably distinguishing himself in this task.' This is clearly drawn from Fantoni's *Storia universale del canto*, i, p. 153: 'ten years after his [Claudio Monteverdi's] death in 1643, he did him the great honour of adapting to the verses of the *Stabat mater* the music of his *Arianna*, set to music 33 years before for the Dukes of Mantua, and repeated in that ancient and illustrious Accademia dei Concordi in Rovigo'. This story was discounted in Vogel, 'Claudio Monteverdi' p. 403. A list of the manuscript sources of the *Lamento d'Arianna* can be found in Cavicchi's review of *C. Monteverdi: Lamento d'Arianna*, ed. Anfuso & Gianuario, p. 309.

155 Pirrotta, 'Monteverdi e i problemi dell'opera', pp. 335–6 ('Monteverdi and the Problems of Opera', p. 247).

156 Bianconi, *Il Seicento*, p. 217 (*Music in the Seventeenth Century*, p. 218).

157 Solerti, *Le origini del melodramma*, p. 214. The same idea (albeit put more vindictively) appears in Doni's letter (in French) to Marin Mersenne from Rome, 27 February 1636 (in De Waard (ed.), *Correspondance du p. Marin Mersenne religieux minime*, vi, pp. 30–31):

> I will send you a copy of *Arianna*, which is not the whole drama (because it was not printed), but its principal part, that is the *Lamento d'Arianna* or the chief scene, which is truly well done and the best piece that we have in this genre, since it is well developed, no less thanks to the continual assistance and labour of the poet (that is, Signor Ottavio Rinuccini, a very accomplished gentleman who was among those of the chamber of the former king) than to the musician Monteverde, who is, for the rest, as nearly all of them, of little intelligence, something which turns out exactly the opposite of the ancients, who were commonly men of distinction and among the most lively and distinguished intellects of that time …

Pietro della Valle is of a similar – if not quite so malevolent – opinion (in Solerti, *Le origini del melodramma*, pp. 153–4):

> The first compositions of value which we heard in this form were *Dafne*, *Arianna*, *Euridice* and other works from Florence and Mantua. The first who in Italy had worthily followed this path, as I said to Your Lordship, were the Prince of Venosa, who perhaps showed the light to all the others in affective singing, and Claudio Monteverde and Jacopo Peri in the above works. But [they] were in fact guided by Rinuccini, author of the verse; by Bardi, most skilled in ancient music; by Corsi, most expert in the practice of music and a great patron and benefactor of its professors; and by those other erudite gentlemen of Tuscany who oversaw with superintendence their compositions and very often made them write them in their own manner,

> whenceforth one sees how much that same Monteverde improved in his latest works, which were very different from his first ones …

158 Doni, *Trattato della musica scenica* (1633–5), in Solerti, *Le origini del melodramma*, p. 213. See also the account by Filippo Vitali in the preface to his *Aretusa* (1620), given in ibid., pp. 96–97: 'This offspring [*Dafne*] grew notably in beauty in *Euridice*, by the same artists, and in *Arianna* by Signor Claudio Monteverde, today *maestro di cappella* of St Mark's in Venice, who, having received it, also competed to embellish and adorn it with his most rich and unusual ideas.'

159 Bonini, *Discorsi e regole sovra la musica*, ed. M. A. Bonino, p. 151 (MS, fol. 87v), also given in Solerti, *Le origini del melodramma*, p. 139.

160 See Chapter III, n. 31.

161 In Monteverdi, *12 composizioni vocali profane e sacre*, ed. W. Osthoff. This setting has nothing more than the *incipit* 'Voglio, voglio morire' in common with the setting titled *L'amante segreto* included in Barbara Strozzi's *Cantate, ariette e duetti* (Venice, Francesco Magni ['Stampa del Gardano'], 1651). Bianconi, *Il Seicento*, pp. 211–12 (*Music in the Seventeenth Century*, pp. 212–13), discusses the lament further, also noting the dependence of the opening on the model of the *Lamento d'Arianna* and therefore placing in doubt the question of its authenticity in terms of its attribution to Monteverdi. This is also the opinion developed in Danckwardt, 'Das Lamento d'Olimpia "Voglio voglio morir"'.

162 Both letters are given in Solerti, *Gli albori del melodramma*, i, pp. 102–3.

163 Mantua, Archivio di Stato, Raccolta d'autografi, Busta 6, from Baldassare Monteverdi (partly given in Vogel, 'Claudio Monteverdi', p. 428).

164 Ibid., (cited in Vogel, 'Claudio Monteverdi', p. 353).

165 Vogel, 'Claudio Monteverdi', p. 430.

166 Now in University of California, Berkeley, Music Library; see MacClintock, 'New Sources of Mantuan Music'. The identification of the madrigal by Cavaletta is made in Il Verso, *Madrigali a tre (libro II, 1605) e a cinque voci (libro XV—opera XXXVI, 1619)*, ed. Bianconi, p. xl.

167 Sartori, 'Monteverdiana', p. 406. On 26 March 1609, Coppini wrote (in Latin) from Pavia to Pier Francesco Villani (given in ibid., p. 404):

> The third book, which contains divine harmonies, is in press. I have laboured hard on this book, but it seems to me to have succeeded to some extent in terms of matching with my words the force of the music. I have dedicated it to the Prince of Mantua, to whom I learn that this book would be welcome both for the musical genre and also for the texts devised by me for the task. Claudio Monteverdi has written something on this to me from Mantua.

Adriano Banchieri, who is included in Coppini's collection, sent the poet a letter of thanks, later published in his *Lettere armoniche* (1628), p. 120 (given in ibid., p. 405): 'Among the illustrious collection which Your Lordship has produced of madrigals for five voices by Claudio Monteverde and other modern composers of our times, and these at the request of the Most Illustrious Lord Cardinal Federico Borromeo, archbishop of Milan, Your Lordship has been pleased to include one of mine.'

168 Banchieri, *Conclusioni nel suono dell'organo* (1609), pp. 58–60 (see Vecchi, *Le accademie musicali del primo Seicento e Monteverdi a Bologna*, pp. 131–3).

169 See Assandri, *Gli atti della nobiliss.ᵃ academia di Cremona*, fol. 18v (in Sommi Picenardi, 'Claudio Monteverdi a Cremona', p. 517).

170 See Guerrini, 'Canzoni spirituali del Cinquecento', pp. 6–7; Kurtzman, 'An Early 17th-Century Manuscript of *Canzonette e madrigaletti spirituali*'.

171 Vogel, 'Claudio Monteverdi', p. 430.

172 See Pirrotta, 'Scelte poetiche', p. 41 ('Monteverdi's Poetic Choices', p. 294).

173 See Davari, 'Notizie biografiche del distinto maestro di musica Claudio Monteverdi', p. 100, and Vogel, 'Claudio Monteverdi', p. 356. A portion (the *altus* part of the Mass) of the copy sent personally to the dedicatee survives, as identified in Annibaldi, 'L'archivio musicale Doria Pamphilj', p. 291.

174 Gombert, *Opera omnia*, ed. Schmidt-Görg, ix, pp. 13–19.

175 Gallico, *Monteverdi*, p. 113.

176 See Kurtzman, 'Some Historical Perspectives on the Monteverdi Vespers', pp. 46–48. For the liturgical issues, see Bonta, 'Liturgical Problems in Monteverdi's Marian Vespers'. Elsewhere, the suggestion has been made – but without any secure documentary foundation, and indeed as seemingly contradicted by the official account of those festivities – that Monteverdi's collection brings together pieces used in 1608 for the institution of the military Order of the Redentore, the consecration of which took place in the church of S. Andrea (see Fenlon, 'The Monteverdi Vespers'). Further possibilities are raised in Dixon, 'Monteverdi's Vespers of 1610'. However, Hucke, 'Die fälsich so genannten "Marien"-Vesper von Claudio Monteverdi', offers a timely emphasis on the general nature of the work and on its character as being more devotional than liturgical.

177 For the relevant titles, see the Bibliography. It should be added, however, that Bonta ('Liturgical Problems in Monteverdi's Marian Vespers', pp. 97–101) proposes that an instrumental canzona should be added in the place of the missing Magnificat antiphon.

178 Schrade, *Monteverdi*, p. 253. Blazey, 'A Liturgical Role for Monteverdi's *Sonata sopra Sancta Maria*', suggests that the *Sonata* is an antiphon-substitute for the Magnificat.

179 See Kurtzman, 'Some Historical Perspectives on the Monteverdi Vespers', pp. 34–35.

180 Ibid., pp. 40, 49–61.

181 Ibid., pp. 62–63.

182 Ibid., pp. 62–63.

183 Ibid., pp. 63–64.

184 Ademollo, *La bell'Adriana ed altre virtuose del suo tempo alla corte di Mantova*, p. 155.

185 Davari, 'Notizie biografiche del distinto maestro di musica Claudio Monteverdi', p. 93; Bertolotti, *Musici alla corte dei Gonzaga in Mantova dal secolo XV al XVIII*, p. 91.

186 A. Grillo, *Delle lettere*, ii (1616), pp. 137–8, given in part in Neri, 'Gabriello Chiabrera e la corte di Mantova', p. 337, and in English translation in Einstein, 'Abbot Angelo Grillo's Letters as Source Material for Music History', pp. 176–7 (the present translation differs).

187 Usually and wrongly referred to as 'Dixit a 5' (see L.11); the correct reading is noted in Stevens, *Monteverdi*, p. 85.

188 Stevens (trans.), *The Letters of Claudio Monteverdi*, p. 80, suggests that the Elevation refers to the Elevation of the Host in the Mass, and that the motet is 'O bone Jesu' (published by Donfried in 1622) or 'Venite sitientes' (published by Calvi in 1624).

189 Roncaglia, 'Di Bellerofonte Castaldi', p. 121.

190 Vogel, 'Claudio Monteverdi', p. 375, and H. Osthoff, 'Gedichte von Tomaso Stigliani auf Giulio Caccini, Claudio Monteverdi, Santino Garsi da Parma und Claudio Merulo', p. 617.

191 Cited in Canal, *Della musica in Mantova*, p. 106.

192 Segarizzi (ed.), *Relazioni degli ambasciatori veneti al senato*, pp. 119–20.

193 Ibid., p. 118.

194 De' Paoli, *Monteverdi* (1979), p. 265 (also cited in Davari, 'Notizie biografiche del distinto maestro di musica Claudio Monteverdi', p. 100).

195 Vogel, 'Claudio Monteverdi', p. 358 (also cited in Davari, 'Notizie biografiche del distinto maestro di musica Claudio Monteverdi', p. 103). For further details of Monteverdi's dismissal from Mantua, see Parisi, '*Licenza alla Mantovana*'.

196 Davari, 'Notizie biografiche del distinto maestro di musica Claudio Monteverdi', p. 105.

197 Davari, 'Notizie biografiche del distinto maestro di musica Claudio Monteverdi', p. 105. The correspondence relating to Marsolo's self-application can be read in Marsolo, *Secondo libro dei madrigali a quattro voci, opera decima*, ed. Bianconi, pp. xxxii–xxxv.

198 Davari, 'Notizie biografiche del distinto maestro di musica Claudio Monteverdi', p. 104 (and Vogel, 'Claudio Monteverdi', p. 430).

199 Davari, 'Notizie biografiche del distinto maestro di musica Claudio Monteverdi', p. 104.

200 Arnold, *Monteverdi* (2nd edn. 1975), pp. 202–3.

201 Ibid., p. 202.

202 Venice, Archivio di Stato, Procuratia *de supra*, No. 140 (*Decreti e terminazioni 1607–1614*), fols. 148v–149r (Vogel, 'Claudio Monteverdi', pp. 431–2).

Venice

1 See Caffi, *Storia della musica sacra nella già cappella ducale di San Marco in Venezia dal 1318 al 1797*. Also relevant is the list of 'Musical Staff of the Basilica of San Marco' given as an appendix in Selfridge-Field, *Venetian Instrumental Music from Gabrieli to Vivaldi*, pp. 292–308.

2 Barblan, 'La vita di Claudio Monteverdi', p. 88.

3 Caffi, *Storia della musica sacra nella già cappella ducale di San Marco in Venezia dal 1318 al 1797*, i, pp. 198–9, 211–12. See also the following documents: Venice, Archivio di Stato, Procuratia *de supra*, Busta 91, Processi 205 (for the vice-*maestri di cappella*) and 207 (for the organists). Negri, a singer as well as vice-*maestro*, is also cited in Venice, Archivio di Stato, Procuratia *de supra*, No. 141 (*Decreti e terminazioni 1614–1620*), fol. 15v (2 April 1615). Here (and for the same date) mention is also made of Don Vito Rovetta from Piove di Sacco, called an organist, perhaps to assist the elderly Giusti (elsewhere Rovetta is called simply a singer, as in Procuratia *de supra*, Nos. 142 (*Atti e terminazioni 1620–1629*), fol. 5r (3 January 1621); 143 (*Atti e terminazioni 1629–1637*), fol. 39r (1 January 1632)). Savi is cited in Procuratia *de supra*, No. 141 (*Decreti e terminazioni 1614–1620*), fol. 16r (2 April 1615).

4 Venice, Archivio di Stato, Procuratia *de supra*, No. 141 (*Decreti e terminazioni 1614–1620*), fol. 9v. Ibid., No. 143 (*Atti e terminazioni 1629–1637*), fol. 124r (29 July 1635) provides another list of instrumentalists active in St Mark's, each of whom were given a one-off gift of 5 ducats, including 'Pietro Loschi, Zuane Caspan, pre Mattio, Pietro Furlan, Bastian de Pelegrin, ms. Antonio Zorzi, Bernardo Tedesco, Marco Martelli, Battista Galli, Francesco Negroponte'. An attempt was made to reintroduce the cornett in St Mark's – the instrument had evidently fallen into disuse – on 8 July 1640 (Procuratia *de supra*, No. 144 (*Atti e terminazioni 1637–1648*), fol. 60):

> Since for much time past has been abandoned the playing in the *concerti* which are performed in the church of St Mark and in the whole city of the instrument of the cornett, which used to offer very grateful harmony and to complete satisfaction, and the Most Excellent Lord Procurators desirous of turning to revive this instrument, and having been informed of the great labour which is necessary for those who wish to play it, have (thus to encourage present performers, and likewise those who wish to address themselves to it) agreed that to [the salary of] Piero Furlan, at present ordinary instrumentalist in the church, should be added 15 ducats per year, and to [that of] Marco, ordinary singer, be given another 15 ducats, with the requirement that both of them be obliged in the music which will be performed in the said church, and always when they will be ordered to do so by the *maestro di cappella*, to play the said cornett, making every effort to make themselves better, and this as it pleases Their Most Excellent Lordships, also being required to fulfil the duties which they have in the said church according to their appointment. [Votes:] 3–0

See also Caffi, *Storia della musica sacra nella già cappella ducale di San Marco in Venezia dal 1318 al 1797*, ii, p. 59.

5 Vogel, 'Claudio Monteverdi', p. 364.

6 Fabbri, 'Inediti monteverdiani', p. 80.

7 The following entries come from Venice, Archivio di Stato, Procuratia *de supra*, No. 141 (*Decreti e terminazioni 1614–1620*), fols. 105v–106r (19 February 1619), 124r (26 January 1620), 121v (30 December 1619). For Grillo, see also Caffi, *Storia della musica sacra nella già cappella ducale di San Marco in Venezia dal 1318 al 1797*, i, pp. 249–50.

8 Cavalli is listed as a soprano in 1616, as a tenor in 1635, and as organist in 1642; see Bianconi, 'Caletti [Caletti-Bruni], Pietro Francesco, detto Cavalli', p. 686. Berti is given as a singer in Venice, Archivio di Stato, Procuratia *de supra*, No. 142 (*Atti e terminazioni 1620–1629*), fol. 84r (17 December 1623) and as organist in ibid., fol. 109r ((18 October 1624); see also Procuratia *de supra*, Nos. 143 (*Atti e terminazioni 1629–1637*), fol. 113v (22 March 1635); 144 (*Atti e terminazioni 1637–1648*),

fol. 15v (17 January 1636). See also Caffi, *Storia della musica sacra nella già cappella ducale di San Marco in Venezia dal 1318 al 1797*, i, pp. 264, 272. For Fillago, see ibid., i, pp. 254–5, and also Venice, Archivio di Stato, Procuratia *de supra*, Busta 91, Processi 207; Procuratia *de supra*, Nos. 142 (*Atti e terminazioni 1620–1629*), fols. 84r (17 December 1623), 109r (18 October 1624), 167r (30 January 1628); 143 (*Atti e terminazioni 1629–1637*), fol. 122r (25 July 1635); 144 (*Atti e terminazioni 1637–1648*), fol. 46r (9 October 1639).

9 Venice, Archivio di Stato, Procuratia *de supra*, No. 142 (*Atti e terminazioni 1620–1629*), fol. 104v (16 September 1624).

10 Procuratia *de supra*, No. 144 (*Atti e terminazioni 1637–1648*), fol. 35r (23 January 1639).

11 Caffi, *Storia della musica sacra nella già cappella ducale di San Marco in Venezia dal 1318 al 1797*, i, pp. 250, 265–6. See also Venice, Archivio di Stato, Procuratia *de supra*, Busta 91, Processi 205. For Grandi as a singer, see ibid., No. 142 (*Atti e terminazioni 1620–1629*), fols. 2v–3r (17 November 1620). Rovetta, too, rose from the ranks of the singers, where he served as a bass, see ibid., fol. 83v (17 December 1623); ibid., No. 143 (*Atti e terminazioni 1629–1637*), fol. 113r (21 March 1635); ibid., No. 144 (*Atti e terminazioni 1637–1648*), fols. 52v (28 March 1640), 94r (1 March 1642), 150r (3 January 1644).

12 Caberloti, *Laconismo delle alte qualità di Claudio Monteverde* (1644), pp. 8–9.

13 The following entries come from Venice, Archivio di Stato, Procuratia *de supra*, No. 141 (*Decreti e terminazioni 1614–1620*), fols. 1v–2r (6 April 1614), 6v (2 September 1614); Caffi, *Storia della musica sacra nella già cappella ducale di San Marco in Venezia dal 1318 al 1797*, ii, p. 97.

14 In Venice, Archivio di Stato, Procuratia *de supra*, No. 141 (*Decreti e terminazioni 1614–1620*), fols. 7v (5 October 1614), 16r (2 April 1615), 113v (7 July 1619).

15 Caffi, *Storia della musica sacra nella già cappella ducale di San Marco in Venezia dal 1318 al 1797*, i, pp. 233, 404–12 (particularly pp. 410–12).

16 Venice, Archivio di Stato, Procuratia *de supra*, No. 141 (*Decreti e terminazioni 1614–1620*), fols. 19v–20r (14 June 1615).

17 Venice, Archivio di Stato, Procuratia *de supra*, No. 142 (*Atti e terminazioni 1620–1629*), fol. 94v (28 April 1624). During Monteverdi's period of service in Venice, as well as the vice-*maestri*, organists and musicians listed above – plus Francesco Monteverdi, to be discussed below – the following singers and instrumentalists are known to have been members of the *cappella* of St Mark's (the sources in this list are made up of Venice, Archivio di Stato, Procuratia *de supra*, Nos. 140 (*Decreti e terminazioni 1607–1614*), 141 (*Decreti e terminazioni 1614–1620*), 142 (*Atti e terminazioni 1620–1629*), 143 (*Atti e terminazioni 1629–1637*) and 144 (*Atti e terminazioni 1637–1648*): Orazio Rossi piemontese, castrato (No. 140, fol. 149r, 19 August 1613); Romano Micheli, *maestro di canto* (No. 141, fol. 5v, 25 July 1614); Domenico Aldegati, bass (No. 141, fol. 8v, 12 December 1614; No. 142, fol. 185v, 18 February 1629); Francesco Rossi, bass (No. 141, fol. 16r, 2 April 1615; No. 144, fol. 91r, 19 January 1642); Bortolo Strambali, contralto (No. 141, fol. 16r, 2 April 1615); Giacomo Macabressa dalla Tisana, castrato (No. 141, fols. 33v–34r, 27 February 1616; No. 142, fol. 1v, 28 October 1620); Francesco Castigliano, castrato (No. 141, fols. 33v–34r, 27 February 1616; No. 142, fol. 181r, 21 January 1629); Felice Cazzeleri da Pistoia, castrato (No. 141, fols. 33v–34r, 27 February 1616); Leonardo Simonetti, castrato (No. 141, fol. 12r, 31 January 1615; No. 142,

fol. 138r, 16 April 1626); Lucio Mora, singer (No. 141, fol. 45r, 3 July 1616); Giovanni Arzignan, singer (No. 141, fol. 106v, 22 February 1619); Fr. Bernardino Pomeli, contralto (No. 141, fol. 112v, 1 July 1619); Giovanni Arrigoni, bass (No. 141, fol. 113v, 7 July 1619); Prospero Arrigoni, castrato (No. 141, fol. 128r, 5 April 1620); Giulio Medici da Treviso, bass (No. 141, fol. 128r, 5 April 1620); Fr. Francesco Nardi, bass (No. 141, fol. 128r, 5 April 1620; No. 142, fol. 145r, 27 September 1627); Paolo Romano, singer (No. 141, fol. 138r, 28 July 1620); Felice Luino da Milano, bass (No. 142, fol. 3v, 29 December 1620); Antonio Zanotti, instrumentalist (No. 142, fol. 47v, 26 April 1622); Don Eleuterio Guazzi da Parma, tenor (No. 142, fol. 50r, 20 May 1622); Don Giovanni Battista Camarella, contralto (No. 142, fol. 50r, 20 May 1622); Stefano Monti, tenor (No. 142, fol. 79r, 6 July 1623); Giovan Battista Marinoni, tenor (No. 142, fols. 79r, 6 July 1623; 136r, 31 March 1626; No. 144, fol. 117r, 11 January 1642); Giovan Battista Pescara, tenor (No. 142, fol. 79r, 6 July 1623); Fra Bernardino Centuron da Trento, contralto (No. 142, fol. 79r, 6 July 1623); Fra Matteo Saracea, trombone and singer (No. 142, fols. 90v, 2 April 1624; 112v, 18 January 1625); Pier Francesco Castello, trombone (No. 142, fol. 92v, 14 April 1624); Fra Giovanni Strambali, contralto (No. 142, fol. 93r, 21 April 1624); Fr. Giovanni Bafini, singer (No. 142, fol. 131v, 19 January 1626); Fra Vincenzo da Valenza, singer (No. 142, fol. 131v, 19 January 1626); Fra Pietro Bertolini, singer (No. 142, fol. 131v, 19 January 1626); Fra Angelo Colombo, singer (No. 142, fol. 131v, 19 January 1626); Felice Sonzi, singer (No. 142, fols. 138v, 16 April 1626; 180r, 14 January 1629); Don Girolamo Rossi (No. 142, fol. 139r, 16 April 1626; No. 143, fols. 6r, 2 April 1630; 36v, 23 December 1631; 42r, 31 January 1632; 105v, 14 January 1635; 134v, 6 April 1636); Fra Enrico Tura, singer (No. 142, fol. 165r, 8 January 1627); Giovan Battista Bisucci, bass (No. 142, fol. 166v, 23 January 1628; No. 143, fols. 39v, 4 January 1632; 105v, 1 January 1635); Alessandro da Napoli, falsetto (No. 142, fols. 166v, 23 January 1628; 179r, 7 January 1629); Fra Benedetto dei Frari, contralto (No. 142, fol. 166v, 23 January 1628); Fr. Francesco da S. Agnese, singer (No. 142, fol. 166v, 23 January 1628; No. 143, fol. 154r, 25 January 1637); Fra Stefano da Ferrara, singer (No. 142, fol. 167r, 30 January 1628); Francesco Bonfante, head of the instrumentalists (No. 142, fol. 168v, 2 April 1628); Fra Giuseppe Maria Amadessi, tenor (No. 142, fol. 176r, 3 December 1628); Frate di S. Stefano, singer (No. 142, fol. 179r, 7 January 1629); Don Giacomo [Rapallino] da Mantova, bass (No. 142, fol. 179r, 7 January 1629); Fra Francesco Rossi, soprano (No. 142, fol. 198v, 21 November 1629); Fra Francesco da Vercelli, singer (No. 143, fol. 12r, 8 October 1630); Domenico Obizzi, singer (No. 143, fol. 12r, 8 October 1630); Girolamo Maggi da Venezia, soprano and tenor (No. 143, fols. 35r, 26 October 1631; 119r, 29 May 1635); Francesco Arzignan, contralto (No. 143, fol. 36r, 28 October 1631; No. 144, fol. 42v, 3 July 1639); Don Bonfiglio Zamberlini, contralto (No. 143, fol. 73r, 10 July 1633); Fra Taddeo da Pesaro, tenor (No. 143, fol. 83r, 2 April 1634); Daniel Bodè, bass (No. 143, fol. 83r, 2 April 1634; No. 144, fol. 30r, 31 October 1638); Marco Pellegrini, soprano, contralto and violin (No. 143, fol. 83v, 2 April 1634; No. 144, fols. 28v, 3 October 1638; 90v, 17 January 1642; 143r, 25 October 1643); Girolamo Medici da Roma, soprano (No. 143, fols. 83v, 2 April 1634; 111v, 25 January 1635; No. 144, fols. 15v, 17 January 1638; 42v, 3 July 1639; 108r, 26 October 1642); Anselmo Marconi, falsetto (No. 143, fols. 106r, 21 January 1635; 111v, 25 January 1635); Fr. Orazio Abbiosi, soprano (No. 143, fol. 135r, 6 April 1636); Filippo Bertolini, soprano (No. 143, fol. 135r, 6 April 1636); Ulderico Borletta, soprano (No. 143, fol. 138r, 22 June 1636; No. 144, fol. 35v, 27 January 1639); Don Annibale Grasselli, tenor (No. 143, fol. 138r, 22 June 1636); Fr. Giovan Battista Faccini, tenor (No. 143, fol. 138r, 22 June 1636; No. 144, fol. 30r, 31 October 1638); Girolamo called 'Marte' [? = Girolamo Medici] (No. 143, fol. 138r,

22 June 1636); Guido Antonio Boretti, contralto (No. 143, fol. 152v, 17 January 1637); Stefano Riccieri, singer (No. 144, fol. 4v, 5 July 1637); Fra Alberto Lazzari, bass (No. 144, fol. 7r, 22 July 1637); Don Giulio Mattioli da Bologna, bass (No. 144, fol. 15v, 17 January 1638); Fr. Francesco Spada, tenor (No. 144, fols. 15v, 17 January 1638; 108r, 26 October 1642); Bonivento Boniventi, contralto (No. 144, fol. 15v, 17 January 1638); Francesco Pesarin, tenor (No. 144, fol. 15v, 17 January 1638); Fr. Gian Domenico Caenazzo, bass (No. 144, fol. 15v, 17 January 1638); Opilio Morlacchini, violone (No. 144, fol. 29v, 24 October 1638); Fr. Natale Monferrato, singer (No. 144, fol. 38r, 22 February 1639); Francesco Santi da Perugia, soprano (No. 144, fol. 46r, 9 October 1639); Venanzio Leopardi, tenor (No. 144, fol. 46r, 9 October 1639); Battista Padoan, trombone (No. 144, fol. 46r, 9 October 1639); Pietro Marizza, instrumentalist (No. 144, fol. 55v, 19 April 1640); Marcantonio Brocca, contralto (No. 144, fol. 65r, 4 October 1640); Don Giovan Pietro Finotti, singer (No. 144, fol. 68v; 10 November 1640); Fr. Giovan Battista Castello, bassoon (No. 144, fol. 77r, 21 April 1641); Francesco Donadoni, instrumentalist (No. 144, fol. 82v, 28 July 1641); Fra Doroteo, bass (No. 144, fol. 91r, 19 January 1642); Giovan Pietro Orcelli, violin (No. 144, fol. 94r, 1 March 1642); Fr. Francesco Facchinetti, singer (No. 144, fol. 98v, 15 April 1642); Francesco (No. 144, fol. 100v, 23 April 1642); Bonifacio Ceretti, contralto (No. 144, fol. 100v, 23 April 1642); Lodovico Porta, contralto (No. 144, fol. 100v, 23 April 1642); Fr. Stefano Boni da Caorle, tenor (No. 144, fol. 100v, 23 April 1642); Fra Piero, contralto (No. 144, fol. 100v, 23 April 1642); Don Giacomo, tenor (No. 144, fol. 100v, 23 April 1642); Giovan Benedetto Tagliavacche (No. 144, fol. 100v, 23 April 1642); Giacomo Maffei, tenor (No. 144, fol. 100v, 23 April 1642); Pietro Tamburlin, contralto (No. 144, fol. 113r, 14 December 1642); Iseppo Mafazzoni, tenor (No. 144, fol. 115r, 4 January 1643); Antonio Rizzo, soprano (No. 144, fol. 115r, 4 January 1643); Paolo Agatea, soprano (No. 144, fol. 115r, 4 January 1643); Giuseppe Valente da Napoli, soprano (No. 144, fols. 115r, 4 January 1643; 127r, 26 April 1643); Giovanni Marchetti, instrumentalist (No. 144, fol. 134r, 23 July 1643).

18 Monteverdi also refers to his duties for Christmas in L.35, 13 December 1619.

19 The festivities for Holy Week and Easter are also mentioned in L.29 (21 April 1618), L.49 [50] (17 March 1620), L.50 [51] (21 March 1620).

20 Culley, *Jesuits and Music*, i, pp. 332–3 (translated in ibid., pp. 185–7).

21 Venice, Archivio di Stato, Procuratia *de supra*, No. 141 (*Decreti e terminazioni 1614–1620*), fol. 17r (20 April 1615), and Busta 90, Processi 204, fol. 12v (24 August 1616; see also fol. 2r). This last document is also cited in Vogel, 'Claudio Monteverdi', p. 367. Francesco Monteverdi was also employed on an occasional basis in St Mark's for Christmas Eve 1618 to sing a *lectio* in Matins, see Arnold, *Monteverdi* (3rd edn. 1990), p. 34.

22 Bianconi, *Il Seicento*, p. 21 (*Music in the Seventeenth Century*, p. 21).

23 Vogel, 'Claudio Monteverdi', p. 430.

24 See above, p. 84.

25 Both Pirrotta ('Scelte poetiche di Monteverdi', p. 232; 'Monteverdi's Poetic Choices', p. 300) and Gallico (*Monteverdi*, p. 27) date the first and third of these three madrigals back to 1607–8 for other reasons.

26 See pp. 84, 117, and Pirrotta, 'Scelte poetiche di Monteverdi', p. 234 ('Monteverdi's Poetic Choices', p. 301).

27 For Marino and his importance for the early seventeenth-century madrigal, see Bianconi, *Il Seicento*, pp. 9ff. (*Music in the Seventeenth Century*, pp. 8ff.), and Pirrotta, 'Scelte poetiche di Monteverdi', p. 237 ('Monteverdi's Poetic Choices', p. 304), as well as Simon-Gidrol, 'Appunti sulle relazioni tra l'opera poetica di G. B. Marino e la musica del suo tempo'.

28 Bianconi, *Il Seicento*, p. 22 (*Music in the Seventeenth Century*, p. 22).

29 Pirrotta, 'Scelte poetiche di Monteverdi', p. 229 ('Monteverdi's Poetic Choices', p. 298), but what follows there should be modified in the light of Gallico, *Monteverdi*, pp. 29–30.

30 Doni, *Trattato della musica scenica* (1633–5), in id., *De' trattati di musica ... tomo secondo* (1763), p. 98: 'consider the passages and motions of the *Lamento d'Arianna* for solo voice, and the same composed for several voices by the same Monteverde at the request of a noble Venetian, and it will be seen that the solo voice always sings well and with good air, but in the *concerto* for several voices, often one hears certain passages which are less than graceful and accommodated to the words, as is the case in the beginning of the bass'. See also ibid., p. 61 of the Appendix, speaking of the need for good progressions and for a melody proportionate to the subject: 'which in singing so many arias together cannot be done. Evidence of this is Signor Claudio's *Arianna*, revised for several parts as three madrigals, where everyone can see if the beginning of the bass has the melody appropriate to those words "Lasciatemi morire" ["Let me die"; a music example follows]. How much better would it have been if that Venetian gentleman, instead of making Signor Claudio revise that *Arianna* – truly the joy of his compositions – as madrigals, had had him write an accompaniment for four instrumental parts in the best manner possible to accompany with this that most beautiful aria in one solo voice?' See also Redlich, *Claudio Monteverdi*, i, p. 136. In the above-mentioned letter of 24 August 1609 (L.7), Monteverdi had similarly spoken of a composition 'for a solo voice, but if later on His Most Serene Highness orders me to rearrange the air for five voices, this I shall do'.

31 On Antonelli and his setting (in manuscript), see Barblan, 'Un ignoto "Lamento d'Arianna" mantovano'. For the Sicilian settings, see Carapezza, 'L'ultimo oltramontano o vero l'antimonteverdi'; Pari, *Il lamento d'Arianna*, ed. Carapezza; Carapezza, '"O soave armonia"'; Il Verso, *Madrigali a tre (libro II, 1605) e a cinque voci (libro XV – opera XXXVI, 1619)*, ed. Bianconi.

32 A. Grillo, *Delle lettere*, iii (1616), pp. 127–8. Partial translations of this and the following letters can be found in Einstein, 'Abbot Angelo Grillo's Letters as Source Material for Music History', pp. 177–8 (the present translation differs).

33 A. Grillo, *Delle lettere*, iii (1616), p. 124.

34 Ibid., p. 322.

35 Ibid., p. 128.

36 Davari, 'Notizie biografiche del distinto maestro di musica Claudio Monteverdi', p. 47. The letter is also given in Solerti, *Gli albori del melodramma*, i, p. 116. Solerti relates it to a presumed Florentine performance of *Arianna* at the Convertite (see the prologue in ibid., p. 188) which therefore took place in 1614. But that prologue could also have been used for the play *Arianna*, the war-horse of the celebrated actress Marina Dorotea Antonazzoni, who, for example, performed it in Florence

in 1616; see Evangelista, 'Il teatro della Dogana detto di Baldracca', p. 372. A letter from Sante Orlandi cited in Solerti, *Gli albori del melodramma*, i, p. 117, seems to refer to a projected Mantuan performance of *Arianna* in 1612.

37 See Federhofer, 'Graz Court Musicians and their Contributions to the "Parnassus Musicus Ferdinandaeus" (1615)'.

38 From the *relazione* of the Venetian ambassador in Mantua, Giovanni da Mulla, of 1615, in Segarizzi (ed.), *Relazioni degli ambasciatori veneti al senato*, pp. 139–41.

39 Mantua, Archivio di Stato, Archivio Gonzaga, Busta 2735 (cited in Davari, 'Notizie biografiche del distinto maestro di musica Claudio Monteverdi', p. 112).

40 Mantua, Archivio di Stato, Archivio Gonzaga, Busta 2735 (cited in De' Paoli, *Monteverdi* (1945), p. 215; Fabbri, 'Tasso, Guarini e il "divino Claudio"', p. 249).

41 Davari, 'Notizie biografiche del distinto maestro di musica Claudio Monteverdi', pp. 40–42; see also Solerti, *Gli albori del melodramma*, i, p. 119; iii, p. 107.

42 Canal, *Della musica in Mantova*, p. 117; Bevilacqua, 'Giambattista Andreini e la compagnia dei "Fedeli"', pp. 98–101.

43 See Solerti, *Gli albori del melodramma*, i, p. 139.

44 See Rosenthal, 'Monteverdi's "Andromeda"', reporting the discovery of *La favola di Andromeda fatta rappresentare in musica dall'ecc.^{mo} sig. principe D. Vincenzo Gonzaga Il Carnevale del M.DC.XX* (Mantua, Fratelli Osanna, n.d.).

45 See Pirrotta, 'Scelte poetiche di Monteverdi', p. 238 ('Monteverdi's Poetic Choices', p. 305).

46 Ibid., p. 243 ('Monteverdi's Poetic Choices', p. 308). Concerning this piece, Strohm ('Osservazioni su "Tempo la cetra"', p. 364) suggests that 'it was composed for a stage performance [accompanied by dance]. But this is not necessarily to say that this performance was ever realized.'

47 Pirrotta, 'Scelte poetiche di Monteverdi', p. 239 ('Monteverdi's Poetic Choices', p. 305).

48 Solerti, *Gli albori del melodramma*, i, p. 115.

49 It appears in the second edition of the poem (Venice, Girolamo Piuti, 1626), XII.43; cited in Bianconi, *Il Seicento*, pp. 14–15 (*Music in the Seventeenth Century*, p. 14).

50 Fabbri, 'Inediti monteverdiani', p. 73.

51 Doni, *Trattato della musica scenica* (1633–5), in id., *De' trattati di musica ... tomo secondo* (1763), pp. 29–30. See also Gallico, 'La "Lettera amorosa" di Monteverdi e lo stile rappresentativo'; Fabbri, 'Lessico monteverdiano'. Doni was in contact with Pietro de' Bardi, and received his account of early Florentine endeavours (given in Solerti, *Le origini del melodramma*, pp. 143–6).

52 See Fabbri, Pompilio & Vassalli, 'Frescobaldi e le raccolte con composizioni a voce sola del primo Seicento'.

53 Gallico, 'La "Lettera amorosa" di Monteverdi e lo stile rappresentativo', p. 287. Achillini's text had already appeared in 1612 with the title *L'amorosa ambasciatrice* (*The amorous ambassadress*). Preti's poem (in *Idilli e rime*, Venice, T. Bortoloti, 1614) is called an 'idillio': 'a lover no longer able to hide his love, decides in the end to reveal it to his beloved by writing this idyll'.

54 See Pannain, 'Studi monteverdiani: ix', p. 25.

55 Redlich, *Claudio Monteverdi*, i, p. 135.

56 Doni, *Trattato della musica scenica* (1633–5), in id., *De' trattati di musica … tomo secondo* (1763), p. 27, transcribed in Solerti, *Le origini del melodramma*, pp. 218–19.

57 For this affair, see Stevens, 'Monteverdi, Petratti, and the Duke of Bracciano', pp. 286–7. Here Stevens publishes a hitherto unknown letter from Monteverdi (also included in Stevens (trans.), *The Letters of Claudio Monteverdi*, No. 40); other letters that concern Monteverdi's links with the duke are L.36, 37 and 46 [47].

58 This suggestion is made, for different reasons, in Stevens (trans.), *The Letters of Claudio Monteverdi*, p. 172.

59 Vecchi, *Le accademie musicali del primo Seicento e Monteverdi a Bologna*, p. 91.

60 Banchieri, *Lettere armoniche* (1628), p. 141 (cited in Vogel, 'Claudio Monteverdi, pp. 433–4, and in Vecchi, *Le accademie musicali del primo Seicento e Monteverdi a Bologna*, p. 82). In his *Cartella musicale* (1614), Banchieri gives the *Capitoli esigibili nell'Accademia dei Fioriti* (reproduced in Vecchi, *Le accademie musicali del primo Seicento e Monteverdi a Bologna*, pp. 134–41). The seventh chapter, 'What is to be done on the day of the Academy', reads:

> On the day of the Academy (as has been said), after Vespers the Beadle will inform the Very Reverend Father Lector and then will sound 25 strokes of the bell. On hearing this, all the novices will transfer to the room of the aforesaid Father Lector to accompany him to the Academy. Having arrived and on being seated, there will be performed for their delight a *concerto* for voices with spinet, at the end of which the chairman will deliver the speech, introducing the first speaker. Then will be sung a motet or serious spiritual madrigal, as for example those by Orlando Lasso, Palest[r]ina or others, with the opportunity of singing also one of those madrigals by that sweetest modern composer, Claudio Monteverde, at present most worthy *maestro di cappella* of St Mark's in Venice, which have been turned into motets by Aquilino Coppini at the request of the Most Illustrious Lord Cardinal Federico Borromeo, and this will be sung without instruments at the little table, at the end of which the second speaker will take the floor, and after the third and last speaker [there will be] a *concerto* as required. Then the chairman, with two words of thanks, will place a sonnet or madrigal, or Latin verses, in the hand of the chancellor, which will be read aloud and presented to the Very Reverend Father Prelate or the Superior if he is present in the Academy; that done the *Principe preterito*, taking the chair, will read a case of conscience to which (if it pleases) each can give his opinion …

61 Noske, 'An Unknown Work by Monteverdi', p. 119.

62 The suggestion is made in Barblan, 'La vita di Claudio Monteverdi', p. 103.

63 In a poem dedicated to Monteverdi, Rinuccini called him a 'cigno canoro, ammirato dall'Adria, / alla cui dotta lira ogni musa cedeva il canto' ('a singing swan, admired by the Adriatic, / to whose learned lyre each muse yielded the palm'), in *Rime* (Florence, 1652), p. 175, cited in Canal, *Della musica in Mantova*, p. 106.

64 See Bevilacqua, 'Giambattista Andreini e la compagnia dei "Fedeli"', pp. 117–18, and Muraro, 'Venezia', col. 1545.

65 L.71 [72], 21 October 1622; other letters referring to the matter are L.72 [73] (19 November 1622), 73 [74] (3 December 1622), 74 [75] (10 December 1622) and 75 [76] (31 December 1622).

66 L.77 [78], 10 February 1623; reference is also made to the recruitment of singers in L.80 [81] of 2 March 1624.

67 Ademollo, *La bell'Adriana ed altre virtuose del suo tempo alla corte di Mantova*, p. 271. The duke and duchess's stay in Venice is described in ibid., pp. 271–80.

68 Ibid., p. 272.

69 Venice, Biblioteca Nazionale Marciana, MS It. VI.304(= 5986), fol. 30r (see also Ademollo, *La bell'Adriana ed altre virtuose del suo tempo alla corte di Mantova*, p. 277).

70 Ibid., fol. 36r.

71 Ademollo, *La bell'Adriana ed altre virtuose del suo tempo alla corte di Mantova*, pp. 280–87, speaks of the success of Basile in Venice – she was Mocenigo's guest – and of the verses written in her honour, in large part collected in the *Teatro delle glorie della signora Adriana Basile* (Venice, Evangelista Deuchino, 1623). To these should be added Gabriele Zinano's canzona 'O nel giardin d'Amore', contained in his *Rime diverse* (Venice, Evangelista Deuchino, 1627), pp. 40–44, and dedicated 'To the mouth of Signora Andriana Basile, while she was staying to sing in the presence of a large number of the nobility in the palace of Signor Gironimo Mocenigo, Venetian gentleman, at the request of Signor Mutio Barone, her husband.' On ibid., pp. 28–29, is a sonnet 'Veggonsi piaggie, e in un giardini e prati', addressed 'Al signor Claudio Monte Verde mastro di capella di S. Marco in Venetia'.

72 Venice, Archivio di Stato, Procuratia *de supra*, Nos. 142 (*Atti e terminazioni 1620–1629*), fol. 79r (6 July 1623); 143 (*Atti e terminazioni 1629–1637*), fol. 2v (27 January 1630). See also Petrobelli, 'L'"Ermiona" di Pio Enea degli Obizzi ed i primi spettacoli d'opera veneziani', p. 139.

73 For all the issues concerning Monteverdi's links with the court in Modena, see Fabbri, 'Inediti monteverdiani'. The unpublished letter by Monteverdi given there on p. 76, which I suggested had been enclosed in a letter from the Estense resident in Venice dated 11 March 1623, should instead be considered a response to the one dated 7 April 1623 summarized in Prunières, *La vie et l'oeuvre de Claudio Monteverdi*, p. 307 (*Monteverdi, his Life and Work*, p. 217 n. 159).

74 Arnold, *Monteverdi* (2nd edn. 1975), p. 202; ibid., (3rd edn. 1990), p. 35; and see Vio, 'Ultimi ragguagli monteverdiani', p. 359 (which also notes payments for 1627).

75 Monteverdi, *Tutte le opere*, ed. Malipiero, viii/1, pp. 132–3. On the possible meanings of the term 'cavallo Mariano', see Gallico, 'La "Lettera amorosa" di Monteverdi e lo stile rappresentativo', p. 297.

76 Pirrotta, 'Scelte poetiche di Monteverdi', p. 30 ('Monteverdi's Poetic Choices', p. 288); the principal variants are listed in ibid., pp. 30–31 ('Monteverdi's Poetic Choices, p. 433 n. 37).

77 The translation of the preface to the Eighth Book here and below is taken from Strunk, *Source Readings in Music History*, pp. 413–15.

78 Fortune, 'Italian Secular Monody from 1600 to 1635', p. 185.

79 See Gallico, '"Contra Claudium Montiuiridum"'. Reference to this litigation is also made in L.81–84 [82–85] of 1625.

80 See Fabbri, 'Il soggiorno veneziano di Ladislao, principe di Polonia'.

81 So wrote the Cremonese Giuseppe Bresciani in the seventeenth century (see Sommi Picenardi, 'Claudio Monteverdi a Cremona', p. 518). On this episode, see also the comments of Ansaldo Cotta (cited here in the Introduction, n. 7) and Bellerofonte Castaldi (see Fabbri, 'Inediti monteverdiani', p. 82).

82 For both documents given below, see Vogel, 'Claudio Monteverdi', pp. 373, 433–4.

83 Banchieri, *Lettere* (1630), pp. 34–5.

84 Ortolani, 'Venezia al tempo di Monteverdi', p. 472. The following material is drawn from Preto, 'Una denuncia anonima contro Claudio Monteverdi', and Glixon, 'Was Monteverdi a Traitor?'.

85 Vecchi, *Le accademie musicali del primo Seicento e Monteverdi a Bologna*, p. 91.

86 Arisi, *Cremona literata*, iii (1741), p. 231.

87 Pontiroli, 'Notizie sui Monteverdi, su personaggi ed artisti del loro ambiente e la casa natale di Claudio', p. 174.

88 Monteverdi, *12 composizioni vocali profane e sacre*, ed. W. Osthoff, No. 7.

89 L.94 [95], 24 May 1627. See also the discussion in Tomlinson, 'Twice Bitten, Thrice Shy'.

90 L.95 [96], 5 June 1627; reference to *Licori* is also made in L.96 [97] of 13 June 1627.

91 L.104 [106]. Reference to the copying of the text is also made in L.101 [102] (31 July 1627), 102 [103] (17 August 1627) and 103 [104] (28 August 1627).

92 Reference to this is probably made in L.111 [112] of 2 October 1627.

93 For the identity of what Monteverdi calls the 'Sereniss.ᵐᵒ Prencipe di Noimburgh', see De' Paoli (ed.), *Claudio Monteverdi: lettere, dediche e prefazioni*, p. 268; Stevens (trans.), *The Letters of Claudio Monteverdi*, pp. 338–9.

94 For the festivities in Parma, see Vogel, 'Claudio Monteverdi', pp. 385–90; Solerti, *Musica, ballo e drammatica alla corte medicea dal 1600 al 1637*, pp. 193–4, 409–518; Lavin, 'Lettres de Parmes (1618, 1627–28) et débuts du théâtre baroque'; Reiner, 'Preparations in Parma'; Vitali, 'Una lettera vivaldiana perduta e ritrovata, un inedito monteverdiano del 1630 e altri carteggi di musicisti celebri', pp. 410–12; *Il corago, o vero alcune osservazioni per metter bene in scena le composizioni drammatiche*, ed. Fabbri & Pompilio, pp. 40, 117–18, 121, 125. The list of Goretti's letters hitherto known and published – either complete or in part – including those lost after the dispersal of private collections which contained them (see the Catalogue of the Succi sale [1888], No. 481, and Kinsky, *Versteigerung von Musikbüchern praktischer Musik und Musiker-Autographen des 16. bis 18. Jahrhunderts aus dem Nachlass des Herrn Kommerzienrates Wilhelm Heyer in Köln*, No. 457) can be seen in Stevens (trans.), *The Letters of Claudio Monteverdi*, p. 344.

95 L.105, 10 September 1627, to Bentivoglio. On 4 September, the latter had written to the duke: 'I cannot say how pleased I am at the decision to make use of Signor Monteverdi, both for the rare qualities of that man as for being able to get down to business' (given in Solerti, *Musica, ballo e drammatica alla corte medicea dal 1600 al 1637*, p. 193).

96 L.107 [109], 18 September 1627.

97 Ferrara, Biblioteca Comunale Ariostea, Antonelli No. 660: Lettere di Antonio Goretti, from Parma, 1 October 1627.

98 Ferrara, Archivio di Stato, Archivio Bentivoglio, Busta 210, fols. 382–3, letter from Parma, 28 October 1627.

99 Ferrara, Biblioteca Comunale Ariostea, Antonelli No. 660: Lettere di Antonio Goretti, from Parma, 29 October 1627 (the final part is cited in Lavin, 'Lettres de Parmes (1618, 1627–28) et débuts du théâtre baroque', p. 146). Similarly, Mar-

gherita Farnese noted Monteverdi's arrival personally to Marquis Bentivoglio on 2 November 1627, in Ferrara, Archivio di Stato, Archivio Bentivoglio, Mazzo 130:

> I find myself with two letters from Your Lordship, the first of the 19th of last month given to me by Count Fabio after he had recovered from his illness, and the other of the 24th, sent to me with the arrival of Monteverde and Goretti . . . Monteverdi is here and attends to his work with much diligence and enthusiasm, nor does he wish Your Lordship to be disabused of the good reports that you have given of him, since he truly succeeds in all aspects as most welcome and most discrete, nor have we failed to treat him kindly as he deserves.

100 Ferrara, Biblioteca Comunale Ariostea, Antonelli No. 660: Lettere di Antonio Goretti, from Parma, 2 November 1627 (the final section is cited in Lavin, 'Lettres de Parmes (1618, 1627–28) et débuts du théâtre baroque', p. 146; another section is quoted in Fabbri, *Tre secoli di musica a Ravenna dalla Controriforma alla caduta dell'Antico Regime*, p. 157).

101 Ferrara, Biblioteca Comunale Ariostea, Antonelli No. 660: Lettere di Antonio Goretti, from Parma, 5 November 1627.

102 Ferrara, Archivio di Stato, Archivio Bentivoglio, Busta 210, fols. 108–9, letter from Parma dated 6 November 1627.

103 On the position of the orchestra in sixteenth- and seventeenth-century Italy, see – in addition to what is said below – Pirrotta, 'Il luogo dell'orchestra', and also *Il corago, o vero alcune osservazioni per metter bene in scena le composizioni drammatiche*, ed. Fabbri & Pompilio, Chapter x.

104 Ferrara, Biblioteca Comunale Ariostea, Antonelli No. 660: Lettere di Antonio Goretti, from Parma, 9 November 1627.

105 Ibid., from Parma, 16 November 1627 (the final section is cited in Lavin, 'Lettres de Parmes (1618, 1627–28) et débuts du théâtre baroque', p. 148).

106 Ferrara, Archivio di Stato, Archivio Bentivoglio, Busta 210, fols. 401–2, letter from Antonio Goretti from Parma, 20 November 1620. The matter of fixing the singers was also brought before Margherita Farnese, who on 18 December 1627 wrote to Enzo Bentivoglio (ibid., Mazzo 130, fol. 329): 'As for what Your Lordship says to me concerning the musicians, I have left it to Monteverdi to please himself in allocating the parts, and if anything should not be to the liking of Your Lordship, I will not blame you in any way.'

107 Lavin, 'Lettres de Parmes (1618, 1627–28) et débuts du théâtre baroque', p. 131.

108 Ferrara, Biblioteca Comunale Ariostea, Antonelli No. 660: Lettere di Antonio Goretti, from Parma, 26 November 1627 (another part of this letter is cited in Lavin, 'Lettres de Parmes (1618, 1627–28) et débuts du théâtre baroque', p. 147). A letter from Lazzarini dated 26 November 1627 once existed in the Heyer Collection (see Kinsky, *Versteigerung von Musikbüchern praktischer Musik und Musiker-Autographen des 16. bis 18. Jahrhunderts aus dem Nachlass des Herrn Kommerzienrates Wilhelm Heyer in Köln*, No. 510), the catalogue of which gives some fragments indicating that the singer was discussing therein questions concerning his role, in particular in the love scene with Diana (evidently he played Endymion), which in Monteverdi's view was the best part: 'it is said to me by Monteverdi . . . that this was the most beautiful section of that part' (in Kinsky, *Versteigerung von Musikbüchern*, p. 94, given in Stevens (trans.), *The Letters of Claudio Monteverdi*, p. 378).

109 Ferrara, Archivio di Stato, Archivio Bentivoglio, Busta 210, fols. 502–3, letter from Parma, 27 November 1627, given almost complete in Italian in De' Paoli, *Monteverdi* (1979), p. 400, and in English translation in Reiner, 'Preparations in Parma', p. 301.

110 Arnold, *Monteverdi* (3rd edn. 1990), p. 38 n. 18. His return was requested by the procurators on 27 November 1627.

111 Ferrara, Biblioteca Comunale Ariostea, Antonelli No. 660: Lettere di Antonio Goretti, from Parma, 7 December 1627 (given in part in Lavin, 'Lettres de Parmes (1618, 1627–28) et débuts du thèâtre baroque', p. 147).

112 Venice, Archivio di Stato, Collegio, Sezione III (*Secreta*), Lettere principi, Filza 58, 9 December 1627 (see Canal, *Della musica in Mantova*, pp. 119–20). The forthcoming 'arrival of Signor Claudio Monteverdi, a most tasteful [*garbatissimo*] gentleman and the greatest virtuoso in his profession' had been announced to the duke by Marquis Bentivoglio on 24 December 1627 (see Solerti, *Musica, ballo e drammatica alla corte medicea dal 1600 al 1637*, p. 193).

113 Ferrara, Biblioteca Comunale Ariostea, Antonelli No. 660: Lettere di Antonio Goretti, from Parma, 21 January 1628.

114 Lavin, 'Lettres de Parmes (1618, 1627–28) et débuts du théâtre baroque', pp. 126, 147. In ibid., p. 148, there is another letter from Goretti dated 25 February 1628: 'We are here with no hope of coming, since for finishing the work and arranging the instruments in the *salone*, which is no little thing, and for rehearsing, there is no chance of coming. The instruments were first found a place in the arch in the middle of the stairway in front of the stage, and then two little organs have been placed in the boxes in front.'

115 Ghisi, 'Firenze', col. 380, and *Il luogo teatrale a Firenze*, p. 88.

116 Povoledo, 'Guitti, Francesco', col. 71, and 'Orchestra', col. 1388.

117 Ferrara, Biblioteca Comunale Ariostea, Antonelli No. 660: Lettere di Antonio Goretti, from Parma, 18 February 1628 (given in part in Lavin, 'Lettres de Parmes (1618, 1627–28) et débuts du théâtre baroque', p. 147).

118 Lavin, 'Lettres de Parmes (1618, 1627–28) et débuts du théâtre baroque', p. 126: letter from Francesco Guitti, Parma, 3 March 1628.

119 Ibid., p. 127: letter from Francesco Guitti, Parma, 15 March 1628.

120 Ferrara, Biblioteca Comunale Ariostea, Antonelli No. 660: Lettere di Antonio Goretti, from Parma, 8 November 1628.

121 Lavin, 'Lettres de Parmes (1618, 1627–28) et débuts du théâtre baroque', p. 148.

122 The texts set by Monteverdi are given in Solerti, *Musica, ballo e drammatica alla corte medicea dal 1600 al 1637*, pp. 409–518.

123 Arnold, *Monteverdi* (3rd edn. 1990), p. 40 n. 21.

124 Vogel, 'Claudio Monteverdi', p. 391.

125 A copy is in Pesaro, Biblioteca Oliveriana, A.ɪɪ.b.7.M.X, but sadly it lacks the final page. The incipit of the fifth sonnet can be reconstructed given that each text begins with the last line of the previous one. I have not been able to consult the copy in Florence, Biblioteca Nazionale Centrale, Magliabechiano XIX.10 cust., given that it was damaged in the 1966 flood. There is no evidence to support the attribution to Monteverdi by Caffi (*Storia della musica sacra nella già cappella ducale*

di San Marco in Venezia dal 1318 al 1797, i, p. 229) of the cantata 'Rosaio fiorito' for the birth of a son of the governor of Rovigo, Vito Morosini, in 1629 (see Vogel, 'Claudio Monteverdi', p. 391): its text has no connection with Monteverdi.

126 A later edition – from the seventeenth century but with no indication of printer, etc. – is noted in Vogel, 'Claudio Monteverdi', p. 425.

127 Monteverdi, *12 composizioni vocali profane e sacre*, ed. W. Osthoff, No. 6. Organ intabulations of Monteverdi's sacred music are contained in manuscripts similarly surviving in Lüneburg, see Basso, *Frau Musika*, i, p. 227. According to Osthoff:

> The motet 'Exulta filia Sion' also survives in Lüneburg, Ratsbücherei, MS Mus. ant. pract. K.N. 206. The manuscript, dated 'Hamburgi 15 Junij 1647' contains a mono-gram and some insertions perhaps attributable to Heinrich Scheidemann (c.1596–1663), Hamburg organist and composer, and also later annotations in the hand of Matthias Weckmann (1621–1674), the pupil of Heinrich Schütz. In this manuscript, as well as compositions by German authors, we find a significant group of pieces by Italians, including among others A. Banchieri, A. Grandi, T. Merula, Giovanni Valentini and Monteverdi; by the last there are 18 sacred pieces, corresponding to the same number of pieces in Vols. 15/16 of *Tutte le opere*, a sacred contrafactum of 'Altri canti di Marte' (*Tutte le opere*, viii, pp. 181ff.) and finally the present motet (see F. Welter, *Katalog der Musikalien der Ratsbücherei Lüneburg*, Lippstadt, 1950, pp. 35, 248–50). This manuscript offers significant evidence of the diffusion of Italian music, and particularly by Monteverdi, in northern Germany.

128 See Vitali, 'Una lettera vivaldiana perduta e ritrovata, un inedito monteverdiano del 1630 e altri carteggi di musicisti celebri', p. 411.

129 Ibid., pp. 411–12.

130 Priuli, *Diari*, fol. 98, given in Zoppelli, 'Il rapto perfettissimo', p. 343.

131 The identification is made in Walker, 'Gli errori di "Minerva al tavolino"', p. 13.

132 See Chapter II, n. 149.

133 Preto, 'Le grandi pesti dell'età moderna', p. 124. Some sources (wrongly?) give the date of Striggio's death as 15–16 June.

134 Mueller & Preto, 'Peste e demografia', pp. 96, 98.

135 Niero, 'I templi del Redentore e della Salute', pp. 304ff.

136 Venice, Archivio di Stato, Cerimoniali, III, fol. 72v.

137 Venice, Archivio di Stato, Cerimoniali, III, fol. 72v.

138 Ibid., fols. 78–79r.

139 Ibid., fol. 83v.

140 Ibid., fol. 83v.

141 M. Ginammi, *La liberatione di Venetia* (Venice, G. B. Conzato, 1631), fol. [4r], cited (with some errors) in Vogel, 'Claudio Monteverdi', p. 393 and emended in Moore, '*Venezia favorita da Maria*', p. 324 n. 94. Moore's article offers a systematic analysis, with full documentation, of all the celebrations associated with the foundation of S. Maria della Salute, suggesting that Monteverdi wrote variously for this occasion some pieces later included in the *Selva morale* (Nos. 6–11, 35–40). *Trombe squarciate* are ceremonial trumpets.

142 Tiepolo, 'Minima monteverdiana', pp. 138–9.

143 Arnold, *Monteverdi* (2nd edn. 1975), pp. 203–4.

144 Caberloti, *Laconismo delle alte qualità di Claudio Monteverde* (1644), pp. 9–10.

145 See Vio, 'Ultimi ragguagli monteverdiani', which contains a deal of new information on Monteverdi in Venice from which I am glad to have profited.

146 See Pompilio, 'Editoria musicale a Napoli e in Italia nel Cinque–Seicento', and Fabbri, 'Politica editoriale e musica strumentale in Italia dal Cinque al Settecento'.

147 Caberloti, *Laconismo delle alte qualità di Claudio Monteverde* (1644), p. 10.

148 This suggestion is made in Prunières, *La vie et l'oeuvre de Claudio Monteverdi*, p. 211 (*Monteverdi, his Life and Work*, p. 218 n. 168).

149 De Waard (ed.), *Correspondance du p. Marin Mersenne religieux minime*, iv, p. 7.

150 Ibid., vi, pp. 17–18. See also Chapter II, n. 157: this evidence, from 1636, is also significantly later than the publication and sending to Monteverdi of the *Compendio* whence arose Doni's disfavour. In ibid., p. 73, is another letter from Doni in Rome to Mersenne, perhaps dating from May 1636, concerning the sending of concerted madrigals by Monteverdi: 'Monsieur Meliand is indeed a fine messenger, who gave you just the letter, without the six parts of Monteverde's madrigals: you should at least say something to him.' This followed another letter, of 27 February 1636 (ibid., p. 17): 'I am indeed astonished that Monsieur Meliand did not give you those madrigals in six parts by Monteverdi which I had sent you as being the best pieces which he had done, and I find it very strange that since he had undertaken to do it he did not say a word to you about it. If it pleases you, you could remark on it to him with surprise to know at least what happened to them.' In the *Compendio* (p. 16), Doni had written: 'So today we do not find true chromatic compositions – still less enharmonic ones – except for a few which have some mixture, like that most artful madrigal by the Prince [of Venosa, Gesualdo] "Resta di darmi noia" and the *Lamento d'Arianna* by Monteverdi, even though greater is the mixture therein of several modes.' The passage in Mersenne to which Doni alludes is instead the following: 'As for the praises of old Adriano [Willaert], whose works in part served as a model for Du Caurroy, and of other excellent composers, both from Germany and the Low Countries and from Italy, among whom one includes Lucas Marenzio, Fresco Baldi, Claude Monteverde and several others, I leave that concern to others who have known them.'

151 Jonckbloet & Land (eds.), *Musique et musiciens au XVIIe siècle*, p. lxiii (partially given in Vogel, 'Claudio Monteverdi', p. 400).

152 Imperiale, *Viaggi*, ed. Barrili, p. 272 (cited in Bianconi & Walker, 'Production, Consumption and Political Function of Seventeenth-Century Opera', p. 213 n. 8).

153 See Fabbri, 'Inediti monteverdiani'.

154 De' Paoli (ed.), *Claudio Monteverdi: lettere, dediche e prefazioni*, pp. 337–8, translated in Stevens (trans.), *The Letters of Claudio Monteverdi*, pp. 419–20.

155 Liberati, *Lettere scritta . . . in risposta ad una del sig. Ovidio Persapegi* (1685), p. 39, cited in Monteverdi, *12 composizioni vocali profane e sacre*, ed. W. Osthoff.

156 Venice, Archivio di Stato, Procuratia *de supra*, Busta 91, fols. 96r–103v.

157 Ibid., fol. 102r.

158 Ibid., fol. 97r.

159 Ibid., fol. 100r.

160 The manuscript survives in Venice, Biblioteca Nazionale Marciana, It. x.115(= 7193).

161 Ibid., fols. 59r–61v: the latter part is also given in Rosand, 'Barbara Strozzi, "virtuosissima cantatrice"', p. 251 n. 34.

162 Pirrotta, 'Scelte poetiche di Monteverdi', pp. 246–7 ('Monteverdi's Poetic Choices', p. 449 n. 128).

163 Stevens, '"Madrigali Guerrieri, et Amorosi"', p. 245.

164 [A. Maugars], *Response faite à un curieux sur le sentiment de la musique d'Italie, escrite à Rome le premier octobre 1639* (n.p., n.d. [Paris, 1639 or 1640]), see Thoinan, *André Maugars*; Vogel, 'Claudio Monteverdi', p. 400. For a likely citation of the *Combattimento* in the *intermedio*, *La fiera di Farfa*, for the revival of *Chi soffre speri* in 1639, see Bianconi & Walker, 'Production, Consumption and Political Function of Seventeenth-Century Opera', pp. 220–21.

165 Ban, *Zangh-Bloemzel*, cited and translated into German in Vogel, 'Claudio Monteverdi', pp. 399–400.

166 Schütz is called a pupil of Monteverdi in the funeral oration by Martin Geyer of 1672, published, among other things, together with a commemorative poem by David Schirmer, which includes: 'Der edle Mont de Verd wies ihn mit Freuden an / und zeigt ihm voller Lust die oft gesuchte Bahn' ('The noble Monteverdi gladly instructed him, / and showed him with genuine delight the course he so often sought after'), given in Stevens (trans.), *The Letters of Claudio Monteverdi*, p. 400.

167 Schuetz [Schütz], *Sämmtliche Werke*, ed. Spitta, ii.

168 See Pirrotta, 'Scelte poetiche di Monteverdi', p. 244 ('Monteverdi's Poetic Choices', p. 309); Stevens, '"Madrigali Guerrieri, et Amorosi"', p. 239.

169 Solerti, *Le origini del melodramma*, p. 171.

170 Bonini, *Discorsi e regole sovra la musica*, ed. M. A. Bonino, pp. 100–1 (MS, fol. 57). See also the dedication to Adriano Banchieri's *Saviezza giovenile* (Venice, Gardano [Bartolomeo Magni], 1628): 'It seems that the music of today brings little honour to composers unless it is used on the stage in the representative style, and whoever stands on the foundations of the good rules and observed counterpoint is struck from the list of musicians and included in that of the antiquarians.'

171 Fabbri, 'Inediti monteverdiani', pp. 80–81.

172 Ibid., p. 81. The sonnet continues: 'La cagion chi la vuole / saper è perch'ei dia tanto diletto / la tiorba il dirà c'ha sempre al petto' ('The reason, whoever wishes / to know it, why he gives such delight / will say that it is that he has the theorbo always to his breast'). Obviously the notion of Monteverdi always having the theorbo in hand is not without prejudice, given Castaldi's predilection for the instrument.

173 Doubt is cast on the traditional dating of Autumn 1639 in Pirrotta, 'Early Venetian Libretti at Los Angeles', p. 238 (id., *Music and Culture in Italy from the Middle Ages to the Baroque*, pp. 320–21).

174 See Petrobelli, 'L'"Ermiona" di Pio Enea degli Obizzi ed i primi spettacoli d'opera veneziani', pp. 125–41.

175 Ibid., and see also De' Paoli (ed.), *Claudio Monteverdi: lettere, dediche e prefazioni*, p. 245; Povoledo, 'Una rappresentazione accademica a Venezia nel 1634', p. 122.

176 Petrobelli, 'Francesco Manelli', pp. 55–57.

177 Povoledo, 'Una rappresentazione accademica a Venezia nel 1634', pp. 122, 165–6, 166.

178 See De' Paoli, *Monteverdi* (1979), pp. 455–6.

179 See, for example, Benvenuti, 'Il ritorno di Ulisse in patria non è di Monteverdi'. The librettos which have survived (listed in Redlich, 'Monteverdi', col. 518) are likewise in manuscript.

180 W. Osthoff, 'Zu den Quellen von Monteverdis "Ritorno di Ulisse in patria"', pp. 73–74.

181 Id., 'Zur Bologneser Aufführung von Monteverdis "Ritorno di Ulisse" im Jahre 1640'. Manuscript librettos of *Il ritorno d'Ulisse in patria* and *Le nozze d'Enea in Lavinia* dated 1641 are listed in Henze-Doehring, 'Eine Libretti Sammlung in der Musikgeschichtlichen Abteilung des Deutschen Historischen Instituts in Rom', pp. 202–3.

182 See Vio, 'Musici veneziani dei primi decenni del Seicento', pp. 382–5.

183 Solerti, 'Un balletto musicato da Claudio Monteverdi sconosciuto a' suoi biografi', gives complete the description by Morando cited here. The poet gave details of this entertainment and of his literary involvement in it to his friend and colleague Gian Vincenzo Imperiale, resident in Genoa, in a letter from Piacenza dated 10 February 1641 (see Martinoni, 'Lettere di Bernardo Morando a Gian Vincenzo Imperiale', p. 212), which says, among other things:

> Last Thursday a *balletto* was performed at court, the description of which will be seen in a little book by me enclosed. The verses were mine, and as a result, they are worth little in themselves; but accompanied by the music it was miraculous, and they were made worthy of extraordinary applause on the part of His Highness and others. I could not write the description in my own way, for His Highness had commanded me to do it very clearly, so that it might serve as a simple outline of the plot for those who were at the entertainment.

184 The attribution was refuted simultaneously by Walker, 'Gli errori di "Minerva al tavolino"', pp. 11–12, and Szweykowska, 'Le due poetiche venete e le ultime opera di Claudio Monteverdi', pp. 149–50; the latter also analyses the poetics implied within the theoretical statements of the anonymous author.

185 As is pointed out in the articles cited in the preceding note. A copy of the *Argomento* is in Venice, Biblioteca Nazionale Marciana, Dramm. 909.3, while a seventeenth-century manuscript copy of the libretto is in ibid., Dramm. 909.4.

186 *Argomento et scenario* (Venice, n.p., 1640), pp. 1–2.

187 Ibid., p. 18.

188 W. Osthoff, 'Maske und Musik'; Bianconi & Walker, 'Dalla "Finta pazza" alla "Veremonda"', pp. 412–13.

189 *Argomento et scenario* (1640), pp. 23–4. Elsewhere (p. 5), the anonymous author states:

> As subject, I then decided to choose the nuptials of Aeneas and Lavinia, not knowing that it had been treated dramatically by others. Certainly I was told afterwards that it had been adopted by others, but since by last carnival I revealed the plan of my work, and then the building was constructed upon it, it did not seem appropriate to me to abandon it, rejoicing, rather, that the fact that the same material was in the hands of a

most noble and most virtuous knight showed that I had had good judgement in my choice.

The 'cavalier' could be Busenello, who in Carnival 1641 at the Teatro S. Cassiano had staged *La Didone* with music by Cavalli, another opera taken from Virgil, in the light of which the present author perhaps had cause to think again to avoid duplication.

190 Ibid., p. 3.

191 See Bianconi & Walker, 'Dalla "Finta pazza" alla "Veremonda"', pp. 410ff.

192 *Argomento et scenario* (1640), pp. 14–15, 19–20, 24–26.

193 The traditional date, 1642, should probably be taken *more veneto*, or else in view of the fact that the carnival season began in the last days of December (from the 26th) of the preceding year (thus, for example, carnival 1643 begins on 26 December 1642). In fact, the *Scenario* published in place of the libretto has the date 1643; see Pirrotta, 'Early Venetian Libretti at Los Angeles', p. 239 (id., *Music and Culture in Italy from the Middle Ages to the Baroque*, p. 454 n. 16).

194 See W. Osthoff, 'Neue Beobachtungen zu Quellen und Geschichte von Monteverdis "Incoronazione di Poppea"', pp. 134–7, and Sartori, 'La prima diva della lirica italiana', p. 446. Note, however, that the parts of Nero and Valletto were written for castratos, see Arnold, 'Monteverdi's Singers'.

195 See Chiarelli, *'L'incoronazione di Poppea o Il Nerone'*. I have most recently discussed this material in 'New Sources for "Poppea"'.

196 Chiarelli, *'L'incoronazione di Poppea o Il Nerone'*, pp. 149–51, and Bianconi, *Il Seicento*, pp. 195–6 (*Music in the Seventeenth Century*, pp. 194–5). The latest survey of the musical sources for *Poppea* – Curtis, 'La Poppea Impasticciata, or Who Wrote the Music to *L'Incoronazione* (1643)?' – comes down strongly in favour of Sacrati. A textual echo of this duet can be found in the quartet which concludes Giacomo Castoreo's *Pericle effeminato* (Venice, Giacomo Batti, 1653), performed in Venice at the Teatro S. Apollinare in 1653 with music by Francesco Luccio.

197 Bianconi, *Il Seicento*, p. 196 (*Music in the Seventeenth Century*, pp. 195–6).

198 See Von Fischer, 'Ein wenig beachtete Quelle zu Busenellos "L'incoronazione di Poppea"'.

199 Bianconi & Walker, 'Dalla "Finta pazza" alla "Veremonda"', p. 422. Badoaro and Busenello's membership of this academy is noted in ibid., pp. 421–2.

200 Brizi, 'Teoria e prassi melodrammatica di G. F. Busenello e "L'incoronazione di Poppea"', pp. 63–68. Act III scenes 2–4 includes a real trial that makes much use of legal terminology.

201 Caberloti, *Laconismo delle alte qualità di Claudio Monteverde* (1644), pp. 6–8.

202 Ibid., p. 10.

203 Ibid., pp. 10–11.

204 Sommi Picenardi, 'D'alcuni documenti concernenti Claudio Monteverde', p. 160.

205 Caberloti, *Laconismo delle alte qualità di Claudio Monteverde* (1644), pp. 11–12.

206 See Arnold, 'The Monteverdian Succession at St. Mark's'.

207 Venice, Archivio di Stato, Procuratia *de supra*, No. 144 (*Atti e terminazioni 1637–1648*), fols. 157v–158r.

208 Boschini, *La carta del navegar pitoresco* (1660), p. 364 (cited in Canal, *Della musica in Mantova*, p. 94; Vogel, 'Claudio Monteverdi', p. 406).

209 Mortari, 'Il ritratto di Claudio Monteverdi di Bernardo Strozzi'.

210 Mortari, 'Su Bernardo Strozzi', pp. 324, 330. See also id., *Bernardo Strozzi*, pp. 66, 73, 139 (Pl. 436); *La pittura a Genova e in Liguria*, ii, pp. 61, 316. Is this the portrait of Monteverdi (purchased between 1614 and 1629) that together with thirteen other portraits likewise representing celebrated composers was in the collection which decorated the music room of the electoral residence at Dresden (see Moser, *Heinrich Schütz*, p. 138, cited in Stevens (trans.), *The Letters of Claudio Monteverdi*, p. 339)?

211 Lesure, 'Un nouveau portrait de Monteverdi', p. 60.

212 Santoro, *Iconografia monteverdiana*, Pl. 2. This little portrait, which shows Monteverdi in full length, is accompanied by a dedication 'To the reverend and virtuous Don Francesco Tondini we give the pleasure of looking upon the true image and clothes of the most celebrated *maestro* who has ever flourished here for the direction of the music', and a note:

> Older than the preceding one is this *maestro* who lived a century ago, most virtuous for song, instrumental music and published compositions. Here is his portrait, taken from a painting, that is, that of the very reverend priest Claudio Monteverde, priest of Cremona, a city always inclined towards the name of the Veneto. Let us discuss him elsewhere, so much as is necessary to the glory of his merit. Claudio died in the times of Doge Erizzo, indeed in the same year as Louis XIII, King of France, departed this world, on 1 December 1643, and he was buried in S. Maria Gloriosa, called 'dei Frari', in the chapel and tomb of the Milanesi.

213 Mortari, 'Il ritratto di Claudio Monteverdi di Bernardo Strozzi', p. 206. In 1639, Paolo del Sera and his brother, Alessandro, were the dedicatees of the 'poema drammatico' for music, *La Delia o sia La Sera sposa del Sole* by Giulio Strozzi, performed at the Teatro Grimani with music by Francesco Sacrati (the libretto with the dedication was published in Venice by Giovan Pietro Pinelli in 1639).

214 Mortari, *Bernardo Strozzi*, pp. 62, 143 (Pl. 358).

215 Mortari, 'Il ritratto di Claudio Monteverdi di Bernardo Strozzi', p. 206.

216 See De Logu, 'An Unknown Portrait of Monteverdi by Domenico Feti'. Similarly unfounded is the suggestion made in Sartori, 'Nuovo volto di Monteverdi', that the picture of an unknown musician published in Einstein, *The Italian Madrigal*, ii, facing p. 724, is in fact Monteverdi.

217 Bianconi & Walker, 'Dalla "Finta pazza" alla "Veremonda"', p. 420.

218 Caffi, *Storia della musica sacra nella già cappella ducale di San Marco in Venezia dal 1318 al 1797*, i, p. 224; ii, p. 100.

219 See Chapter III, n. 131.

220 The same contrast can be found in arias by Frescobaldi (1630), Piazza (1633) and in part, Anglesi (1635), see Fabbri, Pompilio & Vassalli, 'Frescobaldi e le raccolte con composizioni a voce sola del primo Seicento'.

221 Caffi, *Storia della musica sacra nella già cappella ducale di San Marco in Venezia dal 1318 al 1797*, i, p. 251.

Works cited

Pre-1825 texts (and modern editions thereof)

Arisi F., *Cremona literata*, iii (Cremona, Pietro Ricchini, 1741)

Arrivabene L., *Della origine de' cavaglieri del Tosone e di altri ordini, de' simboli e delle imprese* (Mantua, Giacomo Ruffinello, 1589)

Arteaga S., *Le rivoluzioni del teatro musicale italiana dalla sua origine fino al presente*, i (Bologna, Carlo Trenti, 1783)

Artusi G. M., *L'Artusi, overo Delle imperfettioni della moderna musica* (Venice, Giacomo Vincenti, 1600; repr. Bologna, Forni, 1968)
  Seconda parte dell'Artusi overo Delle imperfettioni della moderna musica (Venice, Giacomo Vincenti, 1603; repr. Bologna, Forni, 1968)
  see also A. Braccino da Todi

Assandri G. B., *Gli atti della nobiliss.ᵃ academia di Cremona*, MS in Cremona, Biblioteca Governativa, Libreria Civica, Aa 4.4

Ban J. A., *Zangh-Bloemzel* (Amsterdam, Louys Elzevier, 1642); ed. F. Noske (Amsterdam, Knuf, 1969)

Banchieri A., *Conclusioni nel suono dell'organo* (Bologna, Eredi di Giovanni Rossi, 1609; repr. Bologna, Forni, 1981)
  Cartella musicale nel canto figurato fermo, et contrapunto (3rd edn. Venice, Giacomo Vincenti, 1614; repr. Bologna, Forni, 1968)
  Lettere armoniche (Bologna, Girolamo Mascherino, 1628; repr. Bologna, Forni, 1968)
  Lettere (Bologna, Nicolò Tebaldini, 1630)

Berardi A., *Ragionamenti musicali* (Bologna, Giacomo Monti, 1681)

Bettinelli S., *Delle lettere e delle arti mantovane* (Mantua, Erede di A. Pazzoni, 1774)

Bonini S., *Discorsi e regole sovra la musica*, ed. M. A. Bonino (Provo, Brigham Young University Press, 1979)

Boschini M., *La carta del navegar pitoresco* (Venice, Baba, 1660)

Braccino da Todi A. [? = G. M. Artusi], *Discorso secondo musicale* (Venice, Giacomo Vincenti, 1608; repr. Bologna, Forni, 1968)

Breve descrittione delle feste fatte dal serenissimo sig. prencipe di Mantova nel giorno natale della serenissima infanta Margherita, et nella venuta delli serenissimi prencipi di Savoia nella città di Casale per veder detta signora, et il sig. prencipe prima della lor partita per Mantova (Casale, Pantaleone Goffi, 1611)

Burney C., *A General History of Music* (London, 1789)

Caberloti M., *Laconismo delle alte qualità di Claudio Monteverde*, in G. B. Marinoni (ed.), *Fiori poetici* (Venice, Francesco Miloco, 1644), pp. 5–12

Caccini G., *Le nuove musiche (1602)*, ed. H. Wiley Hitchcock, 'Recent Researches in the Music of the Baroque Era', ix (Madison, A-R Editions, 1970)

Cerone P., *El melopeo y maestro* (Naples, I. B. Gargano & L. Nucci, 1613; repr. Bologna, Forni, 1969))

Chiabrera G., *Canzonette, rime varie, dialoghi*, ed. L. Negri (Turin, UTET, 1952)

De' Paoli D. (ed.), *Claudio Monteverdi: lettere, dediche e prefazioni* (Rome, De Santis, 1973)

De Waard C. (ed.), *Correspondance du p. Marin Mersenne religieux minime*, iv, vi (Paris, Presses Universitaires de France, 1955, 1960)

Doni G. B., *Compendio del trattato de' generi e de' modi della musica* (Rome, Andrea Fei, 1635)

    De praestantia musicae veteris libri tres (Florence, Amadore Massi, 1647; repr. Bologna, Forni, 1970; Hildesheim, Olms, 1986)

    De' trattati di musica ... tomo secondo, ed. A. F. Gori (Florence, Stamperia Imperiale, 1763)

Gerber E. L., *Historisch-biographisches Lexicon der Tonkünstler*, i (Leipzig, Breitkopf, 1790)

    Neues historisch-biographisches Lexicon der Tonkünstler, iii (Leipzig, A. Kühnel, 1813)

Gombert N., *Opera omnia*, ed. J. Schmidt-Görg, ix ('Corpus mensurabilis musicae', vi; American Institute of Musicology, 1974)

Grillo A., *Delle lettere* (Venice, Evangelista Deuchino, 1616)

Grillo G. B., *Breve trattato di quanto successe alla maestà della regina d. Margherita d'Austria* (Naples, Costantino Vitale, 1604)

Hawkins J., *A General History of the Science and Practice of Music* (London, 1776, repr. 1853)

Il corago, o vero alcune osservazioni per metter bene in scena le composizioni drammatiche, ed. P. Fabbri & A. Pompilio, 'Studi e testi per la storia della musica', iv (Florence, Olschki, 1983)

Il Verso A., *Madrigali a tre (libro II, 1605) e a cinque voci (libro XV—opera XXXVI, 1619)*, ed. L. Bianconi, 'Musiche rinascimentali siciliane', viii (Florence, Olschki, 1978)

Kircher A., *Musurgia universalis*, i (Rome, Heirs of Francesco Corbelletti, 1650)

Liberati A., *Lettere scritta ... in risposta ad una del sig. Ovidio Persapegi* (Rome, Mascardi, 1685)

MacClintock C. (trans.), *Hercole Bottrigari, 'Il Desiderio ...'; Vincenzo Giustiniani, 'Discorso sopra la musica'*, 'Musicological Studies and Documents', ix (American Institute of Musicology, 1962)

Magone G. B., *Ghirlanda mosicale* (Pavia, Giovanni Negri, 1615)

Marinoni G. B., *Fiori poetici* (Venice, Francesco Miloco, 1644)

Marsolo P. M., *Secondo libro dei madrigali a quattro voci, opera decima—1614: un madrigale a cinque voci—1604; sei concerti a una, due e tre voci—1620/24*, ed. L. Bianconi, 'Musiche rinascimentali siciliane', iv (Rome, De Santis, 1973)

Martini G. B., *Storia della musica*, ii (Bologna, Lelio Dalla Volpe, 1770)

    Esemplare o sia saggio fondamentale pratico di contrappunto sopra il canto fermo, ii (Bologna, L. Dalla Volpe, 1774; repr. Farnborough, Gregg, 1965)

Menestrier C., *Des representations en musique anciennes et modernes* (Paris, René Guignard, 1681; repr. Geneva, Minkoff, 1972)

Mersenne M., *see* De Waard

Monteverdi C., *Tutte le opere*, ed. G. F. Malipiero, 17 vols. (2/Vienna, Universal Edition, 1954–68)

    12 composizioni vocali profane e sacre (inedite) con e senza basso continuo, ed. W. Osthoff (2/Milan, 1978)

    Madrigali a 5 voci: libro secondo, ed. A. M. Monterosso Vacchelli (Cremona, Fondazione Claudio Monteverdi, 1979)

    see De' Paoli; Stevens

Pari C., *Il lamento d'Arianna: quarto libro dei madrigali a cinque voci (1619)*, ed. P. E. Carapezza (Rome, De Santis, 1970)

Pitoni G. O., *Guida armonica . . . Libro primo* (Rome, c.1690)

Priuli G., *Diari*, MS in Venice, Biblioteca Nazionale Marciana, MS It. VII.2492(= 10145)

Quadrio F. S., *Della storia e della ragione d'ogni poesia*, v (Milan, Francesco Agnelli, 1744); vii (Milan, Antonio Agnelli, 1752)

Schuetz [Schütz] H., *Sämmtliche Werke*, ed. P. Spitta, ii (Leipzig, Breitkopf & Härtel, 1888)

Segarizzi A. (ed.), *Relazioni degli ambasciatori veneti al senato* (Bari, Laterza, 1913)

Solerti A. (ed.), *Le rime di Torquato Tasso: edizione critica su i manoscritti e le antiche stampe* (Bologna, Romagnoli–Dall'Acqua, 1898)

Spagna A., *Oratorii overo melodrammi sacri con un discorso dogmatico intorno l'istessa materia*, i (Rome, Buagni, 1706)

Stevens D. (trans.), *The Letters of Claudio Monteverdi* (London, Faber, 1980)

Strozzi G. B. 'il vecchio', *Madrigali inediti*, ed. M. Ariani (Urbino, Argalia, 1975)

Tevo Z., *Il musico testore* (Venice, Antonio Bartoli, 1706)

Vasari G., *Le vite de' più eccellenti pittori, scultori ed architettori*, ed. G. Milanesi, vi (Florence, Sansoni, 1906)

Zacconi L., *Prattica di musica*, i (Venice, Girolamo Polo, 1592); ii (Venice, Alessandro Vincenti, 1622; repr. Hildesheim, Olms, 1982)

Post-1825 texts

Ademollo A., *La bell'Adriana ed altre virtuose del suo tempo alla corte di Mantova* (Città di Castello, 1888)

Annibaldi C., 'L'archivio musicale Doria Pamphilj: saggio sulla cultura aristocratica a Rome fra 16° e 19° secolo', *Studi musicali*, xi (1982), 91–120; 277–344

Antonicek T., 'Claudio Monteverdi und Österreich', *Österreichische Musikzeitschrift*, xxvi (1971), 266–71

Arkwright G. E. P., 'An English Pupil of Monteverdi', *The Musical Antiquary*, iv (1912–13), 236–41

Arnold D., 'The Monteverdian Succession at St. Mark's', *Music & Letters*, xlii (1961), 205–11

'Monteverdi's Singers', *The Musical Times*, cxi (1970), 982–5

Monteverdi (2nd edn. London, Dent, 1975; 3rd edn. rev. Tim Carter, London, Dent, 1990)

Arnold D. & Fortune N. (eds.), *The Monteverdi Companion* (London, Faber, 1968); rev. as *The New Monteverdi Companion* (London, Faber, 1985)

Barblan G., 'La vita di Claudio Monteverdi', in *Claudio Monteverdi nel quarto centenario della nascita* (Turin, ERI, 1967), pp. 7–148

'Un ignoto "Lamento d'Arianna" mantovano', *Rivista italiana di musicologia*, ii (1967), 217–28

Basso A., *Frau Musika: la vita e le opere di J. S. Bach* (Turin, EDT, 1979)

Becker H. (ed.), *Quellentexte zur Konzeption der europäischen Oper im 17. Jahrhundert* (Kassel, Bärenreiter, 1981)

Benvenuti G., 'Il ritorno di Ulisse in patria non è di Monteverdi', *Il gazzettino*, 17 May 1942

Bertolotti A., *Musici alla corte dei Gonzaga in Mantova dal secolo XV al XVIII: notizie e documenti raccolti negli archivi mantovani* (Milan, Ricordi, [1890]; repr. Bologna, Forni, 1969)

Bevilacqua E., 'Giambattista Andreini e la Compagnia dei "Fedeli"', *Giornale storico della letteratura italiana*, xxiii (1894), 76–155; xxiv (1894), 82–165

Bianconi L., 'Caletti [Caletti–Bruni], Pietro Francesco, detto Cavalli', in *Dizionario biografico degli italiani*, xvi (Rome, Instituto per l'Enciclopedia italiana, 1973), pp. 686–96

'*Ah dolente partita*: espressione ed artificio', *Studi musicali*, iii (1974), 105–30

'Claudio Monteverdi', in *Enciclopedia europea*, vii (Milan, Garzanti, 1978), pp. 771–3

Il Seicento (Turin, Edizioni di Torino, 1982); trans. David Bryant as *Music in the Seventeenth Century* (Cambridge University Press, 1987)

Bianconi L. & Walker T., 'Dalla "Finta pazza" alla "Veremonda": storie di Febi-armonici', *Rivista italiana di musicologia*, x (1975), 379–454

'Production, Consumption and Political Function of Seventeenth-Century Opera', *Early Music History*, iv (1984), 209–96

Biella G., 'La "Messa", il "Vespro" e i "Sacri concenti" di Claudio Monteverdi nella stampa Amadino dell'anno 1610', *Musica sacra*, II/ix (1964), 104–15

Blazey David, 'A Liturgical Role for Monteverdi's *Sonata sopra Sancta Maria*', *Early Music*, xvii (1989), 175–82

Bonta S., 'Liturgical Problems in Monteverdi's Marian Vespers', *Journal of the American Musicological Society*, xx (1967), 87–106

Brizi B., 'Teoria e prassi melodrammatica di G. F. Busenello e "L'incoronazione di Poppea"', in Muraro (ed.), *Venezia e il melodramma nel Seicento*, pp. 51–74

Caffi F., *Storia della musica sacra nella già cappella ducale di San Marco in Venezia dal 1318 al 1797* (Venice, G. Antonelli, 1854–55)

Canal P., *Della musica in Mantova: notizie tratte principalmente dall'archivio Gonzaga* (2nd edn. Venice, 1881; repr. Bologna, Forni, 1977)

Carapezza P. E., 'L'ultimo oltramontano o vero l'antimonteverdi', *Nuova rivista musicale italiana*, iv (1970), 213–43, 411–44

'"O soave armonia": classicità maniera e barocco nella scuola polifonica siciliana', *Studi musicali*, iii (1974), 347–90

Carter T., 'A Florentine Wedding of 1608', *Acta musicologica*, lv (1983), 89–107

'Artusi, Monteverdi, and the Poetics of Modern Music', in N. K. Baker and B. R. Hanning (eds.), *Musical Humanism and its Legacy: Essays in Honor of Claude V. Palisca* (Stuyvesant, New York, Pendragon, 1992), pp. 171–94

Cavicchi A., review of *C. Monteverdi: Lamento d'Arianna*, ed. N. Anfuso & A. Gianuario (Florence, OTOS, 1969), in *Rivista italiana di musicologia*, ix (1974), 306–12

'Per far piú grande la meraviglia dell'arte', in *Frescobaldi e il suo tempo nel quarto centenario della nascita* (Venice, Marsilio, 1983), pp. 15–39

Cesari G. (ed.), *La musica in Cremona nella seconda metà del secolo XVI e i primordi dell'arte monteverdiana* (Milan, Ricordi, 1939)

Chabod F., *Lo stato e la vita religiosa a Milano nell'epoca di Carlo V* (Turin, Einaudi, 1971)

Chiarelli A., '*L'incoronazione di Poppea* o *Il Nerone*: problemi di filologia testuale', *Rivista italiana di musicologia*, ix (1974), 117–51

Cicogna E. A., *Saggio di bibliografia veneziana* (Venice, Merlo, 1847)

Culley T. D., *Jesuits and Music*, i: *A Study of the Musicians Connected with the German College in Rome during the 17th Century and of their Activities in Northern Europe* (Rome, Jesuit Historical Institute, 1970)

Curtis A., '*La Poppea Impasticciata*, or Who Wrote the Music to *L'incoronazione* (1643)?', *Journal of the American Musicological Society*, xlii (1989), 23–54

Danckwardt M., 'Das Lamento d'Olimpia "Voglio voglio morir": Eine Komposition Claudio Monteverdis?', *Archiv für Musikwissenschaft*, xli (1984), 149–75

Davari S., 'Notizie biografiche del distinto maestro di musica Claudio Monteverdi, desunte dai documenti dell'Archivio storico Gonzaga', *Atti e memorie della R. Accademia virgiliana di Mantova*, x (1884–5), 79–183

De Logu G., 'An Unknown Portrait of Monteverdi by Domenico Feti', *The Burlington Magazine*, cix (1967), 706–9

De' Paoli D., *Monteverdi* (Milan, Hoepli, 1945)
Monteverdi (Milan, Rusconi, 1979)

Dixon G., 'Monteverdi's Vespers of 1610: "della Beata Vergine"?', *Early Music*, xv (1987), 386–9

Durante S., 'La "Guida armonica" di Giuseppe Ottavio Pitoni: un documento sugli stili musicali in uso a Roma al tempo di Corelli', in S. Durante & P. Petrobelli (eds.), *Nuovissimi studi corelliani: atti del terzo congresso internazionale (Fusignano, 4–7 Settembre 1980)* (Florence, Olschki, 1982), pp. 285–327

Einstein A., *The Italian Madrigal* (Princeton University Press, 1949)
'Abbot Angelo Grillo's Letters as Source Material for Music History', in id., *Essays on Music* (2nd edn. London, 1958), pp. 159–78

Engel H., 'Marc Antonio Ingegneri' in *Die Musik in Geschichte und Gegenwart*, vi (Kassel, Bärenreiter, 1957), coll. 1210–15

Errante V., 'Forse che sí, forse che no', *Archivio storico lombardo*, xlii (1915), 15–114

Evangelista A., 'Il teatro della Dogana detto di Baldracca', in *Il potere e lo spazio: la scena del principe* (Florence, Electa, 1980), pp. 370–74

Fabbri P., *Gusto scenico a Mantova nel tardo rinascimento* (Padua, Liviana, 1974)
'Tasso, Guarini e il "divino Claudio": componenti manieristiche nella poetica di Monteverdi', *Studi musicali*, iii (1974), 233–54
'Inediti monteverdiani', *Rivista italiana di musicologia*, xv (1980), 71–85
'Il soggiorno veneziano di Ladislao, principe di Polonia: un incontro con Claudio Monteverdi', *Subsidia musica veneta*, iii (1982), 27–52
Tre secoli di musica a Ravenna dalla Controriforma alla caduta dell'Antico Regime (Ravenna, Longo, 1983)
'Lessico monteverdiano: intorno al "genere rappresentativo"', in F. Passadore (ed.), *La musica nel veneto dal XVI al XVIII secolo* (Adria, AMIS, 1984), pp. 89–97
'Striggio e l'*Orfeo*', in L. Berio (ed.), *Musicacittà* (Rome–Bari, Laterza, 1984), pp. 203–13
'I Campi e la Cremona musicale del Cinquecento', in *I Campi e la cultura artistica cremonese del Cinquecento* (Milan, Electa, 1985), pp. 19–24
'Politica editoriale e musica strumentale in Italia dal Cinque al Settecento', *Recercare*, iii (1991), 202–16
'New Sources for "Poppea"', *Music & Letters*, lxxiv (1993), 16–23

Fabbri P., Pompilio A. & Vassalli A., 'Frescobaldi e le raccolte con composizioni a voce sola del primo Seicento', in S. Durante & D. Fabris (eds.), *Girolamo Frescobaldi nel IV centenario della nascita: atti del convegno internazionale di studi (Ferrara, 9–14 settembre 1983)* (Florence, Olschki, 1986), pp. 233–60

Faccioli E. (ed.), *Mantova: le lettere*, ii (Mantua, Istituto Carlo d'Arco per la Storia di Mantova, 1962)

Fantoni G., *Storia universale del canto*, i (Milan, Battezzati, 1873)

Federhofer H., 'Graz Court Musicians and their Contributions to the "Parnassus Musicus Ferdinandaeus" (1615)', *Musica disciplina*, ix (1955), 167–244

Fenlon I., 'The Monteverdi Vespers: Suggested Answers to Some Fundamental Questions', *Early Music*, v (1977), 380–87
'Monteverdi's Mantuan *Orfeo*: Some New Documentation', *Early Music*, xii (1984), 163–72

Ferrari Barassi E., 'Il madrigale spirituale nel Cinquecento e la raccolta monteverdiana del 1583', in Monterosso (ed.), *Congresso internazionale sul tema 'Claudio Monteverdi e il suo tempo'*, pp. 217–52

Fétis F.-J., *Biographie universelle des musiciens et bibliographie générale de la musique*, i (2nd edn. Paris, Didot, 1860)

Finscher L. (ed.), *Claudio Monteverdi: Festschrift Reinhold Hammerstein zum 70. Geburtstag* (Laaber, Laaber-Verlag, 1986)

Von Fischer K., 'Ein wenig beachtete Quelle zu Busenellos "L'incoronazione di Poppea"', in Monterosso (ed.), *Congresso internazionale sul tema 'Claudio Monteverdi e il suo tempo'*, pp. 75–80

Fortune N., 'Italian Secular Monody from 1600 to 1635: an Introductory Survey', *The Musical Quarterly*, xxxix (1953), 171–95

Gallico C., 'Newly Discovered Documents Concerning Monteverdi', *The Musical Quarterly*, xlviii (1962), 68–72

'Dimore mantovane di Claudio Monteverdi', *Civiltà mantovana*, i/1 (1966), 27–31

'Monteverdi e i dazi di Viadana', *Rivista italiana di musicologia*, i (1966), 242–5

'Emblemi strumentali negli "Scherzi" di Monteverdi', *Rivista italiana di musicologia*, ii (1967), 54–73

'La "Lettera amorosa" di Monteverdi e lo stile rappresentativo', *Nuova rivista musicala italiana*, i (1967), 287–302

'"Contra Claudium Montiuiridum"', *Rivista italiana di musicologia*, x (1975), 346–59

'Guglielmo Gonzaga signore della musica', *Nuova rivista musicale italiana*, xi (1977), 321–34

Monteverdi: poesia musicale, teatro e musica sacra (Turin, Einaudi, 1979)

Damon pastor gentil: idilli cortesi e voci popolari nelle 'Villotte mantovane' (1583) (Mantua, Arcari, 1980)

Ghisi F., 'Firenze', in *Enciclopedia dello spettacolo*, v (Rome, Le Maschere, 1958), coll. 372–95

Gianturco C., *Claudio Monteverdi: stile e struttura* (Pisa, Editrice Tecnico-Scientifica, 1978)

Giazotto R., *La musica a Genova nella vita pubblica e privata dal XIII al XVIII secolo* (Genoa, Comune di Genova, 1951)

Quattro secoli di storia dell'Accademia Nazionale di Santa Cecilia (Rome, Accademia Nazionale di Santa Cecilia, 1970)

Glixon J., 'Was Monteverdi a Traitor?', *Music & Letters*, lxxii (1991), 404–6

Guerrini P., 'Canzoni spirituali del Cinquecento', *Santa Cecilia*, xxiv (1922), 6–8

Hanning B. R., 'Alessandro Striggio', in S. Sadie (ed.), *The New Grove Dictionary of Music and Musicians* (London, Macmillan, 1980), xviii, p. 274

Henze-Doehring S., 'Eine Libretti Sammlung in der Musikgeschichtlichen Abteilung des Deutschen Historischen Instituts in Rom', *Die Musikforschung*, xxxviii (1985), 202–3

Hucke H., 'Die fälslich so genannten "Marien"-Vesper von Claudio Monteverdi', in C. H. Mahling & S. Wiesmann (eds.), *Bericht über den internationalen musikwissenschaftlichen Kongress Bayreuth 1981* (Kassel & Basel, Bärenreiter, [1983]), pp. 295–305

Hughes C. W., 'Porter, Pupil of Monteverdi', *The Musical Quarterly*, xx (1934), 278–88

Il luogo teatrale a Firenze (Milan, Electa, 1975)

Imperiale G. V., *Viaggi*, ed. A. G. Barrili, 'Atti della Società Ligure di Storia Patria', xxix (1898), 5–279

Ivaldi A. F., 'Gli Adorno e l'hostaria–teatro del Falcone di Genova (1600–1680)', *Rivista italiana di musicologia*, xv (1980), 87–152

Jonckbloet W. J. A. & Land J. P. N. (eds.), *Musique et musiciens au XVIIe siècle: correspondance et oeuvre musicales de Constantin Huygens* (Leyden, Brill, 1882)

Kinsky G., *Versteigerung von Musikbüchern praktischer Musik und Musiker-Autographen des 16. bis 18. Jahrhunderts aus dem Nachlass des Herrn Kommerzienrates Wilhelm Heyer in Köln* (Berlin, 1927)

Kirkendale W., 'Zur Biographie des ersten Orfeo, Francesco Rasi', in Finscher (ed.), *Claudio Monteverdi*, pp. 297–335

Kurtzman J. G., 'An Early 17th-Century Manuscript of *Canzonette e madrigaletti spirituali*', *Studi musicali*, viii (1979), 149–71

'Some Historical Perspectives on the Monteverdi Vespers', *Analecta musicologica*, xv (1975), 29–86 (a version is also in id., *Essays on the Monteverdi Mass and Vespers of 1610* (Houston, Rice University Press, 1979), pp. 123–82)

La pittura a Genova e in Liguria, ii (Genoa, Sagep, 1971)

Lavin I., 'Lettres de Parmes (1618, 1627–28) et débuts du théâtre baroque', in J. Jacquot (ed.), *Le Lieu théâtral à la Renaissance* (Paris, Centre National de la Recerche Scientifique, 1964), pp. 105–58

Lesure F., 'Un nouveau portrait de Monteverdi', *Revue de musicologie*, liii (1967), 60

MacClintock C., *Giaches de Wert (1535–1596): Life and Works*, 'Musicological Studies and Documents', xvii (American Institute of Musicology, 1966)

'New Sources of Mantuan Music', *Journal of the American Musicological Society*, xxii (1969), 508–11

Marani E. & Perina C. (eds.), *Mantova: le arti*, iii (Mantua, Istituto Carlo d'Arco per la Storia di Mantova, 1965)

Martini A., 'Ritratto del madrigale poetico fra Cinque e Seicento', *Lettere italiane*, xxxiii (1981), 529–48

Martinoni R., 'Lettere di Bernardo Morando a Gian Vincenzo Imperiale', *Studi secenteschi*, xxiv (1983), 187–219

Maylender M., *Storia delle accademie d'Italia*, iii (Bologna, Cappelli, 1929)

Mazzoldi L., Giusti R. & Salvatori R. (eds.), *Mantova: la storia*, iii (Mantua, Istituto Carlo d'Arco per la Storia di Mantova, 1963)

Medici M. & Conati M. (eds.), *Carteggio Verdi–Boito* (Parma, Istituto di Studi Verdiani, 1978)

Mischiati O., *La prassi musicale presso i Canonici regolari del Ss. Salvatore nei secoli XVI e XVII e i manoscritti polifonici della biblioteca musicale 'G. B. Martini' di Bologna* (Rome, Edizioni Torre d'Orfeo, 1985)

Monterosso R. (ed.), *Congresso internazionale sul tema 'Claudio Monteverdi e il suo tempo': relazioni e comunicazioni* (Venice, Mantua & Cremona, 1968)

Monterosso R. et al. (eds.), *Mostra bibliografica dei musicisti cremonesi* (Cremona, Biblioteca Governativa e Libreria Civica, 1951)

Moore J. H., '*Venezia favorita da Maria*: Music for the Madonna Nicopeia and Santa Maria della Salute', *Journal of the American Musicological Society*, xxxvii (1984), 299–355

Mortari L., 'Su Bernardo Strozzi', *Bollettino d'arte*, xl (1955), 311–31

Bernardo Strozzi (Rome, De Luca, 1966)

'Il ritratto di Claudio Monteverdi di Bernardo Strozzi', *Arte veneta*, xxxi (1977), 205–7

Moser H. J., *Heinrich Schütz: his Life and Work* (St Louis, 1959)

Mueller R. C. & Preto P., 'Peste e demografia', in *Venezia e la peste: 1348–1797* (Venice, Marsilio, 1979), pp. 93–98

Müller-Blattau J. M. (ed.), *Die Kompositionslehre Heinrich Schützens in der Fassung seines Schülers Christoph Bernhard* (Leipzig, Breitkopf & Härtel, 1926)

M[uraro] M. T., 'Venezia', in *Enciclopedia dello spettacolo*, ix (Rome, Le Maschere, 1962), coll. 1530–57

Muraro M. T. (ed.), *Studi sul teatro veneto fra rinascimento ed età barocca*, 'Civiltà veneziana studi', xxiv (Florence, Olschki, 1971)

Venezia e il melodramma nel Seicento, 'Studi di musica veneta', v (Florence, Olschki, 1976)

Neri A., 'Gabriello Chiabrera e la corte di Mantova', *Giornale storico della letteratura italiana*, vii (1886), 317–44

'Gli "Intermezzi" del "Pastor Fido"', *Giornale storico della letteratura italiana*, xi (1888), 405–15

Newcomb A., 'Alfonso Fontanelli and the Ancestry of the Seconda Pratica Madrigal', in R. L. Marshall (ed.), *Studies in Renaissance and Baroque Music in Honor of Arthur Mendel* (Kassel, Bärenreiter, 1974), pp. 47–68

The Madrigal at Ferrara, 1579–1597 (Princeton University Press, 1980)

Niero A., 'I templi del Redentore e della Salute: motivazioni teologiche', in *Venezia e la peste: 1348–1797* (Venice, Marsilio, 1979), pp. 294–8

Noske F., 'An Unknown Work by Monteverdi: the Vespers of St. John the Baptist', *Music & Letters*, lxvi (1985), 118–22

Ortolani G., 'Venezia al tempo di Monteverdi', *La rassegna musicale*, ii (1929), 469–82

Osthoff H., 'Gedichte von Tomaso Stigliani auf Giulio Caccini, Claudio Monteverdi, Santino Garsi da Parma und Claudio Merulo', in *Miscelànea en homenaje a monseñor Higinio Anglés* (Barcelona, Consejo superior de investigaziones cientificas, 1958–61), ii, pp. 615–21

Osthoff W., 'Zu den Quellen von Monteverdis "Ritorno di Ulisse in patria"', *Studien zur Musikwissenschaft*, xxiii (1956), 67–78

'Neue Beobachtungen zu Quellen und Geschichte von Monteverdis "Incoronazione di Poppea"', *Die Musikforschung*, xi (1958), 129–38

'Zur Bologneser Aufführung von Monteverdis "Ritorno di Ulisse" im Jahre 1640', *Österreichische Akademie der Wissenschaften: Anzeiger der phil.–hist. Klasse*, xcv (1958), 155–60

'Maske und Musik: die Gestaltwerdung der Oper in Venedig', *Castrum Peregrini*, lxv (1964), 10–49 (translated into Italian as 'Maschera e musica', *Nuova rivista musicale italiana*, i (1967), pp. 16–44)

'Unità liturgica e artistica nei "Vespri" del 1610', *Rivista italiana di musicologia*, ii (1967), 314–27

Paganuzzi E., 'Medioevo e Rinascimento', in *La musica a Verona* (Verona, Banca Mutua Popolare di Verona, 1976)

Palisca C. V., 'Marco Scacchi's Defense of Modern Music (1649)', in L. Berman (ed.), *Words and Music, the Scholar's View: a Medley of Problems and Solutions Compiled in Honor of A. Tillmann Merritt by Sundry Hands* (Cambridge, Mass., Department of Music, Harvard University, 1972), pp. 189–235

'The Artusi–Monteverdi Controversy' in Arnold & Fortune (eds.), *The New Monteverdi Companion*, pp. 127–58

Pannain G., 'Studi monteverdiani: ix', *La rassegna musicale*, xxx (1960), 24–32

Parisi S., 'Licenza alla Mantovana: Frescobaldi and the Recruitment of Musicians for Mantua, 1612–15', in A. Silberger (ed.), *Frescobaldi Studies* (Durham, NC, Duke University Press, 1987), pp. 55–91

Ducal Patronage of Music in Mantua, 1587–1627: an Archival Study (Ph.D. dissertation, University of Illinois, 1989)

Petrobelli P., 'L'"Ermiona" di Pio Enea degli Obizzi ed i primi spettacoli d'opera veneziani', *Quaderni della Rassegna musicale*, iii (1965), 125–41

'Francesco Manelli: documenti e osservazioni', *Chigiana*, xxiv (1967), 43–66

'"Ah, dolente partita": Marenzio, Wert, Monteverdi', in Monterosso (ed.), *Congresso internazionale sul tema 'Claudio Monteverdi e il suo tempo'*, pp. 361–76

Pirrotta N., 'Scelte poetiche di Monteverdi', *Nuova rivista musicale italiana*, ii (1968), 10–42, 226–54; trans. as 'Monteverdi's Poetic Choices' in *Music and Culture in Italy from the Middle Ages to the Baroque*, pp. 271–316

'Teatro, scene e musica nelle opere di Monteverdi', in Monterosso (ed.), *Congresso internazionale sul tema 'Claudio Monteverdi e il suo tempo'*, pp. 45–67; trans. as 'Theater, Sets, and Music in Monteverdi's Operas' in *Music and Culture in Italy from the Middle Ages to the Baroque*, pp. 254–70

'Early Venetian Libretti at Los Angeles', in G. Reese & R. J. Snow (eds.), *Essays in*

Musicology in Honor of Dragan Plamenac on his 70th Birthday (Pittsburgh, University of Pittsburgh Press, 1969; repr. New York, Da Capo, 1977), pp. 233–43; also in *Music and Culture in Italy from the Middle Ages to the Baroque*, pp. 317–24

'Monteverdi e i problemi dell'opera', in Muraro (ed.), *Studi sul teatro veneto fra rinascimento ed età barocca*, pp. 321–43; trans. as 'Monteverdi and the Problems of Opera' in *Music and Culture in Italy from the Middle Ages to the Baroque*, pp. 235–53

Li due Orfei: da Poliziano a Monteverdi (2nd edn. Turin, Einaudi, 1975); trans. by K. Eales as *Music and Theatre from Poliziano to Monteverdi* (Cambridge University Press, 1980)

'Il luogo dell'orchestra', in F. Mancini, M. T. Muraro & E. Povoledo (eds.), *Illusione e pratica teatrale: proposte per una lettura dello spazio scenico dagli intermedi fiorentini all'opera comica veneziana* (Vicenza, Neri Pozza, 1975), pp. 137–43

Music and Culture in Italy from the Middle Ages to the Baroque: a Collection of Essays (Cambridge, Mass., Harvard University Press, 1984): including (pp. 217–34) 'Temperaments and Tendencies in the Florentine Camerata'; (pp. 235–53) 'Monteverdi and the Problems of Opera'; (pp. 254–70) 'Theater, Sets, and Music in Monteverdi's Operas'; (pp. 271–316) 'Monteverdi's Poetic Choices'

Pompilio A., 'Editoria musicale a Napoli e in Italia nel Cinque–Seicento', in L. Bianconi & R. Bossa (eds.), *Musica e cultura a Napoli dal XV al XIX secolo* (Florence, Olschki, 1983), pp. 79–102

Pontiroli G., 'Notizie di musicisti cremonesi nel secoli XVI e XVII', *Bollettino storico cremonese*, xxii (1961–4), 149–92

'Notizie sui Monteverdi, su personaggi ed artisti del loro ambiente e la casa natale di Claudio: spogli d'archivio', *Bollettino storico cremonese*, xxiii (1965–8), 157–221

'Casa natale de Claudio Monteverdi e ampliamento dell'albero genealogico della famiglia Monteverdi', *Archivio storico lombardo*, v–vi (1966–7), 248–58

'Nuove ricerche sui Monteverdi: Filippo, fratello del musico Claudio, chirurgo maggiore dell'Ospedale "S. Maria di Pietà" in Cremona', *Bollettino storico cremonese*, xxiv (1969), 267–77

'Della famiglia di Claudio Monteverdi: parentele e relazioni', *Bollettino storico cremonese*, xxv (1970–71), 45–68

Povoledo E., 'Ferrara', in *Enciclopedia dello spettacolo*, v (Rome, Le Maschere, 1958), coll. 173–85

'Guitti, Francesco', in *Enciclopedia dello spettacolo*, vi (Rome, Le Maschere, 1959), coll. 68–72

'Una rappresentazione accademica a Venezia nel 1634', in Muraro (ed.), *Studi sul teatro veneto fra rinascimento ed età barocca*, pp. 119–69

Povoledo E. *et al.*, 'Orchestra', in *Enciclopedia dello spettacolo*, vii (Rome, Le Maschere, 1960), coll. 1386–96

Preto P., 'Le grandi pesti dell'età moderna: 1575–77 e 1630–31', in *Venezia e la peste: 1348–1797* (Venice, Marsilio, 1979), pp. 123–6

'Una denuncia anonima contro Claudio Monteverdi', *Rassegna veneta di studi musicali*, v–vi (1989–90), 371–3

Prunières H., 'Monteverdi and French Music', *The Sackbut*, iii (1922–3), 98–110

La vie et l'oeuvre de Claudio Monteverdi (Paris, Librairie de France, 1926); trans. Marie D. Mackie as *Monteverdi, his Life and Work* (London, Dent, 1926; repr. New York, Dover, 1972)

'Monteverdi e la musica francese del suo tempo', *La rassegna musicale*, ii (1929), 483–93

Redlich H. F., *Claudio Monteverdi: ein formgeschichtlicher Versuch; das Madrigalwerk*, i (Berlin, 1932)

'Monteverdi', in *Die Musik in Geschichte und Gegenwart*, ix (Kassel, Bärenreiter, 1961), coll. 511–31

Reese G., *Music in the Renaissance* (New York, Norton, 1954)

Reiner S., 'Preparations in Parma – 1618, 1627–28', *The Music Review*, xxv (1964), 273–301

'La vag'Angioletta (and others): i', *Analecta Musicologica*, xiv (1974), 26–88

Roncaglia G., 'Di Bellerofonte Castaldi (con un documento inedito)', *Deputazione di storia patria per le antiche provincie modenesi: atti e memorie*, viii/x (1958), 117–23

Rosand E., 'Barbara Strozzi, "virtuosissima cantatrice": the Composer's Voice', *Journal of the American Musicological Society*, xxxi (1978), 241–81

Rosenthal A., 'Monteverdi's "Andromeda": a Lost Libretto Found', *Music & Letters*, lxvi (1985), 1–8

Rossetti A. M., 'Una corrispondenza inedita di Marco da Gagliano', unpublished paper

Santoro E., *La famiglia e la formazione di Claudio Monteverdi: note biografiche con documenti inediti*, 'Annali della Biblioteca governativa e libreria civica di Cremona', xviii (Cremona, Athenaeum cremonense, 1967)

Iconografia monteverdiana, 'Annali della Biblioteca governativa e libreria civica di Cremona', xix (Cremona, Athenaeum cremonense, 1968)

'La casa natale dei Monteverdi nel quartiere Piazano', *Colloqui cremonesi*, i (1968), 35–47

Sartori C., 'Monteverdiana', *The Musical Quarterly*, xxxviii (1952), 399–413

'Nuovo volto di Monteverdi', *La Scala*, iv (1952), 46–48

'Mantua', in *Die Musik in Geschichte und Gegenwart*, viii (Kassel, Bärenreiter, 1960), coll. 1602–5

'La prima diva della lirica italiana: Anna Renzi', *Nuova rivista musicale italiana*, ii (1968), 430–52

Schizzerotto G., *Rubens a Mantova fra gesuiti, principi e pittori, con spigolature sul suo soggiorno italiano (1600–1608)* (Mantua, 1979)

Schrade L., *Monteverdi: Creator of Modern Music* (New York, Norton, 1950; repr. New York, 1979)

Seifert H., 'Marcus Sitticus von Hohenems und Mantua', *Studien zur Musik im Bodenseeraum*, forthcoming

Selfridge-Field E., *Venetian Instrumental Music from Gabrieli to Vivaldi* (Oxford, Blackwell, 1975)

Simon-Gidrol R., 'Appunti sulle relazioni tra l'opera poetica di G. B. Marino e la musica del suo tempo', *Studi secenteschi*, xiv (1973), 81–187

Solerti A., *Gli albori del melodramma* (Turin, Bocca, 1903; repr. Hildesheim, G. Olms, 1969)

Le origini del melodramma; testimonianze dei contemporanei (Turin, Bocca, 1903; repr. Hildesheim, G. Olms, 1969)

'Precedenti del melodramma', *Rivista musicale italiana*, x (1903), 225–30

'Un balletto musicato da Claudio Monteverdi sconosciuto a' suoi biografi', *Rivista musicale italiana*, vii (1904), 24–34

Musica, ballo e drammatica alla corte medicea dal 1600 al 1637 (Florence, Bemporad, 1905; repr. Hildesheim, G. Olms, 1969)

Sommi Picenardi G., 'D'alcuni documenti concernenti Claudio Monteverde', *Archivio storico lombardo*, xxii/4 (1895), 154–62

'Claudio Monteverdi a Cremona', *Gazzetta musicale di Milano*, li (1896), 473–6, 490–92, 501–3, 517–19

Stevens D., '"Madrigali Guerrieri, et Amorosi"', in Arnold & Fortune (eds.), *The Monteverdi Companion*, pp. 227–54

Monteverdi: Sacred, Secular, and Occasional Music (Cranbury, N.J., & London, Associated University Press, 1978)

'Monteverdi, Petratti, and the Duke of Bracciano', *The Musical Quarterly*, lxiv (1978), 275–94

Strainchamps E., 'The Life and Death of Caterina Martinelli: New Light on Monteverdi's "Arianna"', *Early Music History*, v (1985), 155–86

Strohm R., 'Osservazioni su "Tempo la cetra"', *Rivista italiana di musicologia*, ii (1967), 357–64

Strunk O., *Source Readings in Music History* (London, Faber, 1952)

Szweykowska A., 'Le due poetiche venete e le ultime opera di Claudio Monteverdi', *Quadrivium*, xx (1977), 149–57

Szweykowski Z. M., '"Ah, dolente partita": Monteverdi–Scacchi', *Quadrivium*, xii/2 (1971), 59–76

Tagmann P., *Archivalische Studien zur Musikpflege am Dom von Mantua (1500–1627)* (Bern–Stuttgart, Haupt, 1967)

'La cappella dei maestri cantori della basilica palatina di Santa Barbara a Mantova (1565–1630): nuovo materiale scoperto negli archivi mantovani', *Civiltà mantovana*, iv (1969), 376–400

'The Palace Church of Santa Barbara in Mantua, and Monteverdi's Relationship to its Liturgy', in B. L. Karson (ed), *Festival Essays for Pauline Alderman* (Brigham Young University Press, 1976), pp. 53–60

Thoinan E., *André Maugars* (Paris, Claudin, 1865)

Tiepolo M. F., 'Minima monteverdiana', *Rassegna degli archivi di stato*, xxix (1969), 135–43

Tomlinson G., 'Twice Bitten, Thrice Shy: Monteverdi's "finta" *Finta pazza*', *Journal of the American Musicological Society*, xxxvi (1983), 303–11

Vecchi G., *Le accademie musicali del primo Seicento e Monteverdi a Bologna* (Bologna, AMIS, 1969)

Vio G., 'Ultimi ragguagli monteverdiani', *Rassegna veneta di studi musicali*, ii–iii (1986–7), 347–64

'Musici veneziani dei primi decenni del Seicento: discordie e bustarelle', *Rassegna veneta di studi musicali*, v–vi (1989–90), 375–85

Vitali C., 'Una lettera vivaldiana perduta e ritrovata, un inedito monteverdiano del 1630 e altri carteggi di musicisti celebri, ovvero splendori e nefandezze del collezionismo di autografi', *Nuova rivista musicale italiana*, xiv (1980), 404–12

Vita religiosa a Cremona nel Cinquecento: mostra di documenti e arredi sacri (Cremona, Archivio di Stato e Archivio della Curia Vescovile, 1985)

Vogel E., 'Claudio Monteverdi: Leben, Wirken im Lichte der zeitgenössischen Kritik und Verzeichnis seiner im Druck erschienenen Werke', *Vierteljahrsschrift für Musikwissenschaft*, iii (1887), 315–450

'Marco da Gagliano: zur Geschichte des florentiner Musiklebens von 1570–1650', *Vierteljahrsschrift für Musikwissenschaft*, v (1889), 396–442, 509–68

Walker T., 'Gli errori di "Minerva al tavolino"', in Muraro (ed.), *Venezia e il melodramma nel Seicento*, pp. 7–20

Willetts P. J., 'A Neglected Source of Monody and Madrigal', *Music & Letters*, xliii (1962), 329–39

Z[anetti] E., 'Virginia A[ndreini] Ramponi', in *Enciclopedia dello spettacolo*, i (Rome, Le Maschere, 1954), coll. 564–5

Zoppelli L., 'Il rapto perfettissimo: un'inedita testimonianza sulla "Proserpina" di Monteverdi', *Rassegna veneta di studi musicali*, ii–iii (1986–7), 343–5

Index of Monteverdi's works

This index fulfils a double function, providing references to Monteverdi's works mentioned in this book, and serving as an integrated list of those works in alphabetical order of first lines (including the few not discussed here). It gives only principal sources: fuller details (and other sources) can be found in Manfred Stattkus, *Claudio Monteverdi: Verzeichnis der erhaltenen Werke* (Bergkamen, Musikverlag Stattkus, 1985). The *sigla* for referring to prints (all printed in Venice except where stated otherwise) and manuscripts follow Stattkus where possible.

Prints

ADD	Alessandro Vincenti (ed.), *Arie de diversi* (1634)
ARV	Carlo Milanuzzi, *Quarto scherzo delle ariose vaghezze ... à voce sola* (1624)
CAN	Monteverdi, *Canzonette e tre voci ... libro primo* (1584)
CGC	Ambrosius Profe, *Corollarium geistlicher collectaneorum* (Leipzig, 1649)
CMO	Antonio Morsolino, *Il primo libro delle canzonette a tre voci* (1594)
COE	Giovan Battista Ala, *Primo libro delli concerti ecclesiastici a una, due, tre e quattro voci* (Milan, 1618)
COS	Pietro Lappi (ed.), *Concerti sacri a 1.2.3.4.5.6.7. voci. Libro secondo* (1623)
FDG	*Fiori del giardino di diversi eccellentissimi autori à quattro, cinque, sei, sette, otto & nove voci* (Nuremberg, 1597)
GC1	Ambrosius Profe (ed.), *Erster Theil geistlicher Concerten und Harmonien à 1.2.3.4.5.6.7. & c. Vocibus, cum & sine Sinfoniis, & Basso ad Organa* (Breslau, 1641)
GC2	Ambrosius Profe (ed.), *Ander Theil geistlicher Concerten und Harmonien, à 1.2.3.4.5.6.7. Voc. cum & sine Violinis, & Basso ad Organa* (Leipzig, 1641)
GC3	Ambrosius Profe (ed.), *Dritter Theil geistlicher Concerten und Harmonien, a 1.2.3.4.5. etc. Voc. cum & sine Violinis, & Basso ad Organa* (Leipzig, 1642)
GHS	Leonardo Simonetti (ed.), *Ghirlanda sacra scielta da diversi eccellentissimi compositori de varij motetti à voce sola* (1625)
LDA	Monteverdi, *Lamento d'Arianna ... Et con due Lettere amorose in genere rapresentativo* (1623)
MA1	Monteverdi, *Madrigali a cinque voci ... Libro primo* (1587)
MA2	Monteverdi, *Il secondo libro de madrigali a cinque voci* (1590)
MA3	Monteverdi, *Il terzo libro de madrigali a cinque voci* (1592)
MA4	Monteverdi, *Il quarto libro de madrigali a cinque voci* (1603)
MA5	Monteverdi, *Il quinto libro de madrigali a cinque voci* (1605)
MA6	Monteverdi, *Il sesto libro de madrigali a cinque voci* (1614)
MA7	Monteverdi, *Concerto: settimo libro de madrigali a 1.2.3.4. & sei voci* (1619)
MA8	Monteverdi, *Madrigali guerrieri, et amorosi ... Libro ottavo* (1638)
MA9	Monteverdi, *Madrigali e canzonette a due, e tre, voci ... Libro nono* (1651)

MAA   *Madrigali del signor cavaliere Anselmi ... posti in musica da diversi eccellentissimi spiriti a 2.3.4.5. voci* (1624)

MAC   Giovan Battista Camarella, *Madrigali et arie* (1633)

MAS   Monteverdi, *Madrigali spirituali a quattro voci* (Brescia, 1583)

MAV   Monteverdi, *Sanctissimae Virgini missa senis vocibus, ac vesperae pluribus decantandae* (1610)

MAW   Giaches de Wert, *Il duodecimo libro de madrigali ... a 4. a 5. a 6. & 7. Con alcuni altri de diversi eccellentissimi autori* (1608)

MES   Monteverdi, *Messa a quattro voci, et salmi a una, due, tre, quattro, cinque, sei, sette, & otto voci* (1650)

MO1   Giulio Cesare Bianchi, *Libro primo de motetti ... a una, due, tre, quattro, cinque, e à otto voci con il basso generale ... con un altro à cinque, e tre à sei del Sig. Claudio Monteverde* (1620)

MO2   Giulio Cesare Bianchi (ed.), *Libro secondo de motetti ... a' una, due, tre, quattro, e cinque voci* (1620)

MOC   Gasparo Casati, *Raccolta di motetti a 1.2.3. voci* (1651)

MU1   Aquilino Coppini (ed.), *Musica tolta da i madrigali di Claudio Monteverdi, e d'altri autori, a cinque, et a sei voci, e fatta spirituale* (Milan, 1607)

MU2   Aquilino Coppini (ed.), *Il secondo libro della musica di Claudio Monteverdi e d'altri autori a cinque voci fatta spirituale* (Milan, 1608)

MU3   Aquilino Coppini (ed.), *Il terzo libro della musica di Claudio Monteverdi a cinque voci fatta spirituale* (Milan, 1609)

MVS   *Motetti a voce sola de diversi eccellentissimi autori* (1645)

NFM   Amante Franzoni, *I nuovi fioretti musicali a tre voci* (1605)

PDV   Giovanni Maria Sabino, *Psalmi de vespere a quattro voci* (Naples, 1627)

PM1   Johannes Donfried (ed.), *Promptuarii musici, concentus ecclesiasticos II. III. et IV. vocum cum basso continuo & generali ... pars prima* (Strasbourg, 1622)

PMF   Giovan Battista Bonometti (ed.), *Parnassus musicus ferdinandaeus ... 1.2.3.4.5. vocum* (1615)

ROL   Lorenzo Calvi (ed.), *Rosarium litaniarum Beatae V. Mariae ternis, quaternis, quinis, senis, septenis, et octonis vocibus concinandarum* (1626)

SAA   Francesco Sammaruco, *Sacri affetti ... a2 a3. a4* (Rome, 1625)

SAC   Monteverdi, *Sacrae cantiunculae tribus vocibus* (1582)

SC2   Lorenzo Calvi (ed.), *Seconda raccolta de sacri canti a una, due, tre, et quattro voci de diversi eccellentissimi autori* (1624)

SC4   Lorenzo Calvi (ed.), *Quarta raccolta de sacri canti a una, due, tre, et quattro voci* (1629)

SDM   Lorenzo Calvi (ed.), *Symbolae diversorum musicorum binis, ternis, quaternis, & quinis vocibus, cantandae* (1620–21)

SM1   Monteverdi, *Scherzi musicali a tre voci* (1607)

SM2   Monteverdi, *Scherzi musicali ... a 1. & 2. voci* (1632)

SMS   Monteverdi, *Selva morale e spirituale* (1640–1)

VFM   Pietro Milioni & Lodovico Monte, *Vero e facil modo d'imparare a sonare, et accordare da se medesimo la chitarra spagnola* (repr. Rome/Macerata, 1637)

Manuscripts

H11   Kassel, Murhardsche Bibliothek der Stadt und Landesbibliothek, 2° MS Mus. 51v

H14   Kassel, Murhardsche Bibliothek der Stadt und Landesbibliothek, 2° MS Mus. 58j

H15   Lüneberg, Ratsbücherei, MS Mus. Ant. Pract. K.N.206

Index of names